The Great Deception

A SECRET HISTORY OF
THE EUROPEAN UNION

The Great Deception

A SECRET HISTORY OF THE EUROPEAN UNION

Christopher Booker
and
Richard North

continuum
LONDON • NEW YORK

CONTINUUM

The Tower Building, 11 York Road, London SE1 7NX

15 East 26th Street, New York, NY 10010

www.continuumbooks.com

First published 2003
Reprinted 2003, 2004
This paperback edition published 2005

British Library Cataloguing-in-Publication Data
A catalogue record for this book is available from the British Library.

ISBN: 0-8264-7652-X

Typeset in Adobe Minion by Tony Lansbury, Tonbridge, Kent
Printed and bound in Great Britain by The Cromwell Press, Trowbridge, Wiltshire

Contents

Acknowledgements

The idea that we should one day carry out a full investigation of the history of the 'European project' has been with us for some years. Since our collaboration began in 1992, we have spent much time investigating and reporting in detail on the practical impact of 'Europe' on British life. It soon became obvious to us that this was bringing about a much more far-reaching revolution in the way Britain was governed than was generally realised: as we began to explore in two earlier books, *The Mad Officials* (1994) and *The Castle of Lies* (1996).

Clearly the timing of this much more substantial book, to coincide with the debate over 'Europe's Constitution', is not accidental, not least because it seeks to answer the rather deeper question: how did we, and everyone else in the European Union, arrive at such a fateful moment in our collective history? But the immediate trigger for the intensive programme of research on which *The Great Deception* is based was a cinema commercial put out in 2002 by the organisation leading the campaign against Britain joining the single currency. Featuring a comedian Rik Mayall, in a parody of Hitler, proclaiming '*ein volk, ein Reich, ein euro*', this played on a widespread popular prejudice that European integration was somehow rooted in a desire for German domination. It was this prejudice in turn which had already encouraged some British Eurosceptics to argue that the EU's ideological origins lay in Nazi plans during World War Two to set up a 'European Economic Community'.

We were already aware that this was based on a fundamental misreading of both the nature and the history of the 'project', and that its origins went considerably further back than the Nazi period. But when we embarked on a systematic historical investigation, drawing ultimately on thousands of books, documents, academic papers and other sources, it soon became clear that it was not only the adherents of the 'Nazi origins' theory who had got the history of the European Union fundamentally wrong. So, it turned out, had everyone else who had attempted to reconstruct the story: Eurosceptics and Europhiles alike. And it was not least because of their failure to grasp the 'project's' true origins that historians had misunderstood and misrepresented so much that followed.

The foundation of our researches lay in uncovering for the first time just how directly the European Union drew its inspiration from events during and after the First World War; in particular from the thinking of two friends who held senior posts in the League of Nations, the Frenchman Jean Monnet and his English colleague Arthur Salter. The irony will not be lost on some readers that the original blueprint for what was to become the European Union was sketched out by a British civil servant.

Acknowledgements

Behind the scenes the role of Salter's friend Monnet in the evolution of the 'European project' was to remain so central, right up to the time of his death in the late 1970s, that inevitably some of our most illuminating sources were books relating directly to his part in the story. These included not only biographies of Monnet and his own memoirs, but also references made to their collaboration with him in the memoirs of other key figures, such as Winston Churchill, Paul-Henri Spaak, Harold Macmillan, Edward Heath, Roy Jenkins and George W. Ball.

Apart from the need to correct the historical record on how the 'project' began, not least the official 'myth' which has been spun round the 'Schuman Declaration' in 1950, no major component in the story has been subject to more distortion than the part played in it by Britain. Here, to reach a proper understanding, it has proved necessary to revise whole *tranches* of the 'pseudo-history' produced by writers accepted until now as authorities on this aspect of the story, notably Hugo Young, Roy Denman and, most recently, the author of the British official history, Professor David Milward.

None of these would-be historians have begun to grasp the real story behind de Gaulle's determination to keep Britain out of the Common Market in the 1960s; and for helping to bring this to light we are particularly indebted to the researches of Professor Andrew Moravcsik of Harvard University.

One reason why it would not have been possible to write this book before is that so much of the evidence crucial to establishing a clearer perspective on the past few decades has only been published comparatively recently. This includes not only Moravcsik's own work, but also the wealth of confidential papers relating to Britain's application for entry in 1970–1972 which have only lately become available under the 30-year rule (along with Con O'Neill's official 'insider's' account of the negotiations published in 2000).

Inevitably in reconstructing the events of the 1970s, 1980s and 1990s, the memoirs of British politicians proved an invaluable source: even though to reach a clear understanding of particular episodes it was often necessary to 'triangulate' between the contradictory accounts provided by different participants, such as Lady Thatcher, Nigel Lawson and Geoffrey Howe. On the whole, Thatcher's version of events proved most reliable and illuminating (not least in revealing how poorly she was served in crucial respects by her colleagues). But John Major's memoirs paint a vivid picture of how he became so overwhelmed by the contradictions of 'Europe' that this was a central factor in the disintegration of his premiership.

For help in bringing to light another little-known episode, the hugely significant part played in relaunching the 'project' in the early 1980s by Altiero Spinelli, which was to lead to the transformation of the European Community into the 'European Union', we are grateful to Richard Balfe MEP, who was centrally involved.

Another reason why it would not have been possible to write this book earlier had been the crucial part played in our researches by the internet. This has made it infinitely easier and quicker than before to track down myriad sources, ranging from books long out-of-print to obscure documents produced by the European Commission which would otherwise have been unobtainable. For personal help in this respect we are particularly grateful to the diligent staff of DG4, the archivists of the European Parliament.

The internet has also proved invaluable in reconstructing the history of recent years, for which it is not yet possible to draw on the evidence of historical accounts or political memoirs. But here we also owe a special debt to Brigadier Anthony Cowgill of the British Management Data Foundation, not least for his unique consolidated and annotated editions of the various European treaties, without which serious students of European affairs in the past decade (even including not a few from other EU countries) would have been hopelessly at sea.

For particular insights, documents and other help, we also owe thanks to Charlotte Horsfield, Dr Saul Kelly, John Ashworth, Derek Bennett, Jens-Peter Bonde MEP, Nicholas Booker, Heather Conyngham, Nigel Farage MEP (for underlining the significance of Verdun), Jim McCue, Bill Jamieson, Lord Pearson of Rannoch, Nigel Spearing, the readers of the *Sunday Telegraph*; and, not least, Mary and Peter North for their tireless quest through Yorkshire's second-hand bookstalls, for ever more obscure old books which might shed a further chink of light on one of the most labyrinthine political stories the human mind has yet produced.

Our thanks are also due to our publisher Robin Baird-Smith for his unfailing encouragement, and to his staff at Continuum. No one but ourselves can be blamed for any mistakes which will inevitably have crept into such a complex narrative. And finally, as always, we must thank Mary and Valerie for their patience over our perpetual preoccupation with that other planet which is 'Europe'. Whether it can support 'sustainable life' is a mystery which history has yet to reveal.

Bibliography

Aldrich, Richard L. (2001), *The Hidden Hand – Britain, America and Cold War Secret Intelligence* (London, John Murray (Publishers) Ltd).

Algazy, J. (1984), *La Tentation Neo-fasciste En France 1944–65* (Paris, Fayard).

Almond, Mark (1998), *Europe's Backyard War – The War in the Balkans* (London, Heinemann).

Atkinson, Rodney, and McWhirter, Norris (1994), *Treason At Maastricht* (Newcastle upon Tyne, Compuprint Publishing).

Atkinson, Rodney (1996), *Europe's Full Circle* (Newcastle upon Tyne, Compuprint Publishing).

Ball, George (1982), *The Past Has Another Pattern* (New York, Norton and Co.).

Bell, Lionel (1995), *The Throw That Failed* (London, New European Publications).

Benn, Tony (1995), *The Benn Diaries* (single volume edition) (London, Random House).

Booker, Christopher (1969), *The Neophiliacs* (London, Collins).

Booker, Christopher, and North, Richard (1994), *The Mad Officials* (London, Constable).

Booker, Christopher, and North, Richard (1996), *The Castle of Lies* (London, Duckworth).

Boothby, Lord (1978), *Boothby – Recollections Of A Rebel* (London, Hutchinson).

Brinkley, Douglas, and Hackett, Clifford (eds.) (1991), *Jean Monnet: The Path To European Unity* (New York, St Martin's Press).

Brivate, Brian, and Jones, Harriet (eds.) (1993), *From Reconstruction to Integration: Britain in Europe since 1945* (London, Continuum International).

Bromberger, Merry and Serge (1969), *Jean Monnet And The United States of Europe* (New York, Coward-McCann).

Brugmans, Dr Henri (1948), *Fundamentals Of European Federalism*, with a foreword by Lord Layton (London, The Federal Union).

Burgess, M. (1989), *Federalism And The European Union: Political Ideas, Influence And Strategy* (London, Routledge).

Burleigh, Michael (2000), *The Third Reich – A New History* (London, Macmillan).

Butler, David, and Pinto-Duschinski, Michael (1971), *The British General Election Of 1970* (London, Macmillan).

Butler, David, and Kitzinger, Uwe (1976), *The 1975 Referendum* (London, Macmillan).

Callaghan, James (1987), *Time And Chance* (London, Collins).

Calvocoressi, Peter (1955), *Survey Of International Affairs – 1952* (London, Oxford University Press).

Campbell, John (1993), *Edward Heath – A Biography* (London, Jonathan Cape).

Camps, Miriam (1964), *Britain And The European Community 1955–1963* (London, Oxford University Press).

Camps, Miriam (1965), *What Kind Of Europe? The Community Since De Gaulle's Veto*, Chatham House Essays (London, Oxford University Press).

Carrington, Lord (1988), *Reflections On Things Past* (London, Collins).

Carls, Stephen Douglas (1993), *Louis Loucheur And The Shaping Of Modern France 1916–1931* (Baton Rouge, Louisiana State University Press).

Churchill, W. S. (1948), *The Second World War, Vol. I – The Gathering Storm* (London, Cassell).

Churchill, W. S. (1952), *The Second World War, Vol. II – Their Finest Hour* (London, Cassell).

Churchill, W. S. (1976), *Collected Essays Of Winston Churchill, Volume II, Churchill And Politics* (London, Library of Imperial History).

Clark, Alan (1993), *Diaries* (London, Weidenfeld and Nicolson).

Cole, John (1995), *As It Seemed To Me – Political Memoirs* (London, Weidenfeld & Nicolson).

Coleman, Peter (1989), *The Liberal Conspiracy: The Congress For Cultural Freedom And The Struggle For The Mind Of Europe* (New York, The Free Press).

Connolly, Bernard (1995), *The Rotten Heart of Europe – The Dirty War For Europe's Money* (London, Faber and Faber).

Corbett, Richard (2001), *The European Parliament's Role In Closer EU Integration* (London, Palgrave).

Cowgill, Anthony (1992), *The Maastricht Treaty in Perspective – the Consolidated Treaty on European Union* (Stroud, British Management Data Foundation).

Crossman, Richard (1976), *The Diaries Of A Cabinet Minister* (volume two) (London, Hamish Hamilton).

De Gaulle, Charles (1971), *Memoirs Of Hope – Renewal 1958–1962* (London, Weidenfeld and Nicolson).

Dell, Edmund (1995), *The Schuman Plan And The British Abdication Of Leadership In Europe* (Oxford, Clarendon Press).

Delors, Jacques (1991), *Le Nouveau Concert Européen* (Paris, Odile Jacob).

Denman, Roy (1996), *Missed Chances – Britain And Europe In The Twentieth Century* (London, Cassell).

Dictionary of National Biography 1971–80 (1985), Oxford University Press.

Duchêne, François (1994), *Jean Monnet – The First Statesman Of Interdependence* (New York, W. W. Norton and Co.).

Eden, Anthony (1960), *Memoirs, Full Circle* (London, Cassell).

Edwards, Geoffrey, and Pijpers, Alfred (1997), *The Politics Of European Treaty Reform – The 1996 Intergovernmental Conference And Beyond* (London, Cassell).

European Parliament (1982), *Selection of texts concerning institutional matters on the Community from 1950 to 1982* (Luxembourg, Committee on Institutional Affairs).

Forster, Anthony (2002), *Euroscepticism In Contemporary British Politics – Opposition To Europe In The British Conservative And Labour Parties Since 1945* (London, Routledge).

Fransen, Frederic (2001), *The Supranational Politics Of Jean Monnet: Ideas And Origins Of The European Community* (Connecticut, Greenwood Press).

Friedman, Milton and Rosie (1980), *Free to Choose* (London, Pan Books).

George, Stephen (1990), *An Awkward Partner – Britain In The European Community* (3rd ed.) (Oxford University Press).

Gladwyn, Lord (1966), *The European Idea* (London, Weidenfeld & Nicolson).

Goldschmidt, B. (1982), *The Atomic Complex: A Worldwide Political History Of Nuclear Energy* (La Grange Park, Illinois American Nuclear Society).

Gorman, Teresa (1993), *Bastards* (London, Pan Books).

Grant, Charles (1994), *Delors – Inside The House That Jacques Built* (London, Nicholas Brearley).

Gren, Jörgen (1999), *The New Regionalism In The EU* (Stockholm, Fritzes Offentliga Publikationer).

Griffiths, Richard T. (2000), *Europe's First Constitution – The European Political Community, 1952–1954* (London, Federal Trust).

Healey, Dennis (1989), *The Time Of My Life* (London, Michael Joseph).

Heath, Edward (1998), *The Course Of My Life* (London, Hodder and Stoughton).

Henderson, Nicholas (1987), *Channels And Tunnels* (London, Weidenfeld and Nicolson).

Heseltine, M. (1987), *Where There's A Will* (London, Hutchinson).

Heseltine, M. (2000), *Life In The Jungle* (London, Hodder and Stoughton).

Hillman, Judy, and Clarke, Peter (1988), *Geoffrey Howe – A Quiet Revolutionary* (London, Weidenfeld & Nicolson).

Hogg, Sarah, and Hill, Jonathan (1995), *Too Close To Call: Power And Politics – John Major in No. 10* (London, Little, Brown and Company).

Holland, Martin (1993), *European Integration – From Community To Union* (London, Pinter Publishers).

Holmes, Martin (ed.) (1966), *The Eurosceptic Reader* (London, Macmillan).

Horne, Alistair (1988), *Macmillan 1894–1956* (London, Macmillan).

Howe, Geoffrey (1994), *Conflict Of Loyalty* (London, Macmillan).

Hugh-Jones, Wynn (2002), *Diplomacy To Politics* (Spennymore, Co. Durham, The Memoir Club).

Jamieson, Bill (1994), *Britain Beyond Europe* (London, Duckworth).

Jenkins, Lindsay (1996), *Godfather Of The European Union – Altiero Spinelli* (London, Bruges Group).

Jenkins, Roy (1991), *A Life At The Centre* (London, Macmillan).

Judd, Dennis (1996), *Empire – The British Imperial Experience From 1765 To The Present* (London, Harper Collins).

Kaiser, Wolfram (1996), *Using Europe, Abusing The Europeans – Britain And European Integration, 1945–63* (London, Macmillan).

Kitzinger, Uwe (1973), *Diplomacy And Persuasion – How Britain Joined The Common Market* (London, Thames and Hudson).

Lamont, Norman (1995), *Sovereign Britain* (London, Duckworth).

Lawson, Nigel (1992), *The View From No. 11 – Memoirs Of A Tory Radical* (London, Bantam Press).

Laughland, John (1997), *The Tainted Source – The Undemocratic Origins Of The European Idea* (London, Warner Books).

Lipgens, Walter (1985) *Documents on the History of European Integration. Volume 1, Continental Plans for European Union 1939–1945* (Berlin, Walter de Gruyter).

Lloyd George, David (1938), *The Truth About The Peace Treaties* (volume 1) (London).

Lochner, Louis P. (editor and translator) (1948), *The Goebbels Diaries 1942–43* (New York, Doubleday).

Loth, Wilfried, Wallace, William, and Wessels, Wolfgang (1998), *Walter Hallstein – The Forgotten European?* (London, Macmillan).

Ludlow, Piers (1997), *Dealing With Britain – The Six And The First UK Application To The EEC* (Cambridge University Press).

Maclean, Donald (1970) *British Foreign Policy Since Suez 1956–1968* (London, Hodder & Stoughton).

Macmillan, Harold (1971), *Riding The Storm – 1956–1959* (London, Macmillan).

Macmillan, Harold (1973), *At The End Of The Day – 1961–63* (London, Macmillan).

Major, John (1999), *John Major – The Autobiography* (London, HarperCollins).

Mansergh, Nicholas (1963), *Documents and Speeches on Commonwealth Affairs, 1952–1962* (London, Oxford University Press).

Marijnissen, Jan (1996), *Enough! A Socialist Bites Back* (Netherlands, Socialistische Partij).

Marriott, John (1941), *The Tragedy Of Europe* (London, Blackie and Son Ltd).

Mather, Graham (intr.) (1990), *Europe's Constitutional Future* (London, Institute of Economic Affairs).

McAllister, Richard (1997), *From EC To EU – A Historical And Political Survey* (London, Routledge).

McCue, Jim (1997), *Edmund Burke & Our Present Discontents* (London, The Claridge Press).

Milward, A. S. (2002), *The Rise And Fall Of A National Strategy* (London, Frank Cass).

Mitterrand, F. (1985), *Réflexions Sur La Politique Extérieure De La France. Introduction à 25 discours, 1981–1985* (Paris, Fayard).

Monnet, Jean (1978) *Memoirs* (London, Collins).

Moravcsik, Andrew (1998), *The Choice Of Europe: Social Purpose And State Power: From Messina To Maastricht* (London, UCL).

Moravcsik, Andrew (2000), 'De Gaulle Between Grain and Grandeur: The Political Economy of French EC Policy, 1958–1970' (Pt. 2) in *Journal of Cold War Studies*, Vol. 2, No. 3 (Fall).

Mote, Ashley (2001), *Vigilance* (Petersfield, Hampshire, Tanner Publishing).

North, Richard (2001), *The Death Of British Agriculture* (London, Duckworth).

Novick, Peter (1968), *Resistance Versus Vichy* (London, Chatto & Windus).

O'Neill, Con (2000), *Britain's Entry Into The European Community – Report On The Negotiations Of 1970–1972* (London, Frank Cass).

Owen, David (1992), *Time To Declare* (London, Penguin Books).

Page, Edward C. (1997), *People Who Run Europe* (Oxford, Clarendon Press).

Peyrefitte, Alain (1994), *C'était De Gaulle* (volume 1) (Paris, Fayard).

Salmon, Trevor, and Nicoll, William (1997), *Building European Union – A documentary history and analysis* (Manchester University Press).

Salter, Arthur (1931), *The United States of Europe* (London, George, Allen & Unwin).

Salter, Arthur (1961), *The Slave Of The Lamp* (London, Weidenfeld & Nicolson).

Salter, Arthur (1961), *Memoirs Of A Public Servant* (London, Weidenfeld & Nicolson).

Sampson, Anthony (1968), *The New Europeans* (London, Hodder and Stoughton).

Schwartz, H. (1997), *Konrad Adenauer: German Politician and Statesman In A Period Of War, Revolution And Reconstruction, Vol 2: The Statesman, 1952–1967* (Oxford, Berghahn).

Sharp, P. (1999), *Thatcher's Diplomacy: The Revival Of British Foreign Policy* (London, Macmillan).

Shore, Peter (2000), *Separate Ways – The Heart Of Europe* (London, Duckworth).

Spaak, Paul-Henri (1971), *The Continuing Battle: Memoirs Of A European* (Boston, Little, Brown and Company).

Stephens, Philip (1996), *Politics And The Pound* (London, Macmillan).

Stirk, Peter M. R. (1996), *A History of European Integration Since 1914* (London, Pinter).

Street, C. J. C. (1924), *The Treachery Of France* (Bedford, The Sidney Press).

Thatcher, Margaret (1992), *The Downing Street Years* (London, HarperCollins).

Thatcher, Margaret (2002), *Statecraft – Strategies For A Changing World* (London, HarperCollins).

The New Cambridge Modern History (1960), *The Era Of Violence*, Vol. XII (Cambridge University Press).

Urwin, Derek W. (1995), *The Community Of Europe – A History Of European Integration Since 1945* (second edition) (London, Longman).

van Buitenen, Paul (2000), *Blowing the Whistle – One man's fight against fraud in the European Commission* (London, Politico's).

Vaughan, Richard (1976), *Post-war Integration In Europe* (London, Edward Arnold).

Watkins, Alan (1992), *A Conservative Coup – The Fall Of Margaret Thatcher* (second edition) (London, Duckworth).

Weatherill, Stephen, and Beaumont, Paul (1995), *EC Law – The Essential Guide to the Legal Workings of the European Community* (second edition) (London, Penguin Books).

Werth, Alexander (1957), *France 1940–1955* (London, Robert Hale).

Williams, Charles (2000), *Adenauer – Father Of The New Germany* (London, Little, Brown and Company).

Williams, Neville (1967), *Chronology Of The Modern World 1763–1965* (New York, David McKay Co.).

Wilson, Harold (1979), *Final Term – The Labour Government 1974–1976* (London, Weidenfeld & Nicolson).

Winand, Pascaline (1993), *Eisenhower, Kennedy And The United States Of Europe* (New York, St Martin's Press).

Woodhouse C. M. (1961), *British Foreign Policy Since The Second World War* (London, Hutchinson & Co.).

Worcester, Robert M. (2000), *How To Win The Euro Referendum: Lessons From 1975* (London, Foreign Policy Centre).

Young, Hugo (1990), *One Of Us* (London, Pan Books).

Young, Hugo (1998), *This Blessed Plot – Britain And Europe, From Churchill To Blair* (London, Routledge).

Young, Lord (1990), *The Enterprise Years – A Businessman In The Cabinet* (London, Headline).

Introduction

'The sovereign nations of the past can no longer solve the problems of the present: they cannot ensure their own progress or control their own future. And the Community itself is only a stage on the way to the organised world of tomorrow.'   Closing Words of Jean Monnet's Memoirs

This book tells the story of the most extraordinary political project in history. From small beginnings, it has developed over many decades to the point where, at the start of the 21st century, it seems on the brink of bringing together more than two thirds of the nations of Europe under a unique form of government, like nothing the world has seen before.

Through most of that time it was not generally obvious that this was where this process was heading, not least because it was a cardinal principle of the project's founders that, for a long time, its real nature and purpose should not be brought too obviously out into the open.

Even now, that system of government is veiled in such labyrinthine complexity that, although it has come to rule over hundreds of millions of people, few have any comprehensive knowledge of how it actually works, how it evolved or what an important part it has come to play in their lives.

Only in recent years has the project become so far advanced that its underlying purpose can no longer be hidden. That is why it is now of the highest priority that the peoples of Europe should realise at last what has been and is being done in their name.

It is impossible to understand the true nature of what came to be known as 'the European project' without appreciating how it was set in train by a single guiding idea; an idea which originally crystallised back in the 1920s in the minds of two men. One, eventually to become well-known, was a French former brandy salesman, Jean Monnet. The other, whose name is now almost wholly forgotten, was his close friend Arthur Salter, an English civil servant.

When these two men first conceived their dream of a 'United States of Europe', absolutely central to it was the prospect of setting up an entirely new form of government: one which was 'supra-national', beyond the control of national governments, politicians or electorates. Nation states, governments and parliaments could be left in place: but only so that they could gradually become subordinated to a new supranational government which was above them all.

1

Long before there was any realistic prospect of putting such an audacious idea into practice, Salter dropped out of the story. But Monnet's determination to bring it about never faltered. By the time in the 1940s when he had reached a position of sufficient influence to set their project on its way, he was aware it could never be realised if its true purpose was made too explicit. His ultimate goal could only be achieved if it was worked for by stealth, step by step, over many years, until enough of the machinery of the new form of government was in place for its purpose to be brought fully into the open.

Quite independently of Monnet, another man in the 1940s was also dreaming of a future 'United States of Europe'. Languishing in a Fascist prison, an obscure Italian Communist, Altiero Spinelli, also recognised that, to bring his vision about, it would be necessary to conceal from the peoples of Europe just what was being done in their name until the process was so far advanced that it had become irreversible. Not least because Monnet disliked him, Spinelli was to remain relatively anonymous for many years until, in the last decade of his life, he emerged from the shadows to play a crucially influential role in shepherding the project towards its conclusion.

Apart from these three original visionaries, a fourth man, Paul-Henri Spaak, a prime minister of Belgium, also made his own crucial contribution. It was he who urged on his friend Monnet the idea that, initially, the most effective way to disguise their project's political purpose was to conceal it behind a pretence that it was concerned only with economic co-operation, based on dismantling trade barriers: a 'common market'.

Only after many decades was the project finally ready to declare its real intention. On 26 February 2002, delegates from 25 countries gathered in the largest complex of office buildings in Europe, the headquarters of the European Parliament in Brussels, for the opening of a convention to draft the constitution for a 'United Europe'. Explicit in many of their minds was a direct parallel between what they were doing and the convention which had gathered in Philadelphia in the summer of 1787 to draw up a constitution for the United States of America. They were only too conscious of the thought that, like their American predecessors, they were present at an extraordinary moment in history: the crowning event in the creation of a new state.

When the 105 appointed delegates, watched by a host of functionaries and observers, took their places in the chamber of the Parliament, the huge glass and steel building in which they sat was named after Paul-Henri Spaak. It was overshadowed from next door by an even vaster office block named after Altiero Spinelli: the man who had first suggested 60 years earlier how drafting a constitution for the 'United States of Europe' should be the final symbolic act in its process of political integration.

No more than a handful of delegates had any proper understanding of the part played by these two men in the convoluted process which, over 50 years, had brought them to where they were; any more than did all but an even tinier fraction of the 500 million people across Europe in whose supposed interest all this was taking place.

It was also somehow appropriate that the one name not commemorated in the colossal structures where these events were unfolding was that of the man who more than anyone else had set this process on its way half a century before. Even though he had long since been honoured as 'the Father of Europe', Jean Monnet had always preferred to work behind the scenes, away from the limelight. He knew that, only by operating in the shadows, behind a cloak of obscurity, could he one day realise his dream. What he pulled off, as this book will show, was to amount to a slow-motion *coup d'etat*: the most spectacular *coup d'etat* in history.

Yet even as this process seemed to be nearing its completion, like the putting into place of the final pieces of some vast and complex jigsaw puzzle, fundamental questions were emerging. After 50 years of slowly and painfully assembling the puzzle, was it possible that the pieces were not in fact going to fit together after all?

It was one thing to dream of a continent in which nation states could be persuaded to surrender their power of self-government to a new type of supranational government. But, when it came to the final crunch, was that what their leaders and peoples really wanted?

It was one thing to dream of a Europe in which the richer nations of the west could at last be united with poorer nations to the east which for decades had suffered under Communism. But in practice could that effectively be achieved in a way which would leave all the parties feeling they had been fairly treated?

It was one thing to dream of a single government for a Europe of 500 million people of different nationalities, speaking different languages, coming from wholly different cultural and historical traditions. But in practice could such a government in any meaningful sense remain democratic? Indeed, did that matter?

It was one thing to dream of a Europe sharing a single political and economic system. But on the evidence of its record to date, what were the prospects of that system actually delivering on the promises that were made for it?

As the governments of Europe gathered in the autumn of 2003 to discuss the constitution intended to bind their nations irrevocably together, it was hard not to reflect that the process set in train by Jean Monnet 50 years before had amounted to an immense gamble, one of the most daring political gambles in history. The real question hanging over Europe at this time was: would that gamble come off? And what would happen if it did not?

In arriving at an informed answer to these questions, nothing could be more vital than to understand just how this fateful moment in Europe's collective history had come about.

Hence the purpose of this book.

Chapter 1

The Birth of an Idea: 1918–1932

'Europe is being liquidated, and the League of Nations must be the heir to this great estate.'   Jan Smuts (1918)[1]

'The United States of Europe must be a political reality or it cannot be an economic one.'   Arthur Salter, *The United States of Europe* (1931)

On 11 November 1984, two portly middle-aged men stood holding hands in front of the largest pile of human bones in Europe. One was the President of France, François Mitterrand; the other the Chancellor of Germany, Helmut Kohl. The reason why the two most powerful political leaders in western Europe were staging an act of reconciliation before tens of thousands of graves was that the site of this ceremony was the ossuary at Douaumont, just outside Verdun in eastern France. And if there was one historical event which more than any other inspired what was eventually to become the European Union, it was the battle which had raged around Verdun in the First World War.

For the British the defining battle of that war was the Somme in the summer of 1916. For France and Germany it was the colossal battle of attrition launched in February the same year, when the French commander, General Philippe Petain, pronounced that the fortresses on the hills overlooking Verdun on the River Meuse were where the advance of German armies into his country would be brought to a halt. His legendary words *'Ils ne passeront pas'* were endorsed the same day by France's prime minister, Aristide Briand.

For nearly a year, the French and German armies battered each other to destruction in the most intense and prolonged concentration of violence the world had ever seen. French artillery alone fired more than twelve million shells, the German guns considerably more. The number of dead and wounded on both sides exceeded 700,000.

The impact of this battle on France was profound. Because of the way in which her citizen soldiers were rotated through the front line, scarcely a town or village in France was untouched by the slaughter. Among the two and a half million Frenchmen who fought in the battle were France's future President, Charles de Gaulle, and Louis Delors, whose son Jacques would one day be President of the European Commission. Present for several months fighting for the other side was the father of Germany's future Chancellor, Helmut Kohl.

---

1 Quoted by Lloyd George, David (1938), *The Truth About The Peace Treaties* (London, Victor Gollancz), vol. 1, p. 80.

So deep was the wound Verdun inflicted on the psyche of France that the following year her army was brought to mutiny. Its morale would never fully recover. And from this blow were to emerge two abiding lessons.

The first was a conviction that such a suicidal clash of national armies must never be repeated. The second was much more specific and immediate. It came from the realisation that the war had been shaped more than anything else by industrial power. As the battle for Verdun had developed into a remorseless artillery duel, trainloads of German shells were arriving at the front still warm from the factories of the Ruhr. The battle, and the war itself, became less a trial of men and human resolve than of two rival industrial systems. And the French system had been found sorely wanting.

Particularly inferior had been the heavy guns, many dating back to the 1870s, able to fire shells at only a seventh of the rate of their German counterparts. More and better guns became vital. But, as France's politicians found to their consternation, manufacturing them and the huge quantities of ammunition needed was beyond the capacity of an industry which compared equally poorly with Germany's. This had since August 1914, under the inspiration of Walter Rathenau, been put on a fully integrated war footing, under the control of a War Raw Materials Department.[2]

In the summer of 1916, therefore, a crisis-stricken French government gave an industrialist, Louis Loucheur, near-dictatorial powers to reform and develop the manufacturing base. Before the war, Loucheur had been one of the early pioneers in the use of reinforced concrete. In a national economy dominated by artisan manufacture, he was one of the few French technocrats familiar with the techniques of mass production.

With all the power of the state behind him, Loucheur succeeded in his initial task, even building new factories to make the new guns. But improvements in production precipitated critical shortages of steel and coal, exacerbated by the German seizure in the first weeks of the war of around half France's industrial base in the north-east of the country.[3]

Remedying these shortages required massive imports from Britain, and then from the United States. In turn, this placed considerable demands on shipping. All this required unprecedented economic co-operation between the Western Allies, leading Loucheur to conclude, like Rathenau before him, how far success in modern warfare demanded industrial organisation.

Thus, Loucheur came to reflect, industrial organisation was the key to waging war.[4] From this he developed the idea that, if key industries from different countries, above all their coal and steel industries on which modern warfare so much depended, were removed from the control of individual nations and vested in a 'higher authority', this might be the means of preserving peace.

---

2 The New Cambridge Modern History (1960), *The Era Of Violence* (Cambridge, Cambridge University Press), Vol. XII, p. 509.

3 Carls, Stephen Douglas (1993), *Louis Loucheur And The Shaping Of Modern France 1916–1931* (Baton Rouge, Louisiana State University Press), p. 33.

4 Carls, *op. cit.*, p. 264.

Building the world anew

When the First World War ended on 11 November 1918, much of the pre-war world which had brought it about had already slipped into history. Four great empires had fallen apart: that of Germany itself, and those of Austria-Hungary, Russia and the Ottoman Turks who had ruled over so much of the Middle East. There followed a general sense that the world must be rebuilt, in a way which might ensure that such a catastrophe could never be repeated. But this determination took two competing forms: one was idealistic, the other vengeful.

Post-war idealism was symbolised by US President Woodrow Wilson, whose country's intervention in the last year of the war had finally tipped the military balance against Germany, bringing about her political collapse. Wilson's famous 'Fourteen Point Declaration', supporting the right of peoples to self-determination, guided the post-war settlement agreed at the Paris peace conference in 1919. New nations arose in the former lands of now-defunct empires, their borders supposedly guaranteed by Wilson's supreme embodiment of post-war idealism, the League of Nations. This would keep the peace, by providing a forum for resolving disputes and, if this failed, a mechanism for collective intervention.

In the early stages of the post-war era, however, this mood of idealism was undermined by two rude shocks. The first, following opposition from the US Senate and Woodrow Wilson's succession by President Harding, was the US's withdrawal from the League. America's retreat into isolationism left the new international forum largely a European body, dominated by Britain, France and Italy (neither Germany nor Russia, now locked in the civil war which followed the 1917 Bolshevik revolution, were initially admitted as members). The second was France's determination to wreak vengeance on Germany, the country held chiefly responsible for the catastrophe, and to ensure that it would never again be strong enough to endanger the peace.

Largely as a result of French pressure, therefore, the 1919 Treaty of Versailles imposed on defeated Germany fearsome punishments. She lost more than an eighth of her land area and all her overseas empire. Alsace and Lorraine were returned to France in perpetuity, along with the Saar, rich in coal and iron, pending a plebiscite after 15 years. The Rhineland was to remain under allied occupation. Germany's army was limited to 100,000 men and she was prohibited from producing heavy guns, tanks or military aircraft. Most damaging of all, she was required to pay crippling reparations to the Western allies, in money and goods, amounting eventually to £6.6 billion. Germany was to be humiliated and emasculated.

In January 1923, the screw was tightened still further. Taking as excuse the late delivery of a small quantity of timber for telegraph poles due under the reparations settlement, followed by a default on deliveries of coal (at a time when coal was in surplus), France and Belgium sent 70,000 armed men to occupy the Ruhr, Germany's industrial heartland.

The French contingent included a large number of colonial troops who were allowed to run amok. Their activities triggered a widespread campaign of passive resistance, which the French countered by deposing or imprisoning the ring-leaders and expelling nearly 150,000 people from the district. These included over 46,000 German officials and their families. Confronted by non co-operation and episodes of sabotage, the French authorities resorted to hostage-taking and collective fines. They also conducted aggressive house searches, identity checks and summary executions.[5]

The effect was catastrophic. Industrial output collapsed, causing mass unemployment. When the German government guaranteed the wages of workers dispossessed by the Franco-Belgian action, hyper-inflation ensued. By November 1923, this had so devalued the currency that a single US dollar could buy 4.2 *trillion* German marks. This led to widespread unrest and disorder, attempts at revolution, an unsuccessful putsch in Bavaria by Adolf Hitler and his followers, and moves to create a separate Rhineland republic, the latter financed by French agents, using money stolen from German municipalities.

Few details of this episode, which sent a wave of shock across the non-French world, survive in modern textbooks on European history.[6] At the time, it was clear that French policy was directed at destabilising the German nation. The French occupation force actively interfered in German civil administration, in violation of Versailles Treaty, and sponsored the deliberate wrecking of Germany's infrastructure, particularly its railway system. An American academic at the time, Professor Schevill, who held the chair in modern European history at Chicago, observed:

'France ... is the spoiled child of Europe, privileged to indulge her most capricious desire. Her European allies and friendly America may offer a mild remonstrance over unreasonable and wilful actions of which they do not approve, but they lack the heart to be severe. Since 1919 France has therefore had her way. She alone has made the pacification of Europe impossible.'[7]

Nevertheless, the speed of Germany's recovery from this catastrophe was one of the miracles of 20th century history. Its hero was Gustav Stresemann, founder and leader of the German People's Party, who on 13 August 1924 became Chancellor of a coalition government. Although he held office only until 23 November, in those 100 days he dealt firmly with an insurrection in Saxony, restored order in Bavaria after Hitler's *putsch*, ended the passive resistance in the Ruhr, and began the task of stabilising the currency.

On 30 November, the French government agreed to an inquiry, presided over by an American general Charles Dawes, into the whole question of German reparations. Under what became known as the Dawes Plan, not only was Germany's debt drastically reduced, she was also given a huge foreign loan, raised mainly in

---

5 Marriott, Sir John (1941), *The Tragedy Of Europe* (London, Blackie and Son Ltd), p. 87.

6 In the later decades of the 20th century, after the 'European idea' had became the prevailing ideology, it became noticeable how books mentioning the French military occupation of the Rhineland presented only a heavily sanitised version of what had happened. These airbrushed out the more unsavoury details of how aggressively France's occupying forces behaved, and limited coverage of the episode to little more than cursory acknowledgement that the occupation had taken place.

7 Street, C. J. C. (1924), *The Treachery Of France* (Bedford, The Sidney Press), p. 159.

the US. This enabled her to meet her payments (a deal for which in 1925 Dawes was awarded the Nobel peace prize and became US vice-president under Calvin Coolidge).

So highly regarded was Stresemann that his successor as German Chancellor in November 1924 chose him as foreign affairs minister, an office he was to hold with distinction under four governments. He established a warm friendship with Aristide Briand, now France's foreign minister, and with him, in 1925, became co-author of the Locarno Treaty, supported by Britain, Italy and Belgium, which guaranteed mutual security for France and Germany. For this achievement, the two men were awarded the Nobel Peace Prize. Thus did western Europe emerge into what Winston Churchill was to describe as 'the pale sunlight of Locarno'.[8]

The following year, 1926, Germany was admitted to the League of Nations. A week later Stresemann and Briand, celebrating over a private lunch, 'waxed expansive over Stresemann's favourite theme of Franco-German economic collaboration'.[9] It was no accident that both men had become active supporters of a movement which had lately become remarkably fashionable, calling for a 'United States of Europe'.

The age of the utopians

By the mid-1920s there was a heady sense that the shadows of the previous decade had at last receded. Mankind seemed to be moving forward into a new world, in keeping with technological innovations – the radio, the cinema, motor cars, aeroplanes – which were marking out the 20th century as different from anything seen before.

In America it was Scott Fitzgerald's Jazz Age, a time of unprecedented prosperity, of soaring skyscrapers, Henry Ford's 'Model T', 'flappers' and the Charleston, the first heyday of Hollywood, and on Wall Street the start of the greatest stock boom in history. In the new Soviet Union the triumphant Bolsheviks, having torn down almost every vestige of the old aristocratic, religious autarchy of Tsarist times, seemed to be constructing an extraordinary new society, based on the radiant vision of a Communist Utopia.

In Paris a young Swiss architect, Le Corbusier, was gripped by a quite different Utopian vision, but one which was also to have profound influence on the 20th century. As he argued in *Towards A New Architecture* (1924) and *The City of the Future* (1925), the true social revolution would come from having the courage to tear down the dirty, unplanned cities of the past, which were making humanity unhappy and unhealthy, to replace them with the 'radiant city' of the future, planned down to the tiniest detail: gleaming tower blocks standing amid trees and grass, constructed from the building material of the new age, reinforced concrete.

Amid this euphoria and idealism, all over western Europe leading politicians, businessmen and intellectuals were also becoming seized by another heady vision:

---

8 Churchill, W. S. (1948), *The Second World War, Vol. I, The Gathering Storm* (London, Cassell), p. 63.
9 New Cambridge Modern History, *op. cit.*, p. 467.

that of building a 'United States of Europe'. In 1918, even before the war had ended, the Italian industrialist, Giovanni Agnelli, founder of the Fiat empire, had published a book entitled *European Federation or League of Nations*, arguing that the only effective antidote to destructive nationalism was a federal Europe. But the young man who truly caught the mood of the moment was Count Richard Coudenhove Kalergi, born in Tokyo in 1894 to a diplomat in the Austro-Hungarian embassy and a Japanese mother.

In 1922, still in his late twenties, he published his book *Pan Europa*, launching a movement under the same name. His vision, like that of Louis Loucheur, was that, to maintain peace, the German coal and French steel industries should be merged into a single 'pan-European' industry. They would form the basis for a federal 'United States of Europe' on the American model. Two years later he developed this by supporting the suggestion of a French economist, Charles Gide, that Europe should form a customs union.[10] However, Coudenhove was emphatic that the purpose of his federation would not be to eradicate national identities or reduce the sovereignty of its members, but to celebrate the 'spirit of Europe' by providing a framework in which they could co-operate for the common good.

The speed with which Coudenhove's vision attracted the support of many of Europe's leading figures was remarkable. Among them were Albert Einstein, Pablo Picasso, and French writers such as Paul Valery, Guillaume Apollinaire and St John Perse. Businessmen and left-wing thinkers joined the cause, including, in Italy, Giovanni Agnelli and Professor Luigi Einaudi, a left-wing lawyer who had formerly edited *La Stampa*; in Holland, Edo Fimmen, chairman of the International Transport Workers' Federation; and in Germany, Karl Tucholsky, one of the leading left-wing intellectuals of the Weimar Republic.[11]

However, the most significant headway made by Coudenhove's campaign was among Europe's politicians: not only those already in senior positions, but others, such as the mayor of Cologne, Konrad Adenauer, who would play a crucial role in shaping Europe in the future. One influential convert was Gustav Stresemann, co-author of the Locarno Pact, whose party in the same year agreed to adopt support for a 'United States of Europe' as its official policy. Another in France was Prime Minister Edouard Herriot, who had briefly been munitions minister during

10 In the same year, 1924, Sir Max Waechter, a German-born British industrialist, published *How To Abolish War: The United States of Europe*, in which he independently proposed that the way to European federation could lie through establishing a customs union or 'common market', not least because this would be the only way for Europe to continue competing economically with America and, before long, Japan. He founded a European Unity League to advance his ideas, but this made little impact.

11 Like many supporters of a 'United States of Europe', Tucholsky regarded narrow-minded, aggressive nationalism as the real threat to peace. In 1928 he was to write 'May the thought of the United States of Europe triumph over the nationalistic German and petty Bavarian thoughtlessness of the absolute sovereignty of individual states.' Two years earlier, in an essay on 'Foreign and Domestic Policy' in the pacifist journal *Friedenswarte*, he wrote 'We no longer live in the individual fortresses of the Middle Ages. We live in a house and the name of that house is Europe.' Tucholsky was naturally violently opposed to the rising tide of Nazism, and when Hitler took power the Nazis stripped him of his citizenship, burned his books and gloated over the news of his suicide. (King, Ian (2001), *Kurt Tucholsky as Prophet of European Unity*, European Paper 5/2001 (London, South Bank University).)

Verdun (in 1931 he was to publish a book, *The United States of Europe*). Another convert later to become prime minister was Leon Blum. But *Pan Europa's* most committed supporter was France's foreign minister, Aristide Briand, who had been France's prime minister eleven times and who was now with Stresemann the co-author of the Locarno Pact.

It was the sight of these two major figures joining in support of the 'pan-European' vision which, on 24 June 1925, inspired Winston Churchill, then Chancellor of the Exchequer, to tell members of the House of Commons, as he later recalled, how:

'... the aim of ending the thousand-year strife between France and Germany seemed a supreme object. If only we could weave Gaul and Teuton so closely together economically, socially and morally as to prevent the occasion of new quarrels and make old antagonisms die in the realisation of mutual prosperity and interdependence, Europe would rise again.'[12]

In October 1926, Coudenhove's vision enjoyed its moment of greatest triumph when, at the age of 32, he staged a European Congress in Vienna, attended by more than 2,000 politicians, academics, businessmen, representatives of the professions and journalists. Among them was Briand, who in 1927 became *Pan-Europa's* honorary president. In the same year, as a fervent supporter of the League of Nations, he proposed to the US Secretary of State Kellogg a 'non-aggression pact', whereby their two countries would renounce war as an instrument of policy for-ever. Kellogg's response was to propose what became known as the 'Kellogg-Briand Pact', under which, in 1929, 15 nations, including France and Germany, signed up to similar terms.[13] On 7 September that year, following discussions with Stresemann, at which he cited the 'menace of American economic power' as one of the greatest threats Europe now faced, Briand presented the League of Nations with a dramatic new proposal. 'I think', he said,

'that among peoples who are geographically grouped together like the peoples of Europe there must exist a kind of federal link... Evidently the association will act mainly in the economic sphere ... but I am sure also that from a political point of view, and from a social point of view, the federal link, without infringing the sovereignty of any of the nations tak-ing part, could be beneficial.'[14]

On 20 May 1930, three days after French troops began their final evacuation of the German Rhineland (under the Young Plan), Briand circulated the govern-ments of Europe with a 'Memorandum on a European Federal Union'.[15] He pro-posed that, 'in the interests alike of the peace and of the economic and social well-

---

12 Churchill W. S. (1948), *The Second World War, Vol. II, The Gathering Storm* (London, Cassell), pp. 40–41.

13 In 1929 Coudenhove Kalergi adopted the theme of the last movement of Beethoven's Ninth Symphony as *Pan Europa's* 'anthem'. He was to organise further congresses in Berlin (1930), Basel (1932) and Vienna (1935), but none had the impact of his first Vienna congress in 1926.

14 Gladwyn, Lord (1966), *The European Idea* (London, Weidenfeld & Nicolson), p. 43.

15 Summarised in Arthur Salter's *The United States of Europe* (1931) (George Allen & Unwin), pp. 106–107. See also Keeton, Edward David (1987), *Briand's Locarno Policy: French Economics, Politics And Diplomacy 1925–1929* (New York). Cited in Carls, *op. cit.*, p. 272.

being of the continent', Europe should be given 'something in the nature of a federal organisation'. This would be implemented within the framework of the League of Nations and would 'respect national sovereignties'. But it would centre on 'the conception of European political co-operation', subordinating 'the economic to the political problem', and it should be concerned with co-operation on 'economic policy, transport, finance, labour, health and intellectual co-operation'.

Briand's proposal had already received its warmest welcome from Winston Churchill, now out of office, who told readers of the New York *Saturday Evening Post* on 13 February 1930:

'the mass of Europe once united, once federalised or partly federalised, once continentally self-conscious, would constitute an organism beyond compare ...'

But then, as later, Churchill saw no place in such a federation for his own island, with its world-wide empire. Speaking for Britain, his article went on:

'We are with Europe but not of it. We are linked but not comprised. We are interested and associated but not absorbed. And should the European statesmen address us in the words which were used of old, "Wouldest thou be spoken for to the King, or the captain of the Host?", we should reply with the Shunamite woman. "Nay sir, for we dwell among our own people". We must build a kind of United States of Europe. Great Britain, the British Commonwealth of Nations, mighty America must be friends and sponsors of the new Europe.'[16]

Of the responses eventually received from 26 European governments, almost all 'expressed full agreement with the idea of closer European co-operation'. Only Britain rejected Briand's proposals outright. All the states except Holland insisted that such an association must be 'on the plane of absolute sovereignty and of entire political independence'.[17]

Despite its support, Briand's initiative failed. By now it was clear that the mood of Europe was changing. The previous autumn, only weeks after the death in October of Briand's closest ally, Stresemann, the Wall Street crash had heralded the slide of the world's economies into their greatest slump in history. In Germany's elections of 14 September 1930, fuelled by soaring unemployment and continuing nationalist resentment at the humiliations of the Versailles Treaty, votes for the National Socialist Party had soared from 810,000 to six and a half million. Hitler won over 100 seats in the Reichstag. The following year the Japanese invasion of Manchuria was to expose the League of Nations as no more than a talking shop.

Those brave Utopian dreams of the 1920s were fading rapidly. But all this time a much smaller group of men, watching the events of the 1920s at close quarters, had begun to think that, if the goal of a United States of Europe was ever to be achieved, it would require a different strategy altogether.

---

16 Churchill, W. S. (1976), *Collected Essays Of Winston Churchill, Vol. II, Churchill And Politics* (London Library of Imperial History), pp. 176–186.
17 Salter, *op. cit.*, p. 123.

Enter the supranationalists

One thing the Utopian visions of the 1920s all had in common, from the League of Nations itself, to *Pan Europa* and Briand's European Federal Union, was that they were all based on the idea of nations coming together to co-operate on an 'intergovernmental' basis. This was the road to universal peace: governments should learn how to work willingly together for the common good, but without abandoning their sovereignty.

Curiously enough this posed a problem which had already exercised one of the finest minds Europe has ever produced, six centuries earlier. In 1308, exiled from his native Florence, the poet and statesman Dante Alighieri had, in his treatise *De Monarchia*, addressed the question of how Europe might overcome the endless wars and conflicts produced by a multitude of nations and city states. As an admirer of the Holy Roman Empire, he suggested that there must be one 'empire' above them all, with the power to control their actions in the common interest. Such a power would be 'supranational'.

Over the following centuries, many thinkers offered further proposals for the political unification of Europe, from Leibniz, Kant and the Dutch lawyer Grotius, to Rousseau, Jeremy Bentham and Victor Hugo. The French King Henry IV's minister, Sully, suggested that Europe should be divided into 15 states, governed by a council, and with a European army of 100,000 men to keep the peace. William Penn, who gave his name to Pennsylvania, proposed an 'Assembly of the United Europe', taking its decisions by what would later be called 'qualified majority voting', weighted accorded to national population sizes and economic importance. In the 18th century, the French Abbé de Saint-Pierre suggested rule by a 'European Senate', also with a form of qualified majority voting according to size and the power to summon a European army. In the 19th century the Comte de Saint-Simon proposed a political union of Europe based on the union of England and France, with a bi-cameral parliament, the upper chamber chosen by governments, the lower elected by universal suffrage. The French revolutionary Proudhon, at the end of his life, published *The Federal Principle* (1863), attacking nationalism as the supreme evil which leads inevitably to war, and arguing not only that nation states should be welded together in a European federation, but that the states themselves should be broken up into regional governments.[18]

What all these proposals had in common, with the possible exception of the last, was that they were all ultimately 'intergovernmental', based on the willing co-operation of sovereign states. The first formal example based on Dante's principle of an authority which was 'supranational' (apart perhaps from the mediaeval Papacy) was put forward in the 1920s by Louis Loucheur.

During the Paris peace conference of 1919, Loucheur acted as chief economic adviser to the French prime minister Clemenceau. Drawing on the lessons of trying to integrate France's military production during the war, he urged that the key to peace would be to integrate the economies of France and Germany, particularly

---

18 For an admirable historical summary of proposals for a united Europe, see Gladwyn, *op. cit.*, pp. 33–42.

those industries central to waging war, coal and steel. In the early days of the reparations programme, its secretary-general, British civil servant Arthur Salter, later recalled how Loucheur and his wartime opposite number Walter Rathenau had tried to use German skilled labour to help rebuild the French economy; only for their efforts to be sabotaged by French industrialists.[19]

Finally in 1925, just when the vogue for 'intergovernmental' European co-operation was reaching its height at Locarno, Loucheur's vision of integrating Europe's coal and steel industries was given practical expression, by Emil Mayrisch, head of the giant Luxembourg-based steel combine, ARBED. He brokered an 'International Steel Agreement', covering the steel industries of France, Germany, Belgium, Luxembourg and the Saar. This was hailed by Gustav Stresemann as 'a landmark of international economic policy, the importance of which cannot be overestimated',[20] not least because it had the power to reduce over-capacity by imposing production quotas for each member country. It also had a central 'treasury' with power to levy surcharges on members who broke the rules.

Loucheur's steel agreement had created Europe's first, albeit embryonic 'supra-national' authority. Mayrisch hoped it would be a model for similar schemes. It would certainly later be remembered by Konrad Adenauer and others as the model for the European Coal and Steel Community which was to be the embryo of the European Union. Loucheur himself, before his death in 1931, would in 1927 propose at a League of Nations-sponsored conference the setting up of an 'economic League of Nations' based on a customs union or 'common market'.

But it was not Loucheur who would one day be remembered as 'the Father of Europe'. That title would be reserved for a younger man who watched what Loucheur was doing in the 1920s, but who alone would crack the secret of how to get that 'United States of Europe' finally launched on its way.

Enter Monsieur Monnet

Among the senior figures in the League of Nations at its foundation were two who were already close friends. One was Arthur Salter, the British civil servant who ran the Reparations Commission. His friend Jean Monnet, younger by seven years but appointed aged only 31 to be the League's deputy-secretary general, was a small, self-effacing Frenchman with a moustache, who decades later would be described as looking like Hercule Poirot.[21]

So crucial a part was Monnet to play in this story that it is relevant to know something of his origins. He was born in Cognac in 1888, the son of a wealthy brandy-maker. He left school at sixteen without academic qualifications, to work in his father's firm, J. G. Monnet. After a short apprenticeship, from 1906 to 1914 he represented the firm abroad, spending more time in North America, England, Scandinavia, Russia and Egypt than in France.

19 Salter, Arthur (1961), *The Slave Of The Lamp* (London, Weidenfeld & Nicolson), p. 86.
20 Hexner, Ervin (1943), *International Steel Cartels* (Durham, N. C.). Cited in Carls, *op. cit.*, p. 266.
21 Sampson, Anthony (1968), *The New Europeans* (London, Hodder and Stoughton), p. 7.

In 1914, the outbreak of war found Monnet, at the age of 26, back in France, but unfit for military service. What he did then was to set in train a sequence of events which was to change the course of European history. But, as was to become typical of Monnet, the exact circumstances remain obscure. There are two versions, one set down 60 years later in his memoirs, the other reconstructed from other sources.

According his memoirs, a month after the start of hostilities the young man realised that the Allied supply system was breaking down. Through his father's company lawyer, he sought 'out of the blue' an interview with France's prime minister, René Viviani, meeting him in September 1914 in Bordeaux – to where the French government had fled from the approaching German armies. Monnet proposed a plan to co-ordinate the use of Allied ships bringing supplies to beleaguered France.[22] As a result, he was sent to London to help set up an International Supply Commission, which organised an Anglo-French pool of ships to supply the Allied forces.

The alternative version of these events is rather murkier. One of Monnet's chief pre-war customers had been the Hudson Bay Company of Canada, which bought large quantities of brandy from him, much of which was then sold on to the native Indians, a trade prohibited by law.[23] Monnet was grateful for this, since he found it hard to compete in the legal market with better-known firms such as Hennessy.

As the prospect of a European war loomed in 1914, Monnet had discussed with the Hudson Bay Company the vital and potentially lucrative role that could be played by a major international trading concern. According to this version, it was Hudson Bay which arranged through its influential French contacts for the young man to meet France's prime minister. Certainly when Monnet was sent to London to set up his shipping pool, he arranged a huge £150 million contract for Hudson Bay to ship 13m tons of goods from Canada to France, on which the company would take one percent commission. Monnet received no payment, but it placed the Hudson Bay Company in his debt, in a way which would later be handsomely repaid.[24]

By 1916, the year of Verdun, Monnet was working in Paris as *chef de cabinet* to France's economics minister Clementel. Later, he recorded his shock at finding just how disorganised were France's shipping arrangements, at much the same time as Loucheur was finding similar chaos in her munitions production. The French government had not even managed to acquire powers to requisition ships for the war effort, and Monnet recalls how he became determined to see the organisation of shipping turned into 'the nerve centre of the Allies' economic organisation'.[25]

---

22 Monnet, Jean (1978) *Memoirs* (London, Collins), pp. 49–52.
23 Fransen, Frederic (2001), *The Supranational Politics Of Jean Monnet: Ideas And Origins Of The European Community* (Connecticut, Greenwood Press), p. 15.
24 Duchêne, François (1994), *Jean Monnet – The First Statesman Of Interdependence* (New York, W. W. Norton and Co.), p. 35.
25 Monnet, *op. cit.*, p. 63. Loucheur met and took an intense dislike to Monnet, and tried to arrange his transfer to the front. After intense lobbying by Monnet, which reached Cabinet level, he retained his position.

In 1917 a number of meetings were arranged in Paris to discuss how this could be achieved, and here Monnet met up again with Arthur Salter. Their first encounter had been in London in 1914 when Salter had been put in charge of requisitioning merchant shipping for the Admiralty. He was later to recall the central part the two of them played in finding a solution, and how the key decision was taken 'at a small dinner discussion in October 1917'.[26] The outcome was the setting up of the Inter-Allied Maritime Transport Council, charged with co-ordinating the use of Allied shipping, relying on the co-operation of the British, French and American governments. Monnet had wanted to go further. Instead of relying on co-operation, he pressed for the creation of an 'international council' with full authority (*pleins pouvoirs*) to dictate the Allied shipping arrangements. Even though he did not get his way, for the first time in his life he had conceived of a body which was 'supranational'. It was an idea he found particularly appealing.[27]

One of Monnet's skills throughout his life was to make influential friends. He was a born behind-the-scenes operator, persuading others to help advance projects on which he had set his heart. Salter was one such friend, and when the war was over, and the statesmen and civil servants of the victorious powers gathered in Paris for the peace conference, Monnet made many more who would become useful allies, including a young American lawyer John Foster Dulles. After tireless lobbying, when the new League of Nations was established, the young Frenchman became its deputy-secretary-general, under the British head of its secretariat, Sir Eric Drummond.

For three years Monnet worked at the centre of the new organisation. With its Secretariat, its Council, its Assembly and its new Court of International Justice, he was initially highly optimistic that the League could impose its benevolent will on the world 'by its moral force, by appealing to public opinion and thanks to customs which would ultimately prevail'.[28] He admired the internationalist idealism of his colleagues ('Drummond had decided from the outset that the Secretariat of the League ... was not to consist of national delegates but of international servants whose first loyalty was to the League')[29]; and one with whom he worked closely was his old friend Salter, who was now administering German reparations through the League.

But increasingly Monnet became frustrated by one particular feature of the League: every member state had the power of veto, so decisions could only be taken unanimously. As he was later to put it 'the veto is the profound cause and at the same time the symbol of the impossibility of overcoming national egoism'.[30] He summed up his feelings:

---

26 Salter, Arthur (1961), *Memoirs Of A Public Servant* (London, Weidenfeld & Nicolson), p. 113.
27 Fransen, *op. cit.*, p. 24.
28 *Jean Monnet, A Short Biography* (Altiero Spinelli Institute for Federalist Studies). *www.eurplace.org/federal/monnet.*
29 New Cambridge Modern History, *op. cit.*, p. 477.
30 This is the version given in *Jean Monnet, A Short Biography, op. cit.* The English translation of Monnet's *Memoirs* (*op. cit.*, p. 97), is rather more pedestrian: 'the veto was at once the cause and the symbol of this inability to go beyond national self-interest'.

'... I was impressed with the power of a nation that can say no to an international body that has no supranational power. Goodwill between men, between nations, is not enough. One must also have *international laws and institutions* [our italics]. Except for certain practical but limited activities in which I participated, the League of Nations was a disappointment.' [31]

In 1923, Monnet was prevailed upon by his sister to rescue the family business from a financial crisis. He resigned from the League and called in the favour owed him by the Hudson Bay Company, asking it for a loan. It advanced him two million francs, which he was told he could treat as a gift (he did repay it, seven years later, but in a devalued currency worth less than 40 percent of the original loan plus interest). Having restored the family business, Monnet moved to America, to become a partner in the New York merchant bank Blair and Co. There he made a fortune, but lost much of it in the Wall Street crash. To stay solvent, he again relied on the Hudson Bay Company. Sir Robert Kindersley, a former Hudson Bay Company governor, arranged for him a large, unsecured loan from Lazards Bank, which Monnet was able to repay fully only 30 years later.

In 1932 his role as banker took him for a year to China, where he arranged finance for the reconstruction of the railways. In the freewheeling and corrupt world of Shanghai in the 1930s, Monnet negotiated substantial loans to influential backers of the Chiang-Kai-Shek government, some of whom were distinctly 'shady'. [32] But as he watched the League of Nations stand impotently by as China slid towards chaos – not least after the Japanese invasion of Manchuria in 1931 – he reaffirmed his conviction that, ultimately, international peace and security could only be guaranteed by supranational institutions. One old friend of like mind whom he had followed to China was Arthur Salter, who had advised its government on reorganising the railways.

If Monnet's mind had for some years been largely on other matters, Salter had become increasingly preoccupied with how a 'United States of Europe' might be established. In 1931 he published a collection of papers under the title *The United States of Europe*, in which he addressed the possibility of building a federal Europe within the framework of the League of Nations itself. Because the League, had become largely a regional organisation, Salter saw that it might be adapted to provide a framework for a politically united Europe. In an essay entitled '*The United States of Europe' Idea* he drew on the model of how Germany had been politically united in the 19th century, through establishing a *Zollverein*, a 'common market'. His 'United States' would work in the same way, raising its funding through a common tariff on all goods imported from outside. This, like Germany, would need 'a political instrument to determine how the distribution [of those funds] should be made'. He went on to say that:

'the commercial and tariff policy of European States is so central and crucial a part of their general policy, the receipts from Customs are so central and substantial a part of their

31 Bromberger, Merry and Serge (1969), *Jean Monnet And The United States of Europe* (New York, Coward-McCann), p. 19.
32 Fransen, *op. cit.*, p. 17.

revenues, that a common political authority, deciding for all Europe what tariffs should be imposed and how they should be distributed, would be for every country almost as important as, or even more important than, the national Governments, and would in effect reduce the latter to the status of municipal authorities.'[33]

'In other words' he went on, 'the United States of Europe must be a political reality'. Its organisation could be based on that of the League of Nations, with a Secretariat, a Council of Ministers, an Assembly and a Court – but with one crucial proviso. The central source of authority in this new body, Salter urged, must be reserved for the 'Secretariat', the permanent body of international civil servants, loyal to the new organisation, not to the member countries. The problem with giving too much power to a Council was that they would always remain motivated primarily by national interest:

'In face of a permanent corps of Ministers, meeting in committees and "shadow councils", and in direct contact with their Foreign Office, the Secretariat will necessarily sink in status, in influence, and in the character of its personnel, to clerks responsible only for routine duties. They will cease to be an element of importance in the formation or maintenance of the League's traditions.'[34]

The Secretariat, Salter argued, would be above the power of national ministers, run by people who no longer owed any national loyalty. 'The new international officer needed for the League's task' he wrote, 'is something new in the world's history.'[35]

What Salter was describing, of course, was precisely the 'supranational' principle by which nearly three decades later Monnet would inspire the setting up of the European Economic Community, deliberately intended as an embryonic 'United States of Europe'. He even envisaged that another way to erode nationalism might be to split up its member states into regions. The only term in Salter's blueprint which needed changing was 'Secretariat'; and as it happened, in describing reactions to Briand's proposal in 1930 for a 'European Federal Union', he was able to record that the League of Nations had already set up a 'European Commission'.[36]

By now, however, as Europe plunged into the Great Depression, the shadows were gathering over such dreams: 1932 saw the death of Briand himself, the most distinguished champion a 'United States of Europe' had yet won to its cause. The next year brought the rise to power of Adolf Hitler. His idea of how Europe might be united was very different.

---

33 Salter, Arthur (1931), *The United States Of Europe*, George (London, Allen & Unwin), p. 92.
34 Salter, *op. cit.*, p. 134.
35 Salter, *op. cit.*, p. 136.
36 Salter, *op. cit.*, p. 124.

Chapter 2

The Nazi Cul-de-Sac: 1933–1945

'We are perhaps more interested in Europe than other countries need to be.'
Adolf Hitler, speech at Nuremberg Rally, 1937

On 13 December 1941, when Hitler's armies were at the gates of Moscow, the magazine *Picture Post*, then in its heyday as Britain's leading mass-circulation weekly, gave prominence to an article by its proprietor Edward Hulton headed 'How The Nazis Promise Europe a New Heaven'.

In his article, Hulton reported on how a 'grand assembly of puppet powers' had recently taken place in Berlin, to be told that it would be the Nazis' purpose after the war to unite Europe as the richest economic entity in the world. 'Up to now,' a senior Nazi economist Werner Daitz had proclaimed, 'Europe has not been able to take advantage of her wonderful natural opportunities. This because her different states have refused to work together.' But under the Nazi 'New Order', a united Europe would 'use her economic strength as a political lever' to assert her proper influence in the world. To illustrate the Nazi plan for a 'new Europe' the magazine published a map of the trans-continental railway system, quoting Josef Goebbels: 'a Europe without frontiers can make proper use of its communications'.

Half a century later, in the 1990s, a number of books appeared by British Eurosceptics arguing that the origins of the European Union lay in ideas put forward by the Nazis during World War Two.[1] This belief arose because their authors had noted what appeared to be a striking resemblance between some of those ideas and features of the 'European project' as it had developed in the decades after the war. In particular they were struck by Nazi references during the war years to setting up a 'European economic community' and a single European currency.

The very fact that such an argument could be put forward was in itself a testament to the remarkable lack of knowledge, both among Eurosceptics and Europhiles, as how the post-war 'European project' actually came about. In particular it reflected a near-universal failure to understand how directly that 'project'

---

1 These included: Laughland, John (1997), *The Tainted Source – The Undemocratic Origins Of The European Idea* (London, Warner Books); Atkinson, Rodney, and McWhirter, Norris (1994), *Treason At Maastricht* (Newcastle-upon-Tyne, Compuprint); Atkinson, Rodney (1996), *Europe's Full Circle* (Newcastle-upon-Tyne, Compuprint); Mote, Ashley (2001), *Vigilance* (Hampshire, Tanner Publishing).

stemmed from ideas which long predated the rise of Nazism, and which were already well-established in the minds of men such as Salter and Monnet before the end of the 1920s. Certainly the re-emergence of the campaign to built a 'United States of Europe' in the years after the Second World War owed a great debt to ideas developed during the years of Hitler's dominance. But these drew nothing from the Nazis. They were developed by men fiercely opposed to Nazism: not least by some of those whose thinking had already been moving in this direction for over 20 years.

There was only one moment when it had seemed possible that the Nazi Party might embrace the cause of a 'United States of Europe'. This long preceded the Nazis' arrival in power in 1933, happening during the only period in the party's history when Hitler himself faced a serious rival for his leadership. In 1924, he had been imprisoned in the castle of Landsberg for his part in the previous year's abortive Munich *putsch* and, in his absence, his deputy Gregor Strasser, a talented organiser, had led the party to its first electoral success, winning 32 seats in the *Reichstag*.

Strasser was insistent that the Nazis must broaden out their base from Bavaria to other parts of Germany. In particular he won support from the then-young, left wing-inclined Josef Goebbels, for his view that the National Socialist Party must become both more national and more socialist in its appeal. In 1925 when the two men drew up a party programme, this reflected the cause then being promoted by Stresemann and Briand by calling for a 'United States of Europe', including a proposal for a single European currency.

In 1926, however, Hitler re-asserted his authority over the party, during a conference in Bamberg. Goebbels switched his loyalty from Strasser back to Hitler; Strasser's 'Programme for National Socialism' was rejected. Hitler was to eliminate his erstwhile rival in the 'Night of the Long Knives' in 1934. He himself never showed the slightest interest in any idea of a 'united Europe', other than one united under his own leadership by force of arms. Once he had risen to power in 1933, the only value he attached to the concept of 'Europe' was as the matrix of German culture, illustrated by his declaration at the Nuremberg Rally of 1937:

'Our country, our people, our culture and our economy have grown out of general European conditions. We must therefore be the enemy of any attempt to introduce elements of discord and destruction into this European family of peoples.' [2]

Embodying that desire to re-assert his nation's identity which was an inevitable reaction to the humiliations forced on Germany by France at Versailles, Hitler had already reversed one of those humiliations by marching his troops into the 'demilitarised' Rhineland in 1936. He was about to introduce further 'elements of discord' into the European family by his expansion into those other legacies of Versailles, Austria and Czechoslovakia, in 1938–1939. In September 1939, he advanced across another Versailles frontier, into the former German lands ceded to Poland in 1919. By the following spring and summer, as his armies swept through

2 Laughland, *op. cit.* p. 11.

Denmark, Norway, Belgium, Holland, Luxembourg and France, he was well on the way to building a 'united Europe' by means which would have had those 1920s idealists Stresemann and Briand recoiling in horror.

The twilight years of 'Europeanism'

As the twin shadows of Nazism and Fascism lengthened over Europe in the immediate pre-war years, the futility of the League of Nations had become ever more cruelly exposed, firstly by its failure to prevent Japan attacking Manchuria and China, by Italy seizing Abyssinia and then Hitler marching into the Rhineland, Austria and Czechoslovakia.

Coudenhove nevertheless continued his campaign for a 'United States of Europe' until a few months after the German-Austrian *anschluss* in 1938. Two years later, after the war had begun, he took refuge in New York, where he was to spend the war years proselytising for European unity, in a way which was to have considerable influence on post-war American attitudes to Europe.

In Britain some of the old League of Nations insiders who had been most enthusiastic for a 'United States of Europe' in the 1920s remained in close touch. Salter, who continued to work for the League until 1930, became in 1934 the Gladstone Professor of Politics at Oxford and a fellow of All Souls. In 1937 he was elected an independent MP for Oxford University. One close friend, since they met at the Paris peace conference of 1919, was the economist John Maynard Keynes; and he was later to recall how, during the 1930s, they had both been members of a 'small and secret committee' of leading economists which continued to advise successive prime ministers up to the outbreak of war.[3]

When the war started, Salter recalled, Keynes held weekly meetings at his house where they were joined by William Beveridge, the civil servant who was to shape the post-war expansion of the welfare state, and Walter Layton. He was economist, who in the early 1920s had been director of the League of Nations' Economic and Financial Section.[4] From 1923 to 1939 Layton had been an influential editor of *The Economist* and a fervent enthusiast for a federal Europe, a crusade he was to continue into the post-war era.

A like-minded friend of this circle was Lionel Curtis, who had been a leading member of the British delegation concerned at the Paris conference with setting up the League of Nations. At that time, he had invited a number of British and American delegates, mainly from Woodrow Wilson's League of Nations team, to form an Anglo-American society, out of which had come two 'think tanks', each destined to play an important behind-the-scenes role in lobbying for European integration over the following decades. In London in 1920 Curtis set up the Royal Institute of International Affairs, known as Chatham House. Its Washington counterpart was the Council on Foreign Relations (CFR).

In 1940, when Coudenhove arrived in the USA as a refugee, it was the CFR which arranged a position for him at New York University, where he held

3 Salter, *The Slave Of The Lamp, op. cit.* p. 85.
4 Salter, *op. cit.* p. 88.

graduate seminars on the problems of European federation. Through CFR contacts, he was given regular coverage in the *New York Times* and the *New York Herald Tribune*, whereby the idea of a 'United States of Europe' was during the war years to become increasingly familiar to influential American opinion.[5]

Another old friend with whom Salter was re-united shortly after the outbreak of war was Monnet. Following his lucrative spell in China, Monnet's career as a merchant banker had continued to be murky. On his return to America he had been investigated for tax evasion. In 1938 his company had even come under suspicion by the FBI for having laundered Nazi money, although this inquiry was called off without any charges being laid.[6]

At the outbreak of war in 1939, however, Monnet was back in Europe, where he was appointed chairman of the Franco-British Economic Co-ordination Committee, with the task of arranging contracts for war supplies in America and their shipment across the Atlantic. His vice-chairman, as parliamentary secretary to the new Ministry of Shipping, was Arthur Salter. Just as in 1914, the outbreak of war had brought the two men together in London and again for a very similar purpose.

In the spring of 1940, their task was made suddenly more urgent by the *blitzkrieg* launched by Hitler, first on Denmark and Norway, then on 10 May on Holland, Belgium and France. That morning Churchill became Britain's prime minister. Three weeks later came the Dunkirk evacuation and by mid-June it was clear France was going to fall. At this critical moment, Monnet came to play a central role in one of the more curious episodes of the war.[7]

On 14 June, General Charles de Gaulle, France's under-secretary for war, had arrived in London to arrange for shipping to transport the French government and as many French troops as possible to North Africa, to enable them to continue the war. There he met Monnet, who came up with the even more daring proposal that, to symbolise their determination to fight on, France and Britain should declare 'a Franco-British Union'. The two nations should be joined indissolubly as one, complete with a single government, joint armed forces, common citizenship and even a single currency.

The two men, along with Monnet's colleague Rene Pleven, had discussed this proposal with Sir Robert Vansittart, the former permanent head of the Foreign Office. The following day Vansittart, Foreign Secretary Lord Halifax and others put the plan to Churchill over lunch at the Carlton Club. Churchill was far from convinced, but when he raised it at Cabinet later that afternoon, he was surprised 'to see the staid, stolid, experienced politicians of all parties engage themselves so passionately in an immense design whose implications and consequences were not in any way thought out'.

The following morning, 16 June, the Cabinet met again to discuss the collapse of France, which was becoming more alarming by the hour. At any time, it

5 Jasper, William F. (1989), 'United States of Europe', *New American*, 5 (8), 10 April.
6 Fransen, *op. cit.*, p. 144.
7 This episode is largely reconstructed from the full account given by Churchill, W. S. (1952) in *The Second World War, Vol. II, Their Finest Hour* (London, Cassell), pp. 176–184.

seemed, the French government might surrender, and not least of the Cabinet's concerns was that this might give Hitler control of France's naval fleet, the fourth largest in the world. By the time the Cabinet reassembled that afternoon, Churchill had seen de Gaulle, now wholly behind Monnet's proposal and viewing such a dramatic gesture as the only hope of strengthening the hand of the French prime minister Paul Reynaud in stiffening his government's resolve. Halifax reported that Vansittart had again been in consultation with de Gaulle, Monnet and Pleven, and that they had produced a draft declaration, which de Gaulle was ready to take back that night to present to the French government.

Churchill's War Cabinet discussed the draft 'proclamation of an Anglo-French Union'. Only one substantive change was made to a text which had originated largely from Monnet, with Salter's assistance. Churchill struck out his reference to Britain and France adopting 'a common currency'. But otherwise the declaration was much as Monnet originally conceived it, including a provision for joint organs of defence, foreign, financial and economic policies. The two countries would have 'a single War Cabinet, and all the forces of Britain and France, whether on land, sea or in the air, will be placed under its direction'.[8]

After the draft had been approved by the War Cabinet, Churchill describes how he took it into the next room, where de Gaulle was waiting with Vansittart. 'The General read it with an air of unwonted enthusiasm', and communicated it by telephone to Reynaud at Bordeaux. If the French government approved, Churchill was ready to fly out with senior colleagues to discuss it the following day. But Reynaud's colleagues, led by Marshal Petain, reacted with violent hostility to what they saw as a trick to reduce France to the status of a mere 'British dominion'. A wave of anti-British feeling had swept official circles and public opinion in the wake of Dunkirk. 'We would rather have Hitler than be the slaves of England', some shouted in the halls of the prefecture of Bordeaux, again the temporary seat of the French government.[9]

Petain himself described it as 'fusion with a corpse': the corpse in his eyes being a doomed Britain. Admitting defeat, Reynaud resigned. He was succeeded by Petain, who promptly sued with Germany for a humiliating peace. It was thus Monnet's proposal which provided the final catalyst for France's surrender.[10]

Following France's fall, Monnet threw himself into transferring French contracts with America to the British war effort. Although he was now technically an 'enemy

---

8 The text of the Declaration Of Union is given by Churchill, *op. cit.*, p. 179. The draft showing a line through Monnet's proposal for a single currency is in the Public Record Office and was shown in the BBC documentary series *A Poisoned Chalice*, 1995.

9 Brombergers, *op. cit.*, p. 29.

10 Churchill describes how later that day he was visited by Monnet and de Gaulle in the Cabinet Room. Monnet did most of the talking, pleading that Britain should immediately send all her remaining fighter squadrons to France. Churchill 'could not do anything to oblige him'. As the two men left, de Gaulle, 'who had scarcely uttered a single word', turned back to Churchill, saying in English 'you are right'. Churchill thought to himself 'here is the Constable of France'. Little could he have guessed that, of the two Frenchmen, it would not be de Gaulle who would have the greater part in shaping the future history of Britain and Europe, but his voluble, intense colleague, whose suggestion, if accepted, could only have ensured defeat in the Battle of Britain. Behind the apparent altruism of his 'Anglo-French union', Monnet's real concern was the interest of France.

alien', Churchill appointed him as a member of the British Supply Council in Washington, personally signing his passport to give him entry to the US. There he was able to continue liaising with Salter on arranging contracts for war supplies in America for the British government.

In 1941 Churchill appointed Salter to head a British mission to Washington, to press on the Americans the need for a vast programme of new shipbuilding (this would eventually lead to the 'Liberty ships' which were to provide Britain with such a vital lifeline).[11] Between 1940 and 1943 (and again in 1944 to 1945) Monnet was based in Washington, where his talent for 'networking' soon won him influential friends in the US establishment, from Justice Felix Frankfurter of the Supreme Court to Dean Acheson, later to become US Secretary of State. Both men would lend active support to his European integrationist campaign in the post-war era. While in Washington in 1941, he met Paul-Henri Spaak. To him, he expounded his underlying philosophy for a united Europe and explained in rough outline plans for a European coal and steel union.[12]

As the tide of war swung in the Allies' favour, Monnet's attention turned increasingly to the shape of the Europe he wished to see emerging in the post-war era. At the end of February 1943, after the Allies had retaken French North Africa, he was sent by President Roosevelt to Algiers to arrange for arms shipments to the Free French forces. Here he found bitter rivalry developing between the two French generals who could claim to act as leader of the Free French, de Gaulle and Giraud. In his efforts to resolve this dispute, Monnet formed a close alliance with the politician sent out by Churchill to act as the British Cabinet's Political Representative in the Mediterranean, Harold Macmillan.

Macmillan records how he and Monnet had extensive conversations about the future of France and post-war Europe, and despite their reservations about de Gaulle's high-handedness, agreed he was the only man of sufficient stature to lead a government in exile. Between them they laid the foundations for what amounted to a provisional French government, the *Comité Francais de Libération Nationale* (CFLN), to be led by de Gaulle. Monnet was co-opted as a member, and for one of its early meetings, on 5 August 1943, he produced a memorandum which declared:

'There will be no peace in Europe, if the states are reconstituted on the basis of national sovereignty with all that implies in terms of prestige politics and economic protectionism. If the nations of Europe adopt defensive positions again, huge armies will be necessary again. Under the future peace treaty, some nations will be allowed to re-arm; others will not. That was tried in 1919; we all know the result....

The nations of Europe are too circumscribed to give their peoples the prosperity made possible, and hence necessary, by modern conditions. They will need larger markets. And they will have to refrain from using a major proportion of their resources to maintain "key" industries needed for national defence....

Prosperity and vital social progress will remain elusive until the nations of Europe form a federation of a "European entity" which will forge them into a single economic unit...

11 *Dictionary of National Biography 1971–80* (1985) (Oxford, Oxford University Press).
12 Spaak, Paul-Henri (1971), *The Continuing Battle: Memoirs Of A European* (Boston, Little, Brown and Company), p. 213.

Our concern is a solution to the European problem. The British, the Americans, the Russians have worlds of their own into which they can temporarily retreat. France cannot opt out, for her very existence hinges on a solution to the European problem....'[13]

Again Monnet was developing his vision of a Europe which could achieve lasting peace only if organised under a supranational authority sufficient to overrule the fractious impulses of national sovereignty. This would forge the member states into a 'single economic unit', based on integrating those 'key industries needed for national defence', such as coal and steel. It would also be a Europe in which he no more imagined the direct involvement of Britain than that of America or Russia.[14]

Festung Europa

In the late summer of 1942, Europe was politically more united than she had ever been. From the North Cape to the Mani in southern Greece, from the fishing ports of Brittany to the snowcapped peaks of the Caucasus 2,000 miles to the east, an unprecedented area was under the sway of a single political system. But within Hitler's 'Fortress Europe' three different groups of people were discussing the value of a 'united Europe' which might emerge after the war, each for their own reasons.

Hitler himself regarded talk of post-war European unity as a 'presumptuous irrelevance'. He had loathed the early European unity movement, despised the Briand-Stresemann policy of *rapprochement* and dismissed Coudenhove as 'everybody's bastard'.[15] He had banned 'European unity' associations as soon as he had the chance, together with the Esperanto language.

Lower down the Nazi hierarchy, however, there were some who spent the war years conceiving plans for the kind of unity to which Europe might aspire when the war was over. One such was Werner Daitz, a leading Nazi economist. He launched a Society for European Economic Planning and Macroeconomics (*Grossraumwirtschaft*), and produced a book, *What the New Order in Europe Brings to the European Peoples*. He was also one of many ideologues of the time who attacked the 'outmoded' notions of national sovereignty and the nation state. In 1938 Daitz had declared that the idea of the state derived from British political theory and the French Revolution. He held the nation to be small and selfish compared with the 'great common undertaking' which was Europe. 'The common interests of Europe take precedence over the selfish interests of nations', he declared.[16]

Another enthusiast for European unity was Hitler's foreign minister Joachim von Ribbentrop. In late 1942, he headed a Committee on the Restructuring of Europe, giving a number of academics and politicians free reign to create different scenarios for Europe's future development. But they did not represent official

13 Fontaine, Pascal (ed.) (1988), *Jean Monnet: A Grand Design for Europe* (Luxembourg, OOP).

14 Fransen, *op. cit.*, p. 89. Fransen read through the Monnet papers in Lucerne and records that it was at this time that Monnet first committed to paper his idea of creating a 'European state of heavy metallurgy'.

15 Lipgens, Walter (1985) *Documents on the History of European Integration. Volume 1, Continental Plans for European Union 1939–1945* (Berlin, Walter de Gruyter), p. 37. He cites *Hitlers Zweites Buch. Ein Dokument aus dem Jahr 1928*, p. 131.

16 Laughland, *op. cit.*, p. 14.

Nazi thinking. Nevertheless, Ribbentrop persevered, and in March 1943 he proposed inviting all heads of state of the occupied countries, along with Franco's Spain, to sign an instrument setting up a 'European confederation'.[17] Hitler's contemptuous response was to issue a decree requiring that 'the planning, preparation and execution of demonstrations of a European or international kind ... must cease'.[18]

A third Nazi functionary to favour European unity was Hitler's finance minister, Walther Funk. Like Daitz, he held that 'common interests' had to take precedence over particular ones. 'There must be a readiness to subordinate one's own interests in certain cases to that of the European community', he declared. He was charged with planning the reconstruction of the post-war economy within the framework of a 'New European Order' and a new world economy. To this effect he chaired a committee which produced a series of essays, which were still coming out as late as January 1945. These set out ideas for a *Europaische Wirtschaftgemeinschaft* (European Economic Community), strictly under German leadership and including a proposal for a single currency.[19]

Funk's proposals were widely publicised in the occupied countries, to persuade their peoples that co-operation with Germany could reap economic benefits in the future. There was no evidence, however, of any systematic attempt to put them into practice. Indeed any attempt to impose on Europe a common currency would have caused Germany serious problems. The occupied countries were being charged the costs of their occupation: in the case of France twenty million Reichsmarks per day. Repayments were calculated at a much-devalued exchange rate, magnifying the debt to such an extent that forty-two percent of the total foreign contribution to the German war-time economy ended up coming from France.[20] A single currency would seriously have undermined this advantageous arrangement.

Whatever the rhetoric of some of his followers, Hitler had not the slightest intention of giving up control. As Goebbels put it: 'It is only right and just that we take the leadership of Europe definitely into our hands... The German people ... have actually won the hegemony of Europe and have a moral right to it'.[21] Nevertheless, as the Germans came to terms with having to wage a prolonged war, Goebbels recognised that the rhetoric of 'Europeanism' could serve a useful propaganda purpose. He wrote in his diary on 12 April 1943:

17 Adolf Hitler: decree, 4 November 1942. *Akten zur Deutschen auswärtigen Politik* (ADAP), E, IV, pp. 222–224, extract reproduced in Lipgens, *op. cit.*, p. 109.

18 Laughland, *op. cit.*, pp. 29–30.

19 It was the use of this term which was to prompt some Eurosceptic writers to claim a direct parallel between Funk's 'European Economic Community' and the 'European Economic Community' set up in 1957. But this is based on an imprecision of terminology. Funk's word *gemeinschaft* is used to describe a community which has a sense of 'belonging together', sharing values, loyalties and perhaps kinship. This aptly describes what the Nazis had in mind, bringing together the Aryan peoples in a Germanic empire, with the outer regions pressed into service as vassals. The later 'European Economic Community' was not so much a *gemeinschaft* as a *gesellschaft*, a society of equals, based on the same framework of rules to control their competing interests.

20 Burleigh, Michael (2000), *The Third Reich – A New History* (London, Macmillan), p. 278.

21 Lochner, Louis P. (editor and translator) (1948), *The Goebbels Diaries 1942–43* (New York, Doubleday & Company Inc.), p. 83.

'It is a curious fact that we shun the phrase "European co-operation", just as the devil shuns Holy Water. I can't understand why that is true. So obvious a political and propaganda slogan ought really to become a general theme for public discussion in Europe. Instead, we avoid it wherever possible.'[22]

The purpose, as he conceived it, was to create a sense of 'European identity', to make 'Europeans' aware of their collective difference from the alien cultures with which they were at war, those of Britain, the United States and above all Stalin's Soviet Union. The further the tide of war turned, the more prominent this theme became, projecting Germany as the protector of the 'European' culture against the barbarians from the east. But such professed enthusiasm for the 'European ideal' was simply a device to encourage occupied countries to 'volunteer' their young men to join the *Waffen-SS* and to mobilise their economies against the Bolshevik hordes in what was increasingly styled a 'European war of liberation'.[23]

The propaganda had its effect. In June 1944, Fernand de Brinon, Vichy's Secretary of State, affirmed: 'We will help Germany on every front and in every way to preserve the West, its enlightenment, its culture, its traditions'.[24] Admittedly this came from a man known before the war as a 'crook with an irresistible love of money', who, as the Allies invaded France in 1944, escaped to Germany with four million francs in bank notes and a sizeable quantity of jewellery.[25] He was executed by the French in early 1947.[26] Nevertheless, in the end, 50,000 non-Germans from every part of occupied Europe fought on the Eastern front, under the banner of the *Waffen-SS*. Many believed they were defending 'Europe', rather than serving the interests of Germany.[27]

Fascists and collaborators

Despite the tendency of some post-war writers to see the Nazis and their various allies across Axis-dominated Europe as a homogenous entity, the many disparate groups had their own distinct ideologies and ambitions. Nevertheless running through their rhetoric on the theme of European unity were two persistent themes. The first was a desire to proclaim the end of the nation state and its absorption into a greater European identity; the other a sense that the emerging 'New Europe' could now recover its old self-confidence and compete with any power in the world.

In 1943, for instance, Mussolini's education minister Giuseppe Bottai wrote of nationalism being 'the ossification of a political principle that has served its time ... it acts as a hindrance to the general advance of civilisation'.[28] Italy's finance minister Alberto de Stefani wrote:

22 *Op. cit.*, p. 325.
23 Burleigh, *op. cit.*, p. 430.
24 Algazy, J. (1984), *La Tentation Neo-fasciste En France 1944–65* (Paris, Fayard), p. 56.
25 Werth, Alexander (1957), *France 1940–1955* (London, Robert Hale), p. 127.
26 Novick, Peter (1968), *Resistance Versus Vichy* (London, Chatto & Windus), p. 184.
27 Burleigh, *op. cit.*, pp. 430–431.
28 Cited in Laughland, *op. cit.*, pp. 17–18.

'Nationalities do not form a sound basis for the planned new order ... there is only hope for peace by means of a process which on the one hand respects the inalienable, fundamental patrimony of every nation but, on the other, moderates these and subordinates them to a continental policy... A European Union could not be subject to the variations of internal policy that are characteristic of liberal regimes.'[29]

Stephani's reference here to 'liberal regimes' was essentially a code for Britain and America. Thus he was simply reiterating the general line of Fascist propaganda, dressed in 'European' clothes. This is more evident in the views of another Fascist opponent of the nation-state, Camillo Pellizzi, editor of the magazine *Civiltà Fascista*. He believed the Fascist principle would overcome the 'particularism' of Europe's nation-states, writing:

'The Axis is, or can be, the first definite step towards surmounting ... that typically European phenomenon which we call the nation, with its inevitable, one might say physiological corollary of nationalism... One cannot 'create Europe' without the nations or against them: we must create it from the different nations, while subduing national particularism as far as may be necessary.[30]

In the occupied countries, many politicians and intellectuals who had advocated the cause of European unity since the 1920s now convinced themselves working with the Nazis was the way to achieve it. Thus, one of the leading collaborators in Vichy France, Jacques Benoist-Mechin, secretary of state for Franco-German relations from June 1941 to September 1942, declared that France's policy of collaboration required 'the abandonment of old illusions'. She would be able to join the new Europe, he asserted, 'only when she abandons all crumbling forms of nationalism – which was itself in reality only an anachronistic particularism – and when she takes her place in the European community with honour'.

Similarly, another ardent Vichyite, the writer and philosopher Pierre Drieu La Rochelle, who had been a strong supporter of European unity since the early 1920s, espoused the Fascist cause. He argued that 'it is the only way of defending Europe against itself and against other human groups'. However, before committing suicide at the time of the liberation of France, he wrote, 'Perhaps all this is a lot of eyewash: the truth may be that I'm scared of being kicked around by the police'.[31]

In Belgium, the Walloon collaborator Léon Degrelle, a leader of the Fascist Rexist movement, saw his country becoming part of a recreated Burgundy (the 'middle kingdom' between France and Germany) and a full partner of the Third Reich. Yet his original pre-war credo had been ultra-nationalistic and he had became overtly Fascist only in 1939. Under the Nazi occupation his brand of Fascism mutated into unashamed collaborationism, proclaiming a pan-European vision of the New Order.[32] Another Rexist leader, Pierre Daye, in 1942 wrote a tract, *Europe for the Europeans*, in which he saw Nazi Europe not as a political

---

29 *Op. cit.*, p. 18.
30 *Op. cit.*, p. 19.
31 Werth, *op. cit.*, p. 126.
32 Griffin, Roger (1993), 'Europe for The Europeans: Fascist Myths of the New Order 1922–1992', Occasional Paper (No. 1) by the Humanities Research Centre (Oxford, Oxford Brookes University).

entity in its own right but more as a bastion against Communism and the divisive foreign policies of Great Britain.

Vidkun Quisling, the Norwegian collaborationist leader, argued that Europe would be strong and peaceful only if united: 'We must create a Europe that does not squander its blood and strength in internecine conflict, but forms a compact unity. In this way it will become richer, stronger and more civilised, and will recover its old place in the world.' He wanted to see a Pan-Germanic Federation with a federal flag and the Fuhrer as president.[33]

Nothing in all this flood of rhetoric, however, provided any practical model for the type of political integration which was to emerge after the war. As one historian put it:

'Such pan-European illusions were actively fostered by the Nazis themselves. Clearly the bulk of the Third Reich statements relating to pan-Europeanism disseminated by the Nazis in the occupied territories can be dismissed as cynical propaganda calculated to encourage, if not the active co-operation, then the passive acquiescence of the new vassals. Neither Hitler, nor many of his leading hierarchs such as Goebbels, had the slightest intention to compromise absolute German hegemony through the creation of a European confederation, "subsidiary" or otherwise.'[34]

Thus, the collaborationists' real purpose was to clamber onto the sledge of Europe's ruling power in the hope of being given a share in the spoils. There was nothing in their rhetoric which would spill over into the movement for European integration as it was to develop in the post-war years. Nazi thinking was an ideological *cul-de-sac*. The practical steps to realise the dream of a 'United States of Europe' would derive their inspiration from those who, during the war, regarded themselves as the Nazis' sworn enemies. Some of those ideas were to emerge from within occupied Europe itself, from those who spent the war years most obviously at odds with everything Nazism and Fascism stood for.

The resistance

Outside the grip of the Nazis and their allies, the inter-war dreams of European unity did not die. They went underground. In each occupied country resistance movements emerged. If this movement as a whole had any unifying philosophy, it was a determination to seek a new beginning in the post-war reconstruction of Europe. Central to this was the concept of a united Europe. In common with the pre-war 'Pan-Europeanists' (and that of the Nazis when it suited them), they held nationalism and national pride to be responsible for past European wars. The prevailing ethos supported the creation of new structures to transcend historical boundaries.

This much was openly declared, long before the end of the war, by resistance groups in Czechoslovakia, France, Italy, the Netherlands, Poland and Yugoslavia, and even in Germany itself. But the most strident supporters of European unity were the Italian Communists, who were at the core of the anti-Fascist movement.

33 Cited in Laughland, *op.cit.*, p. 16.
34 Griffin, *op. cit.*

In this respect the major figure to emerge during the war years, who was eventually to make a very significant contribution to the development of the European Union, was the Italian, Altiero Spinelli. Born in 1907, he joined the Communists at the age of 17 and had been active in opposing Mussolini's Fascism. In 1928, he was arrested and imprisoned, spending 12 years in jail before eventually being sent to a prison on the Mediterranean island of Ventotene, 30 miles west of Naples. While in prison, he broke with Communism and embraced the cause of European unity, composing in 1941 what became known as the 'Ventotene Manifesto', under the title *Towards a Free and United Europe*.[35] This was to become one of the basic texts of the European federalist movement.

Spinelli's text addressed the familiar theme of creating a 'federal' Europe, but now in terms of exploiting the continent-wide chaos which he predicted would inevitably arise when the war was over. Like so many others, Spinelli wanted to see 'the definitive abolition of the division of Europe into national, sovereign states'. To achieve this, he called on his followers to foment revolution. True to his political ideology, he proclaimed, 'the European revolution must be socialist: i.e., its goal must be the emancipation of the working classes and the creation of more humane conditions for them'.

Spinelli was coy about the structures of his 'European federation' but definitely had in mind an all-powerful, supranational authority. This he saw developing into a 'United States of Europe', with its own constitution and armed forces. It would have the power to ensure that its 'deliberations for the maintenance of common order are executed in the individual federal states'. In turgid prose, he argued that this state would only retain the autonomy it needed 'for a plastic articulation and development of political life according to the particular characteristics of the various peoples'. His views on the part played by democracy, however, were very clear: 'During revolutionary times, when institutions are not simply to be administered but created' he insisted, 'democratic procedures fail miserably'.

For a model of how Spinelli's 'European Federation' would come about, one need look no further than this passage of the Ventotene Manifesto:

'During the revolutionary crisis, this movement will have the task of organising and guiding progressive forces, using all the popular bodies which form spontaneously, incandescent melting pots in which the revolutionary masses are mixed, not for the creation of plebiscites, but rather waiting to be guided.

It derives its vision and certainty of what must be done from the knowledge that it represents the deepest needs of modern society and not from any previous recognition by popular will, as yet non-existent. In this way it issues the basic guidelines of the new order, the first social discipline directed to the unformed masses. By this dictatorship of the revolutionary party a new State will be formed, and around this State new, genuine democracy will grow.' [36]

35 Jenkins, Lindsay (1996), *Godfather Of The European Union – Altiero Spinelli* (London, Bruges Group).
36 Leiden University History Department History of European Integration, *www.let.leidenuniv.nl/history/rtg/res1/index.htm*

In other words, 'the people' were not to be involved in the construction of the new state. Popular assent would be sought only when the project was all but complete. At that moment their 'crowning dream' would be the calling of a 'constituent assembly', to 'decide upon the constitution they want'. The drawing up of the constitution would be the final act in the emergence of the 'United States of Europe'. Only then, within the framework of the new state which had been brought into being, would 'democracy' be permitted to resume.

In July 1941, Spinelli's manifesto was smuggled to the mainland. His ideas came to be adopted by the Communist-dominated Italian Resistance as a whole, leading to the formation in 1943 of the European Federalist Movement. This spread the message to groups in other countries, giving rise to a series of meetings in neutral Switzerland, culminating in a major conference in Geneva in July 1944, attended by activists from Denmark, France, Italy, Norway, the Netherlands, Poland, Czechoslovakia and Yugoslavia. There was even a representative from a secret anti-Nazi group within Germany itself.

At the Geneva conference, the collective resistance movements produced a declaration which claimed that their wartime struggle would give their countries 'the right to take part in the reconstruction of Europe on the same basis as the other victorious powers'. In those countries, they declared, 'the life of the peoples which they represent must be based on respect of the human individual, on security, on social justice, on the complete utilisation of economic resources for the benefit of the whole and on the autonomous development of national life'.[37]

These aims, the conference considered, 'cannot be fulfilled unless the different countries of the world agree to go beyond the dogma of the absolute sovereignty of the state and unite in a single federal organisation'. However, injecting a faint note of reality, the declaration went on: 'The lack of unity and cohesion that still exists between the different parts of the world will not allow us to achieve immediately an organisation that unites all civilisations under a single federal government'. This meant that, in the immediate post-war period, 'the European problem must be given a more direct and more radical solution'.[38]

This 'direct solution' would consist of a European 'Federal Union'. Only thus could the German people be allowed to participate in the life of the new Europe without endangering the rest. As before, the 'Union' would have its written constitution and a supranational government directly responsible to the peoples of Europe. It would control its own army, with no national armies permitted. It would also have its own court, with sole jurisdiction over constitutional matters and exclusive rights to arbitrate in conflicts between the central authority and member states.

It would be another 40 years before Spinelli would make his central contribution to the shape of the European Union as it finally emerged. But the ideas on which this was based were all there in the declaration of 1944, originating from the few pages he had scribbled in his island prison, at a time when Hitler's 'Thousand Year Reich' had seemed the undisputed master of Europe.

---

37 Vaughan, Richard (1976), *Post-war Integration In Europe* (London, Edward Arnold), p. 17.
38 *Ibid.*

Chapter 3

Two Tries That Failed: 1945–1949

'More than ever we are convinced that we are right in proclaiming the necessity
for complete European Union. But ... it is a disgrace that Europe had to wait for
a word of command from the other side of the Atlantic before she realised where
her own duty and interest lay.'

Dr Henri Brugmans, Chairman of the European
Union of Federalists, August 1947

The official history of the European Union, as can be seen from the European
Commission's *Europa* website and any number of other publications, invariably
begins with the period immediately after the Second World War. The Commission's version opens with the historic speech made by Winston Churchill in
the Great Hall of Zurich University on 19 September 1946. After painting a
typically robust picture of the 'plight to which Europe has been reduced' by the
'frightful nationalistic quarrels originated by the Teutonic nations', Britain's
revered wartime leader held out his vision of how the hundreds of millions of
inhabitants of this unhappy and ruined continent might 'regain the simple joys
and hopes which make life worth living'. To achieve peace, freedom and an end to
'all the crimes and follies of the past', he said, 'we must build a kind of United
States of Europe'.[1]

Churchill was to renew his message in three more major speeches in the years
that followed, in London in 1947, at The Hague in 1948, and in Strasbourg in
1949. These rallying calls by Europe's only statesman at that time of world stature
would later be claimed as having been the inspiration for the steps which eventually led to the European Union: a project in which it would also be claimed that
Churchill wished Britain to play a central part. In every respect this is based on a
misreading of the facts.

For a start there was a crucial distinction between the type of united Europe
envisioned by Churchill and that which would begin to take shape in the 1950s.
He made this clear by his references at Zurich to the 'pan-European union' which
had been worked for by that 'famous French patriot and statesman Aristide
Briand', and to that 'immense body which was brought into being amidst high
hopes after the First World War – the League of Nations'. At all times, Churchill
was essentially looking back to that internationalist idealism of the 1920s, associated with Briand, Stresemann and Coudenhove: a 'United States of Europe' based
on an alliance of sovereign states.

1 *The Times*, 20 September 1946.

As we shall see, however, it was precisely this type of 'intergovernmentalism' which the founders of what was to be the European Union regarded as their greatest obstacle. Indeed, when their project was finally launched, the man chiefly responsible for it was openly dismissive of Churchill's type of 'United Europe'. Monnet was convinced that the goal could only be reached in a wholly different way.

Secondly, as Churchill consistently made clear both at Zurich and later, he saw any 'united Europe' rooted in 'a partnership between France and Germany'. There was no question of Britain's direct participation. 'In all this urgent work', as he put it,

'France and Germany must take the lead together. Great Britain, the British Commonwealth of Nations, mighty America, and, I trust, Soviet Russia … must be the friends and sponsors of the new Europe, and must champion its right to live.'

In 1947, at the Albert Hall in London, he conjured up his vision of a 'Temple of World Peace', which would have 'four pillars': the USA; the Soviet Union; a 'United States of Europe'; and, quite separately, 'the British Empire and Commonwealth'. Ironically, this was almost the only point on which Churchill and Monnet were agreed. If a 'United States of Europe' was to be brought about, it would be without Britain.

However, the most fundamental misconception about how the European Union came into being stems from the myth that its intellectual genesis emerged after the Second World War. All the essential ideas which lay behind the moves to unite Europe at that time had in fact been conceived in the 1920s, before the rise of Hitler, as a way to prevent a recurrence of the First World War. In that sense they had already failed in their original purpose, in that they had been unable to prevent the Second World War.

More significantly, by the time these ideas were disinterred after 1945, the political balance of Europe and the world had changed out of all recognition. The chief problem they were designed to solve, the national rivalry between France and Germany, paled into insignificance beside a new, much greater threat, identified by Churchill in his other famous speech of 1946, given at Fulton, Missouri. Then he spoke of how, from Stettin on the Baltic to Trieste on the Adriatic, 'an iron curtain has descended across the Continent'.[2] In that respect, the efforts to dissolve Europe's ancient national enmities in a new union were specifically addressed to solving a problem which no longer existed.

---

2 Although it was Churchill's Fulton speech on 5 March 1946 which made this phrase famous, the term 'iron curtain' had been used many times before, not least in a widely reported article by Josef Goebbels in *Das Reich* on 25 February 1945, in which he warned that German surrender would lead to Soviet occupation of most of the Reich and eastern Europe, dividing the continent by 'an iron curtain' of 'enormous dimensions'. Churchill himself, in a cable to President Truman on 4 June 1945, wrote 'I view with profound misgivings … the descent of an iron curtain between us and everything to the eastward'. Another phrase was given general currency through the Fulton speech when Churchill urged the continuation of 'a special relationship between the British Commonwealth and Empire and the United States'.

The golden age of inter-governmentalism

As the world emerged into an uncertain peace, following the dropping of the first nuclear weapons on Japan in August 1945, there was a general mood of cautious optimism, expressed above all in a renaissance of internationalist idealism. The defeat of the Axis powers had required international co-operation on an unprecedented scale. Reflected in the famous picture taken in February that year at Yalta, showing Stalin seated alongside the dying President Roosevelt and Winston Churchill, the world political scene was dominated by what were known as the 'Big Three', the three powers which had played the leading role in the allied victory: the USSR, the US and Britain with her Commonwealth.[3]

The end of World War Two was to act as even more a spur to schemes of international co-operation than the end of the Great War 25 years earlier. Many of the international institutions which were to provide a framework for the post-war world were called into being at this time. Foremost among them was the United Nations, set up in 1945 to replace the League of Nations (which was only formally dissolved in 1946).

The first UN General Assembly was held in London in January 1946 under the presidency of Belgium's foreign minister Paul-Henri Spaak. From the Bretton Woods conference of 1944, as instruments of post-war financial and economic reconstruction, came the International Monetary Fund and the World Bank. In October 1947, indirectly through the UN, came the signing of the General Agreement on Trade and Tariffs (GATT) designed to work for the progressive liberalisation of world trade.

All these were intergovernmental structures based on co-operation between sovereign governments. As with the League of Nations before them, their prime mover, closely supported by Britain, was the United States of America. But, this time, there was to be no American retreat into isolationism. The US was firmly committed to play a central role, as was symbolised by the fact that the permanent headquarters chosen for the new United Nations was not in neutral Switzerland, like that of the defunct League. It was in the heart of New York (where its General Assembly building on the East River was to be designed by that most Utopian of all 1920s architects, Le Corbusier).

There was of course one reason above all why the US was to find it impossible to repeat its 1920 retreat into 'splendid isolation'. The Second World War had produced a complete reshaping of the balance of power. At the start of that war the leading western European nations, with their imperial possessions scattered across every continent, were still powers which, politically and militarily, were of world-rank. But by the war's end, the world was bestridden by the two new super-powers, the US and the USSR: one already armed with nuclear weapons, the other soon to possess them, representing two political ideologies in potentially deadly

---

3 The scale of the contribution made by Britain and the Commonwealth was reflected in the fact that by 1944 the Commonwealth armed forces totalled 8.7 million, of which Britain contributed 4.5 million. This compared with US armed forces of 7.2 million. (Williams, Neville (1967), *Chronology of the Modern World 1763–1965* (New York, David McKay Co.).

conflict. Nowhere was this more obvious than on the continent of Europe which, far from being the centre of world politics, was to become merely the central cockpit in which that greater rivalry was acted out.

However, it was not yet evident just how deep this division of Europe was to become. Initially, it had been agreed at the Moscow conference of October 1944 that most of central and eastern Europe, then being liberated from Nazi occupation by the Red Army, would fall after the war into 'the Soviet sphere of influence'. But when hostilities ended several of Europe's pre-war democracies, including Czechoslovakia, Poland, Hungary and Romania, re-established democratic, multi-party forms of government. Only in Bulgaria were the political intentions of the Communists, under the shadow of Soviet occupation, already more obvious. Yugoslavia was placed under one-party Communist rule by Tito, then still Stalin's ally. Albania followed suit, and played an active part in promoting an attempted Communist take-over of Greece only narrowly averted by Britain's armed intervention in the Greek civil war of 1944–1945.

The immediate task confronting the western half of the continent, including all those occupied countries which had been liberated by the Western allies, was to re-establish self-governing institutions and to rebuild their economies. Here too, there initially seemed grounds for optimism, despite the presence in Italy and France of large Communist parties, which were to provide a constant reminder of how fragile the re-born democracies of western Europe might prove if economic recovery was not successful.

An early reflection of that optimism was contained in a confidential paper presented to the British Cabinet in the summer of 1945 by none other than Arthur Salter, who had now become Churchill's Chancellor of the Duchy of Lancaster in the post-war 'caretaker government'. His chief task had been to report on the state of the economies of 'liberated Europe'.

Salter's conclusions were surprising. After touring western Europe, he reported that 'the material destruction is much less, and the resources available for restoration are much greater, than could have been anticipated'. Except in 'the limited areas of actual conflict', he had found the industrial infrastructures of France, Holland, Belgium and even Germany itself still surprisingly intact. In general, western Europe had enough food, coal, port facilities and other raw materials to meet its essential needs. The most serious obstacle to recovery was the breakdown of the distribution system, in particular the extensive damage to railways. This, he suggested, could be overcome by use of surplus army trucks. 'All that liberated Europe needs', he concluded, 'represents an effort, in terms of manpower and materials, which is small by comparison with what was required by actual combat.'[4]

Scarcely had Salter presented his report, however, than the government to which he belonged was replaced in the electoral landslide which, in July 1945, dismissed Churchill from office. The Labour victory, on the most radical Socialist programme ever presented to the British electorate, was itself a vivid expression of

---

4 Salter, *The Slave Of The Lamp*, *op. cit.*, pp. 207–211.

the post-war mood of idealism. The vision held out to the British people was that a new and better world could now be created, based on international co-operation and, at home, a massive expansion of state ownership and state controls. Its aim was to build a 'better, fairer and more efficient society'. The peace was to be 'planned' just as had been the victory.

Britain's new government, under Clement Attlee, launched a radical restructuring of Britain's economy, based on the belief in centralised planning and nationalisation. The Bank of England and a wide range of basic industries, including coal, iron and steel, the railways and public transport, were taken into public ownership.

An equally ambitious and in some ways very similar programme was being launched in France. The man in charge was Salter's old friend, Monnet. As a member of de Gaulle's National Liberation Committee, in 1943 he had been appointed as 'Commissioner for Armament, Supplies and Reconstruction'.[5] On 30 August 1944, when General de Gaulle set up a provisional French government in newly-liberated Paris, Monnet was full of ideas on how to restructure the French economy.

After VE Day in May 1945, he realised that a key would be American financial help. He therefore returned to Washington for some months, where, by effective lobbying, he talked the US government into providing a loan of $550 million. A useful ally in this was a young Washington lawyer, George W. Ball, who in the years that lay ahead was to become one of his closest and most useful collaborators.[6]

Armed with this aid, Monnet was able to return to France in November 1945, in charge of the new *Commissariat du Plan*, set to implement a four-year programme of reconstruction and modernisation. As in Britain, the 'Monnet Plan', as he himself called it, was based on state planning, controls and wholesale nationalisation, starting with the Bank of France and the railways. After de Gaulle stepped down as France's President in January 1946, Monnet had become arguably the most powerful man in France.[7]

However, fully engaged in reconstruction as they were, in the first two years after the end of the war, there was little talk of bringing about 'European unity' from the governments of western Europe. The exception was a plan agreed by the governments-in-exile of Holland, Belgium and Luxembourg, to set up a common customs area between their three countries, Benelux. The idea had been inspired by Monnet's attempt at Anglo-French union in 1940,[8] and was finally ratified on 29 October 1947.

During these two years, however, the vision of creating a 'United States of Europe' did break into the headlines, from two unexpected directions. One was the speech made in Zurich in September 1946 by Churchill himself, now out of power and not averse to creating a stir on the international stage. He came up with

---

5 Taken from Monnet's own entries to *Who's Who* (London, A. & C. Black).
6 Ball, George (1982), *The Past Has Another Pattern* (New York, Norton and Co.), p. 77.
7 Milward, A. S. (2002), *The Rise And Fall Of A National Strategy* (London, Frank Cass), p. 37.
8 Brombergers, *op. cit.*, p. 31.

a startlingly unconventional proposal: the setting up of a 'Council of Europe'. The other, not dissimilar proposal came from the country which over the next few years was to play a key part in promoting Europe's political integration: the United States of America. That it should have come from America itself was partly the result of the inter-war idealism when a group of internationally-minded Americans had set up the Council for Foreign Relations (CFR) in 1920.

The CFR prospered during the years of America's isolationism, perversely, as a consequence of the State Department's withdrawal from world affairs. This had led to serious under-staffing and the CFR had begun to fill the gap with a series of position-papers addressing major foreign policy issues of the day. Generously funded by the Rockefeller Foundation and other industrial corporations, it had carried out detailed examinations of 'mechanisms for the economic integration of Europe'. Over 120 influential figures, including academics, business leaders, politicians and civil servants drawn from across the Roosevelt administration, were involved in this programme, holding 362 meetings and producing no fewer than 682 documents.

In 1939, it set up a series of 'War and Peace Study Groups', and when Coudenhove Kalergi had arrived in New York as a refugee from Hitler, the CFR arranged for him to spend the war years teaching 'European integration' at New York University.

The cause of European unity was also actively promoted in Washington in the early war years by Monnet. Not only did he win sympathy from such key US establishment figures as Dean Acheson, George Kennan and Justice Felix Frankfurter, but several times met President Roosevelt himself.

As peace approached, and Washington began to think about how Europe might be rebuilt, politically and economically, the 'Europeanists' had succeeded in convincing established liberal opinion that the solution to Europe's post-war problems would lie in some form of political unification. There was, however, an important proviso: the US would not be prepared to support continued European colonialism.[9] Europe had to learn to live within her own boundaries.

All this was reflected when, in 1946, one of the CFR's study teams, headed by David Rockefeller and Charles M. Spofford, a senior lawyer, produced a paper entitled 'The Reconstruction of Europe', which was widely circulated in US government circles. In March 1947, after active lobbying by Coudenhove, two Senators, William Fullbright and Elbert D. Thomas, piloted a resolution through both houses of the US legislature that 'Congress favours the creation of a United States of Europe'.

To attract public support for the resolution, CFR members orchestrated an intensive media campaign. On 17 March, *Life* magazine, whose publisher, Henry Luce, was a leading CFR member, proclaimed: 'our policy should be to help the nations of Europe federate as our states federated in 1787'. Sumner Wells (CFR) of the *Washington Post*, owned by another CFR member, Eurgen Meyer, wrote:

---

9 An exception to this was the loan negotiated by Monnet for French reconstruction in 1946 (Ball, *op. cit.*, p. 77.)

'Europe desperately needs some effective form of political and economic federation.' Boston's *Christian Science Monitor*, another strong CFR supporter, advised: 'the US could hardly impose federation on Europe, but it could counsel … It could mould its leading and occupational policies towards upbuilding a single continental economy'. The *New York Times*, the most influential CFR mouthpiece of all, produced on 18 April a magisterial editorial proclaiming: 'Europe must federate or perish'; while the *St Louis Post Dispatch* declared that 'for Europe it is a case of join – or die'.[10]

However, what gave the real impetus to American support for European integration was the darkening international climate, and it was this which was bring the United States fully into the European arena.

The Marshall Plan: The first try that failed

The trigger for US interest was primarily its fear of Communist take-overs in Italy and France, where the Communists briefly became the largest single party in the Assembly. At its root was the economic dislocation caused by the unusually severe winter of 1946–1947, which undermined that initial post-war optimism about the potential for recovery of western Europe's economies. Washington began to sense serious concern over Communist ambitions in Europe.

Ironically, however, the first country to run into real economic crisis was Britain: over-stretched by her still enormous military commitments and by the efforts her people had made through six years of war, much of it financed by huge American loans under the wartime 'Lend-Lease' programme which had cost the US $48.5 billion.

No sooner had the Japanese war come to an end in August 1945 than the US government abruptly terminated Lend-Lease. The impact on Britain's economy was compared by John Maynard Keynes to that of 'a financial Dunkirk'. Keynes himself, then the most respected economist in the western world, was dispatched to America to negotiate a replacement. In December 1945, he managed to secure loans of $3.75 billion from the US and a further $1.25 billion from Canada. But the terms were harsh, demanding that sterling be made freely convertible with the dollar, thus seriously undermining Britain's special trading relationships with her colonies and Commonwealth.

In the first year after the war, Britain's adverse trade balance soared to a then-enormous £298 million (the following year it was to rise still further, to £443 million). So grave did the situation become that, over that freezing winter of 1946–1947, the Labour government was forced to export coal to reduce the balance of payment crisis. Yet fuel stocks in England were so low that power stations had to cut back drastically on generating hours or shut down altogether. Factories producing goods for export had to stop work or curtail production. For the ordinary citizen, the austerities of everyday life were now even more exacting than they had been

10 Jasper, William F. (1989) 'United States of Europe' in *New American*, 5 (8), 10 April.

during the war, the drastic rationing of clothing and food now being extended even to bread.

Already, as this financial crisis mounted, a government committee had reported in July 1946 that the cost of supporting the British zone of Germany in the year 1946–1947 would be over £80 million,[11] a sum Britain could not afford. The only remedy was economic integration of the occupation zones. The British and US authorities had already begun the rebuilding of German self-government centred on the *Länder*, the regional divisions of Germany dating back to the Weimar Republic. They now agreed that the British and American zones should be fused, creating the so-called 'bizone' from 1 January 1947, with the US paying for three-quarters of its financing.[12]

Further burdened by the costs of her military and political responsibilities in the Eastern Mediterranean, Britain then informed Washington on 21 February 1947 that she could no longer continue providing financial aid to the governments of Greece and Turkey (in addition to her substantial military commitment to Palestine, where the British mandate was now coming under severe strain from the campaign by Jewish nationalists and terrorist groups to set up a state of Israel).

This precipitated crisis meetings between members of Congress and State Department officials. Their outcome was a statement by Truman's Under-Secretary of State Dean Acheson propounding what would later become known as the 'domino theory'. Facing the possibility of a Communist take-over in both Greece and Turkey, he declared that more was at stake than just those countries. If they fell, Communism might spread south to Iran and even perhaps to India.

A support package was hastily devised and, addressing a joint session of Congress on 12 March 1947, Truman asked for approval for $400 million in military and economic assistance for Greece and Turkey. 'It must be the policy of the United States', he declared, 'to support free peoples who are resisting attempted subjugation by armed minorities or by outside pressures.' He thus established what became known as the 'Truman Doctrine', which was to guide US diplomacy for the next 40 years.

This also marked the beginning of America's cold war foreign policy, at a time when the fragile *détente* between the Western allies and the Soviet Union was visibly crumbling. The events of 1947 were to mark a decisive turning point in the relations between Communist 'East' and non-Communist 'West'. As local Communist parties registered significant gains in elections in Romania, Hungary and Czechoslovakia, it had become clear that Stalin had every intention of turning the countries of central Europe into a Soviet empire. In October a Warsaw conference was to set up the 'Cominform' (Communist Information Bureau), to co-ordinate the activities of all Europe's Communist parties. The so-called 'Big Three' negotiations between America, the Soviet Union and Britain on the future of Germany were getting nowhere, and in December 1947 the talks were

11 Approximately £2 billion at 2003 values.
12 Woodhouse, C. M. (1961), *British Foreign Policy Since The Second World War* (London, Hutchinson & Co.), pp. 16–18 and pp. 110–112.

to collapse irrevocably, over Soviet demands that Germany should pay massive reparations.

It was against this background of a Europe rapidly polarising between Communist and Western camps that the US Secretary of State George Marshall early in 1947 organised a team of officials, led by one of his most senior advisers, George Kennan. His task was to map out an ambitious new strategy for Europe's economic support. Three of the key figures in putting together this study were members of the Council of Foreign Relations, Dean Acheson, Will Clayton and George Kennan.[13] In particular Kennan and Clayton had extensive consultations with the man now in charge of France's economy, their wartime Washington friend Jean Monnet.[14] From their combined efforts came the European Recovery Programme, better known as the 'Marshall Plan'. This was announced by Marshall on 5 June 1947, in a speech at Harvard University. Crucially, to avoid any appearance of the US dictating European policy, Marshall couched the offer of help in these terms:

'It is already evident that, before the United States government can proceed much further in its efforts to alleviate the situation and help start the European world on the way to recovery, there must be some agreement among the countries of Europe as to the requirements of the situation and the part those countries themselves will take in order to give proper effect to whatever action might be undertaken by this government. It would be neither fitting nor proper for this government to undertake to draw up unilaterally a programme designed to place Europe on its feet economically. This is the business of the Europeans. The initiative, I think, must come from Europe. The role of this country should consist of friendly aid in the drafting of a European programme and the later support of such a programme so far as it may be practical for us to do so. The programme should be a joint one, agreed by a number, if not all of the European nations.'[15]

In response to Marshall's declaration, 16 European nations agreed to attend a conference in Paris on 12 July 1947, to form a group known as the Committee for European Economic Co-operation (CEEC). The CEEC's chairman was a British civil servant, Oliver Franks. But its key figure was his vice-chairman Jean Monnet, aided by his deputy Robert Marjolin and his former Washington lawyer George Ball, who had come to Paris in August to work for Monnet, advising how the CEEC case for economic aid could most effectively be presented to Washington.[16] The result of their work was a report on 12 December that, to cover the period 1948–1951, the 16 nations would need $19.1 billion. Seven days later, on 19 December, after making provision for emergency aid to France, Italy and Austria, President Truman submitted to Congress his 'European Recovery Bill', requesting $17 billion over four years.

The Marshall Plan has generally been viewed as an altruistic gesture by the USA to help its impoverished Western allies in their hour of need. However, also under-

13 Bundy, William P., *www.foreignaffairs.org/generalInfo/history.html.*
14 Brombergers, *op. cit.*, p. 62.
15 *www.marshallfoundation.org/about_gcm/marshall_plan.htm*
16 Ball, *op. cit.*, pp. 77–78.

lying it were strong commercial interests. Europe represented for America 'an enormous market, of several hundred million persons' which she could not afford to lose.[17] Economic support for Europe thus represented an opportunity for US manufacturers and suppliers desperate to find outlets for their production after orders for war *materiel* had dried up. As with the earlier Truman package for Greece and Turkey, the proffered aid was by no means solely financial. It included grain, machinery and vehicles produced in America.

Additionally, US corporations had recognised that there was an opportunity to buy up valuable European assets at knock-down prices: a form of intervention at which de Gaulle expressed particular alarm. Europe's economic weakness might also enable the US government to exert pressure on European governments to adopt more 'liberal' trading rules, thus easing the path for American exports.

An even more significant element in the Marshall Plan, however, was that, from the outset, it included a major political component. Despite its apparent 'hands off' approach, the conditions imposed on recipient countries were deliberately designed to promote a federal Europe, the creation of which had for the State Department now become a Holy Grail. At one bound, thanks not least to effective lobbying by the CEEC's vice-chairman Monnet, the most enthusiastic integrationist power in post-war Europe had become the United States.[18]

No sooner had the Marshall Plan been announced than it was greeted with particular excitement by many groups which, since Churchill's Zurich speech in September 1946, had been evangelising for the cause of European political and economic unity. In Britain itself, on 14 May 1947, Churchill had launched at the Albert Hall his all-party United Europe Movement, with his son-in-law, Duncan Sandys MP, as its president, and a committee which included two members of the Labour Cabinet and several future Conservative Cabinet ministers, among them Macmillan. Churchill repeated his call for a 'United States of Europe', of which the USA, the USSR and Britain could be sponsors, and advocated the re-integration of Germany into the Western world.

Similar associations had been formed in France and Germany. A European Union of Federalists had been set up, under the chairmanship of a leading Dutch Socialist and pacifist, Dr Henri Brugmans. Its objective was to bring together groups in Britain, Belgium, France, Italy, Luxembourg, the Netherlands and Switzerland, under the aegis of a new committee, the International Co-ordination of Movements for the Unification of Europe Committee.

When Marshall announced his Plan in June, support for it was quickly orchestrated across western Europe. Among those most active in this operation were several figures who had been enthusiasts for the integrationist cause since they were wartime exiles in London. These included Paul van Zeeland, more than once Belgium's prime minister, and Joseph Retinger, a Polish émigré, who early in 1947

---

17 Brugmans, Dr Henri (1948), *Fundamentals Of European Federalism*, foreword by Lord Layton (London, The Federal Union), p. 4.

18 Aldrich, Richard L. (2001), *The Hidden Hand – Britain, America and Cold War Secret Intelligence*. (London, John Murray (Publishers) Ltd), pp. 342 and 344. Aldridge also cites Thorne's *American Political Culture*, pp. 316–320 and Hogan's *Marshall Plan*, pp. 213–214 and 332–333.

had formed an Independent League for Economic Co-operation (ELEC). In March 1947, ELEC's leaders, headed by Van Zeeland, had already met in New York to discuss closer links with the United States, and they were now recruited to promote the Marshall Plan. A memorandum supporting the Plan was approved by ELEC on 30 June 1947 in Paris and sent to all European governments.

Another prominent advocate for the Plan was Brugmans, who, addressing a conference of his Union in August 1947, said, after referring to the Marshall Plan:

'More than ever we are convinced that we are right in proclaiming the necessity for complete European Union. But…it is a disgrace that Europe had to wait for a word of command from the other side of the Atlantic before she realised where her own duty and interest lay.'[19]

Within months Brugmans' speech was being widely circulated among 'European federalists', updated with a reference to the three events of 1947 which had 'determined international life: the Marshall Plan, the breakdown of the Conference of the Big Three and the setting up of "Cominform".'

Citing Proudhon's plea of 1866 that 'to end the irreparable abuse of sovereignty' what was needed above all was 'the dismemberment of sovereignty', Brugmans called for the setting up of 'supranational' authorities. They would administer hydro-electric power from the Alps, the European railway system and 'the first nucleus of autonomous European administration of coal and heavy industry'. This call was echoed in a foreword to the British edition of Brugman's speech by Arthur Salter's friend Lord Layton, who wrote that 'the whole of Western Europe can in fact be regarded as a single, highly interdependent industrial unit' crying out for supranational control.

Despite this orchestrated support from Europe and intense lobbying in Washington, the US Congress remained hostile to Marshall's proposal. Again it was pressure from events elsewhere which turned the tide. In February 1948, the 'Prague coup' established complete Communist control over Czechoslovakia. This event had profound repercussions throughout the Western world, lending substance to Acheson's 'domino theory'. Congressional resistance to the Marshall Plan collapsed. On 13 March, it was supported by the Senate and on 2 April it was approved by the House of Representatives with a massive 329:74 majority. Nevertheless, Congress refused to write a blank cheque. Aid was limited to $5.3 billion for one year, at the end of which approval had to be sought for continued funding.

For pro-integrationist lobbyists on both sides of the Atlantic, an important lesson had been learned: rhetoric on protecting western Europe from the threat of Communism was likely to be the most effective shaping American opinion. John McCloy, soon to become US High Commissioner for Germany (and later chairman of the CFR, from 1953 to 1970), admitted: 'one way to assure that a viewpoint gets noticed is to cast it in terms of resisting the spread of Communism'.[20] The

19 Brugmans, *op. cit.*, pp. 3–4.
20 Cited in Jasper, *op. cit.*

French also found the Communist threat highly advantageous. Mendès-France commented: 'The Communists are rendering us a great service. Because we have a "Communist danger", the Americans are making a tremendous effort to help us. We must keep up this indispensable Communist scare'.[21]

The chief instrument chosen by Washington to promote its new policy of European integration was a new organisation, formed on 16 April 1948, to administer the distribution of Marshall Plan funding. This was the Organisation of European Economic Co-operation (OEEC). The French government, heavily influenced by Monnet, pushed for the new body to be given an executive council with supranational powers and a permanent secretariat. The committed integrationist Paul-Henri Spaak, now once again Belgium's prime minister, was appointed its director general. This was vociferously opposed by the British Foreign Secretary, Ernest Bevin, supported by Sweden and Switzerland, who also had serious reservations about the 'political' components of the plan.

Through their efforts, the OEEC remained strictly intergovernmental, controlled by a 'Council of Ministers' making decisions on the basis of unanimity. Monnet's verdict could not have been more withering: 'the OEEC's nothing: it's only a watered-down British approach to Europe – talk, consultation, action only by unanimity. That's no way to make Europe.'[22] The first serious attempt to set up a large-scale supranational European organisation had failed.

The Council of Europe: the second try that failed

In 1948, following the breakdown of the 'Big Three' talks on the future of Germany, relations between 'East' and 'West' in Europe seemed to be worsening by the month. Less than a month after the Prague Coup, on 17 March, Britain, France and the three 'Benelux' countries signed a mutual defence treaty in Brussels. Three months later, in June, the great powers were to be plunged, over Berlin, into their most serious crisis since the end of the war.

Before the eruption of this crisis, however, came another significant landmark in the campaign for European political unity. In May 1948, Brugmans and his European Union of Federalists organised in The Hague a vast 'European Congress', which to their delight was chaired by Winston Churchill. Among the 800 delegates attending were several former and future prime ministers, including Alcide de Gasperi of Italy, Robert Schuman of France and Harold Macmillan of Britain; 29 former foreign ministers; and even a delegation from west Germany, led by the man soon to become its first Chancellor, Dr Konrad Adenauer.[23]

Taking up Churchill's proposal in Zurich, the congress called for the creation of a Council of Europe, to draw up plans for the political and economic integration of Europe. The congress was too large and unwieldy to reach any firm decision on

---

21 Galtier-Bossiérer, J. (1950), *Mon journal dans la grande pagaie* (Paris), p. 187. Cited in: Werth, *op. cit.*, p. 351.
22 Ball, *op. cit.*, p. 81.
23 Horne, *Macmillan 1894–1856, op. cit.*, pp. 313–314.

the composition of such a Council and no formal proposals were adopted. One thing, however, was agreed: that a European Movement should be set up, to co-ordinate on an international basis the different groups now promoting European integration, its task to 'break down national sovereignty by concrete practical action in the political and economic spheres'.[24]

This decision was indirectly to trigger one of the more curious episodes in the history of the European integration movement. Shortly after The Hague Congress, two of the most active campaigners for integration, Josef Retinger and Churchill's son-in-law Duncan Sandys, went to America to lobby for support for their campaign for European unity. Here they met two key figures, William J. 'Wild Bill' Donovan, founder in 1947 of the CIA, and his colleague Allen Dulles, later to become head of the CIA under President Eisenhower (and whose brother John Foster Dulles was to be Eisenhower's Secretary of State). These two very senior members of the US intelligence community had recently joined in support of Coudenhove to form a Committee for a Free and United Europe. But, as a result of the meetings with Sandys and Retinger, Coudenhove, who considered that he alone should lead any unity movement, was now dropped, amid some acrimony. A new organisation was set up, the American Committee on United Europe (ACUE).

From this time on, as recent academic research has established,[25] the ACUE was used as a conduit to provide covert CIA funds, augmented by contributions from private foundations such as the Ford Foundation and the Rockefeller Institute, to promote the State Department's obsession with a united Europe, in what one historian has called a 'liberal conspiracy'.[26]

Over the next few years, ACUE funding was secretly channelled to a range of individuals and organisations working for European integration, from politicians such as Paul-Henri Spaak and trade unions to such influential British magazines as Lord Layton's *The Economist* and the intellectual monthly *Encounter*. However, the major beneficiary of ACUE funding was the European Movement. Between 1949 and 1960, it was kept afloat almost entirely on $4 million of CIA money, these contributions amounting to between half and two-thirds of the Movement's income.[27]

Even while these negotiations were secretly afoot in Washington, however, the eyes of the world were suddenly focused in June 1948 on the most serious international crisis since the Cold War began. In January 1948, the British and US authorities in Germany had proposed that western Germany must move towards

24 Boothby, Lord (1978), *Boothby – Recollections Of A Rebel* (London, Hutchinson), p. 264.
25 *Cf.* Joshua Paul of Georgetown University, Washington, reported in *Daily Telegraph*, 19 September 2000, and Richard Aldrich, *The Hidden Hand, op. cit.*
26 See Coleman, Peter (1989), *The Liberal Conspiracy: The Congress For Cultural Freedom And The Struggle For The Mind Of Europe* (New York, The Free Press).
27 ACUE funds were also used for a range of other purposes in Europe, including the financing of anti-Communist parties. In 1948, for instance, the CIA paid $10 million to support the Italian electoral campaign of Alcide de Gasperi a staunch supporter of European integration. This substantial contribution was intended to help avert an Italian civil war in which the Communists might prevail.

full self-government, based initially on the German-run economic council they had set up in their biozone, with a second chamber consisting of representatives of the *Länder*.

To meet French objections to this move, a six-nation conference was called in London, attended by representatives of the three occupying powers and the Benelux countries. On 7 June, it agreed to proposals for west Germany's political development on a federal system, based on the *Länder*, along with a new single currency, the *Deutschmark*. On French insistence, it also agreed to an International Ruhr Authority, to control the coal and steel industries of the Ruhr.

What provoked the crisis was the decision of the three allied powers to introduce the *Deutschmark* into West Berlin. In those pre-Wall days, access to the different zones was not restricted. The Soviet authorities, fearful that the new currency would soon come to be used throughout the city, and aware that control of a currency brought economic control,[28] imposed a blockade, cutting off road and rail access to the three western zones. Disaster for millions of West Berliners was only averted by the Allies, who for nearly a year would manage to keep the city's population alive by flying in immense quantities of food, fuel and other vital supplies in what became known as the Berlin airlift.

This first 'Berlin crisis' confirmed how serious the Soviet threat at the heart of Europe had become and triggered negotiations on a comprehensive solution to the whole question of Western Europe's security. Even the French government recognised that the Soviets presented a greater threat than a resurgent Germany, and pressed for greater US involvement in the defence of Europe. This was to lead to the signing in Washington on 4 April 1949 of the North Atlantic Treaty, committing the US, Canada, Britain, France, Italy, the Benelux countries and four other western European nations (Norway, Denmark, Portugal and Iceland) to set up an integrated military organisation for the defence of non-Communist Europe.

It was the resultant organisation, NATO, the North Atlantic Treaty Organisation, with its headquarters in Fontainebleau, which was to guarantee the peace of Europe for the next 40 years. And its successful establishment was above all a triumph of intergovernmentalism: independent nations co-operating in a way which did not detract from their sovereignty.

While the NATO negotiations had been proceeding, active steps had also been taken to set up the Council of Europe called for by the conference of The Hague. This was the first time since the 1920s that a proposal put forward by Europe's various federalist groups had been taken up at government level when, in January 1949, the governments of France, Great Britain and the Benelux countries, together with Denmark, Ireland, Italy Norway and Switzerland, began talks on the form such a Council might take.

Ernest Bevin and the British government were extremely sceptical of its overall aim, and the discussions were led by the French, aided by the European Movement, with discreet off-stage encouragement from Monnet's old friend Dean

---

28 This was a lesson the advocates of a European 'single currency' were quickly to learn.

Acheson. Himself a fervent integrationist, he had succeeded Marshall as US Secretary of State on 7 January. Britain sought to dilute the proposals, arguing instead for a permanent conference of foreign ministers. In order to encourage British participation, which was regarded as essential, not least by Washington, a compromise was reached. The Council would divide its role: one part would be a Committee of Ministers, meeting behind closed doors, the other a Consultative Assembly, drawn largely from members of existing national parliaments, meeting in public.

On 5 May 1949, the Statute of the Council was signed in London by the 10 governments of the United Kingdom, France, Belgium, The Netherlands, Luxembourg, Italy, Ireland, Denmark, Norway, and Sweden. In the same month the European Movement formally came into being. Duncan Sandys and Leon Jouhaux of France became co-presidents; Josef Retinger its secretary-general.[29]

The first session of the Council began in Strasbourg on 10 August 1949. It was attended by senior politicians from each of the participating countries, including leading members of the British and other governments. The star was indisputably Churchill, who was given the freedom of the city and made a memorable speech to a rapturous crowd of 50,000 in Strasbourg's main square (telling his fellow delegate Harold Macmillan 'this is the best fun I've had for years and years').[30]

The first president of the Assembly was Spaak, who had resigned as Belgian prime minister after a defeat in the general election only a week before the first session. He took his seat to preside over a series of discussions on how the Council could further the cause of integration,[31] keen on the one hand to promote integration but, on the other hand, anxious not to lose touch with the British. With the exception of Richard Mackay, an Australian-born Labour MP, none of the British delegation advocated British entry into a Federal Europe.[32]

In the second session, the 'federalists' launched a 'major offensive', seeking to establish supranational authorities in the 'key sectors' of defence, human rights, coal, steel and power. But it was from the debates that clear divisions began to emerge, with sustained opposition to integration from British and Scandinavian delegates. Macmillan, then one of the Conservative delegates. explained that the British opposition was, above all else, 'a matter of temperament', a preference to

---

29 Retinger was also given CIA funding to set up an organisation known, from the Dutch hotel in which it first met in May 1954, as the Bilderberg Group. The purpose of this organisation, which continues to this day, was to stage regular meetings, deliberately shrouded in secrecy, between top politicians, businessmen and lawyers, to strengthen links between the US and western Europe. Among those who attended the first meeting, as guests of Prince Bernhard of the Netherlands, were senior European politicians and, from the US, David Rockefeller of the CFR and George Ball. Many of its members played an active role in the history of European integration and decades later the supposed influence of the Group was to become the focus of a popular conspiracy theory. But, as such, the Group played no direct part whatever in the integration process which began with Monnet's 'Schuman Plan' in 1950, four years before the first Bilderberg meeting took place.

30 Horne, Alistair (1988), *Macmillan 1894–1956* (London, Macmillan), p. 315.

31 Urwin, Derek W. (1995), *The Community Of Europe – A History Of European Integration Since 1945* (second edition) (London, Longman), p. 35.

32 Spaak, *op. cit.*, p. 209. See also, Aldrich, *op. cit.*, pp. 355–356. Mackay's activities were funded generously by the ACUE, with CIA approval.

work empirically when dealing with practical problems, rather than setting out 'general principles' which were then applied to practical issues. The British took the view that those who wished to take the federal path should do so, but they had no intention of following. At that stage, Spaak avers, the idea of 'little Europe' took shape, comprising France, Germany, Italy and the Benelux countries.[33]

By the third session, in the autumn of 1951, when the Conservatives had succeeded Labour and Churchill had replaced Attlee, there were some hopes that his party might be more 'Europe-minded'. But, in power, the Conservatives proved no more enthusiastic for integration than their predecessors. Sir David Maxwell-Fyfe (later to become Lord Kilmuir) broke the news. The Churchill government was ready to give its friendly support to the movement for European integration, but there was no question of the British taking an active part. Spaak finally concluded that the Council would never be anything more than a talking shop and came to realise that 'we must do without Britain's support if we were to make any headway'. He resigned as president on 11 December 1951, by then sharing Monnet's view that Britain would not consider joining until a united Europe was created.[34]

Already, a third bid to give Europe a supranational government was under way; and this one would succeed.

---

33 Spaak, *op. cit.*, pp. 211–212.
34 Spaak, *op. cit.*, pp. 219–220 and p. 225.

Chapter 4

'An Almost Mystical Conception': 1950–1951

'Not just a piece of convenient machinery. It is a revolutionary and almost mystical conception.'   Harold Macmillan on Monnet's 'Schuman Plan'[1]

Through the late 1940s, one man had stood more or less apart from the abortive efforts to set up a 'government for Europe'. Monnet was now nearing the end of implementing his four-year plan for the 'modernisation' of France. But, as he was to recall in his memoirs two decades later, he had watched the successive failures of the OEEC and the Council of Europe with a sense of resigned detachment, only too certain that neither of them could

'... ever give concrete expression to European unity. Amid these vast groupings of countries, the common interest was too indistinct, and common disciplines were too lax. A start would have to be made by doing something more practical and more ambitious. National sovereignty would have to be tackled more boldly and on a narrower front.'[2]

If Monnet was sure that something much 'more practical and ambitious' was needed to achieve the desired goal, however, then events in the late spring of 1950 conspired to create precisely the opportunity he was looking for.

During 1949, West Germany had finally emerged to self-government under the Chancellorship of Konrad Adenauer. Under its Basic Law, passed on 8 May 1949, the new Federal Democratic Republic, or FDR, was based on a federation of the eleven highly decentralised *Land* governments which, on British insistence, retained considerable power, guaranteed by a constitutional court. In crucial respects the federal government, centred in Bonn, could not act without the consent of the *Länder*. In particular, all international treaties had to be ratified by the *Länder* through their legislative assembly, the *Bundesrat*. The largest and most powerful of the *Land*, Bavaria, had actually voted against the new constitution, for not reserving even greater power to the *Länder*. Decades later, this structure was to play a part in the history of the European Union that no one could have foreseen.

At the time, however, the new Germany, under the guidance of Ludwig Erhard, was already showing signs of a remarkable economic recovery. This raised the question of how the new nation should be assimilated into the western European

1 Horne, *op. cit.*, p. 319.
2 Monnet, *op. cit.*, pp. 273–274.

community. At the Council of Europe in August 1949 Churchill had shocked many delegates by proposing that she should be given the warmest of welcomes. Two of the western occupying powers, the USA and Britain, wanted to see her continue on the road towards full economic recovery and nationhood as soon as possible. But this had provoked a deep rift with France, which wanted to continue exercising control over the German economy, for fear that she might once again become too strong a political and economic rival.

The argument centred on that old bone of contention, the coal and steel industries of the Ruhr, heartland of Germany's economy and formerly the arsenal of her war machine. In 1948, France had demanded the setting up of an International Ruhr Authority, which would enable French officials to control Germany's coal and steel production and ensure that a substantial part of that production was diverted to aid French reconstruction. It was a curious echo of France's policy after the First World War. Naturally the new West Germany was bitterly opposed to such an authority. Equally so were the other two occupying powers, America and Britain.

For over two years this dispute had festered, without resolution. But in the spring of 1950 the US Secretary of State Dean Acheson finally lost patience. He issued France with what amounted to an ultimatum. On 11 May there would be a foreign ministers' meeting in London; and unless the French could offer a satisfactory compromise proposal, the USA would impose a solution on all parties.

This gave Monnet the opportunity for which he had been waiting. For years he had dreamed of building a 'United States of Europe', beginning by integrating the coal and steel industries, and setting up a supranational authority to run them. This was the idea first put forward in the 1920s, by Coudenhove and Loucheur, and partly implemented by Mayrisch in 1926. It was the idea Monnet himself had outlined to Spaak in 1941 and in his Algiers memorandum in 1943. But what Monnet had in mind was that the coal and steel industries, not just of France and Germany but of other western European countries, should be placed under the direction of a supranational authority: just as over dinner in Paris in 1917 he and Salter had come up with a similar plan for the control of allied shipping.

When Monnet came to commit his plan to paper, he was obviously troubled by how much he dare reveal of its real underlying purpose. Before getting to its final stage, it went through nine separate drafts. In the first, the pooling of coal and steel was regarded as 'the first step of a Franco-German Union'. The second opened it up to the 'first step of a Franco-German Union and a European federation'. By the fifth draft, this had been changed to 'Europe must be organised on a federal basis. A Franco-German Union is an essential element is this'. The seventh demanded that 'Europe must be organised on a Federal basis'. But, by the final draft, almost all this was missing. All he would allow himself was a reference to the pool being 'the first step of a European federation', a vague term which could mean different things to different people.[3]

Although what Monnet really had in mind was the creation of a European entity with all the attributes of a state, the anodyne phrasing was deliberately chosen

3 Fransen, *op. cit.*, pp. 96–97.

with a view to making it difficult to dilute by converting it into just another inter-governmental body. It was also couched in this fashion so that it would not scare off national governments by emphasising that its purpose was to override their sovereignty.[4]

Once his memorandum was complete, Monnet's next problem was how to get it adopted. He could not act as the champion of his own plan. As a natural behind-the-scenes operator, his style was always to act indirectly. He needed to win over very senior support in the French government. His initial thought was the prime minister, George Bidault, and he therefore handed his memorandum to Bidault's closest aide, asking for it to passed on. In the memorandum, Monnet wrote of the 'German situation' becoming a cancer that would be dangerous to peace. For future peace, he wrote, the creation of a dynamic Europe is indispensable:

'We must therefore abandon the forms of the past and enter the path of transformation, both by creating common basic economic conditions and by setting up new authorities accepted by the sovereign nations. Europe has never existed. It is not the addition of sovereign nations met together in councils that makes an entity of them. We must genuinely create Europe; it must become manifest to itself...'[5]

Alas for Bidault, who thereby missed his chance of immortality, the memorandum did not reach him. Frustrated, because time was short, Monnet looked around for another candidate. On 4 May, he lunched with Bernard Clappier, chief assistant to Robert Schuman, France's foreign minister. The meeting was fortuitous. Clappier and his master were well aware that the foreign ministers' meeting set for 11 May was only a week away, and Schuman still had no idea of what to offer to placate Acheson. His own officials had only been able to offer a version of that solution to the 'Ruhr problem' which had been imposed in 1919. Monnet knew that, if Schuman could be presented with a more imaginative proposal, he might welcome it with huge relief.

As a potential advocate, Schuman had other advantages. Born in 1886 in Luxembourg to a German mother, he was fluent in both German and French, having read law at the universities of Berlin, Munich and Bonn. He had then moved to Alsace Lorraine when it was under German rule, which meant that in 1914 he had been recruited into the German army. Yet in the Second World War, when Alsace Lorraine was again part of Germany, he had, as a French citizen, been arrested by the Gestapo. He was thus a perfect witness to the need to resolve the Franco-German conflict.

Clappier agreed to pass Monnet's memorandum to his minister as soon as possible, catching him while he was sitting in a train on his way to Metz for the weekend. When Schuman returned to Paris, after studying the document, he had adopted the plan wholeheartedly. It had now become the 'Schuman Plan', although in reality it was not his at all. In the final analysis, he was not even committed to it, except as a device to get him off a hook.[6]

---

4 *Ibid.*
5 Reproduced in Vaughan, *op. cit.*, p. 55.
6 Fransen, *op. cit.*, p. 97.

Once Schuman had agreed, the contents of the Plan were passed by his office in great secrecy to the German chancellor, Konrad Adenauer, in the hope of securing his provisional agreement. Other governments, especially the British, were not told. According to Professor Bernard Lavergne, a prominent political commentator of the time, who was to publish a highly critical study of the plan:

'The curious thing was that M. Bidault, the Premier, was – at least, at first – not at all favourable to the Plan which, in early May, was suddenly sprung on him by his Foreign Minister, M. Schuman. And oddly enough – though this was typical of M. Schuman's furtive statesmanship and diplomacy – neither was M. François-Poncet, the French High Commissioner, nor the Quay d'Orsay, or even the French Government, properly informed of what was going on during the days that preceded the "Schuman bombshell" of 9 May.'[7]

However, 'as a result of a curious coincidence', Dean Acheson was already on his way to the summit in London, and had decided to go via Paris to confer informally with Schuman. By another 'coincidence', Monnet was present at their meeting. As Monnet disingenuously put it, 'courtesy and honesty obliged us to take Acheson into our confidence'.[8] The Plan was also presented to the French Cabinet, but only in a most perfunctory way:

'Only three or four ministers were informed about it (the Plan), and when, finally, on 8 May, the Council of Ministers met, no serious discussion took place at all. Schuman gave them a rough sketch of the Plan, and, without really knowing what it was all about, they gave it their blessing.'[9]

Schuman then took an audacious step. He would announce 'his' plan by appealing directly to the peoples of Europe, through the media. In a radio broadcast on 9 May 1950 – today officially commemorated as 'Europe Day' – he revealed Monnet's plan to the world. 'World peace', he began,

'... cannot be safeguarded without the making of creative efforts proportionate to the dangers which threaten it. The contribution which an organised and living Europe can bring to civilisation is indispensable to the maintenance of peaceful relations. In taking upon herself for more than 20 years the role of champion of a united Europe, France has always had as her essential aim the service of peace. A united Europe was not achieved and we had war.

Europe will not be made all at once, or according to a single plan. It will be built through concrete achievements which first create a de facto solidarity. The coming together of the nations of Europe requires the elimination of the age-old opposition of France and Germany ...

With this aim in view the French Government proposes that action be taken immediately on one limited but decisive point ... it proposes that Franco-German production of coal and steel as a whole be placed under a common High Authority, within the framework of an organisation open to the participation of the other countries of Europe. The pooling of coal and steel production should immediately provide for the setting up of common foundations for economic development as a first step in the federation of Europe.'

7 Lavergne, Bernard (1952), *Le Plan Schuman* (Paris), pp. 14–15. Cited in Werth, *op. cit.*, pp. 479–480.
8 Monnet, *op. cit.*, p. 301.
9 *Ibid.*

After describing how 'the solidarity in production thus established will make it plain that any war between France and Germany becomes not merely unthinkable, but materially impossible', he went on to say that this would help simply and speedily to achieve 'that fusion of interest which is indispensable to the establishment of a common economic system'.[10]

This was the 'Schuman Declaration' which now occupies pride of place on the EU's *Europa* website as the document 'which led to the creation of what is now the European Union'. Yet, according to one historian, although the plan was immediately greeted with great excitement by the press, the curious thing was that literally nobody knew exactly what it was about, not even Schuman.[11]

According to a much later account by Roy Denman, a senior Foreign Office civil servant and apologist for the European Union, the British prime minister Clement Attlee 'received the French proposal with ill-grace'.[12] In fact, of course, the British government did not 'receive' it at all. They had been sent a summary only hours before the public broadcast and learned of the full text only from the broadcast. Attlee was extremely annoyed, and had every right to be. Not only was France's behaviour wholly undiplomatic, after an earlier incident, Attlee had specifically asked that no decisions involving Germany be taken before the foreign ministers' conference in London, which was about to begin two days later.[13] Furthermore, when he heard that Acheson had been informed about the plan in advance, he suspected – not without justice – that the Americans and the French had been colluding.

Yet, on the basis of these deceptions, what Monnet called his 'silent revolution' had started. There could now be no turning back without massive and adverse political consequences.

The wider response

As Monnet anticipated, Adenauer endorsed the plan. There was little else he could do. To reject what appeared to be a magnanimous offer from the French would have not been politically astute, and there were compelling reasons for its acceptance. Monnet was correct in his assumption that Adenauer saw in the plan a way Germany might reassert partial control of its industry. And, as Monnet also well knew, Adenauer was highly sympathetic to the idea of European unity. In 1948 he had attended the United Europe Congress in The Hague, where the Congress had declared: 'European nations must transfer and merge some of their sovereign rights so as to secure common political and economic action'. Afterwards, Adenauer had observed: 'In truth, in [the unification movement] lies the salvation

---

10 Leiden University History Department History of European Integration site, *op. cit.*
11 Werth, *op. cit.*, p. 478. The 'excitement' was not universal. Journalist Raymond Aron, in the *Manchester Guardian*, wrote: 'One may ask how it is that an idea as banal as this should now be accepted as something vital and new.' (30 May 1950).
12 Denman, Roy (1996), *Missed Chances – Britain And Europe In The Twentieth Century* (London, Cassell Publishers Ltd), p. 187.
13 Duchêne, *op. cit.*, p. 201.

of Europe and the salvation of Germany'.[14] Then, in March 1950, Adenauer had proposed, during an interview with a journalist, that France and Germany should unite as one nation. Their economies would be managed as one, their parliaments merged, their citizenship held in common.[15]

Adenauer's extravagant proposal had not been taken seriously; but two months later came the Schuman Plan. In ensuring a favourable response Monnet's tactics had been immaculate. In fact Adenauer's initial enthusiasm cooled somewhat when he learned that Monnet was behind the Plan, fearing that the real aim was to promote French interests at the expense of Germany. However, during a meeting between the two men on 23 May, Monnet assured him of absolute equality between nations. Only then did Adenauer relax, declaring, 'I regard the implementation of the French proposal as my most important task. If I succeed, I believe my life will not have been wasted'.[16]

Germany would at this stage have welcomed the participation of the British, as a counter to possible French dominance; and a formal invitation was extended to the British government to take part in talks on what was described as 'a plan to have a plan'. Even Schuman would probably have preferred British involvement. But that was the last thing Monnet wanted.

Without prompting, Britain's prime minister Attlee had in any case decided there was no way in which Britain could accept that 'the most vital economic forces of this country should be handed over to an authority that is utterly undemocratic and is responsible to nobody'. The Cabinet minutes of 2 June 1950 stated:

'Our position was different from that of the other European countries by reason of our Commonwealth connections, and we should be slow to accept the principle of the French proposal ... especially as it appeared to involve some surrender of sovereignty.'

The Treasury's view was, 'It is not in our interests to tie ourselves to a corpse.' Labour's National Executive Committee asserted that Western Europe lacked the 'civic and administrative traditions' essential to democratic socialism.[17] A formal note was sent to the French government, stating:

'... it remains the view of His Majesty's Government that to subscribe to the terms of the draft communiqué ... would involve entering into an advance commitment to pool iron and steel resources and to set up an authority, with certain supreme powers, before there had been a full opportunity of considering how these important and far-reaching proposals would work in practice. His Majesty's government are most anxious that these proposals should be discussed and pursued but they feel unable to associate themselves with a communiqué which appears to take decisions prior to, rather than as a result of, intergovernmental discussions ...[18]

---

14 Schwarz, Hans-Peter (1981 and 1983), *Die Ära Adenauer, 1949–1957* and *Die Ära Adenauer 1957–1963*; Vols II and III of *Geschichte der Bundesrepublik Deutschland* (Stuttgart, Deutsche, erlags-Anstalt). Cited in Williams, Charles. (2000), *Adenauer – Father Of The New Germany* (London, Little, Brown and Company), pp. 331–332.

15 Williams, *op. cit.*, p. 358.

16 Monnet, *op. cit.*, p. 311.

17 Labour Party (1950), *European Union* (London), pp. 7 and 9.

18 Cited in *Anglo-French Discussions Regarding French Proposals for the Western European Coal, Iron and Steel Industries* (1950), Command Paper 7970 (London, HMSO).

This was precisely the response Monnet had expected. On the basis of Britain's past record and commitment to intergovernmentalism, he had anticipated that they would oppose the supranational element which was the very core of his plan. He had thus deliberately engineered Britain's exclusion, by the simple expedient of making joining the talks conditional on accepting the supranational principle as non-negotiable, and by setting an impossibly short deadline of 2 June, during the Whitsun holiday, for agreeing to this condition.

History records that, as the deadline approached, Attlee and his Chancellor of the Exchequer, Sir Stafford Cripps, were out of London and could not be contacted. Herbert Morrison, as acting-prime minister, was tracked down to a restaurant after having spent the evening at the theatre. Asked for a decision, he had famously remarked: 'The Durham miners won't wear it.'[19] A thinly attended Cabinet confirmed Morrison's reaction.

In that context, only the previous year the government had nationalised Britain's iron and steel industries. It would seem curiously untimely then to hand over their control to another body, which had no concern for them to be run in Britain's national interest, and wholly unrealistic to expect that a government which had as one of its main priorities full employment to have handed industries employing a total of 1,179,000 workers over to the control of a supranational authority.

Furthermore, the defence ministry was concerned that the Plan might affect the war potential of the country. Bevin agreed, fearing that, if Europe was over-run, and Britain's economy had gone too far down the road of economic integration, she might not be able to function independently. Manny Shinwell, then defence minister, endorsed this concern. The risk of relying on pooled western European resources, some of which might be lost to an invader, was too great.[20] Thus, the central objective of the Plan which made it so attractive its advocates – eliminating the independent war-making capability of member states – was anathema to the British. In view of her Second World War experience and the real possibility of a Soviet land invasion of Europe, the lack of enthusiasm was far from irrational.

Britain was by no means alone in having reservations about 'Le Plan'. French Socialists shared the British concerns; the Communists feared it might allow French industry to be smothered by the Germans, with resultant unemployment. A widely held view, cited by Lavergne, was that:

'From the moment Britain, with her 220 million tons of coal and her 16 million tons of steel was unwilling to join, it should have been a matter of the most elementary prudence for M. Schuman to abandon his Plan.'[21]

However, there was one British MP who was unequivocally in favour of Britain joining the talks. A day after Communist North Korea's armies swept over the frontier into South Korea on 25 June, thus precipitating another major Cold War crisis, the new young Conservative Member for Bexley gave his maiden speech in

19 Cited in Denman; George; Young and others.
20 Milward, *op. cit.*, pp. 41–42 and 52–53.
21 Werth, *op. cit.*, p. 481.

the House of Commons. Ignoring the convention that such speeches should avoid controversial matters, Edward Heath averred that for Britain not to join the talks on the Schuman plan would be a grave error. By standing aside, 'we may be taking a very great risk with our – economy in the coming years – a very great risk indeed'. [22]

Another enthusiast for Britain's involvement was a young Cambridge undergraduate, Geoffrey Howe, destined one day to become Margaret Thatcher's Chancellor and then Foreign Secretary. Writing to a friend on 7 July 1950, he argued that 'active British leadership in a more positive form of European union is essential politically'. This, he added, 'would have the subsidiary advantage of ensuring that any such body that is set up without our help will not be Germany-dominated'. [23]

What neither Heath nor Howe appeared to recognise was that the skill with which Monnet had deliberately managed to exclude the British from the negotiations. It was regarded by many of his colleagues as one of his greatest triumphs. [24] Nor did they seem to take into account the broader strategic, and especially the defence implications.

But many British 'Europeanists' argue to this day that Britain made a fundamental and tragic error in not joining the negotiations, thereby seeking to influence them. Dean Acheson himself was later to describe it as 'the greatest mistake of the post-war period'. [25] Their views, however, are refuted by none other than the British official history of the period, its author writing:

'The conversations and correspondence with French officials and with Schuman between 9 May and 2 June can lend some credence to the idea that the United Kingdom might have obtained an acceptable treaty, meaning one with no subjugation to a High Authority as a promise of closer union… Nevertheless, the outcome of the negotiations suggests that there was no treaty which would have given Britain the economic and political advantages identified by officials, without a supranational authority as embryo and symbol of a European federation. Acceptance of Monnet's non-negotiable principle did require a change of national strategy… It would have meant a commitment of political support … to a reconstruction of the pattern of political power in Europe in which the United Kingdom … could not share.' [26]

In any event, British involvement was precisely what Monnet wanted to avoid. Correctly reading the psychology of the British government, he created a situation it could not have accepted. [27]

---

22 *Hansard*, 26 June 1950, col. 1959.
23 Howe, Geoffrey (1994), *Conflict Of Loyalty* (London, Macmillan), pp. 21–22.
24 Fransen, *op. cit.*, p. 100.
25 Horne, *Macmillan 1894–1956*, *op. cit.*, p. 319. See also Denman, *op. cit.*, p. 188; George, Stephen (1990), *An Awkward Partner – Britain In The European Community* (third ed.) (Oxford, Oxford University Press), p. 5; and Dell, Edmund (1995), *The Schuman Plan And The British Abdication Of Leadership In Europe* (Oxford, Clarendon Press).
26 Milward, *op. cit.*, pp. 61–62.
27 Dell, who argues in his book that the British *were* wanted, nevertheless concedes that, 'Monnet's hyperbole increased the possibility of an adverse British reaction', adding, 'He should not have been surprised. He knew the British too well' (*op. cit.*, pp. 5 and 23.). That itself suggests that Monnet's 'hyperbole' could hardly have been accidental.

Another myth that countless people prefer to believe (as can be seen, for instance, from the Commission's *Europa* website) is that the plan really did originate with Schuman, who has thus become honoured as one of the 'Founding Fathers of Europe'. In fact the historical record unequivocally shows that it was all due to just one man: Jean Monnet. It was an extraordinary testament to his peculiar talents that he had been able to seize the moment to move his project to the centre of the agenda with such dazzling success.

Monnet's 'one-man show'

Launching his plan was only the start of Monnet's achievement. Invitations to discuss it had also been extended to representatives of the three Benelux countries and Italy. By 3 June they had all agreed to take part. Particularly enthusiastic was the Italian premier Alcide de Gasperi. Thus were brought together what were to become known as the 'Six'.

By the time the talks began, Monnet had already engineered another coup. Not only did he get agreement that he should chair the negotiations; he had also managed to convince a French inter-ministerial committee that he should be France's representative at the talks, with power to appoint his own advisors.[28] Thus came about the extraordinary situation whereby, in what were to become one of the most important negotiations in its history, France was represented by a man who was not even a member of its government.

To get the negotiations under way, Monnet produced a *document de travail*, which meant that, in addition to organising the talks, chairing the sessions, and representing France, he also set the agenda. The 'one-man show' was to continue. Nevertheless, it was July before Monnet could produce a working draft for consideration by the governments of the Six, not least because of the incoherence of his original *document*. Belgian prime minister, Paul van Zeeland, described that as 'so vague on essential details that it was impossible to speak definitely about it'.[29]

When it was ready, a summary of Monnet's July text was given to the press, in which he was 'careful to include the following stipulation':

'The withdrawal of a State which has committed itself to the Community should be possible only if all the others agree to such withdrawal and to the conditions in which it takes place. The rule in itself sums up the fundamental transformation which the French proposal seeks to achieve. Over and above coal and steel, it is laying the foundations of a European federation. In a federation, no State can secede by its own unilateral decision. Similarly, there can be no Community except among nations which commit themselves to it with no limit and no looking back.'[30]

After that, wrote Monnet, 'no one could any longer doubt our ambition and our determination'.

---

28 Duchêne, *op. cit.*, p. 209.
29 *Ibid.*
30 Monnet, *op. cit.*, p. 326.

Nevertheless, each of the representatives involved sought to extract the maximum advantage for their nations. Part of the price was a two-percent turnover tax imposed on German collieries to support the decrepit Belgian coal mines; and a preferential ore supply arrangement for Italy, with subsidies for the importing of coal, and special tariffs and quotas to protect its steel industry.[31] These concessions breached Monnet's original concept of 'equal treatment' but they were needed to get agreement.

There were other concessions. Monnet's original plan had focused on that component closest to his heart: the supranational power to be given to his 'High Authority'. At the behest of the Belgians, a Court of Arbitration was added, to adjudicate in case of disputes. The French finance minister had then proposed the inclusion of an Assembly, which would retain the ultimate power to dismiss the High Authority, much as a shareholders' meeting has the power to dismiss a board of directors.

Monnet's supranationalism now came under further attack from those who disliked the idea of his High Authority being free from control by elected politicians. The Dutch chief negotiator, Dirk Spierenburg, called for an intergovernmental 'watchdog' to supervise the High Authority. Monnet resisted this strongly but, in face of continued Dutch insistence, reinterpreted the proposal. He accepted it so long as there was majority voting and no 'veto', insisting that the 'watchdog' should be a 'forum' through which the High Authority could 'play an educating role *viz-à-viz* the governments'.[32]

Thus was born the 'Council of Ministers'. Monnet then set about devising a voting formula, which meant that the combined power of Germany and France could not outvote the remaining members, a system which was to become known as 'qualified majority voting'. Finally, he secured a crucial agreement that, although the Council of Ministers could take part in decision-making, it could not instruct the High Authority. Monnet's 'Authority' was to remain supreme, immune from the interference of nation states. Supranationalism had survived its greatest challenge.

In the first months after Monnet's Plan had been launched, amongst those who had praised it was Macmillan. To the Assembly of the Council of Europe on 15 August 1950, he had described it as being 'not just a piece of convenient machinery. It is a revolutionary and almost mystical conception'.[33] As someone who had enjoyed lengthy discussions with Monnet on his views on the future of Europe during their time together in Algiers in 1943, Macmillan perhaps had a shrewder understanding than most of the intentions which lay behind it. However, in the same speech, he made it clear that it was not for Britain, telling the delegates:

31 Gillingham, John (1991), 'Jean Monnet and the European Coal and Steel Community: A Preliminary Appraisal', in Brinkley, Douglas, and Hackett, Clifford (eds), *Jean Monnet: The Path To European Unity* (New York, St Martin's Press), p. 144.

32 Fransen, *op. cit.*, pp. 106–109.

33 Horne, *Macmillan 1894–1956, op. cit.*, p. 319. It is not clear whether Macmillan was being ironic. Horne portrays his subject as being a more enthusiastic supporter of European integration than other sources.

'At all events, one fact is certain, and we had better face it frankly. Our people will not hand over to a supranational authority the right to close down our pits and steelworks. We shall not permit a supranational authority to reduce a large section of our fellow citizens in Durham, the Midlands, South Wales and Scotland to unemployment. These fears may be imaginary, but their existence is a fact, and a fact moreover, which no British Government can afford to ignore.'[34]

Then, after the negotiations had meandered on for some months, several British delegates to the Council of Europe, including Macmillan, sought to reassert the intergovernmental agenda. They put to the Assembly that the Coal and Steel Community be made an agency of the Council rather than an independent, supranational authority. As always, Monnet reacted sharply. In a letter to Macmillan he strongly denounced the proposal, complaining that it would not offer the creation of a new economic community, 'but merely a mechanism for coordination among nation states', precisely what he was most anxious to avoid.[35]

But this British intervention turned out to be no more than a side-show. By then, the momentum of the Six was unstoppable. Final agreement was reached and formalised by the Treaty of Paris, signed on 18 April 1951, creating the European Coal and Steel Community. It was not until December 1951, however, that the Treaty was ratified, 'in an atmosphere of doubt and resignation, and a good deal of indifference'.[36] The Gaullist deputy Jacques Soustelle thought the Plan was not 'European' but 'anti-European':

'We are all in favour of a European confederation, comprising Germany… But what worries us about the Coal-Steel pool is that instead of bringing us nearer to "Europe", it is taking us away from it. Instead of delegating our powers to a democratic Assembly, we are asked to abandon an important sector of our economy to a stateless and uncontrolled autocracy of experts.'[37]

Professor Lavergne expressed concern about the project's alarming lack of democracy in another respect:

'The French public could not make head or tail of the subsequent negotiations. Parliament, for its part, was presented with the project only very late in the day, and apart from twenty or thirty deputies and senators with sufficient general knowledge to form an opinion of the Plan, few grasped its meaning… In most cases the thing was looked at through the distorting prism of a few slogans or electoral prejudices; in many cases, most of the deputies voted with their eyes shut, and simply obeying the decisions taken by their party.'[38]

But Monnet had got what he wanted. His great project was at last launched. Unsurprisingly, he was also appointed as the new High Authority's first president, based in Luxembourg. As for where it might all lead, he himself left little room for doubt. Addressing the first session of the Community's new assembly, he told the delegates that they were taking part in 'the first government of Europe'.[39]

---

34 Cited in Spaak, *op. cit.*, p. 216.
35 Archives National (A. N.), Paris, 8 August 1950. 81/AJ/158.
36 Werth, *op. cit.*, p. 481.
37 Débats, A. N., 6 December 1951, p. 8881. Cited in Werth, *op. cit.*, p. 550.
38 In Werth, *op. cit.*, p. 480.
39 Duchêne, *op. cit.*, p. 235.

Chapter 5

The Rocky Road to Rome: 1950–1957

'Our Community is not a coal and steel producers association. It is the beginning of Europe.'
Jean Monnet[1]

'Nobody after the first two years of Monnet's presidency at the High Authority would again talk of it or its equivalents as "a European government"... the idea of a Europe in some sense above the nations was no longer stated in the open.'
François Duchêne[2]

One remarkable feature of Monnet's triumph was that, despite the protracted arguments about how his 'government of Europe' should be constructed, the model which finally emerged was almost identical to that outlined by Salter 20 years earlier. Adapting the structure of the League of Nations, Salter had proposed that the government of a 'United States of Europe' should be made up of a Secretariat, with supranational powers; a Council of Ministers representing national governments; an Assembly representing national parliaments; and a Court of Justice. This was precisely the structure, changing 'Secretariat' to 'High Authority' which came together to in the Coal and Steel Community. In due course the same model would be extended to run the 'European Economic Community' and the European Union.

Yet, in previous accounts of the history of the 'European project', this has been overlooked. In vain does one look for any reference to Salter. There is scarcely a mention of the crucial developments in the 1920s, when the key ideas emerged. There may be perfunctory references to Coudenhove Kalergi. But, as with Salter, the name of Loucheur has vanished.

The reason for this is that the 'project' soon came to evolve its own mythology, to explain how it originated. One of the project's central needs was to portray itself as having emerged from the years after 1945. This allowed it to promulgate the myth that it had put an end to European wars, and also allowed it to present itself as a progressive creation of the modern world, rather than as a failed dream of the 1920s. Only as a post-war ideal could it be projected as new and forward-looking, which was perhaps the unconscious reason for writing its true genesis out of the script.[3]

---

1 *Memoirs, op. cit.*, p. 392.
2 *Op. cit.*, p. 288.
3 One unintended by-product of this rewriting of the official chronology was that it would help to reinforce the myth of the EU's 'Nazi origins'; in that the ideas behind it could then be shown to have followed those of the Nazis about European integration rather than having preceded them.

Thus, in the official histories, the project's origins became increasingly veiled in the kind of hagiography accorded in previous ages to saints. Monnet would come to be presented as a visionary figure who had happened to emerge at the right moment after 1945, and whose only concern had been to achieve lasting peace.[4] Spinelli, for all his talk of dictatorships and revolution, would be presented as the man who made the EU democratic. Schuman would be honoured with a reverential plaque in the European Parliament in Strasbourg, describing him as the 'Father of Europe', when his only real contribution had been to act briefly as Monnet's 'front-man'.

This re-writing of history was to become even more glaring when British historians reconstructed the events surrounding Britain's involvement in the project. Two accounts published in the 1990s, to which frequent reference will be made in these pages, were those by *Guardian* journalist Hugo Young and Sir Roy Denman, a former senior civil servant in the Foreign Office.[5]

Young claims that, had Britain pressed for it, Schuman would have been willing to dilute the principle of supranationalism in 'his' proposed High Authority.[6] He thus misses the point that the driving force was not Schuman but Monnet, who was absolutely insistent that the supranational character of his High Authority was non-negotiable.[7] Denman's account of the Schuman Plan negotiations only mentions Monnet once, again falling for the fiction that Schuman was the prime mover. Similarly, though for different reasons, John Laughland in his attempt to ascribe the origins of the EU to Nazi ideology, *The Tainted Source*, only makes four brief references to Monnet, without recognising his pivotal role.

What makes such misunderstanding perverse is that Monnet soon cast off his anonymity as the project's real author and came to London to discuss his plan with civil servants and ministers. As Young himself records, Monnet then made it crystal clear that the autonomy of his High Authority would mean 'the surrender of national sovereignty over a wide strategic and economic field'.[8]

Few at the time had any illusions about this. Con O'Neill, then a young diplomat in Bonn, later recalled, 'The idea that there should be a body with real author-

---

4 A small but revealing instance of this reworking of history is in the attempts to trace the 'theory of European integration' to a book written in 1943: *A Working Peace System* by David Mitrany, a Romanian-born writer, then working at the London School of Economics. In McAllister, Richard (1997) *From EC To EU – A Historical And Political Survey* (London, Routledge), p. 13, the author even suggests that Monnet's thinking must have been influenced by this work. In formulating his theory, however, Mitrany refers to the Allied Control Commission for Shipping in the First World War and similar Allied co-operation in the Second, in both of which Monnet was centrally involved. Rather than Monnet having been influenced by Mitrany, therefore, the truth was the other way round.

5 Young, Hugo (1998), *This Blessed Plot – Britain And Europe, From Churchill To Blair* (London, Routledge); Denman, Roy (1996), *Missed Chances – Britain And Europe In The Twentieth Century* (London, Cassell).

6 *Op. cit.*, p. 65.

7 Young even mocks the 'British *idée fixe*, that the Schuman Plan would lead to a European Federation' (*This Blessed Plot*, p. 60.). Such an analysis, he writes, 'turned out to be premature, if not something of a hallucination'. Young thus completely misses the Plan's central purpose (*cf.* for instance, Monnet's *Memoirs, op. cit.*, p. 326).

8 Young, *op. cit.*, p. 58.

ity over the decisions of national governments was something we felt was grotesque and absurd'.[9] Given Attlee's comments about the 'lack of democracy' in Monnet's project, there can be no doubt that its nature was clear to the British government, which was why Britain could not accept it. Yet some accounts continue to present the Schuman Plan as something the British government could have modified, if only it been sensible enough to attend the talks.

This was to become a persistent theme of the mythology surrounding Britain's involvement with 'Europe' through the decades which followed. It rests on the need to portray the founders of the project as reasonable and open to ideas, whereas the British must invariably be shown as obdurate and lacking in vision. The central, implicit message behind this version of history is: 'Europeans – positive, forward-looking, good; British – negative, backward-looking, bad'.

Nevertheless, despite Monnet having brilliantly pulled off the first step of his grand design, he was now to overreach himself. As a result, the next six years were to prove a rocky road. He would not eventually achieve his goal until his allies had impressed on him the need for their most daring strategy yet: to cloak the 'project' in deceit.

Monnet takes a fall

When the president of the new 'government of Europe' first came before the Assembly of his European Coal and Steel Community, he was quick to tell the 'deputies':

'We can never sufficiently emphasise that the six Community countries are the forerunners of a broader, united Europe, whose bounds are set only by those who have not yet joined. Our Community is not a coal and steel producers' association: it is the beginning of Europe.'[10]

For all his sense of triumphalism, however, events were catching up with M. Monnet. Having so far unfolded his plan so deftly, he now made a near-fatal mistake.

The cause of his near-nemesis was the Korean War, which had broken out on the Sunday after negotiations on the ECSC had opened. Monnet immediately feared that the pressure of this major new Cold War crisis, threatening possible Soviet aggression in Europe itself, might lead the Americans to strengthen their demands for German re-armament. This might reduce the attraction to Adenauer of the Schuman plan, as he might now be able to achieve this key objectives without having to place Germany's coal and steel under the control of the High Authority.

To regain the initiative, Monnet had decided that the original Schuman plan should be widened to include defence, and set about planning what was to emerge as a proposal for a European Defence Community (EDC). This provided for a

---

9 *Op. cit.,* p. 69.
10 Monnet, *op. cit.,* p. 392.

European Army, run by a European minister of defence and a council of ministers, with a common budget and arms procurement. While all other members would be able to maintain separate forces, for colonial and other purposes, Germany would only be allowed to participate in the European Army.

For his advocate this time, Monnet by-passed Schuman, who was strongly opposed to German rearmament. Instead, he sought out a man who had been his assistant during his somewhat murky days as a merchant banker – Rene Pleven. He had also been with him in London in 1940 during that exciting time when he had put to Churchill the plan for Anglo-French union. Fortunately for Monnet, his old subordinate was now in a position of some authority: he had become France's prime minister.

Again the familiar deception was repeated. Although the proposal was entirely Monnet's, he kept in the background and his idea became the 'Pleven Plan'. Pleven outlined it to the French Assembly on 24 October 1950, where it won approval by 343 votes to 220. Nevertheless, during the debates, Pleven made clear that negotiations would not start until the Coal and Steel Treaty had been concluded, thus safeguarding Monnet's original scheme.[11]

Unlike the Schuman Plan, this plan was not well received abroad. The Germans, in particular, were highly suspicious, preferring their forces to be part of NATO. They had good reason for their suspicion. Monnet intended his EDC to be 'a government capable of taking the supreme decisions in the name of all Europeans'. Yet, for that very reason, the Italian premier, de Gasperi, supported the new plan, proclaiming that 'The European Army is not an end in itself; it is the instrument of a patriotic foreign policy. But European patriotism can develop only in a federal Europe'.[12]

Again, the Americans intervened, this time in the form of General Eisenhower, now the first supreme commander of NATO land forces. Meeting with Monnet on 21 June 1951, he agreed that Franco-German reconciliation could only be achieved through a European Army. The Korean War, following the intervention of Communist China, had entered a critical phase. As anticipated, American pressure for German rearmament had intensified, giving Adenauer a powerful negotiating hand. He chose to exploit it, offering in return for his support of the EDC a 'general treaty'. This would recognise West German sovereignty, accept German contingents into the EDC on equal footing, allow West Germany into NATO, end the remnants of allied occupation of his country, and conclude a peace treaty. Ambitious though this proposal was, it was quickly agreed by the Allies and by the end of November 1951 a draft treaty was ready.[13]

In the final stages of the treaty negotiations, the British government had changed. On 25 October 1951, after a general election, Labour had lost to the Conservatives. Churchill was again prime minister, with Anthony Eden as foreign secretary. But the new government was immediately plunged into a balance of payments crisis and economic disaster loomed.

11 Leiden University Historical Institute, History of European Integration site, *op. cit.*
12 Monnet, *op. cit.*, p. 382.
13 Williams, *op. cit.*, pp. 372–373.

Despite some initial hopes that the 'pro-European' Churchill might reverse the Labour's view of the Six's moves to integration, his view that Britain should remain aloof from direct European involvement remained intact. Britain, in Churchill's view, was still one of the international 'Big Three', with her special relationship with America. Although anxious to co-operate with his European neighbours, his policy rested on 'overlapping circles', whereby Britain remained between Europe and the USA.

In opposition Churchill had claimed to favour the idea of a 'European Army', without ever spelling out what this might mean in practice. Back in power, however, orthodoxy re-asserted itself. Now the supranational element of the plan had become clear, he brushed aside any idea of a European army, calling it a 'sludgy amalgam', adding, 'What soldiers want to sing are their own marching songs'. De Gaulle took a similar view.[14]

According to Hugo Young, on 28 November 1952, Eden told a press conference in Rome that no British formations would be available to the new army,[15] which Young describes as an example of British 'perversity'.[16] But the record shows that the new Conservative government did its best to be constructive. At a meeting with Schuman in February 1952, Eden assured the French of a close association with the Defence Community. British forces on the continent would co-operate very closely with 'European forces'.[17] In a further effort to be helpful, Eden proposed in March 1952 that the two Communities of the Six should come under the aegis of the Council of Europe. Monnet, predictably, saw this as a challenge to his supranationalism.[18]

Although nothing further came of Eden's initiative, the French themselves had considerable reservations about the idea of a European army. What most concerned them was the possibility of Germany seceding from the Defence Community, allowing the German units raised to be reconstituted as a national army. Paris therefore pressed for an Anglo-American guarantee against any member's secession. London's response was obliging. Under the 1948 Brussels treaty, Britain was already pledged to give assistance to France and the Benelux countries in the event of war. The Six now asked, on 14 March 1952, that she should extend that guarantee to West Germany and Italy. Responding in a broadcast on 5 April, Eden said it was the duty and intention of the British government to help the people of Europe towards the idea of a united Europe. Great Britain could not join an exclusive European federation, but she could give support and encouragement to both the Coal and Steel and the Defence Communities.[19]

Ten days later, he followed this up with a firm proposal. In the event of an armed attack on any member of the European Defence Community, Britain would give full military and other aid in accordance with article 51 of the United

14 Sampson, *op. cit.*, p. 17.
15 Young, *op. cit.*, p. 76.
16 *Ibid.*
17 Calvocoressi, Peter (1955), *Survey Of International Affairs – 1952* (London, Oxford University Press), pp. 93–94.
18 Documents on British Policy Overseas, Series 2, Vol. 1, doc. 484 (29 August 1952).
19 *Ibid.*

Nations Charter. This offer was well received by the Six. In Germany it was hailed as 'one of the most important political developments of recent times'. [20]

However, this was not an Anglo-American guarantee. The Americans were still putting their faith in the EDC and refused to co-operate. As a result, on 19 May, it was announced that Washington and London were unable to provide a joint guarantee and would instead make a 'declaration of intent'. Talks then became bogged down in arguments about the German contribution to the European defence budget, until the French Cabinet, still dissatisfied by the lack of commitment from the British and Americans, against German withdrawal from the EDC, decided it would not sign the agreements.

Efforts were made to satisfy the French by re-wording the declaration of intent. The USA and Britain finally agreed to regard any action which threatened the integrity of the European Defence Community as a threat to their own security. [21] It was enough. The European Defence Treaty was signed on 27 May 1952, along with a general treaty which effectively restored German sovereignty. [22] This was far from what Monnet had envisaged, with the budget subject still to national veto. Even so, there was still so much opposition in France that her prime minister Antoine Pinay signed the treaty without intending to seek immediate ratification.

It was over ratification that Monnet's scheming began to unravel. Opposition in the French Assembly, far from diminishing, had been hardening. The Socialist group wanted a 'more democratic' EDC, with a European Assembly elected by universal suffrage. This was to prompt Monnet's most daring initiative so far, in concert with the man who over the next few years would be his closest ally, Paul-Henri Spaak. [23]

Spaak proposed setting up a European Political Community (EPC), as a 'common political roof' over the Coal and Steel and the Defence Communities, creating 'an indissoluble supranational political community based on the union of peoples'. Schuman and Adenauer welcomed this, as did Italy's prime minister de Gasperi, who went even further, proposing that a future EDC assembly should prepare a draft European constitution.

In September 1952, Spaak's proposal was jointly endorsed by the foreign ministers of the Six, along with the assemblies of the ECSC and the Council of Europe, and the ECSC Assembly was asked to study the question of creating a 'European Political Authority'. The result, from an *ad hoc* committee under Spaak, was a

---

20 Calvocoressi, *op. cit.*, p. 94. See also Foreign Office Press Release, 15 April 1952, and *The Times*, 16 April 1952, *Le Monde* and *Neue Zeitung*, 17 April 1952.

21 *Op. cit.*, p. 103.

22 *Op. cit.*, p. 126.

23 Not only had Spaak been the US State Department's original nominee as president of the OEEC, and later first president of the Assembly of the Council of Europe, in 1950 he had also become president of the European Movement, following the resignation of Churchill's son-in-law Duncan Sandys. Churchill and Sandys, who believed that the European Movement should represent the aspirations of the whole of Europe, including those central and Eastern European peoples now under Soviet hegemony, had become increasingly disenchanted with the Movement's narrow obsession with integration in western Europe. After a brief hiatus, the Movement was still largely supported by secret funding from the CIA, through ACUE, of which Spaak himself was also a beneficiary.

'Draft Treaty Embodying the Statute of the European Community'. This was nothing less than the first formal attempt to give Europe a constitution. It was submitted by Spaak to the foreign ministers of the Six on 9 March 1953 and to the ECSC Assembly the following day, which approved it by 50 votes, with five abstentions. Introducing his draft 'constitution' to the ECSC Council, Spaak began with the opening words of George Washington's address in presenting the American Constitution to Congress in 1787, going on to express his conviction that, 'with the same audacity', Europe could hope for the same success.[24]

This latest Monnet-Spaak initiative could go no further, however, while the EDC itself was still attracting opposition. Part of the plan was to apply supranational controls on any production of nuclear weapons, which caused the French Atomic Energy Commission, Gaullist in sympathy, to wake up to the implications, should France wish become a nuclear power.[25] By October, deputies in the National Assembly were expressing concern that the treaty gave too many advantages to Germany, which would come to dominate the Community. Objections were also raised that the Treaty was presented as a *fait accompli*, to be accepted or rejected without alteration.[26]

Thus, while the rest of the Six went on to ratify the Defence Treaty, French politics were to prevail. So great did opposition become among both Socialists and Gaullists that the Pinay government was brought down. A new government was formed under Rene Mayer, with Gaullist support, and the 'Europe of Jean Monnet' became almost a term of political abuse. Then, after four months, Mayer was replaced by Joseph Laniel. In the despairing words of Monnet, he 'did nothing'. Despite intense pressure from the United States, with President Eisenhower's Secretary of State John Foster Dulles threatening to cut US aid, France's ratification process had come to a halt.

Outside Parliament, opposition was at least as strong. Army leaders were against it, intellectual groups detested it and de Gaulle, in November 1953, declared himself implacably hostile to it, referring to 'this monstrous treaty' which would rob the French Army of its sovereignty and separate the defence of France from the defence of the French Union. It would go against all her traditions and institutions, and deliver her soldiers to an organism over which France had no control. He blamed this 'and other supranational monstrosities' on 'the Inspirer', M. Jean Monnet. In a bitter parody of Monnet, he declared, 'Since victorious France has an army and defeated Germany has none, let us suppress the French Army'. He went on:

'After that we shall make a stateless army of Frenchmen and Germans, and since there must be a government above this army, we shall make a stateless government, a technocracy. As this may not please everyone, we'll paint a new shop sign and call it "community"; it won't matter, anyway, because the "European Army" will be placed at the entire disposal of the American Commander-in-Chief.'[27]

24 Griffiths, Richard T. (2000), *Europe's First Constitution – The European Political Community, 1952–1954* (London, Federal Trust), p. 93.
25 Duchêne, *op. cit.*, p. 233.
26 Calvocoressi, *op. cit.*, p. 127.
27 Werth, *op. cit.*, pp. 646–647.

What finally brought matters to a head was a quite separate event, the fall to the Communist Viet Minh on 7 May 1954 of the enclave in Dien Bien Phu, in French Indochina. This disaster brought down the government. By 17 June, Laniel had been replaced by Mendès-France, a radical nationalist. He was ambivalent towards the EDC and sought to dilute its supranational element, proposing this to the Six in Brussels on 3 August. Adenauer rejected this out of hand. Spaak, who chaired the conference, made an almost hysterical plea to Mendès-France to support the treaty, clasping him by the arm while telling him that:

'France will be completely isolated … You will be alone. Is that what you want? We must, *must* make Europe. The military side isn't everything. What matters is the integration of Europe. EDC is only the first step in that direction, but if there is no EDC, then everything falls to the ground.'[28]

Brushing aside Spaak's accusations that he was not being 'a good European', Mendès-France also ignored entreaties from the Americans and even Churchill, from whom he sought, unsuccessfully, guarantees of British involvement in the EDC. He thus brought the treaty before a hostile Assembly on 30 August 1954 without endorsement. After a stormy debate, in which the supranational issue predominated, it was rejected by 319 votes to 264. Mendès-France's government abstained. The triumphant majority burst into the Marseillaise.[29] The EDC was dead. The idea of a Political Community soon faded into obscurity.[30] Monnet and his supranationism had suffered a resounding defeat.

Still the problem of German rearmament remained. Eden stepped in to propose an extension of the 1948 Brussels Treaty, bringing Germany and Italy into its scope. This would set up the Western European Union (WEU), organised on an intergovernmental basis. Although for decades it would remain little more than a shadow, since its functions were largely exercised by NATO, the undertaking from Britain that her troops would not leave the continent without agreement from the other members was enough to satisfy French fears of unchecked German power. These fears had in any case lost much of their force. *Le Monde*, which had been strongly opposed to the idea, conceded that 'twelve German divisions mattered little in a world of atomic strategy'.[31] The WEU was soon ratified by all members.[32]

With that, it seemed that progress towards supranational integration had been all but blocked. Intergovernmentalism had triumphed. In December that year, to complete her success, Britain signed an agreement of 'association' with the European Coal and Steel Community, committing her to no more than friendly co-operation.

28 *Op. cit.*, p. 696.
29 Duchêne, *op. cit.*, p. 256.
30 As an example of real perversity, Hugo Young claims that Britain's refusal to place sufficient soldiers under European command 'was, effectively, what drove French parliamentarians to kill the EDC'.
31 Werth, *op. cit.*, p. 700.
32 Nevertheless US Secretary of State Dulles, a supporter of the EDC (and Monnet's friend since 1919) wrote dismissively to Eden about the plans for WEU that he would regard 'any solution which did not provide for the creation of a supranational institution as makeshift'. (Eden, Anthony (1960), *Memoirs, Full Circle* (London, Cassell), p. 159.)

The new strategy: deceit

The effect of the EDC rejection was to be profound and long-lasting. Quite simply, it was at this point that the 'project' went underground. According to Duchêne:

'Nobody after the first two years of Monnet's presidency at the High Authority would again talk of it or its equivalents as a "European government"... Awareness that the French would have to be coaxed into further progress introduced caution into the European vocabulary. The word *federal* was reserved as the political equivalent of Latin for the rare religious occasion. Even *supranational*... tended to be used only when another fig-leaf could not be found. The idea of a Europe in some sense above the nations was no longer stated in the open.'[33]

What had been to date a series of tactical deceptions now became a deliberate attempt to conceal. So far-reaching was this change of strategy to become that, in 1965, when the 'Merger Treaty' was agreed between the Six, combining the executives, councils and assemblies of the three 'Communities' – ECSC, EEC and Euratom – Article 9 of the Coal and Steel treaty, which originally read:

'The members of the High Authority ... shall refrain from any action incompatible with the *supranational* character of their duties.'

would be modified to

'The members of the Commission ... shall refrain from any action incompatible with their duties ...'

Monnet's more immediate reaction to his crushing defeat was to resign as president of the Coal and Steel Community. This meant that arrangements had to be made to fill his post, requiring a meeting of the foreign ministers of the Six. This was originally set for 8 February but, in the interim, Mendès-France's government fell, delaying the meeting. The new French government was led by Edgar Faure, less hostile to European integration.

This gave Monnet some encouragement and he decided that something less ambitious might work. He settled on his earlier strategy of building his 'Europe' through the progressive integration of other economic sectors. In late 1955, from various options, he had chosen as his next target the nuclear industry, then in its early stages of development. It seemed to offer distinct advantages. While coal and steel represented the past, the 'power of the atom' could position 'Europe' as forward-looking and modern. Furthermore, the scale of investment required to develop the industry was so huge that Europe-wide co-operation could be made to seem a logical step.

To present his new plan for what was eventually to become 'Euratom', Monnet, in a pattern now familiar, needed a front-man, a new Schuman or Pleven: particularly since he had now made so many enemies. His choice was his closest ally, Paul-Henri Spaak. This proved sound. The new French prime minister Faure

33 Duchêne, *op. cit.*, p. 256.

proved receptive to overtures from Belgium's respected foreign minister. On 4 April 1955, Spaak sent Monnet's proposals – which encompassed not just nuclear but all forms of energy and also transport – to Adenauer, Pinay – now France's foreign minister – and Italy's foreign minister, Gaetano Martino. In an accompanying letter Spaak suggested the time had now come for a 're-launch' (*relancer*) of the 'European idea'.[34]

There was one highly significant omission from Spaak's letter. Although he and Monnet had already discussed the possibility of a 'customs union' or 'common market' among the Six, Spaak did not mention it. Monnet feared that to raise it so soon after the collapse of the EDC might be going too far.

The German response was not encouraging. Rather than pooling resources through Euratom, Erhard thought Germany would be better off buying technology from the US or Great Britain. France's reaction was even less positive. In a message delivered orally to Spaak via the Belgian ambassador, her foreign minister replied that to 'supranationalise energy and transport might produce another EDC in France'. He added: 'Take care! Edgar Faure does not like Monnet.'[35]

The only positive response came from the Dutch foreign minister, Johan Beyen. He proposed the very idea Monnet had rejected, a 'common market'. Crucially, he suggested that this should not be a free trade area, but a customs union. Duties levied on goods traded between member states would be progressively reduced, then abolished, while a common external tariff wall would be erected against non-members.

All of this precipitated an internal battle between senior political figures of the 'Six', from which three options emerged. One, favoured by Erhard, was a free trade area, using the infrastructure of the intergovernmental OEEC. The second was Beyen's 'common market'. The third was Monnet's strategy, whereby integration would be achieved sector by sector.

Quite how this issue was resolved is not clear.[36] But on 18 May 1955 the Benelux foreign ministers offered a document to their ECSC counterparts known as the 'Benelux Memorandum'. This linked the Beyen and Monnet strategies, in what was to become known as the *junktim*,[37] suggesting that a working group should be set up to draft treaties for a 'common market'. The integration of transport, energy, nuclear energy and social legislation would all be included.[38] Erhard's views had been ignored.

This memorandum had, in fact, been composed by Spaak, based on a draft prepared by himself and Monnet. After Spaak had amended Monnet's version, he sent it back with the note '*Ici votre bébé*' ('Herewith your baby'). The most significant

---

34 Archives of the Ministry of Foreign Affairs, Paris. Europe, 1944–..., Generalities, vol. 110, pp. 109–111.
35 Duchêne, *op. cit.*, p. 271.
36 Duchêne, *op. cit.*, p. 274.
37 European Parliament (2002), *The European Parliament And The Euratom Treaty: Past Present And Future* (Luxembourg, Directorate General for Research), Working Paper, Energy and Research Series, ENER 114EN, p. 9.
38 Bruylant, E. (1987), *Pour Une Communauté Politique Européenne, Travaux Préparatoires (1955–1957)*. Tome II: 1955–1957 (Bruxelles), pp. 25–29.

change was that the words 'United States of Europe' in Monnet's original had been struck out. Spaak was careful to give more emphasis to the idea of an 'economic community'.[39]

Thus did the central deception of the whole story become established. From now on, the real agenda, political integration, was to be deliberately concealed under the guise of economic integration. Building 'Europe' was to be presented as a matter of trade and jobs.

Messina: A close run thing

France was attracted to Euratom, which would enable Germany's nuclear industry to be controlled, and might also assist in the as-yet undeclared objective of producing a French nuclear bomb. On the other hand, with the highest tariffs of the Six, and many other protectionist rules, she was hostile to the idea of a common market. Nevertheless she agreed that there should be 'exploratory discussions' of the Benelux memorandum, during talks on who should replace Monnet as head of the Coal and Steel Community. The Germans had considerable reservations as to whether to proceed at all.

The venue chosen for the talks was Messina, in deference to Italy's foreign minister Gaetano Martino. He was facing an election in Sicily and needed to be near his power base. The dates of 1–2 June 1955 were agreed. A British representative was invited, but Messina was considered too far to go, for what was, ostensibly, only a meeting of Coal and Steel Community ministers.

Before the meeting, Monnet learnt that the French were preparing to bury the Benelux Memorandum under pious resolutions.[40] Conscious that his presence might inflame the situation, he therefore decided not to attend. Spaak, acting as Monnet's front man, chaired the conference. At first, for the supranationalists, the meeting went badly. Monnet was on the telephone constantly, seeking to instruct Spaak. Max Kohnstamm, the Dutch secretary to the High Authority, who had taken a number of calls from Monnet, was eventually driven to tell his old boss: 'Please understand, they are not here to make Europe. They are here to bury you.'[41]

But late at night Spaak had gone to the hotel room of the French foreign minister Pinay. When he emerged in the early hours of the morning, some kind of agreement had been reached. It was enough for Spaak to order a bottle of champagne and greet the dawn with a rendition of *O sole mio*.[42] That morning, ministers adopted a resolution that accepted much of the Benelux Memorandum, some of it word for word. However, the resolution only committed the Six to set up an intergovernmental committee to study how to put the Memorandum into action.[43] The future was far from certain as there was still considerable opposition

39 Monnet, *op. cit.*, p. 403.
40 Duchêne, *op. cit.*, p. 280.
41 *Ibid.*
42 Duchêne, *op. cit.*, p. 281.
43 European Parliament, *Selection of texts concerning institutional matters on the Community from 1950 to 1982* (Luxembourg, Committee on Institutional Affairs), pp. 94–100.

to the proposals. The French had not assented but simply agreed 'not to oppose a continuation of talks'.[44]

Interestingly, Luxembourg's representative, Joseph Bech, said the most significant thing about the meeting was its lack of any 'smell' of a High Authority, Schuman-style, to ruffle French concerns over sovereignty.[45] The deception was continuing.

A translation of the Messina communiqué was despatched to London by the British Embassy in Rome, on 11 June. An accompanying letter from assistant under-secretary, John Coulson, reported 'it looks as though the Ministers had difficulty in reaching agreement on any specific action', adding:

'The Germans were keenly interested in transport, while Benelux wanted to expand the scope of the authority. The Italians went all out for a common market, while the French views were not clear. It is evident that the final communiqué went as far as possible to repeat the views of all the participants without taking any decisions of principle. It will be noticed that all the questions are to be "studied", but there is no indication of how this is to be done.'[46]

The Foreign Office, in fact, had considerable difficulty in finding out what had happened. In a letter to the new foreign secretary, Macmillan, on 15 June, the UK ambassador in Paris referred to the communiqué as 'lengthy but not very informative' suggesting that it was an accurate reflection of the vagueness that had prevailed at the conference. 'There is some evidence for the theory that the six Ministers were unable to get to real grips with the problems they discussed', he wrote. Noting the lack of clarity, he added:

'... the Europeans are having to proceed very cautiously. Their opponents on the other hand, or many of them, do see advantages in some of the schemes now being considered. The practical differences between the two camps are therefore much narrower than the ideological differences. Therefore when M. Pinay says that the new schemes are to be supranational and the Gaullists say they are not, both sides are using contradictory words to express roughly the same issues. M. Boegner, when asked to explain M. Pinay's language, said that he might well be thinking of organisations which had powers of decision (and were therefore supranational) but whose decisions would be reached unanimously (and were therefore intergovernmental). I am aware that this is a quibble. But this sort of double talk does seem to keep the Europeans quiet and if it serves to quieten a largely useless quarrel it has some justification.'[47]

Press coverage was meagre. The Italian newspaper, *Il Tempo*, described the communiqué as 'another unnecessary document'[48] and *Le Monde* reported 'the governments have implicitly abandoned the idea of supranationality'. Macmillan later observed 'the official view seemed to be a confident expectation that nothing would come out of Messina'.[49]

---

44 Duchêne, *op. cit.*, p. 282.
45 Young, *op. cit.*, p. 81.
46 PRO. FO371/11640, pp. 7–9. Letter from J. E. Coulson Esq. to Ashley Clarke.
47 PRO. FO371/116040, pp. 38–43. Letter from Gladwyn Jebb to Harold Macmillan, 15 June 1955.
48 PRO: Coulson, *op. cit.*
49 Macmillan, Harold (1971), *Riding The Storm – 1956-1959* (London, Macmillan), p. 73.

This was to reckon without Monnet. He was working on creating a platform from which he could continue his campaign. This culminated in his setting up an 'Action Committee for the United States of Europe', which issued its inaugural manifesto on 15 October 1955. With funding from the Ford Foundation, arranged by ACUE, its immediate objective was 'to ensure that the Messina resolution... should be translated into a genuine step towards a United States of Europe'. An important adjunct was to give Monnet a 'permanent visiting card' to any head of government. Very much in character, his new role would provide

'... him and his organisation with the advantage of being able to influence political élites directly without having to face the disadvantage of public scrutiny. Europe was being constructed by a remarkably small élite; while public support was welcomed, it was never a prerequisite for Monnet's Europe.'[50]

Thus Spaak would be kept in the limelight, chairing the intergovernmental committee set up at Messina, while Monnet continued to work in the shadows.

The Spaak Committee

The complex drama just beginning, the historical consequences of which were to be immense, essentially involved two separate plots. One was the discussions in Brussels directed by Spaak, mainly conducted through the work of four technical committees. The other centred on the response of Britain, still Europe's most powerful nation and not directly involved.

By this time the principal roles in the British government had changed. The ageing Churchill had retired, succeeded by Anthony Eden, who led his party to election victory in May 1955. Macmillan became Foreign Secretary.

Eden's Cabinet considered the Six's invitation to join the talks just beginning in Brussels. Despite rejecting British participation in any supranational organisation on principle, it decided on 30 June to send Russell Bretherton, an under-secretary of the Board of Trade. Much would later be made that only a civil servant rather than a minister was sent, but the talks were intended to be technical discussions rather than negotiations.

When they began, Bretherton made it clear, under instructions from London, that Britain did not subscribe to the 'Messina goals'. He pursued his government's traditional intergovernmental line, attempting to steer the Six towards a limited alternative, under the aegis of the OEEC, warning that much of what was being proposed would duplicate the OEEC's work. Spaak objected to the OEEC alternative as a 'much more modest enterprise' which 'offered no prospect of a European political union'.[51]

Representatives of the OEEC were present at the talks and the conduct of the meetings alarmed the head of the UK delegation, Hugh Ellis-Rees, who sent a letter of complaint to Macmillan. Stating that warnings of a conflict with the OEEC's work had not been heeded, he wrote:

50 Holland, Martin (1993), *European Integration – From Community To Union* (London, Pinter Publishers), p. 9.
51 Spaak, *op. cit.*, p. 236.

'... the Secretary General has been made to feel most unwelcome ... until representations by Her Majesty's Government to the six Governments concerned brought about a better atmosphere and an opportunity of regular attendance. But there has never been any consultation on the avoidance of duplication: in fact, when a suggestion of this kind was made on one occasion by the United Kingdom observer, it was brushed aside by M. Spaak on the grounds he was obliged to carry out the directives of the Messina Conference. All the evidence here suggests that the OEEC's position will not be considered.' [52]

In a seven-page letter, Ellis-Rees gave numerous examples of how the committee's objectives might duplicate the OEEC's work or cut across it, noting that:

'The whole proceeding has been unusual ... It may be asked ... why the six Member countries did not raise the issues in the Organisation, if they were dissatisfied with the speed of progress ... It would indeed have been courteous if one of their representatives at the Messina Conference had explained to the Council of Ministers of the OEEC, who were meeting a few days afterwards, what they were proposing to do.' [53]

Ellis-Rees then offered an explanation as to why the organisers of the Messina conference had behaved so oddly. It seemed they had 'political objectives':

'It is clear that both the French and German representatives on the Preparatory Committee have no other object in view, since they represent those elements in their respective governments who are in favour, or at least want to appear to be in favour, of European integration; and we are frequently told by representatives of Belgium and the Netherlands that the whole impetus behind this, so far as the Benelux is concerned, can be labelled "political" rather than "economic".'

From Spaak himself, in his memoirs, came an admission that confirmed this impression. With his colleagues, he wrote, 'we realised the political implications of our goal and knew that what we were about to achieve was nothing short of a revolution'. [54] Yet it was clear the British were not alone in having reservations about the talks. The German finance minister Hans Schäffer, took the view that:

'... partial or functional integration in the style of the Iron and Steel Community (*sic*) should not go further, since it was necessarily bound up with supra-national authorities. Instead one should aim for a gradual process towards full integration, making progress, if possible, on many subjects but in every case by co-operation between governments and without developing any further supra-national authorities.' [55]

The note added that it was not possible to judge what sort of agreement was likely to be reached on the setting up of a common market. There were clear 'signs of conflicting interests':

'The Germans, who have been very active in Brussels in supporting the movements towards further integration, have nevertheless been unwilling to make many concessions in the field of agriculture, which, of course, must be a matter of prime concern to the Dutch and the French. There are also signs that the French will be extremely reluctant to go very far very

---

52 PRO. T 232/433, 11 October 1955, pp. 49–55.
53 *Ibid.*
54 Spaak, *op. cit.*, pp. 230–231.
55 PRO. T 232/433, 10 October 1955, pp. 2–4.

fast in the direction of true integration through dismantling of tariffs ... and may try to create a diversion by suggesting integration in particular sectors, notably in transport, energy and the development of atomic energy.'[56]

In parallel with the common market talks, details of the proposals for an 'Atomic Community' were also being discussed, and it emerged that the new organisation would require all fissile materials, including supplies of uranium, to be placed in a common 'European pool' under 'Euratom's full control and ownership. A central intention was to prevent military programmes using them. This was wholly unacceptable to the British, as Europe's only nuclear power,[57] and it was clear that her interdependent civil and military programmes would not fit into this European mould. On 7 September 1955 therefore, Britain had no option but to withdraw from the Euratom talks.

Spaak was formally notified of the reasons for this in a letter from the British Ambassador in Brussels, George Labouchere. Informing Spaak that the UK government recognised 'the strong impetus towards multilateral co-operation in Europe', he pointed out that Britain's civil nuclear operations were so closely integrated with her military programme that there would be 'overriding difficulties in the defence field. These would prevent the UK from putting her resources, including supplies of nuclear material, into the European pool'.[58]

As discussions ground on, Bretherton was told how Spaak intended to organise the final stages of the committee's activities. In late October, there would be a meeting of delegations to hear reports from the committees, restricted only to the Six. Spaak then intended to set up a small drafting group to write the final report, and to hold a meeting of heads of delegations in November, from which Britain would also be excluded. Between these meetings there would be a meeting of the full steering committee, to keep everyone informed of progress. To this Britain was invited.

Britain was to be excluded from the drafting group because it was felt it might thus be possible for the Six to go further than Britain would wish. Her presence 'might in some way act as a brake on the others'.[59] In conclusion, Bretherton was told:

'Monsieur Spaak felt that it was unrealistic to expect that the United Kingdom would become an equal member of the Common Market, which, with the Atomic Energy proposal, represented the most important elements of under consideration. He felt, however, that it was highly desirable that we should be associated with whatever Common Market arrangements emerged ... we should not feel that we were being in any way excluded from the community. The fact that we were not expected to be present at the restricted meetings

---

56 *Ibid.*
57 Britain had exploded her first atomic bomb in 1952, and was well on the way to producing her first hydrogen bomb (tested in 1957). The first US hydrogen bomb test was in 1952. The USSR first detonated a nuclear device in 1949, her first thermo-nuclear test was in 1954. France's first atomic test was not until 1960. Britain was also substantially ahead of the rest of Europe in the development of nuclear power for civil purposes (the world's first large-scale nuclear power station was opened at Calder Hall, Cumberland, in August 1956).
58 PRO. FO 371/116054, pp. 61–63.
59 PRO. T 232/433, 14 October 1955, pp. 56–57.

of heads of delegations was solely designed to ensure that the Six reached as great a measure of agreement among themselves as possible.'[60]

The steering committee meeting was held on 7 November 1955. It was at this
meeting that Bretherton announced that Britain was to withdraw from the talks
on the common market. The way in which he communicated this has become a
legendary episode in the history of Britain's relations with 'Europe', subject to the
most bizarre historical disagreement. According to the account offered by Roy
Denman, Bretherton asked for the floor and spoke 'in the following terms':

'The future treaty which you are discussing has no chance of being agreed; if it was agreed,
it would have no chance of being ratified; and if it were ratified, it would have no chance of
being applied. And if it was applied, it would be totally unacceptable to Britain. You speak
of agriculture, which we don't like, of power over customs, which we take exception to, and
institutions which frighten us. Monsieur le president, messieurs, au revoir et bonne
chance.'[61]

Bretherton then apparently walked out. But to support his version of what happened, Denman, curiously, cites only a secondary source, a book by Charles Grant
published in 1994, nearly forty years after the event.[62] Grant, in turn, can only cite
as his own source Jean François Déniau's *L'Europe Interdite*, quoted in *Le Monde*
in October 1991.

Hugo Young also offers this version of the incident, giving a slightly different
wording, citing Déniau as his source (referring to him as 'J.-F. Denian').[63] Young
claims that Bretherton's text was drafted in Anthony Eden's own hand. But
Wolfram Kaiser, a respected German academic expert on European integration
who writes in detail about Britain's role in the EU, believes the speech to have been
'a Foreign Office statement', which Bretherton read out 'word for word'.[64] As to the
alleged 'walk-out', Young concedes that 'there is no documentary evidence that
anything so exciting occurred'.[65]

Nevertheless, according to Young, after Bretherton delivered his speech, 'Spaak
just blew up', saying: 'I am astonished and very hurt at this. You are just sticking to
your guns. England has not moved at all, and I am not going to move either.'[66]
Kaiser gives a very different account:

'The Six were not surprised. Spaak commented ironically that some governments could not
understand the new context for European integration that had been created by the Messina
conference, but separation was peaceful – as long a Britain refrained from torpedoing the
Messina initiative.'[67]

60 *Ibid.*
61 Denman, Roy, *Missed Chances, op. cit.*, p. 199.
62 Grant, Charles (1994), *Delors – Inside The House That Jacques Built* (London, Nicholas Brearley),
   p. 62.
63 Young, *op. cit.*, p. 93.
64 Kaiser, Wolfram (1996), *Using Europe, Abusing The Europeans – Britain And European Integration,
   1945–63* (London, Macmillan Press), p. 47. He cites as his reference: PRO FO/116055/361
   (7 November 1955). Young cites PRO T/234/181 as the source of a document that Bretherton
   may have used.
65 Young, *op. cit.*, p. 93.
66 *Ibid.*
67 Kaiser, *op. cit.*, p. 47.

While Denman has it that Bretherton walked out and did not return,[68] Young had Bretherton denying that he made 'the spectacular exit legend attributed to him'.[69] In any event, he could hardly have 'returned', since this was the committee's final session and Britain had already been told that it was not invited to the final drafting session. Nor could the Six have had anything to be surprised about. Bretherton had made Britain's position abundantly clear from the outset.

Still more oddly, neither Young nor Denman refer to the account of Miriam Camps,[70] a US State Department observer, although they both cite her as a source elsewhere and list her book in their bibliographies. Young calls her book 'the most authoritative history of the time'.[71] Yet, at the closing meeting of the committee, Camps describes Spaak as having decided to ask for comments only from those who had not accepted the principles of the Messina resolution: 'that is the British representative…' Bretherton, 'when asked for his comments' indicated, 'on instructions from London', that his government 'could not take a definite position on the common market until it knew all the details of the plan': an entirely reasonable point, since the committee had yet to produce its report.

This is echoed by a Treasury memorandum dated 17 November 1955, recording notes of a meeting with Spaak. This stated 'we cannot join Euratom' and then observes *viz-à-viz* British membership of the common market that, until Spaak had produced his report, 'it would be impolitic for us to take a formal position'. It concludes: 'It would indeed be a major reversal of UK policy to say that we should join a common market and the Europeans would be very surprised if we did'.[72] Spaak himself, who does not mention the Bretherton incident in his memoirs, dates Britain's withdrawal from the common market from a memorandum dated 19 December 1955, addressed to the German government. It declared that '…it is our view that Britain cannot join such a project'.[73]

Yet despite Camps's account and all the other evidence, Bretherton's departure is the point at which Denman insists that Britain 'walked out of Europe',[74] and which Young describes as her 'self-exclusion'.[75] Yet Britain had already withdrawn from Monnet's supranational Euratom because she was being asked to accept terms to which she could not possibly agree. And when the proposed treaties on Euratom and the common market became linked, Britain would have found it impossible to proceed. By leaving the Euratom talks, as she had to, Britain had, in effect, been excluded from the common market because of the way the treaties were subsequently linked.

68 Denman, *op. cit.*, p. 199.

69 Young, *op. cit.*, p. 93.

70 Camps, Miriam (1964), *Britain And The European Community 1955–1963* (London, Oxford University Press), p. 66. The book is described as 'a detailed and objective account of the British search for an accommodation with the European Economic Community…' It was lauded by the *Financial Times* as 'far away the most comprehensive and best account', with Roy Jenkins, in the *Daily Telegraph*, describing her degree of objectivity as 'just right'.

71 Young, *op. cit.*, p. 129.

72 PRO. T 234/181, 17 November 1955.

73 Spaak, *op. cit.*, p. 233.

74 Denman, *op. cit.*, p. 201.

75 Young, *op. cit.*, p. 99.

Nevertheless it is important to recognise that – contrary to the version given by Young, Denman and others – Britain made it clear that in every other way she wished to continue co-operating with her European neighbours. On nuclear power, Spaak had been told:

'the United Kingdom would not wish to do anything which would hinder the creation of Euratom if the six Messina countries should decide that their interests would be so met. Her Majesty's Government would in fact be fully prepared to conclude a separate agreement with the European organisation.' [76]

In October 1955, the UK Atomic Energy Authority had already proposed an Anglo-German joint civil nuclear programme and, largely at the behest of Britain, the OEEC had set up a working party on the possibilities of wider nuclear co-operation. Labouchere referred to this, stating that this body:

'seems likely to recommend a flexible system of multilateral co-operation ... the working party may well propose that within the organisation there should be room for agreement on specific projects or for specific purposes between groups of countries which would be neither binding on other countries in the organisation nor subject to their veto. Under such a scheme the countries more advanced in atomic energy could co-operate closely on joint research projects...'

... the OEEC working party reported in December.[77] It advocated the establishment of an OEEC directorate for nuclear energy, to co-ordinate national research and prepare joint projects. A key proposal was to build a plant to give Europe self-sufficiency in enriched uranium. But this was to be an intergovernmental venture, as opposed to Monnet's supranational plan and, although welcomed by Erhard, it created a crisis for Spaak. The combination of Britain's departure, the OEEC proposals and splits in the German delegation put not only the Messina agenda at risk but also Monnet's supranational ambitions.

Nothing better illustrates the gulf between intergovernmentalism and supranationalism than Monnet's response. Instead of welcoming Britain's generous offer, he called on his 'Action Committee' in January 1956 to adopt a declaration emphasising the supranational nature of Euratom and calling on the parliaments of the Six to give it their support. Adenauer also intervened. Unlike Erhard, he strongly favoured the customs union aspect of the common market and, although less keen on Euratom, regarded this as necessary to gain French support for the market. To counter the opposition of Erhard and others he, on 19 January, demanded from all his ministers 'a clear, positive attitude to European integration', stating that the Messina resolution had to be implemented without alteration and delay.[78]

At Monnet's request, President Eisenhower then took a hand. To the end of December, on Monnet's advice, the US had maintained a friendly distance from

76 PRO. FO 371/116054, *op. cit.*
77 Nelsen G. R. (1958), *European Organisation In The Field Of Atomic Energy*. European Yearbook IV, pp. 36–54.
78 Schwartz, H. (1997), *Konrad Adenauer: German Politician and Statesman In A Period Of War, Revolution And Reconstruction, Vol 2: The Statesman, 1952–1967* (Oxford, Berghahn), p. 231.

Euratom. He was conscious that too active a role might upset the French government, which had also seen the project as means whereby Europe might match the industrial power of the United States. Eisenhower now, on 22 February 1956, announced that the US would release 20 tons of enriched uranium (equivalent to 40 million tons of coal) for peaceful use by friendly states. He made it clear that the uranium would be offered on more preferential terms to Euratom than to any individual state. The condition was that Euratom had to have 'effective communal authority and could undertake duties and responsibilities similar to that (*sic*) of national governments'.[79] Again America had backed supranationalism.

Even in Washington, however, signs of division were appearing. According to the British embassy, there was now more enthusiasm for European integration in the State Department than among US economic policy makers, who feared the new common market might discriminate against imports from the dollar area.[80] For the moment, however, Monnet's State Department supporters continued to prevail.

Franco-German musical chairs

Through the first 10 months of 1956 the two main players in the European drama, France and Germany, lumbered through elaborate shifts of policy, ending in each reversing the positions they held at the start of the year. The resultant *impasse* threatened to bring the whole process to a halt.

The year began with a major upset in French domestic politics when, at a general election on 2 January, the Gaullists lost 100 of their 120 seats in the Assembly and most of their influence. The new Socialist prime minister, Guy Mollet, was a committed supranationalist, having been president of the Council of Europe assembly, a delegate to the ECSC assembly and an active member of Monnet's Action Committee. His foreign minister, Christian Pineau, was of like mind.

Despite this, the new French government, now also preoccupied with the rebellion in its Algerian colony, still believed it would have difficulty selling a common market to the French public. On 7 February, Pineau told the American Ambassador that 'a common market would not be possible ... without a great deal of education in France'.[81] The pair therefore agreed the two 'communities' should be separated, allowing Euratom to proceed. This, they thought, would better serve French interests. Germany, however, although still unenthusiastic about Euratom, favoured the common market.

On 21 April, the Spaak Committee finally published its report.[82] Running to 84 pages on the common market and 24 on Euratom, it largely followed the line of the Messina resolution. Crucially, the elements of Euratom which would have made British acceptance impossible remained.

---

79 Goldschmidt, B. (1982), *The Atomic Complex: A Worldwide Political History Of Nuclear Energy* (La Grange Park, Illinois, American Nuclear Society), pp. 293–294.
80 PRO. FO 371/116054, pp. 83–84. Letter from J. H. A. Watson, British Embassy, Washington, to A. J. Edden, Mutual Aid Department, Foreign Office, London, 10 November 1955.
81 Duchêne, *op. cit.*, p. 290.
82 Intergovernmental Committee created by the Messina Conference. *Report of the Heads of Delegation to the Foreign Ministers* (Brussels, Secretariat), 21 April 1956, pp. 9–135.

At Monnet's insistence, in the wake of the EDC debacle, the report made no mention of a 'High Authority', or 'supranational'. [83] It proposed that the new governing authority should be given the more neutral title of 'commission'. According to Camps:

'… great care had been taken to present proposals which could be accepted by the French government without, at the same time, abandoning any of the points of principle to which the "Europeans" attached real importance. Words and phrases such as "supra-nationalism", which in the post-EDC atmosphere were certain to generate unfavourable emotional responses were abandoned in favour of phrases that were neutral emotionally and logically defensible. Thus, on the most difficult aspect of them all, that of institutions, the Benelux memorandum side-stepped the acrimonious "intergovernmental-supra-national" argument but, at the same time, firmly established the central point, that is, that an institution endowed with real power would be required.' [84]

One highly significant new element in the package, added on French insistence, was a common agricultural policy. 'One cannot conceive the establishment of a general Common Market in Europe', said the report, 'without agriculture being included.' The reason for this was that farming, still mainly on peasant smallholdings, accounted for a quarter of France's workforce and was over-represented in parliament.[85] If it was necessary to sell the idea of a common market, a common policy offering French farmers the prospect of a new outlet for their increasing surpluses of grain and sugar beet might be vital.

Nevertheless, France remained opposed to a common market in principle. Her government thus pushed for the two treaties to be 'decoupled', hoping that the common market negotiations could stagnate. Germany could not agree. On 9 May, Adenauer's Cabinet confirmed that the two treaties must be linked.[86] At a foreign ministers meeting in Venice at the end of May, the Germans, with Italy and Benelux, reiterated that the treaties were interdependent and must be negotiated together. The *junktim* became a central feature of the talks, with the reluctant agreement of the French.[87]

France then insisted on another 'linkage' – between the reduction of tariffs between members in a common market and the harmonisation of social costs: overtime, length of paid holidays, and equal pay for men and women.[88] Pineau further proposed that the treaty's scope should be extended to member states' overseas territories. These proposals seemed calculated to provoke disagreement. It was an early example of a French negotiating tactic which was to become only too familiar in the decades ahead whereby, if France wanted to stop something – in this case the common market – it would make demands it knew to be unacceptable. These would provoke a breakdown of negotiations, for which others could be blamed.

---

83 Duchêne, *op. cit.*, p. 257.
84 Camps, *op. cit.*, p. 24.
85 Duchêne, *op. cit.*, p. 291.
86 Stirk, Peter M. R. (1996), *A History of European Integration Since 1914* (London, Pinter), p. 64.
87 Camps, *op. cit.*, p. 66.
88 *Op. cit.*, p. 65.

Nevertheless, the foreign ministers agreed that negotiations should begin. They would be held at the Château Val Duchesse near Brussels, and Spaak's report would provide the basis for discussion.

Histories of these negotiations tend to focus almost entirely on the common market aspects,[89] but the central issue was actually the differences over Euratom. As a recent study by the European Parliament put it:

'The Euratom treaty is often overlooked in the history and operation of the European Union. This neglect is unwarranted. Its tactical pairing with the EEC was a crucial factor in initially persuading and eventually convincing a sceptical French government to engage with European integration after the embittering experience of the aborted European defence community... At the time, in 1955 and early 1956, however, it was widely believed in many quarters that the Euratom proposal held the greater promise of success, while the EEC negotiations faltered.'[90]

Initially, though, it was the Euratom talks that got bogged down. The sticking point was the 'military question', whereby Euratom, as proposed, would prevent France pursuing a military nuclear programme. Although France was already working on a covert nuclear weapons programme, the socialist Mollet was unconcerned. He was happy to renounce nuclear research for military purposes, a position endorsed by Monnet's Action Committee.[91] But the prospect of a prohibition so angered France's nationalists that any Euratom treaty looked destined to follow the EDC. French ratification would never succeed if the impression was given that the treaty would stop France becoming a nuclear power.[92]

By early July, Mollet was forced to tell the National Assembly that Euratom would not stand in the way of French ambitions. With this he secured a vote of 322 to 181 in favour of pursuing negotiations. But that, in turn, strengthened a growing lobby against Euratom in Germany, which now believed it could allow France to restrict Germany's own nuclear ambitions, while pursuing her own. This supposed discrimination now threatened ratification by the *Bundestag*.[93]

The German situation was complex. In June, rumours that Soviet leaders would be invited to Washington DC by Eisenhower had fuelled German fears of a US-Soviet détente, the neutralisation of West Germany and the withdrawal of American troops from Europe. On 13 July, *The New York Times* revealed a plan drawn up by Admiral Radford, chairman of the joint chiefs of staff, which proposed reducing US conventional forces in Europe by 800,000 men. They were to be replaced with tactical nuclear weapons. Adenauer, already nervous about American intentions, had become determined that Germany should now have its own nuclear weapons. Despite the opposition of some of his Cabinet, led by Erhard, he now welcomed Euratom as a means of acquiring them.

---

89 For instance, Hugo Young's *This Blessed Plot, op. cit.*, does not include any references to Euratom in its index. Denman's book, *Missed Chances*, gives it three brief mentions.

90 Directorate General for Research, *op. cit.*, p. vii.

91 Soutou, G. H. (1981), 'The French Military Programme for Nuclear Energy, 1945–1981'. Occasional Paper No. 3, Nuclear History Programme, Maryland.

92 Duchêne, *op. cit.*, p. 295.

93 Duchêne, *op. cit.*, p. 297.

To Adenauer's frustration, the majority of his Cabinet supported Erhard's wish for a free-trade association rather than a common market. Although not an adept politician, Erhard was now a highly respected figure in Germany, because he was identified with the astonishing economic recovery, already known since 1954 as the *wirtschaftwunder* or 'economic miracle', which was rapidly making West Germany the richest and most dynamic country in western Europe.

Adenauer, therefore, had to make tactical concessions. On the common market, he retreated from the concept of Monnet's 'United States of Europe' in favour of Erhard's free market solution. Meanwhile, Monnet himself, as it happened, was doing his best to ditch the common market idea altogether. At a meeting in Bonn on 12 September, he told Adenauer that the French Parliament might not ratify such a treaty. Therefore, Euratom should be the priority.[94] On 20 September, Monnet's Action Committee called for Euratom to be ratified by the end of the year, ahead of any treaty on the common market.

Against this fractious background, on 25 September formal negotiations on both Euratom and the common market began in Brussels. Adenauer, under Erhard's influence, made a speech to the *Grandes Conférences Catholiques* in Brussels, arguing that the first period of European integration had been success-ful in preventing war in Europe and that any further integration should be 'flexi-ble and elastic'. On 5 October, he went further, telling his Cabinet that Euratom would allow West Germany access to the technology necessary to produce atomic warheads as quickly as possible. But the only way to get Euratom was to agree to a 'common market' on Erhard's terms: namely a free trade area.[95]

Perversely, the French had by now begun to warm to the original idea of a full common market, but based on a customs union. The leaders of France's farmers and key French industrialists had come out in favour. But they demanded a price. If high social welfare standards were to be imposed on employers, as France had suggested in the Venice conference as a 'wrecking' tactic, they must be 'har-monised' throughout the new 'community', to avoid the other five member states, especially Germany, gaining a competitive advantage. Predictably, this was entire-ly unacceptable to the Erhard faction.

Thus, from the beginning of the year, the positions of the two main players had become almost wholly reversed. The French, having first supported Euratom and opposed a common market, now opposed Euratom and favoured a common mar-ket. The Germans had now moved to the position abandoned by France.

This provoked a crisis so serious that, at a meeting of the foreign minister of the Six in Paris on 19–20 October, no way forward could be found. Euratom looked doomed. With an impasse on the harmonisation of social policies it seemed the common market would follow. Erhard, for one, was confident that the 'distasteful common market project' was dying, and that the prospects for his chosen alterna-tive, a free trade area, were now looking distinctly hopeful.[96]

---

94 *Ibid.*
95 Williams, *op. cit.*, pp. 439–440.
96 Schwartz, *op. cit.*, p. 240.

At that very moment, however, great events were to rescue the 'project' from oblivion. The irony was that the country whose actions were about to put it firmly back on the rails was Great Britain.

Britain's 'destructive embrace'

Despite Britain's seemingly confident refusal to get drawn into any supranational experiments, some in her government were becoming alarmed that a successful 'customs union' of the Six, based on common tariffs, might be used to exclude British trade.

Following the collapse of the attempts to set up 'Defence' and 'Political' Communities, it had not been unrealistic for the British government to believe that the Messina initiatives would fail. The French Fourth Republic was already a byword for political and economic instability, with 20 changes of government in 10 years. The value of the franc was plummeting, and there was France's humiliating failure to keep control over Indochina, and the running sore of Algeria. In Germany, there was the serious rift between Adenauer and Erhard. Furthermore, following the failure of the EDC, Eden had brought off his triumphant intergovernmental solution with the WEU, enthusiastically accepted by the Six. If the Euratom and common market negotiations failed, there was no reason to believe that British alternatives, based on intergovernmental structures, might not also be accepted.

Nevertheless the British government had given serious thought to the advantages and disadvantages of British membership of a common market, and these had been studied by a working group, set up in June 1955 under a senior Treasury civil servant Burke Trend. When this group submitted its internal report in October 1955, it reflected the dominant British view that a free trade area was preferable to a customs union. Only this option allowed Britain to retain national autonomy in foreign trade policy and to safeguard its Commonwealth preferences. Conscious of the danger of British exclusion from a 'customs union', the report did, however, offer that 'it can be argued, with some reason, that the disadvantages of abstaining would, in the long run, outweigh the advantages'.[97]

The response of the Foreign Office was simply to argue that membership of a common market would be incompatible with Britain's role as a world power.[98] But it also believed that, as with the EDC, the Messina initiative would collapse as a result of French obstruction.[99]

Macmillan accepted the Foreign Office view. But in the autumn of 1955, with the prospect of a more 'Europe-friendly', centre-left government being elected in France, there seemed an increasing chance of a common market succeeding. The civil servants of the economic ministries became more concerned about the dangers of exclusion from 'Europe'. In October 1955, just as the Spaak talks were drawing to

97 PRO. CAB 134/1030/201, 24 October 1955.
98 PRO. CAB 134/1030/200, 24 October 1955.
99 PRO. CAB 134/889, 17 October 1955.

an end, it was agreed they could no longer 'count on the project collapsing of its own accord'. They therefore decided that the common market 'if possible, should be frustrated'.[100]

This represented a significant change in British policy, from the previous stance of 'benign neglect'. The Foreign Office decided to force the issue with a diplomatic offensive. The intention was to divert the 'common market' initiative into the orbit of the OEEC, where the British government could dilute it into something more intergovernmental. The term given to this strategy was 'destructive embrace', taken from a note appended to a memorandum by Gladwyn Jebb, Britain's Ambassador to France.[101]

In pursuit of this strategy, letters from Macmillan were sent to the US and German governments, stressing British displeasure with the Messina initiative and particularly the plan for a customs union. On 14 December 1955, while he was on a visit to Paris to attend a WEU ministerial council and then a North Atlantic Council meeting, Macmillan was still convinced the Messina initiative would fail. He recorded in his diary:

'The French will never go into the "common market" – the German industrialists and economists equally dislike it, although Adenauer is attracted to the idea of closer European unity on political grounds. This, of course, is very important, and I made it clear that we would welcome and assist the plan, although we would not join.'[102]

Inevitably, at the WEU meeting, Macmillan was roundly attacked by the Six, with Spaak 'leading the charge'. Nobody had expected British participation, Spaak had said, but neither had they foreseen a frontal assault by the British government.[103]

The response from the US government was predictably unhelpful. On 12 December Secretary of State Dulles simply affirmed support for the common market. Macmillan aborted his offensive. At the end of 1955 all British embassies were instructed to offer reserved diplomatic support for the common market, to avoid conflict with Washington.[104] According to Kaiser, all Britain had achieved by this 'attempted sabotage' was 'the creation of justified suspicion among the Six as to the British motives in Western Europe… and to raise among the Six the traditional unpleasant spectre of perfidious Albion'.[105]

On 21 December 1955, Macmillan was, somewhat unwillingly, transferred from the Foreign Office to the Treasury. Because of its economic implications, however, he kept some control of the European agenda. And by then he was having serious concerns about the possible success of the 'common market'. 'What then are we to do?' he asked.

---

100 PRO. CAB 134/1026, 27 October 1955.
101 Harold Macmillan Archives. Quoted in Horne, *op. cit.*, p. 363. Gladwyn Jebb appended to a brief on the Common Market the words 'embrace destructively'.
102 Harold Macmillan diaries. Quoted in Horne, *op. cit.*, p. 362.
103 PRO. FO 371/116057/384, 15 December 1955.
104 PRO. FO 371/116057/390, 31 December 1955.
105 Kaiser, *op. cit.*, p. 53.

'Are we just to sit back and hope for the best? If we do it may be very dangerous for us; and perhaps Messina will come off after all and that will mean Western Europe dominated in fact by Germany and used as an instrument for the revival of power through economic means. It really is giving them on a plate what we fought two wars to prevent.'[106]

Despite the failure of his first attempt to subvert the common market, therefore, he sought to regain the diplomatic initiative, instructing his officials to form an inter-ministerial working group to develop possible alternatives. This group was chaired by R. B. W. Clarke, a former *Financial Times* journalist, now head of the Overseas Finance Group in the Treasury. In the spring of 1956, before the ministers of the Six had met in Vienna to agree to formal negotiations, Clarke's committee had produced a number of options, plans 'A to G'. That chosen was 'Plan G', a Free Trade Area (FTA) for manufactured goods only.[107]

Parliament was told what was happening in July 1956, when Sir Edward Boyle, economic secretary to the Treasury, announced that the government was engaged in a major reappraisal of its policy towards the emerging common market. On the European front, approaches were made to the OEEC and, later that month, the OEEC Council responded with a decision to establish a working party to study possible forms of association between the Six and the OEEC, including a possible Europe-wide free trade area.

The new strategy looked promising. The European powers were broadly sympathetic. Erhard was enthusiastic. This was so much closer to his own ideas than any *dirigiste* common market. Macmillan reported that Washington was 'surprisingly positive'. Even Commonwealth leaders were not hostile, seeing in it an opportunity for increased trade with Europe. Duchêne conceded that the FTA was 'a genuine attempt to adapt British interests to the common market'.[108]

Work on 'Plan G' continued through the summer and, to minimise the institutionalisation involved, it was proposed that the FTA be integrated into the existing structures of the OEEC. Formal OEEC negotiations were launched in Paris in October 1956. By that time, common market negotiations looked irretrievably stalled. Erhard was confidently predicting the death of the idea. The Six were in disarray. At that moment, the great events intervened.

Suez: The watershed

On 26 July 1956, Egypt's new leader Colonel Nasser had nationalised the Suez Canal, since its opening in 1869 under Anglo-French ownership. Through the remaining weeks of summer, amid an atmosphere of growing international crisis, Britain and France had assembled a military task force to seize it back. The problem was that this might be viewed as an act of 'colonialist aggression' by the international community, including the USA.

On 23 October, amid intense secrecy, Britain's prime minister Eden therefore sent his foreign secretary to rendezvous in a French villa at Sèvres with Mollet,

---

106 PRO. T 234/100, 1 February 1956. Macmillan to Sir E. Bridges.
107 PRO. BT 11/5715, 10 May 1956.
108 Duchêne, *op. cit.*, p. 320.

Pinay, Israel's prime minister Ben Gurion and his chief of staff, General Dayan. Between them they agreed a plan. Israel would invade Egypt. Anglo-French forces would then intervene in a 'police action' to separate the combatants and seize back the Canal. Nasser would be toppled.

The scheme did not work. On 29 October, Israel invaded Egypt, as planned. But when the following day Britain and France issued an ultimatum, demanding a cease-fire, this provoked a storm of international protest, only complicated by a crisis now blowing up over the Soviet Union's military invasion of Hungary, to suppress the first major popular rising against Communist tyranny in eastern Europe.

This suddenly explosive international situation, possibly threatening a European war, convinced Adenauer more than ever that Germany must have nuclear weapons. In Cabinet on 31 October he put to Erhard that Euratom was now vital to West Germany's security interests. He then added that the only way this treaty could be agreed was if Germany accepted the common market. On 4 November, Soviet tanks rolled into Budapest, where thousands were to die in street battles. Invoking his constitutional right as Chancellor to make policy on matters of national interest, Adenauer bludgeoned his Cabinet into agreeing that he should go to Paris to negotiate, on his own terms, a final settlement on both Euratom and the common market.[109]

Through one of those accidents of history, Adenauer was on the overnight train to Paris on 5 November as the news broke that British and French paratroops had landed in the Canal Zone. When he arrived in the early hours of 6 November at the *Gare de l'Est*, he found half the French Cabinet waiting for him at the station. Adenauer immediately gave his unconditional approval of French actions, thus instantly strengthening Franco-German relations.

As that day unfolded, however, the British Cabinet was also in crisis session over a report from Macmillan that massive selling of sterling had led to an unprecedented collapse in Britain's currency reserves. Washington was furious at Britain's action. So was the Soviet Union, whose prime minister Nikolai Bulganin threatened to shower London and Paris with nuclear missiles. Eden caved in. Unilaterally he decided to abort the Suez campaign. When he telephoned his French opposite number to convey his decision, Mollet was furious at what seemed like betrayal. Seizing the moment, Adenauer advised him to 'make Europe your revenge'.[110]

The Suez crisis, ending in such fiasco, changed everything. In its aftermath, while the Canal remained blocked, oil in Western Europe was in short supply, petrol had to be rationed, roads emptied. This brought home Europe's dependence on Middle East oil, underlining the need for alternative sources of energy. Euratom, with its promise of abundant nuclear power, seemed suddenly an urgent necessity. So dramatic was the impact that a colleague of Monnet suggested, only half-jokingly, that a statue should be erected to Nasser, 'the federator of Europe'.[111]

109 Williams, *op. cit.*, p. 441.
110 Moravcsik, Andrew (1998), *The Choice Of Europe: Social Purpose And State Power: From Messina To Maastricht* (London, UCL), p. 144.
111 Monnet, *op. cit.*, p. 422.

Progress was now rapid. The contentious issue of social harmonisation became a mere trifle. Adenauer removed this previously insurmountable obstacle by agreeing 'in principle' to the French demands and, on 24 January 1957, the Germans also agreed to exclude military installations from Euratom control, clearing the way for the French nuclear weapons programme. By then, Adenauer had already achieved his own nuclear ambitions. In December, a NATO military committee, in a secret directive, had stipulated that 12 West German divisions on the front to the east would be equipped for nuclear warfare. It was assumed that America would supply the firepower, but Adenauer was now satisfied that the way for West Germany to acquire nuclear weapons was clear.[112]

However, the way for the common market was still not entirely open. There were still two issues to be resolved: the problem of overseas territories and the decision-making mechanisms of the two new communities. The key was the overseas territories question. Bled dry by wars in Indochina and Algeria, France could not afford vital modernisation programmes in its territories without German financial support. Post-Suez, Adenauer was willing to contribute nearly half the needed funds.[113] Final agreement was reached in February when any restrictions on the use of fissile material supplied by Euratom were removed.

The Euratom and common market treaties were signed by representatives of the Six governments on 25 March 1957, at a venue carefully chosen for its symbolic significance: the Capitol in Rome, the city which for 2,000 years, under the Roman Empire and the Papacy, had stood at the centre of European history.

The preamble to the treaty setting up the European Economic Community opened with a declaration that it expressed the determination of the 'High Contracting Parties' to 'lay the foundations of an ever-closer union among the peoples of Europe'. In many respects, what followed took the form not so much of a treaty as of a constitution, defining the institutions of a new type of government, with definitions of their purposes and powers. This centred on a new 'European Commission', more an executive than a civil service, which alone would have the right to initiate legislation. Alongside it was to be a 'Council of Ministers', representing the governments of the member states; an 'Assembly', made up of delegates from their national parliaments; and a 'European Court of Justice', with appointees from each member state, entrusted with adjudicating on matters of Community law, in particular where it conflicted with the laws of member states.

The model for this new form of government was already familiar. It was adapted from the Coal and Steel Community. This in turn had been adapted from the League of Nations blueprint sketched out at the end of the 1920s by Monnet's friend Salter in his proposal for a supranational 'United States of Europe'. Crucially, the rule of unanimity which, according to Spaak, had been 'responsible for the bankruptcy of the League of Nations' had been heavily circumscribed. The authors of the Treaty (of which he was one) had been aware of the dangers of

---

112 Williams, *op. cit.*, p. 442.
113 Stirk, *op. cit.*, p. 145. He cites: Küsters, *Fondements de la communauté économique européen,* pp. 257–268.

unanimity and had held that 'the will of the majority should as a rule prevail and that unanimous decisions should only be mandatory in exceptional circumstances'.[114]

Interestingly, Monnet was not invited to Rome for the signing of the new treaties. Both the *Bundestag* and the *Assemblée Nationale* ratified them in the first week of July. Mendès-France voted against ratification. In an earlier debate, he had cautioned, 'France must not be the victim of the Treaty. A democrat may abdicate by giving in to an internal dictatorship, but also by delegating his powers to an external authority'.[115] The last to ratify was Italy, the following December. The European Economic Community was finally born.

It had been a close run thing.

---

114 Spaak, *op. cit.*, p. 250.
115 Monnet, *op. cit.*, p. 425.

Chapter 6

'A Triumph For Monnet': 1958–1961

'Great Britain has lost an empire and not yet found a role.'
Dean Acheson, speech to West Point
Military Academy, 5 December 1962

'No matter how much Macmillan privately asserted that entry into Europe was an act with wide-ranging political consequences, he presented it to the British people as an economic move dictated by commercial imperatives.'
George Ball, *The Past Has Another Pattern*[1]

According to one historian, the governing bodies of the new 'European Economic Community' started work in Brussels on New Year's Day 1958.[2] This was unlikely, and not just because it had been a bank holiday throughout Europe. In what was to become a characteristic of the Community's decision-making process, the foreign ministers of the Six, meeting in Paris on 20 December, had failed to reach an agreement on nominations for the key post of president of the Commission and had adjourned their meeting.

By the time ministers reconvened on 6 January, the decision had been made. The first president was to be a former German law professor, Walter Hallstein.[3] His priority was to turn the Commission, comprising nine members, into an executive body that would 'breathe economic and political life into the product of the Treaty authors'.[4]

The choice of Brussels as headquarters was accidental. Monnet himself still hoped a single site could be found to house all three institutions of the 'Communities', the ECSC, Euratom and the EEC. 'We are building Europe, brick by brick,' he wrote. 'Europe needs a focus to make it tangible and real to people.' He wanted an equivalent to the USA's District of Columbia, giving 'Europe' its own capital.[5] One suggested location had been Compiègne, near Paris, where the 1918 armistice had been signed, and where Hitler humiliated the French government in 1940 by forcing Petain and his colleagues to sign a surrender document in the same railway carriage. In the event, Luxembourg's foreign minister had partly decided the issue, by insisting that ECSC staff stayed in his country while

---

1 Ball, *op. cit.*, p. 217.
2 Duchêne, *op. cit.*, p. 309.
3 Professor Hallstein had been Adenauer's representative at the Schuman Plan talks. He was the second German to hold a senior international post after the war, following the appointment of General Hans Spiedel as commander of Nato land forces in Europe in 1957.
4 Narjes, K. H. (1998), 'Walter Hallstein and the early phase of the EEC', in Wilfried Loth, *et al.*, *Walter Hallstein – The Forgotten European?* (London, Macmillan Press), p. 109. Each country had one Commissioner, plus a second for each of the three largest states – France, Germany and Italy.
5 Duchêne, *op. cit.*, p. 310.

refusing to accept any more Eurocrats apart from the new European Court of Justice. Brussels ended up as a 'provisional' site for the rest, leaving the ECSC in Luxembourg. In the manner of things, 'provisional' was to become permanent.

Initially, the Commission was financed by a loan from the High Authority of the ECSC, which gave it freedom to develop its own agenda. Briefs to individual commissioners were allocated in 10 weeks, the key agricultural portfolio going to a Dutchman, Sicco Mansholt. A crude organisational structure had emerged three weeks later and, by the end of 1958, a thousand officials were at work.

Hallstein was very much in charge, insisting on the right to choose his own staff and resisting pressure from national governments to accept appointees. He enjoyed the trappings of power, receiving emissaries from foreign governments in royal style. One visiting American, Clarence Randall, was heard to complain that Hallstein's officials were 'getting a little stuffy', falling into the habit of addressing each other as 'Your excellency'. Randall recorded that he was tempted to say in a loud voice, 'Nuts!'[6]

One problem was the provision of staff for the Council of Ministers. This need had not been foreseen in the treaties, but member state governments demanded their own permanent staffs in Brussels. On 26 January 1958, therefore, the Six decided to create the Committee of Permanent Representatives (Coreper) to prepare the work of the Councils. Coreper soon began to carry out most of the routine work of examining and discussing Commission proposals, 'preparing' decisions so that they would only have to be 'trimmed' at the full meetings of the Council. Initially, Coreper meetings absorbed much of Hallstein's time until he secured agreement that he could delegate this work to his own directors-general. The Community bureaucracy had developed a life of its own.

Then there was the language problem. It had been agreed that the languages of the member states should be used, although the Commission had rejected a request to treat Dutch and Flemish as separate languages. The very first Council regulation, on 15 April 1958, established French, German, Italian and Dutch as the official languages of the Communities. Nevertheless, French soon became the dominant language. But this multi-lingual approach came at a price. Translation services accounted for approximately 30 percent. of the entire staff expenditure.[7]

On 19 March 1958, the 142-member European Assembly, made up of delegates from national parliaments, convened for the first time in the Council of Europe building in Strasbourg, electing Robert Schuman as its president.[8]

Through those early days of the EEC, Monnet avoided direct involvement in the affairs of the new 'government'. But he was far from idle. Through his Action

6 Winand, Pascaline (1993), *Eisenhower, Kennedy and The United States Of Europe* (New York, St Martin's Press), p. 130.

7 Narjes, *op. cit.*, p. 112.

8 Another 'Community institution' launched at the same time which was to play a far more significant role than its relatively low public profile might suggest was the European Investment Bank (EIB). Drawing on substantial funds guaranteed by member state governments, this was set up to provide low-interest loans to a vast range of projects which might serve the purposes of 'integration'.

Committee, he searched for ways to extend the scope of his 'Communities', in pursuit of his eventual objective of a 'United States of Europe'. One idea which particularly excited him was monetary union. The trigger for his interest had been France's continuing financial crisis, and the plummeting value of the franc, exacerbated by the Algerian war. As always, the solution had to be within a 'European framework'. 'Via money,' as Monnet put it in September 1957, 'Europe could become political in five years.'[9] The following year he wrote to a Dutch politician, suggesting that:

'... the current communities should be completed by a Finance Common Market which would lead us to European economic unity. Only then would ... the mutual commitments make it fairly easy to produce the political union which is the goal.'[10]

Monnet had already suggested a common financial policy to one of France's many prime ministers of the period, Félix Gaillard, yet another of his former assistants who had worked for him in 1945. But Gaillard was to last only five months in office, and no progress was made. Monnet was undismayed. 'There are no premature ideas,' he wrote. 'There are only opportunities for which one must learn to wait.'[11]

As it happened, the chaos of France's finances was about to be brought to a sudden end. The Fourth Republic was in its death throes, torn apart by insurrection in Algeria. On 1 June 1958, in a legal *coup d'état*, brought on by rumours that the Fourth Republic was about to treat with the Algerian independence movement, de Gaulle returned to power, to exercise what Clement Attlee was later to call a 'temporary, semi-dictatorship'.[12] By Christmas, de Gaulle had imposed a series of crisis measures, one of which was to convert every 100 francs (then standing at 1300 to £1) into one. The psychological boost given by the 'New Franc' and other measures transformed France's economy with remarkable speed.

By this time, Monnet had already found another focus for his energies. With his 'supranational government' in place, he felt the need to tackle the only major power in Europe which he thought could pose a threat to it, with its unrepentant belief in 'intergovernmentalism'. He wanted to solve what he saw as the problem of Britain.

The supranationalists' revenge

The political disaster of Suez had dealt Britain's self-confidence a shattering blow. The crisis had fatally weakened Eden, who resigned, pleading ill-health, to be succeeded on 10 January 1957 by Macmillan. By the time the new prime minister was able to re-focus on European affairs, the situation had changed irretrievably. Britain's prestige had suffered a massive blow and the re-orientation of European politics was already well advanced. This was not immediately recognised by

9 Duchêne, *op. cit.*, p. 312.
10 *Ibid.*
11 Monnet, *op. cit.*, p. 428.
12 *Hansard*, House of Lords, 2 August 1962, col. 430.

Macmillan, who later conceded that he failed to recognise the depth of Franco-German reconciliation.[13]

Despite this, Macmillan did make adjustments. With the Common Market and Euratom now looking inevitable, the OEEC had been asked to research options available for Britain's proposed Free Trade Area. In late January, a working party reported that it would be technically possible to establish such an area that would include the Six as a single bloc. Thus, Macmillan, previously having seen the FTA as an alternative to the Common Market, now began to think of it as a 'trade roof' over all the OEEC countries, including the EEC.

After the signing of the Rome treaties, however, Britain's FTA was viewed by the Six without enthusiasm. London therefore offered substantial concessions, not least in allowing the 'supranational' principle of 'majority voting'. Then, in October 1957 the other OEEC members agreed to set up an intergovernmental committee to develop the project further. By now, however, suspicion of the British verged on paranoia and, by February 1958, the French were demanding wholly unacceptable conditions, not least that Britain ended its preferential trading agreements with the Commonwealth.[14]

With the accession of de Gaulle, things got worse. While Erhard had sympathised with the idea of a free trade area, de Gaulle brokered a 'non-intervention' deal with Adenauer, as a result of which, on 14 November, France was able to reject the British plan.[15] *The Times* thundered 'France the Wrecker', but to no avail. The initiative had collapsed. Never again would a free trade proposal on the scale of the FTA become a serious challenge to the Six.

The collapse rocked British industry. Leaders of the Federation of British Industries (later to become the Confederation of British Industry or CBI) now feared they might also be excluded from a second customs union taking shape in Scandinavia, and called on the government to set up a separate European Free Trade Association (EFTA). A new plan was rapidly conceived to group what became known as the 'outer seven', with a format remarkably similar to the abortive 'Plan G'. Negotiations were wrapped up by November 1959, with the initialling of the Stockholm Convention. Great Britain, Denmark, Sweden, Norway, Austria, Portugal and Switzerland had created their own free trade association. Europe was now, literally, at 'Sixes and Sevens'.[16]

Meanwhile, Monnet turned his attention his remaining rival, the OEEC: the jewel in the crown of European intergovernmentalism. As long as it existed, under British chairmanship, it could provide a rallying point for further dissident schemes. It had to be destroyed.

Monnet set about this task in his usual meticulous and devious way, devising as neat an assassination as can be imagined. But nothing of this found its way into

---

13 Horne, *op. cit.*, p. 364.
14 Duchêne, *op. cit.*, p. 321.
15 Wallace, William. 'Walter Hallstein: the British Perspective', in Loth, *et al.*, *op. cit.*, p. 189.
16 Hugo Young fails to understand the difference between the FTA and EFTA, which were two entirely different entities. He therefore compresses the events relating to both, ending up with an entirely fictional account of developments.

his memoirs. The outline of what happened can be reconstructed from Duchêne,[17] with additional detail from Camps. Their accounts give a remarkable insight into the workings of a shrewd, skilled, and ultimately ruthless political operator.

To start the destruction, Monnet used Hallstein to draft a paper on the EEC's policy on external economic relations, stating that there should be no 'regional' association with the FTA. Instead, the EEC should treat all non-member groups and countries on an equal basis, thereby enabling members to be played off against each other, minimising the chances of Britain mobilising yet another coalition against the Common Market. The Council of Ministers adopted the paper on 16 March 1959.

Then, on 27 May, Monnet was in Washington to attend the funeral of his old friend John Foster Dulles. He took the opportunity to see another friend, Douglas Dillon,[18] now Under-Secretary of State for Economic Affairs. Next day he lunched with Eisenhower. Back in Paris on 9 June, he had a long talk with John Tuthill, economics minister at the US embassy. The ground had been prepared.

What Monnet had in mind was a 'reform' of the OEEC, by which he meant its neutralisation or abolition. To dilute Britain's influence, he suggested to Tuthill that the US and Canada should also become members. Ostensibly, this would allow the economic problems of the 'free world' to be discussed on a wider canvas,[19] but the real objective was to weaken Britain's grip on the OEEC.

In his own version of 'shuttle diplomacy', Monnet crossed the Atlantic again, to give Dillon a paper entitled *A New Era in Atlantic Relations*. Then, in July he learned that the US and Canada would join the OEEC. Back in Paris, Monnet saw Tuthill again, this time with a plan to replace the 'discredited' OEEC altogether. On 27 July, Monnet handed a revised version of his original paper to Pinay, now finance minister. Omitted was any reference to the OEEC. He simply proposed an organisation for 'permanent consultations' including the Common Market, the US and Great Britain. True to form, Monnet chose proxies for his idea, suggesting that this proposal should be put jointly by de Gaulle and Adenauer.

In December everything came together. Dillon arrived in Europe for a North Atlantic Council meeting. While in Europe, according to Camps,[20] he 'informed himself' first hand of current thinking on European trade. The impression gained in London was that he was 'cool to an OEEC-wide free trade area', and 'becoming increasingly concerned at the prospect of friction between the two European groups'.[21] However, he seemed to have agreed with British officials that the OEEC 'was the right forum for discussions on European trade', although, without knowing the background, Camps wrote:

'... it seems clear that the Commission of the Community, M. Monnet, and the French government all made it plain during his subsequent discussions with them that they disliked

---

17 *Op. cit.*, pp. 321–323. Despite his detailed account of this episode, Duchêne does not seem fully to have appreciated the wider significance of what his researches had uncovered,

18 Dillon had been US ambassador to France in 1956 when Monnet first met him.

19 *Ibid.*

20 *Op. cit.*, p. 241.

21 *Ibid.*

the OEEC as a forum, particularly as a forum for the discussion of European trade questions.'[22]

Coincidentally, the leaders of the four western powers – Eisenhower, de Gaulle, Adenauer and Macmillan held a summit in Paris on 19 to 21 December 1959, at the end of a NATO council. What clearly was unknown to most commentators was that, prior to this meeting, Monnet had written to Eisenhower. In his letter he had suggested setting up a committee to establish a new 'Organisation for Economic Co-operation and Development' (OECD), stressing how important it was that the Commission was represented on that committee.

Thus was the ambush prepared. During a meeting supposedly about East-West relations, Camps reported that 'rather unexpectedly' trade questions were discussed, 'particularly in the corridors'. She noted that the subsequent communiqué had 'all the marks of a highly negotiated document'.[23] The result was that, on a US initiative, a 'Special Economic Conference' was held in January 1960. Before it had even started, the balance had been tilted against the OEEC. Nearly half the OEEC's representatives were excluded, yet the Commission, United States and Canada were included. Furthermore Douglas Dillon took the chair, annoying the British with his 'obvious support for the French'.[24] When business turned to what was the real reason for the meeting, Dillon suggested that

'The twenty governments who were members or associates of the OEEC should examine the question of whether there should be a 'successor' organisation to the OEEC which should continue those functions of the OEEC that still seemed important, take on appropriate new functions, and be so constructed that the United States and Canada could become full members.'[25]

Now the ambush had been sprung, Dillon then suggested that the OEEC itself should not examine the question. The task should be delegated to a group of three experts, one each from the EFTA countries, the EEC and the USA. Not surprisingly, because of the 'similarity' in the views between the US and the EEC, the Seven thought this group would be 'unbalanced'. The word 'rigged' might have been more appropriate.

Thus, Dillon did not wholly get his way. The committee convened with a Frenchman, an Englishman, an American and a Greek. The conference communiqué, however, gave testament to the underlying power struggle. Wrote Camps:

'To the more ardent "Europeans" the OEEC was the embodiment of the British concept of European unity: co-operation without political commitment. This kind of unity they believed to be inadequate and they feared that if it were allowed to flourish it would undermine the European Community.'[26]

Unsurprisingly, when the expert committee reported, as Camps put it, 'it had not been easy for the Four to find a common view'. The upshot was another committee, chaired by the secretary-general designate of the OEEC's replacement

22 *Op. cit.*, pp. 241–242.
23 *Op. cit.*, p. 243.
24 *Op. cit.*, p. 246.
25 *Op. cit.*, p. 247.
26 *Op. cit.*, p. 248.

organisation, the OECD. The major United States objective, 'fully shared by the French and to a considerable extent by the Six, had been achieved'. The OEEC, and with it Britain's power base in Europe, had been destroyed. Monnet's revenge was complete.

EFTA – the *coup de grâce*

One of the myths assiduously fostered about Britain's post-war attitude towards Europe, before she supposedly showed herself to be more 'outward looking' by joining the Common Market, is that until that time she had somehow remained condescendingly aloof from continental affairs. But the record shows the very opposite. From the moment when her armies had played a vital part in liberating western Europe in 1944–1945, Britain had remained as profoundly involved in the affairs of Europe as she had been for hundreds of years, seeking to assist and co-operate with her nearest geographical neighbours in every conceivable way.

The only reason why this myth of her insular lack of concern later came to be promoted was that it reflected the divergence between those two sharply opposed views of how international co-operation in Europe should best be pursued. Britain's opposition to 'supranationalism' stemmed from a different vision of how Europe should be brought together. Favouring the alternative of 'intergovernmental' co-operation, that was why she had consistently supported or led the way in setting up every kind of intergovernmental organisation, from NATO and the WEU, to the Council of Europe and the OEEC itself.

Another area in which Britain showed tireless zeal for intergovernmental co-operation was civil aviation, where her aircraft industry was still a world leader. She was active in setting up the European Civil Aviation conference in Strasbourg in 1953, which led to the Europe-wide system of air navigation safety known as Eurocontrol (agreed in 1960). In 1956, through the setting up of a Supersonic Transport Aircraft Committee, she took the first steps which were to lead eight years later to a Franco-British agreement to build the world's first supersonic airliner, the Concorde.

To 'supranationalists', these forms of co-operation were viewed with suspicion because they depended on preserving that principle of national sovereignty they so despised. This was why they viewed with particular suspicion the idea of 'free trade', as expressed in the new European Free Trade Area, because it was based on a denial of their credo. And the final step in sabotaging Britain's attempts to maintain European co-operation on an intergovernmental basis came in 1960 when Hallstein masterminded what was to become in effect EFTA's *coup de grâce*.

The Treaty of Rome had laid out a programme for harmonising external tariffs between the Six in three four-year stages, during which time duties on what was called 'intra-community trade' would be abolished. The first stage was due to end on 31 December 1961. But Hallstein proposed that the process should be speeded up. This would mean that low-tariff countries of the Six would have to levy much higher duties on their imports from the outside world, including the EFTA members with whom they did substantial trade.

Decided unilaterally without consulting EFTA, this, as was intended, threw the organisation into disarray, as it had planned to phase its own tariff reductions in line with the EEC. Member states had difficulties in agreeing to match the cuts and, compared with the EEC, the Seven were thus shown to be weak and unco-ordinated.

Eventually, the EFTA members came into line, but not until six months after the EEC changes had come into force, and after Britain had fruitlessly invested considerable diplomatic capital in an unsuccessful bid to pressure Hallstein into reversing his acceleration programme. The delay was a major defeat for the British, who were perceived to be unable to match the cohesion of the EEC.[27] The very future of EFTA seemed in doubt. Relations between Britain and the Six had sunk to an all-time low.

Britain's crisis of confidence

At the start of the 1960s, Macmillan and his colleagues were having to think hard about Britain's position in the world. In the 15 years since the end of the Second World War, this had changed dramatically. In 1945, politically, economically and militarily, she had still been unmistakably a world power. Her empire, including the great English-speaking dominions of Canada, Australia, New Zealand and South Africa, stretched round the globe. The Union Jack still flew over more than a quarter of the human race. The peoples of a fifth of the world's land surface looked to London as the centre of their government. Her influence was supreme across the Middle East. After the USA, she was the second richest nation in the world. In terms of manpower, the contribution of Britain and her Commonwealth to the war effort had been even greater than America's, and her navy was still the second most powerful in existence.

But, in those first post-war years of rationing, austerity and endless economic crises, Britain's real weakness had been cruelly exposed. As a first major step in dismantling her empire, she had in 1947 given independence to the vast Indian sub-continent, including Burma. In 1948, under intense pressure, she had walked away from her UN (formerly League of Nations) mandate over Palestine, allowing the establishment of the state of Israel. In 1949 she was forced into a 30 percent devaluation of sterling, still one of the world major's trading currencies.

In 1951, Britain had been a leading shipbuilding nation. Her car, textile and coal industries were still the largest in Europe. In the early 1950s, as rationing ended and Britain again enjoyed modest prosperity, celebrating the Coronation of a new young queen, she became the world's third nuclear power and pioneered the world's first jet airliner, the Comet. She still took her place at international conference tables as one of the world's 'Big Three'. But all across her empire and spheres of influence troubles were multiplying, as a new spirit of nationalism was on the march in Kenya, Cyprus, Malaya, Persia, Iraq and Egypt.

Then came Suez, which finally brought home to Britain that she was no longer a 'Big Power', scarcely even a power of world rank. In 1957, by granting independ-

---

27 Kaiser, *op. cit.*, p. 105.

ence to Ghana, she launched on the process of abandoning her remaining colonies. Within little more than a dozen years, the transformation of the old British Empire into a Commonwealth was complete. At home, the British discovered 'affluence' and their new prime minister, hailed as 'Supermac', in 1959 won a landslide election victory. But behind the seeming façade of economic well-being, the British were beginning to wake up to some uncomfortable realities.

At the end of 1958 the economic editor of *The Observer*, Andrew Shonfield, published a book called *British Economic Policy Since The War*. Beginning with the question 'why does Britain's wealth grow so much more slowly than the wealth of countries on the continent?', it compared the percentage increases in national output in the countries of Six with Britain, between 1952 and 1956. Production in Germany had risen by 38 percent, in the Netherlands by 27 percent, Italy 26, and France 20. Britain, at a mere 15 percent, beat only Belgium and Luxembourg.

The reasons offered for this by Shonfield, were complex. They ranged from the strain of having to support sterling as a world currency and the military expenditure needed to support her global political commitments, to trade union obstructionism and lack of investment in basic industries.

His underlying message, to be repeated by countless less sophisticated books and press articles over the next few years, was that the British were doomed unless they went through a profound change of attitude. They had to give up global commitments they could no longer afford and they needed to rediscover from their continental neighbours the secret of economic success. For many observers (though not Shonfield in his book), the moral was clear. In abandoning her fading imperial dreams, Britain had to merge her destiny with that of her more dynamic neighbours. By joining their Common Market she might be able to share in their success.

What came to be overlooked in later years, however, was that the success of the Six was unrelated to their membership of the Common Market. Shonfield's figures covered the four years before the Treaty of Rome had been signed. The revival in the fortunes of Germany, Italy and France, helped enormously by Marshall aid and the OEEC, had taken place before the launch of the Common Market.[28]

Thinking the unthinkable

In the early months of 1960 Macmillan's thinking began to move in a direction which even six months before would have seemed unthinkable.

Shortly after the speech in Capetown on 3 February, when he spoke of 'the wind of change' beginning to blow through Africa, he decided to re-examine the validity of the Churchillian doctrine of three interlocking circles, and the assumption that too close a relationship with Europe would necessarily weaken Britain's relationships with the Commonwealth or the US.

---

28 One contemporary politician who did not miss this point was the leader of the Labour Party, Hugh Gaitskell. In his famous conference speech of 1962 (see Chapter 7), he observed 'the rate of expansion in Europe, however you measure it – by industry, by exports, by gross national product – was faster in the five years 1950–1955 than it was in the five years which followed'.

As part of the process, he instructed that the committee originally set up to supervise the FTA negotiations should be renamed the 'European Economic Association Committee'. Macmillan took the chair. Changes were also made to the Whitehall committee structures, from which emerged an Economic Steering (Europe) Committee, chaired by the joint permanent Under-Secretary to the Treasury, Sir Frank Lee. This was to be exclusively responsible for matters of European integration. In March 1960, a supporting committee was set up called the European Economics Questions (Official) Committee, comprised of middle-ranking civil servants. It was to conduct a wide-ranging review to cover a whole spectrum of possibilities, from abandoning attempts to find accommodation with the Six to joining them.

The workhorse of the process was Lee's Economic Steering Committee. On 23 May 1960, on the basis of its deliberations, Lee made a presentation to a special sub-committee of the Cabinet, chaired by Macmillan. His analysis was largely neutral. There were both political and economic advantages in joining the Community, and they would better be obtained by joining the EEC than by some form of 'association', which in any case was unlikely to be offered.[29]

A memorandum was circulated to the Ministerial European Economic Association Committee, appraising the options, including joining the Community or 'near identification' with it, and the consequences which might arise from each. This was discussed at the Committee on 27 May 1960, when Macmillan summed up by saying:

'The basic choice for the government … was between initiating a dramatic change in direction in our domestic, commercial and international policies, and maintaining our traditional policy of remaining aloof from Europe politically while doing all we could to mitigate the economic dangers of a divided Europe. This would be another of the historic moments of history and would need much careful thought.'[30]

The officials were then instructed to consider further questions 'to be indicated by the prime minister'.

There was another reason why Britain might now be reconsidering her involvement with the new 'European Economic Community'. Since the appearance of France's new president in 1958, it seemed the character of the new 'Europe' might be evolving away from dogmatic emphasis on supranationalist technocracy.[31]

Furthermore, in 1958 and 1959 a serious international problem had been arising over the future of Berlin, still occupied by the four 'powers'. The Soviet Union, under its new leader Nikita Khruschev, seemed determined to use the city as the central pawn in his desire to make permanent the separate existence of the USSR's Communist puppet state in East Germany, the German Democratic Republic.

Under what was known as the 'Hallstein doctrine', named after the Commission president from the days when he was Adenauer's foreign minister, West Germany

---

29 Bell, Lionel (1995), *The Throw That Failed* (London, New European Publications), p. 17.

30 PRO. CAB 134/1820, EQ(60)29, reproduced in Bell, *op. cit.*, pp. 140–153.

31 See Milward, *op. cit.*, p. 443. Foreign Office officials used de Gaulle's repeated denunciations of the federal Europe concept to justify 'the lack of discussion about sovereignty'.

claimed to speak for all Germans, in the hope that one day Germany would be reunited. As tension mounted over this issue, at the end of a NATO council meeting in Paris, de Gaulle organised a meeting on 19 December 1959 between himself, Eisenhower and Macmillan, representing the three Western occupying powers, to discuss Berlin. The exclusion of West Germany infuriated Adenauer. He was even more displeased when his three supposed allies agreed to meet Khruschev at an East-West summit the following May, to settle the most important question affecting his country's future.

Thanks not least to de Gaulle's new assertiveness on the international stage, reinforced by France's explosion of her first nuclear device on 13 February 1960, relations between the two leading members of the EEC came under intense strain. As it happened, just two weeks before the arranged summit, on 1 May, an American U-2 'spy plane', flying at 80,000 feet over Sverdlovsk in the heart of the Soviet Union, was shot down by a SAM 2 missile. Amid the resulting furore, an apoplectic Khruschev demanded the summit be postponed until Eisenhower had left the US presidency.

This crisis left Franco-German relations at their lowest ebb since the war, a state of mutual suspicion and hostility which was to last for many months and to lead to both countries threatening to withdraw from NATO. The lowest point of all came with a speech given by de Gaulle at Grenoble in October, when he declared that the only reality in Europe was that of the nation state. This coincided with a visit to Bonn, by France's prime minister and foreign minister. Such was the *froideur* that an official banquet at the Palais Schaumburg had to be delayed for an hour by a blazing row. During the ensuing dinner hosts and guests were scarcely on speaking terms.[32]

This breakdown in relations provided an opportunity for Britain and, against this background, through 1960 and amid intense secrecy, Macmillan and his colleagues meditated on whether to take Britain into 'Europe'. A clue as to his intentions came in a Cabinet reshuffle in July when he appointed the Earl of Home as his foreign secretary, moving his Chief Whip Edward Heath to a new post at the Foreign Office, with responsibility for 'European affairs'. Ever since entering Parliament in 1950, Heath had been a committed 'Europeanist' and an enthusiast for supranationalism. Two other enthusiastic 'Europeanists' were appointed to posts which would be important if Britain applied to join. Duncan Sandys, former president of the European Movement, became Commonwealth Secretary; Christopher Soames, Minister of Agriculture.

One central question was how far they should commit Britain to a 'supranational' form of government, over which Britain might have influence but ultimately no control. When, following the Lee report, civil servants responded to Macmillan's further questions, they qualified their answers with two reservations. The first was that many of the policies of the Six were not yet settled, 'notably on matters left open in the Treaty of Rome'. Secondly, they maintained, if the UK joined the Six, this would 'undoubtedly influence ... the development of these

32 Williams, *op. cit.*, p. 485

policies', although adding, 'it is not possible to judge how great our influence would be'.[33]

So much about where this European project might lead was inevitably unknown. Thus, while some argued that there would be economic advantages to Britain in joining it, these rested on unpredictable factors. At the time, contributions to the EEC budget could not be estimated. What was to become the Community's biggest single expense, initially accounting for over 90 percent of that budget – the Common Agricultural Policy – had yet to be defined. For similar reasons, it was impossible to predict the effects on British agriculture or trade.

Yet Macmillan and his colleagues were in no doubt that the 'Communities' as they stood were intended to lead to full political and economic union. Even before the Treaty of Rome was signed in 1957, the Foreign Office had been briefed that its six signatories intended 'to achieve tighter European integration through the creation of European institutions with supranational powers, beginning in the economic field ... the underlying motive of the Six is, however, essentially political'.[34]

In the summer of 1960 Sir Roderick Barclay, head of the UK delegation to the European Commission in Brussels, sent a despatch to the Foreign Office stressing that the aim of the Community was not merely harmonisation but 'the unification of policies in every field of the economic union, i.e. economic, social, commercial, tariff and fiscal policy. That this was not just "pie in the sky" needed to be made clear to the politicians'.[35]

When Heath, as minister of state for Europe, visited Hallstein in November 1960, his report on the meeting noted how Hallstein had emphasised that joining the Community was not just a matter of adopting a common tariff 'which was the essential hallmark of any "State" (and he regarded the EEC as a potential State)'. It would be necessary, Hallstein had insisted, for any new entrant to accept that the EEC was intended to evolve into something much deeper, 'some form of Federal State', which was what the Commission was working towards.[36]

Particularly revealing in this context was the reply given in December 1960 by the Lord Chancellor, Lord Kilmuir, to a request from Heath, for an opinion on the constitutional implications of signing the Treaty for Britain's sovereignty. Kilmuir responded that loss of sovereignty would in several respects be considerable: by Parliament; by the Crown in terms of Britain's treaty-making powers; and by the courts, which to an extent would become 'subordinate' to the European Court of Justice.[37] On the making of laws, Kilmuir said it was clear that:

'the Council of Ministers would eventually (after the system of qualified majority voting had come into force) make regulations which would be binding on us even against our wishes ... it would in theory be possible for Parliament to enact at the outset legislation

33 PRO. CAB 129/102 pt. 1, C(60)107.
34 PRO/FO 371/150360, cited in Bell, *op. cit.*, p. 1.
35 Paraphrased by Bell, *op. cit.*, p. 22 (based on PRO/FO 371/150363).
36 PRO/FO 371/150369.
37 PRO/FO 371/150369, cited by Bell, *op. cit.*, pp. 36–39.

which would give automatic force of law to any existing or future regulations made by the appropriate organs of the Community. For Parliament to do this would go far beyond the most extensive delegation of powers, even in wartime, that we have ever experienced and I do not think there is any likelihood of this being acceptable to the House of Commons.'

As for the subordination of Britain's courts to the ECJ, Kilmuir wrote:

'I must emphasise that in my view the surrenders of sovereignty involved are serious ones, and I think that, as a matter of practical politics, it will not be easy to persuade Parliament or the British public to accept them. I am sure that it would be a great mistake to under-estimate the force of the objections to them. But these objections should be brought out into the open now because, if we attempt to gloss over them at this stage, those who are opposed to the whole idea of joining the Community will certainly seize on them with more damaging effect later on.'

From the evidence now available, it is clear that Macmillan and his Cabinet were fully aware of the political implications of the decision that lay before them.

But there was still one other consideration which might have to outweigh everything else. If there was one factor above all which set Britain apart from her continental neighbours it was her 'special relationship' with the United States of America. It was on that, and on the fact that, since detonating her first H-bomb in 1957, she had become the world's third thermonuclear power, that Britain's dwindling prestige and influence in the world now rested.

If she were now to throw in her destiny with 'Europe', would all this have to be thrown away? As it happened, this question had suddenly become more acute than ever. The cause was that same incident which brought such an abrupt end to the East-West summit that had in turn provoked such bitter feuding between Germany and France: the shooting down of Gary Powers's U-2 by a Soviet missile.

America lets Macmillan off the hook

To no one did this come as more of a shock than Britain's defence planners. Britain's nuclear deterrent had since 1956 had depended on her force of high-altitude V-bombers. If Soviet ground-to-air missiles were now capable intercepting aircraft at 80,000 feet, any deterrent value had vanished. The only alternative would be a missile, and Britain had been developing two. But the first, Blue Streak, had been cancelled only three weeks before the U-2 incident, because of cost over-runs and, being liquid-fuelled, it was in any case obsolete.[38] The other, Blue Steel, a clearly inadequate air-launched missile with a range of only 100 miles, would be cancelled later in the year. This left Britain with only one hope of preserving her 'independent' deterrent: to buy missiles from the USA – either the air-launched Skybolt or the new Polaris, which would require building a fleet of nuclear sub-marines. Either solution required Washington's agreement.

With 1960 nearing its end, Macmillan's old friend President Eisenhower was soon due to leave office. His successor, elected in November, was the charismatic young senator John F. Kennedy, to whom Macmillan was related by marriage. As

---

38 Given the Soviet ICBM capability, giving only 15 minutes warning, liquid-fuelled missiles took too long to prepare for launch.

the new administration prepared to take office, Macmillan's most urgent priority was to discuss with the new president the two issues at the top of his agenda: 'Europe' and Britain's deterrent.

A US-British 'summit' was fixed for 4 April 1961. Before it took place, much behind the scenes groundwork was necessary. In Washington this centred on a man who had now become one of Kennedy's most trusted advisers, George Ball, his Under-Secretary of State with special responsibility for European affairs. Kennedy had picked him as a key member of his team after hearing him address a conference in New York in January 1960, when Ball spoke of the need for further progress towards political integration in Europe.

Ball was, of course, one of Monnet's closest and most committed allies. They had been working closely together since 1945, not least during the early stages of the Marshall Plan. Although he then returned to private law practice, their close association continued. With the establishment of the ECSC, Monnet had appointed Ball as its legal representative in Washington. In 1954, after the French Parliament had failed to ratify the EDC, Monnet had been so concerned at the effect of this on the US government that he asked Ball to set up a publicity office in Washington. With the advent of the EEC in 1958, this became the Commission's Washington base.[39]

In Ball, Monnet had one of his own men at the heart of the new administration, guiding a president who knew little of contemporary European politics. What was just as significant was that, by this time, Monnet was now convinced that de Gaulle's brand of nationalism required the counter-weight of Britain's membership in his fledgling Community. With this in mind he visited the United States twice in the early months of 1961, when he met Ball and other members of the new administration, and, at Ball's instigation, 'had a long talk with the President'.[40]

Ball himself was by now playing an active part in pushing for British membership. Prior to the planned 'summit' between Macmillan and Kennedy, he flew to London where, on 30 March, at the suggestion of Sir Frank Lee, he met Heath. The three men met in the house of the Earl of Perth, son of Sir Eric Drummond (later the 16th Earl of Perth) who had been Monnet's immediate boss when he was the first general secretary of the League of Nations. Ball intended to encourage Britain to take the plunge. According to his own lengthy account of the meeting, Heath began by confirming that, provided an overall settlement could be found to take care of the Commonwealth, agriculture and EFTA problems, the UK was 'ready to accept a common, or harmonised, tariff'.[41]

In Heath's temporary absence, Lee put the direct question, 'does the United States want the United Kingdom to join the Common Market?' Ball in his reply emphasised that the EEC's institutions should

---

39 Mosettig, Mike (undated), *Building European Ties in Washington – Europe's US Delegation – 40 Years Later*, Delegation of the European Commission to the United States: *www.eurunion.org/delegati/history.htm*

40 Monnet, *op. cit.*, p. 438.

41 Ball, *op. cit.*, p. 211.

'...not become mere technocratic bodies, they should continue to develop politically. If Britain joined the EEC, it should be on the understanding that the present institutions did not form a completed edifice, but would continue to evolve and that the Rome Treaty was not a "frozen document" but a "process".' [42]

Lee's response, according to Ball, was that he fully understood the significance of this, and that although 'the movement towards political federation in Europe' had been temporarily checked, 'he himself did not shrink from the idea of full political union'. When Heath returned to the meeting, Lee summarised what had been said. Heath 'seemed impressed'. Ball 'emerged exhilarated' that 'both Heath and Lee had gone much further than I expected'. [43]

Given the importance of this meeting, and the significance of what was discussed, it may seem strange that Heath was not to mention it in his autobiography: especially as it underlined the expectation that the EEC should eventually evolve into a 'European federation'.

Five days later, on 4 April, Macmillan arrived in Washington for his bilateral summit. When the two men met for their first discussion, sitting across a table with their advisers, 'almost the first question Macmillan asked the President', according to Ball who was sitting with Kennedy, was 'how he and the American government would react if Britain applied to join the European Community'. [44]

'President Kennedy responded briefly, then said "I'll ask Under-Secretary Ball to reply to your question". I then repeated what I had said to Heath in London – that America would welcome it if Britain should apply for full membership in the Community, explicitly recognising that the Rome Treaty was not merely a static document but a process leading towards political unification. I elaborated upon this theme at some length, noting the dangers of a mere commercial arrangement that would drain the EEC of political content. The Prime Minister seemed on the whole pleased and satisfied.' [45]

Macmillan in his memoirs merely records that he was left in no doubt that a decision to join the Six would be welcome.[46] He makes no reference to political unification. Ball recalls that at dinner in the British Embassy next evening, Macmillan twice took him privately aside, seeming 'excited'. 'Yesterday was one of the greatest days of my life,' he said with apparent emotion, 'you know, don't you, that we can now do this thing and that we're going to do it. We're going into Europe.' The only obstacle left was de Gaulle, but Macmillan was convinced 'we're going to do it'. [47]

If Macmillan was elated, he had every reason for so being. Although he had been moving towards the idea of joining the EEC, this might seem to conflict with the 'three circles' doctrine, in that Britain's 'entry into Europe' would detach

42 Ball, *op. cit.*, p. 212.
43 Ball, *op. cit.*, pp. 212–213. Ball quotes 'one of the ablest men in the American Embassy in London upbraiding me for encouraging Britain to move towards Europe'. Despite what had been said, this man implied, with some prescience, 'that he did not believe Britain would ever play more than a foot-dragging role in Europe, resisting any move towards political unity'.
44 Ball, *op. cit.*, p. 214.
45 *Ibid.*
46 Macmillan, *op. cit.*, p. 336.
47 Ball, *op. cit.*, p. 214.

Britain from the United States. Furthermore, it might rule out any hope of US agreement to supply Britain with missiles, eliminating Britain's 'independent deterrent' and all the prestige which went with it. Suddenly, however, that obstacle had been removed. Kennedy's enthusiasm for Britain's entry presented Macmillan with an almost miraculous answer to what had seemed an insoluble problem. Far from entry to the EEC being an obstacle to close relations with the US, it now seemed as if it would strengthen their alliance.

Macmillan's last hurdle was the Cabinet. Back in February Heath had warned Macmillan that its earlier opposition had been so pronounced because, in July 1960, the prime minister had allowed a free debate. Instead, Heath advised, he should now organise the policy-making process in such a way as to lead to the conclusion that the EEC application was 'inevitable'.[48] In the last days of June, therefore, the Cabinet was asked to decide. Macmillan opened the discussion by pointing out that the first question they needed to consider was that 'if we were to sign the Treaty of Rome we should have to accept its political objectives, and although we should be able to influence the political outcome we did not know what this would be'.[49]

He conceded that a decision to enter would 'raise great presentational difficulties'. On the one hand, it would be important to convince the Six that 'we genuinely supported the objectives of the Treaty'. On the other, 'we should have to satisfy public opinion in this country that the implementation of the objectives of the Treaty would not require unacceptable social and other adjustments. The problems of public relations would be considerable.'

The chief way in which these 'problems of public relations' might be overcome would be to stay as quiet as possible about the 'political objectives' of the Treaty, and to sell British membership of the 'Common Market' as if it was primarily a matter of economics: improved trade, more jobs, greater prosperity. It would be yet another victory for that central strategy of deception dating back to 1955, when Spaak had struck out from the 'Benelux memorandum out any references to a 'United States of Europe' and played up the importance of creating an 'economic community'.

The Cabinet voted for entry. To general public astonishment, on 31 July Macmillan announced the decision in the Commons.[50] According to Duchêne, citing a conversation with Camps, the key part played by the US President in bringing about this *volte face* had been no accident. 'There was a "Monnet effect" on Ball and then a "Ball effect" on Kennedy, and then a "Kennedy effect" on Macmillan. It was a triumph for Monnet.'[51]

---

48 PRO. FO 371/158264/12 (7 February 1961), letter from Heath to Macmillan.
49 Bell, *op. cit.*, pp. 59–62.
50 Macmillan, Harold (1973), *At The End Of The Day – 1961–63* (London, Macmillan), p. 1. Macmillan does not quote his statement to the Commons: 'I must remind the House that the EEC is an economic community, not a defence alliance or a foreign policy community' (Ball, *op. cit.*, p. 217).
51 Duchêne, *op. cit.*, pp. 325–326.

Chapter 7

Why de Gaulle Kept Britain Out: 1961–1969

'The French did not wish the British to be at the table taking part in the formative discussions on the CAP, for fear that we might disrupt the very favourable
arrangements they otherwise had every reason to expect.'

Edward Heath[1]

'The importance of the CAP to de Gaulle cannot be overestimated.'

Professor Andrew Moravcsik[2]

It is a familiar fact of history that, during the 1960s, de Gaulle was to slam the door
against Britain's entry to the Common Market, not just once but twice. What has
only recently come fully to light, however, is just why he found it imperative to do
so, as a central plank of his domestic policy for France.

From a British point of view, the generally accepted version of events during
these years begins with the formal acceptance of Britain's application to join by the
EEC Council of Ministers on 26 September 1961. Over the next year, as this version
has it, Heath showed himself highly skilled in negotiating Britain's terms of entry.
But the talks then became mysteriously bogged down. In January 1963, de Gaulle
then startled the world by announcing his personal decision to veto Britain's entry,
claiming that Britain was not yet sufficiently 'European' in her outlook, and still
too closely tied to the USA. This came as a great blow to Macmillan, at the beginning of a year which was to see his government disintegrating amid a welter of
scandals.

In 1965, after a Labour government had taken over under Harold Wilson, Heath
became leader of the Conservative Party: not least thanks to the reputation he had
won as Britain's negotiator in Brussels. When Wilson made a second bid to join
the Common Market in 1967, de Gaulle again blocked British entry, for similarly
idiosyncratic reasons. Only when in 1969 de Gaulle departed from the stage and
was succeeded by Georges Pompidou, this version concludes, did France's attitude
change. Largely thanks to the 'personal chemistry' between Pompidou and Heath,
when he became prime minister in 1970, Britain's third application proved successful.

This construction on what happened turns out to be not just highly misleading
in detail but to have missed the single most important factor in the whole story. It
is true that the key role in the EEC throughout the 1960s was played by de Gaulle.
But what most historians have so far almost totally overlooked is the central

1 Heath, Edward (1998), *The Course Of My Life* (London, Hodder and Stoughton), p. 222.
2 Moravcsik, Andrew (2000), 'De Gaulle Between Grain and Grandeur: The Political Economy of
  French EC Policy, 1958–1970' (Part 1) in *Journal of Cold War Studies*, Vol. 2, No. 2, Spring, p. 34.

underlying reason why France could not yet afford to allow Britain into the Common Market. Yet no sooner was this problem resolved than she then needed Britain to join as soon as possible: for reasons, it turns out, to which the personal views of Heath and Pompidou were irrelevant.

'The Commonwealth problem'

On 16 October 1961, Heath went to Brussels to make an opening statement on why Britain now wished to join the Common Market and three weeks later, on 8 November, the formal negotiations for British entry began.

A common misunderstanding about the 'negotiations' which take place when a new nation joins the European Community is that the applicant country may seek to change the rules to suit its particular needs. But one of the most fundamental principles on which Monnet had established his 'government of Europe' was that, once the supranational body has been granted a particular power or 'competence', this can never be returned. Power can only be handed by individual states to the supranational entity; never the other way round. Once those powers or 'competences' are ceded, either by treaty or by passing laws over a particular area of policy, they constitute the Community's most sacred possession: the so-called '*acquis communautaire*'. This represents the sum of the treaties and the accumulated laws which have been 'acquired' over the years as the Community's 'inalienable possession'. The whole point of the *acquis* is that it is non-negotiable.

All that accession countries can achieve, therefore, are temporary 'derogations' or transitional concessions, designed to make it easier for those country to adjust to the requirements of the *acquis*, with which they will eventually have to comply in full.

When Heath arrived in Brussels on 16 October there was no doubt that the greatest difficulty would be in securing transitional arrangements for the Commonwealth. Addressing the Six, he told them, 'I am sure you will understand that Britain could not join the EEC under conditions in which this trade connection was cut, with grave loss and even ruin for some of the Commonwealth countries.'[3]

Already, when announcing his decision to apply for entry back in July, Macmillan had pledged to the House of Commons that Britain would only join if satisfactory arrangements could be made to meet the special needs of the United Kingdom, of the Commonwealth and of the European Free Trade Association.[4]

By far the greatest problem was the system of 'imperial preference' which had prevailed in Britain's empire and Commonwealth for 60 years and more. Through this, Britain and her Commonwealth partners had established a much larger proportion of their trade with each other than with other countries. In 1961, 43 percent of British exports went to the Commonwealth, as against only 16.7 percent to the Common Market countries and 13.1 percent to her six partners in

---

3 For some reason, this was not reported by *The Times* and other newspapers until 28 November 1961.
4 Macmillan, *At The End of The Day, op. cit.*, p. 22.

EFTA.[5] In 1960, Britain had taken more than half New Zealand's exports and a quarter of those from several other Commonwealth countries, including Australia and India.[6] Yet the essence of joining the Common Market was that Britain would now have to raise tariff barriers against these imports, while her new partners would soon be able to export their goods to Britain tariff-free.

This posed difficulties which no other Common Market country had faced. As the price of Britain's entry, she and her Commonwealth would now be expected to abandon much of their existing trade with each other. In the weeks before his announcement in July of Britain's intention to join, therefore, Macmillan sent several of his Cabinet ministers, led by Duncan Sandys, round the Commonwealth capitals, pleading for their agreement to what he was about to do. These were countries which, less than 20 years before, had sent some four million of their citizens to fight alongside Britain in World War Two. Now they were to be dealt a harsh economic blow.

The response from Ottawa typified the sentiment: 'the Canadian ministers indicated that their Government's assessment of the situation was different from that put forward by Mr Sandys'; and 'expressed grave concern ... about the political and economic effects which British membership in the European Economic Community would have on Canada and on the Commonwealth as a whole'.[7]

The main task confronting Heath as he began formal negotiations in November was to ensure that the damage inflicted on Britain's Commonwealth partners was at least softened. His top priority was to persuade his prospective new partners to grant 'derogations'. These would extend for as long as possible the period in which imports from the Commonwealth could continue, on terms which might protect its producers while they searched for new markets. But, as he got down to detailed, day-by-day argument over arrangements for imports of New Zealand butter or Australian beef, Canadian wheat or West Indian sugar, it was not long before Heath was forced to realise that his new partners were not prepared to make many concessions. The reason was simple. For the Six this was precisely the test of Britain's willingness to abandon her old, traditional role in the world and to demonstrate her willingness now to develop a wholly new loyalties.

What Heath did not realise, however, was that one member of the Six was not only reluctant to make any concessions at all but actually opposed to Britain's entry even before the talks began.

De Gaulle plays his own game

President de Gaulle was unlike any other national leader post-war Europe had known. As Churchill's proud 'Constable of France', he saw himself as the man who had saved his country twice. The first was at the end of the Second World War when he had joined with the Western allies in liberating his country from the

---

5 Figures taken from speech by Hugh Gaitskell to Labour Party Conference, 1962 (Holmes, Martin (ed.) in *The Eurosceptic Reader* (London, Macmillan, 1966), p. 15).

6 *Britain and The European Communities* (London, HMSO), 1962.

7 Mansergh, Nicholas (1963), *Documents and Speeches on Commonwealth Affairs, 1952–1962* (London, Oxford University Press), p. 635.

Germans and restoring her national government; and again in 1958. Then he had rescued France from the chaos of the Fourth Republic to set up his new 'Fifth Republic', the regime which would restore French national self-respect. But with the continuing threat of internal instability being exported back across the Mediterranean from the fearful civil war in Algeria, de Gaulle was aware that any time France might again be plunged into violent chaos. In his 11 years in office he faced no fewer than 34 assassination attempts, more than any other statesman in history.

For these reasons, de Gaulle also saw the 'European Communities' and his country's place in them very differently from any other of their leaders. One of his first acts on becoming France's president in July 1958 had been to arrange a meeting with Adenauer, which took place in September at de Gaulle's home in Colombey-les-Deux-Eglises. They announced that close co-operation between France and Germany was the foundation of 'all constructive endeavour in Europe', and that this should be put on an organised basis.[8] In 1959, de Gaulle's prime minister Michel Debré took this idea forward in a speech proposing that the Six should be aiming not only at economic but also political union. The way to this should be paved by frequent consultations between their leaders.[9] By 1960, both publicly and privately, de Gaulle was canvassing the idea not merely of regular meetings of the Six heads of government but of 'standing commissions' to co-ordinate policies on political, defence and cultural issues, with their own secretariat.[10]

What de Gaulle was here evolving was his vision of a new kind of integration among the Six, shaped not on supranational but intergovernmental lines: his vision of what he was to call a '*Europe des Etats*'.[11] De Gaulle had never been an enthusiast for what he regarded as Monnet's supranational obsessions. As he once remarked 'we are no longer in the era when M. Monnet gave the orders'.[12] Not only did de Gaulle himself seem unsympathetic to Monnet's ideas, but his prime minister Debré so detested them that he would allegedly pass Monnet with averted gaze. A later commentator noted that 'the European reformation had scarcely begun, and the counter-reformation was installed in Paris'.

The impression thus conveyed in 1960, that 'Europe' might now be moving away from supranationalism towards a more intergovernmental approach, had a significant impact on Macmillan and his advisers. It held out the possibility that, by skilful negotiation of her terms of entry, Britain might use her influence to help redirect the EEC onto the path of intergovernmentalism.[13]

---

8 Royal Institute of International Affairs (1959), *Documents on International Affairs, 1958* (London, Chatham House), p. 445. These will subsequently be referred to just as Documents, with relevant dates.
9 *Documents* (1959), *op. cit.*, p. 508–509.
10 See for instance his press conference on 5 September 1960, and *Documents* (1960), pp. 157–158.
11 This came often to be misrepresented as a '*Europe des Patries*', a phrase which de Gaulle himself went out of his way at a press conference to explain that he never used. The misunderstanding arose through a reverse translation back from his original words.
12 This and the two following sentences come from Duchêne, *op. cit.*, p. 315.
13 As the Foreign Secretary Lord Home put it 'if we act quickly now we can go into Europe and help shape the political structure in the way which suits us best. De Gaulle doesn't want a tight European Federation, a Federal Europe. He wants a union of independent states. If we go in now, that is what it will be' (interview in *The Observer*, 23 September 1962).

In February 1961, de Gaulle's proposals for 'closer political co-operation' were discussed at a summit meeting of the Six in Paris, which set up a committee under Christian Fouchet to consider them. These talks had been preceded by a private meeting between de Gaulle and Adenauer, intended to patch up their bitter disagreements the following year over the abortive East-West summit on Berlin.

Adenauer had wanted to clear the air about de Gaulle's seeming desire to emasculate the Community, and also to discuss France's plans regarding NATO. He appeared sufficiently satisfied to agree to de Gaulle's wish for more 'political co-operation'. At the subsequent meeting with their EEC partners, despite a Dutch protest that the rest of the Six should not always be bound by what was agreed between Germany and France, it was resolved that the Fouchet committee should report on further political union. This would not, however, involve any further supranational elements, and would respect national sovereignty with full right of veto.

Fouchet's recommendations were considered at two more heads of government meetings in Bonn, one in May, the second in July. Under discussion were two rival proposals: a 'Union of States', proposed by the French, and a 'union of peoples' preferred by the rest of the Six. Monnet himself had high hopes for the July meeting, noting in his memoirs that 'The first steps towards a European currency now also seemed to be practicable'.[14] His optimism was misplaced, and in his memoirs he plaintively asked why at this time France should have been trying 'to bring back into an intergovernmental framework what had already become a Community?'[15]

Nevertheless the Six did agree on what became known as the Bonn Declaration, announcing on 18 July their decision 'to give shape to the will for political union already implicit in the Treaties establishing the European Communities'.[16] This was just 13 days before Macmillan announced to the world Britain's decision to apply for entry.

Franco-German *rapprochement*

From now on, over the next 17 months two quite different dramas were to unfold simultaneously: in public, it seemed, wholly unrelated, but behind the scenes, in important respects, linked.

The first drama, little understood in Britain, was the coming together of de Gaulle's France and Adenauer's Germany in a new and much closer alliance. It was based on a sense that they shared a European identity in a way which set them apart from the British and even more from the Americans. A powerful trigger for their new sense of common identity was the immense international crisis which blew up on Sunday 13 August 1961, when East Germany sealed off West Berlin's borders with the GDR and began to build the 'Berlin Wall'. The long-simmering East-West tension over Berlin had at last come to a head. When the initial response of the Kennedy government was slow and uncertain, as was that of the British, this

14 Macmillan, *op. cit.*, p. 439.
15 *Op. cit.*, pp. 439–440.
16 *Documents* (1961), pp. 187–189.

reinforced the suspicions of Adenauer and de Gaulle that Anglo-US support could not be relied on.

On 19 October 1961, the French delegation on the Fouchet committee presented a draft treaty to establish a union between the countries of the Six. This proposed severing Europe's dependence for military security on the Atlantic Alliance and the USA, reflecting de Gaulle's wish for Europe to be more self-reliant, centred on a Franco-German alliance. De Gaulle further proposed a radical reconstruction of the EEC, turning it into a voluntary union of independent states. Its secretariat would be based in Paris and there would be extensive national veto powers over all common policies. Effectively, the proposals envisaged a drastic dilution of the powers of the Commission and Council of Ministers, and the subjection of Community law to national law. This was the supreme expression of de Gaulle's vision of a '*Europe des Etats*'. Predictably, the reaction of the other five governments was hostile.

Early in the New Year of 1962, tensions were further exacerbated when the French put forward 'a revised draft treaty' which, far from taking account of the objections of the others, seemed to be worse in many respects than the original.[17] According to one authority, the amended plan had been drawn up in de Gaulle's own hand.[18]

Shortly afterwards, on 9 February 1962, de Gaulle asked for an urgent meeting with Adenauer to discuss his 'Fouchet proposals' and European security. The Chancellor had only recently suffered a heart attack, and was frail, 'tetchy and bad-tempered', although his illness had been kept secret, even from de Gaulle. They met in a hotel in Baden-Baden, where Adenauer refused to support de Gaulle's idea of a looser EEC structure. But the meeting marked a distinct warming in the relationship between the two leaders, not least as they were able to agree on their mistrust of American and British attitudes towards the Soviet Union, and the absolute necessity of avoiding another Franco-German war. Most importantly, de Gaulle was completely at one with Adenauer on the importance of not making deals with the Soviets on Berlin. They shared concern that the Americans and British were prepared to make concession to placate Khrushchev. Adenauer was beginning to look to France as his only reliable ally.

De Gaulle's real agenda

During this time, the negotiations for Britain's entry into the EEC were continuing in Brussels, as if none of these fundamental shifts in thinking about the future of the 'European project' were taking place. Yet the greatest irony was that, at the very time when it seemed de Gaulle was moving away from the concept of supra-nationalism, he was in fact looking to the supranational mechanisms of the EEC to solve a problem which threatened the very existence of the French state.

Nowhere in the mainstream histories of that time or the memoirs of politicians is there any real understanding of just how important to France had become her

17 Camps, *op. cit.*, p. 418.
18 Moravcsik, *De Gaulle, op. cit.*, p. 34.

agriculture, which in 1961 still accounted for 25 percent of all her employment, against only four percent in the United Kingdom. In the years immediately after the war all European countries had introduced state subsidies to their agriculture, to avoid any repetition of the food shortages of the wartime period or the farming depression of the 1930s. But in no country had the subsidy system come to be regarded as politically more important than in France.

Although the effect of subsidies on French agriculture had been a huge boost in output, this had led to persistent downward pressures on prices, which in turn threatened the economic viability of the mass of French farms, many of them small, inefficient peasant holdings. This aroused in the minds of France's politicians a nightmare: the thought of millions of small farmers being displaced from the land and gravitating to towns and cities which could offer them neither jobs nor housing. The fear was that they would lose their naturally conservative political allegiances and become a fertile breeding ground for discontent. In a country where the Communist Party was the largest single political grouping, the spectre of the Communists sweeping to power on the votes of dispossessed agrarian workers was of very great concern. Even armed revolution could not be ruled out. In France's highly unstable political structure, it was vital to the very survival of the state that the farmers and their families should be kept on the land.

To that effect, the Fourth Republic had spent ever-increasing sums on farm subsidies, to the point where this expenditure threatened to bankrupt the state. Yet the subsidies themselves only exacerbated the problem. They drew into production marginal land, while increased income encouraged investment in machinery. In 1950, the number of tractors in the Six as a whole had stood at only 370,000. By 1962 the number had grown to 2,300,000. Wheat production in the mid-1950s increased eightfold. Sugar and wine production rose by over 300 percent. This necessitated ever-larger government-funded stockpiles and export subsidies.[19]

By the early 1960s production was still increasing at a rate of 20 percent per annum. Eleven million of the 24 million dairy cows in the Six were French, each producing less than a quarter of the milk yield of Dutch animals. Dairy subsidies alone were costing the French taxpayer 1.35 billion francs (equivalent to £3 billion a year at 2003 prices), of which 70 million were used to dump powdered milk on the Indian and Mexican markets. Huge further sums were spent on storage and processing, while the surplus 'butter mountain' stood at 200,000 tons.[20] French farm policy was clearly unsustainable. Politically, however, it was essential.[21]

---

19 A widespread subsequent 'myth' about post-war European agriculture was that it was the Common Agricultural Policy which boosted production and made farming prosperous. Decades later a 'Fact Sheet' on the European Parliament website (*The Treaty of Rome and Green Europe*) would, typically, claim that 'the CAP produced spectacular results: the Community was soon able to overcome the food shortages of the 1950s, achieving self-sufficiency and then generating cyclical and structural surpluses'. In fact it was in the 1950s, long before the CAP, that the combination of subsidies and technological innovation had already led to over-production of food, which the CAP only helped to exacerbate.

20 Brombergers, *op. cit.*, pp. 285–286.

21 Moravcsik, *op. cit.*, pp. 3–43.

Only 40 years later, in a meticulously researched academic paper, did an American professor, Andrew Moravcsik,[22] finally bring to light just how crucial this issue had become to the future not just of France but of the European Community. When de Gaulle took power in 1958, France's farm surpluses had already reached crisis point. Attempts to reform the subsidy system had met with stiff opposition, which presented a dangerous threat to his electoral base. De Gaulle was being forced to continue payments on a scale the French government could simply no longer afford. At a crisis Cabinet meeting in August 1962, with the Algerian crisis now largely over, he was to call the 'stabilisation' of agriculture the 'most important problem' facing France. If the problems are not resolved, de Gaulle declared, 'we will have another Algeria on our own soil'.[23]

De Gaulle and his advisers realised there were only two ways to remedy this crisis. The first was to find new export markets for France's massive surpluses. The other was to find an additional source of finance for the subsidies. The answer to both might lie in the EEC. What had become vital, they concluded, was to use it to set up an agricultural policy which could give French farmers access both to external markets and also to additional funding, primarily from Germany. But it was vital that such a policy should be framed above all to meet the needs of France. Thus, despite his overt dislike of supranational institutions, de Gaulle came to regard the EEC as the most essential instrument in furthering France's national interest.

The idea of a 'Common Agricultural Policy' went back to the Spaak report in 1955, and the outline of such a policy had been included in Articles 38 to 45 of the Rome Treaty. But this amounted to no more than vague declarations of contradictory principles, such as commitments 'to ensure a fair standard of living for the agricultural community'; 'to increase agricultural productivity by promoting technical progress'; and 'to ensure the availability of supplies'. There were no indications as to how these ends should be achieved. In 1958, a conference had been held in Stresa in Italy to develop such a policy. But it was to be nearly 11 years before full agreement was reached on the details and the all-important financing arrangements; and this was because the driving force throughout that period, battling to ensure that these met her requirements, was France.

A start had been made in 1960 when the agriculture Commissioner Sicco Mansholt produced a 300-page document, with a deadline for agreement at the end of 1961. The 'Mansholt Plan' proposed replacing all direct national subsidies to agriculture with a system of variable levies and support prices, under the centralised control of the Commission. But, for the next two years, Germany consistently blocked attempts to agree the details. German farm subsidies were the highest in the Six. Any attempt to rationalise and harmonise the support structure would disadvantage her farmers. Only on 14 January 1962, after what Hallstein famously described as '137 hours of discussion, with 214 hours in sub-committee; 582,000 pages of documents; three heart attacks', did the Germans finally agree to

22 *Ibid*. Moravcsik is an Associate Professor of Government at Harvard.
23 *Op. cit.*, pp. 18–19.

give legal effect to the CAP. The clock was 'stopped' for two weeks and the conclusions back-dated to meet the symbolic 31 December deadline.[24]

With the basic principles agreed, however, the next step was to work out the all-important financial mechanisms. At France's insistence, levies on imported goods were to be the main source of income,[25] a provision which particularly favoured her system, as her imports – particularly if her overseas departments were included – were minimal.

This was where France would need to play her hand with infinite subtlety and ruthlessness. Not only would this system ensure the maximum contribution from other members. It would ensure that Britain, which imported a much higher proportion of her food than any of the Six, mainly from the Commonwealth, would be a major contributor. Furthermore, as her main source of supply was eliminated, Britain could provide French farmers with their biggest export market of all.

The central problem for France, however, was that Britain, with the much higher productivity of her own farming sector, would be unwilling to take on the burden of paying for French agriculture. Furthermore, after 1966, it had been agreed that decisions on the future of the CAP would be taken by qualified majority voting. If Britain was allowed to enter before the financial arrangements for the CAP had been settled, she would therefore be likely to side with Germany to block France's proposals. At all costs, Britain had to be excluded from the EEC until those final agreements on the CAP were in place.[26] Therein lay the explanation for the dramas to come.

De Gaulle prepares to veto

By the spring of 1962, de Gaulle had three issues at the top of his agenda. The first was his 'Fouchet proposals' for political union of the Six. On the grounds that these would seriously influence the nature of the union Britain was seeking to join, Heath had made a belated bid for Britain to be involved in the discussions. At a WEU meeting on 10 April, he made plain Britain's assumption that the existing Communities would be the foundation on which 'Europe would be built', but that he hoped their work could be 'knit together with the new political structure in a coherent and effective whole'. There was little need for his concern, because shortly afterwards the proposals collapsed, when France's partners could not agree a way forward.[27]

24 Moravscik, Andrew (1999), *The Choice For Europe* (London, UCL), p. 212.
25 Milward, *op. cit.*, p. 424.
26 Moravscik, Andrew (2000) 'De Gaulle Between Grain and Grandeur: The Political Economy of French EC Policy, 1958–1970 (Pt. 2)', *Journal of Cold War Studies*, Vol. 2, No. 3 (Fall), p. 9. Despite suggestions from the Germans that Britain should participate as observers in discussions about agricultural policy, this never happened. (See also Milward, *op. cit.*, p. 424, and CAB 134/1821.)
27 On 15 May 1962, de Gaulle gave a press conference to explain the collapse, in which he reiterated his view that 'only the States, in this respect, are valid, legitimate, and capable of achieving it (political union). I repeat that at present there is and can be no Europe other than a Europe of States – except of course for myths, fictions, and pageants.' This particularly rankled with Monnet who castigated de Gaulle's comments in his *Memoirs* as having 'travestied' his beloved Community and all that supranationalism stood for.

De Gaulle was anyway by this time becoming more preoccupied by his new alliance with Adenauer. In the same month of April, Adenauer's fears about American policy seemed to be confirmed when the US Secretary of State Dean Rusk came up with a new plan for Berlin, which seemed to propose *de facto* recognition of the GDR. Given only 48 hours to respond, Adenauer had no option but to reject it and, at his request, de Gaulle followed suit. When Kennedy endorsed Rusk's action and criticised Adenauer, affirming that negotiations with the Soviet Union over Berlin would continue, relations between Adenauer and Kennedy became frigid. With this unprecedented rift having developed between West Germany and the United States, de Gaulle moved in to cement the Franco-German axis. He invited Adenauer to make a state visit to France two months later, in July.

The third item on de Gaulle's agenda was Britain's application to join the EEC. By now he was certain Britain would have to be kept out. On 19 May, Macmillan recorded in his diary that the British Ambassador in Paris, Sir Pierson Dixon, conveyed the impression that de Gaulle 'has now definitely decided to exclude us'. Macmillan forlornly noted: 'others (and I am one) do not feel that de Gaulle has definitely made up his mind'. [28]

Throughout, Macmillan remained wholly oblivious to the hidden element in de Gaulle determination to keep Britain out. He was still convinced that the key to changing the General's mind lay in finding some way to offer him help with nuclear weapons: perhaps by talking the Americans into assisting the French (although it had already been made clear to him that this was very unlikely). An alternative was an Anglo-French arrangement for 'joint targeting of nuclear forces', without the direct involvement of the United States. [29]

In pursuit of his fantasy, on 2 to 3 June, Macmillan met with de Gaulle in a beautiful small chateau near Paris, Champs, once the home of Madame de Pompadour. He described his host as playing 'the role of a stately monarch unbending a little to the representative of a once hostile but now friendly country'. But de Gaulle 'repeated his preference for a Six without Britain; first, because British entry would entirely alter the character of the Community'. Only secondly did de Gaulle offer the view that 'Britain was too tied to America'. [30]

The French Ambassador to London, de Courcel, who was present at the discussions, recorded that Macmillan made a direct offer of Franco-British nuclear collaboration as an implied *quid pro quo* for France supporting British EEC entry. But contrary to British expectations, de Gaulle did not react. Instead, he emphasised France's absolute need to export her agricultural surpluses and insistently raised the issue of Commonwealth imports, which he insisted was the 'most fundamental' issue.

---

28 Horne, *op. cit.*, p. 326
29 Letter from Macmillan to Lord Home on 16 May, quoted in Horne, *op. cit.*, pp. 326–327.
30 Horne, *op. cit.*, p. 328. Adenauer had also by this time made clear, in a speech in West Berlin on 11 May, his view that Britain could not possibly join any 'political union' of the Six. In a broadcast on 29 May, he reiterated this, saying that even if Britain did join the Common Market, her interests were so different from those of the Six that she could not join a political union.

Throughout the discussions, Macmillan, completely failed to understand what was at stake. Responding to de Gaulle's demand that Commonwealth imports should be limited to tropical products only, he insisted on transitional arrangements, confirming all de Gaulle's fears. And when Macmillan tried to shift the conversation away from agriculture, de Gaulle kept returning to it.[31] Coming away without the first idea of what had transpired, Macmillan later reported to the Queen that 'the danger of the French opposing a resolute veto to our application has now been avoided, at least for the time being'.[32]

The following month Adenauer paid his state visit to France, the first by a German Chancellor since the war. The six-day visit culminated on 8 July with the two leaders attending High Mass in Rheims cathedral, after having taken the salute at a parade of French and German troops outside the city. It was the first time since the battle of Leipzig in 1813 that French and German troops had been on the same side. In their private discussions, de Gaulle expressed his doubts about Britain joining the EEC. When Adenauer did not disagree, the General knew he had his backing. This had been de Gaulle's real purpose in so assiduously cultivating his alliance with Adenauer. With his flank secure, he now felt able to instruct his negotiators in Brussels to take a harder line with the British.

There were now only four weeks left before the marathon talks in Brussels broke up for the summer. Already the negotiators for the Six had been startled by how many concessions Heath had been prepared to make on Britain's behalf, particularly over Commonwealth imports and even on issues formerly thought to be 'non-negotiable'. This had provoked a joint statement by the prime ministers of Australia and New Zealand, on the eve of Macmillan's visit to Champs, highly critical of Britain's new readiness to abandon imperial preferences.[33]

It was all to no avail. At the final session of the talks, during the night of 4 to 5 August, when everyone was exhausted, the chairman from Luxembourg, Eugène Schaus, had collapsed at two in the morning. Yet the session had continued with Spaak in the chair and, as Heath was to record:

'A little before 4 a.m., the French unexpectedly demanded that we should sign a paper on financing the CAP, committing us to an interpretation of the financial regulation favourable to the French. They wanted a new tariff arrangement on imports from outside the EEC which would maintain the price of domestic produce. The action was self-evidently dilatory in intent, and I refused to be bounced into a snap judgment on such a complex matter. I was supported in this by the Germans and the Dutch, who were as interested as I was. The French redrafted the document twice, but this only hardened my resolve. This was no way to carry on such an important negotiation, and I was having none of it. In response, Couve de Murville said that he would reserve his position regarding food imports from the British Commonwealth, a matter which I had thought to be fully resolved.'[34]

It was a classic negotiating ambush, of a kind which in the years ahead was to become only too familiar. With no agreement possible, the talks had to be

---

31 PRO. PREM 11/3775, pp. 7–9. Record of a conversation at the Château de Champs, 2–3 June 1962.
32 Horne, *op. cit.*, p. 328–329.
33 Horne, *op. cit.*, p. 327.
34 Heath, *op. cit.*, p. 222.

adjourned until the autumn. Then the French would make it clearer than ever that they had no intention of allowing Britain's application to succeed.[35]

The following month, on 5 September, President de Gaulle began a triumphant state visit to the German Federal Republic, regarded as even more successful than his host's visit to France. In their private talks, they agreed that Britain must be excluded, and de Gaulle continued the courtship with a six-page memorandum, suggesting a solemn agreement between the French and German governments to co-ordinate their foreign policy and defence. Without referring to his own Cabinet, Adenauer signalled that such an agreement would be the first priority of his policy.[36]

The *denouement* approaches

In Britain that autumn the Common Market issue briefly moved to the centre of the political stage. Although the Brussels negotiations had been dragging on for a year, they had never attracted much public interest. Now, as one historian put it, they seemed to be 'inexplicably dragging out as if scripted by Kafka. Hours and even days were being taken up by discussion of the tariffs on Indian tea or Australian kangaroo meat'.[37]

Belatedly the newspapers published turgid supplements, trying to explain in laborious detail what joining the Common Market would entail, many to be thrown away unread. Apart from the super-patriotic, right-wing titles owned by the ageing Canadian Lord Beaverbrook, a long-standing champion of the 'Empire', most of the press supported British entry, without showing any understanding of its deeper implications. As the government wanted, the issue was presented almost entirely in terms of economics and the supposed benefits that would follow from British industry being exposed to the 'icy blasts of competition' from the more 'dynamic' economies of the Six.[38]

The greatest enthusiasm for Britain's involvement with 'Europe' was expressed by a group of younger writers and politicians representing what came to be dubbed the 'What's Wrong With Britain School of Journalism'. These publicists, such as Michael Shanks, author of a best-selling paperback *The Stagnant Society*, or the Labour MP Anthony Crosland, a regular contributor to the intellectual monthly *Encounter*, enjoyed contrasting what they saw as a stuffy, tradition-bound, class-ridden, obsolete, inefficient Britain, lost in nostalgia for the days of empire, with what they saw as the newly energetic, innovative, efficient 'Europeans'. These paragons of virtue did not have licensing laws which prevent-

---

35 See Milward, *op. cit.*, pp. 438–441. He takes the view that, had de Gaulle not eventually vetoed Britain's application, the British government would have been forced to break off negotiations over precisely this issue. This view is shared by another historian. He claims that Couve de Murville was convinced that France was within 'striking distance' of forcing Britain to withdraw its application, and was thus reportedly furious with de Gaulle for invoking the veto. (Ludlow, Piers (1997), *Dealing With Britain – The Six And The First UK Application To The EEC* (Cambridge University Press), p. 210.)

36 Williams, *op. cit.*, p. 506.

37 Booker, Christopher (1969), *The Neophiliacs* (London, Collins), p. 183.

38 Or, as Macmillan himself termed it, 'the cold *douche* of competition' (Ball, *op. cit.*, p. 217).

ed drinking after 10.30 at night and had discovered the secret of economic 'dynamism' which Britain had so obviously lost.[39]

This mind-set in turn reflected a much deeper shift in social attitudes which was now evident at all levels of British society. It had first appeared in the late 1950s, in the rise of a new 'youth-culture', centred on rock 'n' roll, an obsessive new fashion-consciousness and a sense of rebellion against everything which seemed identified with Britain's imperial past, from Establishment institutions such as the monarchy to sexual morality. The 1960s had brought a sense that Britain was moving rapidly towards a new kind of society, where all the conventions of belief and behaviour associated with Britain's traditional view of herself suddenly seemed out of date.

Politically this expressed itself in the striking change which had come over the image of Macmillan who, at the time of his election victory in 1959, had been identified with the social changes which were carrying Britain into a new age. But in 1961, with his languid aristocratic style, he had quite suddenly come to be seen as a tired, Edwardian grandfather-figure, particularly when measured against the young and 'dynamic' new President Kennedy across the Atlantic. By a new generation of satirists, in the revue *Beyond The Fringe*, in the new magazine *Private Eye*, and in the BBC's television show *That Was The Week That Was*, Macmillan was made an object of ridicule. He was an antediluvian relic of a past age, out of touch with the 'exciting', 'irreverent' new world now taking shape around him.[40]

Then in early October, the Labour leader Hugh Gaitskell electrified his party's conference at Brighton with a speech wholly dedicated to the Common Market. Lasting 105 minutes, it was arguably the most remarkable speech made to a party conference in the post-war era. He began by observing that the level of debate in the media over this 'crucial, complex and difficult issue' had not been high. He then ranged in magisterial fashion across all the individual issues raised by Britain's application, analysing each in turn, putting the arguments on both sides with devastating clarity, lit by flashes of humour.

He began by discussing at length the economic implications of joining a protectionist trading bloc and abandoning Britain's main trading partners in the Commonwealth and EFTA, although, as he noted, these were now showing a more impressive rate of economic growth than the Six. He pointed out that, as even

---

39 The 'What's Wrong With Britain' vogue had also caught on with the two leading 'trendsetting' glossy magazines of the time, *Queen* and *About Town* (owned by a new young publisher Michael Heseltine). According to a contemporary history: 'It was no accident that it was just these papers which were on the crest of a wave of young, upper-middle class popularity, with their antennae out for any new excitement that happened to be in the air, whether joining the Common Market or candy-striped shirts, economic "growth" or "ton-up kids".' (Booker, *op. cit.*, p. 158.)

40 It was in a full-page strip cartoon in *Private Eye* on 2 November 1962 that Edward Heath was first portrayed as 'Grocer Heath', a nickname which stuck. The sequence of images (drawn by William Rushton to a text by one of the present authors) showed Heath and a senior civil servant, Sir Brussels Sprout, going off to Brussels to negotiate with 'the evil Hallstein gang'. By shouting 'Euratom!', Sprout is transformed into 'Supermarketeer'. He and Heath start laying about them and win 'the Concessions!', such as '2d. off Indian tea' or '4d. off New Zealand butter' (hence 'the Grocer'). Returning home they are acclaimed as heroes, but the final frame records how their 'great victory was nothing more than the graceful surrender that had been inevitable all along'.

Heath was now being forced to admit, as an 'essential part of the Common Market agricultural policy' now taking shape, Britain would be obliged 'to import expensive food from the continent of Europe in place of cheap food from the Commonwealth'.

He addressed the by-now familiar claim that, by joining the EEC, would have a 'home market of 220 million people', pointing out that some of Europe's most successful economies belonged to small countries, such as Switzerland and Sweden, which did not have large home markets. He dismissed the more extravagant claims being made for the economic benefits of joining the EEC as 'rubbish', explaining that Britain would not find a solution to her economic *malaise* simply from joining the Common Market. Ultimately she would only be able to solve it by her own internal efforts.

Gaitskell then turned to the political aspects of merging Britain's destiny with Europe. Here he challenged Macmillan for being nothing like frank enough with the British people. 'We are told,' he said, 'that the Economic Community is not just a customs union, that all who framed it saw it as a stepping stone towards political integration.' But Macmillan was keeping remarkably quiet about the 'serious political obligations' this might imply. What the move towards 'political' or 'federal' union meant, Gaitskell explained, was that powers would be taken from national governments and handed to the new federal government. If Britain was to become part of this, she would be 'no more than a state … in the United States of Europe, such as Texas and California'. If this process was ultimately to lead the British people to hand over all the most important decisions on economic and foreign policy and defence to a 'supranational system', to be decided by a Council of Ministers or a 'federal parliament', Britain would become no more than 'a province of Europe'. It was this which prompted Gaitskell to the most famous passage in his speech, where he said:

'We must be clear about this; it does mean, if this is the idea, the end of Britain as an independent European state … it means the end of a thousand years of history. You may say "let it end". But my goodness, it is a decision which needs a little care and thought.'

Gaitskell ended by pointing out that Macmillan had no mandate for what he was proposing. Indeed it ran contrary to everything the government had told the British people during the 1959 election campaign. Yet they were now, in effect, being told that they were 'not capable of judging his issue – the government knows best, the top people are the only people who can really understand it … the classic argument of every tyranny in history'. The Labour Party proposed that the only honest, democratic way to proceed was to see what terms emerged from the negotiations, then put the most important decision the British people had ever faced to the test of an election.[41] His speech received a tumultuous ovation.

However, not all Labour delegates were impressed. Denis Healey thought the argument exaggerated. He found it 'inconceivable that the Common Market would acquire supranational powers in any major area, still less become a federa-

41 Gaitskell's speech is published in full in *The Eurosceptic Reader, op. cit.*, pp. 15–37.

tion'. He did not share Gaitskell's 'romantic chauvinism' and thought the whole issue 'a futile distraction'. In any case, 'it was certain that de Gaulle would veto Britain's entry'.[42]

Macmillan's response when the Conservatives met for their own conference at Llandudno the following week was to ignore Gaitskell's detailed analysis, and to resort to ridicule. Referring to his passage on the moves towards political union, he said:

'Mr Gaitskell now prattles on about our being reduced to the status of Texas or California. What nonsense!... Certainly if I believed that I would not touch it on any terms... there can be no question of Britain being outvoted into some arrangement which we found incompatible with our needs and responsibilities and traditions.'[43]

But the headlines were reserved for Macmillan's quotation of an old music hall song, in which he sought to contrast his own decisiveness with Gaitskell's lack of courage:

'She wouldn't say "yes", she wouldn't say "no".
She wouldn't say "stay", she wouldn't say "go".
She wanted to climb but she dreaded to fall.
So she bided her time, and clung to the wall.'

The 4,000 Tory delegates, most of whom sported 'Yes' badges handed out by party managers, rocked with laughter and gave Macmillan a standing ovation, to show their backing for a policy which all but a handful of them two years earlier would have rejected as an unthinkable betrayal of their country, the Commonwealth and a thousand years of British history.

The irony was that, although none of those hearing these speeches were aware of it, the die against British entry had already been cast. The day after Macmillan's speech, pictures taken by an American U-2 reconnaissance aircraft identified nuclear-capable Soviet missiles on the Communist island of Cuba, only 90 miles off the Florida coast. So began the 'Cuban Missile Crisis' which, by 25 October had escalated to the point where nuclear war seemed imminent. What emerged was evidence of America's willingness to pursue her own interests, irrespective of the effects on her allies. One effect was to cement the Franco-German relationship.

On 15 December 1962, Macmillan met de Gaulle at Rambouillet. Six weeks after the end of the Cuba crisis, Macmillan was more determined than ever to maintain Britain's independent nuclear deterrent, but he had just learned that the US had cancelled the missile he hoped to buy, Skybolt. Macmillan told de Gaulle that, as a replacement, he planned to ask Kennedy for Polaris. But de Gaulle seemed preoccupied with the Brussels negotiations. 'In the Six', as he was later to reflect, France could say 'no', even against the Germans; she could stop policies with which she disagreed, because of the strength of her position. Once Britain and all the rest joined, things would be different.'[44]

---

42 Healey, Dennis (1989), *The Time Of My Life* (London, Michael Joseph), p. 211.
43 *The Times*, 15 October 1962
44 *Memoirs, op. cit.*, pp. 353–354.

De Gaulle's negative attitude came as a shock to Macmillan. With 'indignation', he accused de Gaulle of putting forward 'a fundamental objection to Britain's application'.[45] He was right. De Gaulle had already decided to turn this 'fundamental objection' into a veto, which he explained to his own Cabinet a few days later, on 19 December 1962:

'If Great Britain and ... the Commonwealth enter, it would be as if the Common Market had ... dissolved within a large free trade area ... Always the same question is posed, but the British don't answer. Instead, they say, "It's the French who don't want it"... To please the British, should we call into question the Common Market and the negotiation of the agricultural regulations that benefit us? All this would be difficult to accept... Britain continues to supply itself cheaply in Canada, New Zealand, Australia, etc. The Germans are dying to do the same in Argentina. The others would follow. What will we do with European, and particularly French surpluses? If we have to spend 500 billion [francs] a year on agricultural subsidies, what will happen if the Common Market can no longer assist us? These eminently practical questions should not be resolved on the basis of sentiments. [Macmillan] is melancholy and so am I. We would prefer Macmillan's Britain to that of Labour, and we would like to help him stay in office. But what can I do? Except to sing him the Edith Piaf song: *Ne pleurez pas, Milord*.'[46]

Still failing to recognise de Gaulle's real concern, Macmillan pursued the acquisition of Polaris during a bilateral summit with Kennedy at Nassau on 18 to 21 December 1962, when he asked Kennedy to make the missile available to both Britain and France. Kennedy was only prepared to say, delphically, that the two countries might be given Polaris on 'similar terms'. He knew that Britain was in a position to make her own thermo-nuclear warheads while France was not; which meant that, even if Congress could be persuaded to approve, there was no way France could be given the missiles. But the point was irrelevant anyway.

On 14 January 1963, under crystal chandeliers in the Elysée Palace in Paris, and without warning his partners in the Six, de Gaulle announced before the world's press that he intended to veto Britain's entry. In the most-quoted passage of his 1500-word statement he declared:

'England, in effect is insular. She is maritime. She is linked through her trade, her markets, her supply lines to the most distant countries. She pursues essentially industrial and commercial activities and only slightly agricultural ones. She has, in all her doings, very marked and very original habits and traditions. In short England's nature, England's structure, England's very situation differs profoundly from those of the Continentals.'

This part of the text has often been interpreted as simply as a nationalistic attack on Britain. Commentators have used it to argue that de Gaulle vetoed the British application because of Macmillan's deal with Kennedy over Polaris. This is cited as evidence of Macmillan's 'Atlanticism' and his preference for the 'special relationship' with the United States. Certainly this weighed heavily with de Gaulle, as he saw the whole philosophy of the British and the Americans as quite different from that of the 'Europeans', characterised above all by France and Germany.

---

45 *Ibid.*
46 Peyrefitte, Alain (1994), *C'était de Gaulle, Vol. 1* (Paris, Fayard), p. 333.

Rarely quoted, however, are the preceding paragraphs, in which de Gaulle could hardly have revealed his real underlying concern more clearly. Referring to the vagueness of the Treaty of Rome on agriculture, he stated that, for France, this had to be 'settled':

'It is obvious that agriculture is an essential element in our national activity as a whole. We cannot conceive of a Common Market in which French agriculture would not find outlets in keeping with its production. And we agree further that, of the Six, we are the country on which this necessity is imposed in the most imperative manner. That is why when, last January, consideration was given to the setting in motion of the second phase of the Treaty – in other words a practical start in its application – we were led to pose the entry of agriculture into the Common Market as a formal condition. This was finally accepted by our partners, but very difficult and very complex arrangements were needed and some rulings are still outstanding.' [47]

In this de Gaulle signalled his concern for the consequences of Britain being allowed to take part in the negotiations before detailed arrangements for the CAP had been finalised. This is confirmed by de Gaulle's own memoirs. Referring to Britain's initial antagonism to the Common Market, and her attempt to set up a rival in EFTA, he says that, by the middle of 1961, the British had 'returned to the offensive':

'Having failed from without to prevent the birth of the Community, they now planned to paralyse it from within. Instead of calling for an end to it, they now declared that they themselves were eager to join, and proposed examining the conditions on which they might do so, "provided that their special relationship with their Commonwealth and their associates in the free trade area were taken into consideration, as well as their special interests in respect of agriculture". To submit to this would obviously have meant abandoning the Common Market as originally conceived ... I could see the day approaching when I should either have to remove the obstruction ... or extricate France from an enterprise which had gone astray almost as soon as it had begun.' [48]

The inescapable inference is that de Gaulle was convinced that Britain's entry would have meant 'abandoning the Common Market as originally conceived', threatening the very core of his survival strategy. She could not be permitted to join until the financial details of the CAP had been settled. At last, it seems, Macmillan began to understand. On 11 February 1963, he told the Commons, 'The end did not come because the discussions were menaced with failure. On the contrary, it was because they threatened to succeed'. [49] In his memoirs, Heath also recognised that agriculture had been a crucial issue, noting that

'... the Community had agreed, largely under pressure from the French, to sort out the framework of the new policy before entering into serious discussions with us on the arrangement for our entry. The French did not wish the British to be at the table taking part

47 In Salmon, Trevor & Nicoll, Sir William (1997), *Building European Union – A Documentary History and Analysis* (Manchester, Manchester University Press), p. 88.
48 *De Gaulle, op. cit.,* pp. 41–42.
49 *Memoirs, 1961–1963, op. cit.,* p. 377.

in the formative discussions on the CAP, for fear that we might disrupt the very favourable arrangements they otherwise had every reason to expect from their partners.'[50]

Despite this, Heath never acknowledged that this very issue lay at the heart of the French veto. After the first three month of negotiations, he expressed his suspicions to one of his senior civil servants that the French seemed to want to drag out the talks as long as possible. He gave three reasons:

'The French expected that opposition would grow in the UK the longer the negotiations progressed; that our own desire to reach an agreement would weaken; and, finally, that something else would turn up to prevent the negotiations being successfully concluded.'[51]

The third reason, Heath suggested, was to prove crucial. The French suspected that our position was becoming progressively weaker economically, politically and militarily, *viz-à-viz* both the Six and the US. In their view, the longer matters were drawn out, the greater the opportunity for securing better terms for the Community and themselves in particular.

There is something of the incurable 'little Englander' in these explanations. Heath's view of the negotiations was wholly Anglocentric. To be fair, wrapped up in the narrow, sterile world of the Brussels negotiating circuit, he could hardly have been expected to have grasped the bigger picture. For that, he was reliant on his officials. Yet the officials themselves were no better informed. A report on the negotiations prepared by the UK delegation was to admit that, during the period between Britain's application and the start of the negotiations, in contrast to the 'intense consultation and discussion' London had enjoyed with Commonwealth countries, contacts with the Six and the Commission had been minimal, and confined only to 'questions of procedure':

'…there was very little knowledge in London of the manner in which the Member Governments, and the Institutions of the Community, were interpreting the provisions of the Treaty of Rome. It is at least possible that, if we had initiated during this period preliminary consultations on matters of substance with Member Governments, and still more with the Commission, we might have acquired information on which we should have been able to base a more informed judgement.'[52]

The real failure, therefore, lay with the Foreign Office. Informed analysis would have indicated that a British application could not succeed. The signals were there. But entirely lacking from the tortuous analyses presented to Macmillan and the Cabinet by the officials was any recognition of the true French agenda. Later commentators such as Denman and Young were to suggest that, if Macmillan's approach had not been so timid and Britain had come forward with more concessions before the 1962 summer break, the negotiations might have succeeded.[53] Of Macmillan, Young writes:

---

50 *Op. cit.*, pp. 216–217.
51 *Op. cit.*, p. 220.
52 O'Neill, Con (2000), *Britain's Entry Into The European Community – Report On The Negotiations Of 1970–1972* (London, Frank Cass Publishers), p. 49.
53 Young, *op. cit.*, pp. 222–226.

'The only future for Britain, it soon turned out, was the one Macmillan sought to bring about. His problem was that he did not try hard enough to achieve it. Even as he plunged towards the future, he was besotted and ensnared by the past.'[54]

Denman and Young praise the prescience of Sir Frank Lee, in 'convincing' Macmillan that Britain should apply to join the EEC. Their books are peppered with praise for the 'brilliance' of the various civil servants who had the 'vision' to appreciate how Britain's way forward lay with 'Europe'. At heart though, both civil servants and commentators were 'little Englanders'. Like Heath, they viewed the continent from an entirely Anglocentric perspective, assuming that, just because Britain wanted to join, the Six would roll over to admit her, wholly failing to grasp why French rejection was inevitable.

When this insular strategy failed and Britain's application was finally rejected, the 'little Englanders' put the blame on the politicians (though not on Heath, whose 'negotiating skills' continued to win admiration). Yet the failure to understand the vital importance of agriculture to France, and how the CAP was then to be weighted so massively in France's favour, led all those responsible for Britain's application to overlook how greatly disadvantaged Britain would be when she was finally to enter. At their door must lie a great deal of the responsibility for the eventual problems in British farming, which by the late 1990s had led to a major social and economic crisis. The fabled 'Rolls-Royce minds' of the Foreign Office and the Home Civil Service had failed in their duty.[55]

As for the other item at the top of de Gaulle's agenda, only a week after he had shocked the world with his veto, Adenauer arrived in Paris for the final negotiations on their planned Franco-German treaty. On 20 January, while Adenauer was dining at the German Embassy, Monnet, Hallstein and the Dutch Commissioner, Blankenhorn, burst in to plead with him to link the Franco-German treaty with an assurance that negotiations with Britain should continue. Here de Gaulle's courtship paid off. Adenauer refused. On 22 January the two men the signed their treaty, in the same Elysée Palace where de Gaulle, nine days earlier, had announced his veto. According to an official summary of the Elysée Treaty:

'It laid the institutional groundwork for biannual summits of heads of state and government, regular consultations at the ministerial level, and generally systematic efforts by French and German policymakers to co-ordinate policies as well as to overcome differences of opinion, to achieve mutually acceptable compromise solutions. The different meetings still go through various fields of work: defence, education, youth affairs and so on, and stand therefore as the milestone of the Franco-German relationship.'[56]

This grand symbol of reconciliation was to be Adenauer's swan song. He had initiated it without consulting his Cabinet and, when it was presented to the

---

54 Young, *op. cit.*, p. 132.
55 Milward (*op. cit.*, pp. 425–426) also remarks that, 'In retrospect, the Ministry of Agriculture's optimism about the role Britain would play in shaping the CAP is hard to explain ... their reports and briefings seemed sometimes wilfully to minimise the problems involved...' and they were '... not based on a full consideration of the way the CAP would also be shaped by political pressures within the Six'.
56 *www.weltpolitik.net/regionen/europa/frankreich/943.html*

Bundestag for ratification, it had been accepted only with the addition of a long, rambling preamble – written by Monnet – which effectively nullified the treaty. This was the last straw for his Christian Democrat Party which, supported by the Free Democrats under Erhard, forced Adenauer to announce his retirement. The following October, at the age of 87, he reluctantly handed over the reins to the minister who had presided over West Germany's 'economic miracle'.

De Gaulle, when told of this response to the treaty was reported to have greeted it with a verbal shrug: 'Treaties are like maidens and roses, they each have their day.' [57] In securing Adenauer's support for his veto, the treaty had already served its original purpose.[58] But its longer-term consequences in placing a Franco-German alliance at the heart of the Community were to be profound.

Into the twilight

The Six formally confirmed Britain's rejection on 28 January 1963. The news came as Britain was enduring the harshest winter of modern times. Much of the island was covered by deep snow from the beginning of January to March. For weeks London was obscured under a thick freezing fog. This helped bring on the sudden death of Gaitskell, from a rare chest disease, at only 56. He was succeeded as Labour leader by Harold Wilson.

Thus began a year in which the mood of English life was to become ever more febrile. Already wild rumours were circulating in London of some immense scandal hanging over the government, which finally broke into the open in June when Macmillan's war minister, John Profumo, admitted he had lied to the Commons about an affair with a girl who was also the mistress of a senior Soviet spy. The headlines were dominated for weeks by further revelations and rumours which threatened to incriminate famous names across the British Establishment.

Equally hypnotic at the same time was the excitement surrounding the emergence of the Beatles, the supreme 'dream heroes' of 1960s popular culture. Their 'irreverence' and 'classlessness' seemed to epitomise the social revolution which had been engulfing Britain since the late 1950s, expressed in everything from the sexual 'new morality' to the rise of 'satire'. The culminatory shock in a year of almost unbroken hysteria in English life was the news on 22 November from across the Atlantic of the assassination of that other supreme 1960s 'dream hero', President Kennedy.

After the dramatic international events of the earlier years of the decade, with the two greatest crises of the Cold War over Berlin and Cuba, the mood of the world itself now changed. America, through the middle years of the 1960s, became increasingly preoccupied by race riots in her cities at home and her ever greater involvement in the Vietnam War abroad. In the Soviet Union in October 1964 Khruschev was overthrown. In Britain, a strange unreality seemed to settle over

---

57 Duchêne, *op. cit.*, p. 330.
58 Spaak confirms de Gaulle's cynicism: Adenauer, he writes, 'failed to resist de Gaulle's deliberate bid to seduce him'. The carefully stage-managed rapprochement at Rheims 'was enough to confuse a man whose advanced age had already weakened his powers of judgement' (Spaak, *op. cit.*, p. 342).

national life, as ever more obsessive attention came to be paid to the new 'pop culture' and the hailing of London as 'the most swinging city in the world'.

Equally unreal seemed the bubble of make-believe surrounding the new government under Wilson, which in October 1964 scraped into power on the promise of creating a 'dynamic' and 'classless' 'New Britain'. Scarcely noticed but with almost frenzied speed, Britain was now freeing herself of almost all her remaining colonies across the globe. When in January 1965 Churchill died at the age of 90, his spectacular state funeral seemed like the nostalgic requiem for a Britain that had already faded into history.

Meanwhile, away from the headlines, in Brussels and Luxembourg the technocrats of western Europe's new supranational institutions were gradually finding their feet.

The supremacy of EC Law

By 1963 the number of European Commission officials was rising towards 2,500. They were now planning for themselves one of the largest office blocks in the world. The immense Berlaymont building on the eastern side of Brussels, designed as 'a symbol of Europe', to provide nearly two million square feet of office space to house 3,000 officials on 13 floors, would not be ready for occupation until 1967.

In the meantime, however, the Commission's first task, to weld the Six into a single trading bloc by creating a common tariff structure against the outside world, was by 1963 almost complete. One of the year's more controversial issues was a new Washington-inspired drive under GATT to lower import duties worldwide, to be agreed through talks known as the 'Kennedy round'. This was meant to be the first time the EEC acted as a single entity in international negotiations. But the US proposals split the Six between the 'free traders', led by Erhard, who supported tariff cuts, and the 'protectionists' led by de Gaulle. The result was a weak compromise.

The Commission's next task was to set about promoting 'ever closer union' between the Six by proposing new laws. In doing so, it employed what came to be known as 'the Monnet method', gradually extending its 'competences' over ever more areas of economic and social activity. Every new initiative would deprive the member states of the right to make their own laws in that area, and thus would the Commission continually strive to enlarge what became known as the 'occupied field'. This was made up of those areas of policy in which the Commission alone had the right to initiate legislation. Regardless of the immediate need cited for introducing any new law, its real purpose was always to transfer ever more power from national parliaments to the supranational centre.

Under the Treaty of Rome, the Community was empowered to pass three main types of law. The first was known in English as a 'directive', although the original French term is simply *loi* or 'law'. This was a general set of instructions which each member state then had to 'transpose' into a national version of its own. The second was the 'regulation', which immediately had the force of law throughout the

Community, exactly as issued. The third was the 'decision', directed to a specific situation, industry or country within the Community, applicable only to those to whom it was addressed. But what these all had in common was that, in keeping with the supranational principle, the right to propose any piece of legislation lay solely with the Commission. Subject to this crucial rule, most laws would then be negotiated between officials of the Commission and those of national governments, for final approval by the politicians on the various Councils of Ministers. But in most cases, thanks to the complexity of much of the legislation going through the system, this political approval was merely a formality. Furthermore the Commission itself would increasingly develop the capacity to issue edicts in its own right, using powers delegated to it by the Councils.[59]

An urgent requirement at this early stage of the Community's development was to establish its legal authority, which the drafting of the Treaty had left ill-defined. This was achieved through the new European Court of Justice based in Luxembourg, the central role of which was to extend and reinforce the supranational authority of the Commission. One of the Court's first objectives was to confirm the supremacy of Community law, which it brought about through two historic judgments in 1963 and 1964.

Both these landmark judgements arose from seemingly trivial cases. The first, known as the *Van Gend en Loos* case, upheld the claim by a Dutch transport company that the Dutch customs authorities had been in breach of the Treaty by raising a duty on imports from Germany.[60] The second, by which the ECJ confirmed its earlier ruling, arose from Italy's nationalisation of her electricity industry in 1962. A shareholder, Mr Costa, protested that the transfer of his shares to the National Electricity Board (ENEL) had deprived him of his dividend. He therefore refused to pay an electricity bill for 1,926 Italian lira, then equivalent to just over £1 sterling. When Mr Costa claimed that the nationalisation infringed the EC Treaty, the case was referred to the ECJ. Again the court seized this opportunity to confirm the supremacy of EC law, stating that:

'By contrast with ordinary international treaties, the EEC Treaty has created its own legal system which … became an integral part of the legal systems of the Member States and which their courts are bound to apply. By creating a Community of unlimited duration, having its own institutions, its own personality, its own legal capacity and capacity of representation on the international plane and, more particularly, real powers stemming from a limitation of sovereignty or a transfer of powers from the States to the Community, the Member States have limited their sovereign rights … and have thus created a body of law which binds both their nationals and themselves.'[61]

The ECJ's conclusions could not have put more clearly where power now lay:

'It follows … that the law stemming from the Treaty, an independent source of law, could not, because of its special and original nature, be overridden by domestic legal provisions,

---

59 In addition to these central types of legislation, both Council and Commission could also issue 'recommendations' and 'opinions', carrying less weight than laws but designed as guidance to be followed by those to whom they were addressed.
60 Case 26/62, *Van Geld en Loos v Nederlandse Belastingadministratie* [1963] CMLR 105.
61 Case 6/64, *Costa v ENEL* [1964] CMLR 425.

however framed, without being deprived of its character as Community law and without the legal basis of the Community itself being called into question. The transfer by the States from their domestic legal system to the Community legal system of the rights and obligations arising under the Treaty carries with it a permanent limitation of their sovereign rights, against which a subsequent unilateral act incompatible with the concept of the Community cannot prevail.'[62]

This ruling, not agreed unanimously by the judges, was years later to be described by one expert observer of EU affairs as a '*coup d'état*'. He recalled that a proposal that Community law must be accepted as superior to national law had actually been rejected in the final drafting of the Treaty of Rome. But now this principle had been established by these two historic cases in the ECJ, it was to provide the foundation on which the whole edifice of supranational government could subsequently be built.[63]

The CAP: the battle continues

There was still one central issue on which the Six were divided. Following his veto of British entry, de Gaulle had become increasingly agitated about the slow progress of the CAP negotiations. At a press conference in July 1963 he warned that unless the Six could meet a new deadline for finalising the budgetary arrangements, the Common Market 'would disappear'. In November, therefore, the Commission tried to force the pace with two proposals, which became known after their author, the agriculture commissioner, as Mansholt I and II. What emerged from these was the Commission's acceptance that farming subsidies should be paid centrally from Community funds.

Although this proposal was intended to break the *impasse*, negotiations immediately stalled, resulting in chaos and confusion. When attempts to introduce standard Community farm prices failed, member states began to make their own bilateral agreements. The different subsidy schemes were still largely financed by national governments, only partly from their contributions to the Community, with no proper budgetary control. Farm surpluses continued to rise.

Monnet, who had not involved himself in the detail of all these negotiations, had become increasingly depressed. By 1965 he felt his Community was stagnating. 'Everywhere' he wrote later, 'there was the danger of a return to separate policies and bilateral agreements; and Germany might well be strongly tempted to compete with France in the quest for national advantage.'[64] But, in December 1965, French presidential elections were due and de Gaulle's attacks on the Community had generated far more opposition in France than expected, especially among farmers.

Capitalising on de Gaulle's weakness, Hallstein proposed that a settlement on CAP finances should be linked with contentious proposals to establish the

62 *Ibid.*
63 Jens-Peter Bonde MEP, Danish leader of the Europe of Democracies and Diversities group in the European Parliament, personal interview, 19 December 2002.
64 Monnet, *op. cit.*, p. 479.

Community's own resources, and stronger powers for the Assembly, all in one package. He believed that, under pressure from the other member states, de Gaulle would be forced to accept the whole package. The Six had already agreed that the decision on CAP finance would be made by the Council of Ministers at the latest by 30 June. But, before the meeting due in Brussels on 28 to 30 June, Hallstein made another tactical error. He submitted the package to the Assembly, which enthusiastically endorsed it.

When the package was presented to the Council on 28 June, the French demanded immediate agreement on CAP funding, only to find that the Germans, Dutch and Italians, not wishing to ignore the Assembly, called for all three issues in the package to be taken as a whole. In the mere 72 hours scheduled for negotiation, this would have been impossible, and effectively amounted to a postponement of any agreement. The French therefore insisted that the CAP funding question should be considered separately, but the other members refused.[65] Right up to the deadline, the stalemate persisted, but when the Commission proposed resort to the now familiar technique of 'stopping the clock', the French representatives would not play. After they had reported back to Paris, de Gaulle ordered his permanent representatives to leave Brussels, and announced a French boycott of all EEC meetings concerned with new policies. The Community had entered what became known as the 'empty chair' crisis.

As France's presidential elections approached, Monnet turned openly against de Gaulle, announcing he would vote against him. The combined pressures put de Gaulle in the humiliating position of winning less than 44 percent in the first round. Monnet then endorsed Mitterrand, the opposition candidate, and de Gaulle only scraped home with a margin of 55 to 45 percent, far short of the huge majorities he was used to.[66]

Once re-elected, however, de Gaulle set out an ambitious price for France's co-operation with the Community. His government called for the Commission to change its name; to refrain from running an information service; abandon diplomatic missions; cease criticising member states' policies in public; submit proposals to the Council before publicising them; and to draft vaguer directives. Most of all, however, De Gaulle demanded explicit recognition of the right of member states to veto any decision arrived at by qualified majority voting (QMV) when they considered their 'vital interests' to be at stake.[67]

The power to override national vetoes lay at the very core of supranationalism and a shocked Monnet wrote in his memoirs how, behind calls for reform of the Commission,

'... could be glimpsed the desire to prevent majority voting becoming normal practice in the Community from January 1966 onwards, as the Treaty laid down. I suspected that this was a goal on which de Gaulle was irrevocably bent...'[68]

---

65 Spaak, *op. cit.*, pp. 481–482.
66 Duchêne, *op. cit.*, p. 332.
67 Moravscik, *De Gaulle*, Part 2, *op. cit.*, p. 36.
68 Monnet, *op. cit.*, pp. 482–483.

Yet, despite de Gaulle's overtly nationalistic stance through the crisis, it was significant that his officials only boycotted discussion on new policies. They continued to participate in the EEC's work on existing policies, including the negotiations on the CAP. In fact the effect of the 'empty chair' policy was to draw the Community more tightly together. Consensus, hitherto elusive, suddenly became easier, and the *impasse* on QMV was resolved in January 1966 with an agreement between France and the others, known as the 'Luxembourg Compromise'. This informal agreement acknowledged that any government which considered its 'vital interests' threatened by EEC legislation could prevent a decision being taken.[69]

Another price extracted for de Gaulle's return to co-operation was the resignation of Hallstein. But his real victory was the protection of 'vital interests', because the particular vital interest de Gaulle had in mind, as he confirmed in his memoirs, was France's agriculture:

'I may say that if, on resuming control of our affairs, I embraced the Common Market forthwith, it was as much because of our position as an agricultural country as for the spur it would give our industry. Certainly I was fully aware that, in order to integrate agriculture effectively into the Community, we should have to work energetically on our partners, whose interests in this matter are not ours. But I considered that this, for France, was a *sine qua non* of membership.'

De Gaulle made clear his conviction that, without a settlement designed to suit France's needs, her agriculture 'would constitute an incubus which would put us in a position of chronic inferiority in relation to others'. Thus he felt obliged to put up 'literally a desperate fight', sometimes going so far as to threaten to withdraw membership.[70]

Moravcsik points out that de Gaulle's confidential discussions and speeches at the time revealed 'a man obsessed with the possibility that QMV might be exploited to undermine carefully negotiated arrangements for fiscal transfers to French farmers'. He repeatedly stressed the need to retain control over three types of votes: those on CAP financing, on GATT negotiations, and on any possible free trade area. His reasoning was simple. Even with the progress already made, the CAP was not yet safe from reversal through the combined efforts of West Germany, Britain, Denmark and the United States, working through GATT. The result might, de Gaulle feared, allow the Americans to swamp the European market with their agricultural produce.[71] He further predicted that, if QMV remained in place, within a year Erhard's West Germany would be sure to call everything into question by calling for a majority vote on the CAP, and France 'would be

69 Spaak (*op. cit.*, p. 471) was surprised to hear de Gaulle insist that 'the European Community, as established under the Treaty of Rome, must be maintained'. He added, 'De Gaulle tends to adopt this rigid stance to prevent Britain's entry into the Common Market; on the other hand he is apt to disregard the Treaty altogether when it is a matter of respecting the powers of the EEC Commission or of submitting to a majority vote.'
70 De Gaulle, Charles (1971), *Memoirs Of Hope – Renewal 1958–1962* (London, Weidenfeld and Nicolson), p. 159.
71 Moravcsik, *De Gaulle*, Part 2, *op. cit.*, p. 40.

unable to do anything'. [72] With the Luxembourg Compromise, he could now protect his CAP agreements. The onward march of the EEC could continue.

Britain's second rebuff

By 1967, the 'project' seemed to be making steady progress. By the so-called 'merger treaty', signed in 1965, the EEC, Euratom and the Coal and Steel Community were now brought together as 'the Communities'. In Brussels the new Berlaymont building was opened and immediately filled by 3,000 Commission officials. On a French initiative, the EEC agreed to adopt a new form of indirect taxation, value added tax or VAT: a percentage of which would be passed to the Commission to provide an additional source of revenue for the CAP. And the output of EEC legislation was quickening. In the early years of the decade, the annual production of new directives and regulations had been around 25 a year. By the middle of the decade this reached 50. Now it was topping 100.[73]

Many of these early directives were dedicated to 'market organisation', requiring the standardisation of a wide range of produce, from eggs to bananas. Everything was geared to promoting uniformity and consistency: an ideology designed to encourage large-scale production but highly damaging to smaller, individual producers.[74]

Then, quite unexpectedly, came a new British application to join the 'Common Market'. In March 1966, Wilson, hitherto a supporter of his predecessor Gaitskell's opposition to entry, had won a landslide election victory over the Conservatives, now led by Heath. So unlikely was it that the Wilson government would apply to join the EEC that, during the election campaign, Nigel Lawson, then editor of *The Spectator*, commented: 'Europe is the supreme issue at this election ... no one who genuinely believes in a European Britain can vote Labour'.[75] Wilson's parliamentary private secretary, Peter Shore, later recalled that he still seemed as hostile to British entry as Gaitskell.[76]

In July 1966, however, only four months after Wilson's election victory, Britain's chronic balance of payments problem came to a head in a major crisis. In the eight years between 1956 and 1964, Britain's economic performance had been lamentable compared with her continental neighbours. The yearly increase in her industrial production had averaged just 2.8 percent, against West Germany's 7.3 percent, Italy's 8.2 percent and France's 6.2 percent. The growth of national *per capita* income had shown Britain similarly lagging behind, her 26.2 percent increase dwarfed by West Germany's 58.2 percent, Italy's 58.3 percent and France's 47.5

72 *Op. cit.*, p. 41.
73 *Official Journal of the European Communities: Directory of Community Legislation In Force and Other Acts of the Community Institutions*, Vol. II, Chronological Index.
74 From this ethos came some of the regulations which in Britain were later to give the EEC's obsession with uniformity a bad name, such as that banning the sale of excessively curved bananas; or the egg marketing regulations which prohibited small free-range producers from selling ungraded eggs to their local shops, thus outlawing the traditional practice of displaying baskets of fresh eggs on the counter.
75 *The Spectator*, 25 March 1966.
76 Shore, Peter (2000), *Separate Ways – The Heart Of Europe* (London, Duckworth), p. 68.

percent.[77] With the pound now under extreme pressure, Wilson introduced panic counter-measures, including a surcharge on imports, which threatened to bring even this modest growth to a halt. His familiar cheery optimism vanished. He began to look around in desperation for some more dramatic solution.

Another factor in his thinking was the growing frustration of his dealings with the Commonwealth. Since the white supremacist regime in Rhodesia had unilaterally declared independence from Britain in 1965, relations with his fellow Commonwealth leaders had become increasingly painful.[78] In addition, as Peter Shore recalled, Wilson had been 'got at' by some of his closest advisers, who were fervently 'pro-European', notably his private secretary, Michael Palliser and his Home Secretary Roy Jenkins, who in the summer of 1967 Wilson was to make chancellor.[79]

In face of all these pressures Wilson made a remarkable *volte face*. By October 1966 he had decided that Britain should make a new application.[80] Although his Cabinet was sharply divided, with ministers such as Denis Healey, Barbara Castle and Douglas Jay strongly opposed, a majority supported his change of policy, on the promise that Wilson and his new Foreign Secretary George Brown would make a 'Grand Tour' of the capitals of the Six to sound out opinion.

The tour started on 15 January 1967, when Wilson was described by his Euro-sceptic back-bencher Michael Foot as trotting round Europe 'like Don Quixote, his Sancho Panza at his side'.[81] The Italians and the Germans supported British entry. But de Gaulle appeared noncommittal. Wilson and Brown nevertheless came away from meeting him optimistic, recommending to their Cabinet colleagues that entry should be pursued. A revealing insight into Wilson's thinking came from his Cabinet colleague, Richard Crossman. In his diary he recorded that Wilson, just back from Adenauer's funeral on 26 April,[82] admitted to the German chancellor Dr Kiesinger that there were 'economic disadvantages in entering the Common Market but they are being overlooked by the British Government because of the tremendous political advantages'.[83]

On 30 April, the Cabinet voted in favour of applying, by 13 votes to eight. On the BBC's *Panorama*, Wilson described the application as 'a great turning point in history', stating that he believed, on balance, 'it will be right economically, but the

---

77 *Britain and Europe: The Future* (1966), London, p. 47, cited in Maclean, Donald (1970) *British Foreign Policy Since Suez 1956–1968* (London, Hodder & Stoughton), p. 80.

78 Shore, *op. cit.*, p. 70.

79 *Op. cit.*, p. 71.

80 US views were no longer a serious factor. Washington was now almost wholly preoccupied with the Vietnam War. Most of the 'Europeanists' in Kennedy's Cabinet had either departed or were otherwise engaged. Even George Ball was now devoting much of his time to Vietnam policy (and was eventually to resign over President Johnson's handling of the war). The State Department's economic bureau was actually hostile to British entry, because it believed that this could threaten the successful conclusion of the 'Kennedy Round' of GATT (Department of State telegramme 186605, 2 May 1967, *Administrative History of the Department of State*, LBJL, cited in Winand, *op. cit.*, p. 362).

81 *The Times*, 9 May 1967.

82 Adenauer died on 19 April 1967.

83 Crossman, Richard (1976), *The Diaries Of A Cabinet Minister*, Vol. II (London, Hamish Hamilton), p. 330.

political argument is stronger'. Britain's role in joining was 'to make Europe stronger, more independent, more decisive in world affairs'.

Monnet's Action Committee had already declared itself 'unanimously in favour' of British entry.[84] In Strasbourg on 9 May, when the European Parliament discussed Britain's application, Fernand Dehousse, a Belgian socialist, declared that it had 'rejoiced our hearts'. But the Gaullists were silent. Then, on 10 May, Britain's entry was discussed by the French Cabinet. Georges Gorse, the minister of information, said afterwards:

'France in the past has sufficiently deplored British insularity not to rejoice over any trend in the opposite direction. I think General de Gaulle will speak about this at his press conference and will be in a position to express the satisfaction provoked in French public opinion by the movement which is pushing Britain towards Europe – a movement we have always hoped for – and the difficult problems raised by a candidature of this importance with everything that implies.'[85]

On 16 May, de Gaulle delivered his verdict: '*Le Grand Non*'. Denman, quoting from the end of his statement, records de Gaulle saying that Britain's entry would only be possible when

'... this great people, so magnificently gifted with ability and courage, should on their own behalf and for themselves achieve a profound economic and political transformation which could allow them to join the Six continentals.'[86]

What he omitted, however, was the long earlier passage in which, by referring to 'the agricultural regulations', de Gaulle gave another indication of his real motives. Britain, he said, 'nourishes herself, to a great extent, on foodstuffs bought inexpensively throughout the world and, particularly, in the Commonwealth'. If she was to submit 'to the rules of the Six', then her 'balance of payments would be crushed' by the duties on her food imports. She would then be forced to raise her food prices to continental levels, causing her even greater problems. But, de Gaulle continued,

'... if she enters the Community without being really subjected to the agricultural system of the Six, the system will thereby collapse, completely upsetting the equilibrium of the Common Market and removing for France one of the main reasons she can have for participating in it.'[87]

Just as in 1963, de Gaulle had laid out with consummate clarity for those with eyes to see why British entry at this stage was out of the question.

Wilson, like Heath and Macmillan before him, showed no signs of understanding de Gaulle's objections. He tabled Britain's application in July 1967, only for this to be formally vetoed five months later. Shore, however, records how Wilson

---

84 Monnet, *op. cit.*, p. 487.
85 *The Times*, 11 May 1967.
86 Denman, *op. cit.*, p. 229.
87 De Gaulle, Charles, fifteenth press conference, 16 May 1967. Text supplied by the French Press and Information Service, New York, available on: *www.fordham.edu/halsall/mod/1967-degaulle-non-uk.html*

then instructed that preparations should be made for another application in the summer of 1970.[88]

In July 1968, Monnet came over to England to meet Wilson, later writing 'rarely had I seen him so determined and so pleased to commit himself to Europe'.[89] Before he left London, Monnet secured agreement from all three main political parties that they should join the Action Committee. Responding to Monnet's formal letter of invitation, Wilson wrote:

'The aims of the Action Committee are in close conformity with those to which the Labour Party subscribes. Our Party believes that European political, economic and technological integration is essential if Europe is to fulfil her great potential and make a unique contribution to secure and maintain world peace.'[90]

Had Wilson won the general election which took place two years later, his conversion to the 'European' cause now seemed so complete that he might well have been the man who took Britain into the EEC.

De Gaulle's final battle

Yet de Gaulle still had not secured his main prize – that financing system for the CAP which would guarantee subsidies for his farmers, with much of the bill picked up by Germany, as the richest country in the EEC, and Germany would also help to absorb France's agricultural surpluses. But this would also be the reason why France would then want British entry. Importing 50 percent of her food, Britain would be cut off from most of her Commonwealth suppliers, EEC import duties making their produce too expensive. She would then have to buy huge quantities of food from her new partners, above all from France.

However the genius which lay at the heart of the budgetary structure was that, since the EEC was a 'customs union', the income from levies on imports would have to be paid to the EEC as its 'own resource'. Once Britain was in, the import duties she collected would be paid straight to Community funds, to help finance the CAP, and therefore the French farmers who would be the chief beneficiaries. France would thus benefit from British entry twice over.

Before he could finally secure this prize, however, de Gaulle unexpectedly found himself faced with two more crises, one from Brussels, the other nearer home. In May 1968, Paris was taken over by crowds of rebellious students, triggering off a wave of strikes and unrest which paralysed the French economy. De Gaulle fled his capital, appealing for support from his army. Invoking fears of a Communist revolution, he called a snap election and won an overwhelming victory.

In Brussels the same year, agriculture commissioner Sicco Mansholt had become seriously disturbed by the way the half-formed version of the CAP was running out of control, with subsidies continuing to soar and food surpluses increasing. As a Dutch free trader, he had originally wanted a liberal, market-

88 Shore, *op. cit.*, p. 70.
89 *Ibid.*
90 Monnet, *op. cit.*, p. 492.

orientated CAP, which would encourage major structural changes to western Europe's agriculture, leading to greater productivity and a substantial drop in employment. What had so far had emerged had been the opposite: high support prices with no spending limits and maximum protection, with prices harmonised at the highest levels, bolstered by subsidised exports of surpluses which were flooding world markets. Thanks above all to de Gaulle, the CAP was more protectionist than the sum of member state policies.

In desperation Mansholt decided to counter attack. He began work on a major CAP reform, the first of what would be many, producing in 1969 the 'second Mansholt Plan'. This concluded:

'The Community is now having to pay so heavy a price for an agricultural production which bears no relation to demand that measures to balance the situation on the market can no longer be avoided...'[91]

He proposed halving the number of farmers; slaughtering millions of farm animals; and turning over seven percent of all agricultural land to forestry. Hundreds of thousands of farmers rioted in Brussels and other capitals and two died. Mansholt's own life was threatened. The Six's agriculture ministers, led by Germany, rejected his proposals out of hand. De Gaulle had now almost completely got his way. France's peasants could stay on the land. The Community, and eventually Britain, would pay the price.

Final victory

In April 1969 de Gaulle held a referendum asking for the French people to approve a *tranche* of radical reforms. When he lost he retired from office, to be succeeded by his prime minister, Georges Pompidou. Valéry Giscard d'Estaing became the new premier. It was this succession which was later to be credited for the shift in French policy which allowed Britain, after Heath's victory in the 1970 general election, to make her third and successful application to join the EEC. Another factor attributed to Heath's eventual success was the arrival of Willy Brandt, a supporter of British entry, as the new German chancellor.

But there was still one vital detail to be settled before Pompidou could allow a further application from Britain or the other three potential applicants – Ireland, Denmark and Norway. He first needed that guarantee on CAP financing. At his first presidential press conference on 10 July 1969, he declared that he had no objection in principle to British accession, but the Six first had to 'reach agreement amongst themselves'. At the same press conference, Pompidou agreed to a summit which had been called for by Brandt and other leaders of the Six, to be held at The Hague in December. There, Pompidou hoped, the arrangements would be finalised.

There was also another important issue on the Six's agenda. There had been a sharp revival of interest among the Six in the idea that the EEC should move

---

91 Commission of the European Communities, *Memorandum on the Reform of Agriculture in the European Economic Community*, Supplement to Bulletin No. 1–69, 1969.

towards economic and monetary union, first mooted by Spaak in his report setting out the framework for the Treaty of Rome. In the early 1960s this had again been advocated by Monnet and Luxembourg's prime minister, Pierre Werner; then again by the European Assembly and the Commission in 1965. Furthermore, the Council of Ministers had already laid the foundations for a common economic policy, by setting up various committees to discuss monetary and economic issues. The most important was Ecofin, at which the finance ministers of the Six held monthly meetings.[92]

In January 1968 Werner formally proposed that the Six should move to full economic and monetary union. This was followed by proposals from Giscard d'Estaing and the Commission.[93] Momentum had now built up to such a degree that Pompidou proposed that the Hague summit, fixed for 1 to 2 December, should link negotiations on the budget and the CAP with talks on monetary integration and 'enlargement'.

When the summit began, Brandt immediately turned the tables on Pompidou, with a thinly veiled threat that, unless there was 'fair play' for the applicant countries, there would be no agreement on the budget. Piet de Jong, the Dutch prime minister, proposed that the Six should discuss enlargement. According to Kitzinger,

'Pompidou, in pained surprise, countered that farming must come first. This was agreed. Everyone knew by this time that that was France's price for lifting the veto.'[94]

Thus the Six agreed to deal with the budget and CAP package first. Farm subsidies would be funded not only from levies on imports from outside the EEC but also from a percentage of VAT receipts levied by each of the member states. This was so radical that it needed a new treaty (to be signed in 1970 as the Luxembourg Treaty).

Only with that settled would France agree to the Six opening negotiations with the four would-be applicants, led by Britain. France did, however, insist on the crucial condition that they would not be allowed to alter the terms of that all-important financial package. As it was later put by a leading Foreign Office civil servant engaged in the subsequent negotiations:

'... the French continued to attach the highest importance to them, and to getting them concluded and ratified by all the existing member states before we could appear on the scene. It was thus a crucial point of the policy with which President Pompidou went to The Hague Summit meeting in December 1969 that, if he had to accept the opening of negotiations on our application, he must ensure that the negotiations did not begin until the Six had completed their agricultural finance regulation, and did not conclude until they had all ratified the resulting Treaty. This was the factor which produced the link, in The Hague Communiqué, between 'the completion of the Community' (*achèvement*) and its enlargement ... *élargissement* was made clearly conditional on *achèvement*.'[95]

---

92 Moravcsik, *op. cit.*, p. 291.
93 The Barre Proposals, named after the then president of the Commission.
94 Kitzinger, Uwe (1973), *Diplomacy and Persuasion – How Britain Joined The Common Market* (London, Thames and Hudson), p. 71.
95 O'Neill, *op. cit.*, p. 169.

In other words, the transition from de Gaulle to Pompidou made no difference to French policy. Throughout the 1960s, it had remained constant. There could be no enlargement until the CAP financial arrangements were in place.

Nevertheless, the budgetary arrangements were not the only unfinished business. The summit's other aim was to plan for further integration: to which effect the heads of government recognised that the Community had now reached a turning point:

'Entering the final phase of the Common Market is not only in fact putting the seal on the irreversible character of the work accomplished by the Communities, it is also preparing the way for a united Europe capable of assuming its responsibilities in the world of tomorrow... Consequently, the Heads of State or Government desire to reaffirm their faith in the political objects which give to the Community its whole meaning and significance, their determination to carry the enterprise through to its conclusion, and their confidence in the final success of their efforts.'[96]

If there had ever any doubt as to where the Six intended to go, there now could be none. To help it on its way, they commissioned two reports. The first, by Pierre Werner, would be on 'economic and monetary union'. The subject of the other, by the Belgian foreign minister Etienne Davignon, was 'political union'. All this was in train before Heath applied for entry to what he would consistently describe to the British people as merely a 'Common Market'.

---

96 Summit communiqué, *Bulletin of the European Communities*, 1–1970: para. 4.

Chapter 8

The Real Deceit of Edward Heath: 1970–1975

'There are some in this country who fear that in going into Europe we shall in some way sacrifice independence and sovereignty. These fears, I need hardly say, are completely unjustified.'

Edward Heath, prime ministerial TV broadcast, January 1973

'The bedrock of European union is the consent of the people.'

Edward Heath, *The Course of My Life*[1]

In April 1970 a Gallup poll showed that only 15 percent of the British electorate were in favour of a further bid to join the Common Market. Nearly three voters in five were opposed. A month later Wilson called a general election which, on 15 June, unexpectedly resulted in Heath becoming prime minister.

The Common Market played virtually no part in the campaign. Sixty-two percent of Conservative candidates made no reference to the EEC in their election addresses and only two percent declared strong support for British entry.[2] Even Heath devoted only three percent of his speeches to the Common Market.[3] His party's manifesto contained only a one-line promise '… to negotiate, no more, no less'.[4] In television and radio coverage, the Common Market did not even rate among the top 12 issues.[5]

It might therefore have come as something of a surprise to most voters to learn that, within two weeks of the election, two of Heath's senior ministers would be in Brussels to begin Britain's negotiations for entry and that, within three years, without any electoral mandate, Britain would have become a full member of the European Community.

'Swallow it whole, and swallow it now'

Just two weeks after Heath became prime minister, his foreign secretary Alec Douglas-Home went to Brussels on 30 June 1970 with his Foreign Office colleague Anthony Barber, to open Britain's negotiations for entry. In the presence of delegations from the three other applicant countries, Ireland, Denmark and Norway, Barber explained that Britain was now ready to accept the Treaties establishing the

---

1 Heath, *op. cit.*, p. 359.
2 Butler, David and Pinto-Duschinski, Michael (1971), *The British General Election of 1970* (London Macmillan), p. 440.
3 *Op. cit.*, p. 444.
4 Conservative Party (1970), *A Better Tomorrow: The Conservative Programme for the Next Five Years*, p. 28.
5 Butler and Pinto-Duschinski, *op. cit.*, pp. 159 and 210.

three European Communities in their entirety, and all 'the decisions that have flowed from them'. As Sir Con O'Neill, the civil servant leading Britain's negotiating team, was to record, this 'had far-reaching implications'. [6]

It was true that, as in 1961, Britain had little choice but to accept the *acquis communautaire*, but the situation was now 'fundamentally altered'. In 1961, the *acquis* had consisted of little more than the treaties themselves. Since then, an 'almost inconceivable flood' of new laws had been enacted,[7] amounting to some 13,000 pages, for many of which the official translations would not be completed until after the treaty of accession had been signed. The *acquis*, O'Neill was to recall, 'haunted us throughout the negotiations':

'Everything, beginning with the Treaties themselves, on which any of the three Communities, through any of their institutions, had ever reached agreement in any form, even if it had never been published, was, provided it had not clearly lapsed or been rescinded, a part of it. And we were asked to endorse, accept and be bound by it all.' [8]

O'Neill himself summed up Britain's negotiating policy: 'swallow the lot, and swallow it now'.[9] The negotiations, therefore, were no more than a façade, to conceal the fact that Heath was determined on entry at almost any price.

As in 1961, Britain could only negotiate transitional concessions or 'derogations'. These centred on the size of Britain's contributions to the Community budget; the difficulties faced by members of the Commonwealth when barriers went up to their exports, notably New Zealand and the Caribbean islands; and what Barber tactfully called 'certain matters of agricultural policy'. Together with fisheries and the role of sterling as a world reserve currency, these issues would define the main scope of the negotiations.

Barber himself was not to lead the British delegation much longer because, following the death in July of Iain Macleod, Heath appointed him as Chancellor of the Exchequer. His place was taken by Geoffrey Rippon QC who led the top-level negotiations in the formal setting of the Council of Ministers chamber in Luxembourg. Detailed day-to-day haggling was conducted by officials meeting in Brussels. O'Neill described the scene:

'In a large room, equipped with simultaneous interpretation, the British Delegation sat at one end of a long hollow rectangle of tables. Opposite them sat the President and the Secretariat. The two longer sides of the rectangle were occupied by the Delegations of the six Member States and of the Commission. There was no lack of people present. In a Ministerial meeting, those present in the room often amounted to one hundred or more; attendance at Deputies meetings fluctuated around seventy or eighty. There was room for

---

6 O'Neill, *op. cit.*, p. 434. As an FCO Under-Secretary, O'Neill was in charge of Britain's negotiating team between 1970 and 1972. When the negotiations were concluded he was commissioned to write a full internal report of 475 pages, which for nearly 30 years remained secret but was finally published in 2000 (having been used by Hugo Young for *This Blessed Plot*). Between 1935 and 1946 O'Neill was a Fellow of All Souls, with Arthur Salter, and served in Brussels as British Ambassador to the European Communities, 1963–1965.

7 O'Neill, *op. cit.*, p. 38.

8 *Ibid.*

9 O'Neill, *op. cit.*, p. 40.

about fifty at the table; the rest sat behind. These large groups of people assembled to listen to a stilted form of dialogue, or rather a series of short and stilted dialogues, between the President of the Community Delegation and the British Delegation.'[10]

The vexed issue which was to dominate the first months of negotiations was Britain's contribution to the Community budget. Thanks to the arrangements for CAP funding devised by the French, her contribution would be out of all proportion to the size of her national income. And, with no less than 91 percent of the EEC's £3 billion budget taken up by funding the CAP, easily the largest share of which went to France, that contribution was likely to be substantial.

Both Britain and the Six were aware that, for political reasons, it might not be advisable for Britain to be seen having to pay her full share immediately: particularly since the shift to more expensive imports from the continent would be increasing food prices in Britain. As Heath himself put it:

'We resolved that we should assume our obligations gradually, because too large a contribution at the beginning, before the dynamic benefits of membership had come through, would have damaged both Britain and the Community as a whole. It would have jeopardised the smooth passage upon which the enlarged Community's successful progress in the first few years would depend.'[11]

Initially, therefore, the Community demanded that Britain should pay 11.5 percent of the Community budget in the first year, rising to 21.5 percent after five years. Even this, the British thought excessive, but it was not until Christmas 1970 that they came back with counter-proposals.

Thus ended the first phase of the negotiations, in which little had been achieved. Elsewhere in Brussels, however, as agreed at The Hague summit, work had been proceeding on the two reports by Werner and Davignon on 'economic and monetary' and 'political' union. As their findings emerged, they threatened to cause Heath considerable embarrassment.

'A federal state with a single currency'

Even before the accession negotiations had started, the Werner committee had, on 20 May 1970, published an interim report bringing about 'economic and monetary union'. When the final report emerged on 8 October, there could be no doubt that its target was an immense leap forward in political integration.[12]

Werner noted that monetary union would mean an irreversible freezing of exchange rates between the EEC's currencies. The introduction of a 'sole Community currency' was optional but 'considerations of a psychological and political nature militate in favour of the adoption of a sole currency which would confirm the irreversibility of the venture'.[13] The economic policies of member

10 O'Neill, *op. cit.*, p. 34.
11 Heath, *op. cit.*, p. 364.
12 Council – Commission of the European Communities (1970), *Report to the Council and the Commission on the Realisation by Stages of Economic and Monetary Union in the Community* (The Werner Report), Supplement to Bulletin 11.
13 *Op. cit.*, p. 10.

states would be centralised in stages, to be completed by 1980, which would also mean centralised co-ordination of regional and structural policies. Werner himself was explicit about the major sacrifice of national sovereignty this would involve. The 'centre of decision for economic policy' would have to be exercised supranationally; and 'in view of the fact that the role of the Community's budget as an economic instrument would be "insufficient", the Community's "centre of decision" would have to be able to influence national budgets. This "Community institution" (foreshadowing the future European Central Bank)

'…will be empowered to take decisions, according to the requirements of the economic situation, in the interests of monetary policy as regards liquidity, rates of interest, and the granting of loans to private and public sectors. In the field of external monetary policy, it will be empowered to intervene in the foreign exchange market and the management of the monetary reserves of the Community.'[14]

Werner conceded that such a massive 'transfer of powers to the Community level from the national centres of decision' would raise 'a certain number of political problems'.[15] These were not lost on Whitehall. The Foreign Office (now the Foreign and Commonwealth Office or FCO) produced an urgent internal report for Heath, copied by the Treasury, noting that

'…the (Werner) plan for economic and monetary union (EMU) has revolutionary long-term implications, both economic and political. It could imply the ultimate creation of a European federal state with a single currency… All the basic instruments of national economic management (fiscal, monetary, incomes and regional policies) would ultimately be handed over to the central federal authorities. The Werner report suggests this radical transformation of the present communities should be accomplished within a decade.'[16]

Monetary union, the FCO noted, 'could become a central point of negotiations over entry…since it will arouse strong feelings about "sovereignty" and provoke vigorous discussions of its implications for future policy…' In some areas, such as taxation, Britain might find it hard to make more compromises than other countries. Nevertheless, the FCO argued, 'we see no real reason why UK interests should significantly suffer'. 'Any problems,' it added optimistically, 'ought not to be incapable of agreed solutions within the community.' But it had to be faced that EMU would lead to the UK and the other EEC countries becoming as

'…interlocked as those of the states of the US. Indeed it could be argued that the independence of the members would be less than that of the (US) states, for the latter have more autonomy over their budgets. The degree of freedom which would then be vested in national governments might indeed be somewhat less than the autonomy enjoyed by the constituent states of the US. There would be relatively little surrender of national sovereignty in the economic field, though as the first stage (of EMU) progressed, sovereignty would pass steadily towards the centre. At the ultimate stage economic sovereignty would

---

14 *Op. cit.*, p. 13.
15 *Ibid.*
16 As reported in the *Guardian*, 1 January 2002. 'Treasury Warned Heath That EMU Plan Could Herald European Superstate'. The Treasury text is essentially the same as the FCO briefing. PRO/ FCO 30/789 (undated).

to all intents and purposes disappear at the national level and the Community would itself be the master of ... economic policy.'[17]

Crucially, the FCO warned, 'there must be no mistake about the final objective; the process of change is "irreversible", and the implications, both economic and political, must be accepted from the outset'.

For Heath and his advisers privately to accept such a plan was one thing. But at a moment when the British people were being assured that the Common Market was really little more than a trading arrangement, any hint that the powers of its member states might be reduced within 10 years to less than that enjoyed by a state of the USA could be political dynamite.

Geoffrey Rippon hurried over to Luxembourg for a personal interview with Werner on 27 October. He congratulated him on his report, assuring him that it 'well stated our common objectives'. But, alarmed at how such a radical step might be received by the British public, he asked that political and economic union might be achieved through a 'step by step approach'. It was 'natural for people to be afraid of change' and 'part of his problem in Britain was to reassure people that their fears were unjustified'.[18]

If Werner's proposals were not enough, three weeks later the foreign ministers of the Six adopted the Davignon Report, on 'the problems of political unification', in what became known as the 'Luxembourg Agreement'.[19] This too was radically integrationist in tone, as Davignon, 'to ensure consistency with the continuity and political purpose of the European design', proposed nothing less than a single European foreign policy. To express 'the will for a political union' it was necessary 'to bring nearer the day when European can speak with one voice'.[20] The governments of the Six had to develop as a common foreign policy in order to 'achieve progress towards political unification'.[21] To implement this plan, the foreign ministers agreed to hold twice-yearly meetings, to co-ordinate the Six's foreign policy, while a committee of senior officials would confer at least four times a year to lay the groundwork for these meetings. Governments undertook to consult on all major foreign policy issues and to 'pursue work on the best way to achieve progress towards political unification'.

In view of the revolutionary contents of the two reports, it must have come as a relief to Heath that virtually no one in Britain noticed them.[22]

17 *Ibid.*
18 From minutes to the meeting recorded by Rippon's private secretary Crispin Tickell (PRO/CAB 164/771). When these were released under the 30-year rule on 1 January 2000, Tickell admitted in a BBC television interview that worries over Britain's loss of sovereignty had been 'very much present in the mind of the negotiators', but that the general line had been 'the less they came out in the open the better'.
19 European Parliament (1982), *Selection Of Texts Concerning Institutional Matters Of The Community From 1950–1982* (Luxembourg), pp. 146–151.
20 *Op. cit.*, p. 147.
21 *Op. cit.*, p. 148.
22 A rare exception was the response to the Werner proposals by a former city editor Nigel Lawson in the *Sunday Times* on 22 November 1970, observing that 'a national currency lies at the very heart of national sovereignty. A common currency is something that can only properly follow political union: it cannot precede it.' Although in later years Werner was to be described as 'the father of the single currency', his report is scarcely mentioned by Hugo Young.

A *coup de théâtre*

The resumed negotiations in January 1971 continued to move with glacial slowness, and the focus remained on Britain's budget contribution. At a press conference on 21 January, Pompidou was asked his opinion of the British position. He replied: 'One must admit that the British have three qualities among others: humour, tenacity and realism. I have the feeling that we are slightly in the humorous stage.' [23] So little had been achieved that O'Neill found it necessary to convey to the officials with whom he was negotiating his 'concern at the pace at which this conference is proceeding'.

The reason for this delay, of course, was that the ratification process for the 1970 Luxembourg Treaty was not yet complete. Until that was safely part of the *acquis*, the French were determined not to risk any upset.[24] Thus, even by the beginning of May little progress was perceptible. Then, suddenly, there seemed to be movement, with simultaneous concessions on both sides. Rippon conceded that British markets would be opened to Community goods from day one of Britain's accession: what was known as 'Community preference' (in contrast to Britain's traditional 'imperial preference').[25] The French agreed 'associated status' for developing Commonwealth countries. As O'Neill put it, the negotiators began to believe there had been a 'decisive move' towards success.[26]

What only a handful of people were aware of was that this 'decisive move' had come as part of a carefully orchestrated strategy. O'Neill's later account of how and why it had come about gives a striking glimpse of how elaborately international affairs can be stage-managed.

Back in January, when there had seemed so little progress, the British embassy in Paris heard reports that senior French officials were speaking freely of a need for a personal 'summit meeting' between Heath and Pompidou. One of Heath's first acts on becoming prime minister the previous June had been to summon the British Ambassador in Paris, Christopher Soames, a fervent 'Europeanist', to ask him to stay on through the negotiations for British entry. Now, in late February 1971, Soames had a long talk with Pompidou's right-hand man, Michel Jobert. He came away persuaded that such a meeting would be useful. But, on 25 February, Soames met Pompidou himself. The French president said nothing about a possible meeting but stressed that the UK must pay a higher percentage of the Community budget after the end of the transitional period than it had so far proposed, and that 'Community preference' must apply from the first day of UK accession. These were France's 'priorities'.

---

23 FCO 30/789, *op. cit.*

24 O'Neill 'wondered to what extent we should attribute the slow progress of the negotiations … to deliberate foot-dragging by the French until ratification should have been completed by their partners', *op. cit.*, p. 172.

25 Defined by O'Neill, *op. cit.*, p. xxvii: 'The mechanism by which European Community agricultural producers were given a market advantage and a degree of protection against agricultural imports from outside the European Community, sometimes by mean of a levy calculated on the basis of the European Community's own guaranteed prices, sometimes by a tariff and sometimes by a combination of the two.'

26 O'Neill, *op. cit.*, p. 73.

On 1 March Soames met Heath in London. On their agenda was a briefing drawn up the previous July by O'Neill's special assistant, John Robinson, in which he had advised on tactics for negotiation over the thorny question of the Community budget:

'We cannot expect to get a satisfactory settlement of this issue within the context of the negotiating procedures which the Community are offering us...the breakthrough will come, if it comes at all, as a result of an appeal to the Six on Community finance at the highest level. This points to a suggestion from our side at the appropriate moment for a summit meeting to settle this issue in principle. It would be important that Pompidou himself should attend such a summit.'[27]

Through Jobert, Pompidou was told that a meeting between himself and Heath 'would be an important element in the negotiations'.[28] By similar circuitous means, the principle of a meeting was agreed, subject to appropriate timing and the effect it would have on the negotiations. It was felt that it would be undesirable for the meeting to take place at a time when the negotiations were deadlocked. This would give the impression that it was a last resort. It would be 'more fruitful' if movement could be seen to have been taken place in the negotiations before the meeting was announced.[29] It was therefore agreed with the French that the summit should be after the ministerial talks in May, which 'should if possible be the occasion of significant progress'.[30] This was why Rippon offered his concession on Community preference while the French gave way on the Commonwealth issue.

But the 'significant progress' still had to be stage-managed. The ministerial meeting on 10 May was deliberately dragged on into the night and beyond, for 13 long hours, before the ritual concessions were made, allowing Rippon to emerge beaming into the daylight to tell a dawn press conference, 'If I were you, I would bet on success.' The French foreign minister, Maurice Schuman, readily agreed, declaring 'without a shadow of doubt', a major breakthrough had been achieved.[31] The news was spread far and wide, even percolating down to Southampton's *Southern Evening Echo*, which proclaimed in bold, front-page headlines: 'On the way to market – Britain and France agree'.[32]

Following this pre-arranged 'success' Pompidou passed the word through 'usual channels' that he was determined his summit with Heath would succeed.[33] It was no coincidence that the Treaty laying down the financial arrangements for the CAP had now been ratified by all the member states and was therefore untouchable.

None of this is reported in Heath's memoirs. He merely observes that the news of his impending summit must have 'contributed to the substantial progress'

27 *Op. cit.*, p. 377.
28 *Op. cit.*, p. 334.
29 *Op. cit.*, p. 335.
30 *Ibid.*
31 *Press Association*, 11 May 1971.
32 *Southern Evening Echo*, 11 May 1971.
33 Heath, *op. cit.*, p. 366.

made in the negotiations. It perhaps shows just how little we should rely for an understanding of history either on political memoirs or on contemporary reporting by the media.

The great 'summit' itself finally took place on 20 and 21 May in the Elysée Palace. Heath was to wax lyrical in his memoirs about the guard at the gate springing to attention on the crisp May morning, and how it was difficult to think of more attractive surroundings in which to conduct talks. Yet to the actual contents of their discussion he gives just a few lines, amid two-and-a-half pages of description:

'... Pompidou had stressed that what he felt was needed was an historic change in the British attitude. Britain was really determined to make this change, France would welcome us into the Community. He regarded his own country and Britain as the only two European countries with what he termed a "world vocation" and said quite explicitly that, if the political and intellectual prestige and authority of Britain were added to those of the Six, the Community would be greatly enriched. My task was to convince him that this was also what we wanted to see... Our purpose was a strong Europe, which could speak with one voice... and could then exert effective influence in different parts of the globe.'[34]

Such was the view of the meeting the media were intended to swallow. Heath had managed to convince Pompidou that 'Britain was genuine in its desire to enter the European family',[35] culminating in a press conference on the Friday evening, when Pompidou gave his own version:

'Many people believed that Great Britain was not and did not wish to become European, and that Britain wanted to enter the Community only so as to destroy it or to divert it from its objectives. Many people thought that France was ready to use every pretext to place in the end a fresh veto on Britain's entry. Well, ladies and gentlemen, you see before you this evening two men who are convinced to the contrary.'[36]

For Heath, this was a 'wildly exciting moment'. He felt it was 'an historic occasion'. But behind all this fluff was the real agenda, only hinted at in the official communiqué: a terse document entirely devoid of flowery rhetoric. Its key passage, the significance of which was missed by almost everyone, declared:

'The President of the Republic and the British Prime Minister considered the range of economic, financial and monetary problems which could arise as a result of enlargement. They also discussed the progress of the European Community towards economic and monetary union, and its implications for existing financial relationships. The Prime Minister reaffirmed the readiness of Britain to participate fully and in a European spirit in this development.'[37]

This was the true, hidden purpose of the meeting: for Pompidou to win Heath's support for his plans to propose the setting up of a common currency. Unknown to all but a very few British, Heath was not just sympathetic. He was eager to participate.

---

34 Heath, *op. cit.*, p. 370.
35 *Op. cit.*, p. 372.
36 *Ibid.*
37 O'Neill, *op. cit.*, p. 436.

The communiqué did nevertheless arouse suspicion that some secret deal had been struck at the summit, to which effect Heath was forced to make a statement to the House of Commons. In what he claimed 'fully explained our position', he told the House:

'We have said that as members of the enlarged Community we would play our full part in the progress towards economic and monetary union. That was confirmed in my talk with President Pompidou… But let me make it clear that we have given no undertakings as to how fast or by what means these developments could or should be brought about. These would be matters for discussion after our entry, when we should be a full member of the Community with all the rights of a member.' [38]

Despite his protestations, Heath was being far from candid. He was asked two questions by Harold Lever: 'What are our intentions on sterling? Could he also clarify whether any question of the parities and fixed parities was decided upon or discussed with the President?' Heath carefully directed his reply only to the second part of Lever's question:

'On the subject of sterling, there was no discussion of parities or items of that kind. It was accepted that this matter only arises in the context of co-ordination of currencies inside an enlarged Community, if we become a member, and is obviously concerned with whatever progress is made on the co-ordination of policies.' [39]

In fact, the deal had already been made. The following year, shortly after Parliament approved Britain's entry, word came from Paris that Pompidou was proposing that member states should make a solemn agreement to 'move irrevocably to economic and monetary union by 1980'. In the 1995 BBC documentary *The Poisoned Chalice*, Sir Roy Denman, present at the time, recalled the Foreign Secretary, Douglas Home, looking askance at this news. He said to Heath, 'The House isn't going to like this.' 'But that,' Denman recalled Heath replying, 'is what it's all about.' When Heath himself was asked in 1995 by the BBC whether he could really have said such a thing, he made no attempt to deny it. His only response, after an unsmiling pause, was, 'well, that's what it *was* about'.

Despite the massive implications of what Heath had now secretly agreed with Pompidou, these never emerged from behind the veils of secrecy during Britain's 'Common Market' debate. When in the 1990s Heath came to be challenged over having concealed his support for a single currency at the time of British entry, his defence was that he had made no secret of his views. His evidence was a Commons speech made at the time of Wilson's application to join in May 1967, when he had declared that 'there can be no doubt that the logical conclusion in a complete market is to move *de facto* or *de jure* to a common currency'. Thus did he dismiss 'those who claim never to have heard of my policy on the matter'. [40]

Shortly after the summit, Geoffrey Rippon on 7 June told the ministers of the Six: 'We shall be ready to discuss after our entry into the Communities what measures might be appropriate in the context of progress towards economic and mon-

---

38 Heath, *op. cit.*, p. 375.
39 *Hansard*, 24 May 1971, cols. 48–49.
40 Heath, *op. cit.*, p. 358.

etary union in the enlarged Community', adding that, to this end, Britain would be prepared after accession to envisage 'an orderly and gradual run-down' of her sterling balances.[41] Again, the significance of this was almost universally missed.

The negotiations are 'successful'

Following the Pompidou summit, French support for British entry was now assured. Considering how little had been achieved in the first nine months, the speed with which all outstanding issues were resolved seemed almost miraculous.[42] But the timing of this had nothing to do with the Heath-Pompidou summit. The most important factor had been the ratification of the Luxembourg treaty. Now the formerly intractable problem of Commonwealth imports could be resolved, with special concessions given for New Zealand butter, although O'Neill reckoned that the terms on which these were granted would add an extra £100 million a year to Britain's budgetary contribution (at 1972 prices). No concessions at all were made for Australia and Canada, although some Caribbean sugar and bananas would still be allowed into Britain under preferential arrangements.

What was looked on as the key meeting took place between 21 and 23 June, when agreement was finally reached on New Zealand dairy products and Britain's contribution to the budget. The 'back of the negotiations was broken' and, after two all-night sessions, when the last meeting ended a little before 5 a.m. on 23 June, 'all were convinced that the negotiations would succeed'.[43] The price was extremely high, but to Heath the agreement was a 'favourable compromise'. Britain was to pay 8.64 percent of the Community budget in year one, rising to 18.92 percent after the transitional period. Even after that there would eventually be no limit to it rising higher.[44] Britain's massive disadvantage was now locked in, leaving her the second highest net contributor after Germany.

Recognising this, Heath's answer was to propose a 'regional policy', through which Britain might win back much of her deficit through subsidies to the regions. Although initially this would fall on deaf ears, in due course Heath's promotion of a 'regional policy' was to have unforeseen consequences.

'Fair and reasonable' terms

With one crucial exception, negotiations were concluded at the June meeting of the Council of Ministers. Heath had achieved the goal on which he had set his heart. The cost to Britain had been enormous. She had been saddled with an enormously expensive CAP, already costing as much each year as the Americans were spending on reaching the moon,[45] and which, with its in-built bias in favour of France, would eventually come to damage so much of British farming.

41 *Op. cit.*, p. 375.
42 Spaak (*op. cit.*, p. 237) was to remark that a lesson he had learnt from earlier negotiations was that, 'Where there is a political will, there are no surmountable technical obstacles. Where such a political will is lacking, every technical obstacle becomes a pretext for those out to wreck whatever negotiations are in progress.' This episode seems to have borne out his view.
43 O'Neill, *op. cit.*, p. 75.
44 Heath, *op. cit.*, pp. 372–373.
45 The *Guardian*, 14 December 1970.

She had agreed to comply with 13,000 pages of legislation which she had no part in framing, and was now committed to enact all future legislation passed by the Community, whether or not in her interest. She had agreed to subordinate her courts to a higher court against which there was no appeal. In anticipation of economic and monetary union, Heath had undertaken to undermine sterling's position as a reserve currency. And, while securing minimal concessions for a few Commonwealth countries, he had committed Britain to make a hugely disproportionate contribution to the budget.

None of this prevented the government setting out to sell its 'achievement' to the British people. The first move came in July 1971 with the publication of a White Paper, *The United Kingdom and the European Communities* (Cmnd 4715). A shortened version, after going through innumerable drafts to ensure that its message was crafted as persuasively as possible, was distributed to every household in the country.

Although the 16-page booklet claimed to set out 'the difficulties as well as the opportunities' of joining, its tone was relentlessly upbeat, starting with a boast that Britain's negotiations had been 'successful'. The essential choice offered was between better security and more prosperity, against having 'in a single generation ... rejected an Imperial past and a European future' and 'found nothing to put in their place'. Membership 'would enable Britain to achieve a higher standard of living'.

Many of the document's claims would become only too familiar in future decades, such as that membership of the Community 'would mean that British manufacturers will be selling their products in a home market five times as large as at present'. Not mentioned was that their continental competitors would be just as free to sell their products in the British market. As for British industry, it was claimed simply that 'the effects of entry will be positive and substantial'.

There was no mention of economic and monetary union. There would be no loss of national identity. Britain's monarchy, parliament and courts would all remain exactly as they were. The legal system would 'continue as before', apart from 'certain changes under the treaties concerning economic and commercial matters'. And in a sentence often quoted later, it was stated that:

'There is no question of Britain losing essential national sovereignty; what is proposed is a sharing and an enlargement of individual national sovereignties in the economic interest.'[46]

---

46 Despite the ambiguous insertion of the word 'essential', the government was fully aware that signing the treaty would involve an immense diminution of Britain's 'sovereignty'. Among the documents which came to light in 2001 under the 30-year rule was a long, confidential paper prepared for the Foreign Office in 1971 analysing 'the implications for British sovereignty of entry into the European Communities'. This concluded that entry would result in very substantial restraints on Britain's powers of self-government, and that over the years this would become ever more obvious. Presciently, the paper also predicted that people would become increasingly alienated from government as it became more bureaucratic and remote, with ever more decisions being taken in Brussels and ever more power being exercised by unelected officials. While recognising this, the paper's chief concern was with how these 'public anxieties' masquerading as concern for 'loss of sovereignty' might be allayed. Various remedies were suggested, such as giving more power to the European Parliament, creating new mechanisms whereby Parliament could scrutinise Community legislation, and strengthening 'regional democratic processes'. It was also suggested that these problems would only become fully evident many years into the future, possibly not until 'the end of the century' (PRO/FCO/30/1048, undated).

Nowhere in the document was there any mention of the word 'supranational'. But there was one further anomaly in the White Paper which at the time attracted little notice. No fewer than three times it made reference to one issue on which final agreement had still to be settled. Under 'Fisheries', the people of Britain were told:

'The Government is determined to secure proper safeguards for the British fishing industry. The Community has recognised the need to change its fisheries policy for an enlarged Community of Ten, particularly in regard to access to fishing grounds.'

This was untrue. The Community had 'recognised' no such thing. On fishing, as the Heath government was already uncomfortably aware, Britain had been very badly caught out.

The great fisheries scandal

With disarming candour, O'Neill was to record that 'when our negotiations opened on 30 June 1970, the problem of fisheries did not exist. It came later the same day. From then on fisheries was a major problem'.[47] What lay behind his words was the most bizarre episode of the negotiations, politically so embarrassing that much of it was kept secret for three decades.

At the centre of this indisputably scandalous story lies the certainty that, some time in the months that preceded the applications for entry by Britain, Ireland, Denmark and Norway, a representative of the Six – the evidence suggests he must have been French – realised that the four new applicants would bring with them the richest, best-conserved fishing waters in Europe.

Furthermore, there was already international pressure for a major revision of the international law of the sea, to extend national control of fisheries to 200 miles (or the 'median line' between two nations). When this took place, the waters of the four applicants would contain well over 90 percent of western Europe's fish, some 80 percent in seas controlled by Britain.[48] It was Nye Bevan who had described Britain as an 'island made of coal, surrounded by a sea of fish'. But potentially, these waters could bring a valuable resource to augment over-fished seas off France, Holland, Belgium and Germany.

What is also evident is that persons unknown within the Community instructed the *Service Juridique* of the Council of Ministers to ascertain whether a way could be devised under the Treaty of Rome to take over the fishing grounds of the applicants as a 'common resource', giving a right of 'equal access' to every member state in the Community. This much emerged from the Foreign Office files released in 2000, which included a legal opinion in French produced by the *Service* on 18 May 1970.[49] The point which its lawyers were asked to address, described as 'extremely delicate', was whether a 'judicial base' could be established on which could rest a 'regulation to give equal access'.

47 O'Neill, *op. cit.*, p. 245.
48 Following declarations of a 200-mile limit by South American countries in 1964 and a 50-mile limit by Iceland, the 200-mile extension was agreed by the United Nations Conference on the Law of the Sea (UNCLOS) between 1972 and 1975. Britain formalised her right to a 200-mile limit in the Fisheries Limits Act 1976, even though by then she had ceded control of fisheries to the EEC.
49 PRO/FCO/30/656.

Every item of Community legislation must be authorised by reference to the powers given to the Community under the treaty, which are referred to at the start of the new law's preamble. The opinion given by the Council lawyers shows that they first considered Article 38 of the treaty, because this mentioned 'fisheries products', the only reference to fish anywhere in the treaty. But 'strict exegesis', they concluded, showed that the article could not 'cover anything outside the products of fishery and not fisheries themselves'. They then turned to Articles 39–43, on agricultural policy, but were forced to conclude that, since these referred only to agriculture, they did not 'constitute perhaps the most appropriate juridical basis for the measure'. The other articles they consulted seemed even more irrelevant. Articles 52–58 on the 'right of establishment' had to be ruled out. To use Articles 59–66 on 'services' would not be 'absolutely satisfactory', because this would require '*un gros effort d'interpretation*'.

Returning to Article 7, which outlawed discrimination between nationals of different countries, they concluded this did not seem, on its own, to 'furnish a sufficient base'. Finally they referred to 'catch-all' Article 235 which permitted passing laws which complied with the 'objectives' of the Treaty but were not specifically authorised elsewhere in the Treaty. 'If one considers that 38–43 of the Treaty do not provide a sufficient legal basis for the Common Fisheries Policy (and the others are unsuitable)', they concluded, 'what about 235?' Given the lack of mention of a fisheries policy, it would be difficult to claim this as an 'objective' of the Treaty.

On the basis of this opinion, it was evident that the treaty offered no justification for what was being planned. Therefore any law enacting it would have no legal base. Despite this, a regulation was drafted to define the 'equal access' principle, with the intention that it should become part of the *acquis* before the four candidates lodged their applications. They would therefore have to accept it, without argument. By any measure this was a trap, aimed at appropriating the applicants' property, to share it between the Community members.

At a hastily arranged meeting of agriculture ministers on 30 June, the principle of equal access to 'Community' fishing waters, 'up to the beaches', was thus agreed, with the intention that a regulation to that effect would follow later. That same day the four entrants lodged their applications.[50]

What was to follow is recounted in dry Foreign Office files, released in 2000 and 2001.[51] Initially the only country fully alive to the implications of the move was Norway. It had already asked to be consulted before the proposal was finalised and been brusquely rebuffed. For months the Foreign Office did not seem to focus on the issue, or make any efforts to ascertain what its consequences might be for Britain's fishermen. Internal notes in July recorded there was 'real doubt about the right of the Community … to regulate access to fishing grounds'. There was 'nowhere any indication that it was the intention … [to] vest in the Community

---

50 According to O'Neill there was a further twist. The Dutch government considered that ambushing 'the Four' in this way would 'look like a kind of insult to the candidate countries' and had decided to block the proposal. But when the 'agriculture council' was hastily arranged, the Dutch official who turned up had not been briefed on this and nodded the proposal through (*op. cit.*, p. 257).
51 PRO/FCO/30/656–659 and FCO/954–978.

the right to exercise extra-territorial competence'. The Ministry of Agriculture and Fisheries told Con O'Neill they could 'not believe the equal access proposals are serious' and suggested they 'must be a basis for bargaining'.

The first warnings were sounded by a trickle of letters from MPs for coastal constituencies, alerted by their local fishermen. Kent and Essex fishermen were warning that, 'if Britain joins the Common Market and French fishermen are given access to inshore waters, they will clean them out'. Throughout the summer such letters continued to arrive, to be side-stepped by Geoffrey Rippon with replies such as 'there is as yet no Common Fisheries Policy in the European Community', or 'we made our interest clear at the start of negotiations on 30 June' (even though a note from O'Neill dated five days earlier had said 'we see no requirement for a special marker to be put down as regards fisheries policy').

In October an FCO briefing for the Permanent Under-Secretary, who was due to meet Heath at a top-level Sunningdale conference, claimed that the legal basis for the CFP was 'Article 38 of the Treaty'. This was despite the EEC's Council Regulation 2141/70, enacting the equal access, having by then been published. Its preamble showed the 'judicial base' was Articles 7, 42, 43 and 235 of the Treaty. Two of these had originally been ruled as irrelevant by the judicial services; the other two had not been considered 'sufficient'. The regulation made no mention of Article 38. Nevertheless, the *canard* that Article 38 was the legal basis for the Common Fisheries Policy became lodged firmly in the official mind and was repeatedly cited over the years by authorities ranging from Con O'Neill to Heath himself.[52]

By now, the MPs' letters were becoming increasingly aggressive in tone. Patrick Wolridge-Gordon, an Aberdeenshire MP, wrote to Rippon on 30 October that there was 'not a fisherman who does not think that if territorial limits are to be abandoned, it means the end of an extremely successful and worthwhile industry for the whole coastline of Scotland. It is indeed unacceptable'. Robert McLennan, MP for Caithness and Sutherland, wrote that the only major herring stocks left in European waters would be 'swept away within a few weeks by their so intensive methods of fishing that have cleaned out the stocks from their own waters'. Jo Grimond, leader of the Liberal Party, MP for Orkney and Shetland, and a keen 'Europeanist' wrote:

'I am perturbed to say the least of it about what is happening over the fishing policy of the Common Market and the curious light it sheds on British diplomacy. I went to Brussels a year ago was told that there was no final policy on fishing but that the Commission would be receptive to the needs of Britain, Norway, Denmark etc. Since then I have been questioning both the Labour and Conservative governments … all I got was flannel.'

The government's response was to work out a formula whereby the protests might be defused. In a memo drafted by D. K. Rowand of the Scottish fisheries

---

52 O'Neill quotes it in his book. Edward Heath, when challenged on the illegality of the CFP in the 1990s, referred to article 38 in the *Sunday Telegraph* (18 February 1996, '*J'Accuse* Booker'); in his memoirs in 1998 (*op. cit.*, p. 70.) and in the House of Commons (*Hansard*, 25 January 2001). Either he had never read the regulation which was the basis of the CFP, or he had not grasped one of the most elementary principles of the way European law is drafted.

department on 9 November, he admitted that the damage to Britain's fishermen would be considerable but argued that Britain could not afford to spend its 'limited negotiating capital' on resisting. He therefore suggested that replies to further letters or Parliamentary questions should indicate that the government was 'aware of the anxieties of the fishing industry' and would 'bear them in mind in the negotiations'. But it was vital not to go into any detail:

'The more one is drawn into such explanations, the more difficult it is to avoid exposing the weaknesses of the inshore fisheries position, the only answer to which may be that in the wider context they must be regarded as expendable.'

From then on, replies to letters by Rippon and others repeated the same formula: 'I can assure you that the Government will take proper account of the importance of the inshore fishing industry to the British economy as a whole.' By this means it was concealed from the public that Britain's fisheries were indeed 'expendable'.

Through the spring of 1971, while the negotiations were still being stalled by France, the FCO was dealing with other issues. But by June, as the deadline for the end of negotiations approached, O'Neill and his team suddenly realised the seriousness of the problem. Ministers took the view, O'Neill was to record, that the ideal solution would be for the Community to suspend its fisheries policy, pending agreement on a suitable regime after British accession. This was ruled out, so Britain sought a compromise, suggesting that the Community could control waters between six and 12 miles off the coast, as long as British fishermen could enjoy exclusive fishing rights out to six miles. Again the Community insisted on control right up to the beaches, offering only a temporary derogation, whereby all member states could keep an exclusive six-mile zone for five years, possibly to be extended to ten, with 'a review' thereafter.

It was on this basis that, with all other issues agreed, the government put out its White Paper in July claiming that 'the Community has recognised the need to change its fisheries policy…' Not for the last time on fisheries, the British public was being seriously misled.

The 'great debate'

Having already agreed to join, without revealing the details of what was involved, the Heath government's next objective was to launch a massive publicity campaign on the merits of entry. Ostensibly this was a campaign to sell the 'Common Market' to the British people, advertised as 'the great debate'. Its real purpose, however, was not to win over the people. In the words of the official appointed as the campaign's co-ordinator, it was 'to convince Members of Parliament that the tide of public opinion was moving in favour of joining the EEC', and thus to win approval for the entry terms from Parliament'.[53]

53 Hugh-Jones, Sir Wynn (2002), *Diplomacy To Politics* (Spennymore, Durham, The Memoir Club), p. 411.

The first serious move in this campaign was the shortened White Paper, circulated at a cost of £2 million to every home in Britain (anti-market Labour MPs asked how taxpayers' money could be spent on what they described as mere 'propaganda'). Ministers were despatched all over the country to sell the 'benefits' of the Common Market on any platform that could be arranged. Between July and October 1971 nearly 300 such speeches were made, Rippon alone making over 50.

One novel feature of the operation was the way pro-market lobby groups were co-ordinated under the umbrella of the European Movement, part-funded by the European Commission, to act as an integral part of the government campaign. Government 'information' services, funded by taxpayers, thus co-ordinated activities with the Trade Union Committee for Europe, the Conservative Political Centre, the Labour Committee for Europe, the CBI and many other organisations, including the National Farmers Union, the Associated Chambers of Commerce and the British Council of Churches.

A key part was played in the campaign by weekly 'media breakfasts' held at the Connaught Hotel, presided over by Geoffrey Tucker, a senior advertising man who had helped to 'sell' Heath and the Tory Party during the 1970 election. Funded by the European Movement, these meetings enabled politicians, representatives of industry, Foreign Office civil servants and influential sympathisers in the media to develop suitable tactics and 'story lines' for the campaign. Journalists were invited to meet the men 'who were actually negotiating in Brussels' and offered 'exclusives' to promote the cause.[54]

'The journalists were able to tell the European Movement and Whitehall frankly what they thought of their public relations efforts and how they could be improved – that such and such a line of argument was too airy-fairy, or that it needed quite a different speaker to put it over if it was ever to get across. Party politicians and industrial representatives would suggest lines of argument for the press to explore.'[55]

Another strategy was a carefully organised campaign based on letters to *The Times*, then still regarded as Britain's most influential newspaper. Pre-written letters were circulated, to be signed by 'top name' individuals or groups of businessmen, to be sent in as if they were the signatories' own work. Particular efforts were made to woo the BBC. One regular breakfast guest was Ian Trethowan, a former political correspondent, now head of BBC Radio. Another was Marshall Stewart, editor of the *Today* programme. Tucker himself later claimed that he had engineered the dismissal of the programme's popular chief presenter, Jack de Manio, a Eurosceptic, to be replaced by the more sympathetic Robert Robinson. 'Nobbling was the name of the game,' as he later put it.[56]

For all this campaigning the European Movement needed money and it did not run short. In the year ending 31 March 1972, it disbursed £550,000, more than five

---

54 BBC Radio 4, Document: *A Letter to Times*, 3 February 2000. Based on interviews of Geoffrey Tucker. Transcript supplied by the British Management Data Foundation.
55 Kitzinger, *op. cit.*, p. 205.
56 *Ibid.*

times its normal budget.[57] But its income, mainly from unnamed donors, reached £915,904, helped by an assurance that the government would increase its annual grant from £7,500 to £20,000.[58]

No attempt was made to give the public objective or factual information. Instead, the Movement used market research to identify issues which might sway public support in favour (the technique later associated with 'focus groups'). The aim was to discover what people wanted to hear, then use it to shape the campaign's propaganda.[59]

In general, the public seemed remarkably ignorant about the EEC and what entry might involve. At one Women's Institute conference, 700 delegates entered a competition to answer five simple questions about the EEC. Only 11 got all the answers right.

The parliamentary campaign

Having negotiated the terms of entry, all Heath wanted was a rubber-stamp from Parliament. He even considered asking it to endorse membership before the summer break. However Francis Pym, the Conservative chief whip, counselled against being seen to rush MPs. Heath thus settled for a 'take note' debate before the summer recess, followed by a full debate and vote in October.

In what was again to become a familiar pattern, the 'pro-Marketeers' went to great lengths to present support for their cause as an issue that transcended party divisions and loyalties. Thus, in defiance of normal practice, Rippon maintained informal contacts with prominent 'pro-Europeans' in the Labour Party, pre-eminently its deputy leader, Roy Jenkins. Labour was deeply divided. Wilson had initially equivocated but, in May, the issue was forced by Jim Callaghan, who famously declared '*non, merci beaucoup*'.[60] To avoid a disastrous split in his party, Wilson finally had to take a stance. Despite a private lecture from Jenkins on the advantages of sticking to the 'pro-European position' he had taken in government,[61] Wilson chose to not challenge the principle, but merely the terms of entry.

The Conservatives, with an overall majority of only 25, also included a sizeable number of dissenters. After calculating that at least 38 of his MPs could not be relied on, Heath decided on the tactical device of a free vote, hoping to recruit Labour pro-marketeers. His resolution was reinforced by the Conservative conference at Brighton on 14 October 1971. Enoch Powell, the most eloquent Tory Euro-sceptic, had pleaded with delegates to reject entry:

'I do not believe that this nation, which has maintained and defended its independence for a thousand years, will now submit to see it merged or lost. Nor did I become a member of

57 Kitzinger, *op. cit.*, p. 208.
58 *Op. cit.*, p. 212.
59 *Op. cit.*, p. 216.
60 Young, *op. cit.*, p. 273.
61 Jenkins, Roy (1991), *A Life At The Centre* (London, Macmillan), p. 319. Jenkins advised Wilson that sticking to the pro-European position would kill his damaging reputation for being 'devious, tricky, opportunistic'.

a sovereign parliament in order to consent to that sovereignty being abated or transferred.'[62]

His speech prompted Heath to call for a vote, which resulted in a huge majority of 2,474 to 324 in favour of entry.

The Commons debate itself was scheduled for six days, culminating in a vote on 28 October. Opening for the government was Foreign Secretary Sir Alec Douglas-Home, who asked the House to approve the decision to join, 'on the basis of the arrangements which have been negotiated' (even though MPs had still not been given a chance to examine the terms). He reminded the House how twice before it had instructed Conservative and Labour governments to negotiate entry, and suggested that, if it were now to change its mind, the international community would look at Britain askance.[63]

Addressing fears of a 'federal Europe', he acknowledged that 'some people might still like to pursue this idea', but claimed that 'political change' in the Community had to be unanimous, and that there was no way any country could be 'dragooned or coerced into a pattern of political association' it did not like.[64] There was no mention of economic and monetary union, or of the Luxembourg agreement committing the Six to work for a common foreign policy. Instead Douglas-Home offered the prospect that, once she was in, Britain could play a part in shaping a new regional policy, which could bring lavish subsidies to boost the poorer areas of the country.

Denis Healey led the attack for Labour, but his speech betrayed a *naiveté* which was to become all-too familiar. He limited his case purely to economic arguments, on the grounds that the Common Market was 'after all an economic community and nothing more'.[65] Wilson also steered firmly away from the political implications of entry. He stuck to attacking what was known of the terms Heath had negotiated, giving notice of how a Labour government would respond if it came into office after accession:

'What we should do ... would be immediately to give notice that we do not accept the terms negotiated by the Conservatives and, in particular, the unacceptable burdens arising out of the CAP, the blows to the Commonwealth, and any threats to our regional policies. If the Community then refused to negotiate ... or if the negotiations were to fail, we should sit down amicably with them and discuss the situation (laughter). We should make it clear that our posture, like that of the French after 1958, would be rigidly directed towards the pursuit of British interests and that other decisions and actions in relation to the Community would be dictated by that determination, until we had secured our terms. They might accept this, or they might decide that we should agree to part; that would depend on them. That is our position.'[66]

After six days of debate, Heath wound up on 28 October. 'Tonight,' he told a packed House,

62 *The Poisoned Chalice*, authors' transcript.
63 *Hansard*, October 1971.
64 *Ibid.*
65 *Ibid.*
66 *Ibid.*

'... the world is ... watching Westminster, waiting to see whether we are going to decide that Western Europe should now move along the path to real unity – or whether the British Parliament, now given the choice, not for the first time but probably the last time for many years to come, will reject the chance of creating a United Europe.'[67]

To their intense frustration, none of the leading Labour pro-marketeers were allowed by the Speaker (in consultation with party managers) to take part. As Roy Jenkins commented later:

'This was supposed to be the great debate of the decade (at least) and we were leaders of one-eighth of the House of Commons ... and, because we were the hinge, were going to make the biggest difference ... Yet of more than one hundred speeches which filled the six days we were not allowed to contribute one.'[68]

Just before the vote, Heath was able to announce that the House of Lords had endorsed his terms by 451 votes to 58, a majority of almost 400. Jenkins led 69 Labour MPs through the 'aye' lobby and, with 20 abstentions, Heath amassed an unexpectedly large Commons majority of 112. Without the support of the Labour pro-marketeers, entry would have been rejected by 36 votes. The result was greeted with pandemonium. Teddy Taylor recalled this as the only time he ever heard bad language openly used in the House. One Labour MP called Jenkins a 'Fascist bastard', and friends advised him to depart quickly, for his own safety.[69] That evening he had the dubious pleasure of reading the *Evening News* front-page headline: 'Witch hunt for Labour traitors'.

After the vote, Heath called in briefly on a private party, where he received warm congratulations from his friend and mentor, Jean Monnet, who had been watching the vote from the public gallery. He then returned to his private sitting room at Number 10, where he played the First Prelude from Book 1 of Bach's *Well-Tempered Clavier* on his clavichord. That night, Macmillan presided over the lighting of a bonfire on the cliffs of Dover. Next morning, the *Sun* proclaimed in bold capitals on its front page: 'IN WE GO'.

Fisheries: the lie direct

Before Heath could fly to Brussels to sign the Treaty of Accession, there was still the issue of fisheries to settle. Having accepted Community control over the fishing waters between six and 12 miles from her coast, Heath still hoped to retain exclusive rights to the six-miles zone. On 18 June, Ireland let it be known that she could not accept the Community's proposals. The Norwegians followed suit three days later. Having given away so much, Britain's negotiators feared that the Community might now offer the other countries concessions it was too late for her to ask for.

The situation became increasingly fraught as Norway passed a law limiting the size of vessels allowed within her 6 to 12 mile limit, thus excluding British deep-

---

67 *Ibid.*
68 Jenkins, Roy, *op. cit.*, p. 330.
69 *The Poisoned Chalice, op. cit.*

water trawlers from one of their most rewarding fishing grounds.[70] Iceland had unilaterally extended its limits to 50 miles, excluding British vessels from another lucrative ground. Pressure began to build for Britain to seek concessions similar to those demanded by the Norwegians. But the political situation was becoming so explosive that O'Neill's team decided to defer further demands until after the Parliamentary debate, lest awkward questions were put by Labour front-benchers. Because the fisheries problem had only come up since Labour's application in 1967, it was the one issue over which Labour spokesmen felt no inhibitions in attacking the government, since they could not be accused of reneging on terms they had been prepared to accept four years earlier.

By the time negotiations were resumed, they became 'so intense, intricate and continuous', according to O'Neill, that he gave up trying to record a step-by-step account.[71] Fisheries had been raised briefly in the debate, prompting Rippon to make the misleading claim that there was now 'a clear understanding' that there would either have to be a wholly new fisheries regulation or the Community would have to accept 'the status quo'.[72]

On 9 November, the Community came up with another minor variation on its earlier proposal, offering member states a 'derogation' adding control up to their 12-mile limits in certain geographical areas. These arrangements would still be subject to review after 10 years, but the decision as to whether they could continue would have to be unanimous. Although O'Neill described this as 'in many respects entirely unsatisfactory', it was to be the basis on which agreement was eventually reached.[73]

The Norwegians were even less happy. Meeting with Rippon, they rejected any solution that was only temporary, insisting that national limits must be permanent. They were unimpressed by his remark that 'it was better when dealing with the Community to go round a problem rather than deal with it head on'. O'Neill regarded the Norwegians as 'stubborn'. Their stance was to bring their relations with the Community to crisis point.[74]

By now Rippon was under almost continuous fire in the Commons, to which he could only respond with evasive or ambiguous answers. As he and his colleagues tried to extract further minor concessions from the Six, centred on those areas where they wanted to retain a 12-mile limit, the Norwegians remained adamant that they must have a permanent 12-mile limit for the whole of their coastline.[75]

---

70 A question which inevitably arises when looking back at the fisheries episode is why Britain and the other applicant countries did not band together to insist that the 'equal access' rule was unacceptable. It is clear from the FCO papers that this was rejected because Britain's distant-water fishing companies, then the biggest players in the fishing industry, saw in 'equal access' a chance to win greater access to Norwegian waters. In the end, of course, Norway did not join and within a few years most of those companies disappeared.

71 O'Neill, *op. cit.*, p. 270.

72 *Hansard*, 25 October 1971, col. 1243.

73 O'Neill, *op. cit.*, p. 272.

74 *Op. cit.*, p. 273.

75 *Op. cit.*, p. 275.

Heath was now worried that, unless the issue could be resolved, his timetable for entering the Community on 1 January 1973 would have to be abandoned. On 29 November, ministers were due to arrive in Brussels for a final marathon session. That morning Heath sent an urgent message to the Norwegian prime minister, Trygve Bratteli. 'You will know,' he wrote, 'that it is very important that we present this question in a manner that will appear satisfactory to our fishing interests.' But Heath went on to say that he was now 'seriously concerned' by the way negotiations were dragging on. If Norway kept up its 'stiff' and 'intransigent' attitude, the Community might lose patience.

It was only because he believed it was of 'the utmost importance' that Norway should join the European Community, wrote Heath, that, 'I dare send you this message today'. It was a great mistake, when dealing with the EEC, he suggested, to make demands 'of a permanent nature', because this 'touches a principle which the EEC considers as fundamental'. If Mr Bratteli could only accept a time-limit, 'subject to revision', Heath suggested, then in practice he would surely find that the EEC would be understanding, and 'will give you the essential concession which you expect'. In other words, so long as the Commission got what it wanted on paper, Heath was sure it would privately allow Norway the *de facto* permanence she wanted. After pleading with Bratteli to instruct his negotiators to give way, Heath ended by threatening, 'with very much regret', that, unless Norway conceded, the other candidate-countries would have to join without her.

When this message was received in Oslo, its contents were swiftly leaked,[76] and word of Heath's intervention soon reached Brussels, just as the crucial meeting was beginning. From the high-handed attitude of the French foreign minister, Maurice Schumann, it was more obvious than ever that the real driving force behind the 'equal access' policy was France. As can be seen from the FCO files, the rest of the Six had all at different times privately indicated unhappiness at the ruthless way this policy was being forced on the applicants. The evening after the Brussels talks ended, the German ambassador to London confessed to Rippon's secretary Crispin Tickell at a private dinner that Schumann's behaviour in Brussels and France's subsequent blocking tactics had been 'deplorable'. 'As seen from here,' he said, 'the Community had behaved at its worst.'[77]

After the fiasco of the Brussels talks, a further meeting was scheduled for Saturday, 11 December. By now the British government's only real concern was to get a formula covering the 12-mile limit which would somehow enable it to defend the policy in Parliament.[78] By Sunday morning, wrote O'Neill, 'we got almost everything we wanted'.[79] The Norwegians still refused to agree.

The following day, 13 December, Rippon made a statement to the House on the outcome of the final meeting. He claimed that 'outstanding problems' on fisheries had been resolved. The Community had been persuaded of the need to protect Britain's vital interests, both by conserving fish stocks and by protecting 'the liveli-

---

76 The full text of Heath's letter appeared in the Oslo newspaper *Aftenposten* on 7 December 1971.
77 Note from Tickell dated 2 December 1971 in the FCO files, *op. cit.*
78 Telegram from Douglas-Home to Soames, 6 December, FCO, *op. cit.*
79 O'Neill, *op. cit.*, p. 277.

hoods of our fishermen'. He then said, 'it is clear that we retain full jurisdiction of the whole of our coastal waters up to 12 miles'.

This was untrue. Firstly, British boats would only have exclusive right to fish out to six miles, and control over access between six and 12 miles would be limited. Secondly, this was permitted only under a 10-year derogation, to expire on 31 December 1982, after which it could only be extended by unanimous agreement of the member states. The derogation could thus be ended by a single veto. Thirdly, Britain had given away entirely the most important principle of all: namely, the Community's power to control her fishing waters, up to the beaches. Even within the six-mile limit, fishermen would still have to comply with Community rules. And when the 200-mile limit came in, the world's richest fishing waters would have been given away *in toto*.

Desperate to hide how much had been conceded, Rippon then said: 'I must emphasise that these are not just transitional arrangements which automatically lapse at the end of a fixed period'. This claim drew fierce challenge from Denis Healey and Peter Shore, both of whom suspected he was lying. What neither had yet seen was the wording of the accession treaty, which MPs would not be allowed to examine until after it was signed a month later. Only when this became available was it was clear that Rippon had told a blatant lie.

The Norwegians continued to refuse the demands of the Six and were to be offered substantial further concessions before they reluctantly reached agreement on 15 January 1971. Their fisheries minister resigned in protest, and this was to play a significant part in the subsequent referendum when, on 25 September 1972, the Norwegian people rejected entry by 52.7 percent to 47.3.

Parliament hands over its power

On 20 January 1972, Labour made a last-ditch bid to stop Heath signing the treaty until Parliament had been given a chance to read the full text. Heath's response was that 'constitutionally there could be no final and authentic text of the Treaty until it had been signed'. He won his vote by 298 to 277. Two days later, his memoirs record, he was given 'a huge ovation' as he entered the great hall of the Palais d'Egmont in Brussels to sign, watched by 'many of those who had played a part in founding and building the European Community', including Monnet and Spaak.

The next great task was to frame the legislation needed to enact the *acquis* into UK law. On the face of it, this seemed an awesome prospect, with 13,000 pages of directives and regulations already in force and an unknown number yet to come.

How this problem was to be solved was given to Heath's Solicitor General, Geoffrey Howe. To work himself into the job, he recalled that he spent a weekend re-reading Enoch Powell's arguments against the legitimacy of the whole exercise. 'Did we', he asked himself, 'really have the authority of the British people to effect such a change. Had we been sufficiently candid about the implications?' In the end, he concluded that these had been fully explained, in documents beginning with those published by the Wilson government in 1967. Apparently ignoring the fact that the British people had been offered no choice in the matter at the 1970 general election, he concluded that the electorate had endorsed the principle of membership. Thus, he believed, the final, crucial stage could properly be entrusted to Parliament.

'For the very sovereignty of Parliament entitled that body to manage or deploy that sovereignty, on behalf of the British people, in partnership with other nations on such terms as Parliament itself might decide.'[80]

Only then did Howe address himself to how this was to be done. Already there had been speculation that any Bill might have to run to thousands of clauses, which Labour's leading dissident, Tony Benn, claimed would never get through Parliament in time for 1 January 1973, when the accession treaty was due to come into force. However, with the help of his senior parliamentary counsel, John Fiennes, Howe produced what he himself described as a *coup de théâtre*: a 'European Communities Bill' of just 12 clauses and four schedules, in a mere 37 pages.

At its heart was one short passage, Section 2, sub-section 2. This used a long-standing device in British law-making, the 'enabling Act' whereby Parliament delegated to ministers the power to enact law directly, without a laborious passage through Parliament. Howe's inspiration was to borrow this device to allow any relevant minister to enact directly into British law any item of Community legislation. In purely constitutional terms, this represented by far the greatest accession of power to the executive in history. As that internal Foreign Office paper on 'sovereignty' had predicted, it would place unprecedented powers in the hands of unelected officials, both in Brussels and Whitehall, who were now in effect being given the right to make laws with only a semblance of democratic accountability.

Howe's next challenge was to persuade Parliament to accept what to a great degree was its own redundancy ticket. Heath's chief whip, Francis Pym, knew that even one amendment could negate the whole accession treaty, putting her entry in jeopardy. In addition, Heath's government had by now become highly unpopular. Inflation was rising rapidly. Wracked by industrial unrest, Britain was in crisis over the miners' strike that was to make Arthr Scargill famous. Trade union power had become one of the most conspicuous features of national life. 'The stakes,' Pym declared, 'couldn't have been higher.'[81]

The debate on the second reading lasted four days, from 16 to 19 February. Wilson accused Howe of imposing, 'literally at a stroke', an alien system of law. With his unrivalled understanding of the constitutional implications, Enoch Powell added a careful analysis of how the Commons was about to lose its supremacy.[82]

Heath knew the vote was going to be difficult, because the Labour Party was officially committed to oppose the Bill, and he could not rely on his own back-

80 *Ibid.*
81 Verbatim account: transcript – *The Poisoned Chalice, op. cit.*
82 *Hansard*, 17 February 1917, cols. 272–273.

benchers. However, faced with the possible collapse of their government, most of the Conservative 'anti-marketeers' gritted their teeth and walked through the 'aye' lobby. Despite that, 15 Tories voted with the opposition. Heath still got his vote, but only by a wafer-thin margin: 309 to 301. The issue had been decided by the four Labour MPs and five Liberals who voted with the government. The hardest part, however, was still to come, as the House embarked on the Committee stage, debating amendments which would involve no fewer than 92 divisions. Again, defeat of any one might negate the treaty.

The story of how the government came through this ordeal was not to emerge for more than 20 years, when several of the MPs involved took part in a BBC documentary. They recounted an unprecedented secret collaboration between the Conservative whips and Labour 'pro-marketeers', who arranged, when necessary, to find pressing engagements elsewhere which would mean their absence from the division lobby. In the words of Shirley Williams:

'... people disappeared. They went to the films, they just didn't show up, and so forth... There was quite a bit of quiet understanding that there were certain amendments where it was better for people to just find themselves... you know, speaking at a meeting at Little Ainsborough or something, so they wouldn't be there.' [83]

At the heart of the plot, according to *The Poisoned Chalice*, was a red book kept by Labour whip John Roper, a 'committed European'. [84] He guaranteed there would be just enough Labour abstentions for the government to win every vote. But to stop the vote-rigging being noticed, and creating embarrassment for the Labour Party, the voting record was kept in Roper's red book so he could vary the abstentions. Francis Pym recalled, looking somewhat uncomfortable: 'it was a secret arrangement. Everybody knew it was happening. How it was happening, nobody quite knew. And that seemed to me very satisfactory.' [85]

After 39 days of debate, the Bill passed its third reading on 13 July by a majority of 17. The way was clear for the United Kingdom to join the EEC. For Howe and Heath it was a triumph. Enoch Powell despaired. 'I don't think people understood,' he said. Tony Benn was more forthright. 'It was a *coup d'état*,' he declared, 'by a political class who did not believe in popular sovereignty.' [86]

83 *The Poisoned Chalice, op. cit.*
84 Heath, *op. cit.*, p. 384.
85 *Ibid.*
86 Both quotations from *The Poisoned Chalice, op. cit.*

Chapter 9

Britain Stays In: 1973–1975

'Do you think that the United Kingdom should stay in the European Community (the Common Market)?'

> Referendum question put to the British people, 5 June 1975

'The result showed conclusively that the British people … wholeheartedly backed the decision taken in 1971 by the British Government, over which I presided, to join the Community.'

> Edward Heath, *The Course of My Life*[1]

'In 1975 I campaigned as a Conservative parliamentary candidate for a "yes" vote in the referendum that kept us in the EC. In retrospect it is abundantly clear that I campaigned on a prospectus that was sufficiently false to ensure that, if the issue had been a public offer in securities, I would face prosecution under the provisions of the Companies Act and I would lose.'

> Tom Benyon, letter to *The Times*, 29 May 2003

To celebrate 'the entry of the United Kingdom into the European Community' on 1 January 1973, the lawyer Lord Goodman, a former chairman of the Arts Council, was invited by his friend Mr Heath to organise a series of nation-wide events under the title 'Fanfare for Europe'. At a gala evening at the Royal Opera House, Covent Garden, prosperous bankers were regaled with operatic hits and guffawed at snippets about foreigners read by actors, while a special arrangement of Beethoven's 'Ode to Joy' modulated into a piece of pseudo-jazz by Michael Tippet. In a darkened room, the Victoria and Albert Museum put on show a tastefully lit selection of art-objects from each member state, such as a pair of Bronze Age wind instruments from a Danish bog. A concert was given in York Minster by the Great Universal Stores Footwear band. The Whitechapel Art Gallery staged an exhibition of sweet-wrappers. Gas and electricity showrooms across the country featured demonstrations of continental cookery.[2]

For many, however, their first experience of 'belonging' to the Common Market came with the arrival of VAT, possibly the most bureaucratic tax system ever devised. Introduced by the EEC in 1967, its advantage to the state was that for the first time millions of businesses would have to act as unpaid tax collectors, charging their customers 10 percent on the cost of all goods and services supplied, then subtracting all the VAT paid to their own suppliers on items not 'zero-rated' or exempt, and sending the difference to the government.

As a reflection of the new system of government the British people were now about to live under, it was a foretaste of much that was to come.

---

1 Heath, *op. cit.*, p. 549.
2 The *Daily Telegraph*, 20 January 1973, 'Lord Goodman's Cultural Circus'.

A 'provisional European government'

Anglocentric histories of the 'European project' usually glide from the signing of Britain's accession treaty in 1972 straight to the attempt by a new Labour government under Wilson in 1974 to renegotiate Britain's terms of entry, leading to the 1975 referendum. Between these events, however, came two developments which were each to have profound long-term significance for the future of European integration.

The first of these began with the Paris summit on 18 October 1972, the day after Heath's European Communities Bill received Royal Assent. The idea for this summit, to celebrate the 'enlargement' of the 'Six' to the 'Nine', originated with Monnet. Pompidou feared it would be merely a public relations exercise, but Heath assured him that it would be a serious occasion where real decisions could be taken: 'for example, that there could be substantial progress towards economic and monetary union'.[3]

Heath also had another objective. Two things were weighing on his mind. The first was the imbalance of the Community budget in favour of agriculture. A second was the rundown of Britain's traditional heavy industries, such as shipbuilding. Germany and other countries had used their Marshall aid after the war to modernise and re-equip, which was one reason why their economies were now so obviously outperforming Britain's. An answer to both problems, thought Heath, would be for the Community to create a proper 'regional policy', whereby Britain could receive subsidies on a scale commensurate with what other countries, such as France, gained for their agriculture. As Heath put it in his memoirs:

'Much time was spent in the Cabinet Office trying to devise a European policy which would help our budgetary imbalance by spending more in the UK than in any other member states, differentiating between our problems of declining industries and high unemployment and the problems faced by other countries. By taking the lead in the development of a Community regional policy we could also demonstrate our avowed intention to play our full part in building up and strengthening the enlarged Community.'[4]

When Heath received Pompidou's draft declaration for the summit, he replied that he 'had always admired the lucidity and clarity of French literature'. He agreed with Chancellor Willy Brandt that Germany and the UK 'would meet Pompidou's wish to underline progress towards monetary integration, provided that the French accepted our wish to give priority to regional and social problems'.[5] On 18 October, Heath met Pompidou before the summit to ask for his support for a 'regional development fund':

'He listened to what I had to say and then remarked that it was not a cause he wished to espouse, because France did not need help. "Moreover," he added, "you have sent me a map showing where the funds would go. I immediately turned my eyes to my own country and looked at my own home, Auvergne, only to find that it would not be getting a penny or a franc. So there is nothing in it for us".'[6]

---

3 Heath, *op. cit.*, p. 387.
4 *Ibid.*
5 Heath, *op. cit.*, p. 389.
6 *Op. cit.*, p. 390.

It was a measure of Heath's single-mindedness that he merely promised to send Pompidou 'a fresh memorandum on the subject ... together with a new, improved map', which he was sure his French colleague would find more acceptable.

In his opening speech at the summit Heath called for 'a clear timetable for economic and monetary union'. He also hoped for commitments on the Community's regional policy and 'a common foreign policy'.[7] The summit's main outcome was an affirmation by the heads of government of their intention to 'transform their relations into a European Union by the end of the decade'.[8] They agreed that 'a European Parliament, elected by universal suffrage, would have to be associated with the development of the European construction'.[9] They also agreed to the setting up of a Regional Development Fund, to be financed by the Community, supported by the European Investment Bank (EIB).

Heath regarded the acceptance of his idea for a Regional Development Fund as a 'major negotiating success'.[10] But by the time it came to be formally approved in December 1974, the funds allocated were only 4.8 percent of the Community's budget, compared with 90 percent for the CAP. Of this comparatively small sum, Britain was to receive just 28 percent while Italy was allocated 40 percent. So much for Heath's 'success'.

Someone else dissatisfied by this summit was Monnet. He felt it had lacked focus and, more importantly, mechanisms for carrying its resolutions forward. His great regret was that it had not established 'a supreme body to steer Europe through the difficult transition from national to collective sovereignty'.[11] By the end of August 1973, therefore, he had produced another of his famous plans, outlining a structure for a 'Provisional European Government'. To carry forward the Paris programme, this body would draw up a plan for 'European Union', to include a 'European Government' and an elected European Assembly. This 'provisional government' would meet regularly and those taking part would keep its deliberations secret.[12]

Monnet came over to England to discuss his proposal with Heath at Chequers on 18 September 1973, telling him 'we must give public opinion the feeling that European affairs are being decided: today, people have the impression that they're merely being discussed'.[13] Heath readily agreed, but had a reservation about making the proposal public 'Let's just do it', he told Monnet.[14] He also worried about the term 'provisional government'. 'That would get me into great difficulties,' he said.

When Monnet approached Pompidou and Brandt, they were equally enthusiastic. Neither shared Heath's reservations about the term 'provisional government'

---

7 *Op. cit.*, p. 391.
8 *Ibid.*
9 Commission of the European Communities (1975), *Eighth General Report of the Activities of the Community, 1974* (Luxembourg), pp. 339–346.
10 *Op. cit.*, p. 392.
11 Monnet, *op. cit.*, p. 503.
12 *Op. cit.*, p. 504.
13 *Ibid.*
14 *Ibid.*

and Pompidou particularly warmed to the name 'European Union'. One of Pompidou's staff was heard to inquire of a *confidant* of Pompidou what this term meant. The reply came 'nothing ... but then that is the beauty of it'.[15]

In late September, Pompidou mentioned Monnet's proposal at a press conference. Heath took up the baton at the Conservative Party conference on 13 October. 'I believe,' he said,

'... that already some of my colleagues as Heads of Government feel the need for us to get together regularly without large staff so that we can jointly guide the Community along the paths we have already set. I would like to see the Heads of Government of the member countries of the Community meeting together, perhaps twice a year, as I have said, alone and without large staffs, with the President of the Commission being present, as he was at the Summit ... our purpose in meeting together would be to lay down the broad direction of European policy.'[16]

Heath failed to mention that he was talking about what was being called a 'provisional government', and said nothing about it being intended to steer Europe through the 'transition from national to collective sovereignty'.

Two weeks later, on 31 October, Pompidou told his Cabinet that regular meetings of heads of states were needed 'with the aim of comparing and harmonising their attitudes in the framework of political co-operation'. He wanted the first meeting to be held before the end of 1973.[17] Monnet was now confident that, despite the turmoil into which the world had suddenly been plunged by the Yom Kippur war in the Middle East, his plan was back on track. Then, as he was to recall, 'when all seemed well, everything was thrown into turmoil'.[18] In the wake of the war, the price of oil quadrupled, threatening chaos to western economies. The governments of the Nine rushed to strike individual deals with the oil sheikhs. Heath was later to write that, at this moment, the Community 'lost sight of the philosophy of Jean Monnet: that the Community exists to find common solutions to common problems'.

'Each member state drifted back to seeking its own, unilateral solutions. So we all had to relearn painfully that there is no solution if we act on our own.'[19]

Despite this, Monnet's plan continued to make progress. By March 1974 he was circulating another paper, proclaiming:

'Existing European practices have proved inadequate as a means of enabling our countries to organise themselves for collective action ... We must break out of this vicious circle, in which the common interests of the Community countries are inadequately served. The existing European institutions are not strong enough today to do it on their own.'[20]

Then, in the three leading Community states, there were changes at the top. After a British general election in February 1974, Heath was replaced by Wilson.

15 Cited in Moravcsik, *op. cit.*, p. 265.
16 Cited in Monnet, *op. cit.*, p. 507.
17 Monnet, *op. cit.*, p. 508.
18 *Op. cit.*, p. 510.
19 Heath, *op. cit.*, p. 395.
20 Monnet, *op. cit.*, p. 511.

In Germany Brandt retired, to be replaced in May by Helmut Schmidt. The same month in France, after Pompidou had died, he was replaced by Valéry Giscard d'Estaing.[21] But the old alliance between Pompidou and Brandt was soon replaced by a similar friendship between Giscard and Schmidt. The two new Franco-German leaders soon agreed that there should be 'no more separate national actions, only European actions'. They accepted Monnet's 'provisional government', giving it the title 'European Council'.[22] The new body was approved at an informal meeting of heads of government at the Elysée on 14 September 1974.

The new European Council's first meeting was in Paris on 9 to 10 December 1974. For Britain, Wilson agreed with his colleagues that:

'The Heads of Government having noted that internal and international difficulties have prevented in 1973 and 1974 the accomplishment of expected progress on the road to EMU affirm ... their will has not weakened and that their objective has not changed...'[23]

The Council also confirmed its determination to work toward a common foreign policy and agreed to 'renounce' the practice, based on the Luxembourg Compromise, of making agreements conditional on unanimous consent. A working party should be set up to study the possibility of introducing a uniform passport for Community citizens.

The main business, however, was to make the Council a permanent institution. Giscard pointed out that there had only been three 'summits' between the heads of government in five years. These needed to be 'more organised' and regular, as Monnet had proposed.[24] Nothing appeared in the communiqué about the Council becoming a 'provisional government', but one of its first actions was to ask the Belgium prime minister, Leo Tindemans, to draft a report on how further integration could be achieved. Giscard brought proceedings to a close with the words: 'The Summit is dead. Long live the European Council.'[25]

Despite this landmark in the evolution of what was now becoming known as 'European construction', journalists and others would continue to refer to meetings of the Council as 'summits'. Even today few realise the significance of what had happened. Monnet himself, however, had no doubts:

'... the European institutions were in charge of immense sectors of activity, over which they exercised the share of sovereignty that had been delegated to them. But if they were to work

---

21 Giscard had been born at Koblenz in Germany in 1926, because his father was finance director of the civil administration by which France ran the occupied Rhineland. The family name was Giscard, but 'd'Estaing', borrowed from an 18th-century French admiral, had officially been added in 1922, to suggest aristocratic origins (The *Daily Telegraph*, 19 May 2003, *The Times*, 20 May 2003).

22 This must not be confused with the Council of Ministers, which had been one of the central components of the EEC structure since 1958 (as of the Coal and Steel Community before that). By institutionalising the earlier 'summits', the European Council was an entirely new concept, which would come to play an increasingly dominant role in Community affairs.

23 European Parliament (1982), Communiqué: Meeting of the Heads of Government of the Community, Paris, 9–10 December 1974. Reproduced in *Selection of Texts Concerning Institutional Matters of the Community from 1950–1982* (Luxembourg), pp. 275–281, para. 14.

24 Wilson, Harold (1979), *Final Term – The Labour Government 1974–1976* (London, Weidenfeld & Nicolson), p. 92.

25 Monnet, *op. cit.*, p. 514.

effectively, the governments had to have the same European will and be prepared, acting together as a collective authority, to transfer the additional sovereignty required to achieve a true European Union. The creation of the European Council supplied the means for reaching that essential decision. A major step had been taken.'[26]

It was, effectively, Monnet's last great *coup*. Retiring to write his memoirs, he was called back to the public stage only once more when, in April 1976, by resolution of the European Council in Luxembourg, he was awarded the title 'Honorary Citizen of Europe'.

The 'sham' of 'renegotiation'

British politics had by now been through turmoil. In the winter of 1973 to 1974, Britain's ailing economy had been plunged into chaos by industrial unrest and a second miners' strike, leading to major power cuts and the 'three day week'. Soaring wage demands and the quadrupling of world oil prices had led to galloping inflation. Heath called an election for 28 February, on the slogan 'Who Governs Britain?' (not, of course, meaning 'Westminster or Brussels' but himself or the unions). Although Heath and Wilson were both unpopular, Labour edged ahead of the Conservatives, by 301 seats to 297. Wilson returned to power. 'Grocer' Heath departed, never again to take centre stage as a national leader.

When Wilson entered Downing Street for his second term as prime minister, he carried with him the baggage of an aggressive Labour manifesto which pledged 'fundamental renegotiation' of Britain's entry terms:

'A profound political mistake made by the Heath government was to accept the terms of entry to the Common Market, and to take us in without the consent of the British people. This has involved the imposition of food taxes on top of rising world prices, crippling fresh burdens on our balance of payments, and a draconian curtailment of the power of the British Parliament to settle questions affecting vital British interests. This is why a Labour government will seek a fundamental renegotiation of the terms of entry.'[27]

Wilson had not promised this from any sense of conviction. He was worried about divisions in his party over the Common Market, even a challenge to his leadership, and because opposition to the Market was strong on the left of the party, he wanted to secure its support. As Bernard Donoughue, then Wilson's senior policy advisor, was to explain, his proposal of a 'renegotiation' was a stratagem to suppress internal party divisions. Now Labour was back in power, he had to deliver.[28]

With Machiavellian skill, he chose Callaghan, his new Foreign Secretary, as the chief negotiator. Regarded as lukewarm on the Community, and an Atlanticist, Callaghan was the leading potential leadership challenger. His direct involvement

---

26 *Op. cit.*, p. 515.
27 Cited in Denman, *op. cit.*, p. 247.
28 Donoughue, Bernard (1993), 'Harold Wilson and the renegotiation of the EEC terms of membership, 1974–1975: a witness account', in Brian Brivate & Harriet Jones (eds), *From Reconstruction to Integration: Britain in Europe since 1945* (London, Continuum International), p. 191.

in the negotiations would make it difficult for him to use the Common Market issue as a stick to beat his leader.

Clearly, what were already known in Brussels as the 'so-called renegotiations' were not Callaghan's idea of pleasure. His experiences of negotiating with Europe as Chancellor had not impressed him. Giscard d'Estaing in particular he found offensively arrogant. When John Cole, the BBC's political editor, suggested that European politics might be fun, Callaghan replied: 'What? Haggling with the French? The French are awful.'[29] According to Cole,

'He recalled his experiences in OECD and other gatherings. He knew it sounded bad, but he feared the French would run rings around the British in the Common Market. He had not enjoyed his hours in the couloirs, while French politicians or diplomats blew cigar smoke over him. Then, when you believed you had agreed on something during the lunch-break, you got back into the meeting to find the French had changed their minds, and though the Germans, Italians and Dutch might talk behind their hands, they would all go along with the French in the end.'[30]

Instructed by the Cabinet to give the impression of taking a tough line, when Callaghan arrived at the Council of Ministers on 1 April 1974 he wanted to read out the aggressive passage from Labour's election manifesto. His officials dissuaded him – this might be impolitic – so it was merely entered into the record. He did, however, declare that the British government reserved the right to propose changes to the treaties as an essential condition of Britain's continued membership, and the right to withdraw if satisfactory terms could not be agreed.[31]

By the time negotiations proper began on 4 June, Giscard had taken up the French presidency. Brandt had been replaced by Schmidt, with Hans Dietrich Genscher as his foreign minister. The Germans were both sympathetic to Britain's position and supportive of moves to reform the CAP. The mood had therefore changed, and Callaghan softened his tone. He put four items on the table: Britain's budgetary contribution; access for Commonwealth produce; CAP reform; and the right of member states to give state aid to industry and the regions without Community interference.

Some progress had already been made on the Commonwealth issue through Judith Hart, minister for overseas development. Although she had opposed British membership, she had brokered what was to become the Lomé convention, signed on 28 February 1975 between the EEC and 46 developing countries in Africa, the Caribbean and the Pacific (ACP). This replaced the earlier Yaoundé agreements, by which the lion's share of EEC overseas aid went to French-speaking Africa.

On CAP reform and state aid, Britain predictably got nowhere. The most contentious issue, however, was the budget contribution. The Treasury had estimated that by 1979, if nothing changed, Britain's share would increase to 21 percent of the budget, against her 14 percent share of Community GNP.[32] Professor Stephen

29 Cole, John (1995), *As It Seemed To Me – Political Memoirs* (London, Weidenfeld & Nicolson), p. 96.
30 *Ibid.*
31 Denman, *op. cit.*, p. 248.
32 George, *op. cit.*, p. 83.

George, a leading advocate of the 'Britain as an awkward partner' school, records that the Commission declined to endorse these calculations and refused to consider any estimate of future contributions. The French refused to recognise levies and tariffs as national contributions, on the grounds that the EEC was a customs union. All such duties must be regarded as the Community's 'own resources' (even though the bill would have to paid by British consumers in higher prices for imported goods). They refused, therefore, to consider any question of a rebate.[33] Despite this, the Commission did propose a form of rebate, but of such complexity that it was not acceptable either to France or Britain.

As the negotiations stalled, the Labour Party held its annual conference, delayed by the year's second general election in which Wilson was returned to power with 319 seats against 277 for Heath's Conservatives. The anti-marketeers narrowly carried a resolution laying down eight conditions for Britain's continued membership, including 'the right of British parliament to reject any European Economic Community legislation, directives or orders, when they are issued, or at any time after'.[34] Next day, however, the German Chancellor Helmut Schmidt charmed delegates with a plea for socialist solidarity, calling on them not to leave the Community. Schmidt then spent the weekend with Wilson at Chequers, where a deal was hatched. Wilson would agree to keep Britain in the Community, and Schmidt would ensure that enough concessions were made at the forthcoming Paris European Council to sustain a claim that renegotiation had succeeded.[35]

In Paris, on 9 to 10 December, Wilson had other ideas. This was his opportunity to show his public that he was looking after their interests. Before leaving London, he had made strong statements about how he 'would accept no nonsense from other member states on the two vital issues yet to be agreed'.[36] But, when discussion turned to the budget, Giscard would not yield an inch. Wilson, 'who had already been very rough on his opponents round the table, said he saw no point in going on'. At dinner that evening, 'd'Estaing softened', thanks to the mediation of Schmidt who, honouring his Chequers promise, persuaded his fellow ministers to examine a formula suggested by British civil servants for a 'correcting mechanism' in relation to the EEC budget.[37]

After three more months of what Callaghan described as 'fraught' negotiations, Wilson headed for the next Council in Dublin on 10 to 11 March 1975, confident that he was in sight of a settlement he could sell at home. On the first day, hours were spent discussing 'a complex and incomprehensible German proposal for implementing the budget correcting mechanism',[38] followed on the second day by similarly arcane debate over complex formulae relating to import quotas for New Zealand butter and cheese.[39] The Belgian prime minister complained about

33 *Op. cit.*, p. 84.
34 Cited in Butler and Kitzinger, *op. cit.*, p. 36: Report of the Seventy-Third Annual Conference of the Labour Party, 1974 (London), pp. 249–260.
35 Based on an interview with Schmidt, *The Poisoned Chalice*.
36 George, *op. cit.*, p. 86.
37 Donoughue, *op. cit.*, p. 196.
38 *Op. cit.*, p. 198.
39 Butler, David, and Kitzinger, Uwe (1976), *The 1975 Referendum* (London, Macmillan), p. 41.

heads of government being reduced to the level of auditors of a supermarket chain.[40]

Nevertheless, a semblance of agreement was reached, enough for Wilson, as planned, to declare the negotiations a success. After lengthy discussions with his Cabinet on 17 to 18 March, he told his ministers that the negotiating objectives had been 'substantially achieved', the Community had changed *de facto* and *de jure* and the attitude of the Commonwealth had changed too. The Commonwealth 'wanted us to stay in'.[41] The Cabinet voted sixteen to seven for staying in. Thus, on 18 March Wilson announced to the Commons that his government would now recommend the electorate to vote in what would be Britain's first-ever referendum, for continued membership on the new terms. Anyone who knew how little had really been achieved would have agreed with Heath's verdict that the renegotiation 'was a sham'.[42] All evidence suggests, however, that the British public were sufficiently impressed by it to achieve the decisive shift in opinion Wilson hoped for.

The people must decide

Holding a referendum on Britain's membership of the Common Market had been first mooted by Tony Benn in 1970 but, at the time, Wilson had flatly rejected one. On 27 May 1970 he told the BBC's Election Forum, when asked whether he would ever change his mind,

'The answer to that is "No". I have given my answer many times, and I don't change it because the polls go either up or down.'[43]

Benn's cause, however, was aided by the unlikely figure of Pompidou who, on 16 March 1972, announced a referendum in France on EEC enlargement. Buoyed by the proposition that what the French people would get should also be given to the British, Benn took his proposition back to the NEC, winning on 22 March 1972 a majority of two for a referendum.

Wilson still opposed the idea. But faced with the Shadow Cabinet favouring the idea, not for the first time on a major issue he changed his mind. A referendum option was approved by eight votes to six. Jenkins resigned as deputy leader, in disgust. 'This was no way to run an opposition,' he said later, 'chopping and changing from ... week to week. And not on any grounds of changed beliefs but on grounds purely of opportunistic politics.'[44]

---

40 *Ibid.*

41 Benn, Tony (1995), *The Benn Diaries* (single volume edition) (London, Random House), p. 313.

42 Heath, *op. cit.*, p. 542. Among those close to the negotiations also later to describe them as a 'sham' was Sir Michael Alexander (at the time Callaghan's assistant private secretary, later ambassador to Nato). Interview recorded for British Diplomatic Oral History Programme, Churchill Archives Centre, Cambridge. The most glaring omission from the issues submitted for re-negotiation was the fisheries policy. Sir Oliver Wright, at the time deputy under-secretary for European Affairs in the FCO (later ambassador to Washington) suggested this was because it would have been impossible to win enough changes to the CFP 'to be able to declare the re-negotiations a success' (Churchill Archive).

43 Cited in Heath, *op. cit.*, p. 540.

44 *The Poisoned Chalice*, authors' transcript.

There the matter rested. But when, in October 1974, Wilson decided to go back to the country in the hope of a larger majority, the option of a referendum was included in Labour's manifesto. Until now opinion polls had for some time shown sizeable majorities in favour of Britain leaving the EEC. But, by November, the polls were beginning to show a significant shift. According to Harris, 53 percent of the electorate said they would be happy to remain in the Community 'on the right terms'. In January 1975 this was even more dramatically confirmed by Gallup. Although a simply majority was still in favour of leaving, when respondents were asked whether 'new terms ... in Britain's interest' would make a difference, 71 percent now preferred to stay in.

With that, on 23 January, Wilson announced his intention to hold a referendum, more than two months before the renegotiation had been concluded. By the time he returned from Dublin to announce that the government would be recommending a 'Yes' vote, the balance had swung decisively in favour, by 66 to 34: almost exactly what the actual vote would be three months later.[45]

When the Referendum Bill was published on 26 March, Heath was strongly opposed, on the grounds, as he explained in his memoirs, that the UK 'had a fully effective parliamentary system for debating and deciding crucial national issues'.[46] He did not explain how the British public could have expressed its views through that system when, since 1964, all three main political parties had supported EEC membership.

Nevertheless Heath was no longer Conservative leader. He had been deposed and replaced by Margaret Thatcher, and it was her role to lead opposition to the Bill. 'There is no power,' as she put it on 11 March,

'under which the British constitution can come into rivalry with the legislative sovereignty of Parliament ... to subject laws retrospectively to a popular vote suggests a serious breach of this principle ... the implications for parliamentary sovereignty are profound.'[47]

Despite his pique at being replaced, Heath warmly approved Thatcher's 'impressive speech'. Yet the remarkable feature of the view shared by Thatcher and Heath was that, although they were both reluctant to share decision-making (i.e., 'sovereignty') with the British people, they seemed quite happy to share it with an unelected law-making body in Brussels.

Battle lines are drawn

Swallowing his objection to the referendum, Heath announced on 19 March that he planned to play a full part in the campaign, on behalf of a new 'all-party' organisation called Britain in Europe (BiE), publicly launched on 26 March. In December 1974, the long-established European Movement had put its own campaign into abeyance, placing all its resources at the disposal of BiE. The new title was chosen

45 Worcester, Robert M. (2000), *How To Win The Euro Referendum: Lessons From 1975* (London, Foreign Policy Centre), p. 12.

46 Heath, *op. cit.*, p. 543.

47 Cited in Heath, *op. cit.*, p. 544.

because it seemed 'crisp' and 'fresh', and because it emphasised that the campaign favoured remaining with the *status quo*. Britain was 'in'. The 'outs' were trying to upset things.[48]

BiE was designed as an umbrella organisation, encompassing the separate Conservative, Labour and Liberal campaigns, along with a Trade Union Alliance for Europe. Its Labour president was Roy Jenkins. Several of its senior staff were seconded from the Labour Party. Its chairman was Sir Con O'Neill, who had retired from the Foreign Office in 1972. Heath was a vice-president, along with the former Liberal leader Jo Grimond, William Whitelaw MP, Lord Feather, former general-secretary of the TUC, and Sir Henry Plumb, president of the National Farmers Union.

As the referendum approached, the Labour Party's fragile unity had begun to unravel. Left-wing MPs, led by Joe Ashton, Tony Benn's PPS, and Ian Mikardo had strongly criticised the terms of the renegotiation and were even calling for the party to campaign for withdrawal from the EEC.[49]

On 22 March, the Scottish Labour Party voted against staying in by 346,000 to 280,000, with Mikardo and others making speeches that bordered on personal abuse of leading members of their own party. Next day, five Cabinet ministers, Benn, Barbara Castle, Michael Foot, Shore and Silkin, issued a statement opposing the government line. Wilson was losing control. He solved the problem by allowing Labour MPs, including ministers, to campaign according to their consciences.

In late March, the government produced a White Paper on the renegotiations, and in a debate on 7 to 9 April recommended Parliament to approve Britain's continued membership on the terms set out. Wilson won by 396 to 170, a majority of 226. But 145 Labour MPs, including 38 ministers, had voted against their own government, with only 137 in support. The day was carried by Conservative MPs, including Heath, only eight Tories voting against. The Referendum Bill had an easier passage, receiving Royal Assent on 8 May.

One bewildering feature of the battle which followed was that, in addition to the official 'Yes' and 'No' campaigns, there were also 'Yes' campaigns for each party. Labour's 'Campaign for Europe' was launched on 8 April, with Shirley Williams as president, and included 88 MPs, 21 peers and 25 trade unionists.[50]

The Conservative 'Yes' campaign was launched by Thatcher on 16 April, at a dinner at the St Ermin's Hotel. She could not have spoken more fervently for the cause.

'It is a fact that there has been peace in Europe for the past quarter of a century, and for that alone I am grateful – grateful that my children have not been embroiled in a European conflict as was their father and as were the children of the two previous generations. We should

48 Butler and Kitzinger, *op. cit.*, p. 72: see n. 39 on p. 165.
49 *Ibid.*
50 The depth of division in the Labour Party was shown by a special conference organised by Labour's NEC in Islington on 26 April, when a motion to approve leaving the EEC was passed (under block voting) by 3.7 million votes to 1.98 million (Donoughue, *op. cit.*, p. 202).

not take that peace which has been secured too much for granted, for it has been secured by the conscious and concerted effort of nations to work together... It is a myth that the Community is simply a bureaucracy with no concern for the individual. The entire staff of the Commission is about 7,000 – smaller than that of the Scottish Office. It is a myth that our membership will suffocate national tradition and culture. Are the Germans any less German for being in the Community, or the French any less French? Of course they are not.'[51]

Despite the Tories having their own 'Yes' campaign, Britain in Europe also relied heavily on the Conservative Party, because it had 'the only effective machinery for putting on a national campaign'.[52] BiE was nevertheless at pains to present itself as an all-embracing body, run by a council of 37 well-known names, including every living ex-prime minister, every ex-foreign secretary (barring Selwyn Lloyd, who as Speaker of the House, had to stay neutral), and other public figures ranging from the television mogul Lew Grade to the former Archbishop of Canterbury, Michael Ramsey. The church was heavily involved, thanks to the efforts of a young Conservative would-be MP, John Selwyn Gummer, who claimed to have the support of over one-quarter of all clergy of all denominations, including almost every Anglican bishop. 'Prayers for Europe' were said in many Anglican churches and supportive items were placed in parish magazines.[53]

Mammon was also well-represented, notably by the enthusiastic support of the CBI. A survey carried out by *The Times* on 9 April showed 415 out of 419 chairmen of major companies wanting Britain to stay in the EEC, and the CBI set up its own European Operations Room, distributing over a million documents.[54]

As during the 'great debate' four years earlier, raising money proved to be no problem for the 'Yes' campaign. Together with the European Movement, BiE were to spend some £1,850,000 on the campaign, nearly 14 times more than the £133,000 available to the 'No' camp.

The 'No' campaign also organised under an umbrella organisation, with the uninspiring title of the National Referendum Campaign (NRC). As most anti-Market groups came from extremes of left and right, it represented an uneasy coalition, covering a wide divergence of individuals and organisations often at odds with one another, as when Tony Benn refused to appear on any public platforms with Conservatives. Tory anti-marketeers were in fact notable by their absence from the 'No' camp. Of the 41 Tory MPs who had defied the whip in 1971 to vote against entry to the EEC, only five played an active role in the NRC, including Richard Body and Teddy Taylor. The rest stayed silent. The few other prominent figures actively supporting the 'No' campaign included the historian Sir Arthur Bryant; journalists Paul Johnson and Peregrine Worsthorne; Patrick Neill QC, a future Warden of All Souls; the economists Lord Kaldor and Robert Neild; and a recently retired permanent secretary of the Ministry of Agriculture, now director of the National Trust, Sir John Winnifrith.

---

51 Cited in Heath, *op. cit.*, p. 546.
52 Butler and Kitzinger, *op. cit.*, p. 78.
53 *Op. cit.*, pp. 82–83.
54 *Op. cit.*, p. 83.

They could scarcely hope to compete with the galaxy of public figures support-ing the 'Yes' bandwagon, which was now ready to roll.

The referendum campaign

A feature of the referendum campaign often overlooked is that it coincided with the worst economic crisis Britain had faced since the war. In June 1975 the infla-tion rate hit 27 percent, the highest level ever recorded. Public spending was out of control and government borrowing was heading towards a record £11 billion. Britain's trade deficit had also reached record levels, not helped by the deficit which since 1973 had opened up in Britain's trade with the rest of the Common Market. This was now running at a yearly rate of £2.6 billion, against the modest surplus Britain had enjoyed before entry.

None of this impinged on the campaign. In fact, the country was almost eerily detached from the mounting financial crisis. Even on 30 June, more than three weeks after the vote, Wilson would still be waving aside any talk of a 'crisis' and dismissing the need for what he called 'panic measures'.

The most tangible evidence of the campaign was the three official booklets sent to every household in the country: two, from BiE and the government, calling for a 'Yes' vote; the third putting the case for a 'No'.

The 'No' leaflet listed benefits which had been promised if Britain joined the Market, from a rapid rise in our living standards and higher investment to more employment and faster industrial growth. In every case, it claimed, government figures showed the opposite result. It tried to evoke the dangers facing Britain from having handed over 'the right to rule ourselves', as her laws increasingly came to be made by 'unelected Commissioners in Brussels'. It claimed that the Market's 'real aim' was eventually to become 'one single country', in which Britain would be a 'mere province'. It rejected the 'scare-mongering of the pro-Marketeers', who claimed that British withdrawal would lead to economic disaster, and called for Britain to negotiate a free-trade agreement with the EEC, like that now enjoyed by Norway, Switzerland and the other members of EFTA.

The BiE case began with simple bullet points summing up the 'real advantages' of staying in. It made 'good sense' for 'our jobs and prosperity', for 'world peace', and 'for our children's future'. But it was the emotional pitch of the BiE case that stood out. It dwelt on how lonely and isolated Britain would be if she was foolish enough to withdraw. Everyone else in the world, it claimed, wanted Britain to stay in, from the USA and the Commonwealth to 'our friends' in the European Community. Outside, 'we should be alone in a cold, harsh world'. Claims that Community was undemocratic and wanted to eliminate national identities were ridiculous. 'All decisions of any importance must be agreed by every member.' Apart from a few new laws needed for 'commercial and industrial purposes', Britain would still retain the rest: 'Trial by jury, presumption of innocence remain unaltered'. The leaflet ended by quoting Heath: 'Are we going to stay on the centre of the stage where we belong, or are we going to shuffle off into the dusty wings of history?'

The government leaflet, *A New Deal in Europe*, emphasised how the re-negoti-ations had brought 'significant improvements' in Britain's terms of membership. Under the heading 'Will Parliament Lose Its Power? What Are The Facts?', voters were again assured 'we cannot go it alone in the modern world'. Membership of 'groupings like the United Nations, NATO and the International Monetary Fund' had not deprived the British of their national identity. It was 'the Council of Ministers' which took all the 'important decisions' in the Common Market, not officials. 'Inside the Market', it concluded, 'we can play a major part' in deciding policies which will 'affect the lives of every family in the country'; 'outside we are on our own'.[55]

The press almost unanimously supported a 'Yes' vote. But inevitably, television set the pace of the campaign. Public meetings, although numerous, were relative-ly sparsely attended. Their primary function, for both camps, was to provide news 'hooks' on which media coverage could be based. This helped to give the cam-paign an air of suffocating unreality, where 'debate' was reduced to little more than slogans and soundbites, a process deliberately encouraged by the tacticians for the 'Yes' camp, who were far more effective than their opponents in setting the level on which the battle was fought. As one commentator observed:

'On both sides, the committed would have liked a political debate about patriotism, sover-eignty and federalism, which is what had moved them to work hard for many years to get Britain into Europe, or keep it from the clutches of Brussels. But, especially on the pro-Community side, practical politicians and campaigners moved in to steer the debate in which prices, income levels and economic security dominated... The familiar bread and butter issues of a British general election took top place in the minds of the publicity men and in the answers pollsters obtained about what the referendum question meant.'[56]

At the centre of the 'Yes' campaign was a unit set up by Jim Callaghan in the Foreign Office, holding daily meetings with his team which, as a senior civil ser-vant Sir Michael Butler was later to recall, included Shirley Williams, head of the Labour 'Yes' campaign, the Head of the News Department, and the Head of the News Department at Number 10, plus one or two other ministers, together with one or two officials. The daily strategy for the campaign was laid down at this meeting.[57]

This unprecedented grouping (Butler himself called it 'an interesting innova-tion') broke protocols by directly involving civil servants in a partisan exercise, although this was excused by the fact that support for 'Europe' was regarded by many senior civil servants as an issue transcending partisan politics.

---

55 One blatantly untruthful claim in the government's leaflet was that: 'There was a threat to employ-ment in Britain from the movement in the Common Market towards an Economic and Monetary Union. This could have forced us to accept fixed exchange rates for the pound, restricting indus-trial growth and putting jobs at risk. This threat has been removed.' Only five months earlier Harold Wilson had agreed with his fellow heads of government in Paris that their will to work towards Economic and Monetary Union had 'not weakened'. Their plans might have been gone into abeyance following the rise in oil prices, but the 'threat' had scarcely been 'removed'.

56 Steed, Michael (1977), 'The Landmarks of the British Referendum', *Parliamentary Affairs*, 30, pp. 130–131. Cited in George, *op. cit.*, p. 93.

57 Churchill College, oral archive, *op. cit.*

Another 'regular' at Callaghan's FCO meetings was the market researcher Bob Worcester, head of Mori International, who played a central part in guiding 'Yes' campaign tactics. In a memorandum to Jim Callaghan on 16 May, he advised the campaign to focus on prices and the cost of living. With inflation heading for 27 percent, the message should be 'that the government will have a better chance of keeping prices down if we stay in the Common Market than if we get out'. He concluded:

'We must not scatter our shots – let the Opposition talk about sovereignty, independence, Britain's role in the world, defence, etc. If they spend two days on this and three days on that between now and the 5 June (polling day), this is the best thing that could happen to us.'[58]

In Worcester's subsequent analysis, he attached particular significance to the public perception of each side's leading figures. Here, it was obvious that the 'No' campaign suffered a marked handicap. Based on subtracting the percentage of the public who liked each figure from the percentage who disliked them, only one of the six leading 'anti-market' personalities registered a small plus rating: Enoch Powell (+2). He compared with Jack Jones (−5), Michael Foot (−9), Tony Benn (−15), Hugh Scanlon (−17) and the Rev. Ian Paisley (−59). All six leading 'Yes' campaigners scored big plus ratings: Reggie Maudling (+12), Wilson (+19), Heath (+21), William Whitelaw (+25), Roy Jenkins (+25), Jeremy Thorpe (+29). With the pro-marketeers occupying the centre ground, there were few figures in the 'No' camp who could be presented as moderate, establishment figures. The media, anyway, liked to focus on the two figures who, to middle-ground opinion, seemed most extreme: Powell and Benn.[59]

After the poll, a Conservative campaigner who had been in the thick of the action, commented on this effect:

'What was notable was the extent to which the referendum ... was not really about Europe at all. It became a straight left versus right battle with the normal dividing line shifting further over than in general elections – hence the Labour split and their discomfiture. In all the speeches I made to Conservative audiences the trump card was always – "beware of Benn, Foot and Castle". It was this, more than anything, which ... increasingly negated the efforts of the anti-EEC Conservatives.'[60]

The 'antis' were never going to succeed. The greatest strength of the 'pros' was the *status quo*: 'If we leave, Britain will be isolated' was their central theme. In addition there was the near-unanimity of establishment opinion in favour of remaining in. The opposition was fatally split and the leading figures of the 'Yes' campaign were vastly more credible than their opponents.[61]

---

58 Worcester, *op. cit.*, pp. 14–15.
59 As public concern mounted at the growth in trade union power, Benn and his anti-market Labour colleagues were seen by many as left-wing bogeymen. This was exacerbated by the extraordinarily high profile given to Benn by the media. Between 1 May and 4 June, he appeared in feature programmes or principal news items 52 times, followed by the almost equally controversial Powell at 23 times. The most prominent 'Yes' campaigner was Jenkins, who appeared 27 times, while Heath equalled Powell on 23. (Worcester, *op. cit.*, p. 194.).
60 Butler and Kitzinger, *op. cit.*, p. 287.
61 For a detailed analysis, see Worcester, *op. cit.*

Unsurprisingly, when 5 June came, the public voted to stay in, by a two-to-one majority. On a 64.5 percent turnout of 29,433,194 electors, 67.2 percent voted 'Yes', 32.8 percent 'No'. Every part of mainland Britain registered a 'Yes' majority, the only exceptions being Shetland (where 56.3 percent voted 'No') and the Western Isles (70.3). After the result had been declared, Thatcher declared:

'The message of the referendum for the government is that the people have looked at the really big issues ... They have looked at what really counts and they have voted that way.'[62]

But it was not only Euro-sceptics who would come to question the outcome. Roy Hattersley, in a BBC radio interview years later, thought it had been 'wrong for us to deal superficially with what Europe involved'. 'We've paid the price for it ever since,' he said, 'because every time there's a crisis in Europe, people say, with some justification, 'well, we wouldn't have been part of this if we'd really known the implications.'[63]

The really significant lesson of that referendum vote, however, was reflected in the fact that, only six months earlier, the opinion polls had consistently been showing majorities in favour of Britain leaving the EEC. What undoubtedly swung public opinion, as the pollsters themselves discovered, was that so many people genuinely believed Wilson had won a better deal. The campaign itself was in this sense wholly irrelevant. The result on 5 June reflected almost exactly what the polls had been showing back in March, after voters had first started telling the pollsters that, if the government now assured them it was in Britain's interest to stay in, they would change their minds. Wilson had swung them round with re-negotiations which everyone who understood them agreed were a 'sham'.

* * * * * *

On 22 November 1974, a piece of history was made in a British court, when for the first time a case had been decided entirely on the basis of the Treaty of Rome. Lord Denning had ruled in favour of a German company which had demanded an English customer should settle his disputed bill in Deutschmarks. In a lower court the company had already been given judgment in sterling, this being previously the only currency in which an English court could legally make an award. But the German firm had appealed because, by then, sterling had been substantially devalued against the mark. Finding for the plaintiff, Denning said:

'This is the first case in which we had actually to apply the Treaty of Rome in these courts. It shows great effect. It has brought about a fundamental change... It has already made us think about our own laws.'[64]

The trouble was that very few others were doing any serious thinking. Britain was sleepwalking into an entirely new situation, the nature of which her people could not yet begin to comprehend.

---

62 *The Times*, 7 June 1975.
63 BBC Radio 4, Document: *A Letter to Times*, 8 p.m., 3 February 2000.
64 *Schorsch Meier GmbH v. Hennin* [1974] 3 W.L.R. 823 (*Weekly Law Reports*, 20 December 1974 issue, pp. 823–831), reprinted in Vaughan, *op. cit.*, pp. 189–194.

Chapter 10

'The Awkward Partner': 1975–1984

'Our decline in relation to our European partners has been so marked that today we are not only no longer a world power, but we are not in the first rank even as a European one.'

Sir Nicholas Henderson, UK Ambassador to France, June 1979[1]

'... the UK really did have a lousy deal. The Agricultural Policy, which we had always known worked against our interests, was out of control ... it was also clear that in a few year's time the UK budgetary contribution would rise so much that we were quite likely to find ourselves the nation making the largest contribution.'[2]

David Owen, Foreign Secretary 1978–1979

'I must be absolutely clear about this... I cannot play Sister Bountiful to the Community while my own electorate are being asked to forego improvements in the fields of health, education, welfare and the rest.'

Margaret Thatcher, 19 June 1979[3]

After endorsing their politicians' decision to commit Britain to a supranational form of government by easily the largest popular vote in their electoral history, the British people emerged from the referendum campaign to a bleak prospect. Twenty-five years earlier Britain had been the second richest country in the world but, in the mid-1970s her industries were inefficient, over-manned and strike-ridden, kept afloat only by annual injections of billions of pounds of taxpayers' money. Nightly familiar on the nation's television screens, trade union leaders such as Jack Jones, Hugh Scanlon and Joe Gormley were viewed as the most powerful men in Britain. Within a year Chancellor Denis Healey would be calling on the International Monetary Fund for the largest loan to which he was entitled. In economic terms, Britain was being scornfully dismissed as 'the sick man of Europe'.

To all these problems, membership of the EEC seemed irrelevant. Although the British people had voted to stay in the Common Market, many imagining that this meant little more than a free trade area, its activities could scarcely have seemed more remote. The overriding concern of the politicians and the media was now again with domestic affairs. So began the period when Britain was to win her reputation as the Community's 'awkward partner'.

Although this would only catch the imagination of the British people a few years later when, in the early 1980s, Thatcher became engaged in her seemingly

---

1 Henderson, Nicholas (1987), *Channels And Tunnels* (London, Weidenfeld and Nicolson), p. 143.
2 Owen, David (1992), *Time To Declare* (London, Penguin Books), pp. 245–246.
3 Thatcher, Margaret (1992), *The Downing Street Years* (London, Harper Collins), p. 79.

174

interminable battle over Britain's budget rebate, the tone was set from the moment Wilson arrived at the first European Council after the referendum. His government, he announced, would stand up for British interests 'no more and no less than our EEC partners'.[4] As recorded by Professor George, this statement was seen in Brussels as alarmingly 'negative'. But all Wilson was suggesting was that, in pursuing her own national interest, Britain now intended to follow the example set most conspicuously by France. Yet, somehow, whenever she did so, it was she alone that was considered awkward, obstructive and not *'communautaire'*.

Odd man out

In 1975, Britain's difficulties in fitting in with her continental 'partners' involved such technical issues that they were scarcely noticed by the media. For instance, the Community proposed to 'harmonise' controls over effluent discharges into rivers. The exacting standards proposed were based on pollution problems associated with such sluggish, slow-flowing rivers as the Rhine. The British pointed out that, for the faster-flowing rivers of their island, such costly standards were not necessary. But it was argued that if Britain was allowed to adopt standards less rigorous than those imposed on the continental, her industries would gain an 'unfair' advantage. Britain's objection was accepted, but the incident left a bad taste.[5]

There was a row over the Regional Development Fund. Under the EEC system, grants from Brussels could only be given under a principle known as 'additionality', whereby the money had to be used for projects 'additional' to those national governments were willing to fund. Given Heath's intention that regional funding should help compensate Britain for the budgetary imbalance, the Treasury wanted to use the money to subsidise projects which would otherwise have been paid for by UK taxpayers. Britain's failure to accept the rules was cited as evidence of a lack of good faith.

A more general charge against the British centred on the attitude shown by Callaghan. According to a contemporary comment:

'The Foreign Secretary's hectoring manner in the Council of Ministers would conspire to lose even a cast-iron case. He's a man to whom rudeness comes naturally in formal negotiations, and is much resented for it. In presentational terms, his arguments in the Council are frequently disastrous.'[6]

This mix of Community sensibilities and supposed British 'awkwardness' took a more serious turn when the Community set out to adopt a 'common policy' on energy.

The problem here was that Britain was just discovering huge reserves of oil and gas in the British waters of the North Sea. Following the world energy crisis which resulted from the quadrupling of oil prices after the Yom Kippur war, the US

---

4 The *Spectator*, 'Unanswered Questions at Wilson's Summit', 26 July 1975, cited in George, Stephen (1990), *An Awkward Partner – Britain In The European Community* (Oxford, Oxford University Press) (third ed.), p. 108.
5 George, *op. cit.*, p. 108.
6 *New Statesman*, 'The Odd Man Out of Europe', 24 October 1975.

Secretary of State Dr Henry Kissinger had called a conference of 13 major oil-consuming nations in Washington, including the EEC Nine, in a bid to establish a common approach to the petroleum cartel, OPEC. Britain, together with seven of the Nine, was prepared to accept the US proposals. The French refused, leading to a theatrical attack on America's position by foreign minister Michel Jobert.

To Kissinger's anger, the French then summoned another conference for Europeans only, in a bid to hatch a separate deal with Arab oil producers. However, the UK government now expected that, within a few years, Britain would be exporting large quantities of oil, thus solving the interminable balance of payments problem which had dogged Britain since the war. This meant that, while her continental partners wanted to see the price of oil reduced, Britain wanted it kept high.

This divergence came to a head through French attempts to hold another conference, in June 1975. They refused to take account of Britain's new status and instead agreed directly with the OPEC oil producers that the rich oil-consuming nations should be represented at the conference only by Japan, the USA and the EEC acting as a single entity. Callaghan, not having been consulted, immediately declared that Britain, with her separate interests, could not be represented by the EEC, with its different interests.

This aroused the ire of her EEC partners. Despite France having blocked the original US-inspired initiative, then having set up its own conference, then having negotiated arrangements without referring to Britain, it was the UK which won odium as the 'awkward partner'. At the European Council meeting in Rome in December, Wilson came under heavy fire from Schmidt, who is reported to have shouted at him that a country with one of the weakest economies in the Community was not in a position to negotiate on such issues without heed to the consequences.[7]

In the end Wilson gave way, accepting EEC representation, but only on an assurance that the Community would argue for a minimum floor price for oil. Though getting what she wanted, as George put it, Britain's stance had cost even more of her diminishing goodwill with her partners. 'The whole episode had been handled badly,' he wrote, 'and it is difficult to see any good reason for this other than stubbornness.'[8] He failed to explain whether, if France had suddenly discovered massive new oil reserves, she would have behaved differently.

Energy was not the only issue now straining relations between Britain and the rest of the Community. There was also the contentious problem of fishing, given fresh impetus on 1 January 1977 when, after the Third United Nations Conference on the Law of the Sea (UNCLOS), the new 200-mile fisheries limit was adopted by most of the world's fishing nations, including the members of the EEC.

The declaration of 200-mile limits by other countries meant that vessels from Community member states would now be excluded from rich fishing grounds off Norway and Iceland. This was of particular relevance to Britain's fishing industry, because a large part of her fleet was made up of 'distant water' trawlers, based in

7 *Op. cit.*, p. 103.
8 *Op. cit.*, p. 104.

ports such as Hull and Fleetwood, fishing across the North Atlantic, from Norway to Iceland and Greenland. One reason why many British fishermen had accepted the Common Fisheries Policy was that they assumed this deep-water fishing could continue. But now, it seemed, these waters could be barred to them. Nineteen seventy-five saw the height of the so-called 'Cod Wars' off Iceland, when British vessels were kept out by Icelandic gunboats. The UK's deep-water fishermen therefore turned their attention to waters nearer home, where, under international law, Britain was about to extend her own limits to 200 miles through the 1976 Fisheries Limits Act.

At a meeting in Edinburgh in April 1975, British fisheries organisations urged that Britain should now press for all non-EEC members to be excluded from its new 200-mile limit, with a 100-mile limit to be reserved for British vessels only. By way of compromise, the government agreed to press for the establishment of exclusive national zones of at least 50 miles. Predictably, the French and the Dutch demanded implementation of 'equal access'.

At this point the full implications of what Heath had given away finally began to dawn on UK fishermen. In February 1976, the Commission proposed that it should manage the fishing resource in all but inshore waters, to be parcelled out on the basis of national quotas. Despite protests from the British and Irish governments, at a final meeting in The Hague in November 1976 the Commission came up with its proposals for a common 'conservation policy'. The seas around Europe would be divided into fishing areas. Every year the tonnage of each species of fish allowed to be caught in each of these areas would be fixed, as the 'Total Allowable Catch', or TAC. This would then be allocated between member states on a quota system.

After fierce argument as to how this should be decided, it was eventually agreed that the divisions should be based on 'historic catches', measured over a specific 'reference period'. This was modified by an additional allowance for areas which particularly depended on fishing for employment, known as the 'Hague preferences'. It was finally agreed that, once national shares of the catch for each species had been established, member states would continue to receive the same proportionate share by a principle known as 'relative stability'.

Bitter squabbling over how all this could be implemented was to continue until 1983. But it was already obvious that the biggest loser would be Britain, which had thus suffered a double blow. Not only was the new 200-mile limit now forcing her deep-water fishing fleet out of business, she was now discovering that, under the same rule, she had lost to the Community waters containing four-fifths of western Europe's fish. They were to be allocated to her 'partners' under the 'equal access' provisions which Heath had conceded and Wilson had made no effort to regain.

'A lousy deal'

On 13 April 1976, Wilson resigned. He was succeeded as prime minister by James Callaghan, who made Anthony Crosland his Foreign Secretary. Among the problems they had to confront was the need to create a fully-elected 'European Parliament'. When the 'Assembly' was set up in 1958, it was made up, like its predecessor in Monnet's Coal and Steel Community, of delegates nominated by national parliaments. But the Treaty of Rome had included a commitment that the Community should have a parliament elected by the people of Europe. When Giscard d'Estaing became president of France he put this on the agenda, and at the European Council in September 1974 it was agreed that the first elections should be held in 1978.

Giscard's conversion to this project, reversing his party's previous policy, stemmed more from political calculation than conviction. For domestic reasons, he needed the support of the smaller independent parties in his National Assembly, for whom 'commitment to European integration was an article of faith'.[9] Offering an elected Parliament for Europe was enough to woo them into his governing coalition. Wilson had agreed to this as part of his renegotiation package, and Callaghan felt obliged to abide by this commitment. He therefore asked a parliamentary committee to look into the mechanics of any election, which duly concluded that a Bill would have to be introduced by the start of 1977 if elections were to be held on the time-scale proposed.

While Giscard had won domestic political advantage by this proposal, however, it soon became clear that the same was not true for Callaghan. At his first Labour Party conference, in October 1976, the left-wing dominated NEC had tabled a resolution rejecting the idea of an elected European Parliament, on the grounds that it would compete with national parliaments. This, they predicted, would strengthen the Commission, thus increasing the power of 'Brussels bureaucrats'.[10] Conference passed the resolution, and, to avoid a damaging row with his own Party, Callaghan put the matter on the back-burner.

It was thus not until late 1977 that a Bill was introduced to permit direct elections, making it impossible to meet the timetable of 1978. There was no time for the Boundary Commission to define the new Euro-constituencies. Callaghan attempted a short-cut, but this evoked threats of resignation from left-wing Cabinet members. Thus, when the Bill came to Parliament, Labour MPs were allowed a free vote. The Conservatives opposition, combined with the votes of 115 Labour 'rebels', defeated it. Callaghan was forced to tell his EEC 'partners' that Britain could not hold direct elections in 1978. 'Because of the priority given to domestic political considerations,' George was to write, 'Britain again appeared to be in breach of the spirit of the Community.'[11] He seemed untroubled that it was only French 'domestic political considerations' which had determined the timetable in the first place.

With Britain thus coming under increasing fire, the next opportunity for her politicians to shine came with the first occasion when she took on the rotating presidency of the Council, from January to June 1977. This began well enough with Wilson's new foreign secretary Anthony Crosland assuring the European Parliament on 12 January of the importance attached by the British government

---

9 *Op. cit.*, p. 118. George cites Jean-Louis Burban. (1977), 'La Dialectique des élections européenes', *Revue française de science politique*, 27, pp. 377–406.

10 *Op. cit.*, p. 118.

11 *Op. cit.*, p. 121.

to the co-ordination of foreign policy – a process that had acquired the title of European Political Co-operation (EPC).

Crosland's deputy was a rising star in Labour's ranks, the 38-year old Dr David Owen. He later recalled that his first task had been to brief himself on the European Community. As he did, he found

'... that the UK really did have a lousy deal. The Agricultural Policy, which we had always known worked against our interests, was out of control – big surpluses were building up in milk products, olive oil and wine and costs were soaring. It was also clear that in a few year's time the UK budgetary contribution would rise so much that we were quite likely to find ourselves the nation making the largest contribution. We also had to cope with a Fishing Policy which had been cobbled up by the Six members on the eve of the Community's expansion and which could hardly have been more unhelpful to UK fishing interests.' [12]

In the early weeks of his new role, as Owen confronted the reality of Britain's membership of the Community, he was tempted to think that Wilson had been right in 1972, and that the terms had been unacceptable.[13] His main problem, however, was his own officials. With 'notable exceptions', he found his senior civil servants so dismissive of the reality that he despaired of being able to develop a tough negotiating stance.[14] The problem, he wrote, was deep-seated.

'Too many Euro-diplomats were reluctant to embark on any course which put us at serious loggerheads with the majority of Community members. They were intelligent people but they never had the tenacity to fight for British interests in the same way as French diplomats fight at every level for France.' [15]

The most contentious issues confronting the British presidency were those to be handled by the Agriculture Council, presided over by Britain's new agriculture minister, John Silkin. At the time, Labour had only a small majority, haemorrhaging through by-election losses, and many fishing constituencies were Labour marginal seats.[16] Silkin, therefore, was eager to show that he was defending Britain's interests, and when the French led opposition to British and Irish demands for exclusive 50-mile fishing zones, he was not prepared to compromise. In the event, no lasting agreements were reached during the British presidency, not least because of what the other member states considered was biased chairmanship. Again, Britain, in defending her national interests, was not being 'communautaire'.

Just as contentious was Silkin's refusal to accept a proposed 1.5 percent increase in CAP funding which, because of the distortions in the system, would have translated into a 3 percent increase in British food prices. This was at a time when the government was struggling to contain price increases through a voluntary pay freeze policy. That the British, because of 'narrow national interests' should block an increase, most of which would go to French farmers, caused further resentment.[17]

12 Owen, *op. cit.*, pp. 245–246.
13 *Op. cit.*, p. 246.
14 *Ibid.*
15 *Ibid.*
16 George, *op. cit.*, p. 123.
17 *Op. cit.*, pp. 123–124.

However, in the fifth month of the presidency, another milestone in Britain's relationship with the Community arrived, one not mentioned by George. On 28 May 1977, the Cabinet committee dealing with Common Market issues was told that the Commission had successfully appealed to the ECJ to have ruled 'out of order' pig meat subsidies paid by the British government, and had instructed that the subsidies be stopped 'forthwith'. Tony Benn was present at the meeting. He asked whether this was the first time that a European Court decision had been taken against the British government and was told it was. In his diaries, he continued:

'Then I asked what would be the political effect of this on pig producers in the UK. John Silkin said it would mean in effect the destruction of our industry, the mass slaughtering of pigs and the abandonment of our processing plants in favour of the Danes... I wanted to be told explicitly – as I was – that I was a member of the first British Government in history to be informed that it was behaving illegally by a court whose ruling you could not alter by changing the law in the House of Commons. It was a turning point ...' [18]

Unsurprisingly, following the British presidency, Callaghan set out to the 1977 Labour Party Conference a six-point plan for British policy towards the EEC, rejecting any increase in powers for the European Parliament, improving the 'scrutiny' procedures of the UK parliament, and asserting the dominance of national regional and industrial policies. However, this only added further fuel to the fire. When he went on to call for the Community to admit Greece, Spain and Portugal because 'the dangers of an over-centralised, over-bureaucratised and over-harmonised Community will be less with twelve than with nine',[19] Britain's disgrace in the eyes of her partners seemed complete.

Towards 'European union'

Away from these difficulties centred on the British, the Community itself was again concerned with its real agenda: ever greater integration. As had been the case ever since the Werner and Davignon reports of 1970, this centred on what were now the Community's two chief aims: to establish economic and monetary union, and a common foreign policy.

In 1971 the USA's abandonment of the 1944 Bretton Woods agreement had thrown international currencies into disarray. In response, most nations had allowed their currencies to 'float' freely against each other on the international markets, but this brought with it the potentially destabilising effect of excessive fluctuations.

To tackle this, Europe's central bankers had met at Basle in 1972 to create a European Exchange Rate Agreement, known as the 'snake'. European currencies would be kept within a band of ±2.25 percent, thus avoiding excessive fluctuations. In addition to the Six, Britain, Sweden, Norway, Denmark and Ireland also

---

18 Benn, *op. cit.*, p. 417.
19 In the 1990s Conservative Party policy on further enlargement would be making exactly the same points.

took part. The 'snake' did not prosper. Britain's participation lasted only six weeks before speculation forced her out. Italy followed shortly afterwards. France left in 1974, rejoined the following year and finally left in 1976. Only West Germany, Benelux and Denmark managed to keep within the margins, creating in effect an expanded Deutschmark zone. By the mid-1970s, therefore, any hope of implementing the Werner proposals for economic and monetary union seemed to have foundered.

Once an idea has entered the collective mind behind the 'European construction', however, it will always re-emerge. In early 1974 the Commission set up a study group to examine the prospects of achieving EMU by 1980. Chaired by Monnet's former close associate, Robert Marjolin, the group included two British representatives, Sir Donald McDougall, the British government's chief economic adviser, and Andrew Shonfield, now director of the Royal Institute of International Affairs. Their report in March 1975 stated uncompromisingly that 'national and economic policies have never in twenty-five years been more discordant, more divergent, than they are today'.[20]

This had led to a succession of monetary crises, and the problem, the group argued, was that there had been a lack of political will by the Community to take advantage of these crises.

'Like all crises, they could have been the occasion of progress, by provoking a crystallisation of latent wills. Great things are almost always done in crises. Those of recent years could have been the occasion for a leap forward.'[21]

This was an early exhortation to use what was to become a major tool of the 'project': the 'beneficial crisis'. Again and again some headline-making crisis would be exploited to justify extending the Community's powers, thus furthering integration.

In this instance, the problems arising from floating exchange rates were used to revive the idea of economic and monetary union. Marjolin's committee was in no doubt of the need to vest in supranational institutions 'all the instruments of monetary policy and of economic policy' currently held by national governments, to exercise these powers 'for the Community as a whole'. The 'common institutions' would have to include a European 'political power', a Community budget and a central banking system, all of which would have to act 'in a comparable way to those of a federal state'.[22] Community taxes would be vital, to enable funding to be transferred to less-developed regions.[23]

The Marjolin Report was soon followed by another, produced by Belgian prime minister, Leo Tindemans. Published on 29 December 1975, it had the beguilingly simple title 'The European Union'. It began by regretting that 'the construction of Europe' seemed to have 'lost its air of adventure'.[24] The 'European idea' was

20 Commission of the European Communities. Report of the Study Group 'Economic and Monetary Union 1980' (EMU – 63), Brussels, March 1975, p. 1.
21 *Op. cit.*, p. 4.
22 *Op. cit.*, pp. 5–6.
23 *Op. cit.*, p. 33.
24 Bulletin of the European Communities, S/1-1976.

'partly the victim of its own successes'. But 'an unfinished structure does not weather well: it must be completed, otherwise it collapses', and one 'basic require-ment for achieving a European Union'[25] was a common economic and monetary policy. But it would also need common foreign and defence policies, complete with a 'European armaments agency'.[26]

Particularly significant was Tindemans' view that, for 'an integrated economic and monetary unit to operate harmoniously', large-scale transfers of funds from the richer areas of the Community to the poorer regions would be needed. This would require a full scale 'regional policy', with much of its funding directed through the Community budget. Tindemans also recommended a policy for forg-ing a 'Peoples' Europe' through 'concrete manifestations of the European solidar-ity in everyday life'.

He wanted to replace both the Council of Ministers and the Commission with a new supranational body. This 'government of Europe' would be responsible to and elected by a more powerful European Parliament, which would include a chamber directly elected by the 'peoples of Europe' and a 'Chamber of States' appointed by national governments. 'A return to intergovernmental co-operation would not help solve European problems,' Tindemans decided.[27] His final pro-posal, to speed up the process of integration, was a two-speed 'Europe', with an inner core moving faster towards political union than those states which were less committed. But this, Tindemans stressed, did not mean a 'Europe *à la carte*'. Every country would have to work towards the same final objective.[28]

Wilson was dismissive of the report, and when it came before the Luxembourg European Council on 1 April 1976, only days before he resigned as prime minis-ter, he recorded that the discussions 'led us nowhere'.[29] Nevertheless, the propos-als were to remain on the Community's long-term agenda.

Enter Roy Jenkins

With talk of a single currency in the air, a central role in what happened next was about to be played by another British politician, whose view of European integra-tion was very different from Wilson's. When, on Wilson's retirement, Roy Jenkins was heavily defeated by Callaghan in his bid to become prime minister, and refused the post of Foreign Secretary, he accepted an invitation to become President of the Commission.

---

25 *Op. cit.*, p. 26.
26 *Op. cit.*, p. 21.
27 *Op. cit.*, p. 45.
28 *Op. cit.*, p. 27.
29 Wilson, *op. cit.*, p. 238. One British MP who welcomed the Tindemans report, however, was Douglas Hurd, then Conservative spokesman for European affairs. He particularly praised the pro-posal for a single 'European foreign policy', emphasising that foreign ministers 'should accept an obligation to reach a common view' (*Hansard*, 17 June 1976, col. 870). However, it did not seem that Hurd grasped the logic of what he was saying, since he went on to observe that this did not mean 'removing the veto by some constitutional piece of surgery. It means creating the habit of agreement.' This was not what the integrationists had in mind. They wanted subordination, not co-operation.

Curiously, this fervent 'Europeanist' was singularly unprepared for his new post. As he wrote in his memoirs:

'My conviction was complete, but my experience was negligible. The only ministerial port-folio that I held after Britain's entry in 1973 was that of Home Department, which as its name implied, and its ethos confirmed, was about as far removed from the business of the Community as any within the compass of the British government. I participated in no Councils of Ministers. I liked to say, only half as a joke, that I kept my European faith burn-ing bright by never visiting Brussels. And this was almost startlingly true. France, Italy, Germany I knew fairly well. But the embryonic capital of Europe I visited only on four occasions between 1945 and the date of my appointment as head of its administration. I was an enthusiast for the *grandes lignes* of Europe but an amateur within the complexities of its signalling system.'[30]

Having started work on 1 January 1977, Jenkins was later to admit that his first six months as President were not a success. In July 1977, after reading criticism to this effect in *The Economist*, he decided a new initiative was necessary. As to the direction it should take, he wrote:

'I was much influenced by ... Jean Monnet ... On at least two occasions his ideas had been spectacularly successful in gaining the initiative, and in the second case he had done so by rebounding from a setback and switching from one blocked avenue to another which was more open ... The lesson he taught me was always to advance along the line of least resist-ance provided that it led in the right general direction.'[31]

Jenkins concluded that he should throw his weight behind monetary union.

In December 1977 the European Council supported Jenkins, and agreed to commission various studies on monetary co-operation. One was produced under the chairmanship of Sir Donald McDougall, head of the British government's eco-nomic service. *The Role of Public Finance in European Integration* was notable for its suggestion that, if the Community was to assume the kind of economic respon-sibilities suggested by the Marjolin report, this would require it, on the model of the federal government in America, to control between 20 and 25 percent of the Community's GDP, amounting even then to hundreds of billions of pounds.[32]

In the absence of any Community action, early in 1978 Giscard and Schmidt decided to back Jenkins. The outcome was to be the European Monetary System (EMS) within which was the Exchange Rate Mechanism (ERM), a more compli-cated version of the 'snake' (and eventual nemesis of the Conservative Party).

The two leaders outlined their ideas to the Copenhagen European Council in April 1978.[33] They stressed the need to insulate a western European bloc from the monetary fluctuations triggered by Japan and the United States, a refrain which

30 Jenkins, Roy, *European Diary*, cited in: Jenkins, *op. cit.*, p. 446. Another 'Europeanist', Lord Carrington, was similarly to recall that, when he became Foreign Secretary in 1979 under Mrs Thatcher: 'I had no great knowledge of the other European statesmen with whom I would be deal-ing, no detailed knowledge of Europe or Community affairs. I had, however, conviction' (Carrington, Lord (1988), *Reflections On Things Past* (London, Collins), pp. 314–315).

31 Jenkins, Roy, *op. cit.*, p. 463.

32 Moravcsik, *op. cit.*, p. 296.

33 Jenkins, *op. cit.*, p. 475.

was persistently to preoccupy European leaders. Their answer was to propose various measures. These ranged from pooling 15 to 20 percent of the official reserves of the member states, to the increased use of a common currency unit in central bank transactions, designed eventually to be the basis for a single currency.[34]

Despite discussion of this 'plan' being a central feature of the Copenhagen Council, no formal decision was made. Instead, secret discussions took place between personal representatives of Giscard, Schmidt, and Callaghan – whose support was being canvassed – in order to forestall opposition from central bankers, finance ministries and, most importantly, the *Bundesbank*. According to one commentator:

'The other six national chief executives, their finance ministers, and central bank presidents, as well as senior officials meeting in the Monetary, Central Bank and ECOFIN committees, were left in complete ignorance. The Danish prime minister, responsible for setting the Council agenda, heard nothing and assumed plans had been abandoned.'[35]

Schmidt was unable to convince Callaghan that Britain should join the EMS. Having just weathered a major sterling crisis, Britain was geared to stimulating economic growth, whereas the German plan was deflationary. In addition Callaghan was more interested in taking intergovernmental action through existing institutions such as the IMF.

At the Bremen European Council in July, therefore, after a series of bad-tempered meetings, Callaghan pulled out altogether. But, by promising additional funds for regional development, particularly to the Italians and the Irish, Schmidt won agreement from the rest of the member states. Jenkins left Bremen 'in a high state of morale' but 'with substantially diminished hope of Britain at last learning its lesson and participating in a European initiative with enthusiasm and from the beginning'. His interest, he wrote, 'became increasingly that of avoiding Britain holding up the advance of others'.[36]

Even without the British, agreement on the details of the new system was reached only with considerable manipulation. Its complexities defy description in a non-technical briefing, replete as they were with such terms as 'parity grid system', 'asymmetrical obligations' and 'variable geometry'. What was significant, however, was that the final details of the agreement, during a bilateral summit between Giscard and Schmidt, were kept secret.

This meeting, in September 1978, was held at Aachen, where Charlemagne had been both born and buried as the first Holy Roman Emperor. Press officials of both governments stressed the historical reverberations of this joint-visit to the throne of Charlemagne, evoking memories of the historic meeting between Adenauer and de Gaulle at Rheims, nearly two decades earlier. Giscard remarked that 'Perhaps when we discussed monetary problems, the spirit of Charlemagne brooded over us'.[37]

34 Moravscik, *op. cit.*, p. 296.
35 Ludlow, Peter, cited in Moravcsik, *op. cit.*, p. 279.
36 Jenkins, Roy, *op. cit.*, p. 481.
37 Cited by Ludlow, in Moravcsik, *op. cit.*, p. 301. It would later be pointed out by Bernard Connolly, a senior Commission economist and the first of the Commission 'whistleblowers', that all this was

The details were agreed at the Brussels European Council on 4 to 5 December 1978. From 1 January 1979, the ERM would come into being. Currencies in the system could join the 'narrow band', in which they would be permitted to keep within a maximum margin of fluctuation of 2.25 percent. When this margin was reached, there would be 'automatic intervention with no limit as to amount'.[38] Member states with floating currencies could opt for a six percent margin, the so-called 'broad band'.

In the communiqué, the political objective was made very clear. The EMS would give 'fresh impetus to the process of European Union'.[39] After the Council, the heads of government and the president of the Commission issued a joint statement, emphasising its importance 'for the future of the building of Europe'.[40]

Despite the euphoria, Britain's refusal to join the ERM had rankled with Giscard. His revenge was to demand that France be given the same share of a planned increase to the Regional Fund as Britain.[41] This effectively blocked any increase whatever, leaving Britain again uncompensated for the disparity of CAP funding. Furthermore Britain's budget contribution was due to rise by nine percent, threatening within five years to make her the Community's largest net contributor.

Of these events, Jenkins later recalled, 'It still seems to me impossible to explain what had come over Giscard.'[42] Were he familiar with the historical record he would have known that, as a French president, Giscard was acting entirely in character. After this 'dismal anti-climax' of a European Council, Jenkins observed, 'the affairs of Europe retreated behind an opaque screen in a way I have never known them do before or since'. The key to what he was describing lay entirely in the conduct of the French government.[43] Yet to Professor George, Britain was the 'awkward partner'.

The 'bloody British question'

The problem of Britain's disproportionate contribution to the Community budget had now become a matter of serious concern to the Labour government. Known by the Community as the BBQ (British Budgetary Question), Jenkins and many others took to calling it the 'Bloody British Question'.[44] It was now poisoning relations between Britain and the Community more than any other issue.

---

based on a deliberate deception. Although designed primarily to meet German needs, the EMS had been carefully dressed up to look more as if it served French interests. This explained the choice of word ECU (European Currency Unit) for the new unit of accounting, because it was reminiscent of the *écu*, a French coin from the time of the Valois. (*Cf.* Connolly, Bernard (1995), *The Rotten Heart Of Europe – The Dirty War For Europe's Money* (London, Faber and Faber), p. 17.)

38 Bulletin of the European Communities, 12-1978, point 1.1.7.
39 *Op. cit.*, point 1.1.10.
40 *Op. cit.*, point 1.1.12.
41 Jenkins, *op. cit.*, p. 485.
42 *Op. cit.*, p. 486.
43 *Op. cit.*, p. 488.
44 *Op. cit.*, p. 489.

By the end of 1976, even while transitional arrangements still applied, Britain was already the third largest net contributor to the budget – after Germany and Belgium. A year later she had become the second largest, and by 1980, it was calculated, she would be the largest, paying subsidies to French farmers while the French blocked increases to regional funds. And now her politicians had the temerity to complain.

Complain they did. At a speech at the Lord Mayor's banquet in the Guildhall in London, on 13 November 1978, Callaghan made it clear Britain as the largest net contributor, with *per capita* income ranking only seventh out of nine, was unacceptable.[45] David Owen, who had taken over as Foreign Secretary after Crosland's untimely death, told the House of Commons next day that even the current situation could not 'be good for the Community, any more than it is for the United Kingdom'.[46]

Predictably, Britain's complaints got short shrift. For sure, she had not been party to the original budgetary negotiations. But had she not accepted the arrangements as part of the *acquis communautaire*? Had there not been renegotiations? Yet now the British were saying, 'no, we still do not like the rules; you must change them to suit us yet again'. The French simply blamed Britain for importing food from the Commonwealth, on which levies had to be paid. They could buy Irish, French or Danish produce. Not to do so was a wilfully anti-Communitarian, and if they wished to reduce their contributions, all they had to do was to exercise Community preference.[47] So it was all Britain's fault. She was, after all, the 'awkward partner'.

'I want my money back!'

March 1979 saw an event which was to transform the politics of Britain and Europe. After the disastrous 'winter of discontent', when Britain had been paralysed by an avalanche of industrial disputes, the Callaghan government was defeated on a vote of confidence in the Commons by just one vote. The general election brought the Conservatives a clear majority of 44 seats. On 4 May 1979, Thatcher walked into 10 Downing Street, where she was to remain for 11 years.

Shortly after she took office, the first direct elections for the European Parliament were held. During the campaign, Thatcher emphasised her 'vision' of the Community, in her words, 'as a force for freedom'.

'We believe in a free Europe, not a standardised Europe. Diminish that variety within the member states, and you impoverish the whole Community... We insist that the institutions of the European Community are managed so that they increase the liberty of the individual throughout the continent. These institutions must not be permitted to dwindle into bureaucracy. Whenever they fail to enlarge freedom the institutions should be criticised and the balance restored.'[48]

45 *The Times*, 14 November, 1978. Cited in George, *op. cit.*, p. 133.
46 *Hansard*, 14 November 1978, col. 214.
47 George, *op. cit.*, p. 134.
48 *Op. cit.*, p. 61.

Yet a smaller percentage of the electorate turned out to vote than anywhere else in the Community and the results simply mirrored the voting pattern of the general election, giving the Conservatives 60 of 78 seats.

The Conservatives' apparent enthusiasm for 'Europe' was seen as 'positive' by many pro-Marketeers. Very quickly, however, Thatcher was thrust into the maelstrom of EEC politics, attending her first European Council on 21 to 22 June 1979. France hosted the talks, choosing Strasbourg as their venue in recognition of the new importance of the European Parliament. Already, there were signs that one issue above all was going to dominate the early days of Thatcher's relationship with the EEC: the budget.

From the first, as Thatcher wrote in her memoirs, 'my policy was to seek to limit the damage and distortions caused by the CAP and to bring financial realities to bear on Community spending'. She had already told Chancellor Schmidt that she would be seeking 'large reductions' and was hoping he would pass the message on to Giscard, who was chairing the Council.[49] Her short term objectives were to have the budget question raised at the Council and to gain acceptance of the need for action, with a firm assurance that, at the next Council meeting in Dublin, the Commission would bring forward proposals to deal with the problem.[50] But, as an indication of what was to come, she observed:

'I knew that Chancellor Schmidt was keen that we should commit sterling to the ERM; but I already had my doubts about the wisdom of this course, which were subsequently reinforced. In any case, my announcement of our intentions as regards the "ecu" swap did not receive much visible welcome from the others: like other such concessions to the *ésprit communautaire*, it appears simply to be pocketed and then forgotten.'[51]

Her disillusionment, however, was quickly reinforced. She knew the budget issue had to be raised on the first day, because the final Council communiqué was always drafted overnight by officials, for discussion on the second and last day. During lunch, she had gained a 'strong impression' from Giscard that he would deal with the budget early on. But, when the meeting resumed, it became clear that Giscard was intent on following the set agenda. By the end of the formal session, almost everything had been discussed, except the one thing Thatcher wanted to talk about. She describes in her memoirs what happened next:

'President Giscard proposed that as time was getting on and we needed to get ready for dinner, the matter of the budget should be discussed the following day. Did the Prime Minister of the United Kingdom agree? And so at my very first European Council I had to say "no".'[52]

However, the lateness of the hour worked in her favour, proximity to dinner concentrating minds. She won agreement that the Commission would be instructed to prepare a proposal for the next Council. Nevertheless, even Jenkins conceded that Thatcher had been 'very oddly treated'.[53] Afterwards, she overheard

49 *Op. cit.*, p. 62.
50 *Op. cit.*, p. 63.
51 *Ibid.*
52 *Op. cit.*, p. 64.
53 Jenkins, *op. cit.*, p. 494.

a foreign government official make a remark that pleased her 'as much as any I can remember'. 'Britain is back,' he said.[54]

The Dublin Council was not due until late November and, in the interim, Thatcher was determined to let the member states know she was serious about the budget. On 18 October, delivering in Luxembourg the Winston Churchill Memorial Lecture, she warned:

'I must be absolutely clear about this. Britain cannot accept the present situation on the Budget. It is demonstrably unjust. It is politically indefensible: I cannot play Sister Bountiful to the Community while my own electorate are being asked to forego improvements in the fields of health, education, welfare and the rest.'[55]

In meetings with Schmidt and Giscard, she brought the topic up again. They 'knew that I meant business', she wrote. In Dublin Castle, after a friendly lunch at the Irish President's official residence, Thatcher set out the British case, emphasising her commitment to the Community and her wish to avoid a crisis. But there was no meeting of minds.

'Some, for example the Dutch prime minister, Mr Andries Van Agt, were reasonable, but most were not. I had the strong feeling that they had decided to test whether I was able and willing to stand up to them. It was quite shameless: they were determined to keep as much of our money as they could.'[56]

By the time the Council broke up, Britain had been offered a £350 million rebate, leaving her net contribution at £650 million. This was simply not enough. Thatcher was not going to accept it. She agreed that there should be another Council to discuss it, but was not over-optimistic that resolution would be reached. Even Hugo Young had to concede, of the others, that:

'... in response to her unsubtle demands for a fair deal, they were rude and derisive, and determined not to meet her anywhere near halfway. Roy Jenkins, a witness, writes that Schmidt feigned sleep during one of her harangues. At another point, Giscard had his motorcade drawn up at the door, engines revving, to signal that he would delay no longer. "I will not allow such a contemptible spectacle to occur again," he said as he departed.'[57]

Young did, however, note that Thatcher had 'broken all the rules': 'the smootheries of conventional diplomacy, the spirit of give-and-take on which the whole European edifice depended, were plainly values she could never be relied on to observe'.[58] But Thatcher was finding that 'give-and-take', in European terms, meant, 'you give, we take'. She could at least take some comfort from *Le Figaro*, which commented:

---

54 *Ibid.*
55 Thatcher, *op. cit.*, p. 79.
56 *Op. cit.*, p. 81. By now Thatcher was becoming known for the phrase 'We want our money back!', and was even sometimes heard to call it 'my money', according to the UK's Commissioner Christopher Tugendhat. (Young, Hugo (1990), *One Of Us* (London, Pan Books), p. 187.)
57 Young, *op. cit.*, p. 314.
58 *Ibid.*

'To accuse Mrs Thatcher of wishing to torpedo Europe because she defends the interests of her country is to question her underlying intentions in the same way that people used to question those of de Gaulle in regard to French interests.'[59]

So the battle continued into 1980. To begin with, Francesco Cossiga, the prime minister of Italy, which had now assumed the rotating presidency, seemed to be working for a solution, under pressure from Thatcher. On 25 February, Schmidt was back in London for talks, which again centred on the budget question, but with Schmidt repeating his wish to see sterling within the ERM. By the next Council, on 27 to 28 April, its venue moved to Luxembourg, Cossiga, after breakfasting with Giscard in Paris, believed that the French were willing to offer a solution: a ceiling on Britain's net contributions for a period of years, subject to a review at the end of that time.

Thatcher was suspicious. On closer examination 'it became clear that what the French really wanted were decisions on their most politically sensitive topics – farm prices in the CAP, lamb and fishing rights – before dealing with the budget'.[60] It gradually emerged that, as so often before, the French proposals were less helpful than at first appeared. After the agriculture ministers had given the French more or less all that they wanted, the *quid pro quo* was merely a modest rebate on Britain's net contribution, for one year only.[61] Thatcher had already made it abundantly clear that she wanted a permanent solution, although she did not dismiss the French response as an insult, although by any reckoning it was. She did nevertheless reject the 'offer', prompting Jenkins to call the meeting a 'fiasco'.[62]

Thatcher still expected a solution, not least because both the French and Germans wanted higher agricultural prices and the British could veto them. If she did, the Community would run out of money by 1982. The French response was to consider abolishing the 'Luxembourg Compromise', to prevent Thatcher using it against them. Introduced by de Gaulle to protect France's 'vital interests', when there was a possibility that Britain might use it, the French wanted it abolished.

By now it was clear there was going to be no quick solution and the complexity of what became a prolonged battle is illustrated by the fact that no historical account of it has ever managed to encompass all its twists and turns.[63] Young's version of the next step in the battle is that, after Thatcher had made such a mess of Dublin, it took clever negotiation by the Foreign Office to come up with a reasonable solution, whereby Britain would be given reduction for two years, with the possibility of this being extended to a third.[64]

Thatcher's version is that her tactics at Dublin and Luxembourg had their desired effect, producing a willingness to solve the budget issue before the next

---

59 Thatcher, *op. cit.*, p. 82.
60 *Op. cit.*, p. 84.
61 *Ibid.*
62 Jenkins, *op. cit.*, p. 504.
63 See, for instance, Young, *op. cit.*, pp. 311–325. He scarcely mentions the Luxembourg Council, skipping directly from Dublin to the foreign ministers meeting which took place the month following (see below).
64 Young, *op. cit.*, p. 317.

European Council, scheduled for Venice in June.[65] She sent her Foreign Secretary Lord Carrington, with his colleague Ian Gilmour, both 'convinced Europeans', to Brussels on Thursday, 29 May, for a special meeting with other foreign ministers. After a marathon 18-hour session, they reached what they considered an acceptable agreement, but Thatcher would not immediately accept it. Only after Gilmour contacted various Sunday newspapers, leaking to them the outcome of the Brussels talks but with heavy spin that it represented a 'Thatcherite triumph', did she agree 'through gritted teeth' to the outcome. In a Cabinet reshuffle soon afterwards Gilmour was dropped.

For continuity it is as well to stay with the story of the rebate battle, because the compromise agreed by the Carrington/Gilmour duo was far from the final solution. The issue would continue to fester on through 1982 and into 1983, until it again became the central bone of contention at a European Council meeting in Stuttgart on 17 to 19 June 1983. By then there had been significant changes at the top table. Following her victory in the Falklands War in 1982, and the beginnings of economic recovery after Britain's deep recession of 1981, Thatcher led the Conservatives to a landslide election victory on 15 June. Giscard and Schmidt, the two dominant figures of the Franco-German alliance, had now been replaced by Mitterrand and Kohl. From Dublin, where Thatcher had been the tyro, she was now the senior figure.

At Stuttgart, Chancellor Kohl was anxious to make a success of his first Council in the chair, but for Thatcher there was only one issue: the need to 'to make as much progress as possible towards a long-term solution to the budget question'. This, she had decided, meant full-scale reform of the Community's finances[66]:

'... the Community was on the edge of bankruptcy: the exhaustion of its "own resources" was only months away and it was possible to increase them only by agreement of all the member states to raise the one percent VAT "ceiling"... The requirement of unanimity gave me a strong hand and they knew that I was not the person to underplay it.'[67]

Thatcher thought the Community could easily have lived within the discipline imposed by the one percent VAT ceiling, if only it would cut out waste, inefficiency and corruption. But she judged that the will was lacking 'and that profligacy and that particular degree of irresponsibility which is bred by unaccountable bureaucracy' would continue for as long as difficult decisions could be postponed.[68] In the event, the Council did postponed a decision on financial reform, agreeing only to further negotiations, the results of which would be presented to the Council in Athens at the end of the year.

When the Council met in Athens in December 1983, under the Greek presidency, Thatcher was well-prepared. But, from the start, things went badly awry. At the first session, Mitterrand seemed unprepared and Kohl seemed unwilling or

---

65 Thatcher, *op. cit.*, p. 85.
66 Young, *op. cit.*, pp. 312–313.
67 *Op. cit.*, p. 313.
68 *Ibid.*

unable to make much effective contribution.[69] Neither was the Greek prime minister, Papandreou, helpful.

Thus, on the first day, nothing was achieved, and it was to get worse. On the Monday morning, to Thatcher's astonishment, Mitterrand announced that his position on the budget had completely changed. He was no longer prepared to support Britain's fight for a long-term budget settlement. Instead, he would sanction only another *ad hoc* payment.[70] Thatcher retaliated by refusing to agree an increase in the Community's 'own resources' unless CAP spending was contained and its overall proportion of the budget reduced. She then demanded that member state contributions should be 'fair and in-line with their ability to pay'. 'The argument continued,' Thatcher wrote, 'but I was clearly getting nowhere.'[71]

No communiqué was issued at the end of another Council generally regarded as 'a fiasco'.[72] Much has been made of Thatcher's supposed 'anti-European' stance during this period, but at the time, she was to recall, she genuinely believed that, once the budget contribution had been sorted out and a framework of financial order had been set in place, Britain would be able to play a strong positive role in the Community. She considered herself a 'European idealist', imbued with a vision of a free-enterprise *Europe des patries*.[73]

Even Professor George, concedes that this 'fiasco' was due almost entirely to Mitterrand. His intervention, George writes, 'was either a terrible error, or an indication of more Machiavellian thinking'. One explanation was that Mitterrand was stalling, so that discussions could be carried over into the French presidency, allowing the French government to claim the credit for reaching an agreement.[74]

Thatcher's Foreign Secretary since the 1983 election had been Geoffrey Howe, a fervent 'Europeanist' since boyhood, and despite witnessing the Athens *debacle*, he was later to write that everything was now 'up to France, which took over the presidency of the Community (sic) for the first half of 1984'.[75] The French, he observed,

'... were ideal negotiating partners for this closing stage of the battle. For they, better than most, could recognise the strength of our determination in defence of national interest. Moreover, they had the intellectual agility to identify, and argue with skill, the points where negotiation could oblige us to temper the strength of our case. We were aiming together to find an answer which the French Presidency could then sell to the other partners and table for acceptance at the Brussels meeting of the European Council on 19th to 20th March 1984, en route for the Fontainebleau Summit [*sic*] in June.'[76]

Despite Howe's glowing testimony to their skills, these 'intellectually agile' French failed to table any proposals for the Brussels Council and were not even

---

69 Thatcher, *op. cit.*, p. 337.
70 George, *op. cit.*, p. 153.
71 Thatcher, *op. cit.*, p. 338.
72 *Ibid.*
73 Thatcher, *op. cit.*, p. 536.
74 George, *op. cit.*, p. 153.
75 Howe, *op. cit.*, p. 398.
76 *Op. cit.*, p. 399.

properly prepared for it. Thatcher was. She had already discussed the issue with Mitterrand, at meetings in January in Paris, and in March at Chequers. In February she talked it over with Kohl at Number 10. She was thus confident that the Brussels Council, at last, would deliver a lasting solution to the 'BBQ'.[77]

When the meeting began, on 19 March, Mitterrand at least started proceedings with a discussion of the budget. Then officials were sent away to work on a text relating to the budget while Mitterrand turned to the issue of the Community 'own resource'. His real agenda now became clear. He wanted to increase contributions from VAT receipts to 1.6 percent, thus increasing CAP funds, from which France would benefit most. The Irish, now the Community's largest net beneficiary per head of population, thanks to the size of their farming sector, wanted an even larger increase.[78]

For once, Thatcher and Kohl had something in common. Both set 1.4 percent as their limit, making even that dependent on satisfactorily resolving the Community spending plan. That was as far as they got and, to Thatcher's frustration, the session the next day began with 'a gush of Euro-idealism'. Kohl and Mitterrand became 'quite lyrical on the subject of getting rid of frontier controls', followed by Mitterrand's urging that Europe should not be left behind by the USA in the space race.[79] When, at last, the heads of government got down to business, 'the high-mindedness quickly disappeared'. When the Irish prime minister failed to win a special exemption from proposed milk quota limits, aimed at trimming the Community's vast milk surplus, he invoked the Luxembourg Compromise and walked out. Only after a long adjournment to discuss the text of the Council communiqué did business resume.

What happened then left Thatcher dumbstruck. Despite their earlier agreement, the Italians and Greeks stood out against giving Thatcher her permanent reduction. Mitterrand seemed to side with them. When Thatcher protested that she had been fighting for five years for a fair and lasting settlement, Kohl, possibly by previous agreement with Mitterrand, offered her 'a 1,000 million ecu rebate for five years'. Even Howe called this proposal 'half-baked'.[80] But, almost immediately, France and the rest agreed with Germany. Naturally Thatcher rejected the 'offer'. The Council broke up without issuing a communiqué, and 'to rub salt into the wound', as Thatcher later described it, France and Italy blocked payment of Britain's 1983 refund.

Back in Britain, Thatcher decided she would stop British payments to the Community, if she had the backing of her MPs. But, she wrote, 'there was a hard core of Euro-enthusiasts... who instinctively supported the Community in any dispute with Britain'. Reluctantly, she abandoned the 'nuclear option'.[81]

Clearly though, the arguments had to end. The next European Council, to be held at Fontainebleau on 25 to 26 June 1984, and chaired by Mitterrand on his

77 Thatcher, *op. cit.*, p. 538.
78 *Ibid.*
79 *Op. cit.*, p. 539.
80 Howe, *op. cit.*, p. 400.
81 Thatcher, *op. cit.*, p. 539.

home ground, had to be 'le grand showdown'. But again, Thatcher was forced to cool her heels. After the obligatory opening lunch, Mitterrand asked her to sum up the results of a recent economic summit in London. Others then joined in to give their views. Two hours passed. Only then did Mitterrand turn to the budget and, no sooner had Thatcher given her views on a formula, he 'remitted' the matter to the foreign ministers for discussion later that evening, and moved on to other business.[82]

During the dinner that evening, at the prestigious Hôtellerie du Bas-Bréau, the heads of government were puzzled to see the foreign ministers assembling on the terrace over their coffee. Initially they assumed their colleagues had completed their work, only to find that they were regaling each other with stories of their foreign travels. Mitterrand did not conceal his displeasure, and chased them back inside to continue discussing the budget.

Throughout the whole budget saga, there had been a central sticking point. Britain had insisted on basing their calculations on the total sum she sent to the Community, which included money collected from tariffs and levies as well as the contribution from VAT. The French, however, still refused to accept customs charges as national contributions, arguing that they constituted the Community's 'own resource'. Doggedly, therefore, they would not allow these sums to be included. Then, at Fontainebleau, the French produced a paper on their views as to how the calculation should be made. Once again, only VAT payments were included.

During the foreign ministers' discussion, all this was again given an airing and Thatcher wearily conceded the point, so long as a formula was arrived at based on a percentage of VAT payments to give Britain the permanent rebate she wanted. All that now had to be agreed was the percentage. Thatcher had in mind 70 percent, but Howe came back with the news that between 50 and 60 percent would be offered, with a 'sweetener' that would bring the rebate up to 1000 million ecus for the first two years. 'How Geoffrey,' Thatcher wrote, 'who had been splendidly staunch in the negotiations so far, had allowed the foreign ministers to reach such a conclusion I could not understand.' [83]

To cut a wearisome story short, Thatcher held out for her 70 percent, Mitterrand stuck at 60 and Kohl said he would accept 65. Then Thatcher went for two-thirds, a round 66 percent. Mitterrand caved in. Faced with an unmoving Thatcher, he told her, 'Of course, Madame Prime Minister, you must have it.' An agreement had been reached.[84] Immediately, however, Kohl announced that, since German money had made the settlement possible, he wanted to pay his farmers extra money from Federal funds. Although this was against the rules, no one had the stomach to oppose him.[85]

Even this was far from the end of the story. Tied up in the small print was the establishment of a 'correction mechanism' for dealing with the continuing budgetary imbalances. Its complexity was such that, according to Hugo Young, it was

82 *Op. cit.*, p. 542.
83 *Op. cit.*, p. 543.
84 *Op. cit.*, p. 544.
85 *Ibid.*

'outside the comprehension of every normal European citizen'.[86] Even the Commission itself was to admit that it 'inhibited transparency in the financial relationships between the Member States and the Community budget'.[87]

In 1988 at the Brussels European Council, further revisions were made to the funding system where what became known as the 'Own Resources Decision' was made. This laid down that VAT would henceforth play a reduced role in funding the Community, and introduced a new, fourth form of 'own resource' whereby each member state would make an additional payment representing a proportion of its Gross National Product (GNP). This, in turn, created new distortions and required a new mechanism to calculate Britain's rebate. So complicated was the calculation that, according to the Commission's own reckoning, it produced *the somewhat surprising result that the United Kingdom appears to participate in the financing of its own rebate* [our emphasis].[88]

While the Commission suggested that this 'self-financing' involved only 'very small amounts', the cumulative effects of the Fontainebleau agreement and the Brussels 'adjustment' were to be substantial. They created a situation whereby, whenever the UK applied for CAP funds over and above a threshold level agreed in 1984, the Commission, through its 'correction mechanism', was (and is) able to 'claw back' a substantial proportion of the funds paid. By 2003 this equated to 71 percent.

Because this meant that, in applying for certain funds from Brussels, the Treasury would end up paying for most of them itself, the British government decided that, having won her rebate, Britain should take maximum advantage from it. Therefore, wherever possible, the UK would refuse to apply for such funds, even though other member states were doing so. This further meant that other countries were able to draw on considerably more money for their farmers from Brussels than was available to British farmers, whose ability to match the prices of their EEC competitors was thus reduced.

By 2003, this would have become a significant contributory factor in the collapse of British agriculture. Thatcher's 'victory' turned out to be a very mixed blessing.

---

86 Young, *op. cit.*, p. 323.
87 Commission of the European Communities (1998), Bulletin EU 10-1998 – Agenda 2000. Financing of the European Union (1998), Luxembourg.
88 Commission of the European Communities. Financing the European Union. Commission report on the operation of the own resources system (1998), Luxembourg.

Chapter 11

Enter Mr Spinelli: 1979–1986

'I recall one low point when nine foreign ministers from the major countries of Europe solemnly assembled in Brussels to spend several hours discussing how to resolve our differences on standardising a fixed position of rear-view mirrors on agricultural tractors.'

James Callaghan[1]

'The Heads of State or Government, on the basis of an awareness of a common destiny and the wish to affirm the European identity, confirm their commitment to progress towards an ever closer union among the peoples and Member States of the European Community.'

Solemn Declaration on European Union, Stuttgart, 19 June 1983

On 16 March 1979, Monnet, the first and at the time only honorary 'Citizen of Europe', died at his home in the French countryside 30 miles outside Paris, at the age of 90 years and four months. Four days later Chancellor Schmidt joined Giscard in the nearby mediaeval church of Montfort l'Amuary for his funeral, along with friends from all over Europe and several of his long-time allies from Washington, led by George Ball. The music chosen for the service included pieces by French, German, Italian and English composers, culminating in a recorded version of all five verses of 'The Battle Hymn of the Republic'.[2] As this rousing American chorus rang through the nave, Giscard wrote later that a Frenchman almost felt left out.[3]

In his brief retirement, according to his biographer, Monnet had 'come to question his life's work'. 'Was European union too narrow for a changing world? Had the Common Market really added to growth?' He hoped Europe had 'at least secured peace between France and Germany'. But even there, it might be argued, 'the American presence in Europe had mattered more than a European Community reduced, it seemed, to a customs union'.

It was true that, in the years immediately preceding Monnet's death, the great advance towards 'ever closer union' seemed to have lost much of its impetus. On the level of 'high politics', those brave dreams of the earlier 1970s, the proposals

---

1 Callaghan, James (1987), *Time And Chance* (London, Collins), p. 304.

2 Ball, *op. cit.*, pp. 98–99.

3 Duchêne, *op. cit.*, p. 340. Duchêne records how, in 1988, to mark the centenary of Monnet's birth, Mitterrand arranged for his ashes to be transferred to the grandiose neo-classical setting of the Pantheon in Paris, to lie alongside the remains of such legendary French heroes as Rousseau, Voltaire, Victor Hugo and Emile Zola. Mitterrand addressed a torchlit ceremony on the steps, attended by Chancellor Kohl and many other European dignitaries, who stood for a performance of the 'European anthem' adapted from Beethoven's Ninth Symphony. Monnet's home at Houjarray was bought by the European Parliament as a shrine to his memory.

for full economic and monetary union by 1980, for political union and a common foreign policy, still seemed as far away as ever.

The only place where the momentum of the 'European construction' seemed unflagging in the late 1970s was on what might be described as the level of 'low politics', where the Commission, in alliance with the European Court of Justice, had now become more active than ever in extending its supranational powers, in the name of 'completing the internal market'.

Once internal tariffs had been removed, though, this served to highlight the 'non-tariff barriers', by which individual states were still able to frustrate the emergence of a true 'common market'. These forms of protectionism ranged from national rules and standards which could be used to exclude imports from other countries, to the various forms of 'state aid' by which governments could give their own producers financial advantage over their competitors. It was on this protectionism that the Commission now launched an assault, and it did so on two main fronts.

The first, using its right to initiate all Community legislation, was through a deluge of new directives and regulations designed to 'harmonise' or 'approximate' the laws of member states'. Each replaced different national laws, imposing a single Community law in their place. By the late 1970s, the output of new Community laws had risen to some 350 a year and, as always, the real agenda was further integration.

Nothing better typifies the way the Commission was now extending its supranational tentacles into every 'nook and cranny' of economic life than the nature of the new laws (each identified by its reference number, accompanied by year of issue), such as:

73/361 Council Directive on the approximation of the laws of the Member States relating to the certification and marking of wire ropes, chains and hooks.

74/409 Council Directive on the harmonisation of the laws of the Member States relating to honey.

74/360 Council Directive on the approximation of the laws of the Member States relating to the interior fittings of motor vehicles (interior parts of the passenger compartment other than the interior rear view mirrors, layout of controls, the roof or sliding roof, the backrest and rear part of the seats).[4]

Reflecting the fact that the CAP was still responsible for 90 percent of the Community budget, it generated more law than any other sector, ranging from a long succession of directives which limited the number of plant varieties permissible in the EEC, to items such as:

Commission Regulation No. 1297/77 amending for the fourth time Regulation No. 1019/70 on detailed rules for establishing free-at-frontier offer prices and fixing the countervailing charge in the wine sector.

---

4 This was just one of what would eventually be more than 450 directives controlling the production of motor vehicles. All details of legislation taken from the *Official Journal of the European Communities: Directory of Community Legislation in Force, op. cit.*

The second front on which the Commission launched its assault on national protectionism was through an attack on the financial assistance given by member states to their own industries. In its efforts to stamp out 'illegal state aid', the Commission intervened to eliminate 'unfair competition' in all kinds of economic activity, from shipbuilding to textiles. It did this partly through legislation, but its most useful ally in this battle was the ECJ, whose chief purpose was to act as the Community's 'Supreme Court' in reinforcing supranationalism.

In 1977, the ECJ confirmed that the Treaty of Rome amounted to the 'internal constitution' of the Community, which member states were bound to obey.[5] One measure of the growing importance of the court's 'constitutional' role was that, in the 10 years before 1979, the number of cases heard annually by the ECJ had averaged 113, whereas in the five years afterwards this figure would more than quadruple, to 514. With the ECJ's aid, for instance, the Commission challenged government monopolies in France and Italy on the sale of tobacco, alcohol and matches. Another landmark was the *Cassis de Dijon* case in 1979, when, with the Commission's support, a German firm challenged the German state authorities. They had refused to allow the import of a French blackcurrant liqueur because its alcohol content of 15–20 percent was lower than the 32 percent prescribed by German law. The ECJ ruled that any product lawfully produced in one country could be legally sold in another, even if there was no Community law specifically related to those products,[6] thus cementing in the doctrine of 'mutual recognition'. No longer could any member state control the flow of goods across its borders by applying its own national standards.

In all this torrent of legislative activity, the role of the third leg of the Community tripod, the Council of Ministers, seemed strangely marginal. Ministers found themselves spending much of their time giving formal approval to a constant stream of directives and regulations, the details of which had been negotiated by officials, the technicalities of which often seemed beyond their comprehension.[7] In 1977, for instance, Britain's Minister of Agriculture, John Silkin, found himself by the accident of Britain's 'presidency' having to sign into law the Sixth VAT directive, a complex attempt to harmonise all the items on which member states would be obliged to levy VAT. It was unlikely that, as farming minister, Silkin was fully *au fait* with the implications of what was to become a significant landmark in the history of the Community's long-term ambition to harmonise taxes, but it is his signature which stands at the bottom of the directive.

Worthy though all these efforts to extend the supranational tentacles of the Community might have seemed, they also gave justification to Monnet's fear that

---

5 CJEC, opinion 1/76 of 26 April 1977, ECR 741.

6 *Rewe-Zentral* v. *Bundesmonopolverwaltung für Branntwein*, Case 120/78 [1979] ECR 649 [1979]3 CMLR 494. See also Weatherill, Stephen, and Beaumont, Paul (1995), *EC Law – The Essential Guide to the Legal Workings of the European Community* (2nd ed.) (London, Penguin Books), pp. 490–542.

7 Callaghan was to record his frustration at this in the passage from his memoirs quoted at the head of this chapter, preceded by recalling his bafflement at finding himself having to correspond with his 'Chancellor, Denis Healey about import levels of apricot halves and canned fruit salad'. (*op. cit.*, p. 304).

his great dream was petering out in a sea of humdrum technocracy. From where was the impetus to come which would breathe new life into his great project? Who would bring it back to its original lofty aim of building a 'United States of Europe'?

The answer was to lie in an event which took place just after his death, with the first elections for the European Parliament. The man who would now take on the baton from Monnet was one of the first members of the elected parliament: Alterio Spinelli. Yet, despite Spinelli having conceived his own vision of a United States of Europe nearly 40 years earlier, when confined to his prison cell on the island of Ventotene, through most of those intervening four decades he had played little active part in the 'project'.

In most accounts of the history of the European Union, the years of the early 1980s are dismissed as a time of 'Eurosclerosis', when the march of integration appeared to have stalled. British accounts of that period are dominated almost entirely by Thatcher's endless battle for her rebate. The moment when the 'project' began to move forward again is generally identified with the arrival of Jacques Delors as Commission president in 1985. Yet it was in the early 1980s that the foundations which enabled Delors to make such an impact were laid. What was being planned was the most dramatic leap forward in integration of all: a 'Treaty on European Union'. This was so ambitious that, for tactical reasons, it was eventually decided that it should be divided into two separate treaties, five years apart. The first would be known as the Single European Act; the second was to become the Treaty of Maastricht. The man responsible for the planning this historic move was Spinelli.

The 'Crocodile Club'

During the decades after the war, although he served as a deputy in the Italian parliament, Spinelli had been effectively excluded from mainstream 'European' politics, not least by Monnet, who had no time for his Communist antecedents. He is not mentioned in Monnet's memoirs, published in 1978, and Duchêne notes, in his only reference to Spinelli, that he was a man 'whom Monnet respected but with whom he did not agree'.[8] The disapproval was mutual. Spinelli once remarked that Monnet had 'the great merit of having built Europe and the great responsibility to have built it badly'.[9]

Spinelli had actually been in Brussels between 1972 and 1976 as one of Italy's two Commissioners, but served without distinction. It was only after Monnet's death in 1979 that he came out of the shadows, at the age of 72, to stand for the European Parliament. He chose to sit as an independent MEP attached to the Communist group. He had at last arrived on the stage for which he had been waiting through much of his life.

Spinelli first showed his hand on 25 June 1980, when the Parliament refused to adopt the Council's draft Community budget. The Council came under fire from

8 Urwin, *op. cit.*, p. 285.
9 Burgess, M. (1989), *Federalism And The European Union: Political Ideas, Influence And Strategy* (London, Routledge), pp. 55–56, cited in McAllister, *op. cit.*, pp. 156–157.

several speakers, but none so aggressive as Spinelli. He told his fellow MEPs that they must now take the destiny of the Community into their hands: 'I do not address the Council of Ministers', he told them, 'because it has demonstrated its total impotence'.[10]

Spinelli was convinced that the only way to bring a federal Europe to fruition was for Parliament to seize the initiative and to work for total reform of the Treaty of Rome. Using a rallying cry that was to become all too familiar in later years, he argued that what now made further integration a matter of urgency was 'enlargement': the prospect that within a few years the Community add three new members, Greece in 1981, soon to be followed by Spain and Portugal, when the 'Nine' would become 'Twelve'.

His first formal step towards his goal came in July 1980 when, with his assistant Pier Virgilio Dastoli,[11] he wrote to his fellow MEPs, inviting their support for a concerted move to further integration. Eight 'eager members' responded to his call, meeting at the prestigious Crocodile restaurant in Strasbourg. These included a German and an Italian Christian Democrat, an Italian Communist, two British Labour MEPs, including Richard Balfe, and a lone British Conservative, Stanley Johnson.[12]

So was born the 'Crocodile Club', a cross-party group open to all MEPs convinced 'of the need for European political reform of great width'. Spinelli aimed to outflank the existing party groupings, which he feared would block his initiative. As he explained later in a letter to a colleague:

'The European Parliament is elected using party electoral machines geared to national elections, which do not have European political programs but a vague trans-national background ... their members were divided substantially into three groups: innovators, eager to advance the union; "immobilists", eager to hold it where it was and to even make it regress; the swamp ... composed of those which do not know what they want. The innovators are conscious that they must rally around a common policy and, by ignoring party loyalties, they would conquer the prevailing influence of "the swamp".'

The Crocodile Club was to be the catalyst for 'awakening the innovators'.

The established parliamentary forum for promoting new ideas was the Political Affairs Committee. But this was dominated by the centre-right European Peoples' Party (EPP), hostile to Communists. Spinelli predicted that the committee would

---

10 The following section of the narrative is constructed from a history of Spinelli's activities of this period, written by Palayret, Jean-Marie (undated), 'Entre cellule Carbonara et conseiller des Princes: Impulsions et limites de la relance européenne dans le projet Spinelli d'Union politique des années 1980'. *users.skynet.be/clubcrocodile/Archive/ProjetSpinelli.htm* (translated by the authors), augmented by interviews with Richard Balfe MEP.

11 Dastoli had been *chef de cabinet* for Spinelli when he was president of the 'Independent Left' group in the Italian parliament. From July 1979 to June 1983, he became Spinelli's parliamentary assistant in the European Parliament. By 2003 he was a senior official of the European Parliament, had been secretary-general of the international European Movement since April 1995 and was a professor of the History of European Integration at Rome University.

12 Johnson had between 1973 and 1979 been a senior official of the European Commission, as head *inter alia* of its Prevention of Pollution and Nuisances Division. In 1984, he resumed his career in the Commission, becoming Director for Energy Policy in 1990. His son Boris was to become a prominent journalist and Conservative MP.

only give his project a 'first class burial'. Instead, he planned an *ad hoc* 'constitutional working group', which he could control. For this he needed a parliamentary resolution, to prepare the ground for which, in October 1980, he launched a 'semi-official periodical', *The Crocodile*.[13]

As expected, his resolution was treated with disdain by the established groups; Spinelli's 'forces of organised immobilism'. Even the Communists were reluctant to back him, and only did so when Spinelli made a direct appeal to Italy's national Communist leader, Enrico Berlinguer. The Christian Democrats, however, proved to be the main obstacle, using a procedural device to delay any vote on Spinelli's resolution, hoping that support would collapse.

Here a British MEP Richard Balfe, acting as Spinelli's 'tactical adviser',[14] took the initiative, launching a covert operation code-named 'Keep Silent'. He gradually enlisted support from his Socialist colleagues. The 'Club' attracted heavyweight support from the Italian prime minister Bettino Craxi, and several leading Social Democrats, including Willy Brandt and Erwin Lange (president of the Parliament's powerful budgets committee). In backing the resolution they were joined by the Liberal group, under its German leader Martin Bangemann, later a commissioner.

By this means the resolution gathered enough support to be passed on 9 July 1981, establishing a 'standing committee for the institutional problems charged to work out a modification of the existing treaties'. Spinelli thus won approval for the parliament 'to assume the initiative fully to give new momentum to the establishment of the European Union'.

By this time various senior national politicians were becoming alarmed at Spinelli's activity. At a national conference of the German Free Democrat party in 1981, Germany's foreign minister, Hans-Dietrich Genscher, put forward a 'gradualist' alternative. He then joined forces with Italy's foreign minister, Emilio Colombo, to produce what became known as the 'Genscher-Colombo Plan', which included a proposal for a new treaty to be known as the 'European Act'. This would formalise 'political co-operation' on foreign policy, binding on all member states, and a 'declaration' on economic integration.[15] They proposed that member states should work towards a European defence policy, independent of Nato.

To justify their proposal for a common foreign policy, Genscher and Colombo referred to a little-publicised meeting of foreign ministers which had taken place in London on 13 October 1981, under the chairmanship of Thatcher's Foreign Secretary Lord Carrington. The ministers had formulated new rules for political co-operation, building on the original agreement in Luxembourg in 1970, which they said had 'contributed to the ultimate objective of the European union'.[16] In London the ministers had already agreed to formalise their co-ordination of

---

13 The magazine survives to this day.
14 Interview with the authors, 2 December 2002.
15 European Parliament (1982), *Selection of Texts Concerning Institutional Matters of the Community from 1950–1982* (Luxembourg), pp. 492–499.
16 Reproduced in *Selection of Texts Concerning Institutional Matters of the Community from 1950–1982, op. cit.*, pp. 539–542.

foreign policy through what were termed 'Gymnich-type meetings',[17] taking place in private, without officials present, the contents of which would remain secret. It was also at this London meeting that arrangements were agreed for the so-called *troika* structure, to become famous during the Yugoslav crisis nine years later, whereby the government acting as president of the Council on the six-monthly rota system would act in concert with those which came before and after.

The Genscher-Colombo plan, incorporating the London agreement, was presented to the European Parliament on 19 November 1981, supported by the EPP. Colombo told the MEPs:

'We are calling for a revival of European integration, we want the institutions strengthened and the decision-making process improved and we want to encourage and extend to a greater degree the pragmatic process whereby political co-operation is achieved among our ten countries. In this way, co-operation will become more widespread on matters ranging from security to culture and law, which will bring us closer to the basic aims of a European union. We will achieve this by adopting a flexible approach and through the mutual support of political, economic and social aspects in turn, and as we gradually progress, it will be possible to set ourselves, and meet, new targets.'[18]

In coded form, the plan's purpose was to pre-empt Spinelli's much bolder initiative by deliberately watering down its 'constitutionalist' agenda. However, when it was presented to the London European Council of 26 to 27 November 1981, the plan received no immediate support and, by being referred back to the foreign ministers, was effectively kicked into touch.

Genscher and Colombo did not immediately give up. Eleven months later, on 14 October 1982, they had a further chance to address the Parliament when it debated an interim report on their plan from its political affairs committee. Colombo was unrepentant: 'History has taught us that European Union cannot be attained by moving too fast or forcing the pace,' he declared.[19] But without support from member states their plan had already effectively been buried.

Spinelli's project, however, was still very much alive. His *ad hoc* 'committee for institutional affairs', elected on 22 January 1982, had now been in place for nearly nine months, with Spinelli as its co-ordinator and Mauro Ferri as its president. To maximise support, at Spinelli's insistence, the committee set up a steering group, to hold hearings for a wide range of politicians, trade union leaders and academics to give their views. The European Movement was recruited to whip up public support.

The committee's task, approved by the European Parliament on 6 July 1983, could not have been more ambitious. It was not simply to amend the existing European treaties but, working through six sub-committees, to produce an entirely new one. Spinelli and his allies had already pulled off a remarkable achievement, in convincing their fellow MEPs that, by supporting his project, they could

---

17 Named after Gymnich Schloss, a palatial German Federal Government guest house near Cologne, used for informal, confidential meetings of foreign ministers. The British equivalent is 'Chatham House Rules'.

18 Debates of the European Parliament, No. 1 289/237.

19 *Ibid.*

win unprecedented new prestige for the Parliament. It would establish it as the prime mover in the integration process; as Spinelli himself was already putting it, by transforming the 'Community' into a 'European Union'.

Barely three weeks before Parliament gave Spinelli the go-ahead, the Genscher-Colombo Plan had been given what amounted to its tombstone, when it was incorporated into another document given the grandiose title of a 'Solemn Declaration on European Union'. Presented to the Stuttgart European Council on 17 to 19 June 1983,[20] this stated in its objectives:

'The Heads of State or Government, on the basis of an awareness of a common destiny and the wish to affirm the European identity, confirm their commitment to progress towards an ever closer union among the peoples and Member States of the European Communities.'[21]

The 'Solemn Declaration' was approved by the heads of government, including Thatcher, now so preoccupied with her battle over the budget rebate that she merely noted it in her memoirs as having been just 'one other aspect' of the Stuttgart meeting.

Only four days earlier, on 15 June, Thatcher had won a landslide election victory over a Labour Party led by Michael Foot, which had included in its manifesto a pledge to take Britain out of the EEC. Among the few new Labour MPs to be elected was the young member for Sedgefield, Tony Blair, who promised in his election address:

'We'll negotiate a withdrawal from the EEC, which has drained our natural resources and destroyed jobs.'[22]

In a dismissive comment on the 'Declaration on European Union', Thatcher noted the 'grandiloquent language' which 'had been used about the subject since before the UK had joined the Community', but took the view that she 'could not quarrel with everything, and the document had no legal force'. Therefore, she 'went along with it'.[23]

When later questioned about the Declaration in the Commons, she replied, 'I must make it quite clear that I do not in any way believe in a federated Europe. Nor does that document'.[24] Her new Foreign Secretary Geoffrey Howe also gave the Declaration only a cursory mention in his memoirs, devoting more space to his visit afterwards to Stuttgart's art gallery. He recalled that 'we attached less importance than most of our colleagues – less than we should have done – to this blueprint of the future'.[25]

Thatcher was certainly right about the 'grandiloquent language' and much of the Declaration's text was in fact taken up with restating principles already agreed elsewhere. Its only real purpose was to head off Spinelli's draft treaty, now in active

20 Commission of the European Communities. European Bulletin, EC 6-1983, points 1.6.1 to 4.3.
21 *Op. cit.*, point 1.1.
22 Blair's 1983 election address was published in fascimile on the No-Euro website, *www.no-euro.com*
23 Thatcher, *op. cit.*, p. 314.
24 *Ibid.*
25 Howe, *op. cit.*, p. 307.

preparation. For precisely that reason Spinelli was angry. His committee president Ferri exploded that, for the Parliament, 'no form of consultation with the Council and the Commission is possible'.[26] If only Thatcher and Howe had been better briefed as to the hidden reason for the Declaration, they might have been better prepared for what was to hit them at the Milan Council two years later.

The first 'federal policy'

Just at this moment when the Community was about to take a further giant step towards integration, there had emerged its first example of a fully-fledged 'federal' or supranational policy. In January 1983, after long and bitter argument, the Community had finally agreed how to apply the rules it had laid down for its Common Fisheries Policy.

After The Hague conference in 1976, when the Community had agreed the broad principles on which its CFP was to be operated, fishing ministers had to decide how the principle of 'equal access', modified by the 'Hague preferences' was to work. A 'free-for-all' could not be allowed, otherwise the resource would be quickly expended, so a conservation strategy had to be devised. The first step was to determine proportion of the Total Allowable Catches (TACs) for each of the main species of fish that would be allocated to each country, under a system of national 'quotas'.

In doing this, the ministers opted to base the divisions on historical records, taking account of where national fleets had fished previously, and the tonnages caught. The crude percentages would then be modified by reference to the 'Hague preferences', which were more or less arbitrarily defined by subtracting parts of various country's allocations in order to give them to others.

Predictably, this led to bitter arguments, firstly over which years should be picked as the historical 'reference points'. Eventually, the period agreed spanned 1973 to 1978, which was particularly disadvantageous to Britain. During that period, most of her fishing effort had been concentrated in North Atlantic waters now closed to her. On the other hand, the period was particularly advantageous to France, since most of her fishing effort in those years had been in waters now within the British 200-mile zone.

Then there were bitter fights about the levels set for the TACs, which were to be agreed every year by fisheries ministers, in the last Council of the preceding year. The fights become an annual ritual and identified a fatal flaw in the conservation system. Ministers, fighting for their national interests, would push the TACs higher than was dictated by scientific data, while continually resisting Commission attempts to take over the process. As a result, Ministers often found themselves arguing about allocations of fish in excess of 100 percent of the quantities theoretically available.

As a 'conservation policy', there was a second flaw: although the rules were agreed centrally, their enforcement remained with member states, which meant

26 Debates of the European Parliament. No. 1/289: 261–2.

that countries adopting a 'light-touch' regime would give their own fishermen a commercial advantage, and themselves short-term economic benefits. Lack of enforcement, and the relative severity of different national systems, became a constant source of aggravation, particularly to British fishermen who, with some justice, felt their own system was the most rigorous in the Community.

A problem also lay with the allocation of national quotas. This led to disputes so fierce and so prolonged that, even though the CFP was originally planned to begin in 1980, the start-date had to be delayed to 1 January 1983. Even then, the deadline was missed and final agreement was not reached until 25 January 1983. When the results of the negotiations were announced, Britain was allocated 37 per-cent of the total catch. British fishermen were initially relieved that their country's contribution of four-fifths of the fish seemed at least to have been partially recog-nised. When, however, the details became available, they showed that the British allowance was very short on high-value species, such as sole, and weighted heavily in favour of lower-value fish, such as cod and haddock. In cash terms, the UK's share of the total catch was only 13 percent.[27]

As so often became the case, the negotiators for member states seemed to have won a much better deal for their own fishermen, notably France, which secured, for instance, an 18,000 tonne cod quota for the English Channel, compared with only 1,750 tonnes allocated to British fishermen.

Another flaw, in conservation terms, was the award of a huge one million-ton quota to Denmark's 'industrial' fishing fleet, nominally to permit harvesting sand eels and pout, used to provide food for pig, poultry or fish farms, or to be used as agricultural fertiliser. But this fleet also caught other species, including juvenile cod, which it was allowed to use under the classification 'by-catch'.

But perhaps the most serious flaw was seen in the very nature of the quota sys-tem itself. Dictating to fishermen the maximum quantities of each species they were permitted to land ignored the most basic realities of fishing. When fishermen hauled in their nets, they often caught a range of species for which they had no quota. Since it would be a criminal offence to land these, their only alternative was return their 'illegal' catch to the sea, by which time the fish would be dead. This practice was to lead within a few years to an ecological disaster, as fishermen were forced to 'discard' billions of fish every year.

The reason why 1 January 1983 had been set as the deadline for introducing the new CFP system was in itself significant, in that this marked the end of the 10-year 'derogations' negotiated in the accession talks in 1971. Now those 10 years were up, it lay with the Community to agree whether these 'transitional arrangements' could continue. The condition it imposed was that Britain must agree to the new CFP system.

But so intractable had the quota negotiations been that, on 1 January 1983, the derogations lapsed. Without the framework of quotas, the 'equal access' rule now prevailed without restriction. A Danish trawler skipper, Kent Kirk, also a Danish

27 Figures confirmed by fisheries commissioner Frans Fischler in reply to a question from Charles Tannoch MEP in 2002.

MEP, sailed into British coastal waters and began fishing. After being arrested, he appealed to the ECJ, which upheld his claim that, in the absence of a fisheries policy, he had been fully entitled to fish 'up to the beaches'. This incident, which caused a widespread stir, helped concentrate the minds of the negotiators, and by 25 January the new quota policy had been agreed. Only then were Britain and other member states given back, for a further 20 years, the concession allowing them continued jurisdiction over their inshore waters. But Rippon's claim in 1971 that this was a permanent right had again been exposed as a lie.

It was not generally understood that even the CFP system introduced in 1983 was itself only intended to be a further 'transitional arrangement', based on 'derogations' which would run out on 31 December 2002. But in one respect this was becoming particularly evident in 1983, as negotiations continued over further 'enlargement' of the Community to admit two new entrants, Spain and Portugal.

Spain and Portugal had applied for membership of the Community in 1977, following the deaths of the two dictators, Franco and Salazar, who for decades had kept their countries isolated from the mainstream of European politics. Negotiations began in 1978 and the nine years of talks reflected the particular difficulties posed by the admission of two relatively impoverished countries with mainly agrarian economies. An attempted military coup in Madrid in February 1981 lent particular urgency to Spain's entry, with the Community now anxious to strengthen her fragile new democracy by bringing her into the fold. But despite this urgency, three central issues could not easily be resolved: agriculture, fisheries and the reduction of trade barriers for Spanish industrial goods.[28]

In some respects the toughest challenge of the three was posed by fisheries, because, for domestic political reasons, Spain had built up her fishing fleet under Franco to become easily the largest in Europe. The accession of Spain and Portugal would increase the Community's total fishing capacity by three-quarters, while bringing little in the way of fishing resource. To allow these vessels immediate access to Community waters would be disastrous, not least because Spanish trawlers, fishing round the world, had already become internationally notorious for their predatory disregard of conservation rules.

To accommodate this 'cuckoo in the nest', ministers of the Ten decided that Spanish and Portuguese access to Community waters must be phased in over a long transitional period, starting with the admission of a limited number of vessels on 1 January 1995. Full integration would not be permitted until 31 December 2002. The newcomers were only persuaded to accept these conditions, however, in return for the Community paying a heavy price. Firstly Spain and Portugal were given substantial aid from the Community's 'structural funds', to enable them to update and expand their fishing fleets. Secondly, the Community also undertook

---

28 There was also, in Community terms, the 'side-issue' of the dispute between Britain and Spain over Britain's colony Gibraltar, and the opening of the land border which had been closed by General Franco since 1969. The border crossing problem was partially resolved in February 1984, after 15 months of bilateral talks, when Geoffrey Howe signed an agreement with Spain to reopen the border, on the promise of holding talks about Gibraltar's sovereignty. *Cf.* Howe, *op. cit.*, p. 407.

to pay out huge sums on buying fishing rights for the Spanish and Portuguese fleets around the coasts of Africa and across the under-developed world, to compensate them for their exclusion from European waters.

This *largesse* was to provoke an unintended consequence at the end of 1984. Thatcher recalled how, at the Dublin Council that December, just when the enlargement negotiations were nearing their conclusion,

'Mr Papandreou, the left-wing Greek prime minister, suddenly treated us to some classic theatre. A charming and agreeable man in private, his whole persona changed when it was a question of getting more money for Greece. He now intervened, effectively vetoing enlargement unless he received an undertaking that Greece should be given huge sums over the next six years.' [29]

Other member states seemed 'curiously reluctant' to defend their financial interests, and the Greek Danegeld had to be paid. The price eventually to be paid by British fishermen would be even higher.

A treaty for 'European union'

With the fisheries drama building up to its crisis, during the second half of 1983, Spinelli and his team in the European Parliament were quietly at work on what was now officially called a 'Draft Treaty Establishing a European Union'.[30] Amongst its innovations was a proposal that citizens of member states should, *ipso facto*, become citizens of the Union, and that they 'shall take part in the political life of the Union', enjoying the rights granted to them by the legal system of the Union while being subject to its laws.[31] A central objective of the European Union, Spinelli declared, should be:

'The attainment of humane and harmonious development of society based principally on endeavours to attain full employment, the progressive elimination of the existing imbalances between the regions, protection and improvement in the quality of the environment, scientific progress and the cultural development of its peoples.' [32]

If Spinelli was at odds with Monnet, he nevertheless recognised his brainchild, the European Council, which his treaty incorporated as a fully-fledged Community institution. The role he envisaged for the Council was straight out of the Monnet handbook on integration, where its main role should be to manage the transition of power from national to supranational authority, a process which must be one-way only. Spinelli's draft also proposed a major expansion of the powers of the Parliament, giving it supervisory powers over the Commission, with the right to veto its political programme.[33]

In addition to the 'internal market', the Community was to assume the responsibility for co-ordinating national laws 'with a view to constituting a homogenous

29 Thatcher, *op. cit.*, p. 545.
30 European Parliament, Directorate-General for Information and Public Relations, Publications and Briefings Division, Luxembourg.
31 *Op. cit.*, Article 3.
32 *Op. cit.*, Article 9.
33 *Op. cit.*, Article 16.

judicial area'; the full co-ordination of economic policy; and the harmonisation of taxes. All member states would be required to participate in the European Monetary System and a law should be enacted governing 'procedures and stages for attaining monetary union', complete with a European central bank.

The Union would have 'concurrent competence' over all social and regional policies and those governing health, consumer protection, the environment, education and research, culture and information. It would have competence in relation to certain aspects of foreign policy, and exclusive competence to make trade deals with third countries. There was provision for the Union to set up its own revenue-collecting authorities and mechanisms for creating new sources of revenue. Finally, if any countries should refuse to ratify such a new treaty, the rest would be entitled to carry on without them, thus creating a 'two-speed Europe'.

The draft was adopted by the Parliament on 14 February 1984 by 237 votes to 31 against, with 43 abstentions. It was addressed directly to the governments and parliaments of the member states, to prevent the Council from blocking it. Despite the support of the Parliament, however, Spinelli knew his treaty stood little chance of being ratified by member states without heavyweight support. He therefore sought Mitterrand's aid, not least because France was then holding the presidency of the Council. Thus, in his speech to the Parliament – in the debate which resulted in his draft treaty being adopted – he exhorted France to take the initiative in winning support for it among other member states.

A month later, on 24 March, Spinelli told delegates to the European Movement congress in Brussels: 'too many times we have heard the heads of State and governments make solemn statements and then we see the intergovernmental and diplomatic machines practically crushing them, reducing them to nothing'. He handed a personal note to that effect to Mitterrand during a short audience in Paris on 16 April 1984, telling him that he hoped the presidency would contribute to the advancement of the project, obliging all member states 'to assume their responsibilities'. In particular, he recommended that such an initiative should be taken 'apart from the Council of Ministers, to circumvent the rule of the unanimity'.[34]

Spinelli got his answer on 24 May 1984. Mitterrand 'made the choice for Europe'. Speaking in Strasbourg, he declared he was in favour of the European Parliament's proposals. A new situation demanded a new treaty, and France was open to such a prospect.[35] He was ready to examine Spinelli's project and suggested 'preparatory discussions' which could lead to a conference of interested member states.[36]

Mitterrand responded so positively to Spinelli's ideas because he greatly needed a European success. France was nearing the end of her presidency, and with her economy in recession, fast-rising unemployment, widespread demonstrations and his party's failure in the European elections, he needed a dramatic gesture before his tenure ended. In the spring of 1984, he conducted a marathon tour of eight

34 Spinelli, Alterio, *Diario Europeo*, *op. cit.*, pp. 976 and 998.
35 See Palayret, *op. cit.* He cites official documents.
36 *Op. cit.*, citing Mitterrand, F. (1985), *Réflexions Sur La Politique Extérieure De La France. Introduction à 25 discours, 1981–1985* (Paris, Fayard), pp. 261–262 and 281.

European capitals and judged that there was strong support for a new European initiative. The moment had come 'to leave the humdrum routine of technical questions' and to give 'the political impetus which could solve Europe's crisis'.[37]

However, Mitterrand's support was by no means unconditional. His own foreign ministry was strongly opposed. His economic advisers therefore suggested that he had two options in responding to the treaty. One would be to split it into two parts. Its economic proposals could be put forward as a first step, and discussion of its more ambitious institutional components could then be deferred for 'five years', when it was already envisaged that the Community would re-examine the Solemn Declaration on the European Union. The second option would be for France to advance her own proposals.[38] In the event, Mitterrand came up with a mixture of the two options, starting with an invitation to heads of government to take part in an 'informal meeting' in Paris in the autumn, to discuss 'political and institutional questions', the application of the Treaty of Rome and any other proposals which might be put forward.

The real significance of the advice given to Mitterrand at this time would only become apparent as events unfolded over the next seven years. It was this which first sowed the idea that the next great step forward in the integration of Europe should be in two stages, beginning with a major 'economic reform', then continuing, five years later, with a more ambitious 'institutional reform'. Herein lay the genesis of the two treaties which would become known as the 'Single European Act', ratified in 1986, and the 'Treaty on European Union' agreed at Maastricht five years later. All this was eventually to flow from Spinelli's 'draft treaty' and from his decision at a timely moment to invite Mitterrand to act as its main sponsor.

One feature of Spinelli's project which particularly appealed to Mitterrand was the idea of a 'two-speed Europe' which could not be blocked by the veto of any country, such as Britain, which might be reluctant to move on to much fuller integration. Mitterrand was to confirm this by his actions at the closing European Council under France's presidency, scheduled for Fontainebleau on 25 to 26 June 1984.

As the heads of government gathered at the ornate chateau, Thatcher was almost entirely focused on what was to be the 'showdown' in the battle to win her rebate. After 'very discreet meetings' the previous day between Mitterrand's and Kohl's advisers, Mitterrand slipped onto the agenda a proposal to set up a 'committee of experts' to consider future institutional reform of the Community. Each of the heads of government would have their own personal representatives. Mitterrand himself already saw this as the equivalent of Spaak's 1955 committee which had drafted the Treaty of Rome. A former Irish foreign minister, James Dooge, was chosen as chairman, for what would soon become known to insiders as the 'Spaak II Committee'. Its task was to make proposals to reform the institutions and to 'improve European co-operation'.

---

37 *Op. cit.*, citing *Dépêche Agence France-Presse*, 21 February 1984, in AN. 5 AG (4) PM 12.
38 AN AG 5 (4) PM 12. *Direction économique et financière, service de coopération économique. Fiche sur 'Présidence française: réforme des institutions (projet Spinelli)'*, 20 December 1983.

In her account of Fontainebleau, Thatcher does not refer to the decision to appoint this committee.[39] Had she known of the reasons for its informal title, this might have warned her just how ambitious her partners had become. She also failed to note another decision at Fontainebleau, in the wake of the June elections to the European Parliament which had produced a 'disappointingly low' poll across the Community, with Britain's 31.8 percent lowest of all. Concern at this apathy moved the Council to set up a committee on how to build 'a people's Europe', to be chaired by an Italian MEP, Pietro Adonnino.

Mitterrand had in fact already allowed for the possibility that Thatcher might veto the setting up of the Dooge committee, in which case he planned to call openly for a new 'Messina conference'. Following Fontainebleau, the Community would finally have had cleared most of the technical issues which dominated its agenda, the conflict over the budget and the thorny issue of the Spanish-Portuguese enlargement. The Community would now be free to launch out on a new stage of institutional reform, and for Mitterrand this had now become an absolute necessity:

'At Twelve, the Community integrates heterogeneous interests, contrary traditions, rival ambitions ... the present Community is more fragile than that of yesterday, and there is no longer just one cure for (all) its ills: For a larger Community, stronger institutions (are needed).'[40]

If Mitterrand had been forced to his 'Plan B', his plan was that the conference would then have worked to a Franco-German document, allowing it 'to study a draft treaty for the creation of the European Union starting from the solemn declaration of Stuttgart, taking account of the European Parliament's project'.[41] But since Thatcher had now given her approval, this 'nuclear option' was not necessary.

Mitterrand ensured that he kept a guiding hand on the committee's work, by nominating as his representative Maurice Faure, a 'convinced European', who became its *rapporteur*, responsible for orchestrating its activities. The committee was essentially controlled by its French and German members, who met in Bonn on 19 September 1984 for 'a confidential working session on the Spaak committee'. Their objective was no more and no less than 'the realisation of the European Union'.

The majority of the committee, in any case, recognised the value of Spinelli's project. They were in favour of a 'true political entity' and wanted an intergovernmental conference (IGC) to prepare a Treaty of European Union. This IGC should take as its starting point 'the spirit and the method of the project voted by the European Parliament'.[42]

---

39 Thatcher, *op. cit.*, p. 546.

40 Mitterrand, *Réflexions, op. cit.*

41 Saunier, G. (2001), 'Prélude à la relance de l'Europe. Le couple franco-allemand et les projets de relance communautaire vus de l'hexagone 1981–1985', in Bitsch, M.T., Le couple France-Allemagne et les Constitutions européennes (Bruxelles, Bruylant), pp. 464–485.

42 AHCE; AS 365, document PE 94.568 : 'Note établissant un parallèle entre le rapport du Comité Dooge et le projet de Traité instituant l'Union européenne', 13 December 1984.

The sole British representative on the Dooge committee was a comparatively inexperienced Foreign Office minister, Malcolm Rifkind. It was not to be apparent from the committee's final report that he made much contribution to its deliberations.

Fog in Channel, Continent cut off

Thatcher was to say that, once the rebate issue was resolved, she had been determined that Britain should reunite with her partners to play a 'strong and positive role in the Community'. Looking back on how events unfolded during the 10 months after the Fontainebleau Council, however, it seems as though Britain and her partners were operating on different planets.

Immediately after Fontainebleau, as Geoffrey Howe was to recall in his memoirs, he had attended the Queen's birthday banquet in honour of the Diplomatic Corps, for which he had arranged: an 'impeccably British function'. The Irish had now taken over the presidency of the Community, for what Howe reported as 'a quiet six months'. One of his few recollections of this period was 'an enjoyable day in Germany' in September, inspecting some of the 60,000 soldiers serving with BAOR (the British Army of the Rhine), who were taking part jointly with the *Bundeswehr* in NATO exercises.

Later that month, he returned to make 'an important speech in Bonn', where he stated that Britain's commitment to Europe was 'profound and irreversible'. Evidently oblivious of the most recent dealings between the French and Germans, he was seeking, according to his own account, to demonstrate 'the range of Britain's European commitment' and, by implication, 'to suggest that the Franco-German relationship should not be seen as the only cornerstone of the European Community'.[43] This, as we will see, was to be the cornerstone of British policy, as successive British governments sought to interpose themselves between the French and the Germans. Thus, as others were to do after him, Howe argued that Britain should be 'a strong voice in the Community', as one of its leading members. 'We have brought to Europe a considerable dowry', he said, 'our markets for agricultural and industrial goods, our fishing grounds, our major contribution to the defence and security of the continent'. He continued:

'It is because we have so much at stake in the Community, because we depend so much on its healthy development and because we believe so wholeheartedly in its future that we have devoted so much effort to the reform of its internal arrangements; to building a better foundation for the future of Europe.' [44]

So important did he consider this speech, along with others he was to deliver in similar vein over the months that followed, that he would eventually publish them in a book entitled *Europe Tomorrow*.

43 Howe, *op. cit.*, pp. 403–404.
44 Cited in Hillman, Judy, and Clarke, Peter (1988), *Geoffrey Howe – A Quiet Revolutionary* (London, Weidenfeld & Nicolson), p. 172.

Meanwhile, Mitterrand was pursuing plans to establish a European 'defence identity' independent of NATO, effectively continuing a French policy objective which stretched back to the time of de Gaulle. The opportunity had been presented by the general European alarm over the announcement by US President Ronald Reagan on 23 October 1983 of his Strategic Defence Initiative (SDI), the proposed anti-ballistic missile system dubbed 'Star Wars'. This had raised the spectre for some of America's European allies of the USA finding a way to make herself immune from the Soviet nuclear threat, and thus becoming less willing to commit her own nuclear deterrent on behalf of her allies.

By February 1984, therefore, Mitterrand felt he could use this opportunity to convince the Community to seek its own independent military capability: independent, that is, of the USA. To achieve his aim, he fastened on the moribund Western European Union, set up on a British initiative in 1954. With a view to reactivating it, he had sent a memorandum to all its other members. The initial response was lukewarm. Thatcher predictably rejected the idea outright. However Howe and Michael Heseltine, now her Secretary of State for Defence, both fervent 'Europeanists', had felt 'a strong instinct towards strengthening our European defence linkage', presumably unaware or heedless of the French agenda. It was, they argued, in America's interest as well as Europe's that Europe should pull its weight.[45] By October 1984, the Community members had been sufficiently won round to Mitterrand's idea for a meeting of foreign and defence ministers to take place in Rome within the WEU framework. On 27 October they agreed a 'founding text' for reactivating the WEU, the 'Rome Declaration', the objectives of which included the establishing of a 'European security identity' and the gradual harmonisation of member states' defence policies.[46]

Two weeks later, on 11 November, took place the ceremony with which this book began, when Mitterrand and Kohl met to hold hands at Verdun, solemnly to reaffirm that indissoluble alliance between France and Germany on which they saw that the whole future of 'European construction' must ultimately be centred.

While all these events were unfolding, the Dooge committee had been hard at work. By December, it had a preliminary report ready for the Dublin European Council, favouring an 'intergovernmental conference' to prepare a new treaty. The UK, Denmark and Greece immediately tabled reservations, opposing institutional reform and any need for such a treaty. But at least agreement was reached on another matter. With strong backing from Mitterrand, Jacques Delors, a leading French *fonctionnaire*,[47] was formally appointed as the new president of the

---

45 Howe, *op. cit.*, p. 386.

46 *www.weu.int*

47 A '*fonctionnaire*' in France is much more than a civil servant. Most of the *fonctionnaire* class which came to rule France in the closing decades of the 20th century were educated at the *Ecole Nationale d'Administration* (ENA), set up by Michel Debré in 1946, and known as '*Enarques*'. The Enarques may play the role of politician and senior official interchangeably. Prominent *Enarques* included Giscard d'Estaing, Jacques Chirac (who first became French prime minister in 1974, when Giscard moved from the premiership to the Presidency), and several French Commissioners, such as Pascal Lamy and Yves Thibault de Silguy, responsible for setting up the single currency. Delors, though unmistakably a *fonctionnaire*, was not an *Enarque*, since he did not attend the ENA.

Commission. On the interim Dooge proposals, Mitterrand could not have made his position clearer. At the press conference immediately after the Council, he declared that 'the institutional debate may now take precedence over the others'.[48]

The significance of this seems to have escaped Thatcher, who only weeks previously had survived a massive IRA bomb attack on her hotel at the Brighton Conservative Party conference, and who was still preoccupied by the tense closing stages of the long-drawn out 1984 miners' strike. Already, in a speech in Avignon in October, she had claimed not to know what 'European Union' meant, preferring 'practical unity' in policies.[49]

A month later, in his New Year message to the German people, Kohl made no secret of his determination, with his ally France, 'to give decisive impetus to the European Union concept' during 1985. This was reinforced by the incoming president of the Council, Italy's foreign minister Giulio Andreotti, who had begun his political career as a *protégé* of Alcide De Gasperi. Setting out to the European Parliament his programme, he declared, 'no effort will be spared in seeking agreement by June on a date for convening an intergovernmental conference with the task of negotiating the Treaty on European Union'.[50] Therein lay the genesis of what was to become known as the 'ambush at Milan'. Howe, aided by the 'Rolls Royce minds' of the Foreign Office, should have picked this up. He did not.

By the time of the Brussels Council, on 29 to 30 March 1985, the Dooge Committee was ready to present its final report. One may imagine Thatcher's eyes glazing over as she read the first paragraph:

'After the Second World War, Europe made a very promising start by setting up, firstly with the European Coal and Steel Community and then with the European Economic Community an unprecedented construction which could not be compared with any existing legal entity. The Community – based on the principles of pluralist democracy and the respect for human rights which constitute essential elements for membership and is one of the constant objectives of its activities throughout the world – answered the complex and deeply felt needs of all our citizens.'[51]

Notwithstanding the unsubstantiated assertion that the EEC answered 'the complex and deeply felt needs of all our citizens', the essence of the report was expressed in the following three paragraphs:

'Although the Community decided to complete this construction as from the Summit in the Hague in 1969 and Paris in 1972, it is now in a state of crisis and suffers from serious deficiencies.

In addition, however, the Member States have become caught up in differences which have obscured the considerable economic advantages which could be obtained from the realisation of the Common Market and for Economic and Monetary Union.

48 *Agence Europe*, No. 3984, 6 December 1984, p. 7.
49 Corbett, Richard (2001), *The European Parliament's Role In Closer EU Integration* (London, Palgrave), p. 205.
50 Debates of the European Parliament, 16 January 1985, No. 2-321, pp. 105-106.
51 Ad Hoc Committee for Institutional Affairs, *Report to the European Council*, SN/1187/85 (SPAAK II), Brussels, 29–30 March 1985, p. 1.

Furthermore, after ten years of crisis, Europe, unlike Japan and the United States, has not achieved a growth rate sufficient to reduce the disturbing figure of almost fourteen million unemployed.'[52]

The Committee's answer was that 'Europe must recover faith in itself' and 'launch itself on a new common venture – the establishment of a political entity based on clearly defined priority objectives coupled with the means of achieving them'. Crucially, in arguing that institutional reform was essential to the Community's future, the Committee proposed that the national veto must in general be abandoned in favour of qualified majority voting.

This was significant because, as Salter had been urging back in the 1920s and as Monnet had constantly insisted throughout his career, the issue of whether or not an organisation allowed the national veto was the key defining characteristic of a supranational organisation. Now, under the inspiration of Spinelli, it seemed the European Community was considering phasing out national vetoes on an unprecedented scale, thus opening out the possibility that it might at last move forward to become genuinely supranational.

The form taken by the Dooge Report was that, throughout its text, any dissenting comments from individual committee members were appended as footnotes. It is therefore possible to see what objections were raised to each point, and on this key proposal the only reservation came from a Dane. He rejected the arguments for a new treaty, on the basis that 'difficulties facing the construction of Europe resulted from a failure to implement the existing Treaties fully' and could be remedied by their being strictly applied.[53] From Rifkind there was no comment, either on this or on the conclusion that member states must demonstrate their 'common political will' by creating 'a genuine political entity', namely 'a European Union'.[54]

Among 'priority objectives' identified by the Committee were measures for the completion of a 'genuine internal market', including the introduction of a 'common transport policy', the opening up of access to public contracts and the elimination of taxation differences 'that impede the achievement of the Community's objectives'. The European Monetary System should be strengthened. The Committee noted that 'the logic of integration' had already led member states to co-operate in fields other than purely economic, and argued that 'the accentuation of this process will give a European dimension to all aspects of collective life in our countries'. Again, Rifkind was silent.

The Committee wanted laws to protect the environment, on the basis that pollution 'does not recognise frontiers', and the gradual creation of a 'European social area'.[55] There should be the 'gradual establishment of a homogenous judicial area', together with measures to promote 'common cultural values' and 'an external identity': i.e., a common foreign policy. This was to be augmented by 'developing

---

52 *Ibid.*
53 *Op. cit.,* p. 2, footnote 1.
54 *Op. cit.,* p. 3.
55 *Op. cit.,* p. 14.

and strengthening consultation on security problems as part of political co-operation'. Picking up on the Rome Declaration, the role of the WEU was identified as working towards a common defence policy, and the report specifically proposed moves towards a fully-integrated European defence industry, with industries from different member states working together on joint projects.[56]

Above all this, however, the report's most significant recommendation was the elimination of the national veto in favour of qualified majority voting. Here, at last, Rifkind was visible. Where a member state considered that 'its very important interests' were at stake, he chipped in, discussion should continue until unanimous agreement was reached.

To achieve the radical changes proposed, the Committee was adamant that a major revision of the treaties would be required. It therefore formally proposed an intergovernmental conference to negotiate a European Union Treaty based on the *acquis communautaire*, the present document and the Stuttgart Solemn Declaration on European Union and guided by the spirit and method of the draft Treaty voted by the European Parliament.[57] 'The very decision' to convene such a conference, the report argued, 'would have a great symbolic value and would represent the initial act of a European Union'. It all seemed a long way from the 'Common Market', for which the British had voted in the 1975 referendum. Yet on this too Rifkind remained silent.

When the Dooge Report was presented to the Brussels Council, no decision was taken. The 'high noon' of political integration would have to wait for the next Council, scheduled for Milan on 28 to 29 June 1985.

Ambush at Milan

Thatcher at this time was focused on a wholly different initiative of her own. Her chief contribution to the Brussels Council had been to propose that the Community should embark on a policy of 'deregulation', to stimulate its development as 'a free trade and free enterprise area'.[58] She was excited by the proposals of Arthur Cockfield, formerly the 'prices commissioner' under Heath's government, whom she had sent to Brussels to become the senior British Commissioner under Delors. Within months of his arrival, he had produced a Commission White Paper entitled *Completing the Internal Market*. This document identified nearly 300 measures by which, Cockfield suggested, the Community could by 1992 achieve the 'completion' of its 'internal market' or 'Single Market'.

In support of this policy, Howe produced a report arguing that it would be impossible to make real progress towards the 'Single Market' as long as the unanimity rule prevailed, allowing national vetoes, but he also argued that a new treaty would not be necessary to reduce the number of issues requiring unanimity. The Treaty of Rome could remain unchanged, but there should be a written agreement that the Single Market could proceed as though the unanimity rule did not

56 *Op. cit.*, pp. 21–22.
57 *Op. cit.*, p. 33.
58 Thatcher, *op. cit.*, p. 546.

apply.[59] Howe also proposed a greater degree of 'political co-operation' on foreign policy and that, if necessary, the Council should be given a political secretariat.[60]

Howe then persuaded Thatcher that she should be the one to launch his report on the European stage and, to pave the way for its acceptance, she should invite Kohl to become a joint sponsor of the scheme. Thus, unprecedently, Kohl was invited for a Saturday afternoon and evening at Chequers, during which Thatcher presented 'her' plan to him. Kohl tucked the paper into his briefcase, promising to look at it.[61] Not only was there no response from him but, two weeks after having seen the report, the Germans produced their own counter-proposal; a Treaty between the Twelve to 'mark a new stage in the progression towards the European Union' and to establish a common foreign and security policy. Then, just as the Milan Council approached, Mitterrand announced that he would support the German proposal, to transform it into a 'Franco-German project'. Once again, the Franco-German 'motor of integration' had asserted its dominance.

Thatcher should not have been surprised, but she was nevertheless not amused when she learned that much of the German paper was so similar to the British proposals that it was tantamount to plagiarism.[62] 'Such were the consequences of prior consultation,' she remarked tartly in her memoirs. According to Howe, she was furious, and so was he. Neither ever received a word of explanation from Kohl or from anyone on his behalf.[63]

Nor was the apparent commonality of approach between France, Germany and Britain all that it seemed. It in fact represented a tactical ploy by Mitterrand. Despite his enthusiasm for further integration, there were internal divisions in Germany's Federal government and, with Thatcher's resistance, he felt that 'ambition would have to be moderated'.[64] It was better to go for a bottom line that everyone could agree on. That 'bottom line' was the Dooge report and, in particular, the completion of the Single Market.[65]

Mitterrand was also aware that expectations of a French success at the Milan Council were high, and a public row would play badly at home. Accordingly, he had decided to take a long view, confiding to his advisor, Jacques Attali, 'France's objective is to create a European Union in the long term; the task is now to define the substance and the stages. If we do not agree (at Milan), nothing will be done.'[66] Thus, a start would be made on 'the construction of a political Europe', and the remaining objectives would be dealt with later.[67] That 'start' would be an increase in majority voting. On that there could be no compromise. And despite their out-

59 *Ibid.*
60 Howe, *op. cit.*, p. 408; Sharp, P. (1999), *Thatcher's Diplomacy: The Revival Of British Foreign Policy* (London, Macmillan), pp. 162–163.
61 Howe, *op. cit.*, p. 409.
62 Thatcher, *op. cit.*, p. 549; McAllistair, *op. cit.*, p. 174.
63 Howe, *op. cit.*, p. 409.
64 Palayret, *op. cit.* He cites AN. 5AG (4) EG 13, '*Note pour le Président*' (E. Guigou) a/s. '*Votre rencontre avec le chancelier Kohl: Que faire pour l'Europe?*', 20 May 1985.
65 Favier, P., and Martin-Rolland, M., *La décennie Mitterrand.* T. II, Les épreuves (1984–1988), p. 215.
66 Attali, Jacques, verbatim account, cited in Palayret, *op. cit.*
67 Attali, in Palayret, *op. cit.*

ward agreement with Thatcher, both Kohl and Mitterrand were adamant that there must be an IGC to push through the necessary changes to the treaties.

Meanwhile, in the months leading up to the Milan Council, others had been active. Although Spinelli recognised that the Dooge Report represented a severe dilution of his proposals, he did not reject it outright. Instead, he toured the European capitals with the president of the Parliament, urging an IGC as soon as possible, continuing to argue that it should work on the basis of his draft treaty. On 18 April 1985 the European Parliament enthusiastically approved a resolution moved by Spinelli insisting that it must be closely associated with the drafting of any new treaty and furthermore that the objections of the UK, Denmark and Greece should not prevent other governments setting up the IGC.

At the same time, as Commission president-designate, Delors had also been touring the capitals, suggesting three themes that were necessary to 'relaunch' Europe: a common defence policy; a single currency; and a change in the legal structure which would lead to political integration. He realised from his discussions that he would not get unanimous agreement on all three. As Milan approached, he therefore reached the same conclusions as Kohl and Mitterrand. The only proposal which would win support from all 10 governments would be the completion of the Single Market. The further moves to integration they all wanted would be channelled through this project.[68] The Single Market was to be the 'bait'.

The trap is sprung

As all the participants headed for Milan, the scene was thus set for a classic confrontation. The Italian 'presidency' had announced the setting of a date for an IGC as their main objective. Kohl, Mitterrand, Delors and the Benelux countries were similarly determined. Against them were ranged the British, the Danes and the Greeks, with the Irish hovering in the middle. Thatcher and Howe in particular were intent on blocking any proposals for a new Treaty and therefore any idea of the IGC needed to bring it into being.

With 50,000 activists mobilised by the European Movement parading through the Milan streets, their banners proclaiming 'down with frontiers', Italy's Socialist prime minister Bettino Craxi in the chair at first tried for a 'common position', supported by his Christian Democrat foreign minister, Giulio Andreotti. But Thatcher argued strongly that the Community had demonstrated its ability to take decisions under the present arrangements, and that the Council should simply agree on the measures necessary to achieve the Single Market and 'political co-operation'. A new treaty was not necessary. Greater use of the existing majority voting articles of the Rome Treaty would suffice.[69]

As Thatcher quickly discovered, her arguments were to no avail. Having come to Milan to argue for closer co-operation, she found herself being bulldozed by a majority which 'included a highly partisan chairman'.[70] Intergovernmentalism

---

68 Grant, *op. cit.*, pp. 66–67.
69 Thatcher, *op. cit.*, p. 559.
70 *Op. cit.*, p. 550

was meeting supranationalism head on, and despite support from Greece and Denmark, intergovernmentalism lost. To Thatcher's astonishment, Craxi invoked his right as chairman to call for a vote: a highly unorthodox move. Thatcher and Howe were startled to hear that, contrary to their understanding of the rules, only a simple majority was needed to carry the day. An IGC was agreed by a vote of seven to three.

At the end of the Council meeting, Craxi, in his role as president of the Council, made a statement:

'Today's decision was a difficult and contested one, but it was eventually carried because of the logic of political will and what is possible under the Treaty. We would have preferred a general consensus and unanimity, but these were not to be had. I believe we shall work steadfastly to overcome the obstacles before us and to achieve the necessary consensus to go forward together towards the objectives of the European Union.'[71]

Delors later told journalists that the Commission endorsed Craxi's initiative. He added, 'At least we know where we stand; if we had waited another year or two, we should not have made any progress.' Belgium's prime minister said the Council had been a 'turning point marking the end of Europe's opposition to progress'. The intergovernmental conference would pave the way for the adjustments which would undoubtedly be necessary in a 12-member Community.[72]

Howe's view, faithfully echoed by Hugo Young in his book,[73] was that Thatcher herself had been partly responsibility for the defeat, Craxi's behaviour having been triggered by 'the sharp tone of the British leadership'. Yet Howe admits to having failed completely to anticipate that the British could be outvoted. Had he been better briefed as to what was going on in the background, he would have known that the moment the heads of government walked into the conference room, there could be only one outcome.

Yet again the success of the 'Milan ambush' demonstrated the 'Little England' insularity of the British participants in the Council, and the inability of either politicians or civil servants to grasp how their 'partners' thought and operated. Young at least quotes the comment of Michael Butler, 'one of the posse of hard-faced Foreign Office men by Thatcher's side', who told him years later: 'I was horrified at my own failure to see that this was what they would do to us if we went on being intransigent.'[74] Thatcher bemoaned the fact that so much of her time had been wasted. She would have to return to the Commons to explain why all the high hopes that had been held of Milan had been dashed. She had not even had time to go to the opera.[75] More to the point, Howe's 'strong voice in Europe' had turned out to be no more than a pathetic bleat.

In all the excitement over Milan's main event, the British team also completely

71 Bulletin of the European Communities, EC 6-1985, point 1.2.10.
72 *Ibid.*
73 Young, *op. cit.*, p. 332.
74 *Ibid.*
75 Thatcher, *op. cit.*, p. 551.

overlooked the significance of another item on the agenda, the presentation and approval of a report by Craxi's representative Pietro Adonnino on 'A People's Europe'. This had been commissioned by the Fontainebleau Council the previous year, in response to the apathy towards 'Europe' shown in the poor turn-out for the elections to the Parliament. It was intended to suggest measures which could be adopted to promote the sense of a 'European identity'.

Although there was nothing in the Treaty of Rome to authorise such a strategy, various gestures had been made towards it over the years, such as the Tindemans Report's recommendation in 1975 for a policy forging a 'people's Europe' through 'concrete manifestations of the European solidarity in everyday life'. The 1983 Stuttgart declaration committed member states to promoting 'cultural co-operation', including such proposals as co-operation between higher education establishments and the dissemination of 'information on Europe's history and culture so as to promote European awareness'. There was also to be an 'examination' of the possibility of promoting joint television and cinema projects.[76] This had led in 1984 to the so-called 'television without frontiers' directive, the importance of which was spelt out by the Commission:

'Information is a decisive, perhaps the most decisive, factor in European unification … European unification will only be achieved if Europeans want it. Europeans will only want it if there is such a thing as a European identity. A European identity will only develop if Europeans are adequately informed. At present, information via the mass media is controlled at national level.'[77]

Thus had a new sphere of Community activity emerged, which had no basis whatever in the Treaties. But the Adonnino Report adopted by the Milan Council carried a determination to lift the 'European identity' onto a new plane.

Perhaps the most significant of its proposals, in terms of psychological impact, was that the European Community should have its own flag and its own anthem, 'to be played at appropriate events and ceremonies'. The flag, carrying the emblem of a ring of 12 gold stars on a blue background, was borrowed from the existing flag of the Council of Europe, and would first be raised as the Community's official flag at a ceremony outside the Berlaymont building in Brussels on 29 May 1986.[78] This was accompanied by a first performance of the new 'European anthem', adapted from the 'Ode To Joy' theme from Beethoven's Ninth Symphony, also borrowed from the Council of Europe and first suggested by Coudenhove Kalergi in 1929.

---

76 European Bulletin, *op. cit.*, point 3.3.

77 Commission of the European Communities, *Television Without Frontiers: Green Paper on the Establishment of the Common Market for Broadcasting especially for Satellite and Cable*, COM(84) final, Luxembourg.

78 The rationale for the ring of stars, according to the Commission, was that: 12 was a symbol of perfection and plenitude, associated equally with the apostles, the sons of Jacob, the tables of the Roman legislator, the labours of Hercules, the hours of the day, the months of the year, or the signs of the Zodiac. Lastly, the circular layout denoted union. The Commission also pointed out that the circle of 12 stars was a Christian symbol representing the Virgin Mary's halo, which was a symbol of European identity and unification.

Adonnino also recommended the adoption by 1 January 1986 of a standard 'Community model' driving licence, following a decision by the Paris European Council in 1984 to adopt a 'Community passport' to replace national passports ('Community' vehicle number plates, bearing the ring of stars, would soon follow). The report proposed other 'concrete measures' to encourage 'the people of Europe' to feel a sense of common identity, ranging from a 'Europe-wide lottery' to an emergency health card, entitling them to medical assistance in any member state. It recommended that the Community should take over the long-established practice of 'town twinning', dating back to the Second World War, and use it to promote the idea of 'European union'. It recommended that 'European' sports teams should compete in international events, wearing the 'ring of stars' rather than national symbols (this would be adopted a few years later by the 'European' golf team competing against the USA for the Ryder Cup).

In the cultural field, the committee recommended the financing of European cinema and television programmes made by at least two member states, and the launch of a 'European television channel'. Moving on to education, it recommended the establishment of a 'European Academy of Science, Technology and Art', to 'highlight the achievements of European science and the originality of European civilisation in all its wealth and diversity'. Arguing that 'the people of Europe' did not 'receive satisfactory information on the construction of Europe', the committee recommended an 'information programme', taking the view that:

'Information about the Community should aim to explain the fundamental themes underlying the crucial importance of the Community for the Member States – the historical events which led to the construction of the Community and which inspire its further development in freedom, peace and security and its achievements and potential in the economic and social field. Member States can show how national action is reinforced by Community action. It is also necessary to point out what the costs would be if the Community did not exist.' [79]

Special attention should be given to educational establishments and the need 'to facilitate the work of schools and teachers', by providing them with books and teaching materials putting across 'the European dimension'. Schools and other institutions should be encouraged each year to celebrate 'Europe Day' on 9 May, to commemorate the 'Schuman Declaration'.

The most obvious feature of the Adonnino report was its overall message that the Community should begin to adopt the symbolic trappings of a nation state (several of which, not least the 'ring of stars', would over the next few years become familiar). Yet for all its significance in the evolution of the European Union, the report is not mentioned by Thatcher or Howe in their memoirs, despite their being present when it was approved by the Council, and even though Thatcher's own senior advisor on European affairs, David Williamson, was a member of the Adonnino committee.[80]

79 Commission, *op. cit.*, p. 13.
80 European Council, Presidency Conclusions, Milan, 28–29 June 1985. Bulletin of the European Parliament, PE 99 511, Luxembourg, p. 7.

The Single European Act

It is interesting to contrast how Britain's two main protagonists at Milan record in their memoirs their immediate response to what had happened to them. Howe does not dwell on the episode. He merely recalls how 'soon the irritations of Milan faded into history'. [81] Thatcher in her own memoirs presents a rather more thoughtful perspective:

'Annoyed as I was with what had happened, I realised that we must make the best of it. I made clear that we would take part in the IGC. I saw no merit in the alternative policy – practised for a time in earlier years by France – of the so-called "empty chair". There has to be a major matter of principle at stake to justify any nation's refusing to take part in Community discussions. That was not the case here: we agreed with the aims of enhanced political co-operation and the Single Market; we disagreed only with the means (i.e., the IGC) to effect them.' [82]

Thus, over the next six months, did Britain for the first time enter into the negotiations for a new 'European' treaty. [83] The intergovernmental conference or 'IGC' which results in a treaty is not so much a single event as a process, lasting many months, encompassing scores of meetings between both officials and ministers. Only after the contents of the treaty have been endlessly thrashed out does the process conclude at a final 'summit', where the heads of government argue over any issues still outstanding. The agreed text is then prepared for signing at a later date, before the final stage of the process in which the treaty is ratified by each of the member states.

A novel feature of the 1985 IGC was that, although the Commission had no formal part in it, its members played a central role. Delors attended the meetings of foreign ministers, where much of the work was done, while his secretary-general, Emile Noël, attended meetings of officials. Delors, Noël and François Lamoureaux, Delors' institutional expert, then used the meetings to saturate the delegates with proposals which 'helped define the agenda and dissuaded many governments from putting forward ideas of their own'. [84] All proposals were drafted by these three, without reference to other Commissioners.

With considerable subtlety, Delors steered the negotiations in his direction by carefully linking the UK objectives, notably the single market, to institutional reform. [85] To get what they wanted, the British would thus be forced to concede that which they least wanted: an extension of qualified majority voting. Delors was

81 Howe, *op. cit.*, p. 447.
82 Thatcher, *op. cit.*, p. 551.
83 Contrary to general understanding, the Single European Act was not to be the first treaty since the Treaties of Rome. There had also been the Treaty of Brussels in 1965, merging the three 'Communities' and the very important Luxembourg Treaty of 1970 establishing the arrangements for the EEC budget and the financing of the CAP, which in turn was superseded by the 1975 Treaty of Brussels (which also introduced the Court of Auditors). In addition to these, the accession treaties each time there was an 'enlargement' could themselves be used to establish new principles of policy which might have repercussions wider than those affecting the applicant countries alone (as in the details of fisheries policy established in 1972).
84 Grant, *op. cit.*, p. 73.
85 Corbett, *op. cit.*, p. 219.

also withering in his scorn for any member state daring to put up objections. While he pressed for what he described as the 'two great dreams' of Europe, an 'area without frontiers' and monetary union, Thatcher wrote that every exemption sought by other countries 'seemed to be regarded as a kind of betrayal'. At one time or another, she observed, Delors had denounced almost every member state except Italy, Belgium and the Netherlands.[86]

Once the mass of paperwork had been distilled to its essentials, the substantive issues emerged. The first two were acceptable to the British: the completion of the Single Market, based on Cockfield's White Paper, and strengthened co-operation on foreign policy. Delors had also put forward 'chapters' on environmental policy, research and 'cohesion' (the so-called 'structural funds' providing regional aid). All of these were important policy areas in which the Commission had already become active without having the legal authorisation to do so under the Treaty of Rome. With the proposed new competence on environmental policy came also an arcane new principle described as 'subsidiarity', the ramifications of which few at the time could have predicted.

The British agreed to all these 'chapters', as they did to a modest extension in the role of the European Parliament. Then, however, came the price Thatcher would have to pay for her Single Market. This would be a significant extension in majority voting, the key supranational principle which was the real reason for the treaty.[87] The final version included 12 policy areas which would now be subject to QMV, including all measures considered necessary to establish the 'internal market', a new competence on 'health and safety', decisions relating to regional development and an extension of Community competence to air and sea transport.[88] Yet, despite being fully aware that this expansion of QMV greatly increased the powers of the Commission, Thatcher seemed determined to believe that it would only be used to promote her Single Market rather than for any other purpose. What the British could not accept at all was Delors' vision of 'space without frontiers', which would effectively mean surrendering immigration policy to the Commission. There were two other battles, one with proposals put forward by Cockfield over tax harmonisation and the other on Economic and Monetary Union (EMU).

The trouble with Cockfield's proposals stemmed from his remarkable transformation from British minister to European Commissioner. Within months of arriving in Brussels, Thatcher's nominee had 'gone native'. In Delors' own words, 'he was more and more pro-European'. He was committed to defending the powers and policies of the Commission at all costs.[89] Cockfield had produced two schemes, one attempting to increase the harmonisation of VAT rates, the other a

---

86 Thatcher, *op. cit.*, p. 351.
87 With the accession of Spain and Portugal in 1986, the number of votes in Council rose to 76: the four biggest countries, France, Germany, Britain and Italy each with 10 votes; Spain with eight; Belgium, Greece, the Netherlands and Portugal with five; Denmark and Ireland with three; and Luxembourg with two.
88 A 'qualified majority' would require 54 of the 76 votes, thus preventing the 'big four' ganging up on the smaller states, but leaving Britain with only just over one-seventh of the vote.
89 *The Poisoned Chalice, op. cit.*, verbatim statement: subtitle translation.

proposal for harmonising excise duties on tobacco and alcohol. Both proved widely unpopular and were eventually abandoned.

The other battle, over EMU, stemmed from Delors' insistence that it be included as a new 'chapter' in the treaty. This Thatcher resolutely opposed, right up until the Luxembourg 'summit' in December which was planned to mark the culmination of the IGC process. On this, she thought she could rely on German support and she certainly had the full support of Lawson, who, according to Thatcher,

'… stressed that it would be essential that the language used should contain no obligation on us to join the ERM, make it clear that exchange rate policy is the responsibility of national authorities, minimise any extension of Community competence and avoid any treaty reference to EMU.' [90]

As the deadline approached, Delors protested at the changes proposed to his cherished 'space without frontiers'. At a meeting of foreign ministers on 25 to 26 November 1985, he complained that his texts now had 'more holes than Gruyère' and stormed off to see Kohl and Mitterrand, with spectacular results. By the next ministerial meeting, a Franco-German initiative had reinstated Delors' proposals.[91]

For Thatcher, things were to get worse. By the time the heads of government met in Luxembourg on 2 to 3 December 1985, the Franco-German axis had also reached an accommodation with Delors on monetary union. Germany, having abandoned Britain, agreed to accept a mention of EMU in return for a concession from the French on another issue to which they had been strongly opposed. This enabled Delors to insert into the preamble of the new treaty a commitment to the 'progressive realisation of economic and monetary union'. [92] The inclusion of this phrase moved Thatcher to consider vetoing the treaty, but she was persuaded to give her assent by the Foreign Office, who assured her the statement had no legal significance. Even then, just before midnight on the second day, when everyone was poised to sign, she thought long and hard before affixing her own name.[93] But, with that, the Ten had formalised the Single European Act: a treaty in which they confirmed their will to transform relations between their nations into 'a European Union'.

Almost as an afterthought, they also signed an intergovernmental treaty on 'co-operation' in foreign policy, enshrining the London agreement of 1981. Without committing themselves to details they had already agreed in principle that regional and development funds would be 'significantly increased in real terms'. They finally agreed to declarations of intent on co-operation in research and the funding of technological development (the so-called 'Eureka' programme). With all that, the 'EEC' or 'Common Market' formally became the 'European Community', a term already informally used for several years.

After the summit, one of the main points of interest was monetary union. Thatcher told journalists that the text on EMU was meaningless, otherwise she

90 Thatcher, *op. cit.*, p. 554.
91 Grant, *op. cit.*, p. 73.
92 *Ibid.*
93 Thatcher, *ibid.*

would not have signed it. Delors had a different perspective. For him, it was a sign-post. 'It's like the story of Tom Thumb lost in the forest, who left white stones so he could be found,' he said. 'I put in white stones so we could find monetary union again.'[94]

Reaction to the treaty elsewhere was generally downbeat. Spinelli declared that 'the mountain' had given 'birth to a mouse'.[95] BBC television news next day reported that ministers had met but 'all that emerged was a few modest reforms of the Treaty of Rome'.[96] The *Guardian* considered Britain had been the victor. The *Economist*, redolent of Spinelli, called the treaty a 'smiling mouse', meaning that it was well-intentioned but too diminutive to make much difference.[97]

The real significance of the Single European Act, however, was conveyed by its title. Although it would be presented as mainly dealing with the Single Market, it was in reality a further crucial step towards building a 'single Europe'. It extended 'Community competences', by taking over from national governments the power to make laws in several important new policy areas, notably the environment. Through the extension of majority voting it added substantially to the supranational nature of the Community. And for those privy to all the plotting and manoeuvring which had brought the treaty about in the first place, there was also the knowledge that this first serious revision of the Treaty of Rome was already intended to pave the way for a second treaty. This would be much more ambitious in its scope. One clue to this had been Delors' insistence on that declaration of intent about 'economic and monetary union'.

Of all this, however, Thatcher herself seemed sublimely unaware. Answering questions in the Commons on her return from Luxembourg, she declared:

'I am constantly saying that I wish they would talk less about European and political union. The terms are not understood in this country. In so far as they are understood over there, they mean a good deal less than some people over here think they mean.'[98]

If she had not yet got the message, neither had Parliament. When the Single European Act came to be ratified, the necessary Bill amending the European Communities Act 1972 was pushed through an often thinly attended Commons in just six days. The main debate was scheduled to begin on a Thursday, in the knowledge that MPs would be reluctant to see it prolonged lest it encroach on their weekend. After only three sessions of the committee stage, the government abruptly curtailed any further discussion by passing a 'guillotine' motion.

On the final reading, so few MPs turned up that the Bill passed by a mere 149 votes to 43. Apart from a tiny minority from both Labour and Tory benches, few MPs appreciated that this was what even Hugo Young would later agree was 'a major constitutional measure'.[99] Peter Tapsell, an unrepentant Eurosceptic who

---

94 Grant, *op. cit.*, p. 74.
95 Palayret, *op. cit.*
96 Shown in *The Poisoned Chalice*, op. cit.
97 Grant, *op. cit.*, p. 74.
98 Thatcher, *op. cit.*, p. 656.
99 Hugo Young, *op. cit.*, p. 334.

within a few years would be prominent in opposing the Maastricht Treaty, later spoke for not a few of his colleagues in recalling how they had eventually become 'ashamed' at having voted for it. 'We didn't give it the attention we should have done,' he said.[100]

The real irony was that, in accepting the treaty as an economic measure, Thatcher had unwittingly placed herself in exactly the same situation as the people who had been deceived by Macmillan and Heath into accepting something which was 'political' as just a matter of economics (of which she had been one). But Milan was the start of a learning curve which was eventually to prove her downfall.

On 23 May 1986, Altiero Spinelli died in Rome in his eightieth year. His dream might not yet have been fully achieved, but his life's work was done.

---

100 *The Poisoned Chalice, op. cit.*

Chapter 12

In a Minority of One: 1986–1988

'The British economy has been transformed in the past twelve years. In the 1960s and 1970s we were the sick man of Europe, at the bottom of the league tables for growth, investment and productivity. In the 1980s we were at the top.'

Conservative Campaign Guide, 1991

One cannot understand the second half of Thatcher's 11-year reign as Britain's longest serving prime minister of the 20th century without appreciating just how significant was the part played in it by 'Europe'. In the years after Milan she found herself increasingly at odds, not just with her Community 'partners' but with her most senior Cabinet colleagues, until they worked to bring about her downfall.

The first signs of this division came from an unexpected direction, when, early in 1985, her Chancellor Nigel Lawson, known as a robust 'Thatcherite', became persuaded that the key to imposing monetary discipline on Britain's economy was to join the Exchange Rate Mechanism. He was soon supported by Howe, but their motives were quite different. Lawson regarded himself as something of a 'sceptic' on European issues. He saw linking the pound to the *Deutschmark*-dominated ERM simply as an economic tool, on the grounds that Germany had become a byword for maintaining price stability and that the move would signal to the markets that the UK had no intention of devaluing her currency.[1] Lawson genuinely believed the ERM was a means by which members of the Community could co-operate to serve a common economic purpose.[2] Howe on the other hand was well aware that the ERM's real purpose was not economic but political: a mechanism designed to promote greater integration.

Thatcher disagreed with both her colleagues. Under the influence of her economic adviser Professor Alan Walters, she was convinced that, if Britain tried to confine the exchange rate of sterling to the levels allowed by the ERM, this would

---

1 Lawson, Nigel (1992), *The View From No. 11 – Memoirs Of A Tory Radical* (London, Bantam Press), p. 419.
2 In this respect, Lawson shared the view originally held by the economist Bernard Connolly, who joined the European Commission in 1978, just when Schmidt and Giscard were finalising the deal which brought the ERM into being. As Connolly recalled in *The Rotten Heart of Europe*, he had also believed that the Community's purpose was to promote international co-operation. But, as head of the unit responsible for monitoring the ERM's performance, he soon became aware that its real purpose was to undermine the political and economic independence of the nation states (Connolly, *op. cit.*, p. xi–xii).

only render the pound vulnerable to speculative pressure.[3] By the summer of 1985, however, as Thatcher became increasingly worried about inflation, the only answer Lawson could offer was his obsession with entry to the ERM. Unable to persuade him to moderate his enthusiasm, Thatcher arranged a seminar at Number 10, attended not only by Lawson and Howe but also Willie Whitelaw, her deputy prime minister, Norman Tebbit, her party chairman, John Wakeham, her chief whip, and John Biffen, as leader of the House. Also present were Treasury officials, all of whom favoured entry, and Robin Leigh-Pemberton, governor of the Bank of England.

Apart from Biffen, all the ministers spoke for entry, even, to Howe's surprise, Tebbit.[4] Whitelaw thought the verdict was clear. 'The Chancellor, the Governor and the Foreign Secretary,' he said, 'have all spoken in favour of joining the EMS. And the policies all point in the same direction. For me that should settle the question.'[5] It did not. The lady said 'no', and meant it. She brought the meeting quickly to a close. Lawson invited Whitelaw, Tebbit and Howe to join him at Number 11. They were 'downcast and dumbfounded'. According to Howe, they asked themselves what had been the point of the meeting, if the prime minister had been unwilling to heed the collective judgment.

'The prime minister, we knew, was *primus inter pares* but this was the first time that any of us had contemplated her exercising a veto of this kind – and against the very principle of a government policy that we had all been proclaiming for years.'[6]

Lawson's first instinct was to resign, but he was dissuaded. The gathering accepted that, for the moment, the topic had been removed from the agenda.[7]

The next, more public challenge came from Thatcher's Defence Secretary, Michael Heseltine. As a fervent 'Europeanist', he was aware of the growing pressure from the continent, expressed in the 'Rome Declaration' and the Dooge report, for integration of the Community's defence industries. In August 1985, he had completed arrangements for Britain's participation in the biggest joint-defence project so far, the 'European Fighter Aircraft', later known as the 'Eurofighter'. The different components of this aircraft, designed for a 'Cold War' role in combating the latest Soviet MIGs, were to be built in Germany, Italy, Spain and the UK.

When the proposal came before Cabinet, Lawson remarked that the cheapest and most reliable way to replace Britain's ageing Phantoms would be to buy the next generation of American aircraft off the peg.[8] Heseltine strongly opposed this and when the choice was finally put between a solely British project or a joint European venture, Heseltine favoured the latter, Thatcher the former. The Cabinet backed Heseltine.[9]

3 Connolly, *op. cit.*, p. 46.
4 Howe, *op. cit.*, p. 450.
5 *Ibid.*
6 *Ibid.*
7 *Ibid.*
8 Lawson, *op. cit.*, p. 674.
9 *Op. cit.*, p. 675.

Four months later, a not unrelated issue came up when Britain's leading heli-copter company, Westland's, which had been in financial difficulties, was having to choose between two rival bidders: one the US corporation which included the world's leading helicopter maker, Sikorsky; the other a Franco-German-Italian consortium. Although Westland was in the early stages of the European helicop-ter project, the EH101, the company itself wanted to go with Sikorsky, since for years its main production had been machines such as the Wessex and Sea King, built under licence from Sikorsky. But at this point, Heseltine intervened.

According to Howe, Heseltine was concerned that acceptance of the Sikorsky deal would damage 'the prospects for collaborative European defence produc-tion',[10] to which end he pressed Westland to accept the European bid. Both Lawson and Thatcher were strongly opposed. As she put it later, 'the closer we looked at the European option the less substantial did it seem'.

'The three European companies concerned – Aérospatiale (France), MBB (West Germany) and Augusta (Italy) – were, as Michael certainly knew, subject to pressure from their own governments. Aérospatiale and Augusta were state owned and MBB was substantially financed by the West German government. All the European countries were short of work and promises of more work for Westland from Europe seemed likely to remain just prom-ises.'[11]

On 9 December 1985, when three ministerial meetings had failed to resolve the issue, Thatcher herself chaired a further meeting at Number 10. Westland's chair-man reiterated his preference for the Sikorsky deal. Heseltine, Howe and Tebbit spoke strongly for the 'European alternative'. The European consortium was there-fore given until the afternoon of Friday, 13 December to come up with a package the Westland board could recommend.

The proposed package arrived in time, co-ordinated by Heseltine, but the Westland board still favoured Sikorsky. So desperate was Heseltine to push his European option that he claimed that British Aerospace was ready to join the European consortium. When its offer was still rejected, he blamed this on the Cabinet Office.[12] He also claimed that the cancellation of a special Cabinet meet-ing scheduled for that Friday had deprived him of the chance to press his case. No one else could recall that such a meeting had been planned and, although Heseltine persisted with this claim in Cabinet on 12 December, his colleagues remained adamant that no such meeting had been agreed.

On 19 December, therefore, the Cabinet endorsed the Westland decision. Thatcher reminded those present, including Heseltine, that ministers were no longer entitled to lobby for an alternative. In defiance of this, Heseltine continued to lobby throughout the Christmas recess in a highly public manner, not only 'making the government look ridiculous',[13] but, as Hugo Young concedes, 'open-ly flouting the rules of collective responsibility'.[14]

10 *Ibid.*
11 Thatcher, *op. cit.*, p. 427–428.
12 Howe, *op. cit.*, p. 463.
13 Thatcher, *op. cit.*, p. 431.
14 Young, *One of Us*, p. 438.

What brought the row to a head was a letter from Heseltine to the bankers for the European consortium on 1 January 1986, stating that a link with Sikorsky would bar Westland from participating in any further European projects. This Young allows, 'was manifestly a ruse: yet another artifice devised by Heseltine brazenly to challenge the prime minister's authority'.[15] Thatcher herself had written to Westland, assuring the company of the government's support, and when Heseltine had published his own letter two days later on 3 January, Thatcher was so furious that, in Howe's words, there was now 'civil war within the Cabinet'.[16]

Thatcher asked the solicitor general, Patrick Mayhew, to write to Heseltine to correct 'material inaccuracies' in his letter. An edited version of Mayhew's response was then 'leaked' to the Press Association and published. When it emerged that the leak had been authorised by the Trade Secretary, Leon Brittan, the resulting furore led eventually to his resignation. So febrile had the atmosphere become that the next day's *Sun* bannered a picture of Heseltine over its front page with the headline: 'You Liar!'

Back in Cabinet on 9 January 1986, Heseltine again tried to put his case, but, as even Howe had to observe, 'the earlier validity of his argument ... seemed to grow less and less as Michael's presentation became more apparently obsessive'.[17] When Thatcher, unmoving, summed up the issue, Heseltine responded that he was unable to accept what she said and ended 'I must therefore leave this Cabinet'. With that, he departed. No one moved to stop him.

The effort Heseltine had focused on seeking a 'European' option for Westland contrasted strangely with his lack of attention to another project which had been particularly concerning Thatcher, the Nimrod Airborne Early Warning System. This would eventually have to be cancelled by Heseltine's successor when its cost reached £1 billion, four times the original estimate. His enthusiasm for the Eurofighter would eventually cost the British taxpayer more than £16 billion, for an aircraft which became obsolete with the end of the Cold War and was still not in service by 2003, nearly two decades later.[18]

As for the Anglo-Italian EH101, by the time it eventually entered service with the Royal Navy, five years late, its soaring costs had made it the most expensive helicopter in the world, at £100 million each. It was only finally rendered operable by the technical assistance of the US Lockheed Martin company. Yet Heseltine blithely asserted in his memoirs that the EH101 'proved the success I forecast'.[19] Clearly his chief concern was not the adequacy of defence equipment. But the main effect of the Westland affair had been to weaken Thatcher and, although she survived the loss of two ministers, in her colleagues' eyes, she was no longer quite the impregnable leader she had been. Nor was it the last she would hear of Heseltine.

---

15 *Op. cit.*, p. 440.
16 Howe, *op. cit.*, pp. 464–465.
17 *Op. cit.*, p. 467.
18 Before this became apparent, Heseltine was to claim that the project had *saved* the defence budget £1000m (Heseltine, M. (1987), *Where There's A Will* (London, Hutchinson), p. 265). He did not repeat this claim in his autobiography.
19 Heseltine, M. (2000), *Life In The Jungle* (London, Hodder and Stoughton), p. 329.

A new enemy

Having made one enemy, Thatcher now made another. In the second half of 1986 Britain held the presidency of the Council of Ministers. Almost the only progress made by the Community during this period was the passing of 47 new directives in support of the Single Market. This was the sort of progress, she argued, that the Community needed, rather than 'flashy, publicity-seeking initiatives which came to nothing or just caused bad feeling'.[20] Howe records the same 'notable achievement' but adds a chilling detail:

'We had been able, in other words, to exploit the full steps agreed at Luxembourg for the enlargement of the Community authority at the expense of "sovereign parliaments". It was an achievement worth recording, not least under this presidency.'[21]

But the most remembered incident of these six months came at the end of its concluding London Council, when Thatcher and Delors gave a press conference. Howe records in loving detail how, with Delors and himself on the podium, Thatcher did most of the talking, leaving Delors little opportunity to speak.[22] Then, suddenly, she ended one answer by inviting Delors to comment. Howe has it that Delors had 'switched off': his concentration had faltered. He then quoted Thatcher's own memoirs, recording how she complained that Delors 'had refused to say anything, even when I asked him to comment on one of my answers'. She eventually remarked, to the laughter of the press corps, 'I had no idea you were the strong silent type.'[23]

According to his biographer, Delors felt 'snubbed and patronised' and thought Thatcher had tried to humiliate him,[24] Howe records that 'Neither side really forgave the other for the "offence" which neither of them had wittingly committed'. It was another step along the road to deeper misunderstanding.[25]

More revealing perhaps were Thatcher's comments about Delors' behaviour during the Council, about which Howe is silent. The Council was notable, Thatcher wrote:

'... for the emergence of M. Delors as a new kind of European Commission President – a major player in the game. I had a brief foretaste of this during the first evening's dinner, when, to my surprise and unconcealed irritation, he used the discussion period before dinner to launch into a long speech about the parlous state in which the Community found itself as a result of the CAP and put forward a range of quite detailed suggestions. I replied that we should have been told this before: it was plain from what he said that the Community was broke... I reflected to myself that no one could have imagined a top British civil servant springing surprises on ministers in this way: it illustrated all too well what was wrong with the Commission – that it was composed of a new breed of unaccountable politicians.'[26]

20 *Ibid.*
21 Howe, *op. cit.*, p. 521.
22 *Op. cit.*, p. 521.
23 Thatcher, *op. cit.*, p. 558.
24 Grant, *op. cit.*, p. 77.
25 Howe, *op. cit.*, p. 521.
26 Thatcher, *op. cit.*, p. 558.

What this illustrated was that Thatcher still had not quite understood what the Community was all about. With then 12 member states in the EC, there were 13 governments, the 13th being the Commission. In status Delors was a 'head of government', in some respects superior to Thatcher. But she saw him as some kind of 'top civil servant', and treated him accordingly. No wonder Delors bridled at her treatment of him.

Thatcher's education was to continue. On 9 December 1986, reporting on the presidency to what she called the 'European Assembly' in Strasbourg.[27] Her speech, she claims, could not have been 'more *communautaire*', although she was barracked by some MEPs.[28] When she sat down, Delors – 'a quite new M. Delors whom I had never seen or heard before' – began to speak, cheered on by members.[29] 'It was Euro-demagogy,' she wrote, 'designed to play to the prejudices of his audience, to belittle the British presidency and to ask for more money.'[30] Thatcher was having none of this. When Delors had finished, she stood up and demanded a right of reply. This was something apparently unknown in this 'Parliament'. Speaking off the cuff,[31] she answered Delors' points, as she had done so many times in wind-up speeches in the Commons. And she did not fail to observe that Delors had said nothing of what he told the 'Parliament' when he had had the chance at the press conference after the Council.[32]

Afterwards she sat next to Cockfield during lunch at the *Orangerie*, a charming restaurant in a park opposite the parliament building. She is said to have fulminated against Delors in language which brought blushes to the commissioner's cheeks.[33] Delors himself came in late, and took his place beside Thatcher. She told him that again and again she had stood up for his position in the Commons, even though under intense pressure. 'Of one thing he could be sure,' she told him, 'that would never happen again.'[34]

Thatcher was indeed learning fast. Although her understanding was not yet complete, she had come a long way from her launch of the 'Yes' campaign for the Conservatives 11 years earlier. In addition to noting the determination of the 'Franco-German bloc' to set the Community's agenda, she observed that the Commission 'was now led by a tough, talented European federalist, whose philosophy justified centralism'. She also recorded how easily the officials of her own Foreign Office seemed to be 'moving to compromise with these new European friends'.[35]

Taking on the Community: Phase one

In the early months of 1987, the British people suddenly began to wake up to the extent to which, in the seven years since Thatcher came to power in 1979, their

27 Thatcher consistently refused to call it a 'parliament', except where she referred to it in inverted commas.
28 Grant, *op. cit.*, p. 77.
29 *Ibid.*
30 Thatcher, *op. cit.*, p. 558.
31 Grant claims she was 'flustered'.
32 Thatcher, *ibid.*
33 Grant, *op. cit.*, p. 77.
34 *Ibid.*
35 Thatcher, *op. cit.*, pp. 558–559.

country's economy had been transformed. Although initially this had been masked by the worst recession since the war, brought about in part by the drastic measures introduced by her government to remedy problems which had beset the economy for decades, it was becoming clear that 'Thatcherism' was producing remarkable results.

The brooding presence of trade union power, which had cast such a shadow over British life in the 1970s, had been vanquished. One after another, her government had sold off state industries which for so long had been draining billions of pounds out of the economy, from British Steel and British Leyland to British Airways and British Telecom. The result of these 'privatisations' had been an extraordinary boost in productivity. British Steel, by cutting its workforce by two-thirds while maintaining the same output, was on the way to becoming by 1988 the most efficient steel company in the world. A similar revolution, after the 1984 miners' strike, was taking place in the coal industry. The newspaper industry was similarly able to cut its workforce by two-thirds, after the power of the printing unions was broken in 1986, allowing its switch to computerised 'new technology'.

After years of decline, the City of London had just been through its own electronic revolution, in the 'Big Bang' which was re-establishing it as one of the three leading financial centres in the world. Across the globe, from oil and pharmaceuticals to civil engineering and telecommunications, British industry was showing itself capable of taking on any competition. Nearer home, a rebirth of British inventiveness and enterprise was creating hundreds of thousands of new small and medium-size businesses. And the impetus for this renaissance was entirely home-grown, unrelated to Britain's membership of the Common Market.

When Lawson came to present his budget in March 1987, no Chancellor in living memory had been able to deliver such an upbeat message. After reaching its highest level since the war in 1981, unemployment had been dropping by the month. Wage increases were running well ahead of inflation. After a range of tax-cuts, people felt better off than at any time for years.[36] The 'feel-good' factor was back. Britain was in the midst of the 'Lawson boom'.

Inspired by this euphoria, Lawson in that same month embarked on a daring initiative. Still smarting from the frustration of his wish 15 months earlier to take Britain into the ERM, he decided to do the next best thing, by secretly allowing the pound to shadow the *Deutschmark*. He would use his power over interest rates and Britain's reserves to keep the levels of sterling and the *Deutschmark* as closely linked as possible. Even the governor of the Bank of England and Thatcher herself were not taken into his confidence. She was left to discover it only months later, when she was told what Lawson was up to by 'journalists from the *Financial Times*'.[37]

Long before this, however, she had been encouraged by the effects of the 'Lawson boom' to call an election on 9 June 1987. After winning for the third time

---

36 George, *op. cit.*, p. 173.
37 Thatcher, *op. cit.*, p. 701

in succession, by an even greater margin than in 1983, she felt ready to take on the rest of the Community, in which she was now the longest-serving head of government, with a new confidence.

Her top priority, in view of Delors' revelations that the Community was facing a growing financial deficit, was to crusade for more effective budgetary discipline, and in particular for limits on its runaway spending on the CAP. By far the most expensive item in the budget, the CAP had become a by-word for inefficiency, fraud and excess. Its subsidy system was creating huge surpluses: the beef and butter 'mountains', the milk and wine 'lakes', much of which were then dumped on third countries, undercutting their markets and causing them immense damage.[38]

Seemingly unworried by such concerns, the European Parliament had in the first half of 1987 launched a new drive to reactivate Spinelli's 'draft treaty on European Union', winning support from the national parliaments of Belgium, Italy, Holland and Ireland.[39]

In response to this relentless obsession with further schemes of integration, Thatcher decided that there was no option but 'to stake out a radically different position from the direction in which most of the Community seemed intent on going'. She was determined to 'raise the flag for national sovereignty, free trade and enterprise'. In this, she knew she was isolated in the Community, but

'taking the wider perspective, the federalists were the real isolationists, clinging grimly to a half-Europe when Europe as a whole was being liberated; toying with protectionism when truly global markets were emerging; obsessed with schemes of centralisation when the great attempt at centralisation – the Soviet Union – was on the point of collapse. If ever there was an idea whose time had come and gone it was surely that of the artificial mega-state.'[40]

This marked the start of a war of attrition which was to dominate her remaining three years in office. While she remained in a permanent minority of one, the issues at stake were much wider than during her earlier isolation in the battle over the rebate. What she now wanted to address was the very nature of the 'Community', and where it was heading. It was a struggle which would unfold through three main phases.

The first began just three weeks after her election victory when, with Howe at her side, she attended the Brussels Council on 29 to 30 June 1987. Delors had written personally, in advance, to every head of government, drawing attention to the parlous state of the Community budget, introducing what became known as the 'Delors package'. He proposed that the budget should be planned five years in advance and that new rules should be adopted to curb CAP spending. But he also proposed that structural or regional funds should be doubled over the next five years. This would require a massive increase in the Community's 'own resources'. That additional income should come not just from increasing the Community's share of VAT proceeds to 1.6 percent, as agreed at Fontainebleau, but also from a new source, representing 1.4 percent of member states' gross national product (GNP).[41]

38 Thatcher, *op. cit.*, p. 728.
39 See Corbett, *op. cit.*, pp. 276–284.
40 Thatcher, *op. cit.*, p. 728.
41 Grant, *op. cit.*, p. 77.

Thatcher favoured the idea of the Community imposing greater financial discipline and a curb on CAP spending, although she thought the Commission's ideas nothing like 'tough enough'. She was profoundly irritated, however, that this financial crisis had evoked from the Commission its 'traditional answer' to any financial problem: an increase in the Community's 'own resources'. When Delors linked this to a proposal that, while Britain must keep her rebate, it should be defined by a new formula, Thatcher suspected he was trying to whittle it away. She was opposed to doubling the 'structural funds', strongly backed by Ireland, Spain, Portugal and Greece, which expected to gain most from this, and hoped that France and Germany would join her in rejecting it. She also strongly opposed a 'blatantly protectionist' French proposal for an 'oil and fat' tax, designed to keep out US imports of oilseed, used for animal feed, of which Britain was the largest customer.

The discussions started badly when the president, the Belgian prime minister, allowed no less than four hours discussion of the 'oil and fat' tax, which Thatcher, the Germans and the Dutch had no intention of accepting. Delors had also talked the Belgians into linking the CAP 'reforms', the increase in 'own resources' and the structural funds into one 'package'.[42] This was a device he was to employ more than once, whereby a group of controversial issues would have to be agreed together, making it difficult to reject an item which was unacceptable without losing those which were favoured. By the second afternoon, as the heads of government sat round the uncleared lunch table, with the air conditioning having failed, Howe recorded that impatience grew as the temperature rose. When there was eventually a call for a vote, it was eleven to one for the package. Thatcher was on her own, blamed for the Council's 'failure'.

Part of Thatcher's problem was that neither Kohl nor Mitterrand, both facing crucial elections at home, could afford to upset their farmers by curbing CAP spending. When battle was rejoined at the Copenhagen Council on 4 to 5 December 1987, again there was no agreement. Thatcher was also now convinced that Delors was working to reduce Britain's rebate. It was decided that the 'package' should finally be resolved by a special Council in Brussels early in 1988.

Before this took place, Thatcher had a private meeting in London with Mitterrand, and his prime minister, Jacques Chirac. According to Thatcher's account, Chirac spoke 'very frankly', saying that, if the British continued to block the settlement on agriculture wanted by 'the rest of the Community' – by which he meant the French and Germans – Britain would be isolated. Attention would then focus on her rebate.[43] Speaking equally frankly, Thatcher told him that ganging up on her would not work. She was adamant that agricultural surpluses must be brought under control. Without a satisfactory resolution on that and the rebate, she would not approve any increase in 'own resources'.[44]

On the eve of the Council, an increasingly gloomy Delors told his fellow Commissioners, on 27 January 1988, that prospects for agreement looked bleak. If his

---

42 Moravcsik, *Choice For Europe*, p. 367.
43 *Op. cit.*, p. 734.
44 *Ibid.*

'package' was not passed, he would resign. He invited them to do the same. When none agreed to do so, he branded them as cowards. During an eruption of bad temper lasting two hours, he lashed out at his colleagues, among other things accusing the Greek Commissioner, Grigoris Varfis, of incompetence and treachery, denouncing him and his directorate-general as *une honte* (shameful) and *une scandale.*[45]

What actually unfolded during the two days of the Brussels Council, on 29 to 30 June 1988, has become the subject of so many conflicting accounts that it is impossible to reconstruct with certainty how its conclusions were reached. No minutes are taken at Council meetings. Even the notes taken by interpreters are burned. But undoubtedly, since Germany held the presidency, a key role was played in behind-the-scenes negotiations by Kohl, of whom Thatcher noted: 'his style of diplomacy is even more direct than mine ... he was never above banging the table and on this occasion he spoke in a parade-ground bellow throughout'.[46]

At the end of what Howe described as 'gruelling and bafflingly complex' negotiations,[47] it seemed agreement had been reached. The Council then reconvened, but 'anyone who imagined that it would all be plain sailing', as Thatcher records, 'under-rated the French'. To general astonishment, Mitterrand and Chirac refused the deal, wanting to go back over ground that had been agreed at Copenhagen. A heated argument ensued, lasting more than four hours. At last the Danes suggested referring the matter to a foreign minister's meeting scheduled for 10 days later. Thatcher agreed, subject to the Copenhagen agreements being honoured. When the foreign ministers met, France gave way.[48]

Thatcher believed that, by sticking to her guns, she had finally achieved most of what she wanted. She had won 'legally binding controls on expenditure' and measures to reduce agricultural surpluses. The oils and fat tax was rejected. Britain's rebate, she thought, was 'secure', despite complex changes to the way in which it was defined which would eventually turn out to be much more damaging to Britain's interests than she realised.[49] In return she had reluctantly agreed to a new ceiling of 1.2 percent of GNP for Community 'own resources'. She had also given way on Delors' demand for a huge increase in regional funds, amounting to a quarter of the Community's new increased budget. This, as Delors later revealed, he regarded as the Brussels Council's most important single achievement.[50] It gave the Commission power, at its own discretion, to control substantial transfers of money within the Community, as was confirmed when a new 'framework' regulation (Council Regulation 2052/88) introduced fundamental changes to the way regional policy was administered.

Until that time, national governments had devised their own schemes for regional funding, then applied for money to the Commission. This was to be

---

45 Grant, *op. cit.*, pp. 78–79.
46 *Ibid.*
47 Howe, *op. cit.*, p. 532.
48 *Op. cit.*, p. 737.
49 Thatcher, *op. cit.*, p. 737.
50 Delors, Jacques (1991), *Le Nouveau Concert Européen* (Paris, Odile Jacob), p. 81.

replaced by a new direct 'partnership' between the Commission and the 'competent authorities' at national, regional or local level. Local authorities and regions were encouraged to prepare their own development plans and negotiate directly with Brussels for their funding. This led to a rush of local and regional authorities opening their own offices in Brussels, so that their staffs could lobby the Commission directly. National governments were thus relegated to the status of passive bystanders, although they would be obliged to match EU funding with payments of their own.

Thus did the Brussels Council pave the way for a revolutionary new regional policy, which not only gave dramatic new powers to the Commission but also actively undermined member state governments. Delors also regarded this new policy as vital to the ultimate success of another project to which his ambitions were now turning: economic and monetary union.[51]

In the final analysis, what Thatcher described as 'better than a draw', had turned out to be a major extension of integration. It was not the only such leap at this time. While Thatcher's attention had been elsewhere, Howe had been busy with an initiative of his own. The genesis of this lay in the Rome Declaration of 1984, where the decision was made to reactivate the WEU. From the evidence of his memoirs, he had become enamoured of the idea of a 'European Defence Pillar', and in 1987 he made several speeches, in Brussels, Chicago and London, arguing for Europe to play a greater part in her own defence, independent of America.[52]

Knowing that 'Margaret could never be trusted not to snort impatiently whenever the three letters WEU crossed her path', he had initially secured her 'reluctant consent'.[53] This much Howe records in his memoirs. He fails to mention a meeting of WEU foreign and defence ministers at The Hague on 27 October 1987, which effectively launched the idea of a 'Community defence policy'. Paragraph two of their agreement read:

'We recall our commitment to build a European Union in accordance with the Single European Act, which we all signed as members of the European Community. We are convinced that the construction of an integrated Europe will remain incomplete as long as it does not include security and defence.'[54]

Whether Thatcher was ever made aware of what her foreign secretary was doing is not recorded. It is unlikely she could have approved of his agreement, since the text unequivocally committed the UK to developing 'a more cohesive European defence identity'. It marked the beginning of another important new strand in 'the European construction'.

---

51 Gren, Jörgen (1999), *The New Regionalism In The EU* (Stockholm, Fritzes Offentliga Publikationer), pp. 16–23. Not least of the 'new regionalism' approach was the insistence on multinational co-operation, bypassing member state central governments, thus breaking down national barriers. This process was given the name 'perforated sovereignty'.
52 Howe, *op. cit.*, p. 543.
53 *Op. cit.*, p. 544.
54 European Parliament, Defence Archives. WEU papers.

Phase two: at odds with everyone

By the summer of 1988, the British government was heavily engaged in preparations for the Single Market. Trade and Industry Secretary Lord Young launched a major marketing campaign to sell the idea of '1992', using the slogan 'Make no mistake. Europe is open for business.' On the *Today* programme, he waxed almost mystical about how it would soon be possible 'to buy a television in Oxford Street, go to Paris, plug it into the wall and get a picture'. One observer noted that he only needed pay nine francs for an adapter to get the same results.[55] However, so enthusiastic was Young in his task that, by the end of the year, *Private Eye* had labelled him 'Lord Suit' and nominated him 'Bore of the Year'. 'I could have asked for nothing more,' he wrote in his memoirs.[56]

However, while the Single European Act was still being sold to the British people as a triumph for Thatcher, the 'colleagues' were planning the next stage in their agenda: the single currency. Lawson was one of the few who realised that it could only be a matter of time before a move was made to realise this objective.[57]

The prime mover, of course, had been Delors who, like Monnet before him, regarded monetary union as the key to political integration. His major 'co-conspirator' was Mitterrand, whose motivation, according to Lawson, was no less than to seize 'the political and intellectual leadership of Europe which France regarded as her birthright'.[58]

'That was threatened by the superior economic strength of Germany and, in particular, the Bundesbank, in the crucial field of economic policy. The only way the French could see of trumping the Bundesbank was to subsume it into a central bank responsible for a single European currency.'[59]

Kohl, Delors' other co-conspirator, under the influence of his foreign minister, Hans-Deitrich Genscher, took the view that a strong Germany aroused too much fear for her to be able to exercise the political power and influence warranted by her economic strength, unless that strength was seen to be under restraint. In a coincidence of interest with the French, therefore, he too saw merit in a single currency and a central bank, which would serve to reassure his neighbours that the German dragon had been tamed.

The opportunity for the triumvirate to pursue their objective came when Germany assumed the rotating Community presidency on 1 January 1988. The Germans let it be known that at the Hanover European Council, scheduled for 27 to 28 June, they would propose setting up a committee of 'wise men', to recommend the best method of establishing a European central bank, as a prelude to launching a single currency. This was such a dramatic move that, as Howe recalls in his memoirs, even he began to 'wobble'. 'I have often found myself wondering,' he wrote,

55 *Daily Telegraph*, 19 April 1988.
56 Young, Lord (1990), *The Enterprise Years – A Businessman In The Cabinet* (London, Headline), pp. 262–264.
57 Lawson, *op. cit.*, p. 901.
58 *Ibid.*
59 *Ibid.*

'... why the European agenda seemed always to be unfolding at such breakneck speed. Why this now, when so much earlier business remained to be concluded? In domestic politics one at least had the feeling of being able to influence the speed and manner in which policies were developed. But in the Community we often seemed to be on a remorselessly moving carpet – bringing forward, in A. J. P. Taylor's words, "one damn thing after another". Some European leaders did appear to be almost personally driven from one "initiative" to another by the fear that if they ever came to a halt they might risk falling over.'[60]

Thatcher had similar presentiments. She later noted that, from this point onwards, 'the agenda in Europe began to take an increasingly unwelcome shape', not least in its pursuit of the single currency.[61]

At a G7 economic summit in Toronto on 18 June 1988, she restated to Kohl her 'undying hostility' to the very concept of a European central bank. At the same time, she had to recognise that her chances of stopping the committee were ebbing away. At least, when the heads of government gathered for dinner the night before the Hanover Council, she was determined that there should be no formal reference to a European bank. Any committee set up should be composed of the governors of central banks, who could be relied on to keep their feet on the ground.[62]

Kohl had already indicated to Thatcher that he favoured such an idea and when she proposed it, the others, according to Lawson, 'must have been amazed at her innocence'. He recounts how, after a sufficiently long argument to enable her to feel that she had scored a signal success, they agreed that a study group should essentially be a committee of the Community's central bank governors, exactly as she had proposed. They then slipped in a proposal that its chairman should be Jacques Delors.[63] Delors himself had already made clear to Kohl, at a meeting on the Sunday before the Council, that he was happy to have a committee of bank governors, but then had suggested that he himself should be the chairman, to which Kohl had agreed.[64]

Strangely unfazed by Delors' coup, Thatcher seems to have felt that, when she got her way over the removal of a reference to a European central bank in his committee's terms of reference, she had won the day. She was relaxed about the make-up of the committee, which would include the governor of the Bank of England, Robin Leigh-Pemberton, and Karl Otto Pöhl, president of the *Bundesbank*, both highly sceptical of EMU. Thatcher felt that between them, they would surely manage to put a spoke in the wheel of 'this particular vehicle of European integration'.

Another decision made at Hanover was the Council's re-election of Delors for an unprecedented second term as Commission president, strongly backed by Kohl and Mitterand. After his name had been put forward, Thatcher somehow found herself, in the name of general amity, seconding him. Nevertheless, there was one casualty. Cockfield had tried Thatcher's patience too often. She decided to replace

60 *Ibid.*
61 Thatcher, *op. cit.*, p. 737.
62 Lawson, *op. cit.*, p. 902.
63 *Op. cit.*, p. 903.
64 Grant, *op. cit.*, p. 119.

him as Britain's senior commissioner with Leon Brittan, on the recommendation of Howe but to the disgust of Heath, who complained that sending a 'discredited minister' to Europe degraded the idea that Commissioners were servants of the whole Community.[65] He need not have worried. Brittan went native even faster than Cockfield, and immediately started pressing Thatcher to join the ERM.

Curiously, the person most disconcerted by the Delors *coup* was the head of the *Bundesbank*, Karl Otto Pöhl. When he heard what had been agreed, he 'raged' that Kohl had reneged on an agreement not to commit Germany to EMU. For a time he considered resigning, particularly over the appointment of Delors.[66]

Also far from pleased was Lawson. When, the day after the Council, Thatcher conveyed to him her achievement in getting 'them' to drop all reference to the European central bank, Lawson told her she had achieved nothing: 'there is no way that a committee with those terms of reference can possibly do anything else than recommend the setting up of a European central bank', he told her. To Lawson, as an unqualified opponent of monetary union, the Council had been a disaster. Of Thatcher, he felt the very least she could have done was to have prevented Delors becoming the committee's chairman. 'Nothing could have been worse,' he wrote in his memoirs.[67]

The following day, when Thatcher was reporting on the Hanover Council to the Commons, Lawson was troubled by her apparent confusion over what she had conceded. Neil Kinnock, as leader of the opposition, reminded her that she had said many times that a European central bank was 'not on the cards'. Her reply was that progress towards 'monetary union' would not 'necessarily involve a single currency or a European central bank'.[68] Lawson thought this answer 'mind boggling'.

'Unlike economic union, monetary union had a clearly defined meaning, which had been established in the Community context by the Werner Report in 1970 and which I had spelled out to her on the eve of the 1985 European Council. Now she appeared to be implying that it meant something completely different and relatively trifling, even though she had not the slightest idea what that might be.'[69]

Thatcher continued to insist that she never wanted to see a European central bank in her lifetime, because, as she told journalists in Italy in October, this could only mean

'surrendering your economic policy to that banking system that is in charge of the maintenance of the value of the currency and must therefore be in charge of the necessary economic policy to achieve that ... what I suspect they will attempt to do is call something a European central bank which it isn't and never can be.'[70]

65 *The Times*, 20 September 1988.
66 Grant, *op. cit.*, pp. 120–121.
67 Lawson, *op. cit.*, p. 903.
68 Cited in Lawson, *op. cit.*, p. 904.
69 *Ibid.* One feature of the German presidency which pleased Lawson was France's agreement to abolish exchange controls. There was a hiccup when a new French finance minister argued that this would lead to a massive loss of tax revenues as savings flooded abroad. He proposed that all the member states should adopt a fifteen percent 'withholding tax' on savings. At the time nothing further came of this, but later events were to confirm that, once a proposal has been made in the Community, it never goes away.
70 The *Independent*, 22 October 1988, cited in George, *op. cit.*, p. 193.

Lawson, however, could see the writing on the wall. When the Delors committee started work in September, he could read copies of the working papers emerging from it. It was only too clear that the committee and the UK government were on a collision course.[71]

There was in fact something of Monnet in the way Delors organised his committee. As *rapporteur* he nominated an Italian economist who had long been an ardent advocate of a single currency. Then, by another technique which was to become only too familiar, he restricted the committee's terms of reference. It was not permitted to consider whether EMU was desirable or not in principle, only how it could be made to work.

Finally, to consolidate his grip on the committee, he formed alliances with two more enthusiastic supporters of a single currency: one was the governor of the Bank of Italy, the other a Danish professor of economics who had been co-opted onto the committee by Delors himself. Delors arranged for his two allies to speak on his behalf during the committee sessions, thus enabling him to maintain the appearance of an independent chairman, while, before each session, he spent a day with them and other advisers, debating tactics.[72] Small wonder Lawson was alarmed at what was being produced.

Delors was also busy elsewhere. On 6 July 1988, shortly after his second term as president had been confirmed, he had addressed the European Parliament at Strasbourg. There, he noted with satisfaction that the Community had passed more laws in the previous six months than in the years between 1974 and 1984. He told MEPs that most parliaments in the member states had not yet woken up to the extent to which the freeing of the internal market 'would involve a seepage of their sovereignty to the Community'. He then went on to predict that in 10 years, 'eighty percent of economic legislation, and perhaps tax and social legislation, will be directed from the Community'. With so many decisions being taken by the Community, he announced, there would be the need, for the sake of efficiency, for the beginnings of a European government by 1995.[73]

Thatcher was outraged. In her memoirs, she noted that 'he had altogether slipped his leash as a *fonctionnaire* and become a fully-fledged political spokesman for federalism'. She decided that the time had come 'to strike out' against what she saw was 'the erosion of democracy by centralisation and bureaucracy' and to set out an alternative view of Europe's future.[74] She commissioned a paper from her officials to spell out in precise detail how the Commission was now pushing forward the frontiers of its competences into all sorts of new areas, including culture, education, health and social security.

'It used a whole range of techniques. It set up "advisory committees" whose membership was neither appointed by, nor answerable to member states and which tended therefore to reach *communautaire* decisions. It carefully built up a library of declaratory language, large-

---

71 Lawson, *op. cit.*, p. 906.
72 Grant, *op. cit.*, pp. 121–123; McAllister, *op. cit.*, pp. 201–202.
73 Grant, *op. cit.*, p. 88; George, *op. cit.*, p. 193.
74 Thatcher, *op. cit.*, p. 742.

ly drawn from the sort of vacuous nonsense that found its way into Council conclusions, in order to justify its subsequent proposals. It used a special budgetary procedure, known as *actions ponctuelles*, which enabled it to finance new projects without a legal base for doing so. But most seriously of all, it consistently misused treaty articles requiring only a qualified majority to issue directives which it could not pass under articles which required unanimity.'[75]

Hugo Young is particularly withering about this passage, describing it as a 'catalogue of disgust'. He scornfully quotes Thatcher recounting how, the more she considered it, 'the greater my frustration and the deeper my anger became ... I had by now heard about as much of the European "ideal" as I could take'.[76] What Young carefully omits, with his row of dots, is the question by which Thatcher explained her frustration, in asking:

'Were British democracy, parliamentary sovereignty, the common law, our traditional sense of fairness, our ability to run our own affairs our own way to be subordinated to the demands of a remote bureaucracy, resting on very different traditions?'[77]

Although Young did not allow Thatcher to articulate her question in his book, he went on to suggest that she decided to express her 'disgust' in 'whatever undiplomatic words she could get away with'.[78] This, in September 1988, was to be her famous Bruges speech.

Even while the speech was still in draft, Delors pulled off another coup. On 8 September 1988, he addressed the annual congress of the TUC in Bournemouth, selling them the 'social dimension' of Europe. In what was clearly intended to be a highly provocative challenge to the very basis of Thatcherism,[79] he told delegates:

'It is impossible to build Europe on only deregulation ... 1992 is much more than the creation of an internal market abolishing barriers to the free movement of goods services and investment ... The internal market should be designed to benefit each and every citizen of the Community. It is therefore necessary to improve workers' living and working conditions, and to provide better protection for their health and safety at work.'[80]

Historically hostile to 'Brussels', the union delegates took to the message with an enthusiasm born of years of being treated with contempt by Thatcher. They cheered 'Frere Jacques' to the rafters. Responding to Delors' closing words, 'Europe needs you', Ron Todd, general secretary of the Transport Workers' Union, told delegates there was not 'a cat in Hell's chance' of getting recognition in Westminster. The 'only game in town at the moment', he said, was in a town called Brussels. The game was 'poker' and the unions had to learn the rules very fast.[81]

Peter Shore was one of many who understood what had happened. 'It had a very remarkable effect on the trade union leaders', he later told the BBC: 'reviled

75 Thatcher, *op. cit.*, p. 743.
76 Young, *op. cit.*, p. 347; Thatcher, *op. cit.*, p. 743.
77 Thatcher, *ibid.*
78 Young, *ibid.*
79 McAllister, *op. cit.*, p. 203.
80 The *Independent*, 9 September 1988.
81 In *The Poison Chalice*, *op. cit.*

and rejected' by their own government, they had been 'treated with respect and welcome, even with affection, by the rulers of Brussels'. Thatcher's reaction, in the words of Charles Powell, was 'volcanic'. 'What really bugged her was seeing the president of the Commission trying to play a political role'. She did not realise at the time that the visit had been arranged with the assistance of her own Foreign Office. 'Somewhat cackhandedly', Lawson recalled, the FCO officials had thought this was a way of improving relations with the French.[82]

The FCO was also responsible, as it happened, for setting up a speaking engagement for Thatcher less than two weeks later, on 20 September 1988, in the Great Hall of the College of Europe in Bruges, the very heart of Euro-federalism. There she told her audience that there was no better place to talk about the future of Europe 'in a building which so gloriously recalls the greatness that Europe had already achieved over six hundred years ago'. To emphasise that she wanted to talk about European civilisation in a rather larger sense, both historically and geographically, than the narrow sense in which the word 'Europe' had commonly come to be used, she said

'Europe is not the creation of the Treaty of Rome. Nor is the European idea the property of any group or institution. We British are as much heirs to the legacy of European culture as any other nation. Our links with the rest of Europe, the continent of Europe, have been the dominant factor in our history. For three hundred years we were part of the Roman Empire and our maps still trace the straight lines of the roads the Romans built. Our ancestors – Celts, Saxons and Danes – came from the continent.'[83]

Emphasising the broad nature of the 'European identity' she went on 'the European Community is one manifestation of that European identity. But it is not the only one'. She reminded her listeners that Europe in its proper sense also included the countries east of the Iron Curtain. 'We shall always look on Warsaw, Prague and Budapest as great European cities'. The core of her speech amplified this theme:

'It is ironic that just when these countries, such as the Soviet Union, which have tried to run everything from the centre, are learning that success depends on dispersing power and decisions away from the centre, some in the Community want to move in the opposite direction. We have not successfully rolled back the frontiers of the state in Britain only to see them re-imposed at a European level, with a European super-state exercising a new dominance from Brussels.'[84]

Moreover, there were, she wrote, powerful non-economic reasons for the retention of sovereignty, setting out her vision for the future:

'Willing and active co-operation between independent sovereign states is the best was to build a successful European Community … Europe will be stronger precisely because it had France as France, Spain as Spain, Britain as Britain, each with its own customs, traditions and identity. It would be folly to fit them into some sort of identikit European personality.'[85]

---

82 *Ibid.*
83 Extracts cited from full text, courtesy of the Bruges Group, London: *www.brugesgroup.com/media centre/index.live?article=92.*
84 Thatcher, *op. cit.*, pp. 744–745.
85 *Op. cit.*, p. 745.

Thatcher admits to not having predicted the furore her speech unleashed. In 'Europeanist' circles, both in Britain and on the continent, the reaction was one of 'stunned outrage'. [86] But one Euro-enthusiastic periodical did not join the chorus of disapproval, the *Economist*. The speech had not been

'... a predictable diatribe against European unity... Predictable the speech was not: it was a thoughtful, elegant essay on the Europe Britain would like to see... Mrs Thatcher set out a more achievable prospect for the mid-1990s than M. Delors has done.' [87]

Howe, of course, was firmly among those who were 'outraged'. The picture of a Europe being 'ossified by endless regulations' was 'sheer fantasy', he felt. The Community trying to impose on Europe some kind of 'identikit' personality was a 'caricature'. To hold out as an alternative the idea that the Community's decisions should be taken simply through 'willing and active co-operation between independent sovereign nation states' showed that Thatcher clearly had no understanding of what the Community was about.[88]

This was the beginning of the end for Howe. To be working alongside Thatcher while she continued to act outwardly as if she was a committed leader of the Community, he now realised, was

'like being married to a clergyman who had suddenly proclaimed his disbelief in God. I can see now that this was probably the moment at which there began to crystallise the conflict of loyalty with which I was to struggle for perhaps too long.' [89]

All Thatcher had really achieved by her Bruges speech was to sow the seeds of that division within her own party which within a few years would bring it almost to the edge of self-destruction. In that sense, the speech marked a turning point; but not one for the 'project' itself. That was to roll on, unchecked.

---

86 Thatcher, *op. cit.*, p. 746.
87 The *Economist*, 24–30 September 1988, p. 16.
88 Howe, *op. cit.*, p. 537.
89 *Op. cit.*, p. 538.

Chapter 13

'No! No! No!': 1988–1990

'I wanted to change the policies, not the leader. But if that meant the leader had to go, then so it had to be.'

Geoffrey Howe, *Conflict of Loyalty*

Thatcher's Bruges speech made little impact on the British public. In the closing months of 1988 and the first half of 1989, interest in 'Europe' was far outweighed by concern over domestic issues. People were vaguely aware of this new entity called 'Brussels', and of stories about bureaucracy, CAP fraud and waste, butter mountains and wine lakes. They were also dimly conscious of sundry other 'threats', such as rumours that the 'Brussels bureaucrats' were poised to metricate pints of beer and road signs. But all this was remote from their lives.

Political news was dominated by worries over NHS reform and water privatisation, by the impending 'poll-tax', and by the hysteria set off by a junior health minister Edwina Currie over salmonella and eggs. Inflation was creeping up, house prices soaring. Thanks to Lawson, interest rates were high and rising. Thatcherism, heavily reliant on the property-owning classes, was running into the sand; and with it went the popularity of her government.

With a new round of elections to the European Parliament due in June 1989, Heath launched a sustained attack on Thatcher, beginning with a speech delivered in Brussels when she was in the same city at a NATO conference. Referring to Bruges, he said that the British public 'reject such false popularism and such distortions of the truth for the patronising and self-serving hypocrisy that they are'.[1]

Although the Conservative Party tried to exploit the aftermath of Bruges with a clumsy poster campaign asking voters whether they wanted to live 'on a diet of Brussels', 'Europe' never really registered. The electorate made its judgement largely on domestic issues, giving Labour 40 percent of the votes against 35 percent for the Conservatives. It was Labour's first victory over the Tories in a national election since 1974.

Meanwhile, behind the scenes, battles of epic proportions on the European front were being fought, the nature of which only a few were even aware. One of these was being fought out in the offices of the Bank of International Settlements in Basel, Switzerland, which had been borrowed by the Delors committee for its

---

1 *The Times*, 30 May 1989.

meetings. During eight sessions of the committee between September 1988 and April 1989, a process was set in train which was to end up with the launch of the 'euro', shaping the economic history of the next 20 years.

Anticipating the worst, Lawson, with his officials, drew up a plan to ensure that the committee's recommendations were 'as modest and as tentative as possible'. Lawson advised Leigh-Pemberton that his tactics should be to assemble 'the widest possible opposition within the committee' to oppose any commitment to a new treaty to introduce monetary union. However the key to Lawson's plan was Pöhl. Without support from the *Bundesbank*, Delors' project would get nowhere. But Delors had anticipated this. Having rigged the committee, he worked on Pöhl, using a mixture of flattery and persuasion. He then turned the central bankers' heads 'with the prospect of a new, Super-Bundesbank at European level, totally independent of governments and consequently able to exercise a degree of power beyond the wildest dreams of many heads of government'.[2]

Instead of blocking monetary union altogether, as expected, Pöhl therefore merely insisted on certain conditions before a European central bank could go ahead. He asked for a commitment that the ECB could not 'bail out' Community governments in financial difficulties; tight limits on the size of budget deficits that countries would be allowed to run; and that all central banks must be made independent before monetary union took place. Delors was happy to oblige.[3] By Pöhl's failure to stand firm, Leigh-Pemberton was left isolated.[4] Unwilling to be the odd man out, he put his name to the final report. This did much to undermine Thatcher's opposition to monetary union.[5]

Lawson now attempted a pre-emptive strike, using a speaking engagement at Chatham House 'to prepare the ground for what seemed Britain's inevitable rejection' of the report. But his other key objective was to draw a clear distinction between ERM and EMU. On the 25 January 1989, therefore, he told his audience that, while monetary union meant handing over control over key economic decisions to a European central bank, ERM was 'an agreement between independent sovereign states'.[6]

Even at this late stage, Lawson still failed to understand that his European colleagues regarded the ERM primarily as the first step towards monetary union, not as a tool for economic management. He could not see that the rules of the game were not about ensuring monetary stability but about forcing currency convergence as a move towards amalgamating the currencies of the member states. What he saw as intergovernmental co-operation was in fact a 'glidepath' to monetary union. Lawson's strange inability to see the political dimension of the ERM is all the more inexplicable when contrasted with his aversion to EMU.

Reading his own account of those years, it seems as though there were two separate sides to his brain: one which could see the perils of EMU, and the other

2 Connolly, *op. cit.*, p. 78.
3 *Op. cit.*, p. 79.
4 Lawson, *op. cit.*, p. 908.
5 Connolly, *op. cit.*, p. 79.
6 Lawson, *op. cit.*, p. 910.

which saw the merits of ERM, neither able to communicate with the other. In this respect, however, as Lawson imagined that the ERM represented the idea of 'co-operative action', he was only suffering from that same delusion which has afflicted generations of British politicians, especially those in the senior ranks of the Conservative Party. They continued to believe that the Community's central purpose was to promote *co-operation*. It was not and never had been. The agenda was *subordination*. Failing to grasp this, Lawson continued in his attempts to lead the UK down the path to ruin, and with it, Mrs Thatcher.

Indeed, while Lawson was carrying out his lone battle against the Delors committee, his personal battle with Thatcher over taking Britain into the ERM was also coming to a head. As ever, he had the ready assistance of Howe. Thus, the three most senior members of the British government were divided on the issue. Thatcher and Lawson were opposed to the idea of a single currency. Howe and Lawson agreed that membership of the ERM was desirable to aid monetary stability. Thatcher alone was opposed to the ERM, while only Howe wanted Britain to join the single currency.[7]

When the Delors report was finally presented to Community finance ministers in April 1989, it recommended that monetary union should be achieved in three stages. In stage one, all countries should join the ERM in what was known as the 'narrow band'. Stage two should see the establishment of the institutions necessary to run the currency, headed by the European Central Bank. Stage three, with exchange rates irrevocably fixed, would see the Central Bank taking over responsibility for monetary policy. Confirming Lawson's and Thatcher's worst fears, the report also insisted that, by embarking on the first stage, the Community would commit itself irrevocably to eventual economic and monetary union.

In Lawson's view, the report affected the question of sterling's membership of ERM in two important ways. Firstly, it gave it the ERM new lease of life but, more importantly, 'it also fatally confused the essentially economic question of the ERM with the fundamentally political argument over EMU'.[8] What it had done, in Lawson's view, was to turn the economic mechanism of the ERM into a political instrument. Yet he still persisted in his delusion that the ERM was an economic measure and in pressing Thatcher to join.

To pursue this aim, Lawson and Howe hatched a scheme to push Thatcher further towards their objective. An attempt to use the Dutch prime minister, Ruud Lubbers, to convince her of the merits of the ERM misfired, but Lubbers did at least inject a note which became Lawson's main argument: that joining the ERM would greatly strengthen Britain's case in resisting the recommendations of the Delors report.[9] At a meeting between himself and Thatcher early in May, Lawson expanded on his theory of how entering stage one of a three-stage process would help resist being drawn into the next two stages. He wanted to argue with the Community that there was no need for monetary union, as the ERM would be

7 Howe, *op. cit.*, p. 534.
8 Lawson, *op. cit.*, p. 913.
9 *Op. cit.*, p. 915.

sufficient.[10] Thatcher would have none of such *naiveté*. Equally, Lawson was not going to give way. Joining the ERM had become a battle of wills.

Nevertheless, it was Howe who made the next move, 'innocently' suggesting to Thatcher that, before the Delors report was presented to the forthcoming Madrid Council, he and his co-conspirator should send her a joint analysis of the economics and politics of the ERM, 'in the context of the new situation created by our need to respond to the threat of EMU'. Lawson doubted the value of this, and their paper went through several drafts, reflecting the difference of view between himself and Howe.

Headed 'EC Issues and Madrid', the final version ran to some length. The conspirators argued that 'if we simply said "no" to EMU at Madrid, the others would go ahead without us, creating a two-tier Europe, which would be damaging to us'. Therefore, Britain should join ERM (stage one) but then try to postpone any progression to stage three.[11] This was a classic Foreign Office ploy, arguing that we should go along with something we did not want because it was the only way to pre-empt something worse.[12]

It also reflected what was to become a prominent theme in Europeanist rhetoric, the use of such metaphors as 'missing the bus', 'missing the train', 'travelling in the slow lane' and many other such clichés, all intended to convey that Britain would be missing out on something, inevitably with dire consequences. No one ever seemed to ask why it was so important to catch this bus, train, or whatever, when its ultimate destination was so uncertain.

Nevertheless, that was the plan. 'If it could be achieved,' wrote Lawson in his memoirs, 'this would head off the intergovernmental conference and subsequent amendments to the Treaty on which the French were so keen. But we could turn the trick only if we convinced a sufficient number of others of our sincerity.'[13] So that was what it was all about: sincerity. To prove her 'sincerity' Britain should give a 'non-legally binding' undertaking to join the ERM by the end of 1992.

At least Lawson had the decency to feel unease. He wrote in his memoirs, 'I had an innate distaste for cabals and plots, and had never been part of one.'[14] With what seemed cautious regard for his own self-protection, he also insisted on some amendments to the 'minute' and, crucially, that it was delivered to Thatcher on Foreign Office paper. Howe agreed and it was forwarded to Number 10 on 14 June with a request for a joint meeting. Lawson records that Thatcher's reluctance to talk was 'extraordinary'. Grudgingly, she agreed to see the conspirators on 20 June, just six days before the Madrid Council.[15]

The meeting was not a success. Thatcher disagreed completely with the Lawson/Howe analysis and was totally opposed to any commitment to joining the ERM by a particular date. The conspirators got nowhere other than an agreement

---

10 *Op. cit.*, p. 917.
11 *Op. cit.*, p. 929.
12 Connolly, *op. cit.*, p. 78, note 6.
13 Lawson, *op. cit.*, p. 929.
14 *Op. cit.*, p. 930.
15 *Op. cit.*, p. 931.

from Thatcher that she would not 'close her mind' and would reflect further on what had been said.[16]

Thatcher had meanwhile received a paper from her advisor, Professor Walters, suggesting a series of virtually impossible conditions which should be met before Britain joined the ERM.[17] When the thrust of this was conveyed to Howe by Charles Powell, he immediately contacted Lawson who considered it 'palpably absurd'. In his view, it was merely another bid to postpone entry into the ERM for as long as possible, if not indefinitely. 'The hand of Alan Walters was all too visible,' he observed.[18] Together he and Howe began plotting what Thatcher termed 'the ambush before Madrid', for which purpose they sent another minute, demanding a further meeting.

Thatcher received it at Chequers on the Saturday morning. Almost immediately, she received a telephone call to ask about a time for the meeting. This, she wrote, 'was extremely inconvenient', as she was due in Madrid the next afternoon. But the plotters were not to be deterred. She offered them late Saturday, or early Sunday morning. They chose the latter. Thatcher later wrote:

'I knew that Geoffrey had put Nigel up to this ... I knew that he had always thought that he might one day become leader of the Conservative Party – an ambition that became more passionate as it was slipping away from him ... this quiet, gentle but deeply ambitious man – with whom my relations had become progressively worse as my exasperation for his insatiable appetite for compromise led me sometimes to lash out at him in front of others – was now out to make trouble for me ... There can be no other explanation for what he now did and put Nigel up to doing.'[19]

The three met at 8.15 on Sunday morning. Howe and Lawson stood each side of the fireplace in Thatcher's study, facing her. Having prepared their tactics beforehand, Howe urged his boss to speak first at Madrid, setting out her conditions for joining ERM and announcing Britain's date of entry. He and Lawson had even worked out a precise formula for her statement. As before, they stood by their argument that this would stop the Delors process from moving to stages two and three. Then came the bombshell. Unless she acceded to their demands, they would both resign.

Even though she doubted that she could afford to lose two senior ministers in one go, Thatcher's would not be blackmailed into a policy she knew to be wrong. She refused point-blank to undertake to set a date, but would reflect further on what to say at Madrid. So the 'nasty little meeting' ended. The conspirators left, 'Geoffrey looking insufferably smug'.[20]

Five hours later Howe and Thatcher met again in an RAF VC10 to Madrid. But they travelled in separate compartments, a drawn curtain between them. On arrival, they went separately to their suites in the Ritz Hotel. When they met again,

16 *Ibid.*
17 Thatcher, *op. cit.*, p. 709.
18 Lawson, *op. cit.*, p. 932.
19 Thatcher, *op. cit.*, p. 712.
20 *Ibid.*

their conversation was 'brittle and businesslike', with neither ERM nor EMU being discussed.[21]

Monetary union was at the top of the Council agenda. Thatcher was expected to 'handbag' the Delors plan but she let others speak first, keeping everyone in suspense, including Howe, who had no idea what she was going to say. When she did speak, she was calm, quiet, and measured. According to Howe, who was no doubt taking careful notes, she told the meeting that, in respect of the Delors Report, 'we should be pragmatic'. 'The Delors Report was right to go for a staged approach to EMU and its analysis was invaluable'. Speaking very deliberately, she then declared: 'I can reaffirm today the United Kingdom's intention to join the ERM.' But she did not give a date. The timing must be for her government alone.

The effect, Howe recalls, was 'electrifying'. At lunch, a number of 'colleagues' commended the 'new, strikingly calm presentation of a much more positive position'. Delors was delighted. Having escaped a 'handbagging', he congratulated Howe 'on having won the intellectual argument within the British government'. Howe too was pleased. Although Thatcher had avoided giving an entry date to ERM, 'we had made an essential breakthrough', he wrote.[22] In the context of his warm relationship with Delors, there can be little doubt as to the identity of the 'we' to which he referred. It was not his own government.

In her memoirs, Thatcher was dismissive of the whole issue. 'I was, of course, opposed root and branch to the whole approach of the Delors Report,' she wrote, 'But I was not in a position to prevent some kind of action being taken on it.'[23]

In fact, a greater concern of Thatcher at the Council had been a second project on which Delors was now pushing hard, his 'Social Charter'. From the moment he had arrived at the Commission, this had been a pet project, balancing the single market, as he put it, with 'an effort to improve the lot of workers'.[24] By 1988, he had promised trades unions a series of Community labour laws, whence the term 'Social Charter' emerged. Thatcher felt this to be 'simply a socialists' charter – devised by socialists in the Commission and favoured predominantly by socialist member states'.[25] When it came to the vote, however, Thatcher was again on her own.

The end of Howe and Lawson

Back in London, there was unfinished business. High on the list was Howe. In the July reshuffle, he was demoted to Leader of the House and the non-job of deputy prime minister. With no very visible qualifications for succeeding him, John Major took over as Foreign Secretary. Thatcher thought this comparatively unknown figure would be more malleable. Nevertheless, the balance of her new Cabinet, with John Gummer and Chris Patten taking over agriculture and the environment, had slipped towards the Euro-enthusiasts. This, she mused, did not matter as long as

21 Howe, *op. cit.*, p. 581.
22 *Op. cit.*, p. 583.
23 Thatcher, *op. cit.*, p. 751.
24 Grant, *op. cit.*, p. 83.
25 Thatcher, *op. cit.*, p. 750.

crises which threatened her authority could be avoided. But, as Thatcher quoted *Lear*, they came not in single spies but in battalions.[26]

The first crisis erupted right next door, at 11 Downing Street. Following the ultimatum on the eve of the Madrid summit, the tension between Thatcher and her Chancellor had not abated. Interest rates were soaring as a result of Lawson shadowing the *Deutschmark* and, just before the Conservative Party conference on 10 October, following a rate rise by the *Bundesbank*, they reached a record 15 per-cent. The *Daily Mail* savaged Lawson as 'this bankrupt chancellor', demanding his resignation. Relations were not helped by a series of critical statements from Walters, prominently reported by a media keen to exploit differences between Lawson and Thatcher's adviser.

Feeling his job was being made impossible, Lawson had by 26 October decided that either Walters should go or he would resign.[27] After being told by Thatcher in the morning that she did not want to lose Walters, Lawson sent round his res-ignation letter that afternoon. To Thatcher's chagrin, when she discussed this with Walters, he too insisted on resigning. For her replacement chancellor, Thatcher chose Major, drafting in Douglas Hurd, another long-time Euro-enthusiast, as Foreign Secretary.

Predictably, the financial markets reacted adversely. The pound fell two cents against the dollar within 10 minutes of the announcement of Lawson's resignation, with a further two cents by the New York close. There was a similar dive against the *Deutschmark*, with the pound falling through the psychologically important DM 3 barrier, bottoming out at DM 2.90. The next day's newspapers reported it as a major crisis. The *Daily Mail* devoted most of its front page to the headline 'Thatcher Day of Disaster' while the *Daily Mirror* screamed 'Thatcher in Crisis'. Only the *Sun* took a contrary view, with the succinct headline 'Good Riddance'.

That weekend Thatcher noted that Howe gave a speech 'of calculated malice', praising Lawson's courage for his fight to get Britain into the ERM. At least she took consolation from the fact that his replacement 'had not got personal capital sunk in past policy errors'. However, she soon found that she had a Chancellor who, as a former whip, favoured entry into the ERM as a way to reduce internal strains within the party. With heavy heart she was prepared to go along with this. But on EMU she remained immovable. This 'went to the heart not just of the debate about Europe's future but about Britain's future as a democratic, sovereign state'. On this, she wrote, there would be no compromise.[28]

But compromise she did. At the behest of Thatcher, the day before he resigned, Lawson had finalised a paper on what became known as the 'hard ecu', an arrange-ment whereby all currencies of the member states should become legal tender throughout the Community. The theory was that the most popular currency would drive out the others, leading to *de facto* monetary union, without loss of sovereignty.

---

26 Thatcher, *op. cit.*, pp. 758–759.
27 Lawson, *op. cit.*, p. 961.
28 Thatcher, *op. cit.*, p. 719.

It fell to Hurd, the new foreign secretary, to unveil this plan at the foreign ministers' Council in Brussels on 26 October 1989. It was immediately seen as a diversionary tactic, scorned by the French finance minister as 'illusory and unacceptable'. Come what may, the other members were determined to proceed with full monetary union. The French prime minister, Michel Rocard warned, 'Britain is like a slow ship in a naval convoy. Sometimes, for the good of all, the last vessel must be abandoned to its tragic destiny.'[29]

Diversion from the east

In the autumn and winter of 1989, Europe was shaken by its greatest political event for decades. The peoples of East Germany, Czechoslovakia, Hungary, Poland, Bulgaria and Romania stumbled out into the dawn of their freedom from the Communism which had held them in its grip for 40 years. It was yet another reminder of just how casually the word Europe had come to be made synonymous only with that 'little Europe' in the west, which covered barely a quarter of the continent's land area.

This was the point Thatcher had tried to make in Bruges the previous year. It was no accident that, of all the leaders of western Europe, she herself was by far the best known to the peoples of central and eastern Europe. As the 'Iron Lady', they had seen her, throughout the 1980s, standing alongside President Reagan as a shining champion of liberty, democracy and the free market, against the state power of the 'evil empire'.

Eventually, the influence of these great events on the future of 'little Europe' was to be enormous. But their most immediate impact came from the dismantling of the Berlin Wall on 9 November. At once this opened up the prospect of a united Germany, bringing together 60 million West Germans with the 20 million in the east, to make what would be easily the largest, richest and most powerful nation in the Community. It was a prospect the rest of Europe viewed with alarm.

For Kohl, however, this unexpected chance to unite his country was the opportunity of a lifetime. When he appeared on the steps of the Schoneberg town hall in Berlin on 10 November, the night after the wall had been breached, he had been jeered by a hostile crowd. But he was determined to make a 'grand gesture'. On 28 November he announced a hugely ambitious plan to bind the two Germanies in a confederation, preceded by free elections in East Germany and a massive infusion of aid. Every weak East German mark would be exchanged for a strong *Deutschmark*. Significantly, Kohl had consulted none of his allies in Washington, Paris or London, or even his own foreign minister. Nevertheless, he insisted that Germany's reunification must be embedded in the 'European' process and that this 'enlargement' would require the Community to be strengthened further.[30]

France now held the presidency, and at the Strasbourg Council on 8 December 1989, Mitterrand set the scene by declaring that 'Rarely has a European Council

29 *Time International*, 20 November 1989, p. 42.
30 McAllister, *op. cit.*, p. 215.

confronted such major issues'.[31] He seized the opportunity to insist that a date must now be set for an IGC on economic and monetary union before the end of 1990. Thatcher, recognising that the Germans had aligned themselves with the French, knew she was on her own and could not block an IGC. Having been relegated to the status of a bystander, she decided to be 'sweetly reasonable'.[32]

Another agenda item was Delors' Social Charter and, on this, Thatcher refused to budge, reinforced by her discovery that the Commission was proposing no fewer than 47 initiatives, including 17 directives, in the areas of policy it covered. From a British point of view, she wrote, that effectively ended discussion on the Charter.[33] Equally, Thatcher remained utterly opposed to 'political union'. Once more she was preparing to place herself in the firing line against the forces of European integration. Her stance was to bring an end to her premiership.

End game

The year 1990 started with a dramatic proposal from Delors. Confident that the integration bandwagon was rolling in earnest, he suggested to the European Parliament on 17 January that there should be not one IGC but two: one concentrating on EMU, the second on other 'institutional questions'. Privately, he harboured ambitions to preside over both. Then, on 23 January, he told French television viewers that:

'My objective is that before the end of the millennium Europe should have a true federation. The Commission should become a political executive which can define essential common interests ... responsible before the European Parliament and before the nation-states represented how you will, by the European Council or by a second chamber of national parliaments.'[34]

For the first time, Delors had openly used the word 'federal'. He later told his biographer that this could not work unless the Twelve had first 'delegated important powers of sovereignty to the centre'.[35]

In March 1990 Delors' position was reinforced when the European Parliament adopted a report produced by its vice-president, the British Socialist MEP David Martin, calling for a transformation of the Community into a 'European Union of a federal type'. Besides monetary union, this advocated the integration of 'political co-operation' (i.e., foreign policy) into the Community framework. He wanted greater powers over social and environmental policy; the incorporation into the treaties of a charter of fundamental rights; the systematic use of majority voting in the Council; and a strengthening of the executive powers of the Commission. With that had to come much more money for the Community budget and, last but not least, increased powers for the Parliament, including the

---

31 Cited in *Time International*, 18 December 1989, p. 17.
32 Thatcher, *op. cit.*, p. 760.
33 *Ibid.*
34 Cited in Grant, *op. cit.*, p. 135.
35 *Ibid.*

right to initiate legislation.[36] Again the Parliament was acting as a driver of integration by putting items on the IGC agenda which would otherwise not have been considered.

The Irish, as holders of the presidency, then intervened by announcing a special European Council on 28 April to discuss German reunification and political union. Just before this, on 18 April, Kohl and Mitterrand jointly published their own ideas for the two IGCs. These effectively supported the Parliament, calling for 'political union' to take effect at the same time as EMU, on 1 January 1993. The two leaders also called on the Community to 'define and implement' a common foreign and security policy.

Thatcher had to concede that, if the Community was moving towards monetary union, then at least 'political union' was logical. A single currency and a single economic policy ultimately implied a single government. However she was particularly cynical about the prospects for a common foreign policy. She noted that, at the same time, Kohl and Mitterrand had sent a joint letter to the president of Lithuania urging him to suspend his country's declaration of independence to ease the way for talks with Moscow. She took pleasure in pointing out in Dublin that this was done without consulting the rest of the Community, let alone NATO. This suggested to her that the likelihood of agreeing a common foreign and security policy was remote.[37]

Her approach to the Council was unorthodox. Giving her speech during a working lunch, she decided on a tongue-in-cheek approach, telling the other heads of government how to dispel fears about what was intended by 'political union'. They should explain that it did not mean a loss of national identity, nor giving up separate heads of state, whether monarchs or presidents, nor the suppression of national parliaments. Nor would the European Parliament gain powers at the expense of national parliaments. Warming to her theme, she suggested that it meant no change to countries' electoral systems, nor changes to the Council of Ministers, and there would be no greater centralisation of powers in Europe at the expense of national governments and parliaments. There would be no weakening of NATO and no attempt to turn foreign policy co-operation into a restriction on the rights of states to conduct their own foreign policies.[38]

What she found remarkable about the response to this semi-satirical *jeu d'esprit* was that the heads of government seemed quite unable to spell out precisely what they meant by 'political union'. Top marks for 'calculated ambiguity' went to Andreotti, who suggested that it would be dangerous to reach a clear-cut definition as to what the term meant.[39]

In May, France further muddied the waters when the foreign ministers met in Ireland. Roland Dumas, the French foreign minister, talked of changing the European Council from a periodic gathering of heads of governments to an institution with its own secretariat. He also suggested that the Council presidency

36 Corbett, *op. cit.*, pp. 284–285.
37 Thatcher, *op. cit.*, p. 761.
38 *Op. cit.*, pp. 761–762.
39 *Op. cit.*, p. 762.

should be strengthened by appointing a president from one country for several years, rather than the six-monthly rotating presidency. This was an idea to which the French were to return and Delors, fearing that this 'intergovernmentalism' might wreck his own plans, began to refer to the next treaty in terms of an *Acte Unique Bis* – A Single Act Part Two – emphasising the need for institutional changes in order to forestall French ambitions.[40]

June 25 brought the heads of government to Dublin again for their regular European Council. Against Thatcher's wishes, but without her trying to block it, the Council declared that the two IGCs would start later in the year, immediately after the October Rome Council. Meanwhile, a committee of national officials would carry out preparatory work on 'political union'. For the rest, Mitterrand and Kohl indulged in grandstanding, proposing a billion-dollar aid programme for the Soviet Union. Thatcher was again cast in the role of objector, arguing that without fundamental market reforms, the money would simply be wasted in propping up a decaying political structure. For once, Delors agreed, and the plan was shelved.[41]

Meanwhile, with the prospect of East Germany becoming an integral part of the Community, Austria and Sweden had tabled applications to join, followed by Malta and Cyprus. Britain in particular favoured their entry on the basis that 'widening' would prevent the 'deepening' of the Community. This was to become a constant refrain, but the Community stood firm. There would be no further enlargement until after the completion of the Single Market in 1992. As for the central European countries, Delors argued that it would take 15 to 20 years of preparation before they would be ready to join.[42]

Back in the UK, the Conservatives were having their own troubles. In the spring, the poll tax had become the focus of growing discontent, triggering a large-scale riot around Trafalgar Square on 31 March. This had been followed in May by the Party's dismal performance in the local government elections. Egged on by the party's Europhiles, these events lent strength to an emerging 'Thatcher must go' caucus, balanced only by what some political commentators were calling the 'Keep Calm Party' headed by Major.[43] His programme was to retain Thatcher as leader but to take the country into the ERM and generally make friendlier noises to the Europeans.[44]

Instrumental in Major's conversion to the ERM had been Hurd, who courted his younger, less experienced colleague over a series of breakfasts at his London residence in Carlton House Gardens. Thatcher was again confronted by an alliance between her two most senior ministers. With Howe also sniping in the background, a glowering Lawson on the back benches and the broadsheet newspapers all pushing for ERM, encouraged by *ex cathedra* statements from the now totally 'native' Leon Brittan, Thatcher was becoming increasingly isolated.

40 Grant, *op. cit.*, p. 142.
41 Thatcher, *op. cit.*, p. 763; Grant, *op. cit.*, p. 143.
42 Grant, *op. cit.*, p. 143.
43 Watkins, Alan (1992), *A Conservative Coup – The Fall Of Margaret Thatcher* (2nd ed.) (London, Duckworth), p. 131.
44 *Ibid.*

One constant friend was her trade and industry secretary, Nicholas Ridley. But, by an error of judgment, he gave the young editor of *The Spectator* – Nigel Lawson's son Dominic – a characteristically outspoken interview on European issues. In the interview, published on 13 July 1990, he observed, *inter alia*: 'I'm not against giving up sovereignty in principle, but not to this lot. You might just as well give it to Adolf Hitler, frankly.' The magazine's cover carried a Garland cartoon showing a small Mr Ridley running away from a big poster of Kohl, having just daubed his face with a moustache to make him look like Hitler. Such was the outcry that Ridley was forced to resign, leaving Thatcher with no committed supporters in her own Cabinet. Her dwindling band of supporters was to be further diminished in tragic circumstances on 30 July when her long-time friend and political ally, Ian Gow, was murdered by an IRA car-bomb.

A few days later, on 2 August, while Thatcher was in Aspen, Colorado, to give a lecture, news came in that Iraq had invaded Kuwait. As it happened, President George Bush was also in Aspen. She immediately urged the strongest possible response, stiffening his resolve by promising large-scale British military support. This did little to increase her domestic popularity; nor did it strengthen her position with her own Cabinet. The eyes of her colleagues were still fixed on Brussels.

In the manner of an infidel embracing Christianity under threat of painful death, Thatcher now accepted that Britain should join the ERM. This was announced by a delighted Major on 5 October 1990, days before the start of the Conservative Party Conference in Bournemouth. In what was to become a key feature of ERM mythology, the joining rate was DM 2.95, later held by ERM apologists to have been 'too high' and the reason why Britain would be forced into a humiliating exit in 1992. Major's decision was immediately backed by Labour, the Liberal Democrats, the trade unions and the CBI. The one person who was furious, according to Connolly, was Delors. By now his main concern was to be free of his most formidable enemy: the one leader who could upset all his plans for the new treaty. Joining the ERM, he feared, might give her a political lifeline. Thatcher had to be removed, quickly.[45]

An opportunity was to hand. A European Council had been scheduled for Rome in late October, under the Italian presidency. It was supposed to clear the decks of other business, notably the GATT talks, so that the Council could then move on to what were seen as the really big issues, the aims and organisation of the forthcoming IGCs.[46]

The GATT talks, involving 125 countries and hailed as 'the biggest negotiating mandate on trade ever agreed', had reached a critical stage. At stake was the so-called 'Uruguay Round' which had started in September 1986, in Punta del Este, Uruguay. The aims were to achieve a drastic further reduction in tariffs on industrial goods across the world, and to open up new areas to freer trade, including

45 Connolly, *op. cit.*, p. 104.
46 *Op. cit.*, p. 105.

agriculture and services. These measures, it was estimated, could increase the world's income by over $200 billion a year.[47]

According to his biographer, GATT brought out the worst in Delors: 'uncontrollable emotion, a Gallic view of the world and a deep mistrust of the Anglo-Saxons'.[48] The term 'liberalise' meant reducing subsidies and preventing 'Europe' from dumping her agricultural surpluses on the world market, thus threatening to undermine the very basis of the CAP. French farmers, predictably, were implacably hostile to the proposed changes.

It was a measure of how far Britain had surrendered her powers that, although she was the world's second largest overseas trader, she no longer had a seat at these talks. Instead the Community negotiated as a single bloc, with the Council hammering out its position from a welter of conflicting interests among the Twelve, then giving the Commission the mandate to undertake negotiations on their behalf. Any deal had finally to be approved by the Council. Britain, Germany, Holland and Denmark generally supported 'liberalisation'. France had tried to obstruct progress at every opportunity. The Commissioner responsible for the negotiations was a Dutchman, Frans Andreissen, disposed towards flexibility, but he was often blocked by the Irish Agriculture Commissioner, Ray MacSharry. When disputes broke out between Andreissen and MacSharry, Delors did nothing to resolve them.[49]

By the summer of 1990, the Community's inability to reach a common view had brought negotiations to an *impasse*. The sticking point was the EEC's refusal to accept US demands for a drastic cut in agricultural subsidies. The GATT secretariat proposed a compromise to break the deadlock but, at a meeting in July with James Baker, the US Secretary of State, Delors threatened to resign rather than accept any compromise.[50]

Community trade and agriculture ministers had then met six more times but, almost entirely due to French intransigence, failed to reach agreement on a counteroffer. Again, Delors did nothing. With final negotiations scheduled for Brussels in December 1990, time was running out. Thatcher was therefore insistent that an issue of such importance to billions of people round the world must be discussed in Rome.

The 'little Europeans', obsessed with their plans for monetary union and the new treaty, would have none of it. As Connolly recorded, 'it became clear that something was in the air' when orders were given within the Commission that at all costs a planned report called *One Market, One Money* must be rushed out in time for the October Council.[51] Connolly described the report as 'propaganda'; 'a set of specious, anti-economic arguments and rigged model simulation results', intended to promote the idea that the Single Market could only work properly with a single currency.[52] The report claimed that a single currency would save the

---

47 Sandiford, Wayne, *GATT and the Uruguay Round* (*www.eccb-centralbank.org/Rsch_Papers/Rpmar94.pdf*).
48 Grant, *op. cit.*, p. 171.
49 *Ibid.*
50 *Op. cit.*, p. 172.
51 Connolly, *op. cit.*, p. 105.
52 *Ibid.*

Community £9–13 billion a year in transaction costs,[53] a sum which, even if not grossly inflated, was dwarfed by the annual benefit potentially available from successful conclusion of the GATT negotiations.

Shortly before the Rome Council began, the Christian Democrat group, led by Andreotti, the Italian prime minister, decided that Thatcher must be ambushed. The Council would refuse to discuss GATT and focus instead on monetary union, with the view to declaring that the final stage of EMU must begin on 1 January 1993. The thinking, according to Connolly, was that

'Mrs Thatcher ... would be forced out into the open; either she would agree, conceding game, set and match ... or, more likely, she would have to refuse, leaving the door open for a strike by her British opponents.'[54]

Then, on 21 October, the Commission issued its opinion on 'political union'. It had adopted most of the Parliament's proposals, including majority voting for foreign policy and the notion of 'European Union citizenship', going on to say that the new treaty would not produce the final shape of the European Union 'but should leave the door open to developments in a federal direction'.[55]

Thatcher herself admits she was quite unprepared for the way things went once the Council opened on Saturday 27 October 1990. As planned, Andreotti made clear at the beginning that there was no intention of discussing the GATT. Thatcher briefly took the heads of government to task for ignoring such a crucial issue, hoping in vain that others would intervene.[56] After bad-tempered discussion about a proposal from Delors that the Council should support the Soviet Union by declaring that its external borders must remain intact, thereby denying independence to the Baltic States, the agenda moved on.

In an increasingly tense atmosphere, the 'Eleven' were determined to insert in the communiqué a statement on political union, which only Thatcher refused to accept. What they were proposing, she told them, pre-empted the conclusions of the IGC. The 'Eleven' then demanded that stage two of monetary union must start on 1 January 1994, a year later than initially proposed. Thatcher could not agree to this either.[57] The trap had snapped shut. A bewildered Thatcher could only write in her memoirs: 'they were not interested in compromise. My objections were heard in stony silence. I now had no support. I just had to say no.' She repeated that 'no' to journalists outside, telling them:

'It seems like cloud cuckoo land ... If anyone is suggesting that I would go to Parliament and suggest the abolition of the pound sterling – no! ... We have made it quite clear that we will not have a single currency imposed on us.'[58]

The following Monday, according to Connolly, a senior French official, debriefing his staff on the outcome of the Council, was asked whether it had been a failure.

53 Grant, *op. cit.*, p. 148.
54 Connolly, *op. cit.*, p. 106.
55 Corbett, *op. cit.*, pp. 300–301.
56 Thatcher, *op. cit.*, pp. 766–767.
57 *Op. cit.*, p. 767.
58 Cited in Watkins, *op. cit.*, p. 142.

'On the contrary,' he replied, 'the Council had been an outstanding success, since it had re-established an eleven-to-one situation in the Community and destabilised Thatcher at home.'[59]

Back home, on 30 October, Thatcher reported to the House on what had happened. At some length, in her opening statement, she expressed her regret that the Council had refused to discuss the GATT talks, an issue of considerable importance to Britain's economy. This passed over the head of Kinnock, who quickly went into full sneering mode:

'Does the Prime Minister not understand that, with her method of conducting affairs, she is throwing away that sound argument and losing both potential allies and necessary influence? Does she not appreciate that, even now, her tantrum tactics will not stop the process of change or change anything in the process of change? All they do is strand Britain in a European second division without the influence over change that we need.'[60]

His long catalogue of personal abuse finally provoked Thatcher into a reply which included one of the most famous lines of her premiership:

'The president of the Commission, Mr Delors, said at a press conference the other day that he wanted the European Parliament to be the democratic body of the Community. He wanted the Commission to be the executive and he wanted the Council of Ministers to be the senate. No. No. No.'[61]

This, in the words of Hugo Young, became 'in its monosyllabic brutality, the rubric of one of her most famous parliamentary moments, leaping with rage, ringing round the chamber, startling those who even in eleven years had much experience on the Thatcher vocabulary on Europe'.[62] What Young was no more able to grasp than Kinnock was the significance of Thatcher's opening statement on GATT. Here she had given an accurate diagnosis of all that was wrong with the Community:

'The Uruguay round of trade negotiations is due to be completed before the end of this year. The outcome will decide whether world trade becomes steadily more open, or we repeat the mistakes of the past and relapse into protectionism.

The most difficult item is agriculture. All the major participants in the Uruguay round committed themselves to table negotiating offers by 15 October. All except the European Community have done so. The Community has been discussing this problem since the round began in the autumn of 1986. It gave an unequivocal commitment in April last year to make substantial and progressive reductions in agricultural support.

That commitment was repeated at the Houston economic summit in July this year ... there have been six sessions of European Community Ministers to discuss the proposal. The most recent, lasting some 16 hours, was on Friday last week. But no agreement has been reached. The main opposition has come from France and Germany.

59 Connolly, *op. cit.*, p. 106.
60 *Hansard*, 30 October 1990, col. 872.
61 *Op. cit.*, col. 873.
62 Young, *Blessed Plot*, *op. cit.*, p. 368.

The Community's failure has harmed its reputation. Negotiations between the leading groups of countries cannot start until the Community's proposals have been tabled ... the European Council requested Ministers to meet again and put the Commission in a position to table a negotiating offer ... but President Mitterrand made it clear that France would continue to vote against those proposals. It remains for Agriculture and Trade Ministers to try yet again to reach a conclusion. If we fail, it will give a signal to the world that the Community is protectionist.' [63]

For a country that had supposedly joined the 'Common Market' to improve trade, Thatcher was dealing with the issue of most immediate concern to her country's prosperity. Yet Kinnock barely mentioned GATT and was wholly unconcerned by French and German obstructionism. His only concern was to push home what he thought would play best to the press gallery.

Another commentator who showed no interest in GATT was Howe, who could only caricature Thatcher's performance in terms of its 'reckless' and 'crude' nationalism, drawing cheers from the 'anti-Europeans' on her back-benches.[64] To what extent Thatcher was indulging in 'nationalist crudity' can best be judged from the Hansard record. Immediately after her reply to Kinnock, for instance, Nicholas Ridley asked whether she thought the 'eleven' were 'intransigent' on GATT. Were they 'deliberately working for the failure of the GATT round in order to achieve their objectives of a fortress Europe'? Thatcher's factual response is worth quoting at length:

'The European community is the only group of nations which, after years of studying the problem, has not tabled an initial negotiating position on agriculture in the GATT round. The United States, Japan, the Cairns group, Canada and Switzerland have tabled theirs, but from the Community – nothing. It really is a disgrace that we have not even been able to agree on a negotiating position, let alone start to negotiate with all the other groups – between now and the end of the year.

Yes, I agree with my right hon. Friend that several countries in the Community are highly protectionist. The common agricultural policy is a protectionist policy, but we will try to reduce the protectionism, first because it would help the third world, secondly because it would mean that we would not have export subsidies – and thereby take business away from other countries – and thirdly because in this country we believe in open trade. This was the most serious matter to be discussed at the European Council, and I most earnestly hope that this time Agriculture Ministers... I mean the French and German Agriculture Ministers, will accept the proposals of the Commission for the negotiating position in the Uruguay round.' [65]

Then it was Paddy Ashdown's turn. Did she realise that she had 'isolated this country in Europe, weakened our voice in Europe, divided the government and betrayed this country's long-term best interests'? Did she realise that 'for as long as she hangs on to power, so long will Britain be held back from its future, and that she no longer speaks for Britain – she speaks for the past'?[66]

63 *Hansard*, 30 October 1990, col. 869.
64 Howe, *op. cit.*, p. 644.
65 *Hansard, op. cit.*, cols. 873–874.
66 *Op. cit.*, col. 874.

Thatcher's answer was typical knockabout politics. Ashdown's policy was 'to abolish the pound sterling, the greatest expression of sovereignty'. It would be 'totally and utterly wrong' to agree to that now. That matter was 'one to be decided by future generations and future Parliaments'. Parliament was supreme, not the leader of the Liberal Democrats.[67]

She was then asked by David Owen whether it was clear that what was being attempted at Rome was a bounce which led only one way, to a federal United States of Europe?

'Is it not vital that, in this House ... it should be possible for a Prime Minister to make it clear, if necessary, that Britain is prepared to stand alone? We should not relish it, but if we were faced with the imposition by treaty of a single currency and with a situation that prevented the enlargement of the Community to include Poland, Hungary and Czechoslovakia, would not Britain be ... right to use the veto?'[68]

Thatcher agreed. 'That is precisely the stance that we took,' she replied.

'The European monetary system to which we belong is designed for twelve sovereign states, in co-operation with one another, to come to an exchange rate mechanism. What is being proposed now – economic and monetary union – is the back door to a federal Europe, which we totally and utterly reject. We prefer greater economic and monetary co-operation, which can be achieved by keeping our sovereignty.'[69]

Asked by a Scottish Labour MP whether she thought she would have had a better response if 'she used the moderate language of a 21st-century European and not the intemperate language of a little Englander', Thatcher asked in her turn:

'Bearing in mind that the hon. Gentleman was not there, will he tell me of any language that was intemperate? Those who seem to know most about this are the people who were not there and heard nothing of what was said or of the way in which it was done.'[70]

If all this was 'nationalist crudity', one suspects that Howe took from the replies what he wanted to hear. Even his own emollient presence, Howe mused, 'was no longer restraining her dangerous anti-Europeanism'.[71] With that, he claims, he resolved to depart and set about drafting his resignation letter. If his resolve needed strengthening, the subsequent front-page of the *Sun* might have helped, with its famous headline 'Up Yours, Delors!'

67 *Ibid.*
68 *Op. cit.*, col. 877.
69 *Ibid.*
70 *Op. cit.*, cols. 878–879. For intemperate language it would be hard to beat the comments offered to Mrs Thatcher later in the debate by Labour MP Andrew Faulds, who asked whether she did not think it would be more 'compassionate' to negotiate with Saddam Hussein over Kuwait rather than consign 'thousands of young men' to their deaths. Mrs Thatcher replied that she had not noticed 'much compassion' in Saddam Hussein's behaviour, and suggested there was 'nothing to negotiate about'. Faulds replied 'there is everything to negotiate about, you stupid woman'. When the Speaker intervened, Faulds repeated 'you stupid, negative woman ... you would love a war. You love war'. Again the Speaker intervened to tell Faulds 'that is very bad behaviour from the Hon. Gentleman ... he must not shout in that way'. But the MP was not reprimanded further and allowed to remain in his place.
71 *Ibid.*

Checkmate

It was not so much Howe's resignation itself which caused a stir, as the statement he read to the Commons to explain it on 13 November. From his subsequent account, his choice had been between a 'damp squib', or a 'sensation'. His fellow-Europeanist Vernon Bogdanor, of Brasenose College, Oxford, advised him to make his 'resignation count, really count'. That meant, in Howe's view, making it clear that 'he could no longer share the prime minister's view of the right approach to the European question'. [72]

In a peroration phrased with feline craft, Howe explained to a silent House that:

'The conflict of loyalty, of loyalty to my Right Honourable friend the Prime Minister – and, after all, in two decades together that instinct is very real – and of loyalty to what I perceive to be the true interests of the nation, has become too great. I no longer believe it is possible to resolve that conflict from within this government. That is why I have resigned. In doing so, I have done what I believe to be right for my party and my country. The time has come for others to consider their own response to the tragic conflict of loyalties with which I myself wrestled for perhaps too long.' [73]

Just as important as the words was the timing. Under the Conservative Party's rules, the annual leadership election was in the offing. It was to present Thatcher with her ultimate test. Waiting in the wings was Howe's ally and the chief pretender to the throne, Heseltine, who had been conducting an unofficial campaign for the leadership ever since he walked out of the Cabinet three years before.

Taking his cue from Howe's elliptic 'the time has now come for others...', Heseltine launched his leadership bid, plunging the parliamentary Conservative party into turmoil. For days the media feasted on the spectacle of Tory MPs queuing to plunge their dagger into the back of the woman whose force of personality and conviction had dominated them for so long. Particularly conspicuous were three of the most fanatical 'Europeanists', who seemed permanently available to the cameras on St Stephen's Green to contribute just the drops of poison the BBC in particular seemed to welcome: Emma Nicolson, Hugh Dykes and Peter Temple-Morris, all three of whom would, within seven years, have defected to other parties.

After beating Heseltine by only 204 votes to 185 on the first round, Thatcher felt she had no option but to resign, which she did on 22 November 1990. When the news came though, Heath rang his office with the gleeful admonition, 'Rejoice, Rejoice', [74] and celebrated by buying his staff champagne. [75] However, Heseltine, the wielder of the knife, was not to gain the crown. That was to be wrested from him by the successor Thatcher herself preferred, John Major.

Howe had achieved precisely what he had hoped for. On the last page of his memoirs he reveals how he wanted:

72 Howe, *op. cit.*, p. 661.
73 *Op. cit.*, p. 667.
74 The words Thatcher used on hearing of the liberation of South Georgia on 26 April 1982.
75 Campbell, John (1993), *Edward Heath – A Biography* (London, Jonathan Cape), p. 787.

'to change the policies, not the leader. But if that meant the leader had to go, then so it had to be. I have no regrets whatsoever about resolving the conflict of loyalty in that way, however deeply I regretted the necessity for having to do so.'[76]

Although Delors too had longed for Thatcher's downfall, when it finally came about his feelings were mixed. She had become the greatest unifying force in the Community. But the Italians, who at the very least had triggered the events which had led to Thatcher's downfall, were 'triumphant'. They immediately set about preparing for the second Rome Council, hoping to give a decisive push to 'political union'.[77] Representing Britain would be Major, determined to be 'at the heart of Europe'. His own education was about to begin.

76 Howe, *op. cit.*, p. 692.
77 Grant, *op. cit.*, p. 150.

Chapter 14

'At the Heart of Europe': 1990–1993

'My aim for Britain in the Community can be simply stated. I want us to be where we belong. At the very heart of Europe.'   John Major, Bonn, 11 March 1991

'This Treaty marks a new stage in the process of creating an ever closer union among the peoples of Europe.'   Maastricht Treaty on European Union, 1992

'Now we've signed it – we had better read it!'
Douglas Hurd, Maastricht, 7 February 1992[1]

When Major became Britain's prime minister, as the least experienced holder of the office since Ramsay Macdonald in 1924, he was faced by three immense challenges. The first was that his country was about to go to war. Fifty thousand British servicemen were assembling in the Gulf, under overall American command, for the liberation of Kuwait. The second was that Britain's economy had entered its sharpest recession since 1945. The 'Lawson boom' had pushed inflation to 10 percent, its highest level for more than a decade, and unemployment was soaring. The conventional remedy would have been to lower interest rates, but the need to maintain the value of the pound at a level required by the straitjacket of the ERM had driven them to record highs, at one point reaching 15 percent.

The third challenge was the Rome European Council, poised to launch the two intergovernmental conferences in preparation for the Treaty on European Union. High on the agenda were two proposals Major knew he would have serious difficulty in persuading his party to accept: the single currency and Delors' 'Social Charter', granting workers' rights which threatened to overturn the reforms by which Britain had in the 1980s curbed the power of the unions.

While Britain's attention was focused on the drama surrounding the downfall of Thatcher, the European Parliament had staged a joint meeting with representatives of national parliaments. Calls were heard for the Community to be remodelled as a 'European Union', centred on a single currency, and for a constitution. This would confirm the Commission as the executive in a government of Europe, with the Council of Ministers and the Parliament itself as the two houses of its legislature.[2] A hybrid between Spinelli's Draft Treaty of 1984 and ideas more recently advanced by Delors, one result of this initiative was that it persuaded Britain's Labour Party to support monetary union, completing its conversion to full integrationism.

Douglas Hurd, retained as Foreign Secretary, made his own pitch for further integration with a speech in Berlin at which he called for a 'distinct European role'

---

1 Jamieson, Bill (1994), *Britain Beyond Europe* (London, Duckworth), p. 72.
2 Corbett, *op. cit.*, pp. 299–300.

in defence, suggesting that the WEU should represent the Community in NATO. This encouraged Delors to argue that the difficulties of trying to run a 'common foreign and security policy' on an intergovernmental basis would lead national governments to hand more powers to the Commission. In an interview he said that, thanks to events in eastern Europe and the Gulf, moves to adopt a common foreign policy were now 'leaping ahead'. 'It is like a chemical experiment', he told his interviewer, who noted that his eyes lit up like a small boy playing with a chemistry set.[3]

One piece of unfinished business scheduled for just before the Rome Council was what was intended to be the final resolution of the GATT talks. On 7 December 1990, 2,000 delegates from 107 countries accounting for 85 percent of world trade gathered at the Heysel conference centre outside Brussels. Outside, 30,000 angry, placard-waving farmers denouncing cuts in agricultural subsidies were greeted by armed riot police and clouds of tear gas, prompting them to run amok, smashing cars and buildings.[4]

Yet again the Community refused to agree to more than a limited subsidy cut and talks collapsed. 'Never have such hopes been so brutally dashed', said Australian trade minister, Neal Blewitt, representing 12 southern hemisphere countries which had formed the Cairns group.[5] Delors' response was to turn his wrath on the country he saw as taking the lead in trying to undermine the CAP:

'The Americans should stop insulting us, I'm not going to be an accomplice to the depopulation of the land. It's not up to the Americans to tell us how to organise our farm policy and the balance of our society. Their attitude is to treat the EC as if it had the plague and then encourage the rest of the world to join in.'[6]

The gulf that divides

When Major arrived at Rome for his first European Council meeting as prime minister, on 14 to 15 December 1990, his fellow heads of government went out of their way to be friendly, as if to demonstrate that previous differences with Britain had all been the fault of Thatcher. But it did not take long for Major to arouse yet another outburst from Delors when, immediately after the Council, the finance ministers embarked on the first of the two intergovernmental conferences, on EMU.

Delors expected them to welcome a draft treaty, largely written by himself, allowing the introduction of the single currency, to begin when eight members were in favour, with no country being obliged to join. This was less warmly received than Delors would have liked, not least because the Dutch and the French suddenly found praise for Major's 'hard ecu'. A petulant Delors stormed at what he considered Major's attempt to sabotage his project. In what was taken as a dark

---

3 The *Independent*, 13 December 1990. Cited in Grant, *op. cit.*, p. 151.
4 *Time International*, 17 December 1990, p. 42.
5 *Ibid.*
6 Grant, *op. cit.*, p. 172.

reference to the part he saw himself as having played in the overthrow of Thatcher, he threatened 'if we have to provoke another crisis, we will'. [7]

However, Major had more pressing concerns than the tantrums of Delors. As the new year of 1991 dawned, the eyes of the world were on the Middle East, where, after the expiry of a United Nations ultimatum to Saddam Hussein to withdraw from Kuwait by 15 January, the US-led coalition two days later launched its spectacular assault.

The Gulf War had already created serious strains within the Community. Initially 'Europe' had put up a common front, with France joining Britain in contributing to the coalition forces. Public opinion in member states, however, varied sharply. Eighty percent of Britons and 65 percent of the French thought the war justified, but in Germany 80 percent were opposed. Banners fashioned from bedsheets festooned windows across the country, proclaiming 'War in the Gulf is genocide! No blood for oil!' The streets of Bonn were jammed by 200,000 protesters. Germany refused not only to commit any troops to the Gulf but even to support its NATO ally, Turkey, which feared incursions from neighbouring Iraq. This drew a sharp rebuke from the Turkish president, Turgut Ozal, when it was discovered that German firms had supplied Iraq with materials for making chemical and biological weapons. On German television, he stormed, 'Who gave them to him? You are responsible. You should come and help us and take your responsibility.' 'Germany,' he complained, 'has become so rich it has completely lost its fighting spirit.' [8] Denmark, Spain, Greece and Holland lined up with Germany. Belgium refused to sell artillery ammunition destined for British forces serving in the Gulf.

Just before the UN ultimatum was due to expire, Major met Mitterrand in Paris on 14 January for an 'amiable and enjoyable discussion', only to find that two hours later French diplomats had launched a separate peace initiative through the United Nations, linking Iraqi withdrawal from Kuwait with a Middle East peace conference. Neither Britain nor America had been informed.[9] Major was furious and said so. When Britain and America blocked the French move, any semblance of a common European foreign policy was again in tatters.

No one was more sensitive to this than Delors. In early February, with the Middle East land war still raging, he addressed the European Parliament with ironic understatement: 'Public opinion senses that Europe has been rather ineffectual,' he told the MEPs. 'We will have to face up to that lesson.' On leaving the chamber, he raised his hand like a pistol to his head, pulling the trigger as a sign of his frustration.[10] Alan Clark, Major's junior defence minister, was more forthright. 'One of the great arguments of the people plugging the whole Euro-unity notion was that we were going to move into common military policy, common foreign policy and common financial policy', he said; but 'at the first major test, they ran for the cellars'.[11]

---

7 Grant, *op. cit.*, p. 151.
8 *Time International*, 4 February 1991, p. 45.
9 Major, John (1999), *John Major – The Autobiography* (London, HarperCollins), pp. 231–232.
10 *Time International*, 11 February 1991, p. 46.
11 *Ibid.*

In March Delors produced his response, in a speech in London to the International Institute for Strategic Studies. It was time, he said, for 'Europe' to 'shoulder its share of the political and military responsibilities of our old nations'. He proposed that the WEU should be reactivated as a Community institution, with its own multilateral forces: an embryonic European army.[12]

To Delors the Community's divisions had become a 'beneficial crisis' to justify a further dramatic move to political union. This was 'the lesson of the Gulf War' he told an American journalist: 'its heart, its motor is the desire to shape a joint foreign and security policy'.[13] In this Delors had already won backing from France and Germany, who in a joint paper were now proposing that the European Council should co-ordinate Community defence policies, with the WEU becoming the 'European pillar' of NATO.[14]

In the wake of the successful liberation of Kuwait, Major took an opportunity to rebuild relations with Germany. After meeting Kohl in late February, when he was invited to review a German guard of honour, he returned to Bonn on 11 March to give a lecture, organised by the British ambassador and attended by Kohl. According to his biographers, this was intended by Major as the moment when he would seize the initiative, by outlining 'his vision of a free-market Europe, based on nation states, open to the new democracies of the east, a bulwark of peace as well as an engine of prosperity'.[15] The key word was 'co-operation': the code-word for doing business outside the 'straitjacket' of the Brussels institutions.[16] With this in mind, he proclaimed what was to become the most familiar expression of how Major wanted to see Britain's relations with 'Europe':

'My aim for Britain in the Community can be simply stated. I want us to be where we belong. At the very heart of Europe. Working with our partners in building the future.'[17]

There, at the heart of his philosophy, was the complete antithesis of the 'Monnet method' and what the European Community was about. It harked back to those post-war days when Britain had so fervently embraced 'intergovernmental co-operation' through the Council of Europe and the OEEC. Now, after the GATT fiasco, where the Community had shown itself the very opposite of a free-market organisation, and the Gulf War, where it had shown itself so split, such an idea of 'partners' working together in harmony was either wildly optimistic or profoundly self-deluding. Wittingly or not, Major was setting himself in direct conflict with Delors, the high priest of supranationalism.

Such was Major's innocence that he thought that his ambition to be 'at the heart of Europe' was an 'unexceptional objective'. He soon realised how wrong he was. 'Few sentiments in recent British political history,' he was to write, 'have provoked such havoc or been so misrepresented.' To Eurosceptics at home, his wish to see

---

12 Grant, *op. cit.*, p. 186.

13 *Time International*, 22 April 1991, p. 24.

14 Grant, *ibid.*

15 Hogg, Sarah, and Hill, Jonathan (1995), *Too Close To Call: Power And Politics – John Major in No. 10* (London, Little, Brown and Company), p. 78.

16 *Ibid.*

17 Major, *op. cit.*, p. 269.

Britain 'at the heart of Europe' was taken to be an unabashed embracing of 'federalism'. But Delors, more practised in reading the runes, could see that Major's real intention, as he himself later confirmed, was to make it 'clear that we would bring our own proposals to the intergovernmental conference at Maastricht, since I didn't like what was on offer'.[18]

By now the presidency was held by tiny Luxembourg. A special European Council was convened on 8 April to discuss what was scathingly described by Belgium's foreign minister as a situation where the EC had shown itself to be 'an economic giant, a political pygmy and a military larva'. At the centre of the discussions was the prospect of a common foreign and defence policy, but their only real outcome was an initiative by Major. This was the creation of a United Nations 'safe haven' in northern Iraq, to protect hundreds of thousands of Kurdish refugees displaced by the Gulf War.

The main task of the Luxembourg presidency was to co-ordinate the proposals for the two IGCs. From over 2,000 pages of submissions emerged a 'global draft' which, in the arcane vocabulary of the Community, was called a 'non-paper'. This proposed a highly radical innovation: the new 'European Union' should rest on what were called three 'pillars'. The first or 'Community 'pillar' would be based on an extended version of the existing treaty, concerned with the Community's core activities, with the Commission playing its classic supranational role. The other two 'pillars' would create a wholly new legal framework, outside the Commission remit, separately to cover foreign affairs and internal security. These would be handled on an intergovernmental basis.

Predictably, this structure attracted considerable criticism but the Luxembourg government stood firm, arguing that its draft was the only one on which there was a chance of unanimous agreement.

Just before this draft was considered by the European Council, which met in Luxembourg on 28 to 29 June, the British parliament was given the opportunity to debate it. To their disgust, most MPs were ill-prepared. The draft, 134 pages long, had only become available at lunchtime, from 'a private, unattributable source'.[19] Nevertheless, Hurd, opening the debate on behalf of the government, set out the central issues:

'Those who favour the creation of a European state want to see all European co-operation ultimately channelled through the institutions established by the treaty of Rome. We do not accept such a model. It is necessary to have common institutions which are to some degree supranational, to develop and administer some common policies. As we have seen, that is true of the rules that govern the single market and its external manifestations in negotiations on world trade. That logic does not apply in areas such as foreign and security policy or in the work of Interior or Justice Ministers. The treaty of Rome remains the bedrock of European integration, but there is nothing intrinsically more European about channelling all co-operation through the institutions of the Community rather than proceeding, where it makes sense, through co-operation between Governments directly accountable to national Parliaments.'[20]

18 *Ibid.*
19 *Hansard*, 26 June 1991, col. 1005.
20 *Op. cit.*, col. 1009.

This was an illuminating contribution. Had MPs been able to understand the nuances of his references to supranationalism and intergovernmentalism, they might have learnt something. In general, however, Hurd's comments sailed over the MPs' heads. Indeed most of the speeches were strikingly superficial and ill-informed, not least those from Gerald Kaufman, Labour's spokesman for foreign affairs, and Paddy Ashdown, the Liberal Democrat leader.

One speaker who did grasp the central point was Thatcher, except that, instead of using the word 'supranational', she used the woollier, more ambiguous term 'federal'. As she tried to explain, there were different ways in which the nations of Europe could express their wish to co-operate together, and it was a great mistake to suppose that the only means of co-operation which was 'European' was supra-nationalism. These 'federalists' invariably tried to

'... pretend that they are somehow more European than the rest of us. They are not; they are just more federal. There is nothing specifically European about a federal structure – indeed, the opposite: it is the nation state which is European.'

She gave examples of other forms of European co-operation which were just as valid, such as the contribution France made to common defence while remaining outside NATO. Yet 'no one says that France is isolated'. Similarly most members of the Community had agreed to reduce their frontier controls, under the Schengen agreement (ratified in 1985). This was appropriate to their needs, because of their geography, just as it was inappropriate to the island of Britain. 'The true Europeans,' she said, 'are those who base themselves on Europe's history ... rather than on constitutional blueprints.' [21]

Here, re-stated yet again, was the fundamental British view of how relations between the European states should be conducted, on a basis of 'flexible co-operation'. Thatcher's was arguing that her approach had just as much right to be seen as 'European' as that of the 'federalists'. But nobody was listening. To her simplistic critics, people were either 'pro-' or 'anti-European'. On that basis Thatcher was to be dismissed as an 'anti'.

At the Luxembourg Council, the draft received less discussion than expected. The heads of government were diverted by a grave new crisis. It was one which was to show up the Community's pretensions to act on a wider stage as an international power in its own right in a humiliating light.

The Yugoslav debacle

On 25 June 1991, two small nations, Slovenia and Croatia, declared their independence from the Federation of Yugoslavia. Tensions between the seven nations making up Yugoslavia had been mounting ever since, in 1987, Slobodan Milosevic had gained control of the Serbian Communist Party, the ruling group in the Serb-dominated federation. As Communism crumbled across central Europe, the

21 *Op. cit.*, cols. 1028–1029.

peoples of Slovenia and Croatia prepared to break loose from the Belgrade government, to set up free, democratic states on what they imagined was the western European model. Belgrade's response on 27 June was to order the Yugoslav National Army, the JNA, into Slovenia to put down the 'rebellion' by force.

As news of the fighting in Slovenia reached the Council meeting, it was greeted as an almost heaven-sent opportunity. Here was a crisis at the heart of Europe which would give the Community an opportunity to intervene as the continent's 'superpower', demonstrating the 'common foreign policy' in action. The Council immediately sent the *troika* to mediate, led by Jacques Poos, Luxembourg's foreign minister. He was joined by Italy's foreign minister, Gianni di Michelis, and the Dutchman Hans van den Broek, chosen because Holland was about to take over the presidency from Luxembourg.

For Poos, the Yugoslav crisis was a sign that 'the hour of Europe has dawned'. He added, 'If one problem can be solved by the Europeans, it is the Yugoslav problem. This is a European country and it is not up to the Americans. It is not up to anybody else.' [22] The line the Community proposed to take had already been set the previous year, when the internal strains now breaking Yugoslavia apart had first appeared. At the first Rome Council the Twelve had declared their support for 'the preservation of the unity and territorial integrity of Yugoslavia'. [23]

The Council was simply unable to grasp why the peoples of Slovenia and Croatia would now do anything to break away from the tyranny of Belgrade which had held them in its grip since 1945. Since the whole purpose of this Council was to discuss building a new federal government for 'Europe', the Twelve could hardly be expected to welcome the idea of another federation collapsing.[24] As president of the European Council, Luxembourg's prime minister Jacques Santer reflected the general view when he told journalists: 'We have to try all means to save the Federation.' Even Major joined in, saying 'the great prize is to hold the federation together'. [25]

So opened the first stage of a tragedy which was to cast a shadow over Europe for 11 years. It was decided that the three foreign ministers should immediately fly to Yugoslavia to mediate between the various parties. The people of Slovenia and Croatia decked their streets and villages with 'ring of stars' flags, imagining that these envoys of the European Community were coming to support them in their wish for freedom, democracy and self-determination.

When the *troika* arrived in Belgrade on 28 June, however, their only purpose was to reassure the Federal authorities of their desire to see Yugoslavia held together. Already the Community had agreed to give the Federal government a huge loan of 700 million ecus. As Poos himself put it, 'the idea of national self-determination is dangerous as a basis for international order... It would release

---

22 Almond, Mark (1998), *Europe's Backyard War – The War in the Balkans* (London, Heinemann), pp. 32–32. See also *The Death of Yugoslavia*.

23 *Op. cit.*, p. 42. It was Britain's Douglas Hurd who had first proposed that the Community should look forward to welcoming the Yugoslav federation as a member.

24 *Ibid.*

25 *Op. cit.*, p. 33.

an explosive development'.[26] He poured scorn on the idea of tiny Slovenia imagining it could survive on its own as a nation, even though its population was six times larger than that of Luxembourg.

They demanded that Slovenia should revoke its declaration of independence as a condition of a ceasefire. So ill-informed were the *troika* ministers, they were not even aware that the Federation had already reconciled itself to Slovenia's secession. At midnight on 30 June, the moment when the EC presidency passed to the Dutch, van den Broek, now leader of the *troika*, raised a glass to the Federal politicians with whom he was sitting in Belgrade to declare that the EC would continue to support Yugoslavia's unity.

By then, the Federal authorities had already lost control of the JNA in Slovenia, which was now running amok. As television pictures of the fighting dominated the weekend news, cracks in the EC façade began to appear. On 3 July, Hurd told the Commons that the conflict appeared to be escalating 'out of control'. He conceded that 'it may no longer be possible to hold the whole country together'. Without apparent irony he declared, 'We have learnt that one cannot suppress nationalist feeling or force it into a framework against which it revolts.'[27]

On 4 July, the EC ministers convened a summit between the Serb and Slovene leaders on Brioni, Tito's luxury island retreat in the Adriatic, with the intention of brokering a peace. But the Serbs and Slovenes had already reached their own agreement. The *troika* was 'kicking at an open door'. The 'Brioni Agreement' on 8 July, in effect, marked formal acknowledgement of the break-up of the federation.

Hailed as a triumph for 'European' diplomacy, the agreement was anything but. Not only did it leave the major issue of Slovenia's sovereignty unresolved; it opened the way for the JNA, now being rapidly turned into a Serb army, to turn on Croatia. By August, just when a popular *coup* in Moscow was marking the fall of Gorbachov and the imminent collapse of that other Communist federation, the Soviet Union, Serb artillery units were bombarding the Croatian town of Vukovar, followed by the even bloodier siege of Osijek, inflicting thousands of military and civilian deaths.

Nevertheless, the European Community continued its futile efforts at mediation, not least with a conference which opened on 17 September, chaired by Britain's former Foreign Secretary Lord Carrington. This aimed to create a new Yugoslavia in the form of a 'union of sovereign republics'.

By now, though, it was clear that the EC's intervention had been a shameful fiasco. On 25 September, the United Nations intervened, with a Security Council Resolution placing an arms embargo on the whole of the former Yugoslavia. On 8 October the UN Secretary-General appointed Cyrus Vance, once US Secretary of State, as his personal envoy to 'former Yugoslavia'. The tragedy still had years to run. But the idea that the European Community could play an effective part in its humane resolution had already been dispelled.

---

26 *Ibid.*
27 *Hansard*, 4 July 1991, col. 328.

Countdown to Maastricht

Compared with such tumultuous events, the efforts of the 'little Europeans' to construct their next treaty might have seemed trivial. But the moment when the heads of government would meet at Maastricht was fast approaching. One point at least they had agreed at the Luxembourg Council was that, in order to secure agreement to economic and monetary union, no country could be compelled to join it. This meant that, although Britain could not prevent other member states adopting a single currency, she herself could not be forced to join it. Major's 'opt-out' was in the making.

It was not until September that the Dutch presidency produced a new draft of the proposed treaty. This confirmed Britain's worst fears. It could not have been more integrationist, proposing a unitary structure for the proposed European Union, bringing foreign policy and internal affairs into the Community frame-work.

Fortunately for Major, the draft met with outright hostility from every country except Belgium. The Dutch even managed to alienate France and Luxembourg, the latter taking offence because its own draft had been so unceremoniously dumped. The Dutch had no option but to revert to the Luxembourg text, proceeding with specific changes on an issue-by-issue basis. Despite two further foreign ministers' meetings in November, agreement on a final text was still not reached.

Even with what was left, Major was still dismayed. Quite apart from his refusal to allow Britain to be forced immediately into a single currency,[28] there was also the 'Social Chapter'. Major felt this would reverse Conservative reforms to the labour market and increase unemployment. He was also adamant that foreign and home affairs should not 'come under the control of Brussels' or that the Commission should have a role in defence policy. As he put it later, 'It was evident that we were bound to play the abominable no-men in the negotiations, and that we would face a domestic cacophony of conflicting advice'.[29]

That 'conflicting advice' was already becoming vocal from within his own party, not least from Thatcher, whose every whisper was passed on to the waiting media.[30]

To flush out parliamentary opposition, Major decided to hold a Commons debate on 20 and 21 November. It was a risky strategy but, if the Commons backed his position, this would lend weight to his negotiating stance at Maastricht. But, if it was an act of courage, it was also, according to an analyst who studied the Eurosceptic movement, 'an act of deception':

'The motion was very weak and almost impossible to oppose unless MPs subscribed to the hard line sceptical position. Major's commitments were remarkably open-ended, carefully constructed to allow him the maximum flexibility in finding a means to agree British support for the treaty. He also talked up his government's opposition to commitments that

---

28 Major, *op. cit.*, p. 271.
29 *Ibid.*
30 *Op. cit.*, p. 274.

were neither in the draft treaties nor even a likely outcome. And he was vague on issues which still had to be decided.'[31]

Reading the debate, which in Hansard ran close to 120,000 words, the length of a sizeable novel, it is hard to detect the passion which was to dog the later debates when the treaty came to be ratified. The single currency was the chief preoccupation, mentioned 233 times, with 'federalism' getting 152 mentions and 'sovereignty' 113. However it was also a debate which showed all three major parties in favour of a treaty of some kind, even though Labour and the Liberal Democrats were keener on the single currency.

Again, a significant contribution came from Thatcher. Picking up on a suggestion from Tony Benn that there should be a referendum on the single currency, she pointed out that if, in future, all three major political parties should agree to monetary union, the British people would have no say in the matter.[32] Yet the constitutional implications of this would be so serious, she argued, quoting the great constitutional authority Dicey, that there should be a referendum. Otherwise they would have no chance to pronounce on whether fundamental rights should be taken away 'not only from them but from future generations, and which, once gone, could not be restored'.[33] 'We should let the people speak,' she concluded. Hurd, Kenneth Clarke and Michael Portillo all spoke against the idea.

If there were reservations about what was to happen at Maastricht from some MPs, they at least had that in common with Delors. Addressing the European Parliament the same day as the second half of the Commons debate, he declared that the Dutch-brokered final draft of the treaty, due to go before the heads of government at Maastricht, was unworkable and 'crippling'.

What worried Delors were the two intergovernmental 'pillars'. Because of the 'likelihood of politicians and bureaucrats striking deals behind closed doors', he said, these components 'will pollute the European Community and roll it back'.[34] 'The plan for the EC to manage external economic relations and for member states to run foreign policy would lead to 'organised schizophrenia,' he declared.[35]

Delors wanted all parts of the treaty to be brought into a 'single institutional framework', run by the 'Community method', with his Commission playing a central role. But he found no backers. To compound his woes, his own headquarters in Brussels, the Berlaymont complex, had to be closed down, after 1,400 tons of asbestos in the building were ruled to be dangerous. More than 3,000 displaced officials had hurriedly to be evacuated and re-housed all across the city.

Maastricht: The birth of European union

As the politicians gathered in the Dutch town of Maastricht on Sunday 8 December 1991, the treaty they were to discuss over the following two days marked the

31 Forster, Anthony (2002), *Euroscepticism In Contemporary British Politics* (London, Routledge), p. 97.
32 *Hansard*, 20 November 1991, cols. 297–298.
33 *Ibid.*
34 Grant, *op. cit.*, p. 197.
35 *Op. cit.*, p. 198.

culmination of the process which had begun in the Crocodile Restaurant in Strasbourg 10 years earlier.

It was Spinelli, the former Communist, who had launched the idea of a Treaty on European Union. It was Mitterrand's advisers who in 1984 had suggested that it should be divided into two parts, starting with what was to become the Single European Act. Now the moment had come to complete that process, in what would mark the most momentous leap forward in 'European' integration since 1957.

As the motorcade carrying Major and his colleagues arrived in the suburbs of Maastricht, their morale was low. Delors had been addressing 'a thousand flag-waving, foot-stamping federalists' in Maastricht's town square, in a last-minute appeal to the 'peoples of Europe', 'Federalism is a guideline, not a pornographic word, you can speak it out loud', he told them. 'We have been focusing too much on a country which has said no, no, no!' [36]

Major himself put the chances of achieving an acceptable agreement only at 50/50. Politically, the position he faced was 'dire'. If he withheld agreement to the treaty, huge ill-will would be caused on the continent and his party at home would be split. On the other hand, if he gave away too much, as he put it:

'I might earn goodwill on the Continent, but the Conservative Party would repudiate it, the Cabinet would split, and the agreement might fail in Parliament. We would then face a general election in the worst possible circumstances. Only if I obtained an agreement that met the objectives I had set out in the Commons could it be satisfactorily presented at home. Few believed that was possible.' [37]

That Sunday evening, as Major and Hurd were meeting with Ruud Lubbers, the Dutch prime minister who was to chair the summit, news came through that Boris Yeltsin, Russia's new president, had joined with the leaders of the newly independent Ukraine and Byelorussia to declare 'the Soviet Union has ceased to exist'. [38] It was curious that, just when one 'Union' had finally collapsed, Europe's politicians should be gathering to create a new one.

Next morning the summit convened in the *Provincienhuis*, an austere modern structure recently erected on 'Government Island' in the River Maas. Across the water several thousand bored journalists waited for any titbits of news which might emerge from the conference room. Sealed from the outside world, the leaders assembled round the table was dominated by its 'big players', Kohl and Mitterrand, with Delors brooding in attendance but not permitted to contribute directly.

As had become customary, the meeting began with a *tour de table*, in which the heads of government set out their positions at length, explaining what they could and could not accept. The presidency would then consider the contributions overnight and produce a text that, in its view, had the best chance of securing agreement.

---

36 *Op. cit.*, p. 200.
37 Major, *op. cit.*, p. 276.
38 Cited in Major, *op. cit.*, p. 277.

Kohl spoke first, telling the heads of government that the single currency was 'crucial' and must be 'irreversible'. Member states must be prepared for monetary union by 1996 to 1997. He was echoed by Wilfred Martens of Belgium. Then Major decided to speak, 'before the tide of enthusiastic agreement rose too high'. His contribution broke the consensus, setting the tone for the rest of the summit. Britain was to be on her own. However it was not Britain's well-known views on the single currency which started the trouble. This came when discussion turned to foreign policy and defence. Martens wanted a common defence policy in the treaty, without a national veto, which would effectively mean that no country could act independently. Again Major had to disagree.

After lunch, discussion moved on to other subjects and Major's account gives a sense of the horse-trading which goes on at European Councils (as in all Community institutions). 'I leavened our determination to keep foreign policy and home affairs for national decision-making,' he wrote, 'by making a series of positive proposals on less emotive subjects.'[39] What he meant was, that to compensate for his 'negative' stance, he was now willing to make concessions. These included substantial extensions of qualified majority voting, greater powers for the European Parliament and 'co-operation' between governments on what was now called 'Justice and Home Affairs'. Major transfers of power to the Community were agreed simply in a bid to appear 'more positive'.

On the second morning, having worked through the night, the Dutch presidency presented its draft conclusions. Major and his team were horrified. Thanks to Belgian pressure, the intergovernmental 'pillar' structure was now to be regarded as a mere transitional stage, before its policy areas were handed over to full 'Community competence'. There was also the Social Chapter, the item which topped the day's agenda. The Dutch had only made minor concessions to the British and, when Mitterrand objected even to these, the rest supported him. Major was again on his own, but here he had no opt-out, leaving him forced to reject the Social Chapter. When Mitterrand countered that, without it, he would block the entire treaty, the issue was deferred for 'bilateral talks'.

Meanwhile there was drama elsewhere in the building where, at a parallel meeting of finance ministers, the British unveiled the opt-out they were demanding on stage three of EMU, the single currency. Drafted in full legal form, this specified all the articles of the treaty which would not apply to the UK. It was 'non-negotiable'.[40]

As the hours dragged on in the main meeting, Lubbers even refused refreshment for the heads of government, assuming that this would speed consent. Gradually agreement was reached on all outstanding points, until the only item left was the Social Chapter. Discussion took six hours, with Major doggedly refusing to allow it into the treaty. Unanimity it had to be and 'eleven to one', as Major pointed out to a pleading Lubbers, was not unanimity.[41]

39 *Op. cit.*, p. 280.
40 *Op. cit.*, p. 284.
41 *Op. cit.*, p. 287.

Eventually, the issue was resolved by a classic fudge. Lubbers proposed an agreement *outside* the treaty which would apply only to the Eleven, but with a protocol allowing Community institutions to be used for its implementation. By this formula, British Commissioners could take a hand in framing legislation under the Chapter and British MEPs could vote on it, but Britain would take no part in Council decisions and they would not apply in the UK. For Major, it was a real achievement.

His other achievement was to refuse to accept Community control over immigration. A common form of visa had been agreed and Britain had already accepted the list of countries whose citizens must apply for them, including those of the Commonwealth, such as Australia and New Zealand. Furthermore, in 1990, Britain had already signed the Dublin Convention, an agreement for dealing with asylum seekers, due to come into force in September 1997 and which would cause the UK immense problems. But Major would not accept Community control over who was or was not allowed to immigrate to Britain. The point was not pressed.[42]

At 1.30 on Wednesday morning, the negotiations finally ended. Major had secured his opt-outs. But behind them a huge amount more had been conceded. For the first time, written into the treaty were common foreign, security and defence policies, and 'co-operation' on 'justice and home affairs'. The member states undertook to support 'the Union's external and security policy actively and unreservedly in a spirit of loyalty and solidarity'. And, in a declaration appended to the Treaty, the WEU was recognised as 'an integral part of the development of the Union'. To all intents and purposes, it was now a Community institution.

In addition, the 300 million inhabitants of the Community, like it or not, became 'citizens of the European Community'. These new 'European citizens' would be allowed to participate in local and European Parliamentary elections, as voters or candidates, anywhere in the Community and would have a Parliamentary Ombudsman. There would also be a Court of Auditors to report on Community finances. In a major extension to the 'structural funds', necessary for the workings of the single currency, the treaty set up a 'cohesion fund', to transfer money from richer countries to poorer. A new 'Committee of the Regions' would be established, made up of representatives from the Community's 111 'regions' who would have to be 'consulted' on legislation. The ECJ was given power to levy fines on member states which failed to implement its rulings.

Perhaps most significant of all, the treaty had also greatly extended the areas of Commission 'competences', along with an extension of qualified majority voting to 30 more areas of policy. Added to those already ceded under the Single European Act were 'broad economic guidelines', social policy, public health, consumer protection, telecommunications, energy, education, culture, vocational training and transport, including measures relating to the 'trans-European network'. There were also major extensions of Community control over environmental law, including for the first time 'town and country planning' and 'measures

---

42 Hogg and Hill, *op. cit.*, p. 155.

which significantly affect a member state's choice between different energy sources'.[43]

A final part of the treaty introduced the principle of 'subsidiarity'. Due to become a major point of contention, this amounted to an agreement whereby the Commission would only take action in areas of policy where it did not already have exclusive competence, when it was considered that this could be done more effectively at 'Community' rather than national level.[44] As Major was to find out, this was as meaningless as it was obscure.

Such was the complexity of the overall treaty, however, that not even Major knew in detail what he had committed his government to signing. In the early hours of Wednesday 11 December, therefore, his first task was to instruct his accompanying officials to summarise the 'bull points', as a guide to what had been agreed. It was to be months before a full printed version of the treaty became available, and even then it would be largely meaningless, because so much would be shown only as 'amendments' to the existing treaties, comprehensible only when cross-referred to earlier texts.

Nevertheless, Major's 'bull points' were enough to be going on with. Exhausted, he flew back to London, to sell to the British people what he had agreed to in their name.

The selling of Maastricht

Considering how little anyone yet knew of what the Treaty actually contained, it was perhaps small wonder that the British media took Major at his own estimation. On 11 December, therefore, *The Times* front-page carried the headline 'Major wins all he asked for at Maastricht'. Next day the newspapers were almost unanimous in praise of what the *Daily Telegraph* called 'Major's success at Maastricht'.

On returning to London, Major on the afternoon of the same day, 11 December, made a statement to the Commons. It was received with acclaim and much waving of order papers. He told MPs:

'This is a treaty which safeguards and advances our national interests. It advances the interests of Europe as a whole. It opens up new ways of co-operating in Europe. It clarifies and contains the powers of the Commission. It will allow the Community to develop in depth. It reaches out to other Europeans – the new democracies who want to share the benefits we already enjoy. It is a good agreement for Europe, and a good agreement for the United Kingdom.'[45]

Yet Major cannot have been wholly unaware what an immense range of powers he had ceded, perhaps indicated by his response to one of his own back-benchers, who asked him to summarise them. His reply was evasive. The detailed informa-

---

43 Cowgill, Anthony (1992), *The Maastricht Treaty in Perspective – the Consolidated Treaty on European Union* (Stroud, British Management Data Foundation), pp. xvii–l.
44 Cited in Grant, *op. cit.*, p. 203.
45 *Hansard*, 11 December 1991, col. 862.

tion 'that my hon. Friend requires' could be found in the Commons library.[46] In fact, it was still to be months before MPs or anyone else would find out just how much had been surrendered.

For the moment, therefore, in Cabinet it was ' sweetness and light'. Hurd and Lamont were rapturously received at meetings of Conservative back-benchers. It was the modern equivalent of a Roman triumph, wrote Major, adding in hindsight 'soon it would all be very different'.[47] But that time had not yet come. In a two-day Commons debate a week later, Major moved his own motion:

'... this House congratulates the Prime Minister on achieving all the negotiating objectives set out in the motion that was supported by the House on 21 November; and warmly endorses the agreement secured by the Government at Maastricht.'[48]

Predictably, he launched the debate with a paean of praise for his own role in the negotiations: 'we ensured a safer Europe, and we reaffirmed the primacy of NATO; we set the framework of a stronger and more coherent European foreign policy, in which our national independence of action is assured' etc. etc.[49] Kinnock, and his opposition colleagues, on the other hand, spent most of their time attacking Major's opt-outs, accusing him of creating 'a two-speed Community' which put Britain 'in the slow lane'.[50]

On the range of new Community competences, almost the only MP to sound the alarm was Tebbit, now a back-bencher. Although conceding that the outcome might have been much worse, he noted that Britain had been fighting a defensive action all the way, against 'federalist follies' which would damage 'not only the United Kingdom but the Community as a whole'. Maastricht had established 'a series of bridgeheads into our constitution, into the powers of this House, and into the lives of individuals and businesses'.[51] Another warning was sounded by the Labour back-bencher Gwyneth Dunwoody:

'People will not accept a system that they do not clearly influence... We are in a dangerous position. The European Community at Maastricht... produced something which many people in this country do not understand. Where they understand it, they do not accept it and where they accept it, they have grave doubts about any elected House which takes them rapidly down the road to federal organisation – by any other name – without having consulted them. No one in the House has a mandate to commit the people of this country to a federal Europe.'[52]

---

46 *Op. cit.*, col. 873.
47 Major, *op. cit.*, p. 288.
48 *Hansard*, 18 December 1991, col. 275.
49 A few days later Germany was to make a mockery of the 'common foreign policy' when, on 23 December, it defied agreed EC policy by unilaterally recognising the independence of Slovenia and Croatia. This might have seemed an admirable recognition of the right of these nations to self-determination, particularly since Croatia was fighting desperately for survival against a ruthless Serb invasion, but it brought much opprobrium on Germany for having broken 'Community solidarity'.
50 *Op. cit.*, col. 292.
51 *Op. cit.*, col. 323.
52 *Op. cit.*, col. 357.

Alan Haselhurst, a Tory, dismissed such fears, pointing out that the people of Britain were largely uninterested by such 'international issues'. For every letter sent by his constituents about Maastricht, he had received 'ten times that number about Sunday trading and similar matters'. [53]

The most passionate speech came from another Conservative back-bencher, Richard Shepherd. He told the House he already belonged to a 'union', the United Kingdom of Great Britain and Northern Ireland, formed by people with one language and united by their will to make it work. He did not know how to relate to a 'union of Europe'. Noting how assiduously Kinnock had avoided speaking about democracy and that there was no mechanism in the treaty for changing the law, he demanded, 'Where is the mechanism whereby we may hold Ministers accountable?'

The British people had already witnessed, he said, the reduction of one 'great Department of State – the Ministry of Agriculture, Fisheries and Food – to a branch office'. When farmers or consumers wanted redress for their problems, they now had to go to Brussels, because there was no longer any way in which MPs or ministers in London could 'satisfy their aspirations'. [54]

Shepherd ended by recalling how the world had watched the peoples of eastern Europe fighting for the 'freedom and the liberty that we enjoy', yet here was the House of Commons talking solemnly as if handing over its powers to run the country was 'merely a question of a pile of money'. 'It is not – it is about the spirit and life of a nation. I cannot let this go down without crying out "it is wrong".' [55]

Despite this, the government won by 339 votes to 253. The Conservatives had endorsed their leader's 'triumph' with scarcely a dissenting voice. The way was clear for Hurd, as foreign secretary, accompanied by Francis Maude as his minister of state, to return to Maastricht on 7 February 1992 for the ceremonial signing of the treaty. Along with representatives of 11 other heads of state, they formally inscribed their names on behalf of Her Majesty Queen Elizabeth II, to the strains of a Mozart string divertimento, K.136. Afterwards Hurd joked to journalists 'now we've signed it, we'd better read it'. [56]

The 'European Union' had been born. All that was now left was the formality of getting the Treaty ratified.

The rise of 'euroscepticism'

In the immediate aftermath of Maastricht, Major was advised that a snap general election might bring a Conservative victory. This was tempting, because Labour had been ahead on the opinion polls for more than two years. But he decided to wait for 9 April, giving time for a tax-cutting budget and the completion of legislation to abolish the unpopular poll tax.

53 *Op. cit.*, col. 378.
54 *Op. cit.*, col. 506.
55 *Op. cit.*, col. 507.
56 Hurd's admission that he had not read the Treaty was later to be more famously echoed by his Cabinet colleague Kenneth Clarke.

The election campaign was strangely unreal. Britain was still in the grip of a recession, the jobless total had risen above two and a half million, and 75,000 homes had been repossessed from those unable to afford the mortgage payments, either because they were out of work or through crippling interest rates.

Much of this agony was directly attributable to the constraints imposed by the ERM, yet the opposition parties could not make this an issue because they too were committed to the ERM. The only difference on 'Europe' in their manifestos was that, whereas the Conservatives rested on the claim that Maastricht had been 'a success both for Britain and for the rest of Europe', Labour and the Lib-Dems were promising to sign up to the single currency and the Social Chapter.

Despite the recession, the most emotive issue in the campaign was a proposal by Labour's shadow Chancellor John Smith to raise £3 billion a year in taxes from the better-off. With polls still predicting a Labour victory, Kinnock also blundered by staging what seemed like a victory rally in Sheffield a week before polling day.

When 9 April came, to general astonishment, the Conservatives took 14,092,891 votes, the largest number ever won by a party at a general election. Within weeks Kinnock was to resign as leader of the opposition, later to become a European Commissioner. He was replaced by the man who more than anyone had lost Labour the election, John Smith. Major remained at Downing Street, albeit with his majority cut to 21 seats.

The first major Bill before the new parliament was the amendment to the European Communities Act, bringing into effect the Maastricht treaty. Not the least remarkable feature of the second reading of this Bill on 20 to 21 May was that MPs were expected to approve the treaty still without having been given a full text. Tristan Garel-Jones, the new Europe minister, believed it would be 'presumptuous' for MPs to have it 'until it had been approved by the House'. Fortunately 1,500 copies of a consolidated edition of the treaty compiled by a tiny private organisation were made available to MPs and peers in time for them to study what they were voting on.[57]

On 20 May the debate ran on until 7.30 the next morning. It recommenced later that day, culminating that evening in a vote. Major's memoirs make no reference to the debate, in which he claimed that:

'The future of Europe is now based on a different foundation. It is based on free trade and competition, on openness to our neighbours, on a proper definition of the limits of the power of the Commission, and on providing a framework for co-operation between member states outside the treaty of Rome.'[58]

According to Major, Maastricht had marked the point at which, for the first time, the centralising trend of the Community had been reversed. This travesty was echoed by Hurd next day, when he declared that it had been 'an important

---

57 It was produced by Brigadier Anthony Cowgill at the British Management Data Foundation. The 1,500 copies were bought by Sir Keith Joseph of the Centre for Policy Studies for distribution. A definitive version with analysis was published in October 1992, and distributed, *inter alia*, by HM Stationery Office, thus giving it semi-official status.

58 *Hansard*, 20 May 1992, col. 270.

step away from an increasingly centralised … Community towards a new Europe in which Britain has a central place'.[59]

What marked out this occasion from previous debates on the issue was the prominence of a new generation of Tory backbench critics, generally described as 'Eurosceptics', although venomously characterised as 'anti-Europeans' by their opponents. During the six months since the treaty had been agreed, an array of new organisations had also been formed, both inside and outside parliament, dedicated to fighting what was seen as its undermining of democracy. After a further year had elapsed, some 27 organisations had been created.[60]

Within the Conservative parliamentary party, a Fresh Start Group was led by Michael Spicer and Bill Cash, himself once an enthusiastic 'Europhile'. Spicer and Jonathan Aitken formed the European Reform Group. One recruit, who made his maiden speech in the debate, was Iain Duncan Smith, Tebbit's successor as MP for Chingford. Many extra-parliamentary organisations were also launched or supported by Tory members in the constituencies. A rift was opening up between grass-roots activists, largely Eurosceptic, and the party leadership.

By now the extent to which Maastricht represented a further leap towards 'federalism' had begun to register with many Conservatives, despite the determination of Major and Hurd to pretend otherwise. Even the new 'pillars' promoting common policies on foreign and home affairs, although intergovernmental in character, potentially represented a major extension of 'Community' influence over the right of nations to run their own affairs. The fact they were to be run by the Council did not rule out the possibility that the powers would later be handed to the supranational Commission. In that sense, the ghost of Monnet must have smiled on Maastricht.

The central plank on which Major rested his claim of a reversal of 'centralism' was the inclusion of 'subsidiarity'. But this was not enough to convince those who had actually studied what was meant by the term. As Bill Cash put it:

'The principle of subsidiarity is a con trick. It is said that there will be a devolution downwards of functions… However, the critical fact is that the main functions will be transferred upwards. One has only to look at the main provisions of the treaty that are taken to the upper tier – economic and monetary union and matters of that kind – to realise that that is where the real power would lie. Apart from the fact that many distinguished jurists have repeatedly rubbished the concept of subsidiarity … the fact remains that this is a concept which, in my judgment, is centralising rather than decentralising. Yet we are being told the opposite.'[61]

If Major and Hurd honestly believed that Maastricht had 'reversed the tide of federalism', they can only have been monumentally self-deceiving. Yet despite evidence that the 'Eurosceptics' were now becoming considerably sharper and better-informed in their criticism, when it came to the crucial vote only 72 MPs voted against the Bill, including 22 Conservatives. By approving the Maastricht treaty in

59 *Op. cit.*, 21 May 1992, col. 519.
60 Forster, *op. cit.*, p. 88.
61 *Hansard*, 20 May 1992, col. 314.

principle, the oldest parliament in Europe had voted for what was potentially an even greater surrender of its powers than that implicit in the original European Communities Act 20 years before.

Scarcely two weeks later, on 2 June, the Danish people in a referendum rejected the treaty by 50.7 to 49.4 percent. Although all the main political parties had been in favour of ratification, a poorly-funded coalition of activists, led by the 'June Movement', had run a spirited *Nej* campaign, aided unwittingly by their government which had circulated 300,000 copies of the treaty, without explanation or summaries. Sight of this unreadable document had been enough to tilt the balance in a country which held its leaders in healthy disrespect. Even Denmark's foreign minister admitted he did not understand it, 'and I negotiated it', he said.[62]

The defeat sent shock waves across Europe. If any member state failed to ratify a treaty, it had to be declared void. But the Danish prime minister, Paul Schluter, disowned the result. 'Can anyone seriously believe,' he said, 'that our small nation with five million people can stop the Great European Express of three hundred million?'[63]

Other governments, supported by Hurd, immediately looked for ways to move the goalposts. The Danes were reviled in the most condescending terms. In the words of Portugal's foreign minister, Sr de Pinheiro, representing the presidency, 'there is something rotten in the state of Denmark'. Either the Danes should be expelled from the Community or they must be forced to reverse their decision. As Pinheiro put it, 'only donkeys don't change their minds'.[64]

Whatever else, the Danish vote presented Major with an immediate problem. Britain was about to take over the presidency so his was the task of rescuing the treaty. And with his own Maastricht Bill about to go to its Commons committee stage and back-bench opposition becoming more organised, something had to give. To allow him to focus on Denmark, he therefore postponed the committee stage.

The response from France was rather more dramatic. Mitterrand announced that he would suspend parliamentary ratification and allow his people a referendum of their own. It was a serious gamble. Mitterrand at the time was unpopular. If French voters followed the Danish lead, Maastricht really would be dead.

Subsidiarity to the rescue

The Community response was to convene a special Foreign Affairs Council on 4 June. Its decision was to continue as before with ratification. The door would be 'left open' for Denmark but there would be no re-negotiation. Kohl was reported as saying that once the Danish 'hiccup' was out of the way, there would be an acceleration of European integration.[65]

---

62 *Time International*, 1 June 1992, p. 70.
63 *Time International*, 15 June 1992, p. 10.
64 Booker, Christopher and North, Richard (1996), *Castle of Lies* (London, Duckworth), p. 179.
65 *The Times*, 8 June 1992.

Over the next few weeks, the Community evolved a more considered answer to the Danish problem, and also to the more general fear that the peoples of Europe were becoming concerned by the shift of power away from nation states. That answer was that magic word 'subsidiarity'. As Hurd explained to the Commons, the plan was to get the European Council to set limits to the powers of the Commission and to take practical steps 'to implement the principle of subsidiarity'. 'We need ... to make it clear to our constituents and others in the Community that matters will improve,' he told the House.[66]

By the time the European Council met to consider this in Lisbon on 26 to 27 June, its members were in happier mood. The Irish referendum had endorsed the treaty with a 69 percent 'yes' vote. The Council welcomed this result. Denmark was not mentioned.[67] Nor was the hardly irrelevant fact that the Irish were now the greatest beneficiaries of Community *largesse*, receiving £6 back from the EC for every £1 they paid in.

Nevertheless a keynote of the Council was a long speech from Delors on the importance of subsidiarity. He had just been subjected to the ordeal of waiting to see whether he would be reappointed president for a further two years. Chastened but relieved, he made it clear, as his biographer puts it, that subsidiarity was now his 'big idea' for 1992.[68] Kohl and Major supported him, agreeing that subsidiarity was the way to reassure public opinion that the European Union was not bent on becoming a 'superstate'. No one demurred.

As Grant later wrote, opposing subsidiarity had, since the Danish vote, become 'no more acceptable than the slaughter of baby seals'. This was echoed in the presidency conclusions, which stated that the 'future development of the Union' would depend 'to a considerable degree on the strict application to existing and future legislation of the principle of subsidiarity'. This would be essential 'to ensure a direction of the European construction which is in conformity with the common wish of the member states and of their citizens'.[69]

It was agreed that Commission and Council should 'undertake urgent work' on steps needed to implement the 'big idea', to be presented at Edinburgh in December, when Major would be in the chair.[70] A truer indication of the real agenda, however, was a resolution tucked away on page 14 of the presidency conclusions, calling for steps to be taken to set up 'Europol', eventually to provide the Union with a supranational police force.

Less than two weeks before, just as little public attention had been given to another dramatic leap forward in the integration process, when defence ministers of the WEU held a meeting in Bonn on 19 June. Although the Maastricht treaty had yet to be ratified, they had already jumped the gun by moving to establish a common defence policy. With Britain represented by Malcolm Rifkind, they drew up what was known as the 'Petersberg Declaration'. In light of 'the progress made

66 *Hansard*, 8 June 1992, col. 37.
67 Bulletin of the European Community, Presidency Conclusions, 29 June 1992, p. 3.
68 Grant, *op. cit.*, p. 217.
69 Bulletin, *op. cit.*, p. 9.
70 *Ibid.*

in developing the role of the WEU as a defence component of the European Union', they agreed that the WEU should move its secretariat from London to Brussels. It would also develop 'its operational capabilities' to allow it to undertake measures of 'conflict prevention and crisis-management'. This was the embryonic 'Rapid Reaction Force', the first step towards giving the European Union its own armed forces.[71] In addition they asked for a report on the setting up of a European Armaments Agency.

Although there was careful emphasis that the WEU would operate in close co-operation with NATO, this was a very significant further step in creating a European 'defence identity'. Yet, although Rifkind advised the Commons that he was to attend the Bonn meeting, no report on what was agreed was made to the House afterwards. Again the stealthy transformation of the WEU had slipped the net of parliamentary scrutiny.

'Black Wednesday'

Long before the Edinburgh Council, the political landscape was to undergo a cataclysmic change. The cause of this was the precipitate departure of the UK from the ERM on 16 September 1992.[72]

Strangely enough, the trigger which set off this explosive event was the Danish 'no' vote, which shattered any assumption that ERM would be a trouble-free glide-path to the single currency. Instead, EMU might be sunk completely, or the 'core' countries might form their own 'mini-Union', outside the framework of Maastricht. Anticipating such possibilities, the financial markets began to reposition themselves.

The first response was that investors who had placed large sums in Spain and Italy, gambling on falling long-term interest rates and firm exchange rates, began to withdraw their money. When Spain made no move to support its currency, it was obvious that devaluation of the *peseta* was inevitable. Italy at last responded with drastic budget cuts, which temporarily stabilised the *lira*. But then Germany, faced with massive new expenditure to pay for reunification, raised its interest rates, careless of the effect this would have on other ERM members. Money flooded into the *Deutschmark*, putting pressure on other countries to raise their interest rates. An immediate casualty was Italy, which in mid-July reluctantly raised its rate by 1.25 percent. But that made it difficult for the government to finance its deficit, negating earlier budget cuts. The *lira* started to slide.

In Britain, the German rate rise also presented problems. Sterling had enjoyed a honeymoon flush after Major's unexpected re-election but was now caught by the rise in the *Deutschmark*. The obvious response would have been to raise interest rates to bolster the value of the pound. But with the UK economy already in

---

71 WEU, Meeting of the Council of Ministers, Bonn, 19 June 1992.
72 The account of this episode is constructed from Connolly, *op. cit.*, contemporary newspaper records, and from Stephens, Philip (1996), *Politics And The Pound* (London, Macmillan), pp. 226–262.

deep recession, and fearful of a further damaging rise in mortgage rates, Lamont chose instead to drop the rate. This sent an alarm signal to the money markets.

During the late summer, as sterling fell to the bottom of its permissible ERM band, the rules demanded a rate rise. But Lamont and Major realised that this would be political suicide. Instead, in an attempt to stave off the inevitable devaluation, they resorted to bravado. The money markets were not impressed.

By late August, as the *Deutschmark* rose to the top of the ERM band, the pound was at its lowest permissible level. The *lira* actually slipped below it. The rules required that the *Deutschmark* should be 'realigned', to release the strain. But this was vetoed by EC finance ministers. Then, fatally, the UK Treasury announced that it had borrowed 10 billion ecu to finance intervention on behalf of the pound. This signalled that the government was now prepared to throw in any money it could find to avoid raising interest rates. Sterling was being set up for the speculators as a target.

In fact it was the *lira* which first came under pressure, after fears of imminent devaluation prompted wholesale selling. As the *Deutschmark* strengthened still further, wiping out gains made by sterling as a result of the borrowing announcement and driving the *lira* against its lower ERM limit, Italian interest rates went through the roof. At an ECOFIN council, the head of the *Bundesbank* came under concerted attack by the finance ministers of Italy, Britain and France, pleading with him to reduce Germany's interest rates. Despite nine hours of heated argument, he refused.

At stake now was more than the ERM. The future of the whole Maastricht treaty was under threat. In a televised debate days earlier, Mitterrand, in support of his 'yes' campaign for the referendum, had effectively rewritten the treaty, claiming that the Council of Ministers could control the proposed European Central Bank. Now, as the world's media looked on, the ECOFIN meeting was poised to break up in disarray, its members unable to prevail over the *Bundesbank*, the natural model for the ECB. This would have told French voters that Mitterrand had no control and ensured a French 'no', consigning the treaty to perdition. For public consumption, therefore, a fudge was arranged, with the Council declaring that the *Bundesbank* had agreed not to raise interest rates, something it had already decided.

Financial commentators soon penetrated the fudge, aided by 'unhelpful' statements from the *Bundesbank*, which also made it clear that Lamont had failed to extract a promise of lower interest rates. Sterling again dropped, and weaker currencies began falling out of the system altogether. First to go was the Finnish *markka*, which put pressure on the Swedish krona, forcing the Swedish central bank to push up overnight interest rates to 24 percent.

There were now eight days to go before 'Black Wednesday' and, after further unhelpful statements from the *Bundesbank*, the *lira* came under massive attack. On the Thursday, with one week to go, Major then made a speech to a Glasgow dinner of the Scottish CBI that was finally to destroy any credibility he had left. He declared that realignment within ERM was the 'soft option, the devaluers' option that would be the betrayal of our future and out children's' future'. All too soon, he was to eat his words.

On Friday 11 September, as the *lira* closed below its permitted ERM floor, Kohl made a secret visit to the *Bundesbank*, hatching a deal that amounted to ditching the 'peripheral' currencies in order to protect the franc. A new Franco-German alliance had been forged, contravening all the ERM rules.

Behind the scenes, George Soros, a hedge fund manager whose name was to become famous, had amassed a 'war chest' of £10 billion with which to attack sterling. The money soon began to have its effect. On the Tuesday, sterling closed at its lowest level since joining the ERM, a mere fifth of a *pfenning* above its ERM floor. After the European markets closed, the pound ran into firestorm selling in New York, plunging it below its ERM limit. The Bank of England intervened but, when European markets reopened the next day, its reserves were leaking at an alarming rate, while sterling remained nailed to the floor. By mid-morning, under ERM rules, there was only one course left to Lamont. He raised interest rates to 12 percent. It had no effect. At 2.00 in the afternoon, he raised them a further three points to 15 percent.

The markets took this as a signal that the game was up. Sterling would have to leave the ERM. Selling increased until, by 4.00 in the afternoon, the Bank had given up. Sterling fell four *pfennings* below the ERM floor. By mid-evening, after panic consultations with the ERM monetary committee, Lamont stumbled out of the Treasury to announce that sterling's membership of the ERM had been suspended. The Italian *lira* was also on its way out, as was the *peseta*. Soros later claimed his activities had netted him a profit of more than £1 billion. The ERM was in tatters. So was the Conservative party. Only five months before it had won the largest popular vote in Britain's electoral history. Over the next 10 years it would never be ahead of Labour in the opinion polls again.[73]

Major's nightmare begins

Despite the ignominious collapse of one of their most ambitious experiments to date, the integrationists scarcely blinked. Four days after 'Black Wednesday', on 20 September, the French people went to the polls. Turnout at 70.5 percent was unusually high, but the treaty was approved only by 51.05 percent to 48.95. With just one vote in 100 going the other way, the treaty would have been dead. Nevertheless, Kohl exulted, 'the positive result of the French referendum ... will give the European integration process a new boost in the other member states'.[74]

This notwithstanding, it gave Major yet another problem. A French 'no' might have given him a way out of Maastricht. Now he had to confront a rebellious party, 71 of his back-benchers having signed an Early Day Motion calling for the government to abandon economic union. At the party conference in Brighton, the newly-ennobled Lord Tebbit won a huge ovation for a defiantly Eurosceptic speech, telling Major to adopt 'policies for Britain first, Britain second, and Britain third'.[75]

73 The only freak exception would be September 2001, due to the fuel-tax protests.
74 The *Guardian*, Special Report, 22 September 1992.
75 Gorman, Teresa (1993), *Bastards* (London, Pan Books), p. 100.

The next step in Major's growing disaster was a Commons debate, triggered by a letter sent to him in October by Neil Kinnock, asking for a report on the significance of Denmark's rejection of Maastricht. Major refused but, unexpectedly, offered a debate when Parliament resumed. What became known as the 'paving debate', on 4 November, gave the Fresh Start Group their opportunity. With 70 or so potential rebels, there was real possibility that, aligned with Labour and the Ulster Unionists, they might defeat the government. It was a threat Major took very seriously. One rebel, Teresa Gorman, recalls a massive 'dirty tricks campaign' by party whips to force recalcitrant MPs into line. Nevertheless there were still sufficient defiant Tories for Major to fear the loss of 'his' treaty.

His life was not made any easier by the new Baroness Thatcher. She attacked Major in a television interview for agreeing to re-appoint Delors and described Maastricht as 'a treaty too far'. On 2 July, in her maiden speech to the Lords, she again called for a referendum and declared that she would vote against ratification.[76]

The 'paving debate' in November thus became a trial of strength between Major and Thatcher supporters, with Major determined to save 'his' treaty. Parliament, he said, had supported, 'indeed acclaimed' the deal when it had first been laid before it.[77] He could not cope with the idea that his MPs had acclaimed it sight unseen, and that when they actually read the treaty they had not liked it. Many now believed they had been sold a false prospectus. Doggedly persisting in his claim that he had reversed the tide of federalism, and determined to resign if parliament now overruled him,[78] Major again stressed the value of subsidiarity. This featured so prominently in the debate that it was mentioned 71 times. It was Major's shield, his 'proof' that Maastricht was a decentralising treaty.

What made this debate different was that Labour, despite supporting the treaty, attempted to beat the government. In the event, with the support of the Liberal Democrats, Major carried the day, but only by 316 votes to 313, a majority of just three. But Major's 'success' was entirely the result of extraordinary pressures put on his rebels by his whips, prompting one commentator to record that the debate:

'...was so unreal that it seemed to be taking place in a fairground hall of mirrors, punctuated only by the distasteful off-stage noises of government managers forcing MPs into voting against what they believed. It was a spectacle that degraded everyone.'[79]

Delors' 'big idea'

In championing subsidiarity as his 'big idea' for 1992, Delors was drawing on his Catholic past, when he had learned of the encyclical *Quadragesimo Anno*. Its intention was to defend people from oppression by Fascist and socialist state authorities, and the poor against 'capitalist exploitation', introducing a philosophy had developed into what became known as 'Personalism'. This held that every task

---

76 *Hansard*, House of Lords, 2 July 1992, cols. 895–901.
77 Major, *op. cit.*, p. 361.
78 *Op. cit.*, p. 363.
79 The *Sunday Telegraph*, 8 November 1992.

should be fulfilled by the smallest social unit capable of carrying it out, beginning with individuals and families, up through larger social units. Only when a task could not be fulfilled on a lower level, should a higher unit step in and take over. But, crucially, the 'sub-units' had no veto. It was up to what Delors called the 'higher agencies' to decide when subsidiarity should apply.[80]

Herein, yawned a gulf between Delors and Major. Major imagined that subsidiarity should allow member states to reclaim power from the Commission. Delors saw it as an instrument of integration. Thus, when he told his officials to produce a list of competences that might be handed back, they failed to find any. One directive, on hunting wild birds, had seemed a suitable candidate, not least because it had provoked enormous hostility in the south-west of France. Clashes between environmentalists and ring-dove hunters, who ignored the directive, were frequent and fierce.[81] Delors had even gone on record saying that the law breached subsidiarity.

'But when he examined the problem in the summer of 1992, he found the directive to be a model of subsidiarity: it laid down the principle that certain species should not be shot while nesting or migrating, and left each government to set dates for the hunting season. Delors learned that the Danes became angry when the French shot ring doves on their way from North Africa to Denmark.'[82]

There was a more intractable problem. Most of the Commission's proposals originated with member states. For instance, a German law requiring mineral water companies to collect used containers suited German companies that used glass bottles, but made it hard for French and Belgian firms which used plastic bottles to compete in Germany. The French and Belgians therefore had asked the Commission to produce uniform rules on mineral water bottles.[83] Delors' team analysed 535 proposals made by the Commission in 1991 and concluded that only 30 had been its own idea (albeit that these had included controversial measures on maternity leave, working time and the liberalisation of energy markets).[84] The result was a report which offered little more than a promise to 'consult more widely before proposing legislation'.[85]

As a gesture, however, Delors withdrew three *proposals* for directives.[86] Two were highly technical, concerning radio frequencies and the third dealt with the 'compulsory indication of nutritional values on the packaging of food'. But a directive on this had already been issued three years earlier.[87] The Commission

---

80 Føllesdal, Andreas (1999), *Subsidiarity and Democratic Deliberation*, ARENA Working Paper 99/21 (*www.arena.uio.no/publications/wp99_21.htm*). See also lecture given by Delors in 1991 (Delors, Jacques, *Subsidiarite: defi du changement*, Institut europeen d'administartion publique, Maastricht, 1991, pp. 8–9.).

81 Grant, *op. cit.*, p. 220.

82 *Ibid.*

83 *Ibid.*

84 *Ibid.*

85 Bulletin, 12 December 1992, Presidency Conclusions. Annex 1 to Part A.

86 Bulletin, *op. cit.*, Annex 2 to Part A, p. 2.

87 Council Directive 90/496/EC of 24 September 1990 on nutrition labelling of foodstuffs. OJ L276, 06/10/1990, pp. 0040–0044.

also *considered* withdrawing 11 other proposals, including one on 'the classification of documents of Community institutions'. But no laws already in the *acquis* were withdrawn. Yet the Edinburgh Council meekly accepted Delors' report. Such was Major's reversal of the tide of 'federalism'.

Major's 'toughest and most vital' task was to find a way of getting the Danes to ratify Maastricht. This he achieved by arranging for the Danish prime minister to 'declare' that the citizenship of the 'Union' did not 'in any way take the place of national citizenship'; that Denmark would not enter the single currency, and that his people would not be expected to become involved in the common defence policy. Eleven leaders then happily incorporated a formal recognition of this statement into a 'solemn declaration'. The point was, of course, that the Danes had not been obliged to opt-in either to the single currency or the common defence policy. Absolutely nothing had changed. Despite that, the 'concessions' were used to convince the Danish people that they could now safely vote for the treaty.

Another Major 'triumph' was the budget increase, from £51 billion in 1992 to £64 billion in 1999. He also kept 'Thatcher's' rebate, although this was nearly blocked by the Spanish who had demanded a doubling of regional aid as the price of agreement. Delors did some swift creative accounting and found an extra seven billion ecus.[88] Also agreed was a start to accession negotiations with Austria, Sweden and Finland in 1993, subject to Maastricht being ratified by all existing members, and the candidate countries accepting the whole of the *acquis*. An application from Norway would also be considered. Germany won an increased number of MEPs, reflecting the addition of East Germany and France got Strasbourg recognised as the official seat of the European Parliament.

When Major reported on his 'successes' to Parliament on 14 December, his line was that the Council had 'agreed a package of measures to reverse centralisation' and that the Commission had produced a list of laws which it believed 'must be simplified or abolished'.[89] This was simply untrue. The Commission had only undertaken to withdraw *proposals* for new laws. But no one challenged him.

Parliamentary ratification: round two

'With the future of the treaty secured,' Major wrote, thinking of his 'success' with the Danes, 'the committee stage of the Bill could begin.'[90] It was taken on the floor of the House. Unlike Thatcher with the Single European Act, Major dare not guillotine these proceedings. They thus became a marathon, opposition being co-ordinated by the Fresh Start Group led by Bill Cash. Under his direction, the group submitted over 500 amendments and 100 new clauses. The debates took over 200 hours, lasting 25 full days.

From Major's perspective, this was a complete waste of time, since there was no way that Parliament could amend the treaty he had agreed. But the Fresh Start

88 Grant, *op. cit.*, p. 229.
89 *Hansard*, 14 December 1992, col. 24.
90 Major, *op. cit.*, p. 372.

Group was unrepentant. Its members wanted to demonstrate the strength and intensity of British Euroscepticism, and perhaps to influence the Danes to vote 'no' in their second referendum. Throughout, both sides allied themselves with opposition forces. The government chief whip, Richard Ryder, regularly met with his Liberal Democrat counterpart, Archie Kirkwood, to agree tactics.[91] Of this arrangement Major heartily approved, but he found the Fresh Start Group's similar dealings with Labour deeply offensive, describing it as 'the sceptics' trickery'.[92]

The Fresh Start Group took a different view. None could have been considered as anything other than mainstream Conservatives. Teresa Gorman, who regarded the Maastricht Bill as 'the greatest threat to Britain's independence since the Second World War', explained that 'confronted with a politician (Major) apparently willing to sacrifice ambition for principle ... our instinct was to band together to save democracy'.[93]

What nearly made the difference, however, was what Major called 'a real bullseye' scored by Labour.[94] It introduced an amendment into the committee stage making ratification of the treaty conditional on accepting the Social Chapter. This amendment was accepted for debate, but the vote on it was to be deferred until after the third reading of the Bill. It became a 'ticking time bomb' which would nearly destroy the treaty.

By late April the Bill had completed its committee stage, but before its third and final reading, three events took place, all in their own ways highly significant. The first was a speech by Major on 22 April to the Conservative Group for Europe, in which he told his audience that Maastricht had been used as a scapegoat for the 'varied and nameless fears about Europe'. Going on to state what was now his party's chief official mantra. Conservatives, he declared:

'... must have the confidence and the sharp-edged determination to stay in the heart of the European debate to win a Community of free, independent members.'[95]

Nevertheless, it was a speech mainly remembered for Major's eulogy about Britain, 'the country of long shadows on county grounds, warm beer, invincible green suburbs, dog lovers and – as George Orwell said – old maids bicycling to Holy Communion through the morning mist'. He claims he was simply reminding his audience that Britain's involvement in Europe did not threaten national distinctiveness, but it became a caricature of his political philosophy.[96]

Next came the Newbury by-election, the first since the ERM debacle, which on 6 May 1993 saw a Tory majority of 12,367 turned into a Lib-Dem majority of 22,055. In local government elections at the same time the Conservatives lost a record 24 county councils. The Tories were starting to pay the price for that catastrophic loss of confidence brought about by the ERM.

91 *Op. cit.*, p. 373.
92 *Op. cit.*, p. 372.
93 Gorman, *op. cit.*, p. xvii.
94 Major, *op. cit.*, p. 374.
95 *Op. cit.*, p. 376.
96 *Ibid.*

The third event was the second Danish referendum, on 18 May, just two days before the third reading. The result was a 'yes' for Maastricht, 57–43 percent, marked by the worst riots Copenhagen had seen since the war. Protesters smashed shop windows, burnt cars and barricaded part of the city, declaring it an 'EC-free zone'. Eleven demonstrators and 26 police were injured.[97] How well the voters understood the arguments was questionable. In one post-referendum poll, only 17 percent knew of the Edinburgh 'concessions'.[98] Others complained that their constitution prohibited holding two votes on the same issue. 'We gave our decision last year,' said cabinetmaker Steen Majlund. 'I thought this was a democracy.'[99]

So, back in the United Kingdom, on 20 May the Maastricht Bill went for its third and final reading, before timorous Conservative MPs, many now fearful for their seats. Labour had already indicated that it intended to abstain and the debate was lacklustre. But Roger Knapman, a member of the Fresh Start Group, gave a portent of things to come. He had discovered that, in the seven months since the paving debate on 4 November, 265 EC regulations and directives had been put before the House, which MPs were virtually powerless to stop.[100]

It was Richard Shepherd, however, who went to the heart of the argument, observing that in all the debates on the Bill, scarcely any speaker had returned to the first principle of democratic government.

'The profound rejection expressed by many people across Europe is based on their belief that it is not a democratic treaty … during all the hours of debate, the occupants of both Front Benches scrupulously moved aside from, and did not discuss, the issue of democratic and accountable government. This House is built on that.'[101]

Hurd's response, echoing Major's speech, was that people were 'not sufficiently confident' in how they regarded the Community. We needed 'to build a more decentralised and diverse Community, outward-looking and free-trading'.[102] By all means, he said,

'… let us reduce and criticise the detail, the regulation and the small-minded acts of interference, but let us do that not in a negative way but to find again the decisive will to act together successfully in the great matters where there is a European interest and where there must be a European effort. Because the Bill enables us to play our full part in reasserting that will power, I commend it to the House.'[103]

Tony Benn was unimpressed. No member had the legal or moral authority to hand over powers borrowed from the electors to people who would not be accountable to them. We were 'handing over the British people, without their consent, to a system that has replaced parliamentary democracy', he said.[104] It was to

97 *Time International*, 31 May 1993, p. 22.
98 Cited in Franklin, Mark, *et al.* (1995), 'Referendum Outcomes and Trust in Government: Public Support for Europe in the Wake of Maastricht' in *West European Politics*, Vol. 18, p. 15.
99 *Time International, op. cit.*
100 *Hansard*, 20 May 1993, col. 391.
101 *Op. cit.*, col. 392.
102 *Op. cit.*, col. 393.
103 *Op. cit.*, cols. 393–394.
104 *Op. cit.*, cols. 418–419.

no avail. The result was pre-ordained. All that was needed was the ritual of the vote to put numbers on the charade. When the House divided, the 'Ayes' came to 292, the 'Noes' 112: a majority of 180 for Maastricht.

The drama was not yet over. There was still Labour's 'ticking time bomb' on the Social Chapter, which was debated on 22 July 1993. Under the arcane rules of the House, Major had to table a motion and then John Smith, as Leader of Opposition, had to move an amendment. This was aimed at preventing the government from depositing the Articles of Ratification of the treaty with the Italian government, until it had notified the EC that it intended to adopt the Social Chapter. Since Major had promised that the Social Chapter would not be adopted, if the opposition motion was carried, the government would have to abandon the treaty. On the other hand, the government's motion had to be carried for the treaty to be ratified. Essentially the government had to win both votes.

It would be wrong to dignify the proceedings on the night with the title 'debate'. As before, only more so, it was pure theatre with the issues being decided on the fringes. Key to the outcome was the Lib-Dems who had decided to swap sides. On the other hand, the Conservative whips had been out in force, using every tactic they knew, short of physical violence, to bring members into line.

The whips' pressure was enough to reduce some of the Fresh Start Group support, to the extent that, on the first vote – the opposition amendment – the result was a dead heat; 317 each. The Speaker Betty Boothroyd, as tradition demanded, cast her vote for the government. Proceedings were being broadcast live on the late television news and, after that cliff-hanger, the next result, on the substantive motion, was cataclysmic. Amid pandemonium, the Speaker called it out: 'Ayes to the right, 316; Noes to the left, 324. The Noes have it'. The government had lost by eight votes.

Even before the vote, Major had decided that, if he lost, he would call for a vote of confidence. For mysterious reasons the Ulster Unionists, until then staunch opponents of the treaty, handed Major their eight votes. They were enough. The vote next day was of dubious constitutional propriety, as the confidence motion sought to overturn the vote of the previous night, technically against the rules. But, facing a general election if the government lost, and with the whiff of Newbury still in the air, the rebels caved in. Every Conservative MP, with the exception of Rupert Allason, voted with the government. At 4.30 in the afternoon, Major won the day by 39 votes. Around him stood the wreckage of the Conservative Party.

Chapter 15

Theory and Practice: 1992–1993

'No longer is European law an incoming tide flowing up the estuaries of England. It is now like a tidal wave bringing down our sea walls and flowing inland over our fields and houses.'

Lord Denning[1]

In November 1992, Colman Twohig, who ran a one-man business in Rochester, Kent, supplying electronic devices for use in dredging work, received a letter from the Department of Trade and Industry. It informed him that he would soon have to comply with new regulations issued under the EEC's 'Electromagnetic Compatibility Directive', 89/336. His products would have to be sent to an autho-rised 'testing house' to ensure they did not cause interference with other electrical items (in which case they would be given a 'CE' mark, for *Communauté Européen*).

Mr Twohig had no argument with the principle behind the regulations. The problem was that the devices he assembled for his customers were 'one-off', each designed for specific tasks, many priced at £50 or less. Yet the cost of individual testing would be £1000 a day, making his business unviable.

Roger Brown, who ran a small garden centre near Appleby, Westmoreland, had for years used a disused quarry on his land as a compost heap. He was now informed that, under new EEC waste regulations, his dead leaves and other com-posting materials constituted 'controlled waste'. Since he did not hold a waste management licence, he would have to hire an authorised contractor to remove them, costing £20,000. He also faced possible prosecution for committing a crim-inal offence.

In Farcet, Huntingdonshire, Tom Chamberlain ran a butchery business, owned by his family for 100 years. In 1992 he was named Champion Sausage Maker at the East of England Show. Soon afterwards he was informed by the Ministry of Agriculture, Fisheries and Food (MAFF) that, under the Fresh Meat (Hygiene and Inspection) Regulations 1992, implementing EC directive 91/497, he must make extensive structural changes to his premises. If he did not, on 1 January 1993, he would lose his licence, forcing him to close his business. Although his butcher's shop was only just across the yard from his slaughterhouse, he would no longer be allowed to carry meat between them unless he built a refrigerated tunnel between the two buildings. Among many other requirements, he would also have

---

1 *H.P. Bulmer Ltd* v. *J. Bollinger S.A.* [1974] Ch. 401.

to build a shower and rest room for 'visiting lorry drivers', even though most animals arriving at his slaughterhouse came from farms within five miles radius. Contemplating the cost of these changes, he concluded over the Christmas that he had no option but to cease trading.[2]

In the closing months of 1992, many such stories began to come to light, from almost every sector of British industry, signalling a new phase in Britain's relationship with what many people still called the 'Common Market'. Until now, 'Europe' had seemed remote from their concerns. Occasionally the media would have fun with some 'crazy new EEC directive', such as the one harmonising laws on jam in 1988 which classified carrots as a 'fruit'.[3] But in general 'Brussels' was viewed as some faraway place which had no impact on everyday life. All of a sudden, however, people running every kind of business were now disconcerted to be told they would now have to comply with new 'EEC regulations'. The most obvious reason was the avalanche of legislation related to the launch of the Single Market on 1 January 1993.

Three things in particular were striking about these new laws. One was the strikingly prescriptive way in which most of them were framed, which was widely perceived to have lost contact with common sense. A second was their draconian nature. Never in history had so many new criminal offences been put on the statute book in so short a time. Again, these often seemed to be related not to correcting genuine problems but simply to failing to comply with bureaucratic procedures, involving reams of paperwork. A third was what was commonly perceived to be a marked change in the attitude of the officials and inspectors responsible for enforcing the new laws. Older people in Britain could remember the 1940s, when 'red tape', official 'snoopers' and state controls had been such a prominent feature of national life during and after the Second World War. But by the mid-1950s this tide had receded and for decades officialdom had generally been much less intrusive. Now, however, it seemed a culture change had taken place. Inflated by their new powers, many of the officials regulating businesses seemed to have become almost routinely aggressive and confrontational.

This change appeared with such speed that, initially, many of those affected thought it was something happening only to them. Only gradually did it dawn that they were caught up in something much wider. Although few realised it, what they were experiencing were the first practical consequences of a dramatic change in the way their country was governed. Until now the emphasis in the story of the 'European project' had been on 'high politics'; on the gradual construction, through interminable 'summits' and treaties, of a new system of government. But this had only been, as it were, the theoretical end of the process. What was now becoming visible was how this new form of government operated in practice.

2 Hundreds of similar examples were reported in by Booker, Christopher and North, Richard (1994), *The Mad Officials* (London, Constable), and *The Castle Of Lies, op. cit.*

3 Council Directive 88/593/EEC of 18 November 1988 amending Directive 79/693/EEC on the approximation of the laws of the Member States relating to fruit jams, jellies and marmalades and chestnut purée. The Directive arose because the Commission wanted to rule that jam could only legally be made from fruit. The Portuguese objected that they also made jam from carrots. By a typical EEC compromise, the Commission's solution was to allow carrots to be deemed as fruit.

From a British point of view, the first thing this represented was a radical change in the way most of their laws were made. For centuries the chief form of lawmaking had been through Acts of Parliament, debated and voted on in public by elected representatives of the people. Now, as ever more areas of lawmaking had passed into Community competence, laws were increasingly coming to be made by a quite different method: one which represented as profound a revolution in the nature of their government as the British people had ever seen.

The façade of democracy

No one could hide the fact that the Community had become a law factory, every year churning out more directives and regulations. But no claim was more persistently made for this process than that it was 'democratic'. And this claim centred on the fact that, although only the Commission had the exclusive right to initiate these laws, the supreme legislative body in the Community was the Council of Ministers. It was the Council, made up of elected politicians answerable to national parliaments, which exercised ultimate democratic control over the whole project. Such was the theory. As for the charge that power in the 'new Europe' lay 'with unelected, faceless bureaucrats',[4] the ritual riposte came back that this was absurd, since the Commission employed fewer officials than any large local authority. As far back as 1975, Thatcher herself had used this argument, pointing out that there were 'only 7,000 officials' working for the Commission, mainly in Brussels. In later years, this number crept up to 'only 15,000 officials', then 'only 18,000', then 'only 22,000', then 'only 25,000'. It was true the number crept inexorably upwards. But to see only these officials as the source of the avalanche of legislation emerging from 'Brussels' was completely to miss the nature of the revolution in government this system had brought about.

The point about 'Brussels' was that it acted as a nexus. It was the centre of a network, linking organisations throughout the Community, not least the civil services of all the member states. On any given day in Brussels would be not only the officials of the Commission itself but also thousands of visiting national civil servants, from every country in the EU, all in one way or another engaged on 'building the Community'. Tens of thousands more were at work in their national capitals, all participating in what had become the most complex legislative machine ever known.[5]

---

4 The European Commission, Representation in the United Kingdom (undated), 'A glossary of eurosceptic beliefs: an exposé of misunderstanding'. *www.cec.org.uk/press/glossary.htm*

5 This point was latterly acknowledged by Thatcher in her book *Statecraft*, published in 2002. She notes that the figure given for the Commission staff – which by then had increased to 30,000 – 'leaves out the much larger number of national officials whose tasks flow from European regulations'. (London, Harper Collins, p. 324.) While not directly comparable, there are plenty of historical examples of very small numbers of people dominating large populations, not least the British Raj. At the end of Queen Victoria's reign, 300 million Indians were ruled by barely 1,500 British administrators of the Indian Civil Service, and perhaps 3,000 British officers in the Indian Army. Excluding British soldiers, there were probably no more than 20,000 Britons engaged in running the whole country – fewer than the number of permanent officials currently employed by the Commission. (Judd, Dennis (1996), *Empire – The British Imperial Experience From 1765 To The Present* (London, Harper Collins), pp. 79–80).

This was first reflected in the bewildering variety of ways by which proposals for Community laws came about in the first place. As Delors' study group on subsidiarity had reported in 1992, only 30 of 535 proposals made by the Commission in the previous year originated with the Commission itself. The rest came from other sources, ranging from civil servants of member states to an array of anonymous committees, made up from professional consultants and academics to environmental pressure groups, NGOs or commercially-funded lobbyists acting on behalf of a particular industry or company. It would later be estimated that there were 1,600 such committees operating in Brussels, and beyond them 170,000 lobbyists of one kind or another across the EU, ranging from pan-European trade associations representing whole industries to the representatives of individual county councils pleading for a share in regional funding.

The second stage of the process came when the Commission formally accepted a proposal for legislation. Again in many cases aided by professional consultants or academics from universities across the Community, who would produce the initial drafts,[6] texts would be negotiated over months or years by a further array of committees, often chaired by officials from the Commission. Some were made up of national officials from the relevant government departments of the member states, formally constituted as regulatory committees, often advised by representatives of interest groups. This was the system which had become known as 'comitology', operating by such arcane rules that few people understood it.

The contributions made to this legislative process by national civil servants would be co-ordinated through Coreper, the Committee of Permanent Representatives, which had been part of the Community's core structure since 1958. It was by the officials of Coreper that, except in rare cases where there was still fundamental disagreement, each new directive or regulation was finally agreed. Only now was the proposal ready to move on to its final stage, its submission for approval by the relevant ministers sitting in the Council of Ministers. It was here, according to the theory, that the whole legislative process was given 'democratic' legitimacy.

Indeed at this stage there might also be added what, according to the theory, was a further element of 'democratic' accountability. Before the Council took its final decision, many proposed new laws would go for consideration by the European Parliament, the role of which had been gradually expanded over the years to create the impression that this gave the peoples of Europe some 'democratic' say in how they were governed. The Parliament would go through its own show of examining and voting on the proposal. But in no conventional sense was this a legislature providing a democratic check on the executive. More often, the Parlia-

---

6 The Commission made widespread use of academic institutes to assist in the drafting of legislation. This was a useful device, since contracts were often issued under the 'research' budget, which automatically compelled member states to contribute 'co-funding'. By this means, not only was the Community able to increase its spending at the expense of member state taxpayers but it was able to call on the services of a much larger workforce than was represented by its own employees. Similarly, much of the technical harmonising legislation was now drafted by European standards institutes, particularly CEN (*Comité Européen de Normalisation*). Because these were funded mainly by national institutes and governments, this also provided the Community's integration process with an extensive hidden subsidy.

ment merely added to the Commission's proposals, or chided it for not moving faster on the path to integration.[7] Similarly where, by the procedure known as 'co-decision', consent for a proposal was required from both Parliament and Council, even where their views differed and further complex procedures had to be invoked to achieve 'conciliation' between them, in practice a proposal was hardly ever significantly changed. Ultimately it was with the Council of Ministers that the power lay, and it was on this that the Community's claim to be subject to 'democratic' control ultimately rested.[8]

In practice, a close appraisal of the workings of the Council of Ministers revealed that there was nothing 'democratic' about it whatever. Not only did its meetings take place behind closed doors, without any public record of what was said or how ministers had voted (as was wryly observed, almost the only countries with a legislative process as secretive as that of the Community were Cuba, North Korea and Iraq). Equally relevant was that 80 percent of proposals which came before the Council were placed on what was known as the 'A list', as items the ministers themselves could not examine and which simply went through on the nod.

One of the few participants who ever publicly described the workings of the Council of Ministers in practice was Alan Clark, who recorded in his diary his first Council as a junior trade minister in February 1986. This began with an account of how, before the meeting, he was coached on 'the line to take' by an official of UKREP, the UK's permanent representation in Brussels, before she then set about rewriting the speech he had been planning to make. 'Not that it makes the slightest difference to the conclusions of a meeting what Ministers say,' he went on:

'... everything is decided, horse-traded off, by officials at Coreper... The Ministers arrive on the scene at the last minute, hot, tired, ill or drunk (sometimes all of these together), read out their piece and depart.'[9]

Another minister described how, when he arrived at his first Council, he was startled to see that the first item on the agenda was the *communiqué* to be issued when the meeting was finished. When he protested to his officials that this should surely come last, after the rest of the agenda had been settled, he was condescendingly told, 'Oh no, Minister, all the other items have already been agreed at last week's Coreper.'[10]

---

7 As early as 1965, Miriam Camps noted that increasing the powers of the European Parliament would not improve matters as 'this would make it even easier for the Commission to manipulate public opinion against the Governments'. (Camps, Miriam (1965), *What Kind Of Europe? The Community Since De Gaulle's Veto* (London, Chatham House Essays, Oxford University Press), p. 91). The same point was made 25 years later by the Deputy Director of the Institute of Economic Affairs. 'Rather than the European Parliament acting to check the Commission,' he wrote, 'the reality is the potential use of the Parliament by the Commission in order to assert its independent policy-making rôle.' (Vibert, Frank (1990), 'Europe's constitutional deficit'. In: Mather, Graham (intr.), *Europe's Constitutional Future* (London, Institute of Economic Affairs), p. 78.)

8 Two further fig-leaves of accountability were reflected in the requirement that many items of legislation should be submitted for 'consultation' to the Economic and Social Committee and the Committee of the Regions. In practice this was merely another empty formality, since neither body had any power and any recommendations they made were politely ignored.

9 Clark, Alan (1993), *Diaries* (London, Weidenfeld and Nicolson), p. 139.

10 Lord Hesketh, Minister of State DTI 1990–1991, in private conversation, 1995.

The volume of business transacted in this way was colossal. By 1998, it was estimated that more than 3,000 meetings of the Council of Ministers took place at ministerial or official level each year, an average of 60 a week.[11]

In Britain, this charade was further compounded by the pretence that no minister could approve an item of legislation in the Council of Ministers unless it had been 'scrutinised' in advance by Parliament. This scrutiny system had been set up under Heath in 1973, and on 24 October 1990 was formally confirmed by a Resolution of the House of Commons, laying down that 'no Minister of the Crown should give agreement in the Council of Ministers to any proposal for European Community legislation which is still subject to scrutiny'. In practice, however, this scrutiny by parliamentary committees appointed for the purpose was no more than an empty ritual. MPs had no influence whatever over what went on in the Council of Ministers. The 1990 Resolution was to be forlornly reprinted year after year in Commons reports, recording innumerable instances where ministers approved items which had not been scrutinised, often because the MPs had not been supplied with the relevant documents in time.[12] The record of most other national parliaments, less than half of which even went through the pretence of examining legislation passed in their name, was even worse.[13]

Once a proposal had become Community law, however, there were still two more stages before the process was complete. The first, in the case of a directive, was that the officials of each member state then had to 'transpose' it into a form they considered appropriate to their own country before it could be passed into national law. In Britain, as we shall see, the civil servants would often add damaging requirements which did not appear in the original directive. Nevertheless it was their wording which would now become the law of the land.

At this point a further curious element was added into the process whereby the proposed new law would be submitted for 'consultation' to organisations representing the industry and other interests which would be affected by it. That this was no more than a further sham of 'accountability' was demonstrated by the fact that in almost no case was the wording of the law ever changed by the 'consultation' process. But it gave the officials warning of any problems which might arise when the new law came to be enforced, and it allowed them to reply, when those problems did arise, that the law had only been introduced after 'full consultation with the industry'.

The act of finally putting the directive into law was achieved in Britain by means of the mechanism devised by Howe in the European Communities Act, whereby the version produced by the civil servants was issued in the form of a 'statutory instrument', using powers 'delegated to the minister'. The officials would present these 'regulations' to the minister for his signature (only rarely did a minister read

11 The European Commission, *op. cit.*

12 See, for instance, the Twenty-Seventh Report of the Select Committee on European Legislation on *The Scrutiny of European Business*, 18 July 1996, the Select Committee on Procedure's Third Report on *European Business*, 12 March 1997, the Seventh Report of the Select Committee on Modernisation of the House of Commons on *The Scrutiny of European Business*, 9 June 1998, all published by HMSO, London.

13 *Cf. The Scrutiny of European Business 1996, op. cit*, p. x.

a statutory instrument before 'signing it into law', let alone query its contents).[14] It would then become law. As a formality, the instrument would be 'laid before Parliament', giving MPs the right to object. But again, this right was only theoretical. In practice the chance of any such 'secondary legislation' implementing EC legislation being rejected was nil.[15]

The most remarkable achievement of this new system of government had thus been the extent to which the power to make the vast majority of laws had been transferred from politicians to officials. The only useful role left to the politicians in this process was to lend it a veneer of democratic legitimacy.

But there was still one final stage to come. This was the way in which these new laws came to be applied in practice. In theory every country in the EC was subject to the same directives and regulations. In practice, however, it would soon emerge that the spirit in which different countries chose to enforce these laws would vary wildly between one member state and another.

It was on this basis that, towards the end of 1992, the British, whether or not they understood how their laws were now made, began to discover to an unprecedented degree what belonging to the European Community was really about.

The unlevel playing field

At midnight on 31 December 1992, Major and Heath joined in London to light a 'beacon' (no more than a puny, oil-fired flame sputtering in the rain), celebrating the launch of the 'Single Market'. For five years, millions of pounds had been spent on telling businesses how this would be the moment when all remaining trade barriers were finally dismantled, 'opening up a new market of 340 million consumers', providing an unprecedented boost to growth, jobs and prosperity.

In practice, as those running businesses had already been discovering for some months, the most obvious consequence of the Single Market was a huge increase in regulation. Far from being a 'free trade area', the new Single Market was now the most highly-regulated economic zone in the world, to set up which had required the issuing of 1,368 EC directives.[16] Their chief purpose had been to integrate the member states by 'harmonising' their laws over almost every aspect of economic activity, from the labelling of fire-extinguishers to the design of teddy bears.

One of the most conspicuous features of this legislation was the way so much of it was portrayed as promoting causes to which no one could possibly object, notably those shibboleths of the modern age 'safety', 'hygiene', 'consumer protection' and 'protecting the environment'. A flagship of the new Single Market laws were six directives on health and safety, governing anything from the prescribed height of

---

14 Information based on interviews with ministers and ex-ministers.
15 When in 1995 a rare attempt, backed by MPs of all parties, was made to halt a statutory instrument, setting up the Meat Hygiene Service to enforce EC rules on the meat industry, ministers merely transferred the 'debate' to a standing committee where it had an in-built majority. Government supporters passed the legislation without contributing to the discussion. One MP ostentatiously dealt with his constituency correspondence throughout the proceedings, before voting for the proposal (authors' observation).
16 *Global Britain*, August/September 1998, p. 8.

office chairs to the number of minutes employees were allowed to spend in front of a computer screen. The purpose of these was supposedly to guarantee that all workers throughout the EU would now enjoy the same high standards of safety.

Another swathe of directives, again in the name of 'safety', introduced new 'harmonised' standards to regulate the manufacture of every conceivable type of product, from machine-tools to children's toys, from climbing equipment to gas heaters, from lifts to cricket pads. Every item which met the new standards of the '*Communauté européen*' had to carry the 'CE' mark, as an outward sign of how the Community was now looking after its citizens.

Another significant attempt to 'open up the market' which had excited British enthusiasts for the Single Market, such as the former trade minister Lord Young, was the policy designed to enable firms from any EC country to bid for all public contracts above a certain size. Under three 'procurement directives', covering utilities, services and public works, whenever a hospital wished to buy a scanner, a local council needed to replace its fire engines or a highways authority wanted to build a bridge, the contract would first have to be advertised in the Community's Official Journal, allowing firms across the EC to compete for the work, with a requirement that the lowest tender must be accepted.

Almost all the laws bringing about this revolution had to be transposed into UK statutory instruments, so that, while Parliament was spending months on the Maastricht treaty, debating whether to give away more power to the European Commission, civil servants were busy drafting an unprecedented quantity of secondary legislation based on the previous treaty, the Single European Act. All this was 'nodded through' Parliament without debate, using powers MPs had already ceded under the European Communities Act.

A measure of just how dramatically the use of this form of lawmaking had been expanded was the increase in the number of statutory instruments issued each year. In the mid-1980s, the annual average had been around 2,300, mostly concerned with routine matters of administration such as teachers' pay or road-closures. By 1990 the number had risen to 2,667. In 1991, as the Single Market approached, this increased to 2,933. In 1992 the total for the first time soared past the 3,000 mark to 3,359. At the same time the number of Bills going through Parliament declined precipitately, from an average of 150–200 a year through much of the post-war period to just 41 in 1993 to 1994.

There was no more immediate example of the contrast between theory and practice in the Single Market than the Commission's constantly repeated boast that it would bring 'the scrapping of 70 million customs forms a year'. The dismantling of customs controls across the EU meant that agents for exporters and importers would no longer have to fill in forms recording the quantities and value of goods as they crossed frontiers. But the Commission still wished to keep statistical records, showing the volume of what it called 'intra-Community trade'. It therefore issued EC Regulation 3330/91 imposing a complex new system known as Intrastats. Responsibility for compiling the data was placed on the traders themselves. In return for the abolition of customs forms, the cost of the new system to UK companies alone was estimated at more than £1 billion a year.

As Britain's businesses tried to cope with this deluge of legislation, certain general categories of complaint emerged about how it worked in practice.

One frequent criticism was that, far from making it easier to export goods into other EU countries, the new system had made it more difficult. Rowland Spencer's Hotbox Heaters in Lymington, Hampshire, was one of only six firms in the EU – all British – making specialised gas heaters for use in greenhouses. He was told that, under a directive on 'liquid gas appliances', 90/396, his products would now have to be sent to a 'testing house' to be given the CE safety mark. When Mr Spencer was eventually awarded his mark, after paying £20,000 to a Dutch-owned test house, he imagined he would now be free to sell his products anywhere in the EC. He was then told that, because EC countries used no fewer than 37 different types of liquid gas, his products would now have to go through the testing procedure 37 times, one for each gas. He decided to abandon his trade with other EC countries and to concentrate his sales on Asia, America and Africa. Within a few years his would be the only one of the six firms left.

A second significant problem which came to light in the run-up to the Single Market was what became known as 'gold plating'. So zealous were Whitehall officials in transposing EC directives into British law that they frequently added onerous requirements not included in the original directive. An example was the toy safety directive, 88/378, which required all new toys made after 1990 to be tested, in order to qualify for a CE mark. When the legislation came to the DTI, however, it chose to extend its application to second-hand toys, which provided a significant source of income to charities. This 'gold plating' meant that many old toys could no longer be sold, depriving charities such as Oxfam of millions of pounds a year.

A third, related problem was the extraordinary zeal often shown by British enforcement officials. At Christmas 1992, Acorn Hobbycraft, a fast-growing company making children's model kits in Ringwood, Hampshire, fell foul of trading standards officers from Barking and Dagenham council for including pipe-cleaners in some of their kits, which the officials considered could be injurious to children's eyes. Although the officials failed in their first attempt to bring a criminal prosecution against the company under the toy safety directive, they then appealed. When in 1993 the case was re-heard, they produced evidence based on prodding pipe-cleaners into the eye of a dead pig, claiming that this showed they might cause similar injury to a child. Judge Fanner accordingly ruled that to sell the pipe-cleaners was a criminal offence. The company, which had spent £350,000 on legal costs, was forced into liquidation, putting 14 people out of work, although 60 million pipe-cleaners continued legally to be sold each year for other purposes.

A fourth widespread problem was the discovery of many British firms that, when they attempted to sell their goods and services to other EC countries, this proved remarkably difficult. The Single Market had far from succeeded in dismantling all protectionist barriers. All too often the promised 'level playing field' was in practice a mirage. French officialdom in particular proved tirelessly ingenious in ensuring that business would continue to be given only to French companies, as was demonstrated in particular by the chaos surrounding the 'procurement directives', intended to ensure that public contracts were thrown open to companies across the EC.

While the new system was rigorously enforced in Britain, adding greatly to the complexity and expense of tendering procedures, other countries were notoriously reluctant to allow contracts to go to outsiders. In 1995, analysis of engineering design contracts advertised in the EC's Official Journal showed that nearly half had been submitted from Britain. Not long after the market was 'opened up' in this way, Renault ambulances, BMW police cars and Volvo fire engines would be racing round British streets, the new Severn Bridge would be built from subsidised Spanish steel, and French catering firms would be serving meals to council officials in English town halls. But many continental authorities found that British products and services never somehow matched their requirements.

A fifth problem in complying with this mass of new legislation was its cost. Not only had it called into being a whole new industry of regulatory consultants and bodies such as those authorised 'testing houses', charging huge sums to certify that products could be given CE marks. The cost of regulation was now greatly exacerbated by the emergence of a new type of public regulatory body, the 'Sefra' or Self-Financing Regulatory Agency, empowered to charge fees for inspections and for the licences which were now becoming required by EC law for many firms to stay in business. These Sefras ranged from the Meat Hygiene Service and the Medicines Control Agency, financed from the millions of pounds it charged pharmaceutical companies to licence their drugs, to the Waste Authorities, set up to enforce a thicket of new EC waste disposal rules, and the quaintly-named Her Majesty's Inspectorate of Pollution, set up to enforce EC directives supposedly designed to curb pollution by industry.

When the Single Market came into effect on 1 January 1993, a £5 million chemical plant on Teesside, one of the most modern in Britain, had for months been standing idle, despite its owners Chemoxy International having spent £120,000 in their efforts to comply with the HMIP's idiosyncratic interpretation of a new EC regulatory system known as Integrated Pollution Prevention and Control (IPPC). The plant's purpose was to recycle and render harmless potentially toxic substances such as anti-freeze mixtures, which it did so effectively that the total quantity of VOCs it emitted in a year was only eight kilograms, mainly consisting of acetic acid (vinegar). This was less than the quantity of VOCs emitted by the exhaust of the HMIP inspector's car on his visits to the factory. The incompetence of the officials in trying to apply legislation they did not understand was costing Chemoxy £60,000 a week.[17]

By the closing months of 1992, the concern aroused by this regulatory explosion was becoming so widespread that the government could no longer ignore it. The District Surveyors' Association estimated that the cost to businesses of just one proposed new set of fire regulations, supposedly implementing two short pas-

---

17 In 1995 HMIP would be joined with the Waste Authorities and the National Rivers Authority to create the Environment Agency, the largest Sefra in Britain, set up almost entirely to enforce EC directives at the expense of the tens of thousands of companies it regulated.

sages from EC health and safety directives, would be £8 billion, making them the most expensive law in British history. The regulations, as drafted by the Home Office, were 20 pages long, accompanied by 100 pages of guidance: 3,500 lines derived from just 34 lines of Commission text. At the last minute, following the public furore created by the revelation of their cost, they were withdrawn, but it was to take four more years and 16 more drafts before the Home Office officials could be persuaded to come up with a more reasonable version.

In September 1992 when, for the first time, the practice of 'gold-plating' was exposed in a newspaper article, this so shocked Major's ministers that they discussed it at a Cabinet meeting. Here were the very ministers who had been signing into law hundreds of regulations, apparently unaware that their own officials had been 'gold plating' directives on such a damaging scale.[18] This prompted Major into making a call 'to lighten the burden of government regulation' the keynote of his party conference speech at Brighton two weeks later. Launching his 'deregulation offensive', he announced that he had appointed his trade and industry minister Michael Heseltine to

'... take responsibility for cutting through this burgeoning maze of regulations – who better for hacking back the jungle. Come on, Michael, out with your club, on with your loin cloth, swing into action.'[19]

Over the next four years Major's 'deregulation initiative', inspired by the gold-plating of EC directives, was to remain a flagship policy. Yet during that time, when his government put its lengthy 'Deregulation Bill' through Parliament, not a single regulation implementing a directive was changed. The annual number of regulations issued by his government, which only topped 3,000 for the first time in 1992, never dropped below that figure. Only at the end of the Bill's passage through Parliament did a junior minister in the House of Lords finally admit that the government had always intended that regulation stemming from the EC should be excluded from deregulation.

CAP 'reform'

Not only industry was being engulfed in 'red tape' at this time. In 1993 the Commission's CAP reforms were taking effect, including compulsory set-aside and a new system of linking subsidy payments to the acreage under cultivation rather than to the quantity of crops grown. This brought a quantum leap in bureaucracy as the new 'Integrated Administration and Control System' (IACS), required British farmers to submit exact details of their field areas. Yet maps of the required precision were often not available and, even when they were, the

---

18 The *Daily Telegraph*, 'Who's That Lurking Behind The Brussels Book Of Rules?' by one of the present authors appeared on 14 September 1992, two days before Britain left the ERM. On 24 November, Hurd referred in the Commons to 'cases where officials in Whitehall take decisions made in Brussels and carry them through in excessive detail'. This was 'known in the jargon', he said, 'as "Bookerism", after the journalist who identified the ill'.

19 Prime Minister's speech, Conservative Party Conference, Brighton, October 1992.

timetable set for the submission of an accompanying 79-page form was impossibly short. In the days before the deadline, long queues of farmers formed outside shops selling maps. In Portugal and Ireland, the equivalent IACS form ran to just two pages. In France the authorities accepted estimates of field areas provided by the local town hall.

In the fruit production sector, as a result of grants offered to fruit-growers to cut back their production, hundreds of British apple-orchards were rooted up, while continental growers preferred to continue to exploit a system under which they were subsidised to grow fruit even if it had to be destroyed. In the year 1994 alone this would result in the destruction of 77 percent of the French apple crop and 73 percent of Italian pears. Greek farmers would receive £89 million from the EC to bulldoze 657,000 tonnes of peaches into the ground. According to Commission figures, EC taxpayers in 1994 paid £439 million to destroy millions of tons of fruit in this way, 94 percent of it going to just four countries, Greece, Italy, France and Spain.[20] The net result of compulsory set-aside, intended to take 15 percent of arable land out of production, was that in the first four years of the scheme, costing EC taxpayers £4 billion, annual production of cereal crops rose by 10 percent.

In addition to the labyrinthine subsidy system, Brussels poured out sheaves of directives and regulations to assert its ever-growing control over almost every aspect of agriculture. The dairy industry alone was subject to more than 1,100 pieces of legislation, covering everything from the insemination of cows to the permissible chemical constituents of cheese. Under EC directive 92/102, sheep and goats each had to be given a numbered ear tag, with written records of every movement off the farm. Under directive 77/93 vegetable seedlings could not be sold for commercial use without a 'plant passport'. Under a directive on 'Forestry Reproductive Materials', 66/404, based on a Nazi forestry law of 1934 and designed to preserve the genetic purity of European oak trees, it became a criminal offence to sell acorns from 'hybridised' trees. The result was that by 1995 more than three-quarters of commercially-grown oaks in Britain had to be imported from eastern Europe, to climatic conditions for which they were unsuited.

One of the Commission's most ambitious schemes involved more than 50 separate directives designed to maintain the health of European vegetables. It became illegal to sell seed-varieties unless they had each been registered at a cost of £3,000, plus a further £700 a year to keep them on the list. This resulted in the disappearance of thousands of traditional plant varieties, including more than 95 percent of the 2,500 known varieties of tomato.

One size fits all – the slaughter of the slaughtermen

There was no more comprehensive instance of the way this tidal wave of EC legislation was imposed by the Major government than the trauma it brought to

---

20 HoL Select Committee on the European Communities, *Report on Reform of the EC Fresh Fruit and Vegetable Regime* (London, HMSO, 19 December 1995).

Britain's meat industry. Before Britain joined the EEC, the Commission had issued Directive 64/433 to harmonise hygiene standards for the production of meat exported across national frontiers. When these rules, based on a 19th-century German code, had been challenged by non-EEC countries, including New Zealand, as being outdated, the Commission had then modified them, producing new, extra-legal guidelines called the *Vade Mecum*.[21]

In the 1980s, the UK Ministry of Agriculture, Fisheries and Food had imposed these 'EC export rules' only on those abattoirs which produced meat for export, also providing grants worth millions of pounds to enable them to comply with the 'structural standards'. The result reinforced the three-tier structure of the industry, which became split between some 80 large 'industrial' abattoirs, mass-producing meat for supermarkets and for export; several hundred medium-size abattoirs, mainly producing for family butchers; and several hundred tiny local slaughterhouses, often serving a single adjoining butcher's shop.

As the Single Market approached, harmonised meat hygiene rules were included in the list of measures to apply even to those producers who did not export. The result was a new directive, 91/497, which was actually little different from the earlier directive, but still posed enormous difficulties for the hundreds of small and medium-size abattoirs. They would now have to make the same hugely expensive structural changes originally required only of industrial meat plants. But unlike their larger competitors, they could expect no financial assistance.

What made the situation worse was that as early as May 1990, long before the new directive was finalised, MAFF veterinary officials began 'advising' abattoir owners on the supposed new legal requirements. These instructions were based not on the directive, which only emerged in July 1991, but on the *Vade Mecum* which had no legal force. Bemused owners were then told that unless they complied with these standards by 1 January 1993, the start of the Single Market, they would be prohibited from trading. They were given just seven months to make often major and expensive structural changes without which they would be refused a licence to operate. Faced with what seemed impossible demands, between 1990 and 1992, 205 businesses – more than a quarter of all the abattoirs in Britain – shut their doors.

The survivors were immediately confronted with another problem. The new directive also imposed a continental system of meat inspection, requiring supervision by veterinary surgeons, to replace the traditional British system of using qualified local authority meat inspectors. Lacking vets qualified to inspect meat, however, MAFF adopted a clumsy compromise of requiring meat to be inspected by meat inspectors under the supervision of veterinary officials. Abattoir owners had to pay for both. From 1 January 1993, slaughterhouse owners were being charged up to £100 per hour for the 'services' of vets, many of them hired from Spain and with little knowledge of practical hygiene.

21 Commission of the European Communities, Directorate General for Agriculture. (1992), 'Guidelines for European Commission Inspections of Fresh Meat Establishments', VI/1111/92-EN Rev. 2. (Several versions were produced – this one was made available to the authors.)

In the first week of January 1993, in the slaughterhouse run by Bob Newman in Farnborough, Hampshire, nine men were present. Three were his slaughtermen. The other six were officials, watching them work. In February Nigel Batts, chairman of Reading abattoir, assembled his 17 employees to tell them that, although the business had been doing well enough to warrant expansion, the excessive cost of the new inspection regime was forcing its closure. 'This was the worst thing I have ever done in my life,' he said.[22] In the months that followed, similar closures took place all over Britain, leaving large areas without an abattoir, forcing some farmers to ship animals over 100 miles to be slaughtered.

When agriculture minister John Gummer was challenged as to why the industry was being so damaged, he initially argued that the closures were necessary for 'hygiene reasons'. When this was disproved, he then repeatedly fell back, in letters to MPs and others, on the curiously disingenuous explanation that the owners had 'taken a commercial decision not to invest in the future of their business'.[23]

An ecological disaster

As minister responsible for agriculture and fisheries, Gummer was also now presiding over the destruction of another British industry. For the first few years after the start of the 20-year transitional stage of the Common Fisheries Policy in 1983, the British fishing industry had not fared too badly, although in 1985 the people of Greenland, previously part of Denmark but now autonomous, became so frustrated at the depredation of fish stocks in their waters by EC trawlers that they withdrew from the Community. In return for allowing EC fishing boats to continue fishing her waters, under strict conservation rules, Greenland was paid by £107 million a year by the EU. By a strange quirk, the withdrawal from the EEC of the largest island in the world halved its total land area overnight.

What did anger British fishermen, as Spain's accession approached, was the practice whereby Spanish fishing companies registered their vessels as British and then bought up UK fishing licences. This entitled them to a share in UK quotas, even though they continued to sail from and land their catches in Spanish ports. Since these vessels operated under the Red Ensign, they became known as 'flag boats', or 'quota hoppers'.

By 1988, two years after Spain's accession, bringing a massive injection of EC funds into the Spanish fishing industry, the problem of these 'quota hoppers' prompted Parliament to pass the Merchant Shipping Act, in a bid to protect UK quotas. To qualify for British quota, they had to be owned and crewed in Britain. In what was to become a historic demonstration of the impotence of Parliament, however, a number of Spanish-owned companies, headed by Factortame Ltd, brought an action under Article 7 of the Treaty of Rome, asking for the Act to be set aside as representing 'national discrimination'.

After hearings in the London High Court and the House of Lords, the case was referred to the ECJ, which ruled in 1991 that 'certain aspects' of the Act were 'not

22 Communication with authors.
23 Multiple copies passed to the authors.

compatible with Community law'.[24] This left the Lords no option but to set aside the will of Parliament. Almost immediately the Spanish companies sued the British government for compensation for the 18 months they had been deprived of fishing rights, eventually resulting in an award of over £100 million.

Meanwhile, the Commission had to come to terms with the failure of its fisheries policy. By 1991 fishing capacity in the Community had substantially increased. Since 1970, the total tonnage of the EC fleets had risen by 153 percent, and fishing capacity by 420 percent.[25] Worse still, the 'conservation' rules, which forced fishermen to 'discard' fish for which they had no quota, was causing an ecological crisis. The Commission's own mid-term review of the CFP admitted that:

'In the North Sea discards of haddock may exceed what is retained from a single trawl; the global estimate for 1985 was 460 million discarded individuals, whereas landings amounted to 500 million. In the Bay of Biscay/Celtic Sea discards of hake were estimated at 130 million individuals, for a landing figure of 110 million.'[26]

Yet in Norwegian waters, where the government was still able to impose its own rules, 'discarding' was illegal.

The Commission's response was to propose reducing 'fishing effort' by 'decommissioning' vessels in each national fleet. Known as the Multi-Annual Guidance Programme (MAGP), the news of this was sneaked out by Mr Gummer on 27 February 1992 by way of a written parliamentary answer. He then tried to claim that the UK fleet reduction would be only 12 percent, but it eventually emerged that the Commission was demanding 19 percent, equivalent to nearly a fifth of the fleet. Yet the cut demanded of the much larger Spanish fleet was only four percent, much of it to be financed from EC structural funds. Of the £25 million allocated to the British scheme, however, £20 million would have to be paid by the Treasury, through the rebate 'claw-back'.[27] In other words, British taxpayers would be paying to make room for the Spanish to fish in British waters.

It had already been recognised by the Commission, however, that in view of the size of the Spanish fleet, the proposed cuts would be insufficient. Thus, the Commission gave notice that further cuts might follow, unless member states took their own measures to reduce fishing effort. The UK response was to introduce the Sea Fish (Conservation) Bill, giving the government unprecedented powers to dictate the terms on which fishermen were permitted to fish (the so-called 'days at sea' restrictions). This would enable the government to squeeze thousands more fishermen out of business, by denying them the right to earn a living without having to pay compensation.

The Bill was rushed through Parliament, with the support of almost every Conservative MP, so fast that it had passed its second reading even before the

---

24 Case C-221/89 *R. v. Secretary of State for Transport, ex parte Factortame* [1991] ECR I-3905; [1991] 3 CMLR 589.

25 Porter, G. (1998), *Estimating Overcapacity in the Global Fishing Fleet*, WWF.

26 Commission of the European Communities, *Report 1991 from the Commission to the Council and the European Parliament on the Common Fisheries Policy*. SEC(91) 2288 final, Brussels, 18 December 1991.

27 *Hansard*, 3 June 1992, col. 52.

deadline for industry 'consultation' had expired. Outraged fishermen challenged the scheme in the courts and it was eventually dropped. But the problem had not disappeared. The fishermen's victory had merely postponed the playing out of their tragedy.

A watershed moment

What was now becoming uncomfortably clear was that, whatever the Community claimed it was trying to do, the result was invariably the opposite. A Single Market claimed to be a great act of 'liberation' and 'deregulation' had produced one of the greatest concentrations of constrictive regulation in history. A 'reform' of the CAP intended to cut back on over-production and misplaced expenditure ended up producing more unwanted food at even greater expense. The CFP, intended to 'conserve Europe's fish stocks', had resulted in an ecological crisis.

At least on balance, it might be argued that Single Market must have achieved its intended purpose of stimulating economic growth and creating jobs. But even that was a mirage. In the three years preceding the launch, average EU growth had been an unimpressive 2.3 percent per annum, while average unemployment had been 8.5 percent. In the four years after January 1993, the growth rate was to slump to 1.67 percent – the poorest performance of any economic bloc in the developed world – while EU unemployment would soar to 10.9 percent, with nearly 20 million people out of work.

The significance of what was happening to the 'European project' in the early 1990s was that from now on, more than ever before, it was going to become increasingly possible to measure all those euphoric, long-familiar promises of the great things it was going to achieve in the indefinite future, against what it was actually achieving in practice. It was a watershed moment.

Chapter 16

Odd Man Out: 1993–1997

'Building the Single Currency is like building the mediaeval cathedrals. It will be as big. It will be as beautiful. It will last as much.'

> *Chef de Cabinet* to Yves-Thibault de Silguy, Commissioner in
> charge of preparations for monetary union, August 1996 [1]

'An economic union will survive only if it is based on a political union.'

> Helmut Kohl, 1993 [2]

'As a former Chancellor, I can only say I cannot pinpoint a single concrete economic advantage that unambiguously comes to this country because of our membership of the European Union.'   Norman Lamont, October 1994

'Unemployment in this country is now the lowest of any major European competitor. We have created more jobs over the past three years than Germany, France, Italy and Spain – indeed, we have created more than Germany, France, Italy and Spain added together.'

> John Major to House of Commons, 24 June 1996

It was a measure of the unease provoked by the Danish '*nej*' and the narrowness of the French vote on Maastricht that Delors, in late 1992, felt it necessary to examine means of 'strengthening the image of Europe'. To do this, he appointed a '*Comité des Sages*', headed by Willy de Clercq, a Belgian MEP, working with a group of advertising executives. Their report was unveiled on 31 March 1993 to a press conference in Brussels by Senhor de Pinheiro, the Commissioner for 'Information, Communications, Culture and Audio-Visual Techniques'.

Nothing could better have demonstrated the gap between the political élites of Europe and the 'citizens' they purported to represent than this 'wise men's' report. They suggested that 'Europe', should be treated as a 'brand', and marketed as such. The Maastricht treaty was too complicated, or as de Clercq put it, 'treaty decisions are far too technical and removed from daily life for people to understand'. Instead of being allowed to read it, the 'citizens' should be fed slogans, such as 'Together For Europe For The Benefit Of Us All' and 'Mother Europe Must Protect Her Children'. The 'sages' also suggested financing 'pan-European television broadcasts' by Delors himself, including a programme 'directed at the women of Europe'. 'This will probably be the first time,' the report intoned, 'that a statesman makes a direct appeal to women.' [3] Similarly the media should paid to take 'a more positive line' about the EU, history books should be rewritten 'to reflect the

---

1 BBC Radio 4, 24 August 1996.
2 The *Financial Times*, 4 January 1993.
3 Reported in the *Daily Telegraph*, 1 April 1993. The report also suggested that young people should be targeted because 'it is strategically judicious to act where resistance is weakest'.

European dimension' and broadcasters should be funded to introduce that 'dimension' into television soap operas and panel games.

Even for a normally quiescent Brussels press corps, this was too much. Amid a 'cacophony of protest', angry journalists walked out and the Greek president of the Brussels association of journalists, Costas Verros, accused the Commission of 'acting like a military junta'.[4]

This curious episode presented something of a contrast to two other events unfolding in Europe in 1993. First there was the tragedy engulfing Bosnia, where Croats, Muslims and Serbs, sponsored by the Belgrade government, were becoming locked in the most murderous civil war Europe had seen since 1945. As rival military forces and marauding gangs laid siege to Sarajevo, Mostar, Banja Luka, Srebrenice and other towns, hundreds of soldiers and civilians were dying each month in the name of 'ethnic cleansing', while blue-helmeted UN 'peacekeepers' looked on, powerless to intervene. Since the fiasco of 1990, it was obvious that those who claimed to represent 'Europe' had no means of influencing these events in any way.

A second shadow over the EU countries themselves was the increasingly dire performance of their economies. Growth, which in the late 1980s had averaged three to four percent, had slipped to one percent in 1992, and was heading for zero. In Germany unemployment had risen to seven percent, in France over 11 percent. Those out of work now numbered 18 million, more than double the level a decade earlier. Yet, maintaining the air of unreality, Delors complained to the European Parliament in Brussels on 4 February that this was due to 'a dangerous back-sliding from Europe's economic strategy: the next stage of economic and monetary union'. More integration was his answer to every problem. And this would now centre on three issues: preparation for economic and monetary union; enlargement; and the need to take on more supranational powers through the 'institutional reforms' enshrined in a new treaty.

Within the bubble

The first European Council of 1993, meeting in Copenhagen on 21 to 22 June, also seemed to be living in its own bubble of unreality. The heads of government applauded their 'success' in the second Danish referendum and set 1 January 1995 as the date for the accession of four more members; Austria, Finland, Sweden and Norway. But also on the horizon was entry of the former Communist countries of central and eastern Europe, a prospect viewed without enthusiasm. To avoid making a firm commitment to their early entry, the Council set out five so-called 'Copenhagen criteria'. These required candidates to have established proper

---

4 Reported by Boris Johnson, the *Daily Telegraph*, 1 April 1993. Three years later a Belgian journalist Gerard de Selys described in the French monthly *Le Monde Diplomatique* (June 1996) how 'many of the 765 journalists accredited in Brussels are offered very generous gifts in the form of reports for which they are paid, and for which tidy sums are also paid as expenses. Alternatively they are offered regular or occasional work for one of the many publications produced essentially by the Commission. For some of them, this work can double or triple their salary'. ('The Propaganda Machine of the Commission', June 1996). *Cf. European Journal*, June 1996, p. 12.

democracy and a free-market economy, protection for minorities and respect for the rule of law and human rights. Membership also presupposed the candidate's 'ability to take on the obligations of membership including adherence to the aims of political, economic and monetary union'.[5] These conditions were widely viewed as a delaying tactic.

Only briefly did the Council touch on the Community's economic plight, asking Delors to prepare a White Paper on 'jobs, competitiveness and growth'. But they did confirm the finance ministers' decision to expand 'structural' funding. For the period 1994–1999 this was to be increased to £30 billion a year, almost on a level with the CAP and equating in real terms to three times the size of the Marshall Aid programme. This was to be Delors' next 'big idea'.

Lower down the agenda was a ticking time bomb. 'To promote confidence in the construction of Europe', as the *communiqué* put it, the Council 'underlined the importance' of continuing to combat Community fraud. Although allegations of fraud had long dogged the Community, these had now become persistent, not least with the mysterious 'suicide' in Brussels on 30 March of Antonio Quatraro, the senior Commission official in charge of CAP tobacco subsidies. Under suspicion for his department's handling of the £800 million a year in payments to Italian and Greek farmers for growing tobacco so low-grade that most of it had either to be destroyed or dumped in eastern Europe and north Africa at giveaway prices, his death added to the sense of unease. But all the Council did was to ask the Commission to produce proposals for an 'anti-fraud strategy' by March 1994.

This was not the only time bomb. As the Council ended, Delors took the opportunity to crow about the healthy state of the ERM.[6] He little realised that it was then only seven weeks away from collapse, torn apart by the contradictory needs of different economies. The *Bundesbank* needed interest rates high, to aid Germany in financing reunification with borrowed money. France needed low rates to boost her ailing economy, yet was forced by the ERM to keep them too high. When in late July Germany ignored French pleas for a rate cut, the markets became convinced France would have to devalue.

In four days leading up to 1 August, 'Black Sunday', France committed $100 million to supporting the franc, before conceding defeat. ERM margins were relaxed from 4.50 to 30 percent, effectively allowing the currencies to float free. 'Stage one' in the glide-path to a single currency existed only in name. For Delors, stricken by sciatica and forced to use a walking stick, the prospects for his monetary union must suddenly have seemed remote.

At the same moment, Major was vacationing in Portugal, meditating on where Britain's involvement with 'Europe' might be leading. It had been 20 years since the UK had joined the Community and Maastricht had proved the 'fork in the road':

5 As was widely observed at the time, considering the undemocratic method whereby the Community made its own laws, it was not obvious that the EC itself met its own criteria for membership. France would have been disqualified in 1958 for her systematic use of torture in Algeria. A similar point was for different reasons made about Italy when she took on the presidency under Berlusconi on 1 July 2003.

6 Cited in Grant, *op. cit.*, p. 262.

'Our partners wanted a single currency. We did not. They wanted a social chapter. We did not. They wanted more harmonisation of policy. We did not. They wanted more Community control of defence. We did not. Increasingly they talked in private of a federal destination, even though in public they were reassuring about a Europe of nation states.'[7]

By now, he had nearly three years' experience at the European 'top table' and the battle scars were showing. He recorded the workings of a European Council in a way Thatcher never attempted. Discussion, he wrote, 'followed a somewhat weary pattern'.

'Everyone around the table laid out their views in a set-piece speech that was frequently more for domestic consumption than a serious attempt to influence discussion. This was often because the decision had already been fashioned in private, and the discussion was merely a prelude to confirming it. Before every summit ... the French and Germans reached agreed positions if at all possible. The Commission was in touch with both groups.

Most decisions were proposed by the Commission, after negotiation with France, Germany and the country holding the Union presidency. The smaller nation-states, all of whom were net beneficiaries of the communal budget, often complained bitterly about this in private, but were consenting adults in public. Whenever I witnessed this phenomenon, Aneurin Bevan's famous explanation of how he persuaded reluctant doctors to join the NHS came unbidden into my mind: "I stuffed their mouths with gold." The glow of precious metal beamed out from the silence of many of the heads of government. Their unwillingness to oppose a Franco-German consensus was striking, and for Britain, highly irritating.

The Commission was rarely challenged; and when it was there was often a cowardice to the criticism: any counter-proposal was preceded by a paean, together with a timid suggestion that, perhaps for the best of reasons, the Commission was wrong. Jacques Delors, confident of his position, brushed aside such half-hearted complaints easily, often with German or, more likely French, support. Others rather smugly joined the consensus. Isolated, and made to feel they had behaved improperly, the critics conceded. It was cruel, and an absurd way to operate.'[8]

Only Britain, Major added, was the grit in the oyster. He could now see why Thatcher had become so unpopular among the 'colleagues'. She had been used to a democratic system where people spoke their minds. But when people spoke the language of Westminster in Brussels, 'it was like spitting in church'.

That autumn, Major contributed an article to the *Economist*, setting out his own 'vision' for 'Europe'. It should focus, he argued, on what its people wanted, not on the institutional reforms that so obsessed its leaders. Our prime concerns, he wrote, should be peace, growth, prosperity and employment. He challenged the prevailing view that 'we had to march forward to ever greater political and economic uniformity'.

'It is for nations to build Europe, not for Europe to attempt to supersede nations. I want to see the Community become a wide union, embracing the whole of democratic Europe, in a single market and with commons security arrangements firmly linked to Nato. I want to see a competitive and confident Europe, generating jobs for its citizens and choice for its

7 Major, *op. cit.*, p. 579.
8 *Op. cit.*, p. 583.

consumers. A community which ceases to nibble at national freedoms and so commands the enthusiasm of its member states.'[9]

As Major soon discovered, his efforts were fruitless. 'I caused a stir,' he recalled, 'but wasted my ink.'[10] In 'Europe' he found himself perpetually in a minority of one for not giving enough. When he returned home, he found himself harried by his back-benchers and even the 'bastards' in his own Cabinet for giving away too much. Meanwhile his party's standing in the opinion polls was at its lowest level in history.

The bubble continues

In Brussels, the air of unreality persisted, the autumn of 1993 bringing a moment of celebration. At last, with a ruling by German's constitutional court in Karlsrühe that the Maastricht treaty did not breach the country's Basic Law, the treaty had come into force. On 29 October, the heads of government were summoned to an 'Extraordinary European Council', to declare that, as from 1 November, the European Community would now be known as 'the European Union'. Triumphantly they proclaimed:

'The citizens of Europe know that the Community has brought them an end of bloody wars, a higher level of prosperity and greater influence. They know that today, even more than yesterday, isolation and retrenchment are false solutions, always illusory and sometimes dangerous. They must also realise that the European Union will help them cope with industrial and social transformation, external challenges and a number of the scourges of our society, starting with unemployment.'[11]

Outside the bubble of self-congratulation, unemployment had reached its highest level since the EEC was founded. As for bringing an end to 'bloody wars', the headlines were daily dominated by the chaos in Bosnia which the Community had been unable to end.[12]

Unreality continued with the next European Council, again in Brussels, on 11 to 12 December. The highlight was Delors' White Paper on how to cure 'Europe's structural unemployment'.[13] His remedy was no more than an 'identikit' list of jargon phrases. He emphasised the need to lay 'the foundations for sustainable development', while the 'major challenge' was naturally 'the need to press on with

---

9 The *Economist*, 25 September 1993, p. 29.

10 Major, *op. cit.*, p. 587.

11 European Council in Brussels, 29 October 1993.

12 Almost the only decision the Community had been able to take over the Yugoslav conflict was to support the international embargo on selling arms to the combatants. This policy was summed up by Douglas Hurd's lofty pronouncement that selling arms would only create 'a level killing field'. Since the Serbs were already well armed, only the Croats and Bosnian Muslims were seriously disadvantaged by the embargo. Hurd would have been more honest to admit that, by depriving non-Serbs of means to defend themselves, he was arguing for an 'unlevel killing field'. Despite the Community's high-minded policy, the Croats and Muslims got round the embargo by smuggling in arms bought on the international black market.

13 Commission of the European Communities. (1993), *White Paper on growth, competitiveness, and employment: The challenges and ways forward into the 21st Century*. COM(93) 700 final Brussels, 5 December.

building a unified Europe'. Spelling out the supposed benefits of 'Community action', he claimed that, between 1986 and 1990, member states had created nine million jobs (despite there now being 18 million unemployed). He also claimed that economic growth had been accelerating by 'half a percentage point each year' (in fact it had dropped to zero).

Behind this self-deceiving rhetoric, however, Delors was proposing a hugely ambitious programme. He wanted the Union to control the Community's research and development policy, so that 'co-operation' directed by the Commission would 'gradually become a basic principle'. Even bigger was a scheme to build the 'trans-European infrastructure', interconnecting energy transmission systems and a series of cross-border road and rail projects, collectively known as the 'Trans-European Network' or 'TEN'. The cost would be 400 billion ecus over 15 years, partly paid from regional funds but mainly by member states, with private finance involvement. The aim was to boost employment by launching a neo-Keynesian public works programme, on 'New Deal' lines, which would also promote integration.

The Council approved Delors' 'road map' in such glowing terms that he described himself 'as proud as a peacock'.[14] Yet when Major returned to explain the White Paper to Parliament, he told MPs how member states were 'now determined to pursue realistic, practical and market-oriented policies to improve Europe's competitiveness'. They had agreed on the need for 'firm control of public spending and low inflation; open markets; deregulation; a more decentralised Europe; flexibility in labour markets and reductions in social costs and the decisive role of private investment in generating economic growth'.[15] No one could have guessed that he and his fellow heads of government had just agreed in principle a programme of state-subsidised public works costing more than £260 billion, equal to the entire annual spending of his own government.

'The poodle of Brussels'

By March 1994, Major was having more problems with 'the colleagues'. After more than a year of negotiations, terms had been agreed for the accession of Austria, Finland, Sweden and Norway, although Norway was still insisting on protection for her fisheries. Spain, as always, demanded her ransom, which had Delors scraping up the money to buy fishing rights for the Spanish fleet from Russia.[16] This left a sombre mood in Brussels, as next in line were the former Communist states of central and eastern Europe.

Major, meanwhile, had been doing his arithmetic and had worked out that, with new countries in the Community, Britain's already minimal voting power would be unacceptably reduced. He decided to make an issue of this. Fully supported by his Cabinet, he gave notice that he would veto enlargement unless the

---

14 *Cf.* Grant, *op. cit.*, p. 268.
15 *Hansard*, 14 December 1993, col. 685.
16 Grant, *op. cit.*, p. 270.

Community retained its existing rule that, under the system of qualified majority voting, 23 votes were sufficient for a 'blocking minority'.

In so doing, Major had touched a nerve. QMV went to the heart of the 'project' as the defining characteristic of supranationalism. As Salter and Monnet had recognised in the 1920s, through QMV, nations could be forced to accept decisions against their national interests. So long as they retained the veto, they could block new laws, which is why the first requirement of a supranational body was the elimination of the veto. But even QMV presented problems as long as a minority could still form blocking alliances. This was precisely what Major recognised. Each 'enlargement' of the Union could be used to increase its supranational powers.

Initially Major relied on support from Germany, France and Spain. But as negotiations progressed and after Spain's support was bought off by the Russian fishing deal, this evaporated. Again Britain was on her own. Thus, when asked in the Commons which was more important to him, the *status quo* on QMV or enlargement, Major could only side-step the question. He was determined 'to fight Britain's corner' just as hard as any other nation would fight for its interests, he declared. This was the difference between his government and Labour, which would 'say yes to everything that comes out of Europe, with no critical examination'. It was the Labour leader Mr Smith, who 'would sign away our votes, our competitiveness and our money', which was why he should be described as 'Monsieur Oui, the poodle of Brussels'.[17]

It was a jibe soon to rebound on Major, as Hurd departed for three days and nights of continuous negotiation with his fellow foreign ministers at Ioannina in Greece. He ended up with a classic 'Euro-fudge'.[18] To save face, 23 votes might still be permitted to hold up a proposal for a short time. Otherwise Britain was forced to concede the point. Smith charged Major with a 'humiliating climbdown'.[19] One of Major's own back-benchers, Tony Marlow, angrily commented that since

'...this so-called compromise has not achieved anything of real value for the United Kingdom, and as of now, my right hon. Friend has no authority, credibility or identifiable policy in this vital area of policy, why does he not stand aside and make way for somebody else who can provide the party and the country with direction and leadership?'[20]

For Major, it was a low point of his premiership. 'The mood in the Party was fierce. The press was hideous. It was an appalling time, made worse by the knowledge that the wound was self-inflicted,' he wrote.[21] On 30 March, the front page of the *Daily Mail* had a cartoon depicting Delors in the high heels and fishnet stockings of a Parisian prostitute, leading a dainty poodle on a leash, its head bearing the face of Major. Another prime minister was on his way to being destroyed by 'Europe'.

17 *Hansard*, 22 March 1994, col. 134.
18 Major, *op. cit.*, p. 589.
19 *Hansard*, 29 March 1994, col. 798.
20 *Op. cit.*, col. 802.
21 Major, *op. cit.*, pp. 589–590.

Humiliation continues

Rather less media attention was paid in Britain to the news from Marrakesh on 15 April 1994. After seven years of tortuous negotiations, the governments of 123 nations had signed the 'Final Act' of the Uruguay GATT Round. The consequences of this deal would be felt all over the globe, not least in the damage it would inflict on the third world. It had been a 'stitch-up' between US and EU negotiators, who, by what was known as the 'Blair House Accord' in November 1992, had agreed to 'fudge' an agreement to reduce subsidies.

Under the 'MacSharry reforms' of the CAP, many EU farm subsidies had indeed been reduced, but farmers were being paid 'compensation' for losing them. By agreement, this 'compensation' had been regarded as a permitted 'fair trade' practice, even though the sums farmers received were larger than before. Similarly, the rich producer-countries could continue dumping 40 million tons of subsidised wheat on the world market, thus driving down the world price, at the same time as GATT was forcing third-world countries to open their markets.[22] Unsurprisingly, 150,000 rioted in New Delhi, complaining that Western imports would ruin Indian farmers and force many industries out of business.

In Britain, rather more notice was taken of the unexpected death on 12 May of John Smith, succeeded as Labour leader by the young and still comparatively unknown Tony Blair. Smith's death delayed the start of the election campaign for the European Parliament and, when it began, the Conservatives ran on the ticket *A Strong Britain in a Strong Europe*. But Major's reputation as the 'poodle of Brussels' destroyed its credibility. The Conservatives' vote plummeted to 27.8 percent, its lowest in a national poll in the 20th century. Labour's 44.2 percent increased its representation from 45 seats to 62. Britain's overall turnout, 36.1 percent, was again the lowest in the EU.

Shortly after the elections, Major was 'bounced' by another incident. On the agenda of the Corfu European Council for 24 to 25 June was a successor to Delors, due to retire at the end of 1994 after a record nine years in office. Kohl and Mitterrand strongly backed a fanatical integrationalist, the prime minister of Belgium, Jean-Luc Dehaene. Major's objections forced Dehaene's withdrawal but, later in the year, at an emergency Council in Brussels, he accepted the compromise candidate, Luxembourg's prime minister, Jacques Santer. The president-elect promptly declared that, in his enthusiasm for integration, there was no difference between himself and Dehaene.[23]

So much did this episode preoccupy Britain's media that scant coverage was given to the rest of the Council agenda, which included endorsing Delors' ambitious 1994–1999 framework programme on scientific and technological research. This greatly extended the reach of the Union's budget since the Commission's own contributions now automatically had to be matched by national governments.[24]

22 See CUTS Centre for International Trade, Economics and Environment, Briefing Paper: *Overdue Reforms in European Agriculture – Implications for Southern Consumers*, 6/1999 – *cuts.org/no6-99.pdf*; Howarth, Richard (2000), *The CAP: History and attempts at reform*, IEA Policy Paper, June.
23 George, *op. cit.*, p. 262.
24 European Council at Corfu, 24–25 June 1994, Presidency Conclusions. *www.europarl.eu.int*

The Council also agreed to a Commission request for extensive new regulatory powers over what it called the 'information society', covering use of computer networks for anything from air traffic control to health care.[25] It accepted a Franco-German 'initiative against racism and xenophobia', extending the reach of the 'Justice and Home Affairs' pillar of Maastricht.[26] Finally the Council agreed to set up a 'Reflection Group', to start work in 1995 on preparing for a new treaty.

Compared with the *communiqué* issued by the first European Council in 1973, covering no more than a couple of pages, it was noticeable how the final documents had grown, to 60 pages or more. But Monnet's 'provisional government' was not behaving entirely as planned. In much of its work, the initiatives, or the responses, increasingly lay with member state governments. This government was beginning to flex its muscles, in a way that was to have profound effects.

Nevertheless Britain's MPs scarcely noticed the increasing role of the Council. When Major reported back to the House on 28 June, their chief concern seemed to be the appointment of the new Commission president. In fact, there was little the MPs could have said or done. The Council had agreed on far too many policies for Major to offer anything but the sketchiest summary, although in past times each might have warranted a full debate. That such policy decisions could now be accepted, without discussion, only reflected how rapidly power was now draining away from Westminster.

Odd man in

It was in the summer of 1994 that sharp-eyed observers began to notice another aspect of just how different was Britain from her European 'partners'. In the two years since her exit from the ERM, her economy had begun to expand faster than any other in the EU. For many, 16 September 1992 was now being looked back on as not 'Black' but 'White' Wednesday, as Britain could again benefit from her economic restructuring in the 1980s. The former 'sick man of Europe', with an economy that had ranked fourth behind Germany, France and Italy, was now moving rapidly back towards second place. In terms of income per head, she had then been almost at the bottom of the European league. She was now moving towards the top.

Also being observed, not least by the respected economic journalist, Bill Jamieson, was the remarkable extent to which Britain's burgeoning new prosperity was due, not to the 44.6 percent of her trade she did with the EU, but to the 55.4 percent she did with the rest of world. Britain was now trading with the rest of the EU at a huge loss, amounting in 1994 to £6.79 billion, against a trading surplus with non-EU countries of £5.1 billion. The EU was the only bloc in the world in which the UK was running a deficit, which since she joined the Common Market in 1973 now amounted cumulatively to £87 billion. Added to her net contributions to the Brussels budget, this made an overall deficit of £108 billion. Fortunately this was

25 *Op. cit.*, point 1.4.
26 *Op. cit.*, Annex III.

counter-balanced by a dramatic growth in her income from outside the EU, not least from her investments in the USA, double those in the EU. Economically, UK membership had been far more advantageous to her EU competitors than to the UK itself.

The constant claim that EU membership was an unalloyed economic 'benefit', vital to Britain's survival, was thus another illusion.[27] Yet so ingrained was it in the minds of the British people that it would still be some years before its implications sunk in. It would not be until 1998 that, according to OECD figures, Britain's economy again became the fourth largest in the world, after those of the USA, Japan and Germany; and not until 2002 that her *per capita* income exceeded Germany's to become the highest in Europe. But already a country becoming economically the most successful in the EU was at the same time becoming politically regarded by her partners, bent on ever greater integration, as no more than a tiresome irrelevance.

This was neatly illustrated in the autumn of 1994 by the startling contrast between two views of Europe's future: one from Germany, the other from Major. In a paper addressed to the forthcoming IGC Reflection Group on 1 September 1994, two leading German politicians, Wolfgang Schäuble, Kohl's heir apparent, and Karl Lamers, warned that the Union was in danger of reverting to 'a loosely knit grouping of states restricted to certain economic aspects': little more than a free trade area. So great was this threat that they called for a redoubled drive for further integration. Centred on the Franco-German alliance, a 'hard core' of six or seven states should lead the way. Echoing Tindemans in 1975 and Delors in 1989, they suggested a constitution, allowing the Commission to take on 'features of a European government', with the European Parliament becoming a genuine law-making body and the Council of Ministers acting as a 'Senate'.[28]

Major responded in a speech in Leiden, Holland, on 7 September. He rejected a 'hard core' and instead offered 'flexibility'. Nations, he said, should not all be forced into the same mould, but should be able to opt out of specific policy areas. Only in certain areas such as the Single Market or the environment was there need for conformity.[29] As before, Major was ignored. Rather greater note was taken of a voice from the past, former French president Giscard d'Estaing. Forget political integration for the time being, was his message. Concentrate on EMU. Achieve this and political union would inevitably follow.[30]

---

27 Jamieson, Bill (1994), *Britain Beyond Europe* (London, Duckworth), pp. 102–103.

28 Christian Democratic Union/Christian Social Union Group in the German Lower House (1994), *Reflections on European Policy*, Bonn, 1 September.

29 Cited in Salmon and Nicoll, *op. cit.*, pp. 261–263. Major was given at this time to using the term 'variable geometry' to describe his notion of a 'Europe of overlapping circles', in which differing groups of nations would co-operate for different purposes. To a limited extent this was how the Union was in fact developing, as different, overlapping groups were brought together by, say, the Schengen agreement, monetary union and defence.

30 Szukala, Andrea and Wessels, Wolfgang (1997), 'The Franco-German Tandem', in Edwards, Geoffrey and Pijpers, Alfred, *The Politics Of European Treaty Reform – The 1996 Intergovernmental Conference And Beyond* (London, Cassell), p. 91.

Assailed from every side

Back home during that autumn of 1994, Major came under mounting pressure from both wings of his Party. His conference in October saw a packed fringe meeting cheering Norman Lamont for the most outspoken attack on the EU ever heard from a senior Conservative politician. 'If Britain was not a member of the European Union today,' he said, 'I do not believe there would be a case to join.' He was not suggesting Britain's withdrawal, but it was 'nonsense' to suggest that Britain could not survive outside the EU. 'The issue,' he warned, 'may well return to the political agenda.'[31]

From the other wing, in November, a carefully co-ordinated campaign was launched by a phalanx of senior political and business figures to pressure Major into taking Britain into the single currency. Leading the way was a CBI survey which, according to its director-general, Howard Davies, showed 'a large majority' of his members wanting Britain to join.[32] The findings were timed to coincide with a well-publicised lecture given in the City by Leon Brittan, the EU's Trade Commissioner, who claimed business support for the single currency.[33] In an echo of tactics used in 1971 and 1975, the BBC was also recruited to the cause. It led its news bulletins with the claim that '84 percent of CBI members are in favour of a single currency', while the *Today* programme allowed Brittan, Davies and others to argue for British membership of the single currency virtually unchallenged.

Close examination of the CBI's survey, however, revealed that only 624 selected companies, from 8,000 members, had been polled. Of those, fewer than a third (206) had replied. Only 59 (28 percent) of those, well under one percent of CBI's membership, positively supported British entry. The rest, 72 percent, was either hostile or lukewarm. Only by adding the 56 percent agreeing that EMU could help business in the long run but 'was not a necessity' to the 28 percent in favour was it possible to reach the '84 percent' reported by the BBC. No mention was made of another finding: that 88 percent of respondents were against 'deepening integration'.[34] Such was the way in which the 'debate' was being presented to the British people.

Added to his troubles, Major now faced, on 28 November, a fractious debate on legislation required to approve an increase in UK contributions to the EU budget. Between 1986 and 1994 the budget had risen by 103 percent. But because Major had agreed in Edinburgh to increase Britain's payments, he now stated that, if the House rejected such a solemn commitment, he would resign.[35]

To make mischief, Labour tabled an amendment linking approval of the Bill to action on cutting EU fraud, which had lately been making more headlines. In July 1994 a House of Lords committee reported that fraud, particularly in the CAP, was

---

31 Lamont, Norman (1995), *Sovereign Britain* (London, Duckworth), p. 29.
32 The CBI was at this time firmly controlled by a group of fervent enthusiasts for EMU, including Lord Marshall of British Airways, Davies himself and three Irishmen, Nial Fitzgerald of Unilever, Peter Sutherland of BP, a former Brussels Commissioner, and Christopher Haskins of Northern Foods.
33 Proudfoot Lecture, given in Plaisterers Hall, 17 November 1994.
34 Analysis from British Management Data Foundation and *Castle of Lies, op. cit.*, p. 168.
35 Major, *op. cit.*, p. 599.

now taking place 'on a monumental and growing scale', amounting to £5 billion a year.[36] A book published across the EU by a French MP, Francois d'Aubert, put the total even higher.[37] The EU's Court of Auditors, in what was to become a yearly ritual, refused to approve the EU's 1993 accounts on the grounds that they contained too many 'irregularities'.

For the government, Chancellor Kenneth Clarke rested his case on claiming that the increased contribution was the necessary price Britain for the benefits of EU membership. 'Our economic well-being' he claimed, 'is dependent in huge part on our membership of the single market'.[38] This was counterpointed by speeches from Eurosceptics, including Norman Lamont, who recalled the time when, during Britain's presidency, he had tried to raise CAP fraud at a special meeting of finance ministers.

They had been circulated with a Court of Auditors report detailing various frauds, including a famous episode when a ship in Hamburg had been loaded and unloaded repeatedly with the same meat, for which export subsidies were claimed several times over. Italy had in 1992 claimed subsidies for 4.3 million acres of durum wheat, used for pasta, although satellite photography showed only 1.9 million acres grown. When Lamont announced that he wished to raise this issue with his colleagues:

'... a number of the ministers did not turn up. I opened the discussion. A large number of ministers just read their newspapers. No one contributed a word to the discussion, then Mr Delors attacked me for being political by introducing the subject of the Court of Auditors.'[39]

Another Conservative back-bencher, John Wilkinson, raised the issue of the fines imposed on Italy and Spain, for allowing their farmers to exceed their EC milk quotas. The two governments had tried to 'blackmail' the Community by threatening to veto the Edinburgh budget agreement unless their fines were remitted. Clarke denied this, claiming that British intervention had caused the original fines of £1.6 billion to be raised by a further £860 million, the largest ever imposed. He omitted to mention that the fines had not been paid (nor ever would be).

John Taylor, an Ulster Unionist, provided a graphic account of how hundreds of millions of pounds-worth of EU regional funds were being wasted in Northern Ireland, on projects ranging from 'butterfly parks' to a golfing video, 'as well as £40,000 on Lord O'Neill's steam engine, which closed down a few months later'. Although money was urgently needed to improve various traffic 'black spots', a condition of the funding was that it could only be spent on cross-border roads to southern Ireland, mostly small and little used.[40]

What came over was the MPs' sense of powerlessness. The deal had been done. Their job was simply to vote it through. Major won a majority of 285, with Labour

---

36 *Financial Control and Fraud in the Community*, HMSO, 1994.
37 D'Aubert, Francois, *Main basse sur l'Europe: Enquete sur les derives de Bruxelles*, quoted in *The European*, 4 November 1994.
38 *Hansard*, 28 November 1994, col. 932.
39 *Op. cit.*, col. 961.
40 *Op. cit.*, col. 987.

abstaining. All he could see, however, was that eight Tories had voted against him. At his insistence the party whip was withdrawn from all eight, including Teddy Taylor, Teresa Gorman, Richard Shepherd, Christopher Gill, John Wilkinson and Tony Marlow. Sir Richard Body, once a fervent Europhile who had long since become an expert critic of the CAP, voluntarily resigned the whip in support.

At least for the Eurosceptics there was compensation. The Norwegians for a second time rejected EC membership in a referendum, by 52.1 percent to 47.9, on a 90.4 percent turnout. Decisive again were the fishing communities, some of which voted 90 percent 'no'.[41] Another feature was the opposition of many young people, one of whom, a pretty blonde, explained to the BBC after the result 'it is the lack of democracy in your system we don't like'. For some British viewers it was chilling to realise that, in speaking of 'your system', she meant one of which Britain was now part.

Spain: cuckoo in the nest

For Major though, there was the European Council treadmill. However, when he went to Essen for the last Council of 1994, hosted by Kohl on 9 to 10 December, he was to recall it as 'mercifully free of the petty wrangles which so often disfigured European summits'.[42] The last Council attended by Delors and Mitterrand, it set 1999 as the date for the launch of the single currency. It agreed that Malta and Cyprus should be allowed to apply to join the EU. And it approved the usual raft of integrationist measures, including five 'key areas' in which the heads of government hoped to tackle the mounting problem of Europe's unemployment.

They instructed themselves, for instance, to increase 'the employment-intensiveness of growth', with more flexible organisation of work 'in a way which fulfils both the wishes of employees and the requirements of competition'. They suggested a wages policy based on 'initiatives, particularly at regional and local level, that create jobs which take account of new requirements, e.g., in the environmental and social-services spheres'. They agreed to 'transpose these recommendations in their individual policies into a multi-annual programme'.[43]

When Major returned home to report to MPs on 12 December, he tried to portray these conclusions as evidence that his colleagues had accepted the need for 'labour market flexibility', 'deregulation' and the need to make Europe 'competitive'. 'Yet again', he claimed, 'policies pioneered by Britain were now accepted 'across the European Union'. One item on which Major was questioned, however, was an opaque passage on fisheries, referring to the Act of Accession of Spain and Portugal. On this, Major reassuringly claimed that it meant 'no great change'.[44] He did not realise it was about to become another serious embarrassment.

What his government had overlooked was that, from 1 January 1995, Spain's accession treaty allowed its fishing vessels limited access to 70,000 square miles of

41 Seierstad, Dag, *Norway – EU, 1961–1994*, February 1997, Based on a speech held at a Trade Union conference at Wakefield, November 1995, *www.aksess.no/nteu/eng/*
42 Major, *op. cit.*, p. 523.
43 Presidency Conclusions, European Council, Essen, 9–10 December 1994, para. 9.
44 *Hansard*, 12 December 1994, col. 625.

waters around the Irish coast known as the 'Irish Box'. The Spanish demanded access for 220 vessels, threatening that, if this was refused, they would block the accession of Austria, Sweden and Finland.

The unfortunate fisheries minister, then William Waldegrave, was thus forced to fight a rearguard action at the Fisheries Council on 22 December. His only hope was to negotiate a tighter limit on the number of Spanish vessels allowed into the Box. Reporting to a crowded House after the Christmas recess on 10 January 1995, he had to confess that, against Britain's wishes, 40 Spanish boats would be permitted entry. Not explaining that these would be large, modern vessels capable of catching more fish than the entire Cornish and Irish fleets combined, he claimed that, 'had we not limited the number of ships', things could have been much worse, so 'we have made considerable gains'.[45]

As a sop to angry Conservative back-benchers, Waldegrave announced a week later that funding to compensate British fishermen for 'decommissioning' their boats would be doubled to £53 million. At the expense of UK taxpayers, several hundred more British fishermen would be bribed to go out of business.

The 'benefits of Britain's membership'

Against this background, it might have seemed scarcely credible that, on 2 January 1995, Douglas Hurd, as Foreign Secretary, chose to issue a statement intended to remind the British people of the 'benefits of Britain's membership of the European Union', urging his party colleagues to follow suit.

For a man not known to be stupid, his catalogue of 'benefits' defied logic. 'First,' he said, 'the EU brings us jobs.' The EU, he claimed, 'now takes 53 percent of our exports' (government data for 1995 showed this figure as only 44.6 percent).[46] 'The French,' he claimed, 'cannot block our lamb, or the Germans our beef.' (He was shortly to discover to the contrary.) 'The Italians and Spaniards pay hefty fines for breaking the rules on milk quotas.' (The fines were never paid.) The EU, and NATO, had brought us 'the priceless gift of nearly 50 years of peace on our continent.' (The Bosnian tragedy was at its height.) 'Membership has enabled us to take the European Commission to the European Court of Justice over the French Government's enormous subsidies to Air France.' (When the ECJ declared this £2.4 billion subsidy illegal, the Commission reformulated its permission, allowing the subsidy to continue.) 'The new principle of subsidiarity enshrined in the Maastricht Treaty is helping to reverse the tide of new EU laws.' (Between 1993 and 1994, the total of new directives and regulations had risen from 1602 to 1800.)[47] 'We have now persuaded our partners that jobs should be top of the EU agenda.' (EU-wide unemployment was now higher than at any time since the 1930s.)

Despite this catalogue of self-deceiving rhetoric, however, Hurd was driven to concede that 'Not everything is rosy':

---

45 *Hansard*, 10 January 1995, cols. 26–27.
46 *The United Kingdom Balance of Payments*, HMSO, 1995.
47 Figures taken from the Commission's CELEX database.

'The last few years have seen a testing time for the EU. We have seen too much windy rhetoric, too little effort to address the concerns of ordinary people. Often it is the image of a remote, interfering and wasteful EU which dominates.'

But this was why 'we need to make real headway in correcting what goes wrong' and why 'we must win the argument for a flexible, decentralised Europe'.[48] Meanwhile, Hurd's 'partners' had never been pushing harder for more centralisation.

Wholly absent from Hurd's message was any mention of the single currency, unsurprising since it still divided his party. While some MPs and ministers were agitating for Britain to enter, others were pressing for Major either to rule out British entry forever or to hold a referendum. Major's response was not to commit himself. He believed 'passionately', as he put it, that a decision should not be made 'until circumstances made it clear how our economic well-being would be affected'.[49] The only passion he could muster, therefore, was over not making a decision. Worse still, Major was trying to position EMU as solely an economic issue, with no constitutional implications.

Confusion intensified when, in a Commons debate on European policy on 1 March 1995, Major was asked by his former Chancellor, Norman Lamont, whether he thought it possible to imagine monetary union without political union. Major's answer was typically opaque:

'No, I do not… With one important qualification: I believe that it is possible to move forward to monetary union without necessarily moving forward to political union, but the qualification depends on the nature and style of monetary union and I will deal with that in a moment.'[50]

When he did return to the point, it was only to observe that he was 'wary of the serious political and constitutional implications'.[51] Blair asked him to define these 'constitutional implications'. He got a 'non-answer':

'At the end of the day, the only thing that matters is the British national interest. We cannot judge that except in the round. We cannot judge that until we have all the information available and we know the consequences of going in and the cost of staying out.'[52]

A day would come when Blair would find himself as prime minister impaled on another version of precisely the same hook.[53]

---

48 *Conservative Party News*, published by Conservative Central Office, 2 January 1995.
49 Major, *op. cit.*, p. 604.
50 *Hansard*, 1 March 1995, col. 1067.
51 *Op. cit.*, col. 1068.
52 *Op. cit.*, col. 1071.
53 At just this time Major and Hurd were receiving a confidential report from Lord Renton, a senior Conservative peer and President of the Statute Law Society, who had attended a conference in Rome on 'Legislation in the EC'. Among the speakers were some of the EC's top lawyers, including Dr Rolf Wagenbaur, head of the Commission's Legal Service. Renton reported that the lectures and discussions had 'revealed a most unsatisfactory situation'. The problem of getting 15 nations with different languages and legal systems to agree on new laws had resulted in 'the astonishing complexity and obscurity' of EC legislation. Delegates had insisted that 'improvements' must be made if EC laws were 'to become respected and enforceable'. It was 'notorious' how 'the governments of Greece, Italy, Portugal, Spain, France and even Belgium frequently fail to comply with EC laws, even when they have ratified them'. The same was true of ECJ rulings. At the end of 1993 'there were 82 outstanding cases where Member States had not complied with judgments given against them, and nine in which a second judgment had also been disregarded' (personal communication).

Divided loyalties

On 9 March 1995 came a crisis which highlighted just how membership of the EU was straining Britain's traditional loyalties. After a four-hour chase and a warning burst of machine gun fire, three Canadian fisheries protection vessels in international waters off the Canadian coast arrested a Spanish trawler, the *Estai*, suspecting of breaking conservation rules. Even before the facts had been established, the EU's fisheries Commissioner Emma Bonino was accusing the Canadian government of 'piracy'. She was backed by the Commission's vice-president Brittan in declaring that:

'…with this action Canada is not only flagrantly violating international law but is failing to observe normal behaviour of responsible states… the arrest is a lawless act against the sovereignty of a member state of the European Community.'[54]

What disturbed many in Britain was the automatic support their government gave the Commission, not least because the truth of this situation was rather more complex than Bonino had allowed for.

The rich fishing grounds off Newfoundland were managed by the intergovernmental North-West Atlantic Fisheries Organisation (NAFO), representing more than 20 nations. For years it had brokered voluntary quotas, which worked relatively well until 1986 when Spain joined the EC. Then, under Spanish pressure, the EC unilaterally set its own quotas, 400 percent higher than those agreed. Between 1986 and 1992, on quotas totalling 162,000 tons, the mainly Spanish EC fleet had then caught 407,000 tons, causing cod and flounder stocks to collapse. NAFO had agreed a complete ban on fishing and Canada closed down much of its fishing industry, putting 50,000 people out of work. In January 1995 NAFO agreed to reopen the fishery to allow the exploitation of the one remaining healthy stock, Greenland halibut or 'mock turbot'. The agreed catch was 27,000 tons, of which 60 percent went to Canada, 12 percent to the EC. The EC refused to accept this, awarding itself 75 percent. In February, Canada stopped three Spanish trawlers, finding catches in each case flagrantly in breach of the rules.[55] Then came the arrest of the *Estai*.

Britain had herself been faced with a similar problem by Spanish over-fishing off the Falkland Islands. With Spain now threatening to send a gunboat to protect its trawlers, anger began to be expressed in Britain at the government's unquestioning support for Spain over the *Estai*, described as a 'betrayal' not only of the Commonwealth, but of 'common sense and decency'.[56] In the Commons on 13 March, Labour back-bencher, Gwyneth Dunwoody, called it a 'disgrace' that 'this House is not prepared to say openly that we are sick of the way the Spanish have consistently broken the rules and it is our intention to support the Canadians'.[57]

At this point, as vitriol continued to pour out of Brussels, Canada's fisheries minister, Brian Tobin, produced evidence to show that that 69 percent of the

54 *The Times*, 11 March 1995.
55 *Sunday Telegraph*, 2 April 1995.
56 Simon Heffer, *Daily Telegraph*, 15 March 1995.
57 *The Times*, 14 March 1995.

Estai's haul was undersized and could only have been caught with illegal nets. Her logbooks were fraudulent. A secret fish hold, hidden behind boxes, had contained 25 tons of banned species. From Newlyn, England's largest fishing port, where Spanish disregard for conservation rules had long aroused anger among local fishermen, a rash of Maple Leaf flags spread across Britain to show support for the Canadians.

Belatedly Major changed tack, indicating that he would veto any move by the EU to impose sanctions against Canada. But the damage had been done. Again his government had been caught by divided loyalties. Spain was not amused. Said her prime minister Felipe Gonzales, 'we are developing a common foreign policy. At some point there will come a time to remind Britain it has to show solidarity always, not just when it suits it.' [58]

The march of integration continues

Now moving rapidly to the top of the EU agenda was the next treaty, work on which began when the Reflection Group symbolically held its first meeting at Messina on 2 June 1995, the 40th anniversary of the Messina conference. Joining them were EU foreign ministers, including Douglas Hurd, who, along with the Commission and the European Parliament, issued a 'Solemn Declaration', 'paying tribute to the courage, strength of conviction and vision of those who paved the way for European integration forty years ago', ending:

'In 1955 the founding States passed a turning point in their pursuit of European integration by adopting an original structure which was unparalleled in the world. Meeting in Messina again in 1995, the representatives of the Governments of the Member States reaffirm their common will to take up the new challenges and to continue the task with the same determination shown by their predecessors forty years ago.' [59]

The integrationist fervour of this document would hardly have pleased Conservative MPs, but they had no chance to air their views. The Declaration was never reported to Parliament.

Anyway, MPs were now preoccupied by excitements nearer home, following Major's decision on 11 June to resign as party leader. Faced with constant sniping from his Eurosceptic back-benchers, he had wished to 'lance the boil' by putting himself up for re-election. His only rival was the Eurosceptic, John Redwood, who resigned from the Cabinet to stand against him. The result would be declared before the summer recess.

Meanwhile Major went off to Cannes for the European Council on 26 to 27 June, chaired by France's new president Jacques Chirac (who had attended his first Council as prime minister in 1974). The most significant decision was an agreement to set up 'Europol', an embryonic EU equivalent of the American FBI.

The creation of this body was classic example of the 'Monnet method', whereby some important new initiative would first be proposed as apparently some-

---

58 The *Daily Telegraph*, 5 April 1995.
59 *www.europa.eu.int/en/agenda/igc-home/key-doc.html*

thing quite small and innocuous which no one could oppose. Once it had been accepted in principle, it could then be gradually expanded, until it emerged as a fully-fledged feature of the Community structure. Using as an excuse the need to fight international drug-trafficking, Europol had originally been set up on an informal basis in The Hague in 1993 as the European Drugs Intelligence Unit. By 1995 it had acquired 80 staff, with a budget of £2.8 million. Now it was to be given permanent status as the 'European Police Office', with a much-expanded remit covering more than 20 areas of 'cross-border crime', from illegal immigration to credit-card fraud.[60]

When Major reported to the Commons on 28 June he said little more about Europol's purpose, other than it would 'reinforce the fight against cross-border crime and drug-trafficking'.[61] When the Convention to establish Europol was signed on 28 July, all was now in place to give the EU its own federal police force.

Once again, however, British interest had been more easily aroused by the outcome on 4 July of the Conservative leadership contest, in which Major easily defeated Redwood by 218 votes to 89. To the last moment, the vote might have been sufficiently close to force Major's resignation, until Heseltine offered to swing 20 of his own supporters behind Major in return for being given the new post of Deputy Prime Minister and First Secretary of State. In a Cabinet reshuffle, a relieved Major replaced Hurd as Foreign Secretary with Malcolm Rifkind.[62]

A 'rock for Europe'

If Major's re-election raised his morale, it did little to improve his grip on reality. In September, he was off to a European Council in Majorca, where the heads of government met in idyllic surroundings to debate Europe's economic strategy. As Major recorded:

'... high taxation and public spending, state regulation, central planning, protectionism and other socialist and corporatist mantras were suddenly unfashionable. I argued for flexible labour markets, to help create real jobs, for less red tape, for affordable social costs and above all for making Europe a competitive, free-trading area...'[63]

Then, Major recalls, 'an unusual thing happened... our partners dared to be seen agreeing with the British prime minister'. Speaker after speaker opened by saying, 'I agree with John.' 'For a brief moment,' he added, 'I knew what it must feel like to be Helmut Kohl.'[64]

60 *New Statesman*, 17 March 1995, p. 10.
61 *Hansard*, 28 June 1995, col. 894.
62 As Foreign Secretary, Rifkind almost immediately faced the crisis which arose when Serb forces massacred 7,000 Bosnian Muslims outside Srebrenice. Dutch troops ordered to guarantee the town as a 'safe haven' for Muslims retreated when the Serbs attacked. The bloodiest incident Europe had seen since World War Two eventually prompted US-led NATO air strikes on the Serbs, paving the way at last for a Bosnian peace settlement. As defence secretary, Rifkind had firmly opposed use of air power, famously declaring 'no war in history has ever been ended by air strikes' (forgetting how history's greatest war was ended at Hiroshima and Nagasaki).
63 Major, *op. cit.*, p. 523.
64 *Op. cit.*, p. 524.

Yet, even as he was speaking, the Reflection Group was working on a report for the Madrid Council on 15 to 16 December which could not have been more diametrically opposed. The creation of jobs, they argued, would best be 'encouraged' by three things: more integration, economic and monetary union and the Social Chapter: the three features of the Union that Major was keenest to avoid. More generally they wanted a 'single institutional framework', absorbing the three Maastricht 'pillars' into a single Community. If Europe was 'getting the message' it was certainly not Major's.

The Madrid Council agreed that the report provided a sound basis for the discussions of the IGC, to begin work in Turin on 29 March 1996. Of more immediate concern, however, was the single currency. Top of the agenda was its name and, with dreary predictability, it became the 'euro'. Portuguese prime minister Antonio Guterres was ecstatic. 'Just as St Peter was the rock on which Christianity was built, so the single currency will be the rock for Europe,' he gushed.[65]

The Council then drew up a timetable for its introduction. On 1 January 1999, the currencies of member states would be irrevocably fixed. On 1 January 2002, notes and coins would be issued and, by 1 July the same year, existing currencies would cease to be legal tender. In March 1998 it would be decided which countries could join in the 'first wave', according to whether their figures for 1997 met the Maastricht 'convergence criteria'.

Already these 'criteria' were posing serious difficulties: not least the requirements that government borrowing should not exceed three percent of spending, and that national debt should not exceed 60 percent of a country's gross domestic product. The national debt of several would-be participants was well above 60 percent. Those of Belgium and Italy were above 120 percent. France was already wracked by strikes against drastic spending cuts designed to reduce her deficit to three percent.

Major remained in his own world. Reporting to MPs on Madrid, he told them 'the drive to promote subsidiarity was again strongly in evidence'. It was 'now widely recognised that the United Kingdom was right to reverse the trend towards greater intrusiveness by the Commission'; and increasing emphasis had been given 'to the need to cut the burden of red tape and over-regulation'.[66]

That same month the Commission was dealing with a score of new proposals for directives, including one 'amending Directive 93/16/EEC', which 'facilitates the free movement of doctors and provides for the mutual recognition of their diplomas, certificates and other evidence of formal qualifications'. This alone was to cause outrage in years to come when it would be discovered that doctors applying to join the NHS from countries such as Spain and Greece could not be examined on their English-speaking skills, even if they could speak no English at all. On the other hand, applicants from Commonwealth countries such as New Zealand would be required to undergo compulsory tests.[67]

---

65 The *Economist*, 23 December 1995, p. 61.
66 *Hansard*, 18 Dec 1995, col. 1222.
67 *Ibid.*

More stinking fish

To British eyes, two events in the autumn of 1995 cast the EU in a particularly unfavourable light. One, in September, was *The Times's* serialisation of a book by a senior Commission official, entitled *The Rotten Heart Of Europe: The Dirty War For Europe's Money.* As head of the division responsible for the ERM and monetary affairs, Bernard Connolly's insider's account of the EU's attempts to work towards monetary union since 1978 gave an insight into the Commission's internal workings like nothing published before. As an economist involved with monetary policy at the highest level, he had finally lost patience with the pretence that the ERM and EMU were economic policies when their only real purpose was political. The ERM, he wrote, was not just 'inefficient' but profoundly 'undemocratic', a 'confidence trick' designed to subordinate the 'economic welfare' and 'democratic rights' of Europe's citizens to the will of a political and bureaucratic elite, bent on creating 'a European superstate'. Few of the 'facts' in his book, as he put it, were not publicly available. But 'one of the astonishing things about the ERM and EMU' was that

'... what needs to be revealed is not the "facts" but their manipulation and distortion. The more blatantly obvious the falsehood, the more insistently its perpetrators repeat it. My own decision to write this book ... was born first of incredulity at the hundreds of "black is white" statements made about the ERM, and then of anger at the treatment of anyone who tries to point out the lies.' [68]

As the first of a succession of 'Brussels whistleblowers', Connolly ended by describing the Commission's fanatical intolerance towards any divergence from its strict 'party line': 'dissent cannot be tolerated'. As if to prove his point, no sooner was his book published than Commission officials put it round that he was 'psychologically unstable' and he was quickly dismissed from his post.

Two months later, on 28 November, uproar broke out over an opinion from the European Court of Justice in the on-going Factortame case. Having been disbarred from fishing for 18 months by the Merchant Shipping Act, the court now held that the Spanish 'flag-boat' companies could claim compensation from the UK government. With at least 90 Spanish vessels claiming from £250,000 to £600,000 per boat, the final bill to UK taxpayers was to top £100 million. The Eurosceptic press was incandescent, summed up in a *Daily Mail* headline: 'They fly our flag, take our fish – and now our money.' [69]

The timing of the Advocate General's opinion was impeccable. In Brussels the annual haggling on quota allocations was due, and the Commission was again proposing that UK quotas should be drastically cut. In a debate before the council, the government spokesman Michael Forsyth fell back on the well-worn mantra that the problem arose from 'too many people chasing too few fish'. [70] He did not, of course, admit that most of the fish were in UK waters and that, only because of the CFP, were there now too many 'Community' fishermen trying to

---

68 Connolly, *op. cit.*, p. xii.
69 1 December 1995, p. 17.
70 *Hansard, op. cit.*, col. 1352.

catch them. Labour pulled out all the stops to exploit Tory divisions, resulting in a government defeat by 297 votes to 299. Ministers would have to negotiate in Brussels without Parliamentary approval.

The cuts they were forced to accept were indeed savage: mackerel down 33 percent, plaice 27 percent, sole 23 percent. But this was hailed by fisheries minister Tony Baldry as a 'famous victory', on the slender basis that he had negotiated slight reductions in the cuts originally proposed (which had been pitched high precisely to allow such face-saving 'concessions' to be made). He told MPs that he had achieved his objective 'of securing the best possible deal' for British fishermen.[71] To politicians bereft of power this seemed all that was left to them: to boast about 'famous victories' when they escaped from Brussels with a disaster slightly less than that predicted.

Let the people decide

At the end of the second month of the New Year, on 28 February 1996, the Commission put forward its proposals for the IGC. Predictably, it wanted to see an IGC 'with real ambitions'. This was the chance 'for a genuine debate on Europe'.[72] Delors, conscious that his brainchild, the single currency, was on its way to becoming a reality, was now ready for the next moves. But it was the same old shopping list. He wanted the Union to have a 'strong political and social identity', a common foreign policy, backed by the ability 'to project credible military force', and 'better integration of the armaments industry'. The treaty should establish an 'area of freedom and security', bringing the Schengen Agreement into Community law and transferring Justice and Home Affairs into the 'Community framework', to form the basis for an EU-wide judicial, legal and policing system.

On classic supranational lines, the Commission argued that, as a general rule, national vetoes must be eliminated in favour of QMV (this should even include future amendments to the Treaty). So long as the veto remained, the Commission argued, the Union would be in danger of 'stagnating'. There should be a wholesale simplifying and restructuring of the treaties, to give the Union a constitution. Finally the Union 'must not be for ever bound to advance at the speed of its slowest members'. 'Flexibility' must be 'organised', to permit some member states to move ahead more quickly than others.

A curious situation was now emerging. The Commission, the European Parliament and nearly all member states were now looking to the IGC for a dramatic advance in integration. When the British government set out its IGC proposals in a White Paper on 12 March, they seemed to come from a different planet. Britain wanted to stem the integrationist tide by reducing the flow of Brussels legislation,

---

71 *The Times*, 23 December 1995.
72 Commission of the European Communities, *Reinforcing political union and preparing for enlargement*, Bulletin 1/2-1996, point 2.2.1.

curbing the powers of the ECJ which had become too 'political'[73]; and reforming the 'irrational' Common Agricultural Policy. She also wanted treaty changes to end the scandal of 'quota hopping' and no absorption of the two 'intergovernmental pillars' into the Community framework. Britain opposed any further erosion of the powers of national parliaments and the creation of a 'United States of Europe'.[74] Her view of 'flexibility' was that it would allow a country to be given permanent 'opt-outs', while Delors and the rest saw 'flexibility' as allowing a 'two-speed' Europe in which, although some countries might move more slowly, all must be headed for the same final destination.[75] On almost every issue the British government was at odds. As a Commons committee put it:

'Ministers have claimed from the start that the IGC would be little more than a 5,000-mile service of the Maastricht treaty. One conclusion jumps out from all the evidence received. That is no longer a valid description of the ambitions and expectations of the large majority of governments represented at the IGC.' [76]

However, so determined was Major to avoid this being made an issue that Commons debate was limited to three hours without a vote. Heath for once spoke for many, complaining that, when Britain entered the Community, Parliament had been given 10 days of debate. He noted the White Paper's claim that it was 'crucial that national parliaments remain the central focus of democratic legitimacy'. 'Is "democratic legitimacy" what we have this evening,' he asked; 'three hours in which to discuss a White Paper containing ten vital subjects?'[77]

Major could afford to ignore Heath; but not so a challenge from the Anglo-French billionaire industrialist Sir James Goldsmith, who sat as a French member in the European Parliament. In October 1995 he had launched a 'Referendum Party' to fight the next general election. On 11 March, on the eve of the White Paper, he challenged Major in full-page newspaper advertisements to allow a referendum not just on the currency but on Britain's continued membership of the EU.

On 4 April, Major tried to neutralise the threat to Tory marginal seats by conceding the demand for a referendum on the currency (proposed by Thatcher in her first back-bench speech in 1990). The Conservatives would be committed not to join the euro without first asking the British people.[78] Seven months later, in November 1996, Gordon Brown would give the same pledge for Labour. These commitments were to play a more crucial part in Britain's future relations with the EU than anyone at the time was aware.

---

73 The British government was irked by several other ECJ rulings which it considered 'political', in terms of their invariable support for Commission supranationalism. Particularly controversial was that upholding the Commission's right to use the 'health and safety' Article 118 of the Treaty to authorise its Working Time ('48-hour week') directive. This should have been issued under the Social Chapter, from which Britain had opted-out, but this ruse was used to ensure that the directive applied to Britain as well. Major protested in a personal letter to President Santer, to no avail.
74 White Paper (1996), *A Partnership of Nations*, Cm. 3181 (London, HMSO).
75 See Rifkind, *Hansard*, 21 March 1996, col. 519.
76 House of Commons Foreign Affairs Committee, Session 1995–1996, 3rd Report, *The Intergovernmental Conference.* HC 306, para. 25.
77 *Hansard*, 21 Mar 1996, col. 541.
78 The *Independent*, 4 April 1996.

More immediately, however, a crisis erupting out of nowhere had already brought Britain's relations with her partners to their lowest point since she joined the Common Market in 1973.

Mad cows and madder politicians

On 20 March 1996, Britain's health secretary Stephen Dorrell gave a statement to a packed House of Commons on the cattle disease Bovine Spongiform Encephalopathy (BSE). After years of denial and confusion about the risks of BSE to human health, what appeared to be a new strain of the related human disease, Creutzfeldt Jacobs Disease (CJD), had, unusually, appeared in a number of young people. The disease pattern in their brains appeared similar to that in the brains of BSE-infected cattle.

Warned by the government's Spongiform Encephalopathy Advisory Committee (SEAC) that this could represent the early stages of a major epidemic, Dorrell told MPs that, although there was still 'no scientific proof' that BSE could be transmitted to man by beef, SEAC had concluded that 'the most likely explanation' for new variant CJD was eating meat before the government had imposed strict regulatory measures in 1989.[79]

His statement set off the greatest food scare in history. Media hysteria knew no bounds. The *Observer* revelled in an apocalyptic vision of Britain in 2015, with thousands of Britons dying from CJD every week, the Channel Tunnel blocked and Britain isolated from the world.[80] On *Newsnight*, SEAC's chairman agreed that there could be half a million victims. Beef sales plummeted, not just in Britain but all over Europe.

One European country after another imposed bans on British beef. On 25 March, the Commission's Standing Veterinary Committee (SVC)[81] voted 14–1 for a world-wide export ban, not just of British beef and cattle but of all their derivatives, from skin creams to wine gums. While Major declared the ban 'well beyond any action justified by the available scientific evidence',[82] MPs were outraged to discover that the EU now had power to prevent Britain selling beef even to countries still willing to buy it.

As the beef industry faced meltdown – exports alone were worth £550 million a year – the priority was to restore confidence. One option was slaughter of the entire 11 million-strong national herd, but this was rejected as too expensive. Another came indirectly from SEAC. On the basis that older cows presented the greatest risk, it had recommended that cattle over 30 months old should be deboned before their meat was sold. This was seized on by supermarkets and the National Farmers Union, whose president David Naish advised agriculture minister Douglas Hogg that, as a confidence-building measure, these older animals

---

79 *Hansard*, 20 Mar 1996, col. 375.
80 *A conspiracy to make us all mad*, 24 March 1996.
81 The SVC includes one senior veterinary official from each EU country.
82 The *Daily Telegraph*, 26 March 1996.

should be removed from the food chain. Major agreed to a three-year plan to destroy an estimated three million cattle, at a cost of £2.4 billion.[83]

His next priority was to get the export ban lifted, and it was agreed that this should be left to the Agriculture Council in Luxembourg on 1 April.[84] In Britain's view, all necessary measures to minimise risk had now been taken. The government had banned the use of meat and bone meal in animal feed and taken measures to remove potentially risky materials at slaughterhouses. Each individual BSE-affected animal was destroyed. But the accepted policy in other member states was quite different. Wherever an infected animal was found, the whole herd must be destroyed.

When Hogg arrived in Luxembourg, looking woebegone in a scruffy mackintosh and battered hat, he offered the destruction of 30-month-old cattle as a confidence-building gesture. But his partners still wanted retrospective whole-herd slaughter. An estimated 147,000 animals had to be found and killed. Britain could not meet this demand. The necessary records had not been kept. Argument raged through three days and a full night, but agreement was impossible. The ministers did, as a gesture, agree to help finance the scheme for destroying 30-month-old cattle, and it was widely publicised that the EC would 'foot 70 percent of the bill'. But this referred only to compensation for the loss of the animals themselves, not the cost of destruction. Under the terms of the UK rebate, it emerged that British taxpayers must contribute 80 percent of the cost of a policy which had done nothing to get the ban lifted.

On 15 April, agriculture commissioner Franz Fischler admitted there had been no public health reasons for the ban. 'I wouldn't hesitate to eat beef in England. I see no medical reason not to,' he told reporters. Its real purpose had been to prevent a collapse in the European beef market. Meanwhile, argument over the 'selective cull' had turned into trench warfare. Already some of Major's Cabinet were demanding that Britain should take retaliatory action, particularly when Santer – now installed as Commission president – confirmed that the ban had not been for public health reasons. Hogg said he would take the ban to the ECJ. Major's private response was to dismiss the 'colleagues' as a 'bunch of shits'. [85]

When further compromise offers were rejected and the SVC again refused on 20 May to accept even partial lifting of the ban, Major told MPs in an emergency statement that Britain would conduct a policy of 'non-cooperation' with the EU. Ministers and officials were told not to participate in any decisions requiring unanimity until the EU made concessions. In four weeks Britain blocked more than 65 legislative proposals, in what the media dubbed the 'beef war', provoking intense resentment in Brussels.

The fieriest of the Commissioners, Emma Bonino, then took retaliatory action of her own, demanding further drastic cuts in the size of Britain's fishing fleet. She announced that Britain had fallen way short of the targets for decommissioning

83 The *Daily Telegraph*, 29 March 1996.
84 The *Independent*, 30 March 1996.
85 The *Daily Telegraph*, 23 April 1996.

fishing vessels, claiming the UK fleet had 'doubled in size' since 1988, from 116,000 to 239,000 tonnes. Yet Commission figures showed there had in fact been only a marginal increase, from 206,000 to 211,000 tonnes, entirely attributable to foreign-owned 'flag boats' joining the UK register after the *Factortame* case.

On the basis of her fictitious claim, Bonino now demanded a further reduction of 60 percent in the British fleet, on top of what Britain had already been asked for. By contrast, EU taxpayers were now providing £739 million over seven years for the 'modernisation' of Spain's fishing fleet, and another £894 million to third-world governments, mainly in Africa, to buy fishing rights for Spain and Portugal. The contribution of UK taxpayers to these programmes was £228 million.[86]

So critical had Britain's *impasse* with her partners become that a deal at the Florence Council on 21 to 22 June was imperative. In the preceding weeks, Britain had vainly offered one compromise after another. At Florence, Major felt he had no option but to give way. He settled for a vague promise that the ban might be gradually relaxed, in return for agreeing to the measure previously ruled out: the 'selective cull' of 147,000 animals.[87] To angry MPs, Major claimed that a start on lifting the ban could be made in the early autumn. When he could not say how long this would take, Blair suggested it was likely to be 'years not months'. To loud Labour cheers, he added: 'Mr Major is now so desperate to extricate himself from this mess that he will settle for anything. There is humiliation in this deal. There is ignominy in this deal. In fact it is no deal at all. It is a rout.'[88]

A rout it was. As Commission officials freely admitted, the 'concessions' had been 'only a sop to John Major to persuade Tory MPs that he had not left the summit empty-handed'. 'It has been very important to me that the Brits got nothing,' said the Danish prime minister Poul Nyrup Rasmussen. To Major, it was 'a vintage piece of back-stabbing'.[89]

The misery was not over. On 12 July, the ECJ rejected Britain's request to overturn the export ban.[90] By 16 September, armed with a scientific paper from *Nature* predicting that, even without the 'selective cull', BSE would be over by 2001, Hogg asked his fellow agriculture ministers for a reduction in the cull. There was no deal. Britain either kept to the Florence agreement or the ban would remain. With his parliament increasingly hostile, Major faced certain defeat if he tried to put the necessary legislation before MPs. Without other options, he abandoned the cull. Fischler responded 'as long as the (the British) do not meet the pre-conditions ... an end to the export ban is simply not a possibility'.[91] Klaus Hänsch, president of the European Parliament, observed that, if Britain could not respect joint decisions, it would be better for her to quit the EU altogether.[92]

86 *Castle of Lies, op. cit.*, pp. 86–87.
87 *Hansard*, 24 June 1996, col. 21.
88 The *Daily Telegraph*, 20 June 1996.
89 Major, *op. cit.*, p. 656.
90 Agence Europe, *Together in Europe* (Newsletter), No. 93, 15 July 1996.
91 Reuters, 20 September 1996.
92 The *Independent*, 21 September 1996.

A change of tune

Around this time there were signs of a distinct change of mood in the EU. Apart from BSE, another topic occupying the Florence Council had been Europe's growing unemployment. This prompted Major to boast to the Commons on his return that Britain had created 'more jobs over the past three years than Germany, France, Italy and Spain' added together.[93] The Germans, on the other hand, led by their foreign minister Klaus Kinkel, had effectively sabotaged the Commission's main initiative on unemployment by refusing to vote funds for Delors' grandiose Trans-European Network. 'The responsibility for tackling unemployment lies with national governments,' Kohl told a press conference.[94]

An effect of this change of mood was Germany's lessening enthusiasm for a 'big bang' solution at the IGC, and a wish to concentrate on preparing for the single currency. Top of the Germans' agenda now, as the country with the strongest currency in the EU, was their idea that countries joining the single currency must sign up to a 'stability pact', imposing heavy fines if members breached the proposed maximum public spending deficit levels of three percent.[95]

By September the Commission was complaining that, with the IGC due to end in less than a year, there was 'no trace of the excitement' for what was 'potentially another historic step on the road to European unity'. Instead, it noted, the mood was morose. Failure to progress seemed 'largely structural'. There was no broad pro-European consensus, 'only fundamental divergences'.[96]

But part of the strategy was a wish to avoid too much debate, until a new, more compliant government was elected in Britain, which seemed increasingly certain. Kohl and Chirac were also now anticipating the next enlargement. The idea was therefore emerging of a 'minimalist' treaty, focusing on institutional and procedural changes, as a prelude to the enlargement negotiations, with possibly a further treaty after that.[97]

Increasingly, however, there were serious problems with preparations for the single currency. In September, a report from the IMF painted a bleak picture of a low-growth Europe 'plagued by sky-high unemployment and boxed in by its drive to launch the single currency'. If growth did not strengthen, it preferred to see European nations temporarily increase their deficits in line with the weakness of their economies, rather than cut them to meet the 'tough Maastricht criteria'.[98] The next month, the Commission itself painted an equally gloomy picture. *Per capita* output in Europe was nearly a third below that of the United States and one-sixth below Japan's. Since 1960 Japan had created twice as many new jobs as Europe, the USA five times as many. As a result, unemployment stood at 11 percent, twice as high as in the United States and three times higher than in Japan.[99]

---

93 *Hansard*, 24 Jun 1996: cols. 22–23.
94 Reuters, 23 June 1996.
95 *Ibid.*
96 Agence Europe, *Together in Europe* (Newsletter), No. 94, 15 September 1996.
97 *Ibid.*
98 *Reuters Business Report*, 25 September 1996.
99 *Reuters Business Report*, 10 October 1996.

The lesson was not lost on Rifkind. In a speech given in Zurich to commemorate the 50th anniversary of Churchill's 1946 speech, he warned that the relentless momentum towards economic and monetary union would split the European Union. 'We should not proceed down a path of integration faster or further than our people are prepared to go,' he warned. Echoing Major, he told his audience that Britain had an alternative vision, based on 'choosing carefully the stepping-stones toward closer co-operation; not jumping blindly toward ever greater integration, flailing for footholds that may prove precarious or illusory'.[100]

Britain's Eurosceptics welcomed this as the most outspoken statement ever made by a foreign secretary. Redwood cheered Rifkind for 'responding to the clear mood of the country', and described the single currency as 'a disaster waiting to happen'.[101] This provoked the familiar claque of EU fellow-travellers, including Brittan, Heath, Howe and Hurd, to protest that ruling out British membership of the euro 'would be to betray our national interest'.[102]

Elsewhere, a meeting of EU finance ministers in Dublin on 20 September reached agreement on the all-important 'stability pact'.[103] But anxiety was now mounting over the way several keen euro-aspirants, such as Spain and Italy, were running such huge budget deficits that they were unlikely to qualify. France was equally suspect. She was preparing to sell her state telephone company France Telecom for a sum equivalent to half a percent of French GDP, simply to achieve a one-off reduction in her deficit. Despite stern warnings from the *Bundesbank* about 'window dressing', it seemed yet another 'Euro-fudge' was in the making, as the Commission signalled that the criteria would be 'flexibly interpreted' to allow as many countries as possible to join in the first wave.[104]

Still the IGC was drifting. On 5 October 1996 an 'Extraordinary' Council was held in Dublin. At the eve of Council press conference, Major again championed his notion of 'flexibility', only for Klaus Hänsch, president of the European Parliament, to tell journalists:

'I fail to see why fourteen governments should always have to sacrifice their vision of Europe, and their principles, to keep on board a government which may jump ship in any case. If one government is clearly out of step with the fourteen others on the main issues … then others may have to look at ways of moving forward … or of postponing final decisions until the government in the minority is prepared to change its position, or until another takes its place.'

Kohl was the driving force, pushing his colleagues into agreeing that the IGC should conclude at Amsterdam in June 1997. Only if that timetable was kept could enlargement negotiations start on time. Otherwise they would be caught up in the

---

100 Speech by Foreign Secretary, Mr Malcolm Rifkind at the Churchill Commemoration, University of Zurich, 18 September 1996, *Europe Fifty Years On, 193.114.50.5/texts/1996/sep/18/rifkind_speech_europe.txt*
101 The *Daily Telegraph*, 19 September 1996.
102 Letter to The *Independent*, 19 September 1996.
103 Agence Europe, *Together in Europe*, (Newsletter), No. 95, 1 October 1996.
104 The *Independent*, 20 September 1996.

launch of the euro. Kohl was already referring to the possibility of what he called 'Maastricht III' to follow 'Maastricht II'. Nevertheless, on behalf of the Parliament, Hänsch warned the Council that, without 'institutional reforms', the Union would 'become a mere free trade area'. It was necessary to make 'institutional sacrifices for enlargement'. As to what this meant, Kohl spelled it out to journalists. There must be a major extension of qualified majority voting. 'Unanimity must go,' he said.[105]

Against this background, 'Europe' that autumn was in turmoil, as France, Germany, Spain and Italy introduced further harsh spending cuts to meet the 'criteria'. In Madrid, thousands of public sector workers, including policemen, chanted slogans outside the economic ministry and tipped a lorry-load of ice in the entrance. In France, tens of thousands of teachers stopped work in protest at job cuts. In Germany members of the largest engineering trade union, IG Metall, went on strike.[106]

France and Germany then produced their joint proposals for the IGC, emphasising the need to include 'enhanced co-operation', allowing member states who wished to do so to move ahead in certain areas without being blocked by others. The 'ins' would become the 'vanguard' while the 'outs' would eventually be marginalised.[107] Major's 'flexibility' was getting left still further behind, with Britain looking more like the 'guard's van'.

On 13 December, Major was back in Dublin for yet another Council, which, according to the *communiqué*, 'achieved further decisive progress' on EMU and 'identified a broad range of measures to be implemented at national and Community level aimed at boosting employment'. With an agreement to add an 'employment chapter' to the new treaty, the Commission thought the Council had been 'an undoubted success'.[108] Major told MPs he saw 'no purpose in an employment chapter. It will not create a single job'. He also saw no need for further qualified majority voting. Yet again he stated:

'Some advocate a more integrated, centralised Europe. I respect that view, but I do not share it. It would not be right for Britain. I believe that the European Union must be a partnership of nation states, with Community competence where it is needed, but only where it is needed. This is more than a free trade area, but very much less than an embryo European state. There is only one way in which those competing visions can be reconciled, and that is through the development of a more flexible Europe.'[109]

Ending the year as he started it, Major was on his own. Even his back-benchers were deserting him. The *Daily Telegraph* reported that 147 of them had decided to oppose the single currency in their election addresses, rejecting his policy that options must be kept open.

---

105 Agence Europe, *Together in Europe* (Newsletter), No. 96, 15 October 1996.
106 The *Independent*, 1 October 1996.
107 The *Independent*, 19 October 1996.
108 Agence Europe, *Together in Europe* (Newsletter), No. 100, 15 December 1996.
109 *Hansard*, 16 December 1996, col. 616.

'Tory splits', again

As 1997 began, acclaimed as 'European Year against Racism and Xenophobia', British opponents of the euro, led by John Redwood, were claiming that a single currency could not work without common taxation and a huge increase in 'regional transfers' around the Union (precisely as was suggested back in the 1970s and by Delors in the 1980s).[110] Furthermore, would-be euro members were still, quite shamelessly fudging the entry criteria. Meanwhile in Brussels, Santer was fighting off French attempts to create a 'stability council' to allow governments to control the proposed European Central Bank, when the whole point of the ECB was that it should be outside political control and supranational.

As Britain's general election approached, it was Labour's turn to set out its stall. Robin Cook, the party's supposedly Eurosceptic foreign affairs spokesman, sought to tease out Tory divisions by hinting that a Labour government might join the euro in the next Parliament. But, once again, it was to be 'on the basis of a hard-headed economic assessment'.[111]

If Cook's purpose was to re-ignite Tory passions, he was successful. On 19 February, Rifkind broke the truce on the *Today* programme. Reacting to a charge that the Tories were 'neutral' on the euro, he snapped: 'No... we are hostile...' This drew a sharp retort from his Cabinet colleague Heseltine. Another, Kenneth Clarke, said 'it was obviously a slip of the tongue under pressure from a very skilful interviewer'. When Major pitched in with the view that 'the balance of proof had tilted against a single currency... it would be wrong until proved right', Blair exulted. On *The World at One*, he crowed: 'We have had three different statements from the three most senior people in the Government... It is a quite extraordinary situation.'[112]

Lord Howe was lured into the fray by *Today*, warning he would find it hard to back a government 'that is in principle hostile to the concept of a single currency'. Blair followed up at prime minister's question time, cornering Major into admitting that his government was 'not hostile' to the euro. Clarke forced Rifkind into making a joint statement that 'we are hostile to the notion that a single currency can proceed at any stage on a non-convergent basis'. Twenty Conservative MPs decided to defy party policy by backing monetary union in their election addresses.[113] Again the Conservatives were in disarray, a former minister observing 'this smells of death wish'.[114]

Rather more significant were events on the continent. One was the decision of the troubled French car-maker, Renault, facing a five billion franc loss, to close its plant in Belgium, making redundant 4,000 employees. Santer called it a 'blow to the European spirit of trust'. But the decision was linked to the French government's earlier refusal to help pay for Renault and Peugeot to shed 40,000 workers through early retirement. France's finance minister explained that, with the need

110 Redwood, John (1997), 'Jobless in Leipzig, taxed in Liverpool' in the *Independent*, 17 January.
111 The *Economist*, 8 February 1997.
112 The *Independent*, 20 February 1997.
113 The *Independent*, 21 February 1997; the *Independent on Sunday*, 23 February 1997.
114 The *Independent*, 3 March 1997.

to meet the convergence criteria, 'the state can no longer afford this kind of subsidy'. With French elections due the following year, the pain had to be exported abroad.[115]

For Major, his time had come for his ordeal at the polls. On 17 March he asked for the dissolution of Parliament. With his party trailing by 22 points, even he realised it was unlikely he would be returning as prime minister after 1 May.[116]

Goodbye xenophobia

The 1997 general election was unique. So great had been the recovery of Britain's economy since 1992 that it was now, by almost any measure, the most successful in the EU, thanks to Thatcherite restructuring in the 1980s, and revenues from North Sea oil. Yet so indelible was the impression of incompetence engendered by the ERM debacle that, after 'White Wednesday', the Tories' standing had never recovered. Never before had the authors of such economic success gone into an election facing certain defeat.

Labour's slogan 'Britain will be better with New Labour' echoed the mood of a nation anxious to see the Conservatives gone. 'Europe' was a peripheral issue, despite the intervention of Goldsmith's Referendum Party. New Labour's manifesto spared it only a few lines:

'We will stand up for Britain's interests in Europe after the shambles of the last six years, but, more than that, we will lead a campaign for reform in Europe. Europe isn't working in the way this country and Europe need. But to lead means to be involved, to be constructive, to be capable of getting our own way... We will give Britain the leadership in Europe which Britain and Europe need.' [117]

The Conservative manifesto echoed Major's familiar line of wanting not a federal European state but 'a partnership of nations', introducing a slogan which would remain an object of ridicule from Eurosceptics: 'we want to be in Europe but not run by Europe'.

Scenting a Labour victory, EU governments, led by the Dutch, planned a post-election 'mini-summit' with Blair, to sort out Britain's new position on what was to be the Amsterdam treaty. Before that, on 25 March, a ceremony was held on the Capitol in Rome to mark the 40th anniversary of the signing of the 1957 Treaty, but it was a lacklustre affair. The Europhile *Economist* asked whether 'Europe' was suffering 'a mid-life crisis'. The gap between 'high-flown Euro-guff' and the concerns of 'disenchanted ordinary folk' seemed yawning ever wider. It noted that 'most Europeans' were not inspired by talk of closer union, or single currencies, let alone IGCs. What the Union needed most was economic growth, which looked unlikely. 'It is not surprising ... that the birthday bash was rather a damp squib'.[118]

---

115 The *European*, 6 March 1997.
116 Major, *op. cit.*, p. 707.
117 *www.psr.keele.ac.uk/area/uk/man/lab97.htm*
118 The *Economist*, 29 March 1997.

Kohl sailed above it all. Architect of many of the economic miseries affecting Germany, he announced on 3 April that he would seek re-election the following year, 'to pursue his dream of a more unified Europe'.[119] Then Chirac, eight months early, unexpectedly announced a French general election. He was worried that his country's worsening economic plight, with unemployment at 12.8 percent and the highest taxes of any large western nation, might soon make it impossible to impose the measures needed to bring down his government's deficit to the three percent required by the 'criteria'.[120]

On 1 May Blair swept to his expected victory. But no one expected the size of his majority: 179 seats. He now headed an army of 418 Labour MPs. The Conservatives lost 178 seats while the Liberal Democrats doubled their representation to 46. The Referendum Party's 810,000 votes was the highest tally by a fourth party in British history but its contribution had already been made. This was the commitment of all three major parties that Britain would not join the euro without a referendum.

The first announcement by Labour's new Chancellor of the Exchequer, Gordon Brown, was that the Bank of England was to be given its independence, free to set the basic national interest rate without reference to the Chancellor. This was in accordance with Article 109e(5) of the Maastricht Treaty which laid down that 'during the second stage' of EMU

'… each Member State shall, as appropriate, start the process leading to the independence of its central bank, in accordance with Article 108.'

The EMU protocol did not give the UK exemption from this requirement, since it was part of stage two and Britain's opt out referred only to stage three.[121] The new Foreign Secretary, Robin Cook, was equally swift, delivering on a commitment stretching back to Maastricht days. On 4 May he announced that Britain would join the Social Chapter.

Blair's victory was greeted with relief by other EU leaders, though none was so triumphalist as Kohl, who described it as a rejection of Euroscepticism: 'this should be a lesson for all those who want to win votes with anti-European polemics', he said.[122] On the Sunday, the front page of the *Observer* greeted the result with the largest headline in its history: 'Goodbye Xenophobia'. The humiliation of the Tories, it suggested, had marked the moment when the British people turned their back on 'little Englander' nationalism forever. The overwhelming victory for Tony Blair meant that Britain would at last be enthusiastically involved with 'Europe' in every way. From now on, everything would be different.

---

119 Associated Press (*Newsday*), 4 April 1997.
120 The *Independent*, 21 April 1997.
121 In response to questions from the authors, both the Treasury and the Commission were eager to emphasise that there was no connection between Brown's granting of independence to the Bank and EMU. But they failed to explain how Brown could have avoided complying with a treaty obligation from which Britain was not exempted.
122 The *International Herald Tribune*, 3 May 1997.

Plus ça change

An early visitor to Downing Street was Wim Kok, inviting Blair to meet his new partners in the seaside town of Noordwijk on 21 May. The agenda would be the rapidly approaching Amsterdam summit.[123] What transpired during this 'informal Council' remains obscure. The *communiqué* was more than usually opaque[124] and, on his return home, Blair chose not to make the usual statement to Parliament. Bill Cash complained of the House being treated with 'contempt'.[125]

If Blair was riding high, not so Chirac. His gamble at the polls badly misfired, losing his centre-right coalition more than 200 of its 464 seats in the parliament. Starting Chirac's nightmare of 'cohabitation', Lionel Jospin became Socialist prime minister, with Communist and Green support. His platform had been a promise of creating 700,000 jobs and reducing France's working week to 35 hours (in the hope that employers would have to take on more workers). The French people had decisively rejected 'further and faster' reforms to prepare for the single currency. Their priority was unemployment. The fate of the Amsterdam treaty was sealed. It was going to be the 'minimal solution'.

Meanwhile Giscard d'Estaing had marked the 50th anniversary of the Marshall Plan with a little-reported speech in Chicago on 14 April. Reviewing the history of post-war Europe, he noted that the 'institutions created by the Treaty of Rome went substantially beyond what was required to reach the economic objective'. In fact, it was the framework of a 'future European federal entity that was being established'. He asked 'will there ever be the equivalent of the Philadelphia miracle for Europe (the 1787 Congress that succeeded in raising the pillars of the US Constitution)?'

'The basic law of the European Union, which would order and rank the various diplomatic treaties since 1957, still remains to be written. Could one imagine the major European leaders devoting a few days, or even a week or two, of their time to come together, far from the public and media gaze ... to debate and draft – no office routine and no lobbies allowed – as they did in former years in Rome and at the Elysée, this charter of the European Union that the peoples of our Continent are anxiously awaiting? You probably will say that would take a miracle. But that is just what miracles are – always improbable, never impossible.'[126]

Giscard would have more to say on this a few years hence.

Seemingly oblivious to the political turmoil on the continent, Blair embarked on a tour of European capitals, preaching his new gospel of the 'third way'. He warned a congress of European centre-left parties in Malmo, Sweden, of the need to ditch outdated economic ideas, prompting the Dutch foreign minister to remark that some things never changed: another British leader was telling Europeans where they were going wrong.[127]

123 *Ibid.*
124 Bulletin EU 5-1997, Intergovernmental Conference (1/2), point I.1
125 *Hansard*, 2 June 1997, col. 20.
126 Giscard d'Estaing, Valéry (1997), 'The Seeds of European Union: Can 1997 Match Initiatives of 1947 and 1957?' in the *International Herald Tribune*, 28 May.
127 Young, *Blessed Plot, op. cit.*, p. 491.

When Blair moved on to Bonn on 6 June, he gave the same 'firm but polite advice' to Kohl,[128] but Kohl had other things on his mind. Having scorned France, Italy and others as they had struggled to meet the Maastricht criteria, finance minister Theo Waigel had now discovered a 19 billion mark (£7 billion) 'hole' in his 1997 budget. He was also out of options. With 4.3 million Germans unemployed, the Social Democrats, with a majority in the *Bundesrat*, were opposed to social security cuts. Reducing investment below the level of new government borrowing was forbidden by the constitution. Tax increases had been vetoed by Kohl's coalition partners, the Free Democrats.[129]

The hapless Waigel hit on the ingenious plan of revaluing the *Bundesbank's* gold and currency reserves and transferring the resulting 'surplus' to the Federal account. The *Bundesbank's* president, Hans Tietmeyer, immediately objected to such a 'blatantly cynical move'. It would damage the credibility of the European currency and set a disastrous example of political interference just when the proposed European Central Bank was to be set up.[130] Even Kohl had to back down. But this attempt to 'fiddle' the figures undermined Germany's credibility with just those countries it had accused of 'creative accounting' over EMU.[131]

Germany's deficit problem still had to be resolved, bringing pressure to delay the introduction of the euro. Adding fuel to the fire, Jospin called for a more flexible interpretation of the criteria, while his finance minister Dominique Strauss-Kahn rejected Germany's stability pact proposals. The timetable for the single currency looked shaky and it took Kohl's intervention to bring it back on track. He announced that he would stake his 'political existence' on keeping to the timetable, even though 82 percent of Germans now wanted a delay if member countries could not meet the entry criteria.[132]

Seemingly indifferent to these problems, Blair publicly set out Britain's position for Amsterdam. As well as wanting 'legally binding rights' to keep frontier controls, he strongly opposed bringing defence under 'Community' control by integrating the WEU into the EU, and insisted that 'enhanced co-operation' should only be allowed if states agreed unanimously. And he was standing by a campaign pledge to Britain's fishermen that he would insist on a treaty change to curb the ability of foreign vessels to fish for British quota.[133]

Thus did the heads of government gather in Amsterdam on 17 June for their summit. But the steam had gone out of the process. As if to set the mood, on 14 June, Amsterdam riot police had battled with 50,000 protesters.[134] When the VIPs arrived, demonstrators destroyed the 'summit logo', made from thousands of flowers, hurling the debris at the Royal Palace where the leaders were to dine.[135]

128 Reuters, 6 June 1997.
129 The *Economist*, 7 June 1997.
130 The *International Herald Tribune*, 2 June 1997.
131 *New Statesman*, 6 June 1997, p. 15.
132 Poll reported by the *International Herald Tribune*, 9 June 1997.
133 The *Independent*, 13 June 1997.
134 Reuters, 14 June 1997.
135 Reuters, 18 June 1997.

Inside the building, there was not much more harmony. The *International Herald Tribune* captured the mood:

'To get a feel for the true state of European politics today, one only had to look at the haggard, disgruntled expressions on the faces of Europe's leaders as they emerged from a final marathon session of constitutional negotiations in the predawn hours of Wednesday morning. Concluding two years of bargaining on a reform package that was supposed to prepare the European Union to expand eastward while simultaneously forging deeper political integration among its existing members, the leaders, by their own definition, fell woefully short of the mark.'[136]

The outcome was a the abolition of the veto in 16 more policy areas, including public health, measures to promote employment, the EU research programme and equality of treatment for men and women. There was a transfer of responsibilities to the 'Community framework', including the free movement of persons, the Schengen Agreement and measures relating to external border controls, asylum, immigration and police co-operation, although for the time being these would remain subject to unanimity. The Common Foreign and Security Policy (CFSP) was to be given 'a face', with the Council's appointment of a 'Mr CFSP', one day intended to become the EU's foreign minister. And, thanks to Britain, the Social Chapter could now be fully integrated into the Treaty.

The verdict of one European official on the treaty was 'no leadership, no appetite'. Kohl was stoical. 'There were too many conflicting interests,' he said. German officials confirmed that Kohl was saving his political capital for the single currency. 'The priority is absolutely with monetary union,' a German diplomat said. 'The rest can come later.'[137] Santer put a brave face on it, proclaiming:

'Nobody can say that we have not launched a new phase in European integration. The pace has been maintained. This was not the moment for grand designs and ambitions. We are advancing step by step.'[138]

The only one who seemed happy was Blair, who had been allowed by his colleagues to 'win' a photo-opportunity bicycle race and who made much of an agreement struck with Bonino on 'quota hopping', allowing his aides to claim that he had also won a 'victory' for British fishermen. Yet he had conceded on integration of the WEU into EU structures. Although he would have preferred the word 'integration' to have been omitted, he had bowed to France and Germany.

Simultaneously with the conclusion of the IGC, the heads of government had been holding a European Council. At France's insistence, the Council issued a Resolution on Growth and Employment, keeping employment at the top of the EU's political agenda. The Council also affirmed that EMU would start in January 1999, and agreed Germany's proposals for regulations on the Stability and Growth Pact. Finally, it endorsed the designs for the euro coins and bank notes to be issued in 2002. The notes showed architectural features and bridges loosely symbolising

136 19 June 1997.
137 *Ibid.*
138 *www.eurunion.org/news/eurecom/1997/ecom0797.htm*

European history through the ages, but carefully intended not to represent any specific place or style too precisely.[139]

The central European countries were troubled at the implications of the treaty for enlargement. A Polish official said 'the problems we hoped would be solved before we start negotiations are not being solved, just suspended'. But a senior EU official explained: 'with French unemployment and German economic stagnation, this is no time to throw open the doors to well-educated cheap labour.' 'If the Czechs, Poles and Hungarians haven't figured that out by now, there's something wrong with their figuring-out capacity'.[140]

Reporting back to MPs on 18 June, Blair singled out the 'real progress' made on the problem of quota hoppers. His officials had 'secured an agreement with the Commission' that there could be an 'economic link between boats using our quotas and Britain', such as requiring that 50 percent of a boat's catch to be landed locally.[141] Major, now leader of the opposition, reminded Blair that, during the election, he had said the problem could only be effectively dealt with by treaty changes, which he had made no effort to secure.[142]

Blair's 'victory', it then emerged, was even more hollow than realised. He had raised the matter in a letter to 'His Excellency M. Jacques Santer', who informed him that the conditions he was asking for had already been EU law since 1989. If he wanted 'any further clarification of the Commission's view' he should contact Commissioner Bonino.[143] Blair had in fact gained nothing and been treated with almost contemptuous condescension into the bargain. A new government might have taken over, but the battles were going to be just the same.

---

139 *Ibid.*
140 The *International Herald Tribune*, 21 June 1997.
141 *Hansard*, 18 Jun 1997, col. 315.
142 *Op. cit.*, col. 318.
143 The *Sunday Telegraph*, 22 June 1997.

Chapter 17

Towards 'Political Unity': 1997–1999

'What disturbs people in Britain and many elsewhere is that they see a constant transfer of power in one direction only. They see all the footprints leading into the cave and none coming out ... where does it end?'

Malcolm Rifkind, 21 February 1997[1]

Forty years on from the Treaty of Rome, the 'project' appeared to have come a long way. It had its own capital city, Brussels, its own citizenship, flag, anthem and passport, even its own driving license. It had assumed powers to control and make laws over many more areas of activity than most of its citizens were aware, from agriculture and fisheries to trade, transport, energy and the environment. Its membership had increased from six nations to 15.

What no one had ever properly explained, however, was where the process of 'ever closer union' was heading. Where was it to end? The time was now approaching when it would be necessary to put into place the final pieces of the jigsaw, and inevitably this was going to prove the most difficult phase of all. It would be the moment when all sorts of contradictions so far left unresolved would finally have to be confronted. Furthermore, in the absence of any agreed definition of that ultimate goal, the different participants were beginning to develop their own ideas as to what it should be, and this would spark fierce and prolonged debate as to what kind of Europe they wanted.

For British observers, this posed a particular problem. In the adversarial style of British politics, political opponents tended to speak their minds, whereas the consensus style of continental politics was carried out in a wholly different way. Confrontations were often cloaked in a semblance of agreement, using language so heavily coded that it was sometimes difficult to recognise the debate for what it was. Crucially, continental politicians used the same words, but attributed different meanings to them. For example, many were to talk about the need for 'further integration', appearing to be in agreement with one other when in fact they each meant something entirely different.

Not surprisingly therefore, the most striking feature of British attitudes towards the European 'project' was how little even its most enthusiastic supporters understood its true nature. When British politicians discussed 'Europe', they seemed to be talking in terms of words and concepts which across the Channel had wholly

1 Speech reported by Conservative Central Office, 21 February 1997.

different meanings. Thus, Major's insistence on a flexible, outward-looking Europe of nation states represented a version of 'Europe' which simply did not exist.

When Blair came to power, proclaiming his determination to play 'a leading role in Europe', he seemed to hold a view of 'Europe' not greatly dissimilar from that of the Conservatives. He too proclaimed a vision of a 'Europe of nation states', seemingly oblivious to the nature of supranationalism which had been central to the 'project' for 40 years. And nothing would more clearly reflect this confusion than Blair's continued inability to admit that the most supranational policy of them all, the single currency, was a political rather than economic venture.

When it came to the wider debate about Europe's future, therefore, the British were rarely to be effective participants. The 'project's' central agenda now was to complete the process whereby the powers of national governments could be transferred to the supranational government. This involved eliminating national vetoes and replacing them with qualified majority voting, thus completing the transformation of the Commission into the 'government of Europe'. Yet what had seemed comparatively easy when it could all be presented in terms of 'low politics' and the powers needed to set up a 'common market', now began to look very different when it reached those areas of policy which lay at the heart of a nation's sense of its own identity.

At issue was the reluctance of member states, which had accepted in principle the idea of common policies encompassing such sensitive issues as foreign affairs, defence and judicial affairs, to hand control of these policies to the Commission. The Maastricht 'pillars' had remained intact and, despite member states paying lip service to supranationalism, in these areas of policy intergovernmentalism was developing a new lease of life, under the aegis of the European Council. Thus were re-emerging tensions which had been at the heart of the 'project' since the days of de Gaulle, when national leaders had first begun to insist on playing a much greater role in managing Community affairs than Monnet had intended.

Now, as other areas of policy-making were also becoming central to the project, such as the developing of common strategies for 'defence' or 'employment', the European Council was keen to hold on to them, and in so doing was challenging the primacy of the Commission. But at the same time the intergovernmental Council lacked the infrastructure and resources necessary to ensure that its 'common policies' were carried through.

Despite these growing contradictions, there was nevertheless a general sense that the process of integration was indeed approaching its final stages, and that the tension between the Commission and the Council would have to be resolved. But disagreement over which organisation should have the right to act as the supreme 'government of Europe' would be disguised as a more general debate about what kind of Europe should eventually emerge.

One example of this would be the continuing debate over the right of the Commission to decide taxation. Such a power was crucial to the Commission in realising its ambitions to become *the* government of Europe, releasing it from the 'tyranny' of the member states who held the purse strings. But the Commission could never openly declare such an ambition, so it relied on elliptical justifications, such as its proposal in 1996 that the 'internal market' could not be completed without a uniform imposition of VAT across the EU. This had met with fierce resistance,[2] not least because the power to decide taxes was viewed as one of the most fundamental components of national sovereignty.

Similarly, the debate on enlargement would have its own undertones. Previously, each time new members had joined, this had been used to justify extending the powers of the 'centre', so that each 'widening' was an excuse for further 'deepening'. But what the European Union now faced the greatest expansion so far, and the most problematic, not least because these impoverished, less developed newcomers would impose immense strains on the EU budget, competing for funds with the poorer existing members, such as Spain, Portugal, Ireland and Greece.

Especially serious would be the strain on the CAP. Poland alone had a million farmers, almost as many as the whole of the existing Union. The dependence of a quarter of her population on agriculture provided a striking echo of France's situation in the 1960s, when the need to manage the drift from the land had been the crucial factor behind the creation of the CAP. But, having manipulated the CAP so that it met her own national interest, it would not be easy for France to accept reforms from which she would be a significant loser. Yet, without radical reform, enlargement would be impossible.

As if these problems were not enough, the member states were also having to confront the reality that existing policies were simply not working. The CAP, imposing a 'one-size-fits-all' farming policy from the Arctic Circle to the arid plains of Andalusia, was almost universally viewed as a bureaucratic disaster, creating wasteful over-production, environmental damage and fraud in almost equal measure. The rigidities of the Common Fisheries Policy were creating an ecological crisis. The 'internal market', far from having achieved its promised boost to trade, growth and jobs, was now the economic blackspot of the developed world. Furthermore, the ultimate 'one-size-fits-all' policy of economic and monetary union was already giving rise to immense stress, as its would-be members struggled to meet the Maastricht 'convergence criteria'; and this was even before the theory of such a hugely ambitious experiment was put to practical test.

Finally, there was what was being described in Community jargon as the 'democratic deficit'. As Community action became more conspicuous and intrusive, the 'citizens of the Union' were increasingly regarding it as remote, bureaucratic, undemocratic and unaccountable. For decades, the idea of 'European co-operation' had inspired idealistic goodwill, but 'Europe' had seemed largely peripheral, apart from those whose livelihoods it directly damaged, such as Britain's fisher-

---

2 This proposal, put forward by Mario Monti, the Commissioner for the internal market, in October 1996 (COM final 328), was that VAT should be harmonised at the same rates across the Union, and that all VAT revenues should be paid direct to Brussels, for re-distribution back to member states at the Commission's discretion. This would particularly disadvantage Britain since, unlike almost every other member state she did not impose VAT on food (which alone would have added £7 billion to UK food bills), newspapers and magazines, children's clothes, public transport fares and new homes.

men, and those who benefited from it financially.[3] But now, disillusionment was setting in, just when the need for popular support was becoming vital.

Such were the themes around which the story was now about to unfold.

Preparing for a straitjacket

After Amsterdam, the debate on 'integration' was not immediately to resume. First, there was essential 'housekeeping' to address. The Commission's priority was to deal with the practical tasks necessary to pave the way for enlargement. The political leaders had to continue their preparations for economic and monetary union.

Dealing with enlargement, on 16 July 1997, Santer announced to the European Parliament that accession negotiations should start with six countries: Poland, Hungary, the Czech Republic, Estonia, Slovenia and Cyprus. Five more, Bulgaria, Latvia, Lithuania, Romania and Slovakia, he maintained, did not meet the 'Copenhagen criteria'. And to deal with the problem of the new entrants' claims on the CAP and structural funds potentially bankrupting the EU, Santer proposed a new plan, which he called 'Agenda 2000'.

The ideas were not entirely new. Santer proposed to continue reducing production support, bringing farm prices more in line with world prices, ending intervention buying and compulsory set-aside. But 'compensation' for not receiving subsidies would increase. He also proposed bringing together existing farm environmental and structural measures into a new 'rural development policy', to be paid for partly by 'capping' payments to larger farmers, a device known as 'modulation'.

There would also have to be sharp reductions in the structural funds, now accounting for £20 billion of the EU's £60 billion budget. Instead of payments going to regions with a lower than average GDP, they would now be made to those with the highest unemployment. Finally, proposed Santer, there should be another IGC to draw up a new treaty in 2000.

Response to his proposals was predictably hostile. Portugal, Greece and Ireland protested strongly at the threat to their structural payments. Spain, with the largest share, even threatened to veto enlargement altogether, unless her payments remained intact.[4] But the biggest loser on both counts would be Britain. Her larger farms would lose more to 'modulation', and her unemployment was much lower than the EU average. The original 'club of Six' were ambivalent about enlargement anyway, concerned that the admission of up to 12 new members would dilute the 'Community spirit'. Smaller countries feared they would lose influence. The strain on the EU's administrative arrangements would be enormous, with the need for as many as 4,000 extra translators to translate every document and speech into 11 new languages. Neither the Commission nor the Parliament buildings could accommodate the additional staff needed.[5]

---

3 The Commission's Eurobarometer polls consistently showed that the countries in which it was most popular, such as Luxembourg, Ireland and Greece, were those which financially were its largest net beneficiaries.

4 The *European*, 25 September 1997.

5 Data drawn from the *Independent*, 20 July 1997.

As for the stresses now arising from the need to prepare for the euro, France's new Socialist prime minister Jospin found he could not reconcile fulfilling the Maastricht criteria with meeting his election promises. He decided to opt for the euro, postponing promised tax cuts and going ahead with the sale of France Telecom, breaking an electoral promise to the Communists. The Parisian air was thick with accusations of backsliding and treachery.[6]

In Germany, the *impasse* on the deficit had reached crisis point. Finance minister Theo Waigel had now decided the only way he could meet the Maastricht criteria was to increase taxes and cut state pension, and cut Germany's payments to the EU budget by seven billion marks. So serious was the crisis that deputies were brought back from holiday for an emergency session of the *Bundestag* on 5 August to debate the measures. The parliament's president described them as 'the biggest challenge Germany has faced in fifty years'.[7] Meanwhile Germany's powerful regional governments, the *Länder*, led by Bavaria's Edmund Stoiber, insisted that the Maastricht criteria must be strictly applied to everyone.[8] But, with polls consistently showing most Germans opposing giving up the *Deutschmark*, when Tietmeyer suggested that it would be 'perfectly possible' to postpone the euro, this was interpreted as a coded signal that it should be abandoned. Coming from Germany's most respected financial figure, it was a serious blow to Kohl's authority.[9]

Detached from all this, Britain's politicians were still preoccupied by whether Britain could be got into the euro in the first place. Blair, with the support of his chief 'spin doctor' Peter Mandelson, considered entry vital to his wish to play a 'leading role in Europe'. But suspicions that his Chancellor was less enthusiastic seemed to be confirmed by *The Times* front-page story on 18 October, headed: 'Brown rules out single currency for lifetime of this parliament'.

When the Commission announced, to no one's surprise, that 14 of 15 member states met the Maastricht criteria (only Greece failing to qualify), Santer stepped up the pressure by warning that, if Britain did not join, she would miss the benefits of being in 'a winning team'.[10] Brown announced to MPs on 27 October that 'five economic tests' must met before the Cabinet could recommend that Britain should join. The decision would be made on 'a hard-headed assessment of Britain's economic interests'. By narrowing the issue down to no more than a matter of economic calculation, Brown had cannily retained for himself the power to decide.[11] It was clear there was going to be no immediate decision.

This left as the most active campaigners for British entry that familiar alliance between a small group of senior Conservatives, at odds with the cautiously

---

6 The *Economist*, 5 July 1997.
7 The *Daily Telegraph*, 29 July 1997.
8 The *European*, 7 August 1997.
9 The *Daily Telegraph*, 4 September 1997
10 The *Independent*, 23 October 1997.
11 The *Independent*, 28 October 1997. Brown's 'five tests' were (i) whether there had been 'sustainable convergence' between the British economy and those of the eurozone; (ii) whether there was 'sufficient flexibility' to cope with economic change; (iii) the effect on overseas investment; (iv) the impact on the City of London; and (v) whether economic and monetary union would be good for employment.

Eurosceptic line taken by their party's new leader William Hague, and those organisations which had long since been carefully corralled into support for the cause, led by the CBI and the TUC. Their greatest asset was still the BBC, which continued to give disproportionate airtime to the views of such spokesmen as Clarke, Heseltine and Brittan, now Commission vice-president. As an example of what was to come, on 30 October, Heseltine was given top spot of the day on the *Today* programme to declare, 'Let's be absolutely clear, there's going to be a single currency ... the only issue is when Britain joins, because join we will.'

The increasing readiness of the leading Conservative Europhiles to defy their party's leadership was again in evidence when on 12 November the ratification of the Amsterdam Treaty came before the Commons for its second reading. For the first time Conservative policy was to oppose the treaty. Yet, despite a three-line whip, three Tories stayed away from the vote: Heath, now 'Father of the House', Heseltine and Clarke. It was precisely the kind of gesture for which they had savaged the 'Maastricht rebels' for gross disloyalty.[12]

December, as a British presidency approached, brought what was seen as a humiliation for Britain when EU finance ministers excluded Brown from a new committee 'Euro-X', to be set up to co-ordinate economic policy in the eurozone. He protested that this could 'split Europe', but Germany's Waigel was unimpressed: 'You cannot be both in and out,' he said. The media recorded this as the first crisis in relations between the Labour government and the rest of Europe.[13]

In a bid to restore his 'European credentials', on 5 December Blair staged a preview of Britain's presidency, amid lavish hype, picking as his venue the London terminal of the Channel Tunnel rail service. As various distinguished continental guests emerged from the train, Blair assured them that Eurostar was 'a symbol of our unbreakable ties with the lands beyond the Channel'.[14] But it was not considered wholly tactful to stage the occasion at a station named after an Anglo-German victory over the French at Waterloo.

Certainly Blair's bid to appear *communautaire* failed to impress other EU leaders. A round of telephone diplomacy, attempting to persuade his partners to reconsider their exclusion of Britain from the proposed Euro-X committee, met with continued rebuffs. He therefore shifted his ground, insisting that the committee must remain subordinate to Ecofin. This time it was Jospin who barred the way, telling the *Financial Times*: 'the rules have yet to be defined but the UK, which invented clubs, should not complain at being excluded'.[15]

At the Luxembourg Council, on 12 to 13 December, Blair fared no better. After five hours of bad-tempered argument, he obtained only a vague promise that Britain and the other 'outs' (or 'pre-ins' as they were now termed) could only participate in discussions of 'common interest' at Euro-X. Kohl rebuked him for 'unnecessarily provoking the French delegation'.[16] Labour's honeymoon with the

---

12 *Op. cit*, col. 928.
13 The *Independent*, 2 December 1997.
14 The *Independent*, 5 December 1997.
15 The *Independent*, 10 December 1997.
16 The *Sunday Telegraph*, 14 December 1997.

EU was over. But nothing of his humiliation on Euro-X was reflected in Blair's report to the Commons on 15 December. 'The Luxembourg summit,' he proclaimed, 'showed again that the government are positively engaged in Europe as a leading and influential player.'[17]

At the end of 1997, to mark 25 years of Britain's membership of the 'Community', the *Sunday Telegraph's* economics editor Bill Jamieson noted that the number of EC directives in force had grown from 221 in 1973 to 10,549. In the eight years since 1989, the number of pages of official documents put out by the EU's publications office had more than doubled, from 886,996 to 1,916,808, and was now rising by 20 percent a year.[18]

The isolated presidency

Britain's six-month presidency between January and July 1998, under the slogan 'bringing Europe closer to the people', was an embarrassment. Inevitably it provoked renewed calls from her partners to join the euro, begun in January by Dutch prime minister Wim Kok,[19] followed by Santer and then his monetary affairs commissioner, Yves-Thibault de Silguy, who warned that, if Britain did not join immediately, she would face a range of problems, from the volatility of sterling to a fall in inward investment. Blair, he suggested, had no chance of 'leading' in Europe until Britain was inside the euro club.[20]

Constrained by Brown's 'five tests', Blair could do no more than express general support for the euro, while denying that there was any constitutional bar to British entry. In an attempt to divert attention from his exclusion for the 'club', the theme he chose for his presidency was 'reforms to tackle unemployment'. He argued that the Union should take his lead in reducing burdens on business and embracing 'much more adaptable labour markets'.[21]

The euro was continuing to give his 'partners' problems of their own, not least in Germany where the *Bundesbank's* Hans Tietmeyer began 1998 by warning that the single currency could not 'on its own' solve the problem of Europe's high unemployment. Four German professors, including three well-known economists, later joined by more than 150 others, launched an action in Germany's constitutional court aimed at stopping the new currency. They feared it would collapse amid 'hatred and envy'. Their plea was rejected.[22]

Another bitter row into which Blair was drawn, despite being outside the euro, centred on France's demand that the head of her central bank, Jean-Claude Trichet, must run the new European Central Bank. Originally it had been agreed that the position would be held for eight years by Wim Duisenberg, formerly head of the Dutch central bank, now running the European Monetary Institute, forerunner to the ECB. The French eventually conceded that Duisenberg could take

17 *Hansard*, 15 December 1997, col. 21.
18 28 December 1997.
19 The *Financial Times*, 21 January 1998.
20 The *Daily Telegraph*, 6 February 1998.
21 The *Financial Times*, 19 January 1998
22 The *Daily Telegraph*, 1 and 2 January 1998.

the post, but only on condition that he resigned after four years to make way for Trichet.[23] The dispute spilled over into the first of the European Councils under Blair's chairmanship, held in Brussels, which turned into 'a day-long squabble'. Amid undignified scenes for which Blair was partly blamed, Duisenberg was pressured into agreeing to 'retire' four years early, so the French could get their way. The Commission could now recommend, on 24 March 1998, that 11 European countries should join the single currency on 1 January 1999.

Blair's 'partners' continued to press home the cost of Britain's self-exclusion from the euro. The French again made the running on this, deliberately engineering an incident centred on the Euro-X committee set up to manage the eurozone. Since it fell to Gordon Brown to chair all Ecofin meetings under the UK presidency, it had been proposed that, to save him embarrassment, the inaugural Euro-X meeting should be delayed until Britain had left the chair. The French now moved that it should be brought forward.[24] At its first session Brown therefore insisted on taking the chair, seeking to ingratiate himself with a 'powerful declaration' of Britain's intention to join EMU. He was then humiliatingly ordered to leave, and replaced by Austria's finance minister Rudolph Edlinger.[25]

A more substantial challenge to Britain came from a Commission proposal in May for a 'tax on savings', the so-called 'withholding tax directive'. This would require member states to levy tax at a minimum of 20 percent on the interest from all bonds and deposits held by nationals of other countries. Its declared purpose was to prevent tax evasion by investors in one member state who chose to keep their money in another. Many Germans, for instance, avoided tax by switching their funds to Luxembourg. In two ways this proposal was anathema to Britain. It was an attempt to breach fiercely-guarded national sovereignty over taxation. More specifically it would damage the City of London as the world's leading capital market. Billions of pounds-worth of business would be moved elsewhere, to jurisdictions such as Switzerland and Hong Kong where the tax did not apply.[26]

Britain was just as obviously isolated from her partners over foreign policy. One embarrassment was an initiative by Britain's Foreign Secretary Robin Cook who, while visiting Israel in his capacity as 'EU President', made an unsanctioned detour into a Palestinian settlement in east Jerusalem. The Israeli government was mortally offended. Cook was snubbed by Israel's prime minister Netanyahu and escorted to Ben Gurion airport without even a handshake from a junior Israeli official.[27]

A longer-term problem was the continuing inability of Britain and her partners to agree over Iraq. After the Gulf War, UN resolutions had called upon Saddam Hussein to disarm and UN inspectors had been appointed to monitor the process.

23 The *Economist*, 17 January 1998.
24 *Ibid*.
25 The *Financial Times*, 4 June 1998; the *Daily Telegraph*, 5 June 1998.
26 The *Financial Times*, 18 May 1998. Britain had only become the centre of the world's international bond market after New York in the 1960s imposed its own version of such a tax. The market moved to London where the tax did not apply.
27 The *Financial Times*, 19 March 1998.

When Saddam refused to co-operate and the inspectors withdrew, this precipitated a crisis. Britain sided with the United States in favouring a military solution. Chirac merely argued for more UN sanctions, although his own country had done as much as any to undermine the existing sanctions regime.

Nevertheless it was Blair who was reprimanded by the European Parliament for not trying to present a 'common European position'[28]; and similar dissension arose over policy towards Milosevic's Yugoslavia, when fighting flared up on the border between Albania and the Serbian province of Kosovo. The EU urged a weak policy towards the Serb leader.[29] Britain alone favoured the military intervention urged by the US, which would lead the following year to war and Milosevic's overthrow.

Blair's more emollient approach to 'Europe' equally failed to reap dividends on the domestic front. His government had been unable to resolve the BSE export ban. Britain's farmers had been plunged into their worst crisis since before World War Two, with farm incomes having dropped by 50 percent in one year. This was due not least to the government's refusal to claim Community funding to compensate for the 'strong pound', because, under the 'Fontainebleau effect', most of this additional money would have then been deducted from the UK rebate. The result was that Britain's farmers had to contend with their much more highly-subsidised EU competitors, who could thus afford to sell their produce in Britain at lower prices.[30]

There was also further evidence of the damage the CFP was inflicting on Britain's fishing industry. On 30 April a parliamentary answer revealed that in just four years between 1993 and 1997 the number of fishing boats on the UK register had dropped by nearly a third, from 11,108 to 7,809. The tonnage of Spanish and Dutch-owned 'flag boats' had actually risen, while 3,300 smaller British vessels and their crews were forced out of business.[31]

On 14 June came the crowning glory of Blair's presidency, the Cardiff European Council. Its slogan 'bringing Europe closer to the people' seemed peculiarly ironic as the city was subjected to a ferocious security clamp-down, designed to keep any potential protesters at least a mile from the conference hall. To create an illusion of popular welcome for the cameras, schoolchildren were bussed in from across south Wales, issued with 'ring of stars' flags to wave at the leaders as they gathered round a specially built table, costing £50,000.

The Council was dismissed by the *Financial Times* as little more than 'an exercise in stage management', its centrepiece a fleeting visit from Nelson Mandela. Blair continued to urge his 'reform' agenda, calling for 'a decentralised Europe', not 'some European federal superstate'.[32] But the main concern of his colleagues was whether Britain would join the euro. With Cook giving 'the strongest signal' that Britain would join 'probably in 2002', Santer proclaimed, 'It is no more a question of if Britain will join the euro, it is only a question of when'.[33]

28 The *Daily Telegraph*, 19 February 1998.
29 *Ibid.*
30 The *Independent*, 27 May 1998.
31 *Hansard*, written answer by Elliott Morley, 30 April 1998.
32 *Associated Press Online*, 15 June 1998.
33 The *Daily Telegraph*, 15 June 1998.

However, when Blair himself ended the Council by endorsing the euro as a 'turning point' for Europe,[34] this provoked a dramatic response from Britain's top-selling tabloid, the *Sun*, hitherto an ardent Blair supporter. On 24 June its front page asked, 'Is this the most dangerous man in Britain?' The next day's front-page carried a massive 'NO'. A 'huge army of *Sun* readers', it claimed, had 'round-ed on Tony Blair for backing plans to ditch the Pound'.[35] Although Downing Street claimed Blair was 'unworried' by this attack from what was seen as politi-cally Britain's most influential newspaper, observers noted he seemed distinctly nervous before, on 30 June, he flew to Frankfurt to mark the end of the UK pres-idency.[36] After music from a Dutch male voice choir, dancing from an Irish ensemble, and lunch in the opera house at three in the afternoon, the farce was over. Down the road the same day the European Central Bank opened for busi-ness.

'Hidden Europe': the elephant in the room

By now the deliberately narrowed focus and trivial nature of the British debate on 'Europe' was becoming painfully obvious. Despite the fact that all three main political parties officially supported Britain's membership, their politicians were remarkably reluctant to defend or explain it in any detail. They confined them-selves to uttering little more than a set of well-worn mantras. Repeatedly, for instance, they would claim that the benefits of membership to Britain were 'self-evident': none more so than that she could now 'trade freely with the largest inter-nal market in the world'.

What no politician ever mentioned, however, was how unbalanced that 'trading advantage' had become. It was in the summer of 1998 that figures published by the OECD showed that the British economy was doing so well that it had now over-hauled that of France to become the fourth largest in the world. But it also emerged that, in the 25 years since Britain joined the Common Market in 1973, she had run up a cumulative balance of payments deficit with her EU partners, through trade and net contributions to the Brussels budget, totalling £170 bil-lion.[37]

Equally curious were the efforts made by ministers to conceal just how many areas of national policy were now being decided in Brussels, by pretending that these decisions were their own. One small instance was the new driver's licence, the design of which, according to a leaflet from the Driver and Vehicle Licensing Agency, had been 'decided by ministers'. Yet every detail of its format, including the EU 'ring of stars' logo, was based on the 'Community model driving licence' made mandatory by directive 91/493/EEC. Similarly there were the complications now involved in carrying out simple banking transactions. Although customers

---

34 The *Daily Telegraph*, 16 June 1998.
35 The *Sun*, 25 June 1998.
36 The *Daily Telegraph*, 25 June 1998.
37 Figures compiled from relevant editions of the 'Pink Book' (*The United Kingdom Balance of Payments*), HMSO.

were often baffled by new procedures they had to follow to prove their identity, it was never explained that these were dictated by a directive on 'money laundering', 91/308/EEC.

Another example emerged in the long-running battle waged by environmental groups over the experimental growing in Britain of genetically modified crops. Ministers went out of their way to avoid admitting that they no longer had any power over this issue, since all competence to decide GM policy had been taken over by Brussels in 1990. Another instance was a much-publicised announcement by John Prescott, as Secretary of State for the Environment, that he had ordered water companies to spend £8.5 billion on 'cleaning up Britain's water'. This was presented as if it was entirely his own personal initiative. Nowhere was it explained that 'his decision' derived solely from the need to comply with Brussels water directives.[38]

In this respect, the influence of Brussels on British life had become like the proverbial 'elephant in the room': an object so huge and amorphous that it was not easy to see it was there. There was no better example of this than another of Prescott's initiatives when, in his capacity as Secretary of State for the Regions, he in 1997 and 1998 put through six new Acts of Parliament. Four of these, hailed as 'devolution measures', were to set up elected assemblies for Scotland, Wales, Northern Ireland and London, based on the continental principle of proportional representation. A fifth set up 'regional development agencies' for eight 'regions' covering the remainder of England, with the provision that they too would eventually become part of elected regional governments.

Prescott presented all these new laws as if they had little or no connection with each other, aided by the fact that 'devolution' for Scotland and Wales had been an issue for years. The new Northern Irish assembly was promoted as a way of returning the province to self-government as part of the 'peace process'. But the undeclared link between these Acts was that they represented a policy to split the UK into 12 regional governments, as part of the grand design for a 'Europe of the regions'.

The story of how regionalisation had come to play a central role in Europe's integration was complex. The original impetus, after World War Two, had come from local government leaders in France and Germany, working through the Council of Europe and latterly through one of its subsidiary bodies, the Council of European Muncipalities and Regions (CEMR), of which the president was Giscard d'Estaing. Quite separately Britain had during the war adopted a skeletal regional structure of her own for administrative purposes, and this it had at various times been suggested should be developed on a more permanent basis. In 1972–1973, it will be recalled, Heath had pressed for a 'regional policy' to compensate Britain for the fact that she would lose so heavily from the CAP; and in 1975 the Tindemans report had urged the need to develop a regional structure across the EEC as a precondition of monetary union, to give a means of redressing economic imbalances between richer and poorer regions.

---

38 One former Conservative minister of state for agriculture privately expressed resentment at the constant pressure she had been put under by officials to conceal that almost all the policy initiatives she was given to propose had originated from Brussels (personal information).

The turning point, however, had come in the late 1980s, when Delors had finally insisted on regionalisation becoming a central policy in the Single European Act. He had then instituted the 1988 'framework' regulation 2052/88, allowing regional or local authorities to negotiate directly with the Commission for structural funds. And it was this new system, requiring that regional authorities must be in place to receive Brussels funding, which in 1994 compelled John Gummer, as Secretary of State for the Environment, to set up a 'Government Office' in each of the English 'regions', thus calling them formally into existence.

This was the baton which Prescott had picked up in 1995 when, in defiance of Labour Party policy (which favoured preserving the powers of local government), he set up his own 'Regional Policy Commission' under Bruce Millan, a former Brussels Commissioner for regional policy. As Prescott later revealed, his enthusiasm for regional government went 'back more than 30 years', to the time when, as a young politician in the 1970s he had been leader of the Labour group in the Council of Europe.[39] And it was Millan's recommendation that England should be given 'regional development agencies' which enabled Prescott to set up the embryo of regional governments in the rest of the UK, alongside the new 'regional parliaments' for Scotland, Wales, Northern Ireland and London.

Although Prescott and his colleagues were determined not to admit the link with European integration, the connection was openly acknowledged in Brussels, as in official maps showing the EU divided into 111 'Euro-regions', including the 12 in the UK. In May 1998, as the first senior UK politician to address the newly formed Committee of the Regions, Prescott said:

'Governments must be as close as possible to their citizens and a Europe of the regions is the best way of doing this. The UK has in the past lagged behind in this area, but the new government has been quick to start to put things right…'[40]

Curiously, the only politician to blow Prescott's cover was Heseltine. To a fringe meeting at the 1998 Conservative Party conference, he announced that there were 'two European agendas'. In one, he said, he profoundly believed. But there was another, 'the agenda of the regions, which says that Brussels will dispose of money to the regions of Europe and ultimately bypass national parliaments'. 'I deplore that agenda,' he declared. Blair, he said, was 'playing into the hands of that agenda with his destruction of the United Kingdom'. If he was to continue this process of 'European federalism' begun in Scotland and Wales by extending it to the English regions, that would 'weaken the UK and centralise power in a way I find totally unacceptable'.[41]

At the same conference, Heseltine was in another respect less in tune with delegates' views. Through the year Conservatives had been embroiled in civil war over the euro. Not only had Heseltine and Clarke openly applauded Blair's stance on 'Europe', urging him to go further and faster, with Hurd, Brittan and Patten, the

---

39 *Hansard*, 9 May 2002, col. 275.
40 *www.cec.org.uk/info/pubs/regional/ea/chap2p2.htm*
41 Speech given to Conservative Mainstream in Bournemouth, 6 October 1998 (transcribed by British Management Data Foundation).

former Party chairman, they had been openly sniping at Hague's sceptical stance. Leading the counter-attack was Michael Portillo, no longer an MP but ambitious to lead the party, supported by Lamont, Tebbit and Thatcher.

But it was Hague himself who in a visit to Fontainebleau in May infuriated the Europhiles still further by the most sceptical speech on 'Europe' from a Conservative leader for years. Further integration without democratic support, he warned, could eventually lead to the kind of violent protest which had just broken out in Indonesia. Of the euro, he said, 'one could find oneself trapped in the economic equivalent of a burning building with no exits'. He predicted that it could herald a political union, with tax and public spending decisions taken in Brussels. 'I fear the European Union is in danger,' he concluded, 'of accepting without debate a political destination agreed 40 years ago.'[42]

Over the summer, Clarke, Heseltine and Brittan leaked plans to launch an all-out assault on Hague's policy at the October party conference. Their aim was to ensure that coverage of the conference would be dominated by the image of a party riven by internecine war.[43] In a bid to outflank them, Hague announced a ballot of all party members to endorse his euro policy,[44] dismissed by Heseltine as a 'total irrelevance'.[45] This was followed by similar outbursts from Brittan and Heath,[46] provoking the shadow cabinet to break silence with a campaign to marginalise Hague's critics. Clarke and Heseltine, they said, were treating members 'with contempt'.[47]

The ballot result, declared in Bournemouth in October, resoundingly endorsed Hague. He was backed by 85 percent of his party. His opponents simply announced that they would fight on, to prevent him leading the party 'into a right-wing bunker of unelectability'. With that, they had succeeded only in reinforcing the general perception of the Tories as hopelessly divided, incapable of effective opposition and preoccupied with an issue still seen by most voters as only of secondary importance.

In another respect, however, that summer had seen a significant reverse for the pro-euro campaigners. In propaganda terms, for four years no organisation had played a more central role for their cause than the CBI, with its annual 'polls' purporting to show a sizeable majority of Britain's businessmen backing British entry. These had invariably been heavily publicised by the BBC, while it ignored a stream of polls by other business organisations, such as the Institute of Directors and the Federation of Small Businesses, showing overwhelming opposition to the euro.

In the summer of 1998 the CBI announced it was to stage its biggest membership 'poll' so far, supervised by Bob Worcester of Mori, famous for his role in the 1975 referendum. The previous surveys having been heavily rigged, Worcester was privately challenged that it would be 'unprofessional' to give his name to a further survey. He withdrew, forcing the CBI in some embarrassment to abandon its poll.

---

42 The *Financial Times*, 19 May 1998.
43 The *Financial Times*, 9 August; the *Daily Telegraph*, 10 August 1998.
44 The *Daily Telegraph*, 8 September 1998.
45 The *Daily Telegraph*, 6 October 1998.
46 The *Financial Times*, 14 September 1998.
47 The *Financial Times*, 17 September 1998.

The bluff of the CBI Europhiles had been finally called.[48] Senior CBI members, led by Stanley Kalms, head of Britain's biggest electrical retail chain, then staged an internal counter-attack. He and his allies set up a rival organisation, Business for Sterling, to campaign against the euro. So powerfully did it challenge the other side's claims that, within months, the CBI's propaganda role had been effectively neutralised. Heseltine, Clarke and Brittan had lost their most useful ally.

A German earthquake

On 30 September 1998, there was a political earthquake in Germany. The Christian Democrat party under Chancellor Kohl suffered a decisive election defeat by a Social Democrat/Green alliance. After years of high unemployment, high taxes and economic decline, the effects of which had been reinforced by the preparations for the euro, Germany was not a happy country. What tipped the balance, however, was a left-wing landslide in the former East Germany. Although it was not immediately apparent, for the first time the passing of Communism in eastern Europe was to have a very significant impact on the 'project's' future.

Before the election, the new Chancellor Gerhard Schröder had projected a Eurosceptic line, even referring to the euro as a 'sickly premature infant, resulting from an over hasty monetary union'.[49] But his show of Euroscepticism was electoral grandstanding, designed mainly to appease the powerful *Länder*, which were increasingly concerned at the encroachment of the EU on their powers and fearful of the effects of the euro.

After the election, having been forced to appoint his left-wing party chairman Oskar Lafontaine as finance minister, and his Green coalition partner Joschka Fischer as foreign minister, both enthusiastic integrationalists, Schröder's line appeared to change. At his inaugural address to the Federal parliament on 10 November, he spoke of the single currency as merely 'an important step on the way to European integration'. He then added, 'Only through the further development of a political union will we succeed in forming a Europe that is close to its citizens.' This must also include harmonisation of taxes.[50]

Not far below the surface, however, was the agenda of the *Länder*, as Schröder devoted an important part of his two-hour speech to describing his vision of 'a federal Europe constructed on German lines'. Buried by the resulting furore over tax harmonisation, notably in Britain, the version of 'Europe's' future Schröder was offering was very different from that favoured by many of his EU colleagues, let alone by the Commission. It was in fact directly from this that there would eventually emerge the key proposal for an EU constitution, with the intention that this should limit the powers of the Commission and protect the autonomy of Europe's regions.

Twelve days later in Brussels, however, 11 socialist finance ministers, including Gordon Brown, gathered to consider a socialist manifesto for Europe. With the

48 Worcester's challenger was Brig. Cowgill of the British Management Data Foundation.
49 *Bild*, 25 March 1998.
50 The *Daily Telegraph*, 11 November 1998.

euro approaching, this was a clarion call for EU tax harmonisation, to provide, as Austria's finance minister Edinger put it, 'a common economic roof' for our 'common house of Europe'.[51] Although Brown signed the document, he immediately caused a storm by stating publicly that Britain would be prepared to use her veto to block any moves towards tax harmonisation.[52]

Over the next few days, the issue of 'Europe' dominated the British press as it had not done for years. First the temperature was raised by statements from three Commissioners. Santer challenged Brown's threat to use the veto by claiming that Britain had already signed up in principle to tax harmonisation the previous December, when EU finance ministers had agreed on the need 'to tackle harmful tax competition', including a specific intention to introduce a 'withholding tax'.[53] But Brown had made clear at the time that this must not damage the City of London's position, not least as easily the largest issuer of Eurobonds. Next day Mario Monti, the single market commissioner, insisted that the Commission would proceed with plans to harmonise rates of VAT, energy taxes and excise duties.[54] Then, on a visit to London, de Silguy, the commissioner for monetary union, predicted that tax harmonisation would ultimately lead to EU-wide rates of income tax.[55] This was reinforced by a promise from Oskar Lafontaine, that tax harmonisation would be a top priority for the forthcoming German presidency, provoking the *Sun* on its front page on 25 November to dub him 'the most dangerous man in Europe'.

The heat was raised still further by two of Lafontaine's colleagues. First, interviewed by a Frankfurt newspaper but widely reported in Britain, Joschka Fischer promised that 'deeper integration' would be the priority of the German presidency in more than just tax matters. 'Just as we worked on the first real transfer of sovereignty in the field of currencies,' he said, 'we ought to work on a common constitution to turn the European Union into an entity under international law.' Asked whether he wanted a European army, Fischer replied 'if it is going to turn into a full union, then one day foreign and defence policy will also have to become Community tasks'.[56] Next day in Brussels, Schröder inspired frenzy in the Eurosceptic British press by reaffirming that the vision of an 'ever more integrated Europe' was an idea which 'unites all German politicians'.[57]

As the *Daily Telegraph* summed up: 'the danger of Britain being subsumed into a not very democratic European superstate suddenly seems more alive than ever before'.[58] What had not been appreciated, however, was that Schröder's idea of an 'ever more integrated Europe' was now aimed at moving the 'project' in an entirely new direction.

Before this could develop further, however, the 'project' was about to hit Europe's front pages for a very different reason.

---

51 The *Daily Telegraph*, 23 November 1998.
52 The *Daily Telegraph*, 24 November 1998.
53 The *Daily Mail*, 25 November 1998.
54 The *Daily Mail*, 26 November 1998.
55 The *Daily Telegraph*, 27 November 1998.
56 The *Daily Telegraph*, 26 November 1998.
57 The *Financial Times*, *The Times*, 27 November 1998.
58 28 November 1998.

The Commission in crisis

Over the next few months coverage of the EU was dominated by an extraordinary crisis. This broke when, on 9 December 1998, Paul van Buitenen, a Dutch accountant employed by the Commission as an assistant auditor, sent MEPs a 34-page letter with 600 pages of supporting documents, detailing instances of corruption he had identified in his work as an auditor. These included cases directly involving two Commissioners.[59]

His charges came as no great surprise. Reports and rumours of wholesale corruption, fraud and financial mismanagement in the Commission had been building up for a long time. In February 1998 the European Parliament's budgetary control committee had accused the Commission of giving misleading information and stalling inquiries into fraud among its officials, involving millions of pounds and dating back to 1989.[60] In August the Court of Auditors published a report criticising the Commission's anti-fraud measures as wholly inadequate, and its anti-fraud unit UCLAF as 'highly inefficient and unprofessional'.[61]

Unlike earlier times, however, the issue had not then just faded away. Next to hit the headlines was a scandal involving the European Community Humanitarian Office (ECHO), run by Commissioner Bonino, in which 500,000 *ecu* (£347,000) in humanitarian aid destined for Rwanda and Burundi had apparently been diverted by contractors to their own pockets, or passed back to the Commission.[62] The Commission's embarrassment was intensified when it was forced to cancel the results of all 30,000 candidates in its *Concours* entrance exams, after questions had been leaked and chaotic supervision led to widespread cheating.

The budget control committee then accused the director-general of administration, Stefan Schmidt, of conducting internal inquiries so close to a whitewash his office had 'lost all credibility'. They demanded that he be fired. The Parliament then threatened to delay discharge of the 1996 budget until the Commission released documents on the suspected fraud cases. When it appeared that £40 million had also gone missing from a programme designed to build relations between the EU and its Mediterranean neighbours, the committee complained that 'in 26 cases, the Commission's financial controllers have refused information or access to relevant documents or that they have not been able to locate the partners associated with these projects'.

Most damaging of all was the case of Edith Cresson, former French prime minister turned Commissioner for research and education. Summoned by the Parliament to answer questions about her relations with Rene Berthelot, a 70-year-old dentist from her home town, who had been given lucrative Commission contracts for Aids-related research, she had refused to appear, sending instead her public relations assistant, who in turn refused to answer questions.[63]

59 Van Buitenen, Paul (2000), *Blowing the Whistle – One Man's Fight Against Fraud in the European Commission* (London, Politico's), p. vii.
60 The *Daily Telegraph*, 5 February 1998.
61 The *Financial Times*, 24 July 1998; the *Daily Telegraph*, 29 July 1998.
62 The *Financial Times*, 17 September 1998.
63 The *Guardian*, 24 September 1998.

In early October, more details emerged of the ECHO scandal, with the leaking of a secret audit report. This was so withering about the lack of reliable financial record-keeping that the Parliament's EPP group voted to freeze £250 million of the ECHO budget until the Commission came 'clean on its own inquiries' into fraud and financial mismanagement.[64]

Under such pressure, Santer reluctantly conceded that he would have to set up an independent fraud investigation office. But, using tactics which were to become familiar, he then rejected MEPs' criticisms of a 'cover-up' as 'an intolerable insinuation'.[65] And while the Commission confirmed that the ECHO office had destroyed documents relating to 2,000 aid contracts worth £800 million,[66] the two Commissioners at the heart of the row, Cresson and Bonino, threatened to sue the *Financial Times* and *Libération* for defamation. UCLAF officials were also accused of conducting a 'whispering campaign' against MEPs who had worked to uncover the scandals. However the media's blood was up. Belgium's *Le Soir* caught the mood with its headline 'The Commission turns into a den of vipers'.[67] So rapidly had the crisis developed that Santer, who had been looking forward to a second term as president, looked doomed. A former Italian prime minister, Romano Prodi, was already being canvassed as a likely successor.[68]

The next came blow in November, when the Court of Auditors for the fifth year running refused to 'sign off' the EU's accounts, on the grounds that they contained too many 'irregularities'. This was followed by a claim by the Court's president Bernhard Friedmann, in an interview with *Stern*, that the scandal could destroy the EU, as he accused the Commission of telling 'untruths' over the misuse of funds.[69]

Yet more details emerged. The head of Air France, a friend of Cresson and former adviser to Mitterrand, had been employed by her in Brussels, but when he had returned to Paris, she kept him on the payroll. The regional Commissioner Monika Wulf-Mathies had appointed a close friend's husband to a £72,000 a year post in charge of 'regional issues', but he now admitted he would never have passed the usual recruitment exams.[70] Nor had the Court of Auditors finished. It branded a £600 million nuclear safety project in eastern Europe a 'dismal failure', so badly run that, by the end of 1997, only just over a third of the money had been spent, much of it going to consultants and companies which had won their contracts without tendering.[71]

Further condemnation came from an unlikely source. Clare Short, Britain's international development Secretary, attacked the EU's £2.7 billion overseas aid programme – to which Britain contributed over £530 million a year, a third of the

---

64 The *Guardian*, 4 October 1998.
65 The *Financial Times*, 6 October 1998.
66 The *Daily Telegraph*, 7 October 1998.
67 The *Daily Telegraph*, 15 October 1998.
68 The *Daily Telegraph*, 26 October 1998.
69 The *Daily Telegraph*, 13 November 1998.
70 The *Scotsman*, 24 November 1998.
71 The *Daily Telegraph*, 18 November 1998.

UK's national aid budget – as 'dreadful', ill-conceived, poorly monitored and damaging to the environment. One EU-funded project to build roads in the Cameroon had led to the part-felling of a rain forest designated a world heritage site, with mass-destruction of wildlife and the bulldozing of a pygmy village. Short's department had refused to fund the project, but it was suspected that the Cameroon government had done a deal with French logging companies versed in how to exploit EU aid funds.[72]

Only days after Short's outburst, on 9 December, van Buitenen had sent his incriminating dossier to an MEP. Rapidly circulated round the Parliament, it had caused a sensation. On 17 December the MEPs voted by 270 to 225 not to discharge the 1996 budget,[73] and then Pauline Green, leader of the Socialists, the Parliament's largest group, tabled a censure motion seeking to dismiss the Commission. But not all was what it seemed. To the jeers of colleagues, Green informed her colleagues that she would vote against her own motion, explaining that she merely wished to establish decisively whether the Commission enjoyed parliament's confidence.[74]

Three's a crowd

Although the fraud row dominated the headlines, the less dramatic but ultimately more important debate continued. In early October, to pave the way for Agenda 2000, the Commission had published a report entitled 'Financing the European Union'.[75] Its strategy was to soften up the member states for a major redistribution of contributions, by showing which countries did well from the existing arrangements and which badly.[76]

Clearly evident was the way France and Ireland benefited disproportionately from the CAP. So was the relatively low proportion of national GDP paid by Britain, thanks to the rebate, and part of the report's purpose was to focus attention on this, as a prelude to calling for the rebate to be scrapped. Predictably, Britain protested that the key figure was net contributions, which showed her faring relatively poorly. However, others also reacted unfavourably. France refused to accept any change to the financing of the CAP, Germany was adamant that she wanted her £7.8 billion net contribution reduced. The Dutch, contributing more *per capita* than any other nation, threatened a first-ever use of their veto unless their payments were reduced. Spain dismissed the report as 'this wretched document'.[77]

---

72 The *Daily Telegraph*, 2 December 1998.
73 The *Guardian*, 18 December 1998.
74 The *Financial Times*, 18 December 1998.
75 Commission of the European Communities, Bulletin EU 12-1998, points 1.5.1–1.5.9.
76 Earlier the budget Commissioner Erkki Likaanen had announced that the Commission was to discontinue publishing member states' budget contributions and receipts, on the grounds that 'budgetary flows do not capture all the benefits of membership' (answer to Caroline Jackson MEP, the *Sunday Telegraph*, 22 March 1998).
77 The *Financial Times*, 16 and 20 October 1998.

Underlining the need for 'reform', however, a Court of Auditors opinion noted the 'spectacular increase in direct aid' in the Agenda 2000 proposals. For the arable regime in particular, 'the budgetary cost would be high... putting the whole reform at risk', and the package as a whole would exceed the budget by billions of pounds if subsidies were paid at full rate to the enlargement countries.[78] Member states, therefore, agreed to conclude the negotiations as a matter of urgency, by no later than 25 March 1999, under the German presidency.[79]

Another Commission report now surfaced, on *Corpus Juris*, a proposal under relatively confidential discussion for several years to transform the EU into a 'common judicial area'. The justification claimed for this was that 'the more the borders of the single market are opened up, the more the persistence of "legal frontiers" proves disastrous'.[80] The plan envisaged setting up a powerful European public prosecutor's office, to which each country's own prosecution service would ultimately be answerable. Initially, the new office would investigate activities against 'the financial interests of the European Union', although it could later be extended to cover the whole of the EU's judicial system. As on other occasions, British ministers weakly tried to brush this initiative aside as merely 'a discussion paper', which could anyway not be adopted without unanimous agreement.[81]

The day after publication of this report, Schröder and Chirac met in Potsdam for their first Franco-German 'summit', continuing the tradition of their predecessors. They made a ritual declaration of intention to put 'fresh wind' into their alliance, but Blair had other ideas. British policy had for some time been focused on the need to drive a wedge into the over-powerful Franco-German alliance. With this in mind, on 3 December, Blair arrived in St Malo for a summit of his own with Chirac, prepared to offer one of his country's greatest assets: Britain's armed forces as the nucleus of an EU military framework.[82] Not only would this lock France into a initiative with Britain that he calculated the anti-militaristic Germany would not follow, it was also a bid to reassert Blair's claim to 'leadership in Europe', compensating for Britain's exclusion from the euro. Blair also hoped it might reduce pressure for 'reform' of Britain's rebate.

Chirac humoured Blair, joining him in issuing a joint declaration committing their two countries to the scheme, if necessary working outside the NATO alliance. Blair pronounced it 'an historic agreement'.[83] But in return he got nothing. Furthermore, following calls from Lafontaine and Schröder for an end to national vetoes over taxation, Chirac wryly observed that Britain 'must also digest this reality'.[84]

---

78 Court of Auditors. Opinion No 10/98 of the European Court of Auditors on certain proposals for regulations within the Agenda 2000 framework. Official Journal, 98/C 401/01, 22 December 1998, paras 6, 82 and 89.

79 The *Daily Telegraph*, 16 November 1998.

80 It had been published commercially in 1997. See: Delmas-Marty, Mireille (ed.) (1997), *Corpus Juris – Introducing Penal Provisions for the Purpose of the Financial Interests of the European Union* (Paris, Direction Général du Contrôle Financier/Economica).

81 The *Daily Telegraph*, 30 November 1998.

82 The *Daily Telegraph*, 1 and 4 December 1998.

83 The *Daily Telegraph*, 4 December; the *Financial Times*, 5 December 1998.

84 The *Financial Times*, 4 December 1998.

Less than a week later, Chirac and Schröder reaffirmed the closeness of their alliance with a joint letter, ahead of the forthcoming Vienna Council, demanding more co-ordination of tax and employment policies at EU level, and reductions in national vetoes. The two leaders also dropped a dark hint about Britain's rebate, calling on 'all member states to make compromises and concessions'.[85] The Franco-German axis seemed as strong as ever and it looked as if the 'big three' were set for a showdown at the forthcoming Vienna Council. However, Vienna was an anticlimax. All the EU leaders managed to do was endorse their determination to agree Agenda 2000 by 25 March 1999.

Any other big decisions were put on hold, because attention was now focused almost entirely on the landmark fast approaching when, on 1 January 1999, 11 nations would irrevocably lock their currencies together for the launch of the euro. With less than a week to go, Yves-Thibault de Silguy added fuel to the fire by claiming that Britain could not survive as a serious international power unless it joined the single currency. 'We can live without you,' he told the British people, 'but you can't live without us.'[86]

No such thing as a free launch

On 1 January 1999, more than 30,000 people joined a street party in front of the European Central Bank in Frankfurt to celebrate the launch of the euro and the first economic union in Europe since the Roman Empire. A band struck up a stirring tune to mark the historic day. Curiously, it was not Beethoven's 'EU Anthem' but *Land Of Hope And Glory*.[87]

As the new currency immediately rose in value by a cent, from $1.17 to $1.18, EU finance ministers predicted that the euro would soon rank alongside the dollar as a world currency.[88] To mark Germany's new presidency, her Europe minister Gunther Verheugen told the BBC 'normally, a single currency is the final step in a process of political integration. This time the single currency isn't the final step but the beginning.'[89]

Behind the euphoria, however, was the shadow of the approaching censure motion in the European Parliament. The Commission chose this moment to announce that it had suspended van Buitenen on half pay.[90] No one relished the idea of a leaderless Commission so soon after the launch of the euro, and Schröder offered a life-line, suggesting the charges should be investigated by an independent committee of inquiry. In a grovelling plea to the Parliament, Santer offered a 'a zero-tolerance policy against fraud'. He was ready to bear his share of responsibility 'for the crisis of confidence that has come between us'.[91]

Just before the vote, however, he reverted to type. Following a *tête-à-tête* with Pauline Green in the Strasbourg Hilton, caught on film by a German television

85 The *Daily Telegraph*, 9 December 1998.
86 The *Sunday Telegraph*, 27 December 1998.
87 The *Guardian*, 2 January 1999.
88 The *Financial Times*, 2 January 1999.
89 The *Daily Telegraph*, 2 January 1999.
90 The *Financial Times*, 5 January 1999.
91 The *Guardian*, 12 January 1999.

crew, he threatened that, if MEPs voted against any individual Commissioners, he would resign, taking his Commission with him. The gamble paid off. Reluctant to provoke such a crisis, Parliament backed away from its motion, settling instead for Schröder's suggestion of a 'Committee of Wise Men' to conduct an inquiry.[92]

The situation thus stabilised, Fischer outlined to the Parliament Germany's plans for its presidency. Referring to the launch of the euro, he said 'this act does indeed create a new political dimension. Currency, security and constitution, those are the three essential components of the sovereignty of modern nation states, and the introduction of the euro constituted the first move towards their communitarisation in the EU'. Now, he continued, 'the greatest deficits within the EU are to be found today in the fields of political integration and European democracy. How can we make headway in these areas? After Maastricht and Amsterdam, the call for a European constitution will be much louder than before.'[93] Within six months Fischer would himself be making that call in a manner which was to alter the entire character of the debate.

For the moment, however, attention was directed at a more immediate crisis, as US-led NATO forces prepared to intervene to save Kosovo from Serb ethnic-cleansing. Tension was also building over Iraq. As US and British aircraft bombed anti-aircraft installations in support of the designated 'no-fly' zones, Chirac was expressing strong opposition to the Anglo-American axis. With Blair due to meet him to discuss the crisis, Hugo Young, in the *Guardian*, offered him advice: 'What Iraq needs badly is a little creative French diplomacy,' he suggested. Chirac could offer 'a different policy', reflecting France's 'intimate commercial and political links with Baghdad'.[94]

A problem nearer home was the need to settle the CAP reforms. As final negotiations took place between EU agriculture ministers, 30,000 angry farmers converged on Brussels, giving serious work to Belgium's battle-hardened riot police. By the time the talks were over, with the French flatly rejecting cuts across the board, reforms designed to cut spending had increased it by £1 billion.[95] Britain's farm minister, Nick Brown, declared it a 'good deal for taxpayers, farmers, consumers and the countryside'.[96] *The Times* declared it 'a mockery'.[97]

Elsewhere, on 11 March, after a stormy German Cabinet meeting, Lafontaine, the chief advocate of EU tax harmonisation, resigned, to the delight of the financial markets. Having lost nearly 10 percent of its value in the three months since its launch, the euro briefly rallied to $1.10.[98]

Then, on 15 March, came the publication of the parliamentary report of the 'Wise Men' on fraud and the Commission. It was a bombshell, essentially confirming all van Buitenen's allegations. Most damning of all, the Wise Men found

---

92 The *Independent*, 13 January 1999.
93 Debates of the European Parliament, 12 January 1999.
94 The *Guardian*, 28 January 1999. After the liberation of Iraq in 2003, large caches of French-made Roland surface-to-air missiles were discovered, delivered after the UN sanctions came into force.
95 The *Daily Telegraph*, 12 March 1999.
96 The *Sun*, 12 March 1999.
97 12 March 1999 (leader).
98 The *Guardian*, 12 March 1999.

'a growing reluctance among the members of the hierarchy to acknowledge their responsibility. It is becoming difficult to find anyone who has even the slightest sense of responsibility.'[99] This was enough. Rather than face the ignominy of a vote, on the morning of 16 March the entire College of Commissioners resigned. As the news flashed round Europe, it was hailed as the EU's 'biggest crisis in its 42-year history'.[100] But, after lunch, led by Santer, the Commissioners resumed work as a 'caretaker Commission'. In terms of any fundamental change in the way the Commission conducted its affairs, their 'resignation' was to prove little more than an extended lunch break.

President Santer, however, had been fatally weakened. The Berlin European Council nine days later therefore agreed to replace him with the only formal candidate, Romano Prodi. Despite being dogged at home by persistent suspicions of corruption, for which he had twice been investigated by local prosecutors, he was universally acclaimed by the Council, not least by Mr Blair, who described him, somewhat oddly, as 'a high-quality person'.[101]

With German farmers driving 400 tractors through Berlin's streets, and 2,000 journalists in the press tent blacked out by a power cut, the Council then got down to Agenda 2000. Aznar held out for additional funding, so agreement, of a sort, was not reached until five in the morning, after a brutal 20 hours of negotiation. The Commission's original 'reform' proposals, already watered down by the Agriculture Council, had been diluted still further, making the result a travesty. Intended to cut spending, not only had it been increased, the settlement had been locked in until 2006, with a 'mid-term review' in 2002, which allowed only for minor 'course corrections'. Any idea of early enlargement seemed to have been ruled out. But at least Blair had kept his rebate.

Europe's 'Mr Clean'

Media attention now turned to the economics professor who was about to take centre-stage as the new head of the Commission. Despite his somewhat chequered past, Prodi was widely welcomed as Europe's 'Mr Clean'. What soon became rather more obvious was that he was as outspoken an advocate for integration as Delors. With war raging in Kosovo, he called for the EU to take control as soon as hostilities were over. He predicted that Britain would not be able to stay out of the euro. And he suggested to the *Financial Times* that, if Blair had hoped his St Malo defence initiative might be accepted as 'a substitute for euro membership' he was mistaken.[102]

---

99 Committee of Independent Experts, First Report on Allegations regarding Fraud, Mismanagement and Nepotism in the European Commission (15 March 1999), *www.europarl.eu.int/experts/pdf/reporten.pdf*, point 9.4.25.
100 The *Telegraph*, 16 March 1999.
101 Various allegations had been made against Prodi, of which the most serious was that in the 1980s, while prime minister, he had attempted to sell off the state-owned food conglomerate, SME, to a political crony at half the price it was worth. Italy's most successful businessman Silvio Berlusconi had stepped in with much higher rival bid, and had apparently bribed a judge to stop the Prodi deal. This had created a lasting feud between the two men.
102 The *Financial Times*, 6 April 1999.

To the European Parliament on 13 April, Prodi set out his own 'vision' of Europe. Without openly declaring it, he was preparing directly to challenge the line now being taken by Schröder and Fischer. 'The Single Market' he proclaimed, 'was the theme of the 80s; the single currency was the theme of the 90s; we must now face the difficult task of moving towards a single economy and political unity.'[103] But as he was to confirm in a series of interviews, he had no doubt as to who should lead Europe towards that 'unity'. Europe, he said, needed a 'strong government' to take 'strong decisions' and 'let's be clear', he added, 'the Commissioners have a political responsibility. They will be the government'.[104] There was no hint here of accepting a 'federal Europe constructed on German lines'.

Where there did seem to be agreement was on the prospect of a European army. Prodi acknowledged that, for the common defence policy, this was a 'logical next step'. One day it would be 'inevitable' that the soldiers of participating states should be called to fight by a European commander, under a European flag. Countries which failed to join would be 'marginalised in the new world history'.[105]

As it happened, the day after this interview appeared EU defence ministers took a further step towards a 'European Defence Identity'. They agreed, on a German initiative, that efforts to co-ordinate their military forces should make 'concrete progress' within 18 months.[106] They also agreed that the WEU should be formally absorbed into the EU.[107] Only two days earlier, Blair himself had been calling for 'greater integration in the defence industry and procurement' and, referring to the war still raging in the Balkans, suggested that 'if we were in any doubts about this before, Kosovo should have removed them'. His comments, made in Aachen where he was receiving the Charlemagne prize for his 'outstanding contribution to European unification', came during what was billed as 'probably the most pro-European speech by a British premier since Sir Edward Heath in the 1970s'.[108]

This theme was taken forward by Schröder and Chirac when they met in Toulouse on 28 and 29 May for the Franco-German summit which preceded every European Council. To Blair's dismay, they joined together in accepting the need for a separate European force – the 'Eurocorps' – suitable for rapid deployment in crisis areas or for peacekeeping missions. This Franco-German hi-jack of what he had intended to be an Anglo-French initiative largely negated his efforts in St Malo.[109] Blair was again being marginalised, this being confirmed when the two leaders also agreed that, to pave the way for the next EU treaty, it would be an error to involve all 15 governments in the early stages of the talks. The best way to proceed would be to set up a small group of 'wise men', to explore what institutional reforms were necessary for enlargement.[110]

103 European Parliament, verbatim record, 13 April 1999.
104 *On the Record, www.BBC.co.uk*, 9 May 1999.
105 The *Financial Times*, 10 May 1999.
106 The *Financial Times*, 11 May 1999.
107 The *Guardian*, 12 May 1999.
108 The *Financial Times*, 14 May 1999.
109 AFX (UK), 30 May 1999.
110 *Ibid.*

After the meeting, Schröder, Chirac and Jospin were in obvious good humour. They told a selected group of journalists that their renewal of Franco-German co-operation would be 'particularly useful when, during the next European summit in Cologne, it will be a question of advancing yet further European integration'. Schröder continued, in a further sideswipe at the British: 'it will be necessary to encourage those member states in this direction who perhaps have not yet gone as far, or do not wish to go so far on the subject of integration'.[111]

Reality gap

The Cologne European Council on 4 to 5 June 1999 provided a vivid picture of the growing gulf between theory and practice. Not least, it hailed the introduction of the euro as a 'success' when at that very moment the euro was facing its first real crisis, triggered by Italy's breach of the budget deficit limit. When Italy was allowed to increase the deficit, this raised fears around the markets that politics would be allowed to undermine the strict disciplines set for managing the new currency.[112] As a result, the euro had fallen below $1.05, bringing its loss in value to 11 percent in five months. Yet the Council proclaimed 'a stable euro will increase Europe's ability to promote growth and employment'.[113] Faced with recession and unemployment, it could only respond with platitudes about the need for 'a sustainable reduction of unemployment' and 'a decrease in the fiscal and social security burden on the labour factor'.[114]

Not for nothing did the president of the Association of European Chambers of Commerce and Industry, Jörg Mittelsten Scheid, comment despairingly that the Council's outcome had been as 'poor as expected'. It had completely failed to address the 'structural problems' which had given the EU the highest labour costs in the world.[115]

Indeed what the Council also showed was the gap between its ambitions and its capability to deliver. This was most evident when the EU leaders came to discussing their 'Common Foreign and Security Policy'. Resolving that the EU must 'play its full role on the international stage', the Council nominated Javier Solana, the Spanish director-general of NATO, as its 'High Representative': in effect the EU's first foreign minister. But it was one thing for the Council to appoint a 'High Representative' and solemnly to consider reports on the EU's expanding role in foreign affairs, ranging from 'summits' planned with Washington and Japan to a Balkan Stability Pact, whereby the EU hoped to control the reconstruction of Yugoslavia after the war had ended. It was another to recognise that the Council on its own simply did not have 'the necessary means and capabilities' to implement all its ambitious new policies.[116]

---

111 Transcript of press conference: BMDF translation, 6 July 1999.
112 The *Financial Times*, 26 May 1999.
113 The *Daily Telegraph*, 5 June 1999.
114 Presidency conclusions, European Council Cologne, 4–5 June 1999, point 6.
115 *European Report*, 12 June 1999.
116 Presidency conclusions, *op. cit.*, Annex III.

Nothing had more cruelly exposed these inadequacies than the war in Kosovo, now nearing its climax. Despite combined defence spending of £120 billion, close to 60 percent of America's, which kept more than two million troops under arms compared with the USA's 1.4 million, their 'out of theatre' capacity was less than 10 percent of America's. Thus, over the preceding weeks, it had been US bombers, with British help, which pounded Milosevic to the peace table, under the aegis of NATO, while the 'Europeans' had merely bickered over what should happen next. Britain was prepared to send in troops, Germany was not, France sat on the fence and Italy suggested a bombing pause. Austria had not even allowed NATO aircraft to use its airspace.

Nor could EU leaders deliver on their ambitions for a 'European navigation satellite system' (Galileo), rivalling America's GPS system. While the US had funded its satellites from tax revenues, giving free access to all comers, the European Council could only hope for finance 'largely from private sources', to be recouped from charging Galileo's users.[117] Similarly, although the Council resolved that the Trans-European Network should be expedited and that every school in the EU should be given internet access 'as soon as possible', its reliance on member states being willing to finance these schemes meant there was little prospect of delivery.

The only issue the Cologne Council could control was the timetable for a new treaty. Without irony, it resolved that, to ensure EU institutions could 'continue to work efficiently after enlargement', the IGC should begin early in 2000 and finish by the end of that year. It would deal with three issues, described as 'the Amsterdam leftovers': the size and composition of the Commission, which would become unwieldy if every state in an EU of 27 was allowed its own Commissioner; adjustment of Council voting to give added weight to larger states; and a 'possible extension of QMV', to reduce still further the number of policy areas on which any country could exercise a veto.

Democratic deficit

A week after Cologne came the European Parliament elections. In the UK these were the first fought under new rules, where voters had to vote under proportional representation for a 'party list' in each of the UK's 12 'Euro-regions'.

Hoping to capitalise on what they saw as the public's Eurosceptic mood, the Conservatives kept their slogan of 'in Europe but not run by Europe'.[118] But Hague was careful not to get involved in admitting just how much Britain already was 'run by Europe', concentrating his appeal on opposition to the euro. The BBC gave disproportionate publicity to a tiny 'Pro-Euro Conservative Party', set up by two former Conservative MEPs whose extreme Europhile views had discounted their re-selection. The Liberal Democrats, despite their vaunted Euro-enthusiasm, curiously concentrated their appeal on health, education and crime, the three areas of national policy least integrated with 'Europe'.

---

117 *Op. cit.*, point 15.
118 The *Daily Telegraph*, 10 May 1999.

On polling day, 10 June, the Conservatives more than doubled their representation, from 17 to 36. The UK Independence Party, committed to Britain's withdrawal from the EU, won three seats; the Greens two. The pro-Euro Conservatives failed to win even one percent. But the overall turnout of 23 percent was by far the lowest ever recorded in a British national election, and easily the lowest in the EU (although most countries also recorded their lowest ever poll at 49 percent, dropping below 50 percent for the first time).

Joining the new Parliament were two members of the disgraced former Commission, Bonino and Santer. Its first business was to approve the 20 members of the new Commission, whom Prodi presented to the MEPs on 21 July 1999 as 'Europe's government'.[119] Ten days earlier, just after he had announced their names, the *Sunday Telegraph's* Julian Coman reported that Prodi was 'planning the biggest centralisation of power in the history of Brussels politics'.[120] He was 'to model his administration on a national government', giving himself 'an unprecedented prime ministerial role at the heart of Europe, making Brussels a power to rival London, Paris and Berlin'.

Prodi had 'abandoned the collegiate idea' and aimed 'to create a European government ... set to become an aggressive promoter of causes such as tax harmonisation and a European army'. Coman did, however, suggest that Prodi's ambitions might conflict with those of France and Germany. Few could have realised just how prescient this was.

---

119 Prodi speech, 21 July 1999, *www.europarl.eu.int.*
120 11 July 1999.

Chapter 18

Which Europe?: 1999–2001

'The present generation should lay the final brick in the edifice of Europe. That is our task and we ought to get down to it.' Joschka Fischer, 6 July 2000[1]

'Europe, yes, but what sort of Europe?' Tony Blair, 6 October 2000[2]

On 15 September 1999 a vast, futuristic building on the edge of Strasbourg was the scene of an unprecedented ceremony. This £300 million complex was one of two newly built venues for the European Parliament (the other, even larger, had just been completed at a cost of £750 million in Brussels). Here politicians, officials and journalists now gathered from all over Europe to see the Commission's new President, flanked by the 19 members of what he liked to call 'my government', appearing before MEPs to be confirmed by acclamation.

Just six months after the former Commissioners had resigned in disgrace (although five had now returned), Prodi's 'coronation' was marked by a strange air of triumphalism. As speaker after speaker enthused over how the EU was about to take over most of Europe and its mission to bring peace to trouble spots across the globe, there was, as one observer put it, 'an unmistakable sense of "today Europe, tomorrow the world"'.[3]

High on Prodi's agenda, however, as he began his acceptance speech, was the need to win back all those 'increasingly disillusioned citizens' who, in June, had so conspicuously stayed away from the polls. What the people of Europe 'persist in demanding', he had suggested, were 'clear answers to the important problems in their everyday lives'.[4] To win 'their hearts and minds', he proposed that the EU must capitalise on popular issues such as the need to reassure the people of Europe about 'the safety of the food we eat'. A top priority, to show how relevant 'Europe' could be to improving their lives, must be to restore 'consumer confidence' by taking over competence for food safety from national governments.[5] Prodi's excuse for singling out this issue was the Belgian 'dioxin scandal', which for months had been making headlines as Europe's biggest food scare since BSE. It had cost Belgium's food industry £1 billion and brought down the government of

1 Speech at Humboldt University, translated by BMDF.
2 Speech at Warsaw Stock Exchange, reported by the *Financial Times*, 7 October 2000.
3 The *Sunday Telegraph*, 19 September 1999.
4 Prodi speech, 21 July 1999, *www.europarl.eu.int*.
5 Prodi speech, 15 September 1999, *www.europarl.eu.int*.

Jean-Luc Dehaene, and provided an example of the type of 'beneficial crisis' the Commission exploited to justify extending its powers.[6]

However Prodi's main theme was the challenge of 'enlargement'. This would create a need for the strengthening of the EU institutions, to allow them to rule effectively over a 'Union' which might include as many as 30 nations.[7] Two weeks earlier he had acted on a Franco-German proposal by appointing three 'eminent persons' to report on the institutional implications of enlargement: Dehaene, the defeated Belgian prime minister; Richard von Weiszacker, formerly president of Germany; and Lord Simon of Highbury, formerly chairman of British Petroleum and until recently Blair's junior trade minister.

Leaving them to their work, Prodi had then made a visit to Poland, where from the prime minister, Jerzy Buzek, he heard the alarming news that support for EU entry was rapidly declining, from 85 percent five years earlier down to 55 percent.[8] A similar message was coming from the Czech Republic and Hungary.[9] Not the least of their concerns was the need to comply with 80,000 pages of *acquis communautaire*, the financial and social cost of entry, and the prospect that, having only recently escaped from Communism, they must now take on the dead weight of another regulatory system.

So strongly was Prodi committed to bring the former Communist nations 'home to Europe', to earn his presidency's place in history,[10] that he decided the process must be speeded up. On 22 September, he proposed that, instead of just six applicants, with six more kept waiting, the EU should go for a 'grand slam'. Bulgaria, Latvia, Lithuania, Malta, Romania and Slovakia should also be invited into active negotiation, expanding the candidates to 12.[11] This had other advantages. Aware that most member states favoured a 'minimalistic' approach to the forthcoming treaty revisions, Prodi knew that a 'big bang' enlargement would increase pressure for the institutional reforms he wanted.

When his three *eminenti* presented their report on 18 October, however, they had little more to offer than had already been suggested by the Santer Commission, responding to the 'Reflection Group' report of 28 February 1996, in the run-up to Amsterdam.[12] Again they proposed a 'reorganisation' of the existing treaties, splitting them into two parts, with a 'basic treaty', amounting to a constitution, setting out the Union's institutional framework.[13] There was the now ritual call for the abolition of national vetoes, and that the two intergovernmental

---

6 What Prodi was not aware, because it had not yet come fully to light, was that the Belgian 'dioxin scandal' turned out to be a classic example of a groundless food scare. It arose when it was discovered that vegetable oil used in poultry feed had become contaminated by industrial oil, but in reality this had posed no risk whatever to human health (for full account see the *Sunday Telegraph*, 11 June 2000).
7 Prodi speech, 21 July 1999, *op. cit.*
8 The *Financial Times*, 9 September 1999. See also: 25 August 1999.
9 *Der Spiegel*, 30 August 1999; MTI news agency, Budapest, 9 September 1999.
10 *Der Spiegel*, 30 August 1999.
11 The *Financial Times*, 22 September 1999.
12 Commission of the European Communities: *Reinforcing political union and preparing for enlargement*, *op. cit.*
13 The University Institute at Florence was then asked to produce a draft treaty along these lines. It was published on 15 May 2000.

'pillars' should be brought into the Community framework, made subject to QMV. Finally the report renewed the idea of allowing 'closer co-operation' between states wishing to move towards integration 'further or faster than others'.

Rather more 'concrete' moves towards further integration had already just been proposed by the European Council. Meeting in Tampere, Finland, on 15 to 16 October, EU leaders had agreed to work towards creating an 'area of freedom, security and justice', with the aim of turning the Union into 'a single judicial space'. They also agreed a 'Charter of Fundamental Rights' to be drafted by a 62-strong Convention deliberately modelled on the Philadelphia convention which drafted the US constitution in 1787. Its members came from the Commission, the European Parliament and national parliaments.

In Britain on 14 October, before leaving for Finland, Blair had appeared on the stage of a London cinema, alongside Brown, Clarke, Heseltine and Charles Kennedy, leader of the Liberal Democrats, to relaunch with a major new propaganda campaign, Britain in Europe, to educate the British people on the 'benefits of being in Europe'.

As Blair called for 'honest, clear debate', the media were circulated with a leaflet headed 'Twenty things you didn't know about Britain and Europe'. Most were only too familiar, but such was the desperation to demonstrate the value of membership that it cited five items relating to the EU's 'generosity' in funding benefits such as 'improved fencing' on Northern Irish farms. It failed to mention that for every pound received in regional grants, UK taxpayers had to contribute up to £2 to Community funds and then another pound in match funding. Finally the leaflet suggested as another 'benefit' that more British people took holidays in Europe than anywhere else in the world.[14]

Such was the Blair's idea of an 'honest, clear debate', and so one-sided that, when the BBC radio's news programme *The World Tonight* made it the centrepiece of its evening news report, every contributor supported the BiE campaign.

'Blair out in the cold'

Across the Channel, Prodi was now focusing on two requirements he saw as intimately related, to both of which Britain presented the main obstacle. One was the abolition of national vetoes; the other was power over taxation. Speaking in Karlsruhe on 12 November, he noted the 'extreme reluctance' of some member states to give up their veto over taxation – an oblique reference to Britain's refusal to accept the 'withholding tax'. How 'much more easily' such matters could be resolved, Prodi suggested, if such a tax 'could be adopted under a QMV arrangement'.[15] With weary constancy, Prodi was using the well-tired tactic of exploiting a genuine problem (for Germany) to promote Community ambitions.

On 1 December, addressing the European Parliament, Prodi returned to the charge. 'The European tax package,' he admitted, 'is now in great difficulty.' Not

---

14 The *Sunday Telegraph*,17 October 1999. Interviewed on BBC radio, John Major suggested that another benefit of being 'in Europe' was that the British could enjoy the music of 'Bellini, Wagner and Mozart'.
15 Prodi speech, 21st Forum on Financial Policy and Taxation, Karlsruhe, BDMF, 12 November 1999.

only was it 'an important initiative to combat harmful tax competition, but also an essential piece of our employment strategy'. So impatient was Prodi at how Europe was being 'handicapped by the unanimity requirement' that he compared it to 'a soldier trying to march with a ball and chain round one leg'.[16]

Even as Prodi spoke, the value of the euro was plummeting. On 3 December it broke through the psychological barrier of parity with the dollar. The ECB's Duisenburg laid the blame squarely on Schröder and his failure to address the need for 'market reforms'. Schröder sought to shift the blame onto Blair for blocking the withholding tax. He told the German parliament, 'I make no secret of the fact that I have little understanding for such blockade tactics that place national interest above the necessary European solidarity.'[17] On the eve of the Helsinki European Council, this issue was now regarded as the 'acid test' of Blair's commitment to European integration. Still, however, Brown remained firm, saying he would be prepared to veto the proposal.[18]

The headline issue in Helsinki was the beef export ban, finally lifted by the Commission on 1 August. Both Germany and France had ignored this, refusing to allow British exports to their countries to resume, and on the eve of the Council Jospin reaffirmed the French ban. Only five years earlier, Hurd had proclaimed as one of the benefits of EU membership, that 'the French cannot block our lamb, or the Germans our beef', a claim Blair had exploited when the BSE crisis broke. Small wonder, at the pre-Council dinner, Jospin and Blair were barely on speaking terms, when Blair had made it a key new Labour policy to lift the ban.

In addition, Blair was refusing to order the proposed European heavy-lift military transport aircraft, not yet off the drawing board, in preference to well-tried and more capable US equivalents.[19] But a heavy airlift capability was an essential part of what the Council formally agreed the next day, its 'Common European Policy on Security and Defence'. To back that up, the Council wanted a 'non-military crisis management capability' to enable it to intervene in trouble spots around the world. Additionally, by 2003, it wanted 'new political and military bodies and structures', within the Council, to enable it to deploy, independently of NATO – its own 'military forces of up to 50,000–60,000 persons'. This was the so-called 'Rapid Reaction Force'. For such high-profile operations, 'national' – i.e., European – pride demanded European aircraft.

More profoundly, the French ambition had re-emerged, dressed up in 'Community' clothes, and the Community itself was dressing up its ambitions for further integration in humanitarian motives.[20]

---

16 Prodi speech, 1 December 1999, *www.europarl.eu.int.*

17 The *Daily Telegraph*, 4 December 1999.

18 The *Daily Telegraph*, 9 December 1999.

19 In terms of its specification, the A400M transport aircraft, to be built by the European Airbus consortium, would, apart from its cost, provide an unhappy compromise between the familiar US-built C130 (Hercules) and the larger C17s, both used by the RAF.

20 There was nothing to stop each or any member state, individually or collectively committing troops to the UN. But, as with so many other issues, the EU was more concerned to superimpose a 'European dimension' on member state activities.

On the tax issue, the Council *communiqué* made impatient reference to continuing failure to make progress. To resolve the problem, a 'High Level Working Group' was to be set up to investigate Britain's proposal that, as an alternative to the 'withholding tax', member states must make full disclosure of banking details to other countries' tax authorities. When Blair was then obliged to sign a 'Millennium Declaration' extolling the benefits of monetary union, *The Times* reported that it had been for him 'a bad summit in anyone's language'.[21] To the *Observer*, Blair was 'left out in the cold'.[22]

At least on some issues there had been agreement, not least on Prodi's call for six more countries be added to the accession negotiations. And it was agreed that the IGC for the next treaty should begin in February 2000. On that rocky road due to end in Nice in December Blair was already trudging a solitary path.

Prodi sets the pace

The year 2000 began with world-wide celebrations for the dawn of a new Millennium. But what few celebrated, and many were to curse was the coming into force on 1 January of regulations implementing two EC directives requiring compulsory use of metric weights and measures for goods sold 'loose from bulk'. For the British to sell each other 'a pound of apples' or 'four ounces of cheese' was now a criminal offence.

On 12 January at a press conference in London an Oxford biologist Sir John Krebs was introduced as the first head of Britain's new Food Standards Agency, long promised by the Labour Party as the 'wholly independent' body which, in the wake of countless food scares, would exercise control over all aspects of food safety law.

Almost simultaneously in Brussels, following up Prodi's pledge in Strasbourg, the Commissioner for consumer protection, David Byrne, announced that the Commission was to take 'competence' over all aspects of food safety law throughout the Union. It would set up its own European Food Safety Authority and launch 84 'initiatives', including a sheaf of new hygiene directives, to restore 'public confidence in food regulation'.[23] Just when the Blair government was proudly unveiling Britain's own agency, Brussels was thus making clear that it would have no power to act except as a branch office for its new masters. Yet, so ingrained now was the deceit that pervaded the British government, that there was no acknowledgement at all of this reality.

* * * * * *

As the new year began significant changes of mood and attitude were taking place at the upper levels of the European Union, not least among representatives of the original Six. There were fears that the 'project' was in danger of losing its way. One

21 11 December 1999.
22 12 December 1999.
23 The *Financial Times*, 13 January 2000, the *Sunday Telegraph*, 16 January 2000.

threat was the chaos which might follow from a too-hasty 'enlargement' which in practical terms was beginning to look ever more unworkable. Another was the hindrance to further integration now being posed by those foot-dragging existing members, notably Britain, who seemed not to understand what integration was about. A third was Prodi's inflated idea of his own role, with his talk of the Commission as 'my government' and his obsession with enlargement.

Behind the scenes a battle was developing, charted by Ferdinando Riccardi, editor of the respected Brussels press agency, *Agence Europe*. An associate of Prodi, he noted that 'certain heads of government had become aware of the dangers surrounding European construction', [24] and it was equally evident that they were briefing against the new president. By mid January, the *Financial Times* was reporting that 'Prodi is starting to look like a man under siege'.[25] He was not helped when former president Delors, in an interview for *Le Monde*, launched 'an unprecedented attack' on Prodi's plans for enlargement, warning that they threatened to 'dilute' economic integration and would hamper the ambitions harboured by the existing member states.[26]

Delors' solution was one he had already put forward in a speech in Berlin on 14 November 1999. 'The new treaty', he had suggested, should allow an *'avant-garde'* of nations to move ahead 'further and faster', to achieve full 'confederation' ahead of the others. This was the only way to stay 'faithful to the ideals and political thinking of the Fathers of Europe, Monnet, Schuman, Adenauer, de Gasperi and Spaak'.[27] In Helsinki this idea had been taken up by Jean-Claude Juncker, prime minister of Luxembourg. The prospect of enlargement, he warned his colleagues, raised 'the disastrous spectre' of Europe disintegrating into no more than 'a free trade area'.[28] This could only be avoided by allowing 'enhanced co-operation' between an *'avant-garde'* of 'member states prepared to go further in integration'.[29]

Subsequently other leaders, including Chirac, had also suggested that Europe could develop on two levels: an inner 'hard core' forging ahead to full integration and an outer Union of the new members, with those 'reluctant' states which had failed to join the euro. The only leaders opposed to including this in the new treaty were Spain's Jose-Maria Aznar and Blair.[30]

When Delors renewed his call for an *avant-garde* in January 2000, his intervention was overshadowed by the resignation of Kohl from the chairmanship of Germany's Christian Democrats, after he had been linked with his party's receipt of millions of pounds in political donations from Mitterand, following the sale of

---

24 *Agence Europe*, 10/11 January 2000.
25 The *Financial Times*, 18 January 2000.
26 The *Scotsman*, 19 January 2000.
27 Speech to the Aspen Institute, Berlin, 'Our Historic Challenge: The Reunification of Europe', 14 November 1999.
28 This was a recurring theme of continental politicians, as in the warning by de Silguy in his book *Le Syndrome de Diplodocus* (1996) that, if EMU did not come about, 'there would be a great danger of seeing Europe drift progressively towards a free trade zone – precisely what we have been trying to avoid for the past 25 years'.
29 *Agence Europe*, 10/11 January 2000
30 *Ibid.*

France's state-owned Elf oil company.[31] This prompted the *Sun* to reprint the famous picture of the pair holding hands at Verdun, embellished with wads of notes passing between them.

Against this background, on 26 January the Commission put forward its proposals for the IGC. Under the title 'Adapting the institutions to make a success of enlargement', it predictably urged that 'qualified majority voting should be the rule and unanimity the exception'. To keep the Commission to a manageable size after enlargement, it should either be limited to 20 members, depriving member states of their automatic right to a Commissioner, or should be split into 'two tiers'. This would inevitably mean 'a stronger President', with an inner cabinet of senior Commissioners to 'co-ordinate' the work of their lesser colleagues. Finally the Commission took on the Delors *avant-garde* agenda, by proposing that 'enhanced co-operation' could take place, as long as it was supported by eight member states.[32]

When Hague suggested in a speech in Poland that the Commission now seemed bent on producing 'the blueprint for a single European state', with 'its own government, its own army, its own taxes, its own foreign policy, its own criminal justice system, its own constitution and its own citizenship, as well as its own currency,[33] Prodi seemed eager to confirm his worst fears. Interviewed by the *Independent*, he claimed that unless the EU's larger states were prepared to join in a political union with its own army, they would 'disappear from the history books'. He emphasised that it was now the Commission which was behaving like a 'growing government' for Europe, although what caught notice was his sardonic insistence that the EU must have its own army:

'I was not joking ... If you don't want to call it a European army, don't call it a European army. You can call it "Margaret", you can call it "Mary-Ann", you can find any name ... ' [34]

Prodi went on to issue a paper setting out his Commission's 'strategic objectives' for the next five years. 'What we are aiming at is a new kind of global governance,' he explained. 'Europe's model of integration, working successfully on a continental scale, is a quarry from which ideas for global governance can and should be drawn.' And in all this, he wished to emphasise, the 'pivotal role' would be played by the Commission, which 'has always been the driving force for European integration'.[35]

'Pure Goebbels'

On 14 February, as the IGC opened in Brussels, the British government gave its own views in a 'White Paper', although this glossy full-colour brochure looked

31 The *Guardian*, 19 January 2000.
32 European Commission (2001), *General Report on the Activities of the European Union 2000* (Luxembourg, Office for Official Publications of the European Communities), pp. 7–8.
33 The *Financial Times*, 29 January 2000.
34 The *Independent*, 4 February 2000.
35 Commission of the European Communities, 'Strategic Objectives 2000–2005: Shaping the New Europe'. COM(2000), 154 final, Brussels, 9 February 2000.

more like an advertising promotion.[36] Its tone was set by a message from Blair that, 'unlike its predecessors', his government was 'unwaveringly pro-European'. Not until nearly half way through its 38 pages did it set out the government's position. This consisted not so much of positive proposals of what it wished to see included in the treaty, as merely a defensive list of items it was not prepared to give away. Britain would fight to retain the national veto over five areas: taxation, social security, defence, border controls and the budget contribution. The only other reservation was Blair's fear that an *avant-garde* might leave Britain behind. But so remote was all this from the debate now raging on the continent that one Lib-Dem MEP observed, 'no wonder our European partners sometimes think we are on another planet'.[37]

As if to confirm the unreality of Britain's 'debate', a curious row blew up four days later over a new campaign about to be launched by Britain in Europe, entitled 'Out of Europe, Out of Work'. On Friday, 18 February, in advance of the launch, headline coverage by the BBC and Europhile newspapers claimed that, according to a new study by the National Institute for Economic and Social Research, up to eight million jobs could be lost if Britain left the EU.[38] Almost immediately NIESR's director, Dr Martin Weale, angrily disowned the campaign, calling its claims 'absurd'. His institute's report had found that British withdrawal would have no long-term impact on employment. 'It's pure Goebbels,' he said, 'in many years of academic research I cannot recall such a wilful distortion of the facts.'[39]

On Monday, 21 February, the BiE's campaign was launched by Trade Secretary Stephen Byers, supported by yet another letter to *The Times* from Heseltine, Clarke and Patten. But the campaign was in total disarray. Hastily BiE published another survey from South Bank University claiming that 3.4 million jobs were related to trade with the EU, and the BBC faithfully reported Byers claiming that 'millions of British jobs depend on Europe'. It had little impact. On 22 February the BBC tried to resuscitate the drive by inviting Gordon Brown onto *Today*, claiming that '750,000 British companies export from Britain to Europe'. When government figures disclosed that the number of companies exporting to Europe was only 18,000, the campaign fizzled out,[40] leaving memories only of yet another deception.

Another telling symptom of the deception that pervaded government – although it was difficult to tell whether it was that, or self-deception – was the response of Blair and his ministers to the Lisbon European Council of 23 to 24 March. Portentously entitled 'Employment, Economic Reform and Social

---

36 Foreign and Commonwealth Office, *IGC, Reform for Enlargement: the British Approach to the EU Intergovernmental Conference*, Cmd 4595, 14 February 2000.

37 Nick Clegg MEP, the *Independent*, 15 February 2000

38 E.g., 'Eight Million Jobs Could Be Lost If Britain Quits EU', the *Independent*, 18 February 2000.

39 *Sunday Business*, 20 February 2000.

40 BiE's embarrassment would not prevent Labour spokesmen, from Keith Vaz to Peter Hain, continuing to claim for years ahead that '3.5 jobs depend on EU membership'. Blair himself in his Party conference speech on 2 October 2001 spoke of '60 percent of our trade dependent on Europe, 3 million jobs...'

Cohesion', this they claimed, would be a demonstration of how they were 'winning the economic argument in Europe'. They were persuading their partners, Blair claimed, to move away from 'heavy-handed intervention and regulation' towards a new agenda of 'jobs, competitiveness, economic change and dynamism'.[41]

It was very hard to see this reflected in a more than usually turgid Council *communiqué*, which predicted that by 2010 the EU would be transformed into the 'most competitive, dynamic and knowledge-based economy in the world'. This miracle would be achieved through such measures as 'a better understanding of social exclusion through continued dialogue and exchanges of information and best practice on the basis of commonly agreed indicators'. There was little hint of 'dynamism' in the Council's solemn resolve that 'the combat against illiteracy must be reinforced', or that a 'European framework' should be established to 'define the new basic skills to be provided through lifelong learning, IT skills, foreign languages, technological culture, entrepreneurship and social skills', complete with a 'European diploma for basic IT skills'.[42]

In fact the real drama lay in how it highlighted the rivalry now emerging between Council and Commission, as to which was the true 'government of Europe'. The decision to hold 'an annual Council to co-ordinate social and economic policies' ('the Lisbon process') was reported in a Portuguese newspaper as 'a sign of the growing influence of EU governments'. Prime minister Antonio Guterres crowed that the European Council was 'taking the lead'. Prodi was considered to be losing ground.[43] *Der Spiegel* picked up this theme, claiming that he was 'under pressure to resign'.[44] After reports of rebellions by his own Commissioners, and crisis meetings with them, it took a 'confirmation of unity' from Prodi's colleagues, after an unprecedented secret meeting when even the interpreters had been excluded, to quell the rumours of his departure.[45]

His base a little more secure, Prodi hit back, calling on France and Germany, as custodians of the 'project', to do their duty. With Schröder preoccupied with domestic affairs and the uneasy 'Left-Right cohabitation' between Jospin and Chirac giving an introspective feel to French politics, the Franco-German 'motor' was idling. Prodi challenged both French and German leaders to rev up the engine, telling *Die Zeit* 'the Germans must remember their European responsibilities', adding that 'progress is only possible when it is driven by a Franco-German initiative'.[46]

Fischer moves the goalposts

Jospin had the first opportunity to respond, when on 9 May – marking the 50th anniversary of the Schuman Declaration – he set out to the French Parliament his plans for France's presidency in the second half of the year.[47] Much of what he had

---

41 The *Economist*, 19 February 2000.
42 Lisbon European Council, Presidency Conclusions, 24 March 2000.
43 *Diario de Noticias*, 24 March; the *Financial Times*, 27 March 2000.
44 3 April 2000.
45 The *Daily Telegraph*, 6 April 2000.
46 The *Daily Telegraph*, 8 April 2000.
47 Speech to French National Assembly, 9 May 2000 (BMDF translation, 9 June 2000).

to say was pedestrian, such as the perennial need to 'avoid paralysis', by removing national vetoes and extending QMV. Jospin also threw his weight behind calls for a 'vanguard' or 'hard core' of member states. That was his answer to preventing an enlarged European Union becoming 'merely a free trade area'.[48]

But the 'big idea' was to include the new Charter of Fundamental Rights in the treaty due to be negotiated at Nice at the end of the year. The draft contained 54 articles, under such headings as 'Dignity', 'Equality' and 'Solidarity'. Included in more controversial provisions were those granting the right to 'equality between men and women' in 'all areas'; the universal right to belong to a trade union and go on strike (thus including the armed forces and essential services). All workers had to be consulted on matters affecting them in their workplace; employees, including part-time workers, had a right to paid holidays; and there was to be a total ban on employing children below school-leaving age. Most controversial of all was that any right could be suspended if this was deemed necessary 'to meet objectives of general interest being pursued by the Union'.

Based loosely on the entirely separate 'European Convention on Human Rights' agreed by the Council of Europe in 1950, France, Germany and the Commission described its Charter as 'the final transformation of European integration from its essentially economic origins to a fully-fledged political union'. As part of the treaty, overriding national law, the ultimate arbiter of the Charter's meaning would be the ECJ, directly challenging the established Court of Human Rights in Strasbourg, an international court working under the aegis of the Council of Europe. The EU was working towards its own 'supreme court', covering all aspects of national law, indeed taking a huge step towards the final goal of political integration. It was opposed by countries such as Sweden, Ireland and Britain.

Overshadowing Jospin, however, on 12 May Germany's foreign minister Joschka Fischer launched a 'ground breaking' speech at Berlin's Humboldt University, offering: 'Thoughts on the finality of Europe.' This was to open out the debate on Europe's future in a wholly new way.[49]

His speech focused on the 'historic challenge of enlargement' and the need to 'place the last brick in the building of European integration, namely political integration'. This process, he pointed out, had already begun. 'The introduction of the euro was not only the crowning point of economic integration,' he said, 'it was also a profoundly political act; because a currency is not just an economic factor but also symbolises the power of the sovereign who guarantees it.' But, with the prospect of enlargement to 30 members, it was vital to recognise that, unless the most radical changes were made, the EU would become unworkable. These must be so far-reaching that, although 'the first step towards reform' might be taken in the forthcoming treaty at Nice, this would 'not in the long term be sufficient'.

---

48 *The Times*, 10 May 2000.
49 Fischer, Joschka, Speech: 'From Confederacy to Federation: Thoughts On The Finality of European Integration', Humboldt University, Berlin, 12 May 2000. Reproduced in Joerges C., Mény, Y. and Weller, J. H. H. (2000), *What Kind of Constitution for What Kind of Polity* (Florence, Robert Schuman Centre for Advanced Studies), pp. 19–30.

It was here that Fischer began to reveal just how radical was the new solution he was proposing. There could only be 'one very simple answer' to Europe's future. It would have to become a Federation, involving:

'... the transition from a union of states to full parliamentarisation as a European Federation, something Robert Schuman demanded fifty years ago. And that means nothing less than a European Parliament and a European Government which really do exercise legislative and executive power within the Federation.'

But this was the first of three proposed 'reforms', a reform intended to solve the 'democracy problem'. He argued that, for the parliamentary structure, a choice would have to be made between the US model, with a Senate comprising 'directly elected senators from the member states', or the German federal model with its federal parliament, the *Bundestag,* and the *Bundesrat,* forming a senate representing the *Länder.* He was open as to the shape of the European executive, offering the options of developing the European council into a government, or taking the existing Commission structure as the starting point.

In his two other reforms, however, lay the nub of his speech. The federation would require the 'fundamental reordering of competences both horizontally, i.e., among the European institutions, and vertically, i.e., between Europe, the nation state and the regions'. All three could only succeed if Europe was 'established anew with a constitution' centred around an equal division of powers between the European institutions and 'a precise delineation between European and nation-state level'.

What Fischer was proposing was intended to mark a decisive break with the 'Monnet method' which had played the central guiding role through the past 50 years. This 'gradual process of integration, with no blueprint for the final state' might have been sufficient for 'the economic integration of a small group of countries', but for the 'political integration' of the whole of Europe it was no longer adequate. The Commission would no longer be able to indulge in the creeping acquisition of powers, exemplified in the open-ended process of *engrenage,* and to be able to decide where competences should rest, under the principle of 'subsidiarity'. Instead, the Commission's powers would be set in stone, and constrained. There was a crucial part of his agenda, developing a theme introduced by Schröder 17 months earlier – the *Länder's* powers would be protected from further encroachment.

Recognising that this quantum leap to full federation might be difficult for all EU members, Fischer conceded that it might it might be necessary to look to a process of 'enhanced co-operation', to produce an 'inner core'. Alternatively, 'a few member states which are staunchly committed to the European ideal' could form a new 'centre of gravity'. 'Such a group of states would conclude a new European framework treaty', on the basis of which 'the Federation would develop its own institutions, establish a government ... a strong parliament and a directly elected president'.

'Mechanisms would have to be developed,' Fischer added, to 'permit the members of the centre of gravity to co-operate smoothly with others in the larger EU.' But 'the steps towards such a constitutional treaty' required 'a deliberate political act to re-establish Europe'. And if Europe's development was to continue 'far beyond the coming decade', 'one thing at least' was certain: 'no European project will succeed in future without the closest Franco-German co-operation.'

The significance of Fischer's speech was immense, but it was not immediately understood. Few outside Germany caught the nuances of his reference to the need to protect the powers of regional governments. But, shortly after the speech, the leaders of the 16 *Länder* demonstrated how seriously they felt about change, telling Prodi they would refuse to ratify the next treaty if their powers were eroded. According to Bremen's mayor Henning Scherf, 'we have sworn to do everything in our power to prevent Germany's federal structure from being dissolved by EU centralisation'.[50]

No one was quicker to recognise the implications of Fischer's speech than the Commission, which could see at once how profoundly it challenged Monnet's central orthodoxy. Within weeks Michel Barnier, the Commissioner responsible for the IGC, responded with a paper entitled *Europe's Future: Two Steps and Three Paths*.[51]

In his paper, he outlined three options for reform. The first was Fischer's 'federal' solution, which Barnier dismissed as 'unworkable'. The second option was the 'intergovernmental' approach, with the EU run by national governments through the Council. This too was fraught with problems. The third option, headed 'Renewal of the Community', Barnier suggested, was that 'the keystone' of EU government should be a strengthened Commission, under an elected President. Unsurprisingly, this was his preferred option.

Barnier made no mention of a constitution, but the Commission's university, the European University Institute in Florence, had just delivered the draft in response to the recommendation of Prodi's 'wise men' the previous year.[52] This proposed splitting the existing treaties into two parts. One part, 'the Basic Treaty', would set out the EU's institutional framework and objectives, in the manner of a constitution. Consigned to a second part would be the rules governing specific policies, such as the CAP and the internal market. An important innovation here was that the second part might be subject to a less strict amendment procedure, one which no longer required the unanimity of an IGC summit. That much had also been proposed in a document produced in 1999 by the Institute at the behest of the European Parliament.[53]

President Chirac's third way

As these conflicting views on Europe's future began to emerge, it might have seemed timely that the EU had now acquired its own motto: *Unité dans la diver-*

50 The *Scotsman*, 27 May 2000.
51 Barnier, Michel, *Europe's Future: Two Steps And Three Paths, a personal note*, European Commission, 8 June 2000.
52 European University Institute, *A Basic Treaty for the European Union – A Study of the Reorganisation of the Treaties*. Report submitted on 15 May 2000 to Mr Romano Prodi, President of the European Commission.
53 Parlement Européen, Direction Générale des Études, Document de travail. *Quelle charte constitutionnelle pour l'Union Européenne? Stratégies et options pour renforcer le caractère constitutionnel des traités*. Série Politique POLI 105 FR, Mai 1999.

site, 'unity in diversity'. This supposedly resulted from a two-year long competition involving schoolchildren all over Europe; but it bore distinct similarity to the motto of the USA: *E pluribus unum*, 'out of many, the one'.[54]

The immediate priority was to draw up the agenda for the Nice treaty, and this dominated the final Council of the Portuguese presidency at Santa Maria da Feira on 19 to 20 June. As agreed, this was to centre on the three 'Amsterdam leftovers', although proposals for extending majority voting now covered an unprecedented new 39 policy areas, including several which were highly sensitive in terms of national sovereignty, such as taxation and social policy.[55] The Council also agreed to 'allow' the Charter of Fundamental Rights to be considered for inclusion. As significantly, it added to the three 'core issues' a fourth: that the agenda should include a proposal on 'flexible co-operation'.

To force the issue, Chirac told his colleagues that such co-operation would take place regardless, whether it was within the EU institutions or not.[56] Battle lines were being drawn. Chirac also spoke in Gaullist terms about 'decommunautarisation',[57] a typical piece of opaque but highly charged jargon which meant that the powers of the Council should be extended and those of the Commission reduced. Observers noted that, as Prodi hovered on the edge of the Feira talks, he had been distinctly marginalised.[58]

No sooner was Feira concluded than Schröder proposed that Nice must be followed by another IGC, to be completed no later than 2004, to tackle the 'big issues'. Echoing Fischer, he said that these must include drawing up a new EU constitution, to replace the existing treaties.[59] It was now clear that Nice would be only a sideshow.

Now, with France's presidency due to start on 1 July, the time had come for Chirac to make his contribution to the debate.[60] On 27 June he was in Berlin as the first foreign leader to address the *Bundestag* in the new *Reichstag* building (designed by an English architect, Norman Foster). His central message was that, once Nice had been got out of the way, then would begin 'what I call the great transition period', its chief theme being 'the initiative of those countries' who 'wish go further or faster'. France and Germany would lead a 'pioneer group' of member states, served by its own 'secretariat', in addressing 'the other institutional issues facing Europe', ranging from re-organising the treaties to clarifying the 'nature of the Charter of Fundamental Rights which I hope we shall have adopted in Nice'. When all this was complete, Chirac predicted, the governments and

54 The *Guardian*, 16 May 2000.
55 The *Financial Times*, 16 Jun 2000.
56 The *Financial Times*, 20 June 2000.
57 The *Financial Times*, 26 June 2000.
58 Under the heading 'A Prodi Problem?', Peter Ludlow, director of the Centre for European Policy Studies, observed after Feira 'there is a Prodi question, and it is most pointed at the European Council, where the Commission President seems to have little impact or none at all', in contrast to the central role played by 'Delors, Jenkins and even Santer'. 'We must hope', he went on, 'that President Prodi can win back the lost ground ... the Commission cannot simply be removed from the scenario' (quoted by *Agence Presse*, 4/5 July 2000).
59 The *Guardian*, 23 June 2000.
60 The *Financial Times*, 27 June 2000.

peoples of Europe 'would be called on to give their verdict on a text which we will then be able to establish as the first "European Constitution"'. Finally, if this 'European enterprise' was to prosper, it was 'the Franco-German friendship which we must first seek constantly to deepen'.

In his breathtaking disregard for all the accepted principles of how Europe's affairs should be run, Chirac's speech was much more aggressive than Fischer's a month earlier. Particularly glaring was the way he brushed aside not only the Commission but also all the other member states, in assuming that Europe's future should be reshaped essentially by a Franco-German alliance. Other states could tag along, but only so far as they accepted French and German leadership of his 'pioneer group'.

At least Fischer's idea of a constitution was one which sought to give Europe a new parliamentary system, and was based on the principle that there must be a clear definition of the powers remaining with nation states and regional governments. For Chirac there were no such constraints. Essentially France and Germany should decide what was to be done, according to a new form of 'intergovernmental' collaboration which gave them the primacy. Only when they and their allies had decided on the constitution they wanted would the governments and peoples of Europe be 'called on to give their verdict', in a way which indicated that there could only be one outcome.

Inevitably Chirac's proposals met a hostile response, not least from his 'cohabitees' in France itself. Foreign minister Hubert Vedrine and Pierre Moscovici, the minister for European affairs, immediately disowned them, making clear that they were in no way endorsed by the Jospin government.[61]

The first response from a member of the Commission came from Mario Monti, alarmed on behalf of both the Commission itself and his own country, Italy. Writing in the *Corriere Della Sera*, he warned that Chirac's approach posed a 'more serious and far reaching' risk than the decision to create the single currency in the 1990s. Italy, he said, should support further European integration only so long as this involved strengthening the EU institutions, such as the Commission, the parliament and the ECJ. Chirac's 'concert of nations' would not be 'based on community rules', policed by the Commission and the ECJ, which ensured that all states, large and small, were treated equally. The interests of countries such as Italy could thus be overridden, in a way which might do them 'grave damage'.[62]

Monti's concern over the danger Chirac's proposals posed to the smaller states was echoed by *The Irish Times*. This noted that, as the big countries came forward with their different visions of Europe, what they had in common was a desire to marginalise the supranational Commission, on which the EU's smaller states relied for protection. Reducing the role of the Commission, the paper argued, must inevitably lead to domination of small nations by their larger, more powerful partners.[63]

---

61 The *Independent*, 30 June 2000, AFP news agency, 29 June 2000.
62 The *Financial Times*, 2 July 2000.
63 *The Irish Times*, 1 July 2000.

In London alarm centred on France's threat 'to forge ahead with a two-speed Europe'. Under the headline 'Fast-Lane Signal Leave Britain Sidelined', *The Times* reported the fear that Britain might be left in 'the EU slow lane as other countries accelerated away'.[64] In general, Chirac's proposals were seen as not dissimilar to Fischer's six weeks earlier, and the British government's response was based on the same failure to recognise just how profoundly different the two speeches were. On a visit to Germany, Blair was reported as assuring Schröder that Britain was ready to show greater flexibility over 'Franco-German' proposals for closer EU integration, as if these were viewed by Downing Street as part of some concerted plan.[65] A rather shrewder appraisal came from the *Financial Times*:

'Chirac's speech was not the manifesto for a federal European state that many in Britain feared and some in Germany hoped for … in some important respects, Paris and Berlin are as divided about the future of Europe as they are united.[66]

Chirac's speech, the *Financial Times* perceived, was inspired not so much by ambition for European unity as by the interests of a 'Gaullist France'. What Chirac was after, it suggested, was 'not a United States of Europe but a United Europe of States' dominated by France.

When Chirac came to Strasbourg on 4 July to address MEPs on the plans for the French presidency, however, he made no reference to his 'pioneer group'. Nevertheless, Prodi lost no time in launching a counter-attack. 'The whole point of what we are aiming for at Nice and beyond', he said, was that 'with 27 or 28 more member states, the Union will need *stronger* institutions, not weaker ones':

'… it is therefore an illusion to believe that the 'Monnet method' is a thing of the past, something that could more effectively be replaced by *ad hoc* arrangements. The European Parliament, the Council, the Commission and the Court are our institutions. They provide the guarantees, the checks and balances, without which nothing lasting will be built. Because they are so essential we must work to improve them and this is the task to which we are all committed at Nice.'[67]

The *Financial Times* hailed it as Prodi's 'finest hour'.[68]

Two days later, on 6 July, Fischer came to Strasbourg, and for the first time gave a public German response to Chirac's proposals. Addressing the parliament's constitutional affairs committee, he gave full backing to the idea of a 'pioneer group' and suggested that its 'obvious core' would be the 11 members of the eurozone. Directly challenging the British government's line that joining the euro was purely an economic issue without constitutional implications, Fischer pointed out that the Maastricht treaty, creating the single currency, had been a 'quantum leap' towards federalism, imposing an inexorable 'federal logic' on its participants:

64 *The Times*, 3 July 2000.
65 The *Guardian*; The *Financial Times*, 30 June 2000.
66 The *Financial Times*, 30 June 2000.
67 Speech by Romano Prodi, President of the European Commission, 'Handing over the Torch', to the European Parliament and the Council President at the start of the French Presidency, Strasbourg, 4 July 2000 (*www.europarl.eu.int*), emphasis in the original.
68 10 July 2000.

'Let us be clear, the eleven countries in the euro have already given up part of their sovereignty. They have transferred it to the EU. Adopting the euro was a step towards a certain objective.'

Of course the best solution, he said, would be 'for all fifteen states to do their historical homework and rise to the challenge together'. But if they could not do that, the 'countries that want to proceed will march on'. He then pointedly told MEPs: 'you can't tie progress in the Union to the slowest ship in the convoy'. There could be little doubt which country Fischer had in mind.[69]

The 'slowest ship in the convoy'

The summer of 2000 had suddenly become as fraught with uncertainty over 'Europe's' future as any time since the 'project' was launched back in the 1950s. Instead of the 'project' inching forward towards its unknown goal according to accepted rules and principles, on the table were three different, fundamentally incompatible views of where the Union should be aiming for.

First there was the 'Community method' championed by Prodi and the Commission, based on Monnet's supranational orthodoxy. Second was the 'federal' solution being advanced by Germany and third, and incompatible with either, was the solution favoured by Chirac. Although its roots went back to de Gaulle's vision of a '*Europe des Etats*', it had lately developed new impetus from the growing role of the European Council as a rival to the Commission as a 'government of Europe'. Chirac's approach represented a developed form of intergovernmentalism. Because this would *de facto* be dominated by France and Germany it was to become known as the '*Directoire*', whereby the 'concert of powers' was controlled by its largest members. The term itself had been current since the late 1960s.

Markedly absent from the debate so far was any contribution from the EU's second richest country, Britain; although, speaking in Ghent in mid-June, Blair had reaffirmed his belief that it was 'Britain's destiny' to be a leading partner in Europe, playing her 'full part'.[70] Replaying a version of history that the Europhiles had so assiduously cultivated over 50 years, and thereby failing to heed Fischer's advice to 'do his historical homework', he claimed that hesitation over Europe had been one of Britain's greatest post war mistakes:

'We opted out of the European Coal and Steel Community. We opted out of the European Economic Community. We opted out of the social chapter. We played little part in the debate over the single currency. When we finally decided to join many of these institutions, we found – unsurprisingly – that they did not reflect British interests or experience.'

But just how Britain could now play that leading role in shaping a Europe which did 'reflect British interests', Blair was unable to explain. As his speech indicated, he was keenly aware that, unless he could somehow persuade the British people to

---

69 The *Daily Telegraph*, 7 July 2000.
70 The *Financial Times*, 26 June 2000.

support entry into the euro, he was destined to remain on the margin, watching the main show develop without him.

The impact of 'low politics'

Britain's isolation in the world of Europe's 'high politics' did not mean that her membership of the EU was not having an ever-growing influence on the way she was governed. When it came to 'low politics', the impact of this new system on the nation's life was becoming increasingly pervasive, as was now brought home in peculiarly symbolic fashion by an incident which took place in a Sunderland market.

On 4 July 2000, council officials, supported by two policemen, converged on a fruit and vegetable stall owned by Steve Thoburn to seize his scales. The offence for which he faced criminal prosecution was to sell his wares by the pound, as his customers preferred, rather than in the metric weights which since 1 January had become compulsory. So alien was this law that, across the country, some 38,000 traders and shopkeepers continued to sell their goods in the measures their customers understood. But this was the first time the new law had been put to the test, and it finally brought to a head the stealthy way by which, over three decades, compulsory metrication had been imposed on Britain without Parliament ever being consulted.

This was a story of two parts, beginning at the time of Britain's first application to join the EEC, which officials of the British Standards Institute saw as an opportunity to convert Britain to the continental metric system. Aware that any attempt to abolish traditional weights and measures would be unpopular, the BSI attempted to recruit support from industry. When they organised two meetings with the Federation of British Industry (forerunner of the CBI), the initial response was far from enthusiastic. Eventually, however, the FBI was persuaded to agree to a lukewarm statement supporting an eventual switch to the metric system. That was enough for the government to announce, in a written answer buried at the back of Hansard on 23 May 1965, its intention that Britain should be converted to the metric system within 10 years. What the officials were anxious to avoid was any debate or vote in Parliament. This was why in 1968, when technology minister Tony Benn confirmed to MPs that plans for metrication would go ahead, he emphasised that 'compulsion is not part of the process'.[71]

The government set up a Metrication Board, to co-ordinate the conversion, industry by industry. In 1972, the Heath government, as part of its preparations for Britain's EEC entry (and aware that the Commission was already considering a metric directive) issued a White Paper confirming its intention that Britain should fully convert to metric. But, in the late 1970s, when metrication faced increasingly hostility, Thatcher reversed its policy and in 1979 the Metrication Board was abolished.[72]

71 A political history of Britain's conversion to the metric system up to 1996 can be found in Booker and North, *The Castle of Lies*, Chapter 8.
72 Heath's White Paper justified the policy by claiming that 'two polls' conducted by the FBI had shown that conversion to the metric system was desired by industry. No such polls had been carried out.

It was here the second part of the story began, when the Commission proposed Directive 80/181/EEC, seeking to harmonise metric weights and measures throughout the Community. The only two countries seriously affected would be Britain and Ireland, since this 'one-size-fits-all' policy would force them to comply with the system long used by all other member states. In keeping with its policy, however, the Thatcher government ignored the directive, much to the frustration of British officials who were keen to see metrication completed.

In 1989 the Commission then proposed a new directive, 89/617/EEC, requiring Britain to comply with the earlier directive (this had been signed by three of Thatcher's ministers, Hurd, Lynda Chalker and Francis Maude). Metrication in Britain would thus become compulsory, backed by criminal sanctions, although, to lessen public resistance, derogations were negotiated permitting the UK to retain traditional measures, such as road distances in miles and selling beer or milk by the pint.

It took until 1995 for a series of statutory instruments to be produced, which compelled the switch to metric across much of British life, including the sale of all packaged goods. The official line, confirmed by Heseltine as the responsible minister, was that these had no connection with 'Europe' and resulted entirely from British policy dating back to the 1960s, even though the regulations were put into British law under the European Communities Act. But in the knowledge that compulsory metrication would meet with most popular resistance when applied to the sale of 'loose goods', such as fruit, vegetables and other foodstuffs, the final step was delayed until 2000.

When Thoburn became the first person in Britain to be charged under the new laws, for the crime of selling 'a pound of bananas', this made front-page news. More to the point, it did as much as any previous episode to bring home to the British people just how far their country was now subject to a new form of government, centred no longer at Westminster but in Brussels.

That was the reality of British membership of what had now become the European Union. But it must have seemed very remote to EU foreign ministers when, after a long summer break, they gathered at the spa town of Evian on 3 September, to resume discussing the Nice treaty. Britain's Robin Cook rejected the visions of 'Europe' put forward by Fischer and Chirac, telling his colleagues 'we need a strong Europe and a strong Europe needs strong nation states'. Referring to parallels now being commonly drawn between the United States of America and the need to create a 'United States of Europe', Cook curiously echoed a comment made by Gaitskell 40 years earlier, when he doubted that 'any member state would wish to find itself in the long run in the situation of California or Texas'.[73] But at least the states of America retained the power to decide their own systems of weights and measures.

A fractious autumn

With just three months to go before Nice, it was clear that not all was well in the European Union. The euro plumbed new lows against the dollar, having lost more

---

73 *Agence Europe*, September 4/5 2000.

than 27 percent of its original value. As world oil prices hit their highest level for a decade, there were widespread popular protests against record levels of tax on petrol and diesel, notably in France and Britain, scarcely helped when it emerged that EU finance ministers had agreed in Versailles on 9 September not to lower fuel taxes for 'environmental' reasons.

On 28 September all this was overshadowed by Denmark's referendum on the single currency. On an 85 percent turnout, the Danes snubbed their political, big business and media establishment in rejecting the euro by 53 to 47 percent. In Italy *La Stampa* called it a tragedy that 'a few thousand Hamlets', voting 'irresponsibly and foolishly', for reasons that were 'both irrational and foolish', had been able to weaken the onward march of integration. In Paris and Brussels, the Danish vote was taken as confirming the drive 'from countries such as Germany and France for a two-speed Europe'.[74]

With Denmark thus consigned to the corner in a dunce's cap, it was time for the main players to resume their battle. In Dresden, at a ceremony to mark 10 years of German reunification, Chirac renewed his call for a Franco-German alliance to lead a core of countries towards deeper integration after the EU had enlarged. Schröder agreed it would be the 'joint efforts' of France and Germany that would ensure agreement on essential EU reforms. Prodi, back in Strasbourg, warned MEPs that moves to strengthen direct co-operation between member states at the expense of the Commission 'undermined the democratic nature of the whole EU structure'. He suggested that the Commission should take over control of EU economic policy from the ECB, and also the role played by Solana for the Council of Ministers as spokesman for EU foreign policy.[75]

It was finally Blair's turn to enter the debate, with a much-trailed speech in Warsaw on 6 October 2000.[76] Predictably he called for an early decision on enlargement, reflecting Britain's wish to see the new member states participating in the next post-Nice IGC. Turning to EU reform, he asked: 'Europe, yes, but what sort of Europe?' He cautiously tried to pick his way between the three main contending arguments without coming down too firmly for or against any of them. He could not see any profit in 'pitting the European institutions against intergovernmental co-operation'. Certainly there was a need for a strong Commission able to act independently, because this gave protection to smaller states and allowed Europe to overcome purely sectional interests. But the Commission and the Council had different roles which should be complementary.

He then moved on to the European Council, the purpose of which, he oddly asserted, had been 'formally' laid down in the Treaty of Rome as being to set 'Europe's' agenda (originating in 1974, the Council was of course not referred to in that treaty). Blair now wanted the Council to set out an 'annual agenda for Europe' in a 'far more organised and structured way', thus effectively displacing the Commission's traditional 'work programme'.

---

74 *The Times*, 30 September 2000 (also including quotations from *La Stampa*).
75 The *Financial Times*, 4 October 2000.
76 *www.number-10.gov.uk/news.asp?NewsId=1341&SectionId=32.*

So far Blair had tried to appease both Prodi and Chirac. He then, however, rejected the calls of both Chirac and Fischer for a constitution, suggesting instead, as a partial nod to Fischer, a 'statement of principles' setting out what was best done at the European level and what should be retained at national level. He also echoed Fischer's suggestion that the European Parliament should be given a second chamber, but only to monitor the application of his 'statement of principles' and the workings of the EU's common foreign and security policy.

On the question of groups of member states moving forward together he had 'no problem'. He then contradicted the very reason why this was so constantly under discussion, by insisting that it 'must not lead to a hard core; a Europe in which some member states create their own … policies and institutions from which others are in practice excluded'. The EU was, Blair concluded, 'building a Europe of equal partners served by institutions which need to be independent but responsive and accountable'. It should aspire to be a 'superpower, but not a super-state'.

This incoherent mish-mash, plagiarised from little bits of everyone else's proposals, stuck together with a few wistful platitudes, perfectly reflected how, for decades, Britain had tried to contribute to a game she did not begin to understand. Appropriately it was hailed by Hugo Young as 'the best of British … practical, constructive, and down to the hard realistic earth'.

'His most contentious proposal was for a further downgrading of the Commission. Though this has been happening, it is not formalised. By proposing an EU agenda driven by national leaders rather than the central bureaucracy, Mr Blair is spitting on the household gods erected by Jean Monnet in 1958, but offering a route, as he believes, towards greater accountability as well as a dynamic that better reflects the power balances between the nation states.'[77]

Predictably, since it offered nothing new, Blair's contribution was ignored. A few days later, the Commission suggested that 'sooner or later' the Charter of Fundamental Rights would be turned into a legally binding document, as the quintessential component of an EU constitution. Responding to the ensuing furore, Blair's minister for Europe, Keith Vaz, dismissed the Charter as having no more legal significance than a copy of the *Beano* or the *Sun*.[78]

'We cannot do business like this'

As the deadline for Nice approached, pre-summit manoeuvring was working itself into a frenzy, with an informal European Council in the casino town of Biarritz on 13 to 14 October in order to settle the final agenda. Both representing the presidency, Chirac and Jospin had been weakened by the guerrilla warfare of 'cohabitation'. Chirac had been damaged by allegations of his links to illicit funding of his Gaullist RPR party and by the indignity of a parliamentary question as to whether

77 7 October 2000.
78 The *Daily Telegraph*, 14 October 2000.

he enjoyed immunity from prosecution as head of state. Jospin had seen his own credibility dented by scandals touching close associates.[79]

The government most under pressure at Biarritz, however, was Britain's, as she again seemed at odds with on a whole *tranche* of issues, from extending QMV and the loss of national vetoes to tax harmonisation, from the constitution to whether the Charter of Fundamental Rights should be included in the treaty. Under continuous sniping from the Conservatives, Blair pledged to veto any attempt to bring the Charter into the treaty, maintaining that it was only a 'declaration' with no legal status. Chirac responded by insisting that the legal status of the text was far from settled. 'We will be proclaiming it at Nice,' he said.[80]

Chirac had also been directing his fire at the 10 smallest countries, charging them with responsibility for the failure of enlargement unless they accepted the big countries' proposals for a smaller Commission, with fewer members than member states. The prime ministers of Finland, Sweden and Luxembourg hit back robustly, joined by Guterres of Portugal, who had earlier spoken for a smaller Commission but now declared this unacceptable. Almost all member states complained that France was conducting its presidency in a high-handed manner.[81] The 'small-fry' were beginning to stir.[82]

Britain again fell out with France for undermining sanctions on Iraq, when a Foreign Office minister Peter Hain described France's conduct in sending flights to Baghdad without UN approval as 'contemptible'.[83] There was another spat about the withholding tax and a controversy about the 'rapid reaction force' replacing NATO. France at the last moment tried to spring a 'social agenda' on the IGC. Then, with weary consistency, the British government began to signal the ground it was prepared to surrender. By the end of November it was reported that Blair was ready to give up 17 British vetoes in 12 areas of EU decision-making. There were only six areas on which he remained immovable: tax, social security, borders, treaty change, raising EU revenue and defence.[84]

Even now, Prodi was not satisfied. His 'shopping list' included abolition of the veto over taxation, social security, border controls, external trade and the EU budget. And Britain was not the only problem. Most member states were fighting to hold on to their veto in one area or another. France was blocking moves to QMV on foreign trade, fearing that French culture would be swamped by Hollywood films. Spain was holding out on regional aid, fearing it would lose billions in subsidies.

---

79 The *Financial Times*, 12 October 2000.

80 The *Daily Telegraph*, 15 October 2000.

81 The *Financial Times*, 16 October 2000.

82 Even the Euro-enthusiastic Irish were now starting to show dissent. On 18 September, Sile de Valera, Ireland's culture minister, warned that 'while the Irish government is promoting policies of decentralisation, in the European Union the opposite is taking place, with the push to closer integration'. Calling on her country 'to express a more vigilant, more questioning attitude to the European Union', Ms de Valera was supported by deputy prime minister Mary Harney, who said 'Ireland favours a Europe of nation states, not a centralised superstate or a United States of Europe' (Press Association, 19 September 2000).

83 The *Financial Times*, 8 November 2000.

84 The *Daily Telegraph*, 30 November 2000.

The Germans were worried about asylum and immigration. Prodi was gloomily forecasting a 50–50 chance of breakdown at the summit.[85]

In a bid to stave off such a humiliation, Chirac embarked on a 15,000-mile odyssey across Europe, to meet every other head of government in ten days.[86] Last on his list was Schröder. Under pressure from the *Länder* to insist on a constitution to define the division of power between the EU and the regions, his central objective was an IGC before enlargement. He was also holding out for greater voting power than France in the Council of Ministers, to reflect Germany's larger population. This was Chirac's nightmare. If he conceded, it would be politically disastrous at home. The two leaders failed to reach agreement. Ominously Chirac commented, 'A solution will come, or not come. But it can only come at the last minute, in Nice.'[87]

So, on Thursday 7 December 2000, began a summit scheduled to last three days. It was the culmination of a process formally begun in February, taking 330 hours of formal negotiation, involving hundreds of ministers and thousands of officials, watched by a similar number of journalists, many of them now present in the resort of Nice. For all this, the 15 member states had not yet reached agreement on any of the main agenda items.

In what was now almost a tradition, thousands of demonstrators gave the local riot police more practice in using tear gas. Blair might have wished for some of it inside the conference room where, right at the start, his colleagues insisted on proclaiming the new Charter of Fundamental Rights. But it was not to be in the treaty – not yet – and, although Blair refused to sign the declaration that accompanied it, he had not heard the last of it.[88] He gained another early success, of sorts, when his colleagues agreed that NATO should remain the cornerstone of Europe's defence. And they agreed that some of the candidate states could become members by mid-2004.[89] But before the leaders got down to the main agenda, 'institutional reform', there was still that central issue – the date of the next IGC.

Despite Blair's Warsaw speech, opposing an EU constitution, he was one of the first to agree to the German demand for a summit by 2004, on the basis that by then the first new entrants would have been admitted. Putting the best gloss he could on his climb-down, he told waiting journalists, 'I don't think we've got anything to fear from that. There is much for us to gain from a conference that sets out clearly where it is that the Brussels Commission operates and where it doesn't.' Hungary's foreign minister was not the only one to voice concern: 'We wouldn't want to see a date set for the next IGC … we want to be involved fully, having equal rights.'[90]

For Blair, however, things were to get worse. Having spent months building alliances so that he would not become 'isolated in Europe' like his predecessors, he

---

85 The *Daily Telegraph*, 1 December 2000.
86 The *Financial Times*, 1 December 2000.
87 The *Financial Times*, 3 December 2000.
88 The *Guardian*, 8 December 2000.
89 The *Financial Times*, 8 December 2000.
90 The *Financial Times*, 8 December 2000.

suddenly became just that. Ally after ally deserted him. Denmark, Britain's leading supporter in stopping harmonisation of social security, backed down after being offered a compromise. Germany, meanwhile, appeared ready to drop its veto on asylum policy, and Sweden edged away from its support on taxation. A senior EU official said the 'moment of truth' had arrived for Blair and other leaders if they were not to block the treaty.[91]

As the summit entered an unprecedented fourth day, a Sunday, tempers were beginning to fray and seasoned summit-watchers were predicting that discussions could fail. One blockage was over re-allocation of voting rights, and the first attempt by France had triggered a mutiny among the smaller countries who believed they were being disadvantaged against Germany, France, Italy and Spain. Furthermore, there was dissatisfaction amongst the accession countries, particularly Poland, which had the same population as Spain yet was to get fewer votes. Nor had Germany got a bigger share of votes than other large countries.[92]

News then began to trickle out of a 'furious confrontation' between Blair and Chirac. The French president, in a move which had 'infuriated and shocked the British delegation', had produced a revised treaty draft which included abandoning the veto on tax and social security. The British spokesman emerged after six hours of discussions to give a strongly worded warning that Blair would wield his veto unless the proposals were abandoned. For once, Blair was not alone. Portugal's Guterres condemned the draft as 'an institutional *coup d'état*' and Ireland's Bertie Ahern was described as going 'ballistic'.

Others were equally unhappy about the voting system. Britain, Spain, Germany, Italy and France had all increased their share of voting power in the Council, but small and medium-sized member states had suffered painful reductions. The Portuguese foreign minister described this as a 'humiliation' and protested: 'our votes are being confiscated'. Negotiations were described by one delegate as 'hand-to-hand fighting', as battle was being fought by a coalition of smaller states, fighting to recalculate their shares. Other stories filtered out about Chirac's 'high-handed behaviour', most notably when he shouted that one of Prodi's aides should not have been allowed to enter the room. When Chirac ordered him out, Prodi was reported to have rejoined, 'I see my civil servants wherever I want and whenever I want.'[93]

The summit was deteriorating into bad-tempered chaos, at times verging on the farcical, as when Chirac put forward proposals which were then promptly vetoed by his own government. 'If this is what a Europe run by the so-called big member states, rather than the Commission and the EU institutions, looks like, we want no part of it,' a senior Finnish diplomat observed.[94]

Eventually, agreement of a sort was reached, despite a Portuguese official complaining, 'this is a profoundly negative treaty that cannot be accepted. It hands power over to the big countries'. The final resolution had delegates turning to

91 The *Daily Telegraph*, 9 December 2000.
92 The *Financial Times*, 10 December 2000.
93 The *Sunday Telegraph*; the *Sunday Mirror*; the *Observer*, 10 December 2000.
94 The *Observer*, *op. cit.*

pocket calculators and computer spreadsheets to decipher complex proposals on voting rights. It worked out that future decisions by qualified majority vote would require a 73 percent share of the total votes, plus a 62 percent minimum representation of the total EU population. Britain would hold 14 percent of the vote.

After all the hyperbole, the final draft maintained voting parity between France and Germany, giving them each 30 votes, along with Britain and Italy. The Netherlands and Poland, two of the fiercest critics of an earlier draft, both won increases. Chirac got his 'enhanced co-operation' and British officials claimed a victory when QMV on tax and social security was dropped. Schröder, despite describing the proceedings as 'utter chaos', got his commitment for an IGC in 2004.

Provisionally, there would be four points on the agenda for the next IGC: the Charter of Rights; simplification of the treaties; clarification of 'competences' between the EU and member states; and a possible second chamber to include representatives of national parliaments. Nevertheless, the underlying feeling had been that the French had made a mess. The 3,500 journalists from across the EU dubbed it 'nightmare in Nice'.[95]

Despite that, it was a confident Tony Blair who reported back to the Commons, defending his decision to surrender some veto powers. Arguing that the new treaty would produce a 'more rational way of decision making', he batted away attacks from Hague that the government had signed up to 'three more major steps to a European superstate'. Hague nonetheless pledged that an incoming Conservative government would not ratify the treaty as it stood, and challenged Blair to hold a referendum on ratification. Blair had 'signed away' Britain's veto in 23 areas, giving European institutions an opportunity to impose further integration against Britain's will. Responding, the prime minister mocked the Tories for a stance which would endanger enlargement, describing Hague's proposal as 'idiocy'.[96]

It was left to Francis Maude, a signatory to the Maastricht Treaty, to tell the *Today* programme: 'what's so disappointing about all this is it all goes in one direction. It is all more political integration, deepening and tightening the integration of Europe, which is the wrong agenda'. Already, however, attention was turning to the next IGC.[97] Blair claimed this would be an opportunity for some of the powers currently exercised at a European level to be repatriated to EU member states.[98]

According to the *Financial Times*, however, there was a growing recognition, in Berlin and Paris as well as in London, that 'transfers of sovereignty' were reaching their popular limits. An opinion poll commissioned by the French foreign ministry, published in *Le Figaro* on the eve of Nice, it showed that 53 percent in France, 56 percent in Germany, and 67 percent in the UK felt national sovereignty should be maintained, even if this meant limiting EU powers. In Sweden, five years after she had joined the EU, voters opposed to EU membership out-

95 The *Daily Telegraph*, 11 December 2000.
96 The *Guardian*, 11 December 2000.
97 The *Daily Telegraph*, 11 December 2000.
98 The *Financial Times*, 11 December 2000.

numbered those in favour, by 43 to 37 percent. Nice had done nothing to resolve the underlying tension between member states. Apart from fiddling with voting weights, all real decisions had been postponed.[99] Prodi was unrepentant. 'I cannot hide a certain dismay that we didn't achieve more,' he said. All Blair could say was, 'we cannot do business like this in future'.[100]

Hangover

For some time into the new year, an air of exhaustion fell over those responsible for guiding the 'project'. After the trauma of Nice, they were aware that just over the horizon was that much more important IGC which by 2005 would give 'Europe' a constitution. They were equally aware that hanging over them was that Damoclean sword of enlargement. Unless by then the constitution was agreed, the new members would be entitled to take part in its drafting, with veto power. Much of 2001 would thus be taken up with the main players simply restating the positions they had laid out in 2000.

In late January Schröder looked forward to a Europe where decisions on tax, defence, health and a plethora of other key policies would be 'defined by the EU and not national governments'. He was supported by Prodi, who warned that intergovernmental co-operation was merely 'a recipe for mutual mistrust between member states'. He in turn was supported by Fischer, who pledged that Germany would 'take courageous steps against the centrifugal forces of the intergovernmentalists'.[101]

Meanwhile, as Germany's economy continued to decline, despite being aided by the weakness of the euro, the days of her 'economic miracle' seemed a distant memory. But the first country seriously to collide with the system now governing the eurozone economies was Ireland. On 24 January Pedro Solbes, the Commissioner for economic and monetary affairs, reprimanded Dublin for making inflationary tax cuts and threatened sanctions unless steps were taken to curb public spending.[102]

In February, Commissioner Barnier announced that the December European Council planned for Laeken, near Brussels, would be the moment when the EU must decide whether it was going to adopt a constitution.[103] Prodi urged 'a frank and fundamental appraisal' of the EU's ultimate purpose, asking MEPs: 'are we all clear that we want to build something that can aspire to be a world power ... not just a trading bloc but a political entity?'[104] Visiting London, Prodi met Blair and lunched with journalists in the House of Commons, to press home his message that Britain's economy could not remain successful so long as she remained outside the euro. 'How can you control your economy being surrounded by the euro and not having your man inside the European Central Bank?' he asked. As for

99 *Op. cit.*
100 The *Financial Times*, 12 December 2000.
101 The *Scotsman*, 23 January 2001.
102 *The Irish Times*, 8 February 2001.
103 The *Financial Times*, 7 February 2001.
104 The *Financial Times*, 14 February 2001.

Blair's pretensions to be at the heart of Europe, he said, 'if you stay out, that's your choice, but you can't then pretend to be in'.[105]

Prodi then took command of the wider EU agenda in a way which was to have huge impact on subsequent events, although at the time his action was scarcely reported. Touring central Europe, he told the Czechs that a 'very probable' date for enlargement was 2004.[106] This would effectively bring forward accession by a year. Unless the timing of the IGC itself was brought forward, the new members would have to be included in the negotiations, with veto power over the constitution. And the fractious issues of CAP reform and regional funding still remained unsettled.

By this time, however, the eyes of Europe were on a crisis which was overshadowing Britain. What few realised was how far it represented a massive failure of the new EU system of government.

An unnecessary crisis

On 19 February 2001, a new strain of foot and mouth disease, Pan-Asian O, was identified in pigs in Essex. Within 10 days, the virus had spread through sheep, cattle and pigs, right down the west side of England, from Cumbria via the Welsh borders to Devon. It was already clear that Britain's farmers faced the worst epidemic of the disease on record.

The timing of this disaster could not have been more unfortunate. Britain's farming industry, once the most efficient and successful in the EU, had already been plunged into the worst depression in its history. Almost every sector of British farming was struggling for survival. The core problem was that UK farmers were unable to compete with the much more highly subsidised farmers of countries such as France and Ireland, whose governments used the CAP so much more effectively in their own national interest. The average subsidy to Irish farmers was twice that received by their British counterparts and France alone was exporting twice as much food to Britain as Britain could sell to France. As a result, 25,000 British farmers were now leaving the industry each year. Since the Second World War, the year when average farm incomes in the UK were in real terms at their highest was 1973, the year of entry to the CAP. Now at last the price was having to be paid for decades of having to hand over twice as much to subsidise farmers in other EU countries as British farmers got back in return.

When the foot and mouth disaster struck, however, what also soon became clear was that the government was not remotely prepared for an epidemic on this scale. As ministry officials began to order huge pyres of dead animals and to designate '3 kilometre protection zones' and '10 kilometre surveillance zones', baffled vets wondered why they seemed to be ignoring every recommendation of a report drawn up after Britain's previous epidemic in 1967 to 1968.

What only gradually emerged, because politicians of all parties were at pains not to advertise the fact, was that during the 1980s, under Directive 85/511, poli-

---

105 The *Guardian*, 16 February 2001.
106 *AFX Europe*, 5 April 2001.

cy on the handling of foot and mouth disease had become a Community competence. The UK government no longer controlled FMD policy. The innovations which puzzled local vets, such as the need to ask the ministry for permission to slaughter and the ban on burying animals on-farm, all derived from EU legislation. By mid-March, when outbreaks topped 300 and were doubling every 10 days, the epidemic was so out of control that a new policy was ordered: a 'pre-emptive cull', under which millions of healthy sheep, cattle and pigs were to be slaughtered simply to prevent the disease spreading. Not only was this against British law (the 1981 Animal Health Act only allowed the killing of infected animals or those directly exposed to infection). It was 'recommended' by inspectors of the EU's Food and Veterinary Office in Dublin, on a visit to Britain between 12 and 16 March.[107]

By now the world's leading veterinary scientists, including Professor Fred Brown, an Englishman working for the US government, and Dr Simon Barteling from Holland, were asking why Britain had not launched an emergency vaccination programme, which could bring the epidemic to a halt within weeks, making the mass-slaughter unnecessary. Until 1990 routine use of vaccination on the continent had eliminated foot and mouth. But it had then, on a British single market initiative, been prohibited by another Directive, 90/423. Nevertheless this recommended use of emergency vaccination when an epidemic ran out of control. Dr Barteling had co-ordinated the drafting of 90/423 and was adamant that the crisis in Britain now met all the criteria which should make vaccination mandatory.

The full story of why Britain had been so ill-prepared for the 2001 epidemic, and why vaccination was not used (although the EU allowed its use to end a smaller, simultaneous series of outbreaks in Holland), only emerged long after the epidemic was over. In 1991, the Commission had instructed member states to draw up contingency plans for any reappearance of FMD and in 1992 had approved these without proper examination. That submitted by Britain had been inadequate, allowing for no more than 150 outbreaks.[108] In 1998, after the EU itself had used emergency vaccination in the Balkans to prevent the new Pan-Asian O strain crossing its borders, the Commission had advised member states to take additional measures 'to prevent a local outbreak becoming a disaster'.[109]

In 1999 it warned that the risks of 'a very large outbreak' in the EU were now 'extraordinarily high' and laid down 10 criteria to guide member states as to when

---

107 The precise recommendation was to 'consider preventative slaughter in certain circumstances in an attempt to "get ahead" of the disease, and to reduce the weight of infection to which the animals are being exposed'. European Commission, Heath and Consumer Protection Directorate. DG (SANCO)/3318/2001-MR final, point 9.1.

108 Based on the assessment of threat determined by the Commission. See Commission working documents VI/5211/95 (Contingency plans for epidemic diseases) and VI/6319/98 (Guidelines for FMD contingency plans in non-vaccinating countries) (redesignated XXIV/2655/1999). The working basis was confirmed by the Commission in its written response to the European Parliament Temporary Committee of Inquiry, Document SANCO/10018/2002 – Rev. 2, Section C. Q3, p. 18.

109 European Commission. Strategy for Emergency Vaccination against Foot and Mouth Disease (FMD). Report of the Scientific Committee on Animal Health and Animal Welfare. Adopted 10 March 1999.

to use emergency vaccination. Within days of the epidemic breaking out in the UK in 2001 at least seven of these criteria had been met. But so totally unprepared was the ministry to meet the epidemic in the way recommended that vaccination was out of the question. On 10 April Commissioner Byrne told agriculture ministers in Sweden that, although there could be no change in policy until 'the present crisis is over', vaccination would play a central role in tackling any future epidemic.[110]

Both London and Brussels had been so hopelessly caught out that they kept very quiet about the extent to which this disaster had stemmed from a massive system failure, costing Britain and the EU at least £8 billion, devastating Britain's rural economy and, incidentally, forcing Blair to postpone a long-planned election campaign. In 2002 the Commission introduced a new directive to ensure that any future epidemic was controlled directly by Brussels, relying on vaccination as its main strategy. In the meantime, however, the only real success chalked up by Britain's 2001 epidemic was how effectively the British people were kept in the dark over the fact that foot and mouth was no longer a 'competence' of their own government. 'Hidden Europe' had won another victory.

The dance continues

On 8 May 2001, at a conference of Europe's left-wing parties in Berlin, the German SPD came up with what was known as the 'Schröder Plan'. This called for a constitution to restructure EU institutions, turning the Commission into a strong executive, but controlled by a Council of Ministers transformed into a 'chamber of European states'. Some responsibilities, including those for agriculture, should be repatriated. This 'hyperactivity', commented the *Financial Times*, reflected the pressure from the leaders of the *Länder*, such as Stoiber, to prevent the EU gradually extending its power at their expense.[111] Belgium's prime minister Guy Verhofstadt, on the other hand, feared that the EU might be dominated by a *'directoire'* of larger states.[112] Italy's prime minister, Giuliano Amato, called for greater public debate to prevent the EU's future being shaped just by national 'elites'. Initial opposition to the Schröder Plan came from Sweden and Denmark but eventually no one was to prove more hostile than the French, as chief champions of both the *'directoire'* model and the existing CAP.[113] The response from Chirac, now faced at home with a threat of impeachment for alleged corruption when he had been mayor of Paris, was to repeat his call for a constitution reconstituting the EU as 'a federation of nation states'. Giscard d'Estaing suggested that the EU should regroup round its six original members, or at most the countries of the eurozone, with a looser structure to accommodate the remainder when the EU enlarged to 27 or more members.[114]

Pressure from the applicant countries was mounting, as when Poland's prime minister, in Brussels on 22 May, announced that his country's target-date for entry

110 *The Irish Times*, 11 April 2001.
111 1 May 2001.
112 *Ibid.*
113 The *Guardian*, 7 May 2001.
114 The *Financial Times*, 10 May 2001.

was 2003.[115] But the EU's Eurobarometer polls were now showing how little public support there was for enlargement across the EU, with only 34 percent in favour.[116] And growing popular distrust of the EU itself was reflected in a second Danish referendum on the euro, which on 7 May confirmed the verdict of the first when, on an 88 percent turnout, the Danes again defied their establishment with a 53.1 percent vote against entry.[117]

Back in Britain, where the foot and mouth epidemic was at last receding, Blair was preoccupied by his election campaign, with polling due on 7 June. Labour's manifesto, 'Ambitions for Britain', made no mention of a European constitution or further integration; but Hague's Conservatives were equally silent. Many Tory activists were frustrated by their party managers' decision that any reference to 'Europe' must concentrate solely on endless repetition of the mantra about 'saving the pound', but this failed to strike any chord with the voters (since the decision was to be put to a referendum, it was not an election issue). When, 10 days before polling, Prodi called for Brussels to be given power to levy a 'Eurotax', to make its citizens 'feel more connected to the EU democratic process',[118] this did cause a *frisson* of excitement in Britain, with Hague claiming that Britain was set to lose ever more of its rights and powers. But Blair insisted that Britain could 'win the argument' if it stuck to his policy of 'constructive engagement'.[119] On 7 June, he stormed to a second overwhelming victory, prompting Hague's resignation as Conservative leader. Politicians and officials across Europe welcomed Blair's victory as a sign that Britain had rejected Euroscepticism. Blair hinted at an early referendum on entry to the euro.[120]

Any euphoria in the 'European camp', however, was diluted by the news, a day later, that Ireland had rejected the Nice treaty, with a 'No' vote of 53.9 percent, albeit on a mere 32 percent turnout. Gone were the days when, as proportionately the largest beneficiary of Brussels *largesse*, the Irish had been the most enthusiastic 'pro-Europeans' of them all. They were fearful of the EU's growing power to interfere in their lives, not least through its control over their economy through the euro, and aware that enlargement threatened their CAP and regional funding. Prodi merely saw the vote as underlining the need 'for greater efforts from all of us to explain Europe to our citizens'.[121] There was no question of renegotiating the treaty.[122] Ireland's prime minister Ahern immediately announced plans for another referendum. Having delivered the wrong result, the Irish must now try again.

So it came to 15 June when EU leaders, in sombre mood, met at Göteborg, for the concluding European Council of a lacklustre Swedish presidency. A leading Dutch politician admitted privately that his country would also have rejected Nice

115 *TV Polonia*, Warsaw, 22 May 2001.
116 The *Scotsman*, 10 May 2001.
117 The *Financial Times*, 8 May 2001.
118 *AFX (UK)*, 29 May 2001.
119 *Op. cit.*
120 The *Financial Times*, 9 Jun 2001.
121 The *Herald*, 9 June 2001.
122 The *Guardian*, 9 June 2001.

had it held a referendum.[123] The Council agreed that enlargement was 'irreversible',[124] but achieved little else. Outside, 15,000 protestors ran amok, with 43 injured and one killed by the police.[125]

Immediately afterwards, Ireland began to receive a stream of high-level visitations from EU dignitaries and MEPs, leading *The Irish Times* to comment, 'they tour EU capitals much as our Cabinet tours the provinces'.[126] When Prodi himself, on a four-day 'listening tour', met leaders of the 'No' campaign, they were not impressed. 'For a listening exercise, he did quite a lot of talking', said one campaigner afterwards.[127]

It was now Belgium's turn to assume the EU presidency, its fervently integrationist prime minister, Verhofstadt, declaring that its most important achievement would be the 'Laeken Declaration' on the constitution at the end of the year. As another Eurobarometer poll showed that only 45 percent of the EU's population now believed that they benefited from EU membership,[128] the Commission, on 25 July, published a long-awaited White Paper on European Governance, setting out Prodi's plans for 'reform' of the EU.[129] This was little noted by the British media, apart from the *Daily Telegraph's* Ambrose Evans-Pritchard. He wrote that its proposals constituted not so much 'reform' as a 'revolution'.[130]

'Networking': the Commission's secret weapon

The White Paper on European Governance was one of the most remarkable documents the Commission had ever published. It represented input not just from the Commission's own staff but from hundreds of academics part-funded by Brussels in universities across Europe. Its purpose was to set out a strategy whereby Europe's 'government' could use its existing powers under the *acquis* to expand its hold over national governments and the lives of hundreds of millions of citizens.

The first issue the paper confronted was the EU's 'democratic deficit': the mounting evidence that the steady march of integration was leaving 'the peoples of Europe' behind. The Commission feared that, unless they were engaged more fully, they might eventually rebel.[131]

The problem, the paper argued, was that there was no genuine European '*demos*'. There was no sense among the EU's individual citizens that they shared the same collective identity. The answer to this must be to create a *demos*, not at an individual but on a collective level, by recruiting support from all the mass of

---

123 The *Irish Independent*, 18 June 2001.
124 Presidency Conclusions, Göteborg European Council, 15–16 June. Bulletin 18.06.2001.
125 The *Financial Times*, 18 June 2001.
126 16 June 2001.
127 *Op. cit.*
128 *De Standaard*, 18 July 2001.
129 COM(2001) 428, Brussels.
130 28 July 2001.
131 Farage, N. (2002), *Democracy in Crisis – The White Paper on European Governance*, Occasional Paper No. 44 (London, The Bruges Group), p. 10.

representative bodies making up what the Commission called 'organised civil society'.[132] These included anything from regional and local authorities to trade unions and trade associations, from churches to women's groups. More than ever, the aim should be to foster Europe-wide 'networks' linking such organisations together, to build up a sense of 'European identity'. Thus could be created a 'transnational political space', free of national loyalties. The aim was to move from 'representative democracy' based on nation states to an EU-wide 'consultative democracy'.

The White Paper's second aim was to suggest ways in which the Commission itself could extend its controlling role in the life of nation states without this being too obvious. One of these was to continue setting up a network of agencies, such as the Food and Veterinary Office, the European Food Standards Authority, the Medicines Evaluation Agency, the Air Safety Agency, the Maritime Safety Agency, through which the Commission could direct and supervise the work of existing national officials, with the added advantage that their salary bill would be picked up by national taxpayers. The Commission would shortly be unveiling a plan whereby the Brussels Commissioner responsible for enforcing competition policy would be able to recruit teams of national civil servants, continuing to work in their own home ministries, but now taking their orders directly from his office. Again the advantage was that their salaries would continue to be paid by national governments, while few would be aware that these national officials were no longer answerable to their own government but to Brussels.

This reflected a third aim of the White Paper, which was that the Commission must increasingly take over from national governments the role of enforcing EU legislation: even if, again, this was done by subordinating national enforcement bodies to the direction of a Commission agency. An example of this to be unveiled in 2002 was a proposal that enforcement of the Common Fisheries Policy should become the responsibility of a European Fisheries Agency. This would have the power to direct the work of national fisheries protection vessels (in Britain's case ships of the Royal Navy), by installing on board an agency official, of a different nationality, with authority to give the captain orders.

Just as remarkable as the White Paper's contents was the method by which it was drafted, through that Europe-wide network of academics whose background role in the work of the Commission was one of the least widely recognised features of how it operated.[133] We have already seen how a crucial part in drafting the Commission's legislation was played by such academics, recruited through hundreds of educational programmes part-funded by Brussels. Central to these was the 'Jean Monnet Project', co-financing 2,319 university teaching schemes across Europe to 'promote European integration'. This had created 491 Jean Monnet Chairs, 102 of them in British universities. Forty-seven universities by 2001 boasted 'European Centres of Excellence', more than a quarter of them in Britain.[134]

---

132 Prodi speech: European Parliament, Strasbourg, 4 September 2001.

133 Much of the background work was carried out by the Commission's own 'think tank', the Forward Studies Unit, headed by two academics.

134 *europa.eu.int/comm/dg10/university/ajm/index_en.html*.

Not only did these and similar schemes provide the Commission with a vast pool of assistants for its own work, but again Brussels was able to get their services on the cheap. The Commission's own grants lasted only three years. But to win them the universities had to guarantee the projects would remain in place for at least four more years.

9/11: A beneficial crisis

On 11 September 2001 New York's World Trade Centre was destroyed by the most dramatic terrorist atrocity in history. In an unprecedented demonstration of solidarity, *Le Monde* proclaimed '*Nous sommes tous Américains*',[135] while the US declared war on the 'Axis of Evil' and prepared to launch military action against Afghanistan, where the fundamentalist Islamic Taliban had harboured the *al-Qa'ida* terrorists responsible. Blair set out on a tour of world capitals, building support for an American-led alliance against terrorism, acting like a US ambassador. Prodi flew to meet the presidents of the USA and Russia, calling for 'international solidarity'. Ostensibly, Europe stood at one with the United States.[136]

The reality was different. Before '9/11', the EU had been starting to shape a distinct 'European' voice on foreign policy issues, not least on the Balkans. But this fragile accord was now unravelling. Power had gone back to capitals, a Commission official complained. 'We have lost the diplomatic initiative.' There were complaints that Prodi had failed to take the lead.[137]

Prodi took this to heart. In a speech on 11 October, he predictably called for more integration. The crisis, he said, had highlighted 'the need for action at a higher level than the national one', calling again for a convention to prepare for EU reform.[138] To reinforce his message, Delors and 12 former European Council members – including Kohl and Dehaene – intervened, pressing for 'a new political project' to 're-float the EU'. Their manifesto entitled 'Let us shake Europe awake' was handed over in front of cameras to Verhofstadt, as EU president, and Prodi. It was no surprise that one of the main elements of the manifesto was a call for an *avant-garde*, although this reference was missing from the English text.[139]

Despite this plea, centrifugal forces were pulling against the integrationists. An informal European Council had been called for 19 October, in Ghent, but to the consternation of Prodi and the fury of the smaller member states, it was upstaged by the 'big three', Blair, Chirac and Schröder, holding their own 'mini-summit'. Theirs were the three nations asked by America to contribute militarily to the fight against terrorism. EU officials were 'disturbed' by this development. Prodi remarked pointedly, 'Where the Commission has a presence, that is where Europe is.'[140] To *Corriere Della Sera*, the Afghan war was breathing new life into the *directoire*.[141]

135 13 September 2001.
136 The *Guardian*, 8 October 2001.
137 The *Financial Times*, 15 October 2001.
138 The *Financial Times*, 12 October 2001; the *Guardian*, 18 October 2001.
139 *De Standaard*, 16 October 2001.
140 The *Independent*, 19 October 2001.
141 19 October 2001.

Attempting to paper over the cracks, the Council unanimously pledged its 'full support' for action in Afghanistan, calling for the *al-Qa'ida* terrorist network to be eliminated.[142] Rancour at having to watch from the sidelines was palpable. However, the crisis did provide the excuse for moves on the internal integration front. The Council dusted down the 'Tampere programme' for an EU-wide system of internal security and justice, which for two years had lain on the shelf. As an EU 'action plan' against terrorism, it launched no fewer than 79 initiatives, including several controversial proposals from Tampere, such as a European arrest warrant.[143] For the integrationists, '9/11' was proving to be the most useful 'beneficial crisis' of them all.

Prelude to Laeken

With the Laeken Council approaching, the next two months were dominated by the jockeying of the main players, each pushing their own agenda. On the sidelines of the Ghent Council, a curious spat had taken place between Verhofstadt and Prodi, reminiscent of the *froideur* between Thatcher and Delors in 1988. During the Council press conferences Prodi complained of Verhofstadt 'hogging' the limelight, to such extent that Prodi had absented himself from the final conference in protest.[144] Commentators saw this as a reflection of the Commission's waning influence,[145] and Prodi issued a statement threatening to boycott Laeken unless it was resolved.[146]

For a while, it was 'open season' on Prodi in much of the European media, but he was soon back on the attack. Europe, he told an Italian paper, must 'speak with one voice' if it wanted to be a leading player on the international stage, and that 'voice' had to be the Commission.[147]

Interestingly, although this was supposed only to be decided at Laeken, Prodi also announced that a convention to draw up a constitution would start 'early next year'. National governments would have to agree this prior to the entry to the EU of its new members, 'scheduled for spring 2004'.[148] Despite Laeken still being two months away, it seemed that, behind the scenes, both the decision to hold a constitutional convention and the accession date of the new members had already been fixed.

None of this as usual was noted by the British media, more interested in a belated attempt by Blair to re-establish his 'leading role' in Europe by summoning a 'council of war' at Downing Street, in anticipation of a ground offensive in Afghanistan. This impromptu 'summit' on 4 November was attended by Chirac and Jospin, Schröder, Verhofstadt, Aznar and Berlusconi. Solana and the Dutch

---

142 The *Independent*, 20 October 2001.
143 The *Financial Times*, 22 October 2001.
144 *De Standaard*, 22 October 2001.
145 For instance, see the *Financial Times*, 25 October 2001.
146 *De Standaard*, 23 October 2001.
147 *Corriere della Sera*, 27 October 2001.
148 *Ibid.*

prime minister, Wim Kok, also asked to attend.[149] Prodi was not invited.[150] He explained that this was because he had earlier told Blair on the telephone not to bother as he would not accept.[151]

Prodi was further embarrassed when the International Securities Market Association revealed that, during his time as prime minister, Italy had 'juggled the books' to hide the true size of its budget deficit to meet the conditions for joining the euro.[152] By a secret arrangement with an unnamed bank, the Italian government had been able to defer payments on its debt in 1996 and 1997, to create the illusion that it had met the three percent deficit target set by Maastricht.[153] Prodi denied any wrongdoing.

Blair's ambitions were meanwhile jolted when Commissioner Barnier scorned his proposal for a second European chamber drawn from national parliaments. Even though this idea had originated with Fischer, Barnier added that Britain might have greater influence if she joined the euro: 'if you are fully on board for a united Europe, your voice will be heard more forcefully'.[154]

On 12 November, in Bruges, Prodi was again claiming that the 9/11 crisis called for an EU-wide police force and tighter border controls, under Commission control. In what was to become a constant refrain, he spoke of the 'Community method' being crucial to 'our security, our well-being and the peace of our continent'.[155] He also wanted the Commission to tighten its grip over tax and spending policies. The growth and stability pact alone did not go far enough to safeguard the euro, he said, proposing that 'a model budget policy' for member states was a crucial next step towards economic union.[156]

Yet, just when Prodi was calling for greater central control over the budgets of member states, the Court of Auditors was yet again reporting five percent of the EU's own budget as unaccounted for.[157] Unabashed, Prodi now pressed member states to speed the economic reforms needed 'to ensure that the EU fulfils its promise of having the world's most competitive economy by 2010'. The 'Lisbon process' had so far achieved nothing. He urged that a 'priority reform package' should be agreed by the Barcelona Council, scheduled for March 2002, to show the EU 'delivering promises'.[158]

Finally, the biggest players of all, Germany and France, despite earlier disagreements, joined in supporting a constitutional convention, even offering a draft 'Laeken Declaration'. Blair, opposed to a constitution, was left stranded. Like it or not, the convention would go ahead, and there was no doubting its objective. Chirac and Schröder jointly declared that a constitution was 'an essential step in

149 The *Guardian*, 5 November 2001.
150 The *Independent*, 3 November 2001.
151 RDP Antena 1 radio, Lisbon, 15 November 2001.
152 ANSA news agency, Rome, 5 November 2001.
153 The *Guardian*, 6 November 2001.
154 The *Guardian*, 6 November 2001.
155 The *Guardian*, 13 November 2001.
156 The *Daily Telegraph*, 13 November 2001.
157 The *Financial Times*, 13 November 2001.
158 *Op. cit.*

the historic process of European integration'.[159] All that remained was the crucial choice of the convention's president. Various names had been suggested, including Delors.[160] But when Schröder moved to back France's choice of Giscard, the result was a foregone conclusion. Europe's central 'motor of integration' was working as smoothly as ever.

The Laeken Council would not be confined just to 'high politics'. Also to be agreed was the siting of the Commission's various new agencies, each bringing with it a lucrative financial spin-off for its host country. Apportioning the spoils would be a difficult and delicate task, stretching the limited diplomatic skills of Verhofstadt. But, giving a rare insight as to how the Union really worked, a 'long-serving diplomat' remarked, 'Verhofstadt needs a balance of dissatisfaction for everyone to make it work'.[161] In other words, so long as everybody was unhappy, a deal could be struck.

Laeken, as arranged

On 14 December, to the ritual accompaniment of shouting demonstrators, the motor cavalcades of the EU leaders swept into the former Royal Palace at Laeken. Perhaps as a testament to the skill of the Belgian police, there were only 40 arrests.[162]

After the sham of negotiation, complete with the ritual drama for the sake of the waiting media, the 'EU leaders' did their stuff and announced what had already been decided weeks and months before. With 'Europe at the cross-roads', there would be a convention, paving the way for a constitution in 2003. Giscard would be its president. The former prime ministers of Italy and Belgium, Amato and Dehaene, were to be his vice-chairmen. And the IGC final summit was brought forward to the end of 2003 which, under an Italian presidency, would end in a new 'treaty of Rome'.

Fischer, who had set the process in motion with his Humboldt University speech over a year previously, stated that the convention was a 'body that is very much prepared for integration'. Schröder hoped it would draft a European constitution 'that deserves the name'. Blair immediately said there was no danger that the decision to set up a convention would lead to a European federalist super-state.[163] The 'horse trading', however, was unsuccessful. The EU leaders failed to agree on how to parcel out the new agencies between the member states.[164]

With the convention launched, thoughts turned to the euro, with the introduction of notes and coins due in less than two weeks. This led a German paper to ask Prodi whether, philosophically, 'could it be said that the euro is a way of buying the European soul?' Prodi's response was revealing: 'Money is not only substance, it is also identity.'[165]

159 The *Daily Telegraph*, 24 November 2001.
160 The *Independent*, 6 December 2001.
161 The *Financial Times*, 13 December 2001.
162 The *Guardian*, 14 December 2001.
163 DDP news agency, Berlin, 15 December 2001.
164 The *Financial Times*, 15 December 2001.
165 *Welt am Sonntag*, Hamburg, 16 December 2001.

At the stroke of midnight on 31 December 2001, the euro 'became tangible'. After three years as a virtual currency it had finally arrived, in the shape of more than 15 billion banknotes and 51 billion coins, soon to be the only legal tender for 306 million people in 12 countries.

Hours before the new money was about to be issued, Prodi stated that Europe's single currency would now make 'common rules' for the running of her economies 'inevitable'.[166] The greatest step so far in the march of integration was now irreversible. The end game was on the horizon.

166 *AFX Europe*, 31 December 2001.

Chapter 19

End Game: 2002–2003

'Their crowning dream is a constituent assembly ... which ... must decide on the constitution they want ...'   Altiero Spinelli, Ventotene Manifesto, 1941

On the morning of 28 February 2002 a mass of politicians, officials and journalists streamed into the European Parliament complex in Brussels for the opening of the Convention which was to draft a 'constitution for Europe'. Appropriately, most entered through the Parliament's vast office block, named after the man who 61 years earlier had first proposed that the drawing-up of a constitution would be the final crowning moment in the creation of a 'United States of Europe': Altiero Spinelli.

They then crossed over to the building next door, named after Paul-Henry Spaak, the man who, more than anyone else, had worked with Monnet to set the supranational 'united Europe' on its way. Here, in the Parliament chamber, the 105 delegates, mostly drawn from national governments and parliaments, were to hold the main sessions where the constitution was to be hammered out.[1]

Dominating the occasion, the convention's 76-year-old president, Giscard d'Estaing, told the packed 'hemicycle' that his task was 'to seek consensus' on a single proposal for 'a constitutional treaty'. The agenda would be controlled by a 12-member 'Praesidium', chosen by himself, on which several smaller member states and the 10 new entrants would not be represented. There would be no vote on the final draft. It would thus be up to Giscard and his colleagues to decide where that 'consensus' lay.[2]

The first speaker after Giscard was Prodi, who lost no time telling delegates he wanted a 'European democracy' based on the peoples and states of Europe rather than just on 'the laws of the few largest, strongest or most senior members'. Nor, he went on, as if speaking for the shade of Monnet, should there be a 'new League of Nations reduced to impotence by selfishness and the right of veto'.[3] Prodi's message was clear: no German 'federal' model; no *directoire*; no intergovernmentalism.

---

1 Apart from the president and his two deputies, the 105 delegates were made up of one from each of 28 governments (including 13 candidate countries), two from each national parliament, 16 MEPs and two representing the Commission.
2 The *Daily Telegraph*, *The Irish Times*, and the *Financial Times*, 1 March 2002.
3 *AFX (UK)*, 28 February 2002.

At this historic moment there had already been much talk of the parallel to the convention which met in Philadelphia in 1787 to draw up a constitution for the United States of America. Giscard himself had first drawn this parallel in 1997, and was to elaborate on it again in Washington in February 2003.[4] But what was striking to anyone familiar with those debates in 1787 was just how fundamentally different the two conventions were.

When representatives of the 13 original states met in Philadelphia, they were guided by three central principles. First, they wished to create a constitution which, to prevent the growth of a one-sided tyranny, was based on 'checks and balances' between its three central state institutions. The power of the executive, the US Presidency, was to be restrained by that of the legislature, the Congress. The powers of both would be kept in check by the judiciary, the Supreme Court.

In the emerging 'United States of Europe' these three central constituents had already shown themselves to be not so much in counterpoise as all on the same side of the scales. The purpose of the executive (Commission), legislature (Parliament) and court (ECJ) was not to act as a check on each other's powers but to reinforce each other's efforts to promote ever-further integration. The equation was further complicated by the European Council and Council of Ministers also playing the roles of executive and legislature, thus setting up in rivalry with both Commission and Parliament.

The second dominant issue in 1787 had been the battle to preserve a balance between the rights of the individual states and the power of the new central government. This was achieved by clearly defining the respective powers of the federal and state governments. By contrast, the whole purpose of the 'European project' had been to transfer ever more powers from the member states to the 'supranational' government. Although influential forces were now in play, not least in Germany, to insist that there must be a limit to this one-way centralisation of power, the instinct of all but a handful of the convention delegates was not so much to restrain this process as to carry it further. Again this was complicated by the pressure to erode the power of national governments from below, by guaranteeing the power of regional governments on the 'German federal' model, based on the *Länder*.

The third issue in Philadelphia had been to achieve a balance between the states themselves, to prevent smaller states being dominated by their larger partners. This was resolved by giving the Congress an upper house, the Senate, in which every state had equal representation, regardless of size, so that tiny Rhode Island stood equal with mighty New York; while in the lower house each state was represented according to population size. Again, in Europe, this was precisely the conflict which had so acutely emerged between the smaller states, seeing the supranational Commission as their protector, and the larger states, led by France, wishing to dominate the rest through the '*directoire*' version of intergovernmentalism,

All these contradictions would be reflected in the deliberations of Giscard's convention. His hardest task would be to try to find a coherent balance between them. At least in Philadelphia the representatives all spoke a common language,

---

4 Henry Kissinger Lecture, Library of Congress, Washington, 11 February 2003.

shared a common legal tradition and political inheritance and were all driven by the same desire to achieve a common goal. In Brussels in 2003, none of these things were true. The previous 18 months had produced three quite different versions of 'Europe', all now being actively promoted and all incompatible with each other.

Was Giscard's task impossible? His greatest advantage was that it would be ultimately up to him what 'consensus' emerged. His greatest disadvantage was that, even after he had come up with his draft constitution, it would still have to be argued over by the IGC which was to follow, before the final version could be agreed. Who could predict what differences of opinion might then emerge, to change the whole picture yet again?

Britain all at sea

As the convention began, only one government really had no idea what kind of constitution it wanted, or whether it wanted a constitution at all. Despite its profound implications for the future, the convention's launch was scarcely noticed in Britain, apart from cursory reporting of the appointment of her three delegates, led by the Foreign Office's Europe minister Peter Hain.[5]

Just before the convention opened, rather more attention was paid to a judgement in the Court of Appeal, which in the future might have some bearing on the issues raised by any attempt to sign Britain up to such a constitution. On 9 April 2001, a Sunderland district judge had given his verdict in the case brought against the market trader Steve Thoburn for selling a 'pound of bananas'. Upholding the prosecution's argument that an EC directive could override an Act of Parliament, Judge Morgan stated that:

'This country quite voluntarily surrendered the once seemingly immortal concept of the sovereignty of parliament and legislative freedom by membership of the European Union ... as a once sovereign power, we have said we want to be bound by Community law.'

Morgan had no doubt that Britain had given away her sovereignty for ever. By November, however, following the conviction of four other traders for defying the compulsory metrication laws, the case of the five 'Metric Martyrs' had come before Lord Justice Laws in the Court of Appeal. In taking an unusual time to compose his judgment, it was clear that Laws was fully aware of its constitutional significance, and in a key passage he was at pains to contradict Morgan's earlier ruling.

On 18 February 2002, Laws ruled that EU law could only override the will of Parliament because Parliament had permitted it to do so through the European Communities Act. But there was nothing in this Act, he explained, which allowed the EU or any of its institutions:

'... to qualify the conditions of Parliament's legislative supremacy in the United Kingdom. Not because the legislature chose not to allow it [but] because by our law it could not allow it ...'

The EU, he explained, could not overrule Parliament, because 'being sovereign it cannot abandon its sovereignty'. Parliament might have lent its power to make

---

5 The two others, representing the Westminster Parliament, were the German-born Labour MP Gisela Stuart and, for the Conservatives, David Heathcoat Amory.

laws. But in no way was it capable of handing over the sovereignty it exercised on behalf of the British people. If ever Parliament wished to reclaim that power by repealing the ECA, Laws emphasised, it was free to do so.

If Laws's view was clear enough, this was far from true of the British government's view of the proposed EU constitution. As ministers now began to demonstrate, they were all over the place. A month before the convention began, Hain made a first pitch by appearing to back the '*directoire*' model, by suggesting an 'inner cabinet' for the European Council comprising Germany, France and the UK.[6] A week before the convention opened, he then gave ground on the constitution itself by accepting that the Charter of Fundamental Rights could be included; but only on condition that it was not enforceable in UK courts. At the same time he claimed that the debate was shifting towards Britain's intergovernmental vision of Europe, rather than 'greater federalism'.[7] In this he was supported by Jack Straw, who claimed the 'constitution' was merely a 'statement of principles', intended to define the division of powers between Brussels and national governments. Just 'because an entity has a constitution', he said, 'doesn't make it a state'.[8]

In February Blair pursued the idea of a tripartite '*directoire*' between Britain, France and Germany when he met Schröder during a weekend summit of centre-left leaders in Stockholm. Although publicly he disguised this by merely calling for a stronger Council, Finland's prime minister was not fooled, complaining: 'there are obvious intentions to change the system into a kind of directorate, where the European Commission and smaller countries will be pushed aside'.[9] A week later Chirac confirmed this by repeating his call for a 'federation of nation states': i.e., a French-dominated '*directoire*'.

By March, when Giscard asked delegates to consider the Europe they wanted in 25 years time. Hain had changed his tune again. Bubbling with an enthusiasm he was later to deny, he told his fellow delegates: 'our task is nothing less than the creation of a new constitutional order for a new united Europe'. He then repeated Blair's call for a stronger Council, but at the same time hedged his bets by calling also for 'a stronger Commission'.[10]

In early April, Blair, in another futile bid to promote an Anglo-German 'axis', met Schröder at Chequers. Only the previous day, however, Schröder had already called on the 'traditional motor of European integration' – the Franco-German axis – to decide 'if the Europe of the future will run on intergovernmental co-operation or if it will be more (federally) integrated'. Again, following his *Länder* agenda, Schröder believed there was 'no reasonable alternative' to the more federal model.[11]

The Commission, France, Germany and the other states all, it seemed, now had a clear view of what they were after. Only Britain, hankering after various half-baked versions not on offer, seemed hopelessly at sea.

---

6 The *Financial Times*, 21 January 2002.
7 The *Financial Times*, 18 February 2002.
8 The *Guardian*, 22 February 2002.
9 The *Guardian*; *La Stampa*; and the *Daily Telegraph*: 26, 27 and 28 February 2002.
10 The *Financial Times*, 22 March 2002.
11 The *Daily Telegraph*; the *Guardian*, 13 April 2002.

Noises off

Chirac, now in the midst of his election campaign, was being accused of paying party activists from public funds; renting out public housing to fund party activities; vote-rigging; 'skimming' public contracts; forging invoices and making false expenses claims. In almost any other western democracy, such charges would have disqualified him for office, but he enjoyed presidential immunity. Despite being dubbed 'Superliar', he had a slight poll lead over Jospin. However, his real opponent, it turned out, was the right-wing nationalist, Jean-Marie Le Pen. In the first round, on 21 April, Le Pen beat Jospin into third place. Humiliated, Jospin immediately announced his retirement. Confronted by a choice between 'the Fascist' and 'the Crook', the French held their noses, giving '*l'escroc*' an unprecedented victory, with an 81.7 percent vote. Hailed as a 'defeat for extremism', it was also a defeat for 'cohabitation'. Chirac was at last free to dictate his own European agenda.[12]

In Brussels, attention turned briefly to fish. At the end of the year, Spain's partial exclusion from 'Community waters' was due to expire. Recognising that giving the Spanish fleet 'equal access' would be disastrous, the Commission used an obscure 'conservation' clause in the Amsterdam treaty to seize almost complete control over fishing policy, shutting out the Council of Ministers. Thousands more boats would have to be scrapped, particularly in Scotland, where 600 'whitefish' boats, fishing for species such as cod and haddock, still formed the largest fleet in northern Europe. But there would also be an end to subsidies for the southern European fleets. The Commission was making a wholesale power grab.[13]

In April a tremendous battle raged behind the scenes, as Spain tried to sabotage the Commission's plans. Under wholly improper pressure from a Spanish commissioner (the rules were clear that Commissioners should not act in a national interest), the top Brussels fisheries official, Stefan Schmidt, a Dane, was forced from his post. Schmidt himself was already accused of favouring Denmark's destructive 'industrial' fishing fleet, which had somehow been exempted from the 'cod ban' under which 40,000 square miles of the North Sea were closed to all other fishing. Although this was supposedly to conserve dwindling cod stocks, it was in fact a 'political' device, to force hundreds more, mainly Scottish boats out of business. Infighting would continue to the end of the year.

But by 1 January 2003, it would be clear that the Commission had won almost all it was after. As yet further crippling restrictions were imposed, it would become clear that the Scottish fleet was doomed.[14] It had taken 30 years for the CFP to destroy the Britain's fishing industry, but by now this had been all but achieved. Soon there would be just one 'Union fleet', fishing 'Union waters', wholly under Brussels control.

In May 2002, there was another ritual attempt to 'bounce' Britain into the one 'federal' policy she had so far escaped: the euro. Prodi began the offensive, joined by Patten, Heseltine and Charles Kennedy. Blair was provoked into telling BBC's *Newsnight* that he would have no problem with history recording him as the man 'who dumped the pound', and rejecting any idea that joining the euro was 'a

12 The *Daily Telegraph*, 22 April 2002; *AFX (UK)*, 5 May 2002.
13 The *Financial Times*, 28 May 2002.
14 The *Scotsman*, 18 December 2002.

betrayal of our national interests'.[15] But Brown's antidote was still his 'five tests'.[16] The offensive petered out.

Brown could have cited a new UN economic survey, which accused Brussels and the ECB of 'policy paralysis'. The EU had done too little to boost world growth, and had added to trade frictions by relying on exports to cushion its own economy, all caused by the eurozone's 'deformed budgetary rules' and 'frictions in policy-making' among the EU's squabbling institutions. Unabashed, Prodi bounced back with a demand for one political voice to speak on behalf of the euro.[17]

Days later, on 6 May, the charismatic Dutch far-Right leader, Pym Fortuyn, was murdered. He had been campaigning on an anti-Islam, anti-immigration ticket, and his party had been expected to hold the balance of power in Holland's forthcoming general election. This prompted much heart-searching on the rise of right-wing parties in the EU, with suggestions that the European project was going too far, too fast. But Prodi disagreed. There was not enough 'Europe'. The day Fortuyn died, Prodi had unveiled plans to set up a 'European Corps of Border Guards', to police the EU's frontiers against illegal immigrants.[18]

The fencing resumes

Having failed to recruit Schröder to his cause, Blair now tried his luck with a newly invigorated Chirac. Debate was now centring on whether there should be a full-time 'President of Europe'; and, if so, should such a dominating figure head the Commission or the Council? Blair put it to Chirac that a Council president should dominate.[19] Prodi reacted sharply, pointing out that the Commission had to be capable of saying 'no' to the likes of Schröder or Aznar whenever the need arose. Otherwise, he warned, 'a different kind of Europe might emerge: an intergovernmental Europe'. Furthermore, his powers on the economy and foreign policy needed strengthening. Asked whether he was suggesting 'fully fledged co-ordination of national policies', his reply was, 'Yes, yes, yes, and yes. Four times yes'.[20]

Prodi formally submitted his ideas to the convention on 21 May 2002, proposing that the Commission should be at the Union's 'centre of gravity', with its own foreign policy. He called for the abolition of all national vetoes and more powers to censure countries for profligate budgets.[21] Predictably his ideas were not well received. A Foreign Office official pronounced them 'dead on arrival'.[22] The French and Germans were equally dismissive.[23]

Try as it might to occupy the high ground, the Commission was still being dragged into the all too familiar mire of corruption and financial irregularity: this time by the 'Andreasen affair' which brought back echoes of Connolly and van

---

15 15 May 2002.
16 The *Independent*, 4 May 2002.
17 The *Daily Telegraph*; *AFX (UK)*, 2 May 2002.
18 *AFX (UK)*, 7 May 2002.
19 The *Financial Times*, 16 May 2002.
20 *La Stampa*, 17 May 2002.
21 The *Financial Times*, 22 May 2002.
22 The *Independent*, 23 May 2002.
23 The *Financial Times*, 29 May 2002.

Buitenen. Marta Andreasen was a Spanish accountant who, in January 2002, had been appointed by the budget and anti-fraud commissioner, Michaele Schreyer, as the Commission's chief accountant, to clean up the Commission's accounts. She quickly found what she called 'serious and glaring' shortcomings. The accounts did not even use double-entry book-keeping. The computer system was open to interference, so that entries could be altered. She reported this to Schreyer, who initially supported her. But she was then put under intense pressure to sign off the Commission's 2001 accounts, which she refused to do, claiming that, since they were incorrect, this would be in breach of the Financial Regulation.

When she still refused, despite being told that this was what she received her 'high pay' to do, she was threatened with dismissal. On 7 May she wrote explaining her concerns to Prodi and his two vice-presidents, including Kinnock, who in 1999 had been charged with reforming the Commission to eradicate corruption. On 22 May, the College of Commissioners agreed to release her from her post. She was so frustrated by this response that, on 24 May, like van Buitenen, she put her case in a letter to MEPs. About to board an airliner from Barcelona back to Brussels, she was presented with a fax from Kinnock, telling her she had been removed from her post. From then on, as with Connolly, the Commission's spin machine went into overdrive to blacken her name. Nevertheless her charges were supported by another 'whistleblower' within the Court of Auditors, Dougal Watt. In April he had independently lodged an official complaint against nepotism, corruption and mismanagement within the Court of Auditors itself, endorsed by 205 colleagues, for which he himself was dismissed from his post.

Such matters were of little concern, however, to the final Council of the Spanish presidency in Seville on 21 to 22 June, where top of the agenda were now the two chief problems which would be created by enlargement. One was that the admission of the eastern European countries would set off a wave of immigration. Germany and Austria in particular feared they might be swamped by migrants looking for work in the richer economies of the west, and were determined to delay as long as possible the moment when the newcomers could claim 'right of establishment', entitling them to residence and jobs.

The other fear was the impossible strain that would be imposed on the EU budget unless a similar delay was imposed on the right of the farmers of Poland and the other countries to claim full subsidies under the CAP.[24] At least Commissioner Fischler had proposed a 'mid-term review' which would cut the overall subsidy bill by reducing subsidies to larger farms. But even this would be nowhere enough to solve the problem, and, anyway, it posed such a threat to East Germany's large former collective farms that Schröder immediately rejected it. He faced an election in September, and this was where his SPD drew much of its support.[25] The additional £3 billion a year Fischer was seeking was more than the EU could afford. Britain, Germany, Holland and Sweden, all net contributors, refused to pay more.[26] The CAP was now poisoning enlargement.

24 The *Guardian*, 6 June 2002.
25 The *Daily Telegraph*, 14 June 2002.
26 The *Daily Telegraph*, 15 June 2002.

Another row was brewing over the growth and stability pact, with public spending in France, Italy and Germany out of control. The row intensified when Chirac's new premier, Jean-Pierre Raffarin, put tax-cuts above the stability pact, stating that the pact was 'not written in stone'. Portugal, whose budget deficit was set to smash through the ceiling within the year, was also causing concern. The stability pact, at the core of the euro project, seemed to be disintegrating.[27]

On 1 July, however, when the Danes took over the presidency from Spain, they named the problems posed by enlargement as their top priority. If the accession talks were not concluded by October the 2004 deadline would be missed.[28] But the new entrants were now beginning to realise that the EU was offering them the worst of all worlds. On one hand they would have to take on all the costs of complying with EU legislation, and open their frontiers to produce and goods from the rest of the EU. On the other, it now looked as if the deal they were to be offered would deny their citizens the right to take jobs in existing EU countries for seven years and would initially give their farmers only 25 percent of the subsidies enjoyed by their western counterparts. Furthermore, this would mean that, initially, they would actually be net contributors to the EU budget.[29] Amid angry murmurs of protest, France then also rejected Fischler's modest plans for CAP reform, sticking to the Berlin agreement which blocked any significant changes until 2006. This was echoed by Stoiber, due to be the right-wing standard bearer in Germany's forthcoming elections. Enlargement looked in serious disarray.[30]

At this point European politics were set to sink into their usual summer torpor. But August 2002 was different. Torrential rain swamped the Rhine and Danube basins, submerging towns and cities in Austria, Germany, Hungary, the Czech Republic and Slovakia. For Schröder, trailing in the polls against Stoiber, it was a godsend. He toured the affected areas, meeting the heads of governments of the countries affected and co-ordinating aid, so capturing the headlines. Prodi was right behind him, offering 1 billion euros from the EU coffers.[31] Stoiber was wrong-footed. He had been on holiday when the 'flood of a century' struck. His occasional clumsy appearances on waterlogged dykes lacked conviction.

Growing international tension over Iraq was also an election issue, with both candidates vying to outdo each other in rejecting war. All this served to divert attention from Germany's dire domestic problems, with four million unemployed and a stagnant economy. Schröder began to pull back.[32]

Flood-free Britain was meanwhile being regaled by Jack Straw arguing that the EU should have a written constitution; setting out 'a simple set of principles' in clear language 'as a means of bringing the Brussels bureaucracy closer to the people'.[33] Presented as if this was all his own idea, it was if the convention in

27 The *Daily Telegraph*, 20 June 2002.
28 *AFX Europe*, 27 June 2002.
29 The *Daily Telegraph*, 2 July 2002.
30 The *Daily Telegraph*, 11 July 2002; the *Financial Times*, 15 July 2002.
31 The *Financial Times*, 17 August 2002.
32 The *Independent*, 17 August 2002.
33 The *Daily Telegraph*, 27 August 2002.

Brussels had never existed. When his opposition counterpart, Michael Ancram, denounced the speech, Straw replied that, since every golf club had a constitution, why should the EU not have one too?[34] Those with longer memories recalled that, in October 2000, Blair had argued that the constitutional debate 'must not necessarily end with a single, legally binding document called a constitution'. It had now been turned into a 'British' idea.

The 'project' begins to unravel

When in early autumn the convention resumed, Britain tried to seize the initiative by proposing a 'President of Europe' elected by national MPs. Chirac and Schröder agreed to an elected head of the Council.[35] Although Schröder called for 'balancing powers' for the Commission, Pascal Lamy, Delors' former *chef de cabinet* and now trade Commissioner, condemned these proposals as the most serious assault on the Commission's power and influence in its history.[36]

Now moving fast up the international agenda, however, was Iraq and its 'weapons of mass destruction'. Again attention turned away from the convention. The US vice-president, Dick Cheney, warned that if the world waited until the Iraqis had developed a nuclear bomb, it would be too late. 'Time is not on our side,' he said. Prodi told Washington to obtain UN support: 'otherwise I fear that the greatest achievement of all will be destroyed, the keystone of US diplomacy after 11 September, which is the global anti-terrorist alliance'.[37] Nevertheless, it was clear that 'decisive action' by the US was only a matter of time. At least for Schröder his Iraq policy contributed to his re-election, albeit on a reduced share of the vote.[38]

Now the stability pact welled up again. Faced with alarming budget deficits in France, Germany and Italy, the Commission caved in to pressure, giving the defaulters until 2006 to balance their budgets. Smaller member states, especially Portugal, were furious,[39] their mood further inflamed when France confirmed public spending plans which made a mockery of the rules. France's finance minister was unapologetic. His government had won the election on spending pledges. The stability pact would have to wait until 2004.[40] Even *Le Monde* regretted France's 'national selfishness'.[41]

Another crack appeared in the façade of European unity when Italy offered the US support on Iraq. Prodi conceded the obvious: 'there are no elements for a common European Union position'.[42] Strangely, it was now that the British government, the USA's strongest supporter, offered yet more concessions to the conven-

34 The *Independent*, 28 August 2002.
35 The *Financial Times*, 10 September 2002.
36 The *Financial Times*, 16 October 2002.
37 The *Independent*, 11 September 2002.
38 The *Independent*, 23 September 2002.
39 The *Financial Times*, 26 September 2002.
40 The *Independent*, 9 October 2002.
41 8 October 2002.
42 *Corriere della Sera*, 24 September 2002.

tion. Even more strangely, its offer was to accept abolition of the national veto in areas of foreign policy, just when the 'colleagues' seemed to be abandoning the idea of a common policy altogether. In addition, Hain conceded that the Charter of Fundamental Rights could have full legal status as part of the new constitution.[43] Whatever thinking lay behind this dramatic U-turn, it emboldened Giscard to assert that his convention's report could be adopted in 2003 with only minimal changes by EU leaders.[44]

This optimism carried over to 9 October when, 13 years after the fall of the Berlin Wall, EU foreign ministers agreed to a 'big bang' enlargement, admitting 10 applicants to the Union. Even though final details on financing had still to be agreed, Prodi ecstatically proclaimed, 'we have rediscovered a historic unity between all our peoples. Our common destiny is to build our future together'.[45] What won more headlines was his intervention on 17 October, when he branded the stability pact as 'stupid'. His point, however, was that the Commission lacked the power to enforce the rules. Prodi was supported by Schröder, Chirac and Gordon Brown. A month later he was proposing a revised stability pact, to give the Commission more powers.[46]

At this point, as Germany's foreign minister, Fischer took over as his country's representative to the convention. The time had come for the senior players to get involved. He immediately reverted to his earlier proposal that that the Commission could evolve into a European government, with a president elected by a US-style electoral college to ensure that smaller states had a fair say.[47]

This came just as one 'smaller state' was having its say, with Ireland's second referendum on the Nice treaty. Pouring vast sums of money into the campaign, the Irish government and its Brussels allies pulled out all the stops. The law requiring equal air-time for both sides had been scrapped. The question had been rigged, so that the Irish could not reject Nice again unless they also voted for Ireland to abandon its traditional neutrality by supporting the EU army. On 19 October, the Irish voted 'yes' to Nice, by 63 to 37 percent, on a turnout of 48 percent.[48]

The crucial link between enlargement and CAP spending was finally reaching crisis point. At an extraordinary Council in Brussels on 24 October, Germany was adamant that CAP costs must go down after the end of the budget period in 2006. Chirac, predictably, refused to agree, demanding instead a cut in Britain's rebate to make up the difference.[49] Blair countered with ideas for cost-cutting which Chirac also opposed. *Impasse* loomed, resolved only by yet another fudge when Chirac and Schröder privately agreed to a ceiling on farm spending from 2007 until 2013. Details were 'sketchy and confused' but were thought to be 'favourable to France'.[50]

43 The *Daily Telegraph*, 4 October 2002.
44 The *Financial Times*, 7 October 2002.
45 The *Independent*, 10 October 2002.
46 The *Financial Times*, 17 October 2002; the *Daily Mail*, 8 November 2002; the *Independent*, 28 November 2002.
47 The *Financial Times*, 18 October 2002.
48 The *Financial Times*; the *Sunday Telegraph*, 20 October 2002.
49 The *Financial Times*, 24 October 2002.
50 The *Guardian*, 25 October 2002.

Blair was furious, but Chirac merely reiterated his demand for a cut in the rebate. Tempers flared and Chirac threatened to cancel a planned Franco-British summit, telling Blair, 'You have been very rude and I have never been spoken to like this before.' 'The problem is that Chirac is Chirac,' said one EU diplomat. 'He has recently been re-elected and he is throwing his weight around. It is all very, very French.'[51] As a result of the upsets, it was not until mid-November that the date for entry of the accession countries was agreed: 1 May 2004.

Another Frenchman throwing his weight around was Giscard who, at the end of October, unveiled a 'skeleton' constitution. His suggestion that the EU could be renamed 'United States of Europe' provoked instant British protest.[52] Nevertheless Hain promptly told a House of Commons scrutiny committee that Britain was 'winning the battle against hard-line European federalists'.[53] Days later Chirac's new foreign minister Dominique de Villepin joined with Fischer to announce proposals for strengthening the EU's defence and security policies, and the creation of a European armaments agency. They were also preparing a separate paper suggesting more EU powers in justice and home affairs.[54] With the 'federalists' rampant, Blair was becoming increasingly marginalised.

Perhaps reflecting this, in a curiously unreported speech in Cardiff on 28 November, Blair set out yet another of his 'visions' of Europe. He wanted 'a Europe of sovereign nations ... co-operating together for mutual good'. We should end the nonsense of 'this far and no further'. There were areas in which Europe 'should and will' integrate more: in fighting crime and illegal immigration; to secure economic reform; in having a more effective defence and security policy. Intergovernmentalism should not be used as a weapon against European institutions. Supranational institutions were needed for Europe to work, and the two were 'not in opposition to each other'. Without QMV and without a strong Commission, able to act independently, reform would never materialise. A weak Commission was 'contrary to our interests'. Thus, Europe had to be strengthened 'at every level'. For that, what was needed was 'a proper Constitution for Europe'.[55]

More than ever, this incoherent mass of contradictions signalled Blair's complete failure to grasp the real issues, and how the whole history of the European Union had been a battle between intergovernmentalism and supranationalism. It also marked a near-total retreat from his Warsaw position a year previously.

Prodi, on the other hand, was planning a surprise. Within the bowels of the Commission, a working group chaired by François Lamoureaux – Delors' former deputy chief of staff – had been working on a project so secret that it was given only a code-name: 'Penelope'. What emerged on 4 December 2002 was a 142-page document setting out the supranational case: separate 'Community taxes'; a European army; a Commission elected by MEPs; national vetoes all but gone. Foreign policy and justice and home affairs should come under 'the Community method'.

51 The *Daily Telegraph*, 29 October 2002.
52 The *Independent*, 29 October 2002.
53 The *Guardian*, 21 November 2002.
54 The *Financial Times*, 23 November 2002.
55 Blair speech, 28 November 2002, *www.number-10.gov.uk*.

Virtually all traces of intergovernmentalism in the existing treaties had been expunged. There was also a 'take it or leave it' clause by which any country blocking adoption of the new treaty would be deemed to have left the Union.[56] In London, officials were scathing. 'This is Lord Prodi of Kamikaze,' said one Whitehall source.[57]

Still the enlargement problem had to be resolved. The EU had imposed ever tougher conditions on its prospective members. Their citizens could not move to find new jobs in the west for seven years. CAP subsidies to their farmers would start at only 25 percent, to be phased in over the same period; by which time hundreds of thousands of eastern European farmers, unable to compete with their much more highly subsidised western counterparts, might have been driven off the land. The only consolation prize on offer was a 1.3 billion euro (£830m) lump sum payment, to tide the new entrants over their first year of accession. A day before the Copenhagen Council, Poland's prime minister, Leszek Miller, pressed for this payment to be increased by an extra 2 billion euros. But all he and his colleagues got was permission to transfer the 1 billion euros already promised from the regional aid fund direct to government coffers. There would be no extra money.[58] With that, 10 more countries were on their way into the EU. As Evans-Pritchard of the *Telegraph* commented, 'it promises to be a loveless marriage'.[59]

As 2002 closed, Italy was looking forward to an IGC summit in Rome 12 months later, when she would hold the presidency. Overwhelmed by the 'powerful symbolism' of being able to host a new Treaty of Rome, her government had decided to take 'no rigid position' on the convention, to ensure this rendezvous with destiny was kept.[60] With a potentially stormy IGC based on Giscard's draft constitution due to start in Thessalonika in June, it was set to be a close run thing.

The Franco-German axis

The new year of 2003 marked the 40th anniversary of the Elysée Treaty, launching the Franco-German alliance. It was also 30 years since Britain joined the 'Common Market'. This scarcely inspired mass-celebrations, although one of the few who might have thought the occasion merited uncorking a bottle of 1961 Chateau Lafite, Lord Jenkins of Hillhead, died a week after New Year's Day aged 82.[61]

For Schröder the year did not start well. Business conditions in the eurozone were deteriorating, not least in Germany, where the recovery of the euro against a deliberately weakened dollar was hitting an already faltering export drive.[62] Now Germany faced official censure for breaching the growth and stability pact. Faced by public spending cuts, 2.8 million public sector workers threatened to strike. Schröder's standing in the polls was plummeting.[63]

---

56 European Commission, 'Feasibility Study: Contribution to a Preliminary Draft – Constitution of the European Union'. Brussels, 4 December 2002.
57 The *Guardian*, 6 December 2002.
58 The *Financial Times*, 10 and 13 December 2002.
59 The *Daily Telegraph*, 12 December 2002.
60 *Il Sole 24 Ore*, 18 December 2002.
61 *The Times*, 7 January 2003.
62 Reuters, 2 January 2003.
63 The *Independent*, 9 January 2003.

Britain, having so far failed to split the Franco-German alliance, now hoped to exploit this situation by working with Germany on economic policy. But, less than a fortnight into the New Year, Schröder and Chirac met for dinner in Paris to celebrate the Elysée Treaty. There, the leaders set out to resolve their differences on the convention. For Chirac, there would be a more powerful Council with a permanent president; for Schröder a more powerful figurehead for the Commission, leading a federal structure. It was another classic fudge. The EU would have in effect two presidents, one leading the Council and the other the Commission, both elected. The former would lead on foreign affairs and give the EU 'strategic direction'. The latter would deal with trade, competition and the internal market.[64] Blair was out in the cold.

For Prodi too this spelt defeat, as Denmark, Spain and even Britain accepted the Franco-German compromise, followed by Giscard himself. Prodi was left grumbling that it would lead to the creation of two 'competing bureaucracies'.[65] Blair later tried to buck the decision, lining up with Aznar to propose a full-time EU 'super-president', appointed for a four-year term,[66] but no one listened. More serious opposition came from the smaller states – now mockingly called the 'seven dwarfs' – who still feared the Council presidency could become a *directoire*. In a bid to assert the primacy of the Commission, Belgian premier Verhofstadt tried to lead a rebellion,[67] but by May the 'dwarfs' would not only have been forced to accept the Franco-German plan; they would also have to concede a reduction in the number of voting Commissioners.[68]

Another long-running saga which by then would have been played out was that of Jean-Claude Trichet, governor of the Bank of France. In January he went on trial, charged with having covered up a scandal at the formerly state-owned Credit Lyonnais bank, involving losses of $20 billion.[69] Few believed he was entirely innocent. In June, however, he would be acquitted of all charges. The European Council would promptly confirm that Duisenberg was to step down to allow him to take over as president of the ECB.[70]

Saddam the 'disintegrator'

By the end of January 2003 only one issue held political attention across the world. It was now evident that the US invasion of Iraq, with full British support, might take place at any time, in the teeth of opposition from most EU members. Solana led the way, declaring that the UN Security Council would need proof of weapons of mass destruction before agreeing to authorise a war. De Villepin called on other European governments to oppose American plans.[71] When Bush declared that UN

---

64 The *Financial Times*, 14 January 2003.
65 The *Guardian*, 16 January 2003.
66 The *Daily Telegraph*, 1 March 2003.
67 *De Standaard*, 13 March 2003.
68 *De Standaard*, 17 May 2003.
69 Bloomberg, 6 January 2003.
70 *EurActiv*, 23 June 2003.
71 The *Independent*, 22 January 2003.

weapons inspections, demanded by the French, the Germans and Putin's Russia, would not work, Schröder lined up with Chirac to refuse backing for a UN resolution.

This led to a startling intervention by the US Secretary of State Donald Rumsfeld, who dismissed the Franco-German alliance as 'old Europe'. The centre of gravity was shifting to the east and those countries were with the United States. A spokesman for Bush said that France and Germany had the 'prerogative … to be on the sideline', but the US would go to war, even without UN authorisation.[72] Rumsfeld's comments signalled a seismic shift in US policy on Europe, unchanged since the Second World War. 'Europe' was no longer seen as a homogenous entity, but as separate nations. If Nasser had been the great 'federator', another Middle East leader, Saddam, promised to be its 'disintegrator'.

Unwittingly the 'Europeans' themselves demonstrated why the United States could not take them seriously. On 28 January, as the US Navy assembled around the Gulf, the most powerful in history, the EU launched its own off the coast of North Africa, to patrol for illegal immigrants.[73] It comprised a small flotilla of motor vessels, manned by sailors of five EU nations. When two days later a letter appeared in *The Times*, signed by eight 'European leaders' from Britain, Spain, Italy, Portugal, Hungary, Poland, Denmark and the Czech Republic, calling on the Continent to 'stand united with America', disunity was there for all to see.[74]

Blair did his best to bring the EU together. Fresh from meeting Bush in Washington, he travelled to Le Touquet to meet Chirac: the summit delayed from the previous autumn after their row over the CAP. But not only did he fail on Iraq, fresh wounds were opened over another contentious issue: Britain's former colony of Zimbabwe. Despite its leader Robert Mugabe pursuing a murderous campaign of terror against both white farmers and the mass of his own African population, the UK had handed all right to make policy on Zimbabwe to the EU, which had reacted only by imposing a travel ban on the country's rulers. But now, ignoring even this sanction, Chirac had invited Mugabe to a summit in Paris, Chirac brushed aside Blair's objections and their press conference lacked even a hint of *entente cordiale*.[75]

Two days later, when Giscard published a draft of the first 16 articles of his constitution. Hain was immediately moved to complain that 'It seems to put the EU in charge of economic and foreign policy, when that was not what had been agreed'.[76] But soon Giscard would be struggling with over 1,000 amendments and pleading for more time.

By now, however, Iraq was dominating the headlines.[77] As mass anti-war demonstrations took place across Europe, EU leaders met at a special Council in Brussels on 17 February, where they agreed that UN weapons inspectors should be given more time to find and destroy Iraq's weapons of mass destruction. War

---

72 The *Daily Telegraph*, 24 January 2003.
73 The *Daily Telegraph*, 29 January 2003.
74 *The Times*, 30 January 2003.
75 The *Guardian*; the *Financial Times*, 5 February 2003.
76 The *Financial Times*, 7 February 2003.
77 The *Guardian*, 7 February 2003.

against Saddam should be a 'last resort'.[78] But this fragile unity was quickly shattered when Chirac condemned the candidate countries for supporting America, telling them they had 'missed a good opportunity to shut up'.[79] Within hours, Blair had exploited this outburst by writing to the objects of Chirac's ire in a bid to present himself as their closest ally in Europe.[80]

In a brief break from the tension, EU leaders took heart from the first of the planned referendums on entry in the ten applicant countries. It was worked out that the £4 million spent by the EU on a massive propaganda blitz in the tiny island of Malta, with its population of only 370,000, equated to more money per voter than the combined total spent by political parties in every election campaign in British history. Such lavish investment was rewarded: 53.5 percent of the Maltese voted 'Yes' to entry, and this was subsequently confirmed in a general election.[81]

Blair still had time to offer a joint paper with Aznar, a fellow supporter of the US stance on Iraq, proposing that the Commission should control policy on immigration and cross-border crime. As with Straw's U-turn on the idea of a constitution, Blair – according to Heathcoat Amory, the Tories' convention delegate – was conceding what he suspected would be inevitable, thus enabling him to claim victory for what had been a British idea all along.[82] Blair was less enthusiastic about a proposed mutual defence pact, but Giscard said he would include this in his draft to see how others reacted.[83] The Irish were unenthusiastic about a reference to 'federal', and suggested it should be struck out 'in the interests of clarity'.[84] Amato pronounced that the EU's power came from member states, not 'from God or Prodi'.[85] No one was certain whether Prodi had been told.

Schröder, conscious of the growing rift between 'old' and 'new' Europe, was warming to Chirac's 'core Europe': a 'coalition of the unwilling'. Giscard contented himself with drafting plans for a European public prosecutor to tackle cross-border crime, which he unveiled on 18 March, to add to Blair's ideas for bringing the justice and home affairs 'pillar' within the Commission competence. The supranational agenda was stacking up.

The UK opposed the prosecutor, but Blair was now waiting to see if the UN would authorise the 'coalition of the willing' to invade Iraq. By 14 March, with France set to use its veto on the Security Council, the US had withdrawn its UN motion and Blair, defying 'old Europe', threw his lot in with Bush. On 17 March Bush delivered an ultimatum to Saddam. On 20 March the invasion began. Three weeks later, on 9 April, US Marines were helping jubilant Iraqis tear down a statue of Saddam Hussein in the centre of Baghdad. The *Daily Mail* summed up the event with one word: 'Toppled'.

---

78 The *Washington Post*, 17 February 2003.
79 Many British newspapers diplomatically reported Chirac's comment as 'keep quiet', but his actual phrase was '*se taire*': colloquially 'shut up!'
80 The *Financial Times*, 19 February 2003.
81 The *Financial Times*, 10 March; the *Sunday Telegraph*, 16 March 2003.
82 The *Daily Telegraph*, 1 March 2003.
83 The *Independent*, 1 March 2003.
84 *The Irish Times*, 4 March 2003.
85 *EU Observer*, 6 March 2003.

Given these events, the atmosphere at the spring European Council was frigid. Blair and Chirac studiously avoided each other. But Blair had not abandoned his strategy of 'constructive engagement'. After post-war talks with Bush, he made a special point of briefing his European colleagues on the outcome, offering honeyed words about the UN having a central role in the reconstruction of Iraq.[86] Solana had meanwhile told *Die Welte* that the lesson of the war was that the EU should in future have only one representative on the UN Security Council: 'imagine what influence Europe could have had if it had spoken with only one voice'.[87]

Giscard was planning to protect his *bébé* by building into the constitution a provision for the approval of treaties without unanimous ratification: the so-called 'exit clause'. This would give member states the choice of accepting new treaties or ceding from the Union. The lessons of Ireland and Nice had not been wasted. Next was 'Europe's tattered common foreign policy', which he had left until the Iraq furore had abated. Now he too was suggesting a single EU foreign minister, merging the roles performed by Solana and Patten. But he ducked the crucial issue of whether he should come under the Commission or the Council.

On 16 April 2003 everything stopped for a grand ceremony at the Parthenon in Athens, when leaders of 'old' and 'new' Europe joined to sign the accession treaties. The 2,500-page document, with multiple cross-references to the *acquis*, was unreadable. Significantly, a month later the Commission urged Poland and five other accession countries to speed up their translation of EU legislation. Only a few hundred of 60,000 EU regulations which had to be translated into Polish had been approved by the Council.[88] Not for the first time, leaders of Europe's ancient nations were signing something they had not read. Subject to ratification, however, the Europe of 15 was now 25. Chirac used the ceremony to reactivate his call for an *avant-garde*, saying an enlarged Europe would lose its vitality unless a core of highly-integrated states was able to press ahead.[89]

In Brussels, the convention was now getting bogged down over the structure of the Commission. Prodi, having lost his bid for an all-powerful presidency, stepped in to offer his earlier idea of a two-tier body. This seemed to engender a 'spirit of compromise'. Giscard took advantage of the new mood, proposing an end to the national veto on tax, to eliminate 'unfair' tax competition.[90]

In Milan, Berlusconi was in court to face charges relating to bribing the judge in the SME affair. He had already pushed through a law giving him immunity as long as he was prime minister. But what excited the European establishment was Berlusconi's claim that the 'grave blame and responsibility' lay with 'Professor Prodi, residing undisturbed in Brussels'.[91] With Italy about to assume the EU presidency, the presidents of the Commission and the Council seemed to be in for an interesting collaboration.

---

86 The *Financial Times*, 1 April 2003.
87 The *Sunday Telegraph*, 30 March 2003
88 *Polish News Bulletin*, 23 May 2003.
89 The *Daily Telegraph*, 17 April 2003.
90 The *Financial Times*, 5 May 2003.
91 The *Independent*, 6 May 2003; the *Financial Times*, 7 May 2003.

Britain wakes up

On 8 May 2003, after more than a year when the convention had been almost entirely ignored by Britain's media, the *Daily Mail* finally woke up, declaring the constitution 'a blueprint for tyranny'. Its columnist Simon Heffer claimed:

'Steadily, slyly, Eurocrats have devised a constitution which – and we do not exaggerate – could soon destroy Britain's nationhood. More far-reaching than Maastricht, it lets Brussels control everything from our borders to our banks.'

The next day the paper blasted 'Non!' in huge capitals across its front page, condemning Blair for being prepared to give the Iraqis a referendum on their constitution but denying the British one on theirs. Then the *Daily Telegraph* ran a leader proclaiming: 'this is it: the moment that we have repeatedly been told would never come about. The EU is about to transform itself, *de jure* and *de facto*, into a single state'.[92] Breaking his party's long self-imposed near-silence on 'Europe', Iain Duncan Smith challenged Blair to hold a referendum. Hain countered that there had been no referendums on the Single European Act or the Maastricht Treaty: 'Those were big constitutional treaties. This is more of a tidying-up exercise,' he said.[93] The words were to haunt him.

Then on 15 May, the *Sun* headlined, 'The biggest betrayal in our history'. Its political editor Trevor Kavanagh, echoing Gaitskell, reported that Blair was 'about to sign away 1,000 years of British sovereignty'. A *Sun* poll had 60 percent against 'surrendering more power to Brussels', 'a whopping 84 percent' wanted a referendum, and 61 percent thought Britain should consider leaving the EU to avoid ceding more power.

In the Commons, Blair claimed referendums were held only when 'exceptional changes in the system of government' were involved. Duncan Smith was ready for him: 'Since you came to power there have been 34 referendums on issues as momentous as Hartlepool having a mayor... But the European constitution will decide how every citizen of this country will be governed. Why won't you simply let the British people have their say?' For once the Tory leader had struck a chord. In a poll next day, 83 percent believed that the British people should decide, rather than the British Government.[94] Hain's reaction was simply to turn on the 'Eurosceptic press', accusing it of publishing 'lurid fantasy', still insisting that the constitution was little more than a 'tidying-up exercise'.[95] Giscard dismissed all this furore.[96] The *Mail's* response, on 16 May, was to offer its own vote on a referendum.

Suddenly, in the midst of all this, there was an awful sense of *déjà vu* as yet another fraud scandal broke cover. Olaf and French prosecutors were investigating 'a vast enterprise of looting' of EU funds after £640,000 had gone missing from

---

92 12 May 2003.
93 The *Financial Times*, 13 May 2003.
94 The *Daily Telegraph*, 15 May 2003.
95 The *Daily Telegraph*, 16 May 2003.
96 The *Financial Times*, 16 May 2003.

the accounts of Eurostat, the EU's statistical organisation. No one had been suspended and the Commission still considering whether to take disciplinary action.[97]
After a month of further inactivity, the Commission would be forced to concede
that the allegations were 'far more significant' than had been known. Schreyer, the
anti-fraud commissioner, admitted her department had received a report in
February 2000 warning of possible fraud.[98] In an uncertain world, there was comfort in the knowledge that some things never changed.

With this to come, Blair was having to defend Hain after reports that Lord
Saatchi, Thatcher's former advertising guru, planned to launch a pro-referendum
campaign. Hain had accused him and others of peddling Eurosceptic 'lies' and
'baloney'. Those campaigning for a vote 'might as well put away their placards and
stop wasting their money because we are not going to do it', he said. The ideas
tabled were merely 'first drafts' that could be vetoed by national governments.[99]

The scrap had come at a sensitive time for Blair. He was meeting Giscard at
Number 10, to tell him that he would not tolerate any erosion of the British veto
on tax or foreign and defence policies: his so-called 'red lines'.[100] Straw, therefore,
took a hand. In a speech to the CBI in Brussels, he argued that changes would not
'remotely be on a par' with the single currency.[101] This was swiftly refuted by Jean-
Luc Dehaene, who told the *Today* programme that the constitution would create
a single 'political Europe' just as Maastricht had created a European economic
entity. On the eve of publishing the first full draft of his constitution, even Giscard
agreed a referendum was necessary. So did Hugo Young. 'The British people need
a new, transparent chance to decide the only big question worth putting: do you
want to remain a member of the European Union, or get out? That is the unspo-
ken agenda ...'[102]

Back in Brussels, before the constitution draft could be finalised, there had to
be a final crisis. That was the European way. It came when Giscard tried to replace
the voting system on the Council with a simple majority vote based on 60 percent
of the Union's population. That smashed the Nice deal and the Spanish, its greatest beneficiaries, blocked the move. Giscard halted the convention, leading to a
stand-off that lasted three days. The deal eventually struck allowed Spain to keep
a veto on allocating structural funding until 2017, allowing her to protect her
funding during the next negotiation round.[103]

Giscard also made a concession to Britain, removing the word 'federal' from his
draft. Much was made of this subsequently by Blair and his allies, as demonstrating that the Union no longer had any ambitions to become a 'federal superstate'.
Amato put it in perspective: 'adjectives are used by commentators; what we are
interested in is the substance'.[104]

97 The *Independent, The Irish Times*, 17 May 2003.
98 The *Financial Times*, 17 June 2003.
99 The *Daily Telegraph*, 19 May 2003.
100 The *Financial Times*, 19 May 2003.
101 The *Independent*, 20 May 2003.
102 The *Guardian*, 27 May 2003.
103 The *Financial Times*, 15 June 2003.
104 *Corriere della Sera*, 29 May 2003.

Gordon Brown was less pleased with Giscard's proposals for the eurozone to have its own 'finance minister'. But France and Britain had prevailed in keeping a foreign policy veto. Giscard acknowledged the brutal truth: 'Europe does not have a common foreign policy.' [105] Hain hailed the concessions. 'All the hype and fantasy and scaremongering and downright lies coming from the embittered Eurosceptics will prove to be unfounded,' he crowed. 'This draft is proof of that.' [106]

But more trouble was stacking up for Blair when he was warned that the Lords might block ratification of any new treaty unless there was a commitment to a referendum.[107] Hain then threw the government's policy into disarray by absurdly suggesting on the *Today* programme that, if voters did not like the constitution, they could vote against the government in the European elections. He added, 'I would be quite happy to fight ... endorsing this treaty, and the Conservatives can oppose it, and then the people will decide.' By lunchtime he had been forced into an embarrassing retraction.

By then Blair was on his way to Kuwait for a 'not-a-victory-tour'. But he was now preoccupied with the same problems that had dogged his predecessors. Soon the two years would be up after which parliament had been promised an assessment of Brown's 'five tests'. The answer was already an open secret, and with the polls consistently showing two-to-one majorities against the euro, the chance of winning a referendum was nil. On the other hand, the chances of winning any referendum on the constitution were no better. But, if left unresolved, the combination of constitution and euro threatened to dominate the next general election, giving the Conservatives an electoral gift. By whatever means, 'Europe' had to be neutralised. On his flight to Kuwait, Blair briefed journalists that the 'hysteria' over the constitution raised the deeper issue of Britain's membership of the EU. 'We should decide as a country whether we want to go forward in the European Union or not,' he said. 'I think the debate really does come to that in the end.' [108] Blair was testing the water for what his staff called the 'nuclear option': a referendum on whether Britain should stay in or leave the EU. This was possibly the only referendum he might hope to win.

Such an option could only have been more attractive when Giscard published the second part of his draft constitution. This included the Charter of Fundamental Rights. A document which was once to have no greater legal status than the *Beano* was now close to becoming Community law. Furthermore, the convention had also called for a European public prosecutor, increases in the power of the European Parliament in more than 30 policy areas and the removal of some 20 more national vetoes.[109] This was far from 'tidying up'. Blair was boxed in.

From Kuwait, his next stop was Warsaw for a speech.[110] He explained why he had refused to hold a referendum on the constitution, by comparing Britain with

105 The *Financial Times*, 26 May 2003.
106 The *Financial Times*, 27 May 2003.
107 The *Financial Times*, 28 May 2003.
108 The *Financial Times*, 28 May 2003.
109 The *Guardian*, 28 May 2003.
110 The full text of the speech is on: *www.downingstreet.gov.uk*. Excerpts in the *Guardian*, *The Times*, the *Daily Telegraph*, and others: 31 May 2003.

Poland. 'I note,' he said, 'that though you here in Poland are having a referendum on membership of the EU, you are not having one on the convention.' Developing this theme, he added, 'Likewise, for us, if we recommend entry to the euro it would be a step of such economic and constitutional significance that a referendum would be sensible and right.' Incredibly, after years of denying the constitutional implications of the euro, Blair was now justifying a referendum on the single currency because of its 'constitutional significance'. The euro was 'constitutionally significant'; the constitution was not.

No only was Blair's position illogical, he was also increasingly isolated. Shortly after his Warsaw speech, Lamberto Dini, former Italian prime minister and member of the convention, accused the British government of deceit: 'Anyone in Britain who claims the constitution will not change things is trying to sweeten the pill for those who don't want to see a bigger role for Europe.' [111] As if to underline Dini's words, the British government had discovered a clause in the constitutional draft, smuggled in at the last minute, which would permit the harmonisation of VAT and customs duties. This was the so-called 'escalator clause' (Article I-24), which permitted the European Council to change the contents of the treaty without resort to an IGC. [112]

From Warsaw, it was to St Petersburg for Blair, to meet world leaders for the city's 300th birthday, then on to Evian for a G8 Summit. There, Bush, who had also come via Poland and Russia, reminded Chirac that all was not forgotten, let alone forgiven. In a deliberate snub, he then left early to attend business in the Middle East. Back at the convention, last-minute negotiations were going on in a race to submit the constitution to the European Council at Thessalonika on 20 June. But they were largely for show. Giscard alone would decide whether consensus had been reached. [113]

Gordon Brown continued the counter-attack on the Eurosceptics. Britishness should no longer be equated with being anti-European, because British ideas and values were setting the pace for reform in the EU, he argued in the *Daily Telegraph*. It was possible to be pro-British and pro-European at the same time. Painting an unrecognisable picture of the EU, he then offered his 'way forward': 'intergovernmental, not federal; mutual recognition, not one-size-fits-all central rules; tax competition, not tax harmonisation, with proper political accountability and subsidiarity, not a superstate'. [114] The deception, or self-deception, was continuing to the end.

The following week, enough Poles gritted their teeth to edge the turnout just over the 50 percent needed to validate their referendum, bringing an 82 percent victory for the 'yes' camp. Millions of despondent or bewildered Poles simply stayed at home. For the Commission, it was 'a turning point in European history', adding to Lithuania, Hungary, Slovenia and Slovakia, all of which had now voted 'yes'. [115] The Czech Republic was to follow. Within weeks, its government would be

---

111 The *Daily Telegraph*, 1 June 2003.
112 *Ibid.*
113 The *Financial Times*, 10 June 2003.
114 3 June 2003.
115 The *Daily Telegraph*, 9 June 2003.

launching an austerity package aimed at cutting the deficit, preparatory to joining the euro. *Lidove Noviny* ran a headline, 'Welcome to the EU and back to reality'.[116]

For Britain 9 June 2003 was decision day on the euro. After years of work by the Treasury, producing 18 studies totalling some 1.5 million words filling over 2,000 pages, Brown's answer – to little surprise – was a positive 'maybe'.[117] The Chancellor offered another review in the autumn, leaving open the remote chance of a referendum in 2004 but he made it clear there was no change in policy.[118] For the time being, Blair's European ambitions were dead.

By then, the action had moved to Luxembourg where Fischler had offered yet another CAP 'reform' package, seeking to shift yet more funds from direct support to 'rural development' to reduce the overall cost. He was fighting for the Community's survival, for otherwise the EU would be bankrupt. There was also the 'Doha Round' of the GATT talks, where a deal on cutting export subsidies was desperately needed to reduce dumping surpluses on world markets.[119]

Yet again France and Germany struck a deal: to the *Financial Times*, 'a contemptible deal'.[120] Germany would help France emasculate Fischler's plan, to protect French farmers, in return for French support in opposing the Commission's plans for a take-over directive which would undermine the powers of the German *Länder*. With awesome symmetry the Franco-German alliance had gone back to its roots. Faced with outrage from other member states, Chirac calmly threatened to invoke the Luxembourg Compromise.[121] Nor did it end there. The expected deficit on the Community budget still had to be met, and an obvious source was the British rebate. To its horror, the Foreign Office had discovered in the 'escalator clause' a backdoor mechanism whereby Britain could be robbed of her most coveted concession.[122] From de Gaulle to Chirac, history had gone full circle.

Elsewhere, asymmetry was manifest. Unlike the French back in the 1960s, the Poles were not to get a cushion for their peasantry. They were to be exposed to the full force of competition from highly-subsidised EU produce, transported faster and cheaper down the Trans-European Network to Warsaw than many local farmers could hope to compete with. The only result could be an accelerated drift to the cities. Yet, the EU had also forced the 'rationalisation' of Poland's core industries, such as steel, intensifying already serious unemployment and wiping out any potential jobs for the dispossessed farmers. Emigration would be the only option, something foreseen by the existing EU member states, most of which had refused to allow rights of establishment for seven years. But not so Britain. Following Ireland's lead, she would allow entry to the eastern Europeans from day one of their accession. Furthermore, they would have the same entitlements to benefits, health care and education as UK nationals.[123] The Home Office believed that only

116 The *Boston Globe*, 22 June 2003.
117 10 June 2003.
118 The *Daily Telegraph*, 19 June 2003.
119 The *Financial Times*, 13 June 2003.
120 The *Financial Times*, 22 June 2003.
121 The *Daily Telegraph*, 21 June 2003.
122 The *Daily Telegraph*, 17 June 2003.
123 *The Times*, 19 and 20 June 2003.

5,000 to 13,000 would take advantage of this, but Migration Watch UK, a specialist think tank, warned that the UK could be facing 2.1 million immigrants by the year 2021.[124]

Rather ominously, it was time for Giscard to unveil his (almost) final draft – it was Friday 13 June. The contentious Part III had yet to be produced, and would have to wait until July. But the former French president held up the incomplete text and, trembling with emotion, declared, 'This result is imperfect but it is more than could have been hoped.' 'Instead of a half-formed Europe, we have a Europe with a legal identity, with a single currency, common justice, a Europe which is about to have its own defence.' Looking around the crowded chamber, he then 'divined' a consensus. Thus spoke the people of Europe.[125]

Jack Straw now decided to attack the Eurosceptic 'myths and hysteria'. 'The treaty confirms the EU as a union of nations, not a superstate,' he declared.[126] That day the *Daily Mail* revealed that of the 1.7 million people who had voted in its poll, 89.8 percent wanted a referendum. In a parallel ICM poll – the 'biggest ever', questioning 54,971 people – 88 percent of respondents agreed. 'Now will you listen Mr Blair?' it demanded.

With an unfortunate sense of timing, John Prescott had just announced referendums for elected assemblies in three northern regions. This was after prolonged 'sounding exercises' which had received backing from a 'derisory' 3,329 people out of a combined population of 14 million. Yet, to Prescott, there was an 'overwhelming case' for referendums in all three regions, proving that his party was one 'which believes in consulting people'.[127]

Shortly afterwards, Blair was on his way to Porto Carras in northern Greece, the Council having been moved seventy miles down the coast to avoid demonstrators. He left behind him in England a piece in the *Daily Mirror* accusing Duncan Smith of a 'hidden agenda to take Britain out of Europe'.[128] Would this be Blair's eventual referendum agenda?

The *Economist* would have made less happy reading for Blair. Its front cover had a picture of a large wastebasket, filled to the brim with paper, with the question 'Where to file Europe's new constitution?' The convention had produced a lamentable piece of work which, in many ways made the Union's constitutional architecture 'harder to understand'. 'That is', wrote the *Economist*, 'an incredible feat'.[129] The criticism was deserved. None of the central issues had been resolved. The institutional structure was still a 'sludgy amalgam' of intergovernmentalism and supranationalism. Germany's calls for clear limits to Commission powers had not been heeded.

Meanwhile, the 2,000-strong press corps waiting in Greece was being entertained by a complaint by Chirac against the Italian premier, who had refused to see Yassir Arafat during a recent visit to Israel. Berlusconi said he had been visiting in

124 The *Sunday Times*, 20 July 2003.
125 The *Financial Times*, 14 June 2003.
126 The *Guardian*, 17 June 2003.
127 *Hansard*, 16 June 2003, Col. 27.
128 19 June 2003.
129 Print edition, 19 June 2003.

his capacity as premier, not as the next holder of the EU presidency. France, he said, 'has lost a good opportunity to keep quiet'.[130] The president-in-waiting was now at odds with one of the EU's most powerful leaders, as well as the Commission president. Later, he was to take on the Parliament, by suggesting that a German MEP would make a good *kommandant* in a film about a concentration camp.

In the morning of 20 June 2003, Giscard handed over a blue leather-bound copy of his work to the heads of government, warning them not to unravel it. It marked, he said, 'an historic step in the direction of furthering the objectives of European integration'.[131] Astonishingly, Blair hailed the draft as 'a victory for Britain', although he conceded that there were still battles to be fought in the IGC, now due to start in October and to end the following spring with what would still, despite the delay, be a new Treaty of Rome.[132]

So far as Blair was concerned, those battles were going to be about 'red lines'. But all he would in fact be arguing about was whether the Charter of Fundamental Rights applied to EU institutions or governments; an EU public prosecutor; the veto on tax and social security; and whether the new 'EU foreign minister' would represent the Council.[133] Everything else had been conceded: not least the extensions of QMV which would bring to exactly 100 the areas of policy where, over the decades, the veto had been abandoned.

When Blair slipped away early, EU officials noted that much of Blair's rhetoric was now eerily similar to that of Thatcher and Major in years gone by.[134] Back home, the *Sunday Times* advised him that, if the new treaty introduced further integrationist measures, the solution was simple: 'Don't sign it'.[135] For the 'Community', there was no simple solution. Eighty years after its intellectual fathers, Salter and Monnet, had first come to believe they had the answer to Europe's problems, a way had still had not been found to resolve the fatal conflict between those two incompatible philosophies, intergovernmentalism and supranationalism. It seemed the strains this made inevitable would continue to undermine the dream of a 'United Europe' just so long as it managed to survive.[136]

---

130 The *Financial Times*, 18 June 2003.
131 The *Guardian*, 21 June 2003; *EurActiv*, 20 June 2003.
132 *The Times*, 21 June 2003.
133 The *Independent*, 20 June 2003.
134 The *Daily Telegraph*, 21 June 2003.
135 Leader, 22 June 2003.
136 The draft constitution would not be complete until 10 July 2003, when Giscard warned EU leaders not to make substantial changes to the 'fragile compromise' he had achieved. 'The consensus reached,' he said, 'far from being the lowest common denominator, represents the maximum that could be achieved'. 'I launch an appeal to politicians in Europe,' he ended. 'Citizens, say yes to our constitution.' At the 27th and last session of the convention, delegates added last-minute changes, including the EU flag, anthem, motto and an EU-wide celebration of 'Europe Day' on 9 May. They also agreed to authorise an EU diplomatic service, based in Brussels, to support the EU's new Foreign Minister (Associated Press, 10 July 2003).

Berlusconi symbolically celebrated the start of the Italian presidency by pushing for a directive to abolish compulsory hallmarking of gold, silver and platinum, thus destroying a system which had guaranteed the value of precious metals in Britain for 700 years. Britain was Europe's largest market for metal jewellery and Italy the largest producer, but much of her trade was dominated by the Mafia, which saw the elimination of hallmarking as a licence for fraud.

Chapter 20

Deception or Self-Deception?

'If you open that Pandora's box, you never know what Trojan 'orses will jump out.'
Ernest Bevin on the Council of Europe[1]

The most obvious reason why the story set out in these pages has never been told in this way before is because one of the triumphs of the 'European project' has been the way it has managed to create its own 'myth'. Not only has it attempted to shape the future. Thanks to an army of sympathetic historians, journalists, politicians and the Commission's own publicity machine, it has been superbly successful in reinventing the past. That is why, when one returns to the documentary record, as we have tried to do in this book, there is almost no episode of the European Union's history which does not emerge looking radically different from the version which has been presented by the 'myth'.

The story we have told could not have unfolded in the way it has without the remarkable gifts of one man. The unique achievement of Jean Monnet was not that he inspired the nations of Europe to an unprecedented degree of peaceful co-operation. Both in the 1920s and again in the late 1940s, many others more prominent than himself were gripped by the vision of creating a 'United States of Europe'. What marked out Monnet and Salter when they first conceived their own version of this dream was their conviction that this could only be brought about in one way: by giving Europe a government that was supranational.

This was why they regarded as their greatest enemy not so much nationalism itself as that rival form of internationalism which might seem to be aspiring to achieve the same ends but in a way they saw as doomed to failure: that voluntary co-operation between sovereign governments, the ineffectuality of which they saw as having destroyed the League of Nations. To Monnet no language of condemnation was strong enough to convey his hatred of 'intergovernmentalism'. It was a 'poison', 'pollution', the ultimate delusion.

Part of Monnet's genius lay in his extraordinary ability, operating behind the scenes, to manipulate other people into doing what he wanted. But the other part of his genius was his realisation that he was never going to win acceptance for what he wanted if he went for it directly and all at once. He instinctively knew he

---

1 Barclay, Sir Roderick, *Ernest Bevin and the Foreign Office 1932–1969* (London, Latimer) (1975), p. 67.

could only achieve his goal by working towards it crabwise, step by step, and by concealing the real nature of that goal behind a pretence that it was something less than what it was. There were heady moments when he was tempted to burst out into the open: most notably in the early 1950s when, carried away by his coup in setting up the Coal and Steel Community, he spoke of it as 'the first government of Europe', and then, two years later, launched his plan for a 'European Political Community'. But, with Spaak's aid, he soon learned from these mistakes. Thus emerged what was perhaps his most influential bequest to the 'European project', that strategy which came to be known as *engrenage* or 'the Monnet method'.

There would never be any single, clear definition of these terms. But every 'project' insider would know what was meant by *engrenage*, or 'gearing'. It provided a blanket word to describe all those various techniques whereby the 'project' could advance what was really its only underlying agenda: a steady, relentless pressure to extend the Commission's supranational powers. Each new advance it made would merely be regarded as a means of gearing up for the next. Each new addition to its competences might begin with a small, innocuous-seeming proposal to which nobody could object: until the principle was conceded and those powers could then be steadily enlarged. Each new problem or setback could be used as a 'beneficial crisis' to justify further extending the Commission's powers to provide the remedy.

Thus, brick by brick, would the great supranational structure be assembled. Above all it would be vital never to define too clearly what was the 'project's' ultimate goal, for fear this would arouse the countervailing forces which might seek to sabotage it before it was complete.

In this sense, an intention to obscure and to deceive was implicit in the nature of the 'project' from the moment it was launched. This habit of concealment was to remain such a defining characteristic of the 'project' that it would come increasingly to affect all those caught in its spell.

The roots of deception

There is no more glaring instance of the way the 'myth' has rewritten history than its reworking of how the project was first launched on the world in 1950. Again and again this is presented as having been essentially the vision of Robert Schuman, coupled with what a long procession of the project's sympathisers up to Tony Blair have followed Acheson in calling Britain's 'worst mistake of the post-war period', by failing to join it at its inception.

As we have seen, the Schuman Declaration perfectly exemplified the 'Monnet method' at work. Using Schuman as little more than a ventriloquist's dummy, he seized the opportunity of a 'beneficial crisis' to implement his long premeditated stratagem, drawn from the thinking of the 1920s, that the project should initially be presented as no more than a plan to set up a supranational authority to control the industries crucial to waging war. But the whole point of this device, as he explained to Spaak in Washington in 1941 and Macmillan in Algiers in 1943, was that it could then be used as the foundation for eventual political union.

In the early post-war years others, inspired by Monnet, made premature bids to turn both the OEEC and the Council of Europe into supranational bodies. In each case these efforts were rebuffed, above all by the country which was the leading advocate of the intergovernmental co-operation Monnet despised, Britain. Nothing was more blatant in Monnet's plan for a Coal and Steel Community than the lengths to which he went to ensure the British were kept out, for fear they might corrupt it with their intergovernmentalism. It was indeed precisely its supranational element which the Attlee government was so quick to recognise and reject.

All this was, of course, to be repeated even more dramatically a few years later when Monnet, now head of his Action Committee for a United States of Europe, began discussing with Spaak the next leap forward. It was Spaak who more than anyone was responsible for guiding the project towards its greatest breakthrough of all, the Treaty of Rome. And it was Spaak who steered Monnet into accepting what was to become the central deception of the whole story, when he urged that all mentions of political or 'federal' union should be suppressed and that the project should be sold to the world as no more than a 'common market', designed to promote peaceful economic co-operation, trade and general prosperity.

Again the 'myth', as developed by British publicists such as Young and Denman, has presented this as the second occasion when Britain 'missed a historic opportunity' to become involved and thus to shape the project in ways which, to quote Blair, might have 'reflected British interests'. But again this is to stand the facts of history on their head. Britain's post-war record in promoting European co-operation on an intergovernmental basis was second to none, from the OEEC and the Council of Europe to NATO and the WEU. This was precisely why Monnet and Spaak were again determined to keep Britain out of their project at all costs: not least by making membership of the EEC conditional on joining Euratom, on terms they knew would make it impossible for the British to accept.

When Britain then persisted in trying to promote intergovernmental co-operation through free trade, the OEEC, the FTA and EFTA, Monnet used all his influence behind the scenes, not least through the USA, to sabotage those efforts. Only when he became seriously alarmed that his old ally de Gaulle was trying to subvert the project from within, by dragging it back towards intergovernmentalism, did Monnet go through that U-turn which led him to want Britain in.

Britain joins the deceit

From Britain's point of view, the story can then be understood better in terms of psychology than of rational political calculation. Britain's change of heart over 'Europe' around 1960 stemmed more than anything from her post-Suez loss of national self-confidence and from the onset of that collective inferiority complex which resulted from comparing the performance of her own faltering, obsolescent economy with the new-found 'dynamism' of her Common Market neighbours.

It was this loss of nerve which led London almost overnight to abandon all its old inhibitions about subordinating Britain's affairs to a supranational form of government. From the Cabinet papers of the time, it is clear that Macmillan and his ministers were fully aware of the wider political implications of what they were doing: that the real purpose of the European project was to work towards ultimate political union, and that this would involve an open-ended commitment to surrendering power from Westminster to Brussels. When Macmillan visited Kennedy in April 1961, he was in effect told by Monnet's friend Ball that Washington would only support Britain's application to join on condition that she accepted that the Common Market's true goal was political integration. Heath had already given Ball assurances to that effect on his visit to London.

What is equally clear, however, is that Macmillan and Heath took a conscious decision not to explain this openly to the British people. For what they called 'presentational' reasons, they would persist in the fiction that the Common Market was essentially only an economic project, concerned with trade and jobs. Similarly they carefully downplayed the hugely damaging consequences for the Commonwealth of Britain's decision to join an essentially inward-looking, protectionist trading bloc, membership of which would force her to turn her back on her main trading partners.

Certainly this amounted to deliberate deception. But what also now emerges from the evidence is the remarkable degree to which the Macmillan government and the Foreign Office officials were themselves deceived in failing to understand de Gaulle's real motives in wishing to keep Britain out. Throughout the 1960s, France was driven by her desire to establish a Common Agricultural Policy which was not really an agricultural policy at all. The CAP was a political and social policy, designed to protect French farmers for the ultimate purpose of protecting the French state.

Only in 1969, when France had finally ensured that other countries would subsidise her farmers, did the French now actively need British entry. This was because, in being forced to impose levies on imports of food from the Commonwealth, the proceeds of which would go direct to Brussels to fund the CAP, Britain would simultaneously be handing over the cash to subsidise French farmers and providing a market for their surpluses (which, thanks to EC subsidies, could be sold in Britain at prices below any Commonwealth competition). There is little evidence that the British understood just how profoundly they had been stitched up twice over by this arrangement, even though it would eventually lead to the battle over Britain's disproportionate contribution to the EC budget. Nothing demonstrates more completely how far the British were deceived by this stratagem than the touching belief of Heath, Young, Denman and others that France's reversal of her opposition to British entry stemmed somehow from the 'personal chemistry' between Heath and Pompidou.

Heath's own bid to join the Common Market began what for the British people was to be the greatest deception of all. Without any electoral mandate, having barely mentioned 'Europe' during his 1970 election campaign, on arriving in office Heath almost immediately applied for entry. What were presented as 'negotiations' were no more than a prolonged act of surrender, on everything from the Commonwealth to the CAP, summed up by Con O'Neill as 'swallow it whole and swallow it now'. Even more blatantly than in 1961, Heath persistently misrepresented Britain's membership of the Common Market as no more than a trading issue, when behind the scenes this was already being given the lie by the Werner and Davignon proposals for monetary and political union.

So misleading was the picture Heath and his ministers gave to Parliament and to the electorate that on occasion they stepped over into direct untruths, as in Rippon's denial of how completely they had given away control of Britain's fishing waters, and their White Paper promise that joining the Community would involve no surrender of 'essential sovereignty'. Only 30 years later would it come to light from the Foreign Office's confidential papers just how conscious were its officials of the extent to which Britain was about to surrender its powers of self-government. None of this was publicly admitted at the time, although the author of the FCO's internal memorandum on 'Sovereignty' justified the concealment by suggesting that the British people would not notice what was happening until the end of the century, by which time it would be too late to protest because the process would have become irreversible.

Other FCO papers released in 2003 were to confirm just how far the 'European' issue was in the early 1970s drawing senior civil servants into abandoning their traditionally strict obligation to remain apart from partisan politics. The part played by FCO officials in the propaganda campaign launched by the government to win support for entry marked the beginning of that 'politicisation' of the civil service which would eventually turn into the 'spin machine' of the Blair era. It was a telling instance of how, even at this early stage, 'Europe' was beginning subtly to erode the established disciplines of British public life.

In 1974 and 1975, the deception continued, firstly with the charade of Wilson's renegotiation, then with the curiously one-sided referendum campaign. For the 'Yes' side, this was directed from the Foreign Office on the advice of a marketing expert who, even 30 years later, would be proudly recalling how he had deliberately steered the campaign away from any serious political debate, in order to concentrate voters' minds on such 'bread and butter' issues as prices and jobs.

Looked back on in light of how 'Europe' was later to develop, it is startling to see how far the 'Yes' campaign's message was characterised by this trivialisation and concealment of the real issues; making nonsense of later claims that the British people only voted for continued membership after the issues had been fully explained to them. Almost everything they were told was either irrelevant or untrue. Wilson's unashamed insistence that any threat of monetary union had been removed, only six months after he had agreed with his fellow heads of government that plans for monetary union should continue, was a measure of just how far 'Europe' was now leading Britain's politicians into a curious new world of make-believe, where conventional standards of truth were slipping below the horizon.

The deception of Thatcher

If her predecessor as Tory leader had deliberately set out to deceive the British people over 'Europe', the odd thing about Mrs Thatcher's role in the story was the extent to which she would eventually find herself more in the position of the British people, as a victim of that deception herself.

When she first took on her party's leadership, she was a typical, naïve enthusiast for 'Europe', knowing little about it but happily spouting the regulation propagandist mantras about the need for peace and international co-operation. Four years later, as prime minister and already a little wiser, she inherited the position established by the Labour government in the second half of the 1970s, where Britain was seen as 'the awkward partner', not seeming quite to fit in with the rest of the Community on anything. Thatcher's indignation at what she saw as Britain's disproportionate budget contribution, resulting directly from the system devised to assist France's farmers, was also inherited from her Labour predecessors, although she set about trying to remedy the 'injustice' with rather more determination. But once the budget issue was resolved, as she put it, she looked forward to Britain playing a full and co-operative part in the Community's affairs.

What she was unaware of was just how fast, in the early 1980s, the momentum was already developing behind the scenes for a further great leap forward in integration, taking the 'project' in directions where she would not wish to follow. With full support from a British Commission president, Jenkins, the ERM had already been launched as a prelude to that single currency which as far back as the late 1950s Monnet had seen as the key to political integration. Spinelli was hard at work building support for his plans to create a 'European Union'. Adonnino had been commissioned to follow up the 'Solemn Declaration on European Union' in 1983 by reporting on ways to promote a sense of 'European identity'.

The real significance of all this, it seems, passed Thatcher by; and a large part of the responsibility for this lay with the failure of her closest advisers properly to brief her on what was going on: most notably, after 1983, her Foreign Secretary Howe and his civil servants. As in the 1960s and the 1970s, those celebrated 'Rolls Royce minds' of the FCO, with their supposedly strong sympathy for 'Europe', were shown up as being out of touch with the arcane manoeuvrings of Community politics.

All this came to a head, of course, at the Milan Council in 1985 when, having been lulled into complaisance by Kohl, Mitterrand and Delors giving support for her initiative on 'the internal market', she was humiliatingly bounced into accepting a new treaty, which she had just explained to her partners she did not think was necessary. What Howe and the FCO had failed to explain, although the evidence was there for them to see, was that the 'Single Act' was already planned to be merely the first of two new treaties: the purpose of which would be to move the Community forward to a wholly new phase of integration as the 'European Union', complete with its own currency, integrated foreign and defence policies and the rest.

Having herself been deceived into accepting a 'Single European Act' which itself represented a considerable extension of the Community's supranational powers, Thatcher now fell back on trying to deceive the British people back home into thinking that the new treaty was really no more than what she had initially wanted: primarily concerned with setting up a 'single market'. In this respect, her government's propaganda machine went into overdrive, proclaiming all the benefits British businesses would derive from the arrival in 1993 of the kind of free-trading area most people thought the 'Common Market' had been intended to be in the first place.

Smarting from the way she had been tricked, however, just when her policies were beginning to transform the British economy into Europe's *wirtschaftwunder* of the late-20th century, Thatcher's eyes were at last being opened to the 'project's' real nature. From now on, as she increasingly tried to rip away the veils of deceit and to proclaim what she saw as the truth, as in her Bruges speech of 1988, the more isolated she became: not just from her 'partners' in Europe but from her colleagues at home.

The most curious episode at this time was the running battle with her two most senior colleagues, Lawson and Howe, over the ERM. As a passionate if largely uncomprehending Europhile, Howe's determination to push Britain into the ERM as a first stage towards the single currency which had been flagged up in the Single European Act was understandable. What made the episode truly bizarre, however, was Lawson's fond illusion that joining the ERM had no connection with the single currency, and would merely provide Britain with a desirable form of financial discipline. In his attempt to smuggle Britain into the ERM by secretly shadowing the *Deutschmark*, without daring to tell Thatcher, Lawson was deceiving not only his prime minister but also himself. When he joined with Howe in threatening their double-resignation unless she agreed to Britain entering the ERM, they were foreshadowing not only their own political downfall but also the disintegration of the Thatcher government. When Lawson's successor Major took Britain into the ERM, he was laying the seeds for the eventual demoralisation of the Conservative Party. And when Howe's petulant resignation speech precipitated Thatcher's own downfall, the ever-increasing web of deception and illusion in which 'Europe' had been wreathing British politics since the 1960s had claimed its most spectacular victim to date.

From now on, Britain's relations with 'Europe' would ever more clearly bear out that ancient truth of human nature: that when people set out to deceive others, they end up only by deceiving themselves.

The 'pro-European' orthodoxy

One of the hardest things for future historians to reconstruct about British attitudes to 'Europe' in the late 1980s and early 1990s will be the peculiar psychological pressure which had by now built up to make the benefits of Britain's membership of the Community an article of faith which no rational person could question. In the worlds of politics, the media and big business, acceptance of 'Europe' had become an unchallenged orthodoxy.

Although to a degree this had been deliberately engineered, by the skilful use of key words and phrases, the mindset it engendered became largely unconscious. One of its most successful tricks had been to make the word 'Europe' itself synonymous with the form of government taking shape just at one end of it; so that any distrust of the political 'Europe' could be portrayed as xenophobic hostility to everything stood for by the wider geographical Europe with all its diverse people and cultures.

To support the 'project' was thus to be seen as 'pro-European', implying that this meant outward-looking, positive, internationalist, progressive, on the side of the future, Any 'anti-European' could be labelled as inward-looking, negative, narrowly nationalistic, fearful of change, belonging to the past. The EU's sympathisers described themselves as 'Europhiles', which sounded upbeat and pleasant. Those opposing it were condemned as 'Europhobes', conveying that they were consumed with negativity. From within the 'pro-European bubble', even the most rational doubts directed at the 'project' condemned the doubter as 'hysterical', 'embittered', 'fanatical' or 'swivel-eyed'.

Effective though this was in propaganda terms, the unwitting confusion of 'political Europe' with the wider geographical and cultural Europe could have surreal consequences: as when in 1999 Tony Blair observed on the BBC *Today* programme that the crisis in the Balkans was 'a tragedy unfolding almost on the doorstep of Europe'. As if fossilised in the perspectives of a previous generation, the 'pro-Europeans' persisted in seeing only the countries of western Europe as the 'wider world', at a time when, thanks to modern travel, ever greater numbers of their fellow-citizens were venturing all over the globe. Yet those who suggested that Britain should be less preoccupied with introverted political experiments in Europe and look out to the wider world of the Americas, Asia and Australasia where Britain did half her trade, might well find themselves scorned as 'xenophobic little Englanders'.

An even odder feature of this psychological phenomenon was how hazy seemed to be the knowledge of many of these self-styled 'pro-Europeans' about the supposed object of their admiration. We saw how Roy Jenkins was honest enough to admit this in his memoirs, when, on becoming President of the Commission, he discovered how little he knew of how the Community worked (he was familiar, as he put it, only with its '*grandes lignes*'). But the same was true of countless other 'Europhiles', from Howe and Heseltine to Blair and Cook. They enjoyed the general sense of moral superiority they associated with being 'in favour of Europe', because this made them feel positive and internationalist. But when it came to showing any real understanding of the political system they championed, they all too often proved startlingly ill-informed.

In one sense this was not surprising. Ever since the early 1960s, the most conspicuous feature of British public discussion of 'Europe' had been its superficiality, and the reluctance of politicians to engage in genuine debate or to explain what British membership really involved. All too often their contributions had run to little more than empty slogans. But their refusal properly to debate the issues in fact disguised a deeper reluctance even to think about them, which was one reason why, to so many people, the 'European' issue had become synonymous with infinite tedium (a famous *Private Eye* cover in 1967 showed a group of people asleep in deckchairs, with the caption 'Common Market – The Great Debate Begins').

But this lack of understanding had been covered up by the emergence of a kind of *bien-pensant* consensus: a prevailing orthodoxy that Britain's involvement in 'Europe' was a good thing which should not be questioned. This had already been evident at the time of the 1975 referendum, when almost the entire political, media and business establishment supported the 'Yes' campaign. By the end of the 1980s the power of this mindset, along with the intolerance it directed towards anyone who could not accept it, was at its height. And there was no clearer example of this than the fashionable momentum which built up in 1989 and 1990 to press for British entry to the ERM. By the time Major took Britain in, he had the almost unanimous support of all establishment opinion, ranging from the leaderships of all three political parties to the CBI, the TUC and the mainstream media.

When Major became prime minister, his eagerness to appease the ruling orthodoxy explained his declaration that he wanted Britain to be 'at the heart of Europe'; even though this was almost immediately belied by the way that, on two of the central issues on the agenda for Maastricht nine months later, EMU and the Social Chapter, he was soon irreconcilably at odds with the rest of the Community.

The immediate response to the Maastricht treaty itself reflected just how shallow was the general British understanding of 'European' politics. As usual, it was reported chiefly in terms of personalities and of how successfully Major had 'defended British interests'. Scarcely noticed was the fact that, as planned since 1984, the Treaty of European Union marked the greatest leap forward in integration since the Treaty of Rome. Even less recognised was the significance of its failure to bring the two new 'pillars' of foreign and defence policy and justice and home affairs into the 'Community' net, thus marking the first serious sign of disintegration in that supranational model which had governed the Community's evolution ever since 1957.

When Tory backbench dissidents attempted the following year to subject the treaty's contents to detailed parliamentary scrutiny, they were scornfully dismissed by the orthodox as no more than a handful of embittered, 'little Englander' malcontents. When in September 1992 Britain was forced out of the ERM, her economy plunged into a recession which had brought misery to millions, this marked the end of the most obviously disastrous venture into which Britain's entanglement with 'Europe' had yet led her. But still so powerful was the spell this had cast over an establishment which had almost unanimously favoured Britain's entry into the ERM that even now the 'pro-Europeans' were unable to see how this horrendous misjudgement had resulted directly from their infatuation with a system the true nature of which they had not begun to grasp. Deception was giving way to self-deception.

The culture of deceit

Something very odd began to happen to British public life in the early 1990s. A gulf was beginning to open up between government and people, between politicians and voters, of a kind which had never been seen before. 'Europe' was not the only cause of this drawing apart, but it was the chief cause; and the cataclysmic collapse in Conservative support which followed the ERM debacle was its first conspicuous symptom.

One reason why the debate over 'Europe' had always been so unreal in Britain was that it had been so abstract and theoretical. For 30 years it had invariably tended to centre on what might or might not happen sometime in the hypothetical future. When such and such thing happens, ran the argument – when Britain enters the Common Market, when the Single Market arrives, when Britain joins the euro – all sorts of benefits will follow. There was little the other side could reply except to predict that these promised benefits were being vastly exaggerated and would probably not materialise at all. The contestants in such debates could never hope to engage, because there was no objective evidence to show which side was right or wrong.

The importance of the launch of the Single Market was that for the first time it was an event directly affecting hundreds of thousands of businesses in such a way that they could soon judge whether all those grandiose claims made for the advantages it would bring were true or not. Very soon, the verdict of countless businesses on the Single Market was that it had been so much hype. They had been faced with an unprecedented avalanche of time-consuming and costly new regulations and bureaucracy. But the benefits promised as their reward turned out in most cases to be non-existent.

For the first time since Britain joined the Common Market, a significant minority of people were able to base their view of 'Europe' on direct experience rather than theory, and their response varied from mere disillusionment to downright hostility. They felt they had been deceived.

What angered many even more was that their frustration met with no sympathy from government whatever. Tory ministers and MPs continued to prattle on about the benefits of the Single Market, seemingly impervious to the fact that it had brought so much pain with little gain. The response of the Europhile business establishment was the same. The CBI in 1994 produced one of its famous 'pro-EU polls', purporting to show that 71 percent of British businesses 'were enjoying greater trading opportunities with Europe, due to the Single Market'. This was heavily publicised by the BBC and Tory ministers. But examined in detail, the survey's findings turned out to show something quite different. Only 27 percent of the firms contacted said they had increased their business as a consequence of the Single Market, while similar percentages complained that they had been damaged either by 'over-zealous implementation of EC legislation' by British officials, or by 'unfair competition' through other EC countries failing to ensure a level playing field. A second survey a year later showed all these negative responses substantially increased, with 44 percent of firms now complaining of the UK's 'over-zealous enforcement' and 41 percent of 'unfair competition'.[2]

Many business people were further disconcerted to find that, when they attempted to raise their problems with MPs and ministers, they would now be told

2 *Castle of Lies, op. cit.*, pp. 167–169.

there was nothing the politicians could do, because this was 'legislation which comes from Europe'. They were making the same discovery as the farmers and the fishermen: that whole sectors of government policy and the power to legislate had been handed over to Brussels. They were learning the hard way what it meant to live under a form of government which was no longer accountable, because their own politicians no longer had any power to help them.

What the British people were beginning to face, in fact, was precisely that situation which had been predicted by the secret Foreign Office memorandum on 'Sovereignty' back in 1971, when, by the end of the century, they would discover that most of their laws were made by anonymous armies of officials over whom their elected representatives had no control. The FCO paper had suggested that this might result in a wholesale sense of alienation by the electorate from the political process. But at least its author had then been able to console himself with the thought that all this was still far in the future. In the 1990s that distant day had now arrived.

The most obvious response by the politicians was to retreat ever further into their bunker and simply to try to gloss over what had happened with more deceit and propaganda. Major's response, as we have seen, was to proclaim a 'deregulation' policy which in five years did nothing whatever to stem the ever greater flow of regulations; and which was barred from even pretending to curb that part of the flood which was having the most damaging impact, the mass of new laws now emanating from Brussels.

In face of mounting public concern, even the most dedicated acolytes champions of the 'project', such as Hurd and Brittan, might try to claim that the flow of regulation was being reduced, or that it could be diminished by 'subsidiarity'. This was a particularly disingenuous form of deception, because producing legislation was what the Commission was for. The whole purpose of that legislation was to pursue the 'project's' central agenda: to promote ever further integration, by replacing national laws with 'European' laws. Such was the essence of 'supranational' government. To ask it to behave any differently, as was observed, would be like someone confronted by an elephant saying he would prefer it to be a sheep.

Another response from British ministers, often unwittingly abetted by the ignorance of the media, was to maintain the fiction that they were still in charge, by deliberately concealing that the laws they were having to introduce originated from Brussels. They now routinely pretended, as John Prescott was to do with his £8.5 billion-worth of water regulations and his policy for regional governments, that these initiatives were all their own idea. The oddest thing about this was it was often these same ministers who were otherwise only too happy to proclaim their enthusiasm for the EU. Logically, they should therefore have been happy to boast that the laws they were introducing had been produced by the system of government they claimed to admire. But when it came to admitting that they themselves no longer had the power to legislate, their willingness to extol the virtues of living under a supranational government evaporated.

One body which had no inhibitions about advertising its virtues was the European Commission itself, which was why it was constantly looking for new ways to advance its cause through different forms of propaganda. Increasingly in the 1990s it poured money into providing the schools of the European Union with books, videos and other teaching materials. These were designed, as Adonnino recommended, to introduce 'a European dimension' into every aspect of the school curriculum, from history and geography to cookery lessons and counting games for the under-5s played with toy euros.

The most conspicuous propaganda vehicle of all, however, was all the different forms of regional aid, by which Brussels showered out more than £20 billion a year on tens of thousands of projects all over the EU, to fund anything from unfinished Greek motorways to the World Disabled Sailing Championships in Rutland to a Michelin two-star restaurant in the Var. Invariably a condition of receiving Brussels funding was that the project should in some way exhibit the telltale 'ring of stars', to convey the subliminal message that this public benefit could only have been achieved through the benevolence of the European Union. What such mandatory publicity never revealed in Britain, however, was that, for every £1 received from Brussels, UK taxpayers had to hand over £2 to Brussels in the first place, and that this had to be topped up with a further £1 in 'match funding'. From the Commission's point of view, it was a very economical form of advertising. But it was equally a very deliberate form of deceit.[3]

Such were some of the hidden realities of the political landscape in which, in the mid-1990s, John Major cut an increasingly forlorn figure. He was presiding over a government more and more of whose activities were now being dictated by another quite different centre of government, in another country; yet a prime concern of his ministers was to pretend this was not happening. He was under constant pressure from senior members of his party to make the greatest and most symbolic surrender of his government's power of all, by joining the euro; yet he felt compelled to pretend that this was only a technical matter of economics, and that handing over control of Britain's money and economic policy to unaccountable officials in Frankfurt had no political or constitutional implications whatever.

On all sides Major was learning what it meant to be leader of a country which had already surrendered much of its powers of self-government to the supranational system Monnet had launched all those years before, and which was now demanding yet more. On the continent he was now continually at odds with a system which was acting in ways he considered to be contrary to his country's interest, from prohibiting Britain's world-wide beef exports to closing down her fishing industry, from damaging Britain's position as the world's leading art market by forcing him to impose VAT on art sales to ordering him through the

---

3 In June 1995, adverse publicity about the size of Britain's budget contribution led David Williamson, the director-general of the European Commission, to claim in a speech in York that the contribution by 'each Briton' was only '2p a week'. This was reported by the *Observer* as 'just 2p per head per year'. The Commission's own figures showed that in 1995 each UK household contributed £345 in taxes to the EC budget, equating to £132 a head or £2.54 a week. The Commission's top civil servant was thus wrong by a factor of 12,700 percent, the *Observer* by 660,000 percent (*Castle of Lies, op. cit.*, p. 225).

ECJ to accept the directive limiting the working week to 48 hours. Yet at home, as he floundered towards another general election with the morale of his party at zero, he weakly continued to protest that he was 'winning the argument' and that Europe was 'coming Britain's way'.

The veils of deception and self-deception were now swirling so thickly around all Major did that it was no longer possible to distinguish one from the other. In personal terms, it must in some ways have seemed a relief to be freed from this prison, as his party went down to its greatest election defeat in history. But, from Britain's point of view, power now passed to a leader for whom deception was so much second nature that it would become the defining characteristic of his government. As Blair declared his wish to play a 'leading role in Europe', He can little have guessed how he was about to be outplayed at his own game, in the 'Europe' in which he now for the first time found himself directly participating.

La grande illusion

In the summer of 2003, half a century after Monnet addressed the assembly of his Coal and Steel Community as 'the first government of Europe', it might have seemed on paper that his project had travelled a very long way down the road towards its intended goal; a surprising amount of this achieved in just the previous few years.

Giscard was handing over the draft constitution of what he wanted to call 'the United States of Europe', as a rival world power to the United States of America. Less than a year ahead this new 'government of Europe' was due to establish its sway over 25 nations, presiding over more of the continent than any power in history, apart from Napoleon and Hitler. It had already now issued its own money, the introduction of which in January 2002 Prodi had described as:

'... not economic at all. It is a completely political step ... the historical significance of the euro is to construct a bipolar economy in the world. The two poles are the dollar and the euro. That is the political meaning of the single European currency. It is a step beyond which there will be others. The euro is just an antipasto.'[4]

Already in Africa the first military units wearing EU insignia were in service, as the embryo of the European Union's own armed forces. In 2002 it had laid claim to control of all air traffic within its borders, in the name of what it called 'the Single European Sky'. It had long since claimed control of all the fish in the seas round its shores, which were now described as 'Union waters' to be fished by a single 'Union fleet'. It had laid plans to rival the USA by launching into space the 34 satellites which would form the Galileo global positioning system, designed, among other things, to give it electronic oversight and potential control of all the traffic on Europe's roads.

Even Monnet himself might have been astonished at the progress his '*bébé*' had made.

---

4 Interview on CNN, 1 January 2002.

In reality, however, all was not as well with the 'project' as its supporters might have wished to pretend. As Giscard's constitution headed off for months of acrimonious haggling behind the closed doors of the intergovernmental conference, it was already clear that his 'consensus' had failed to reconcile any of those fundamentally incompatible views which had been emerging in the previous few years as to which sort of 'Europe' should finally emerge.

The applicant countries might now be recording majorities for entry in their referendums. But once the realities of the price their people would have to pay for membership became evident, it seemed likely that their accession would arouse a backlash of intense resentment at the 'second class' status they had been given.

As for the straitjacket of the euro, it was now by the summer of 2003 imposing increasingly severe strains on the eurozone economies. From Portugal, from Ireland, from Greece, there were cries of anguish that their economies were faced with problems their governments no longer had the power to control. Led by France, Germany and Italy, eurozone members were now flagrantly breaking the rules on government deficits. In the summer of 2003 the entire economy of the eurozone for the first time went formally into recession, with German unemployment figures in the year's second quarter alone rising by 650,000, their highest quarterly rise since unification.[5] Polls showed more than half the voters of Germany, France and Holland wanting to return to their old currencies. The one-size-fit-all currency, administered by a supranational body in Frankfurt, was failing for precisely the reasons almost every informed observer had predicted. But since, in Prodi's words, its purpose had not been 'economic at all' but 'political', this was not surprising.[6]

The dream of a 'European army' had so far generated more new bureaucrats in Brussels than troops on the ground. The 'Single European Sky' was no more than another typically grandiose gesture, since air traffic control in Europe had already been efficiently co-ordinated on an intergovernmental basis since 1960.[7] The only success of the Common Fisheries Policy had been to create an ecological catastrophe of world proportions. As for 'Europe's' dream that its own fleet of satellites might soon be stationed in space around the earth, as another symbol of how it was now a rival to the United States, it somehow took the edge off the glory of this achievement to discover the extent to which this project, using Ariane rockets, was really designed as an enormous £20 billion make-work scheme for France's aerospace industry.

---

5 'Eurozone in the Red As French Economy Shrinks', *The Times*, 1 August 2003.
6 Even Delors was forced to admit that his euro was 'not working', although naturally his remedy was to propose greater integration by means of 'fiscal co-ordination' (the *Financial Times*, 2 April 2003).
7 Air traffic control across Europe had since 1960 been co-ordinated by Eurocontrol, which under its 'Single European Sky' policy, the Commission now sought to place under its proposed new European Air Safety Agency. In its drive for integration, it was now a general strategy of the Commission to take over pan-European bodies run on an intergovernmental basis (including governments still outside the EU). The European Postal Union, co-ordinating postal co-operation between 44 countries, had now been placed under an EC directive. Similar power grabs were made for the Joint Aviation Authority and the European Patents Office. The European activities of the World Health Authority in combating disease were to be taken over by the new European Health Protection Agency, and the work in Europe of Interpol was now being taken over by Europol.

The most obvious problem with the most ambitious political project in Europe's history was that, in practice, like its single most ambitious component, the euro itself, it wasn't working. And the reason for this was quite simple. Everything it had attempted or pretended to do, from its agriculture policy to its overseas aid programme, from its regional policy to its currency, from its regulation of food safety to its regulation of fisheries, from its competition policy to its ever proliferating thickets of rules to protect the environment, it was setting out to do by the same self-defeatingly tortuous bureaucratic methods which were not achieving the intended results.

The immense law factory centred on Brussels was ceaselessly churning out directives, regulations, decisions, recommendation and opinions, all purporting to make 'Europe' a better, safer, fairer, better organised, more environmentally responsible place in which to live. But anyone who studied the workings of this mass of regulation in detail could see that remarkably little of it was actually achieving these desirable ends; and one reason for this was that it was not really intended to. One of the hardest truths for any outsider to grasp about the project was that the real motive for everything it had set its hand to since 1952 was not to create a better world in the interests of 'Europe's' citizens, but simply to promote that ever-greater integration which, ultimately, was the project's only real purpose. Evidence for this could be seen precisely in the extent to which, in practice, its tens of thousands of laws were failing to realise the purposes claimed as the excuse for issuing them.

Central to the Commission's strategy were its efforts to enmesh the governmental systems of the member states so closely together that no national government could any longer hope to work on its own. Economically and industrially the aim was the same: to build up such a state of interdependence that no country could any longer run its economy independently, as was symbolised by those defence projects, such as the Eurofighter and Airbus, where one country was allowed to make the wings, another the engines, a third the fuselage.

Administratively, nothing marked out the Commission's ambitions more clearly in the first years of the new century than its moves to assume control over one sector after another of the member states' own administrative machines, by setting up its own 'European agencies', which, with the Commission, could then from behind the scenes direct national civil servants to do their bidding without the Commission having to foot the bill. The European Foods Safety Authority, the European Environment Agency, the European Fisheries Agency, the European Railways Agency, the European Chemicals Agency, the European Aviation Safety Agency, the European Maritime Safety Agency, the European Health Protection Agency: the list grew ever longer. Thus could the Commission act as a super-government without having to become a super-state, because the nation states were increasingly there just to do its supranational bidding.

Another characteristic of this ever more powerful system of government, however, was the extent to which it could itself be manipulated by powerful lobby groups and commercial or professional interests, to draft legislation which would promote the particular purposes of one group or sector at the expense of others.

Any serious student of the Community's legislative process would soon learn to ask the most significant question: on whose initiative was any law first suggested, and by whom behind the scenes was it being most actively lobbied for: whether it was German bus manufacturers lobbying for a directive harmonising the rules on bus construction; or French and Belgian multi-national manufacturers of asbestos substitutes lobbying for directives banning the use of asbestos; or southern European vegetable growers pressing for a regulation making it difficult to grow lettuces in greenhouses; or environmental lobby groups demanding a directive which would do immense damage to Europe's chemical industry.

The extraordinarily complex, arcane and unaccountable processes whereby the Commission alone could generate new proposals for legislation inevitably laid it open to the potential for corruption on a colossal scale; as did the fact that it was each year responsible for disbursing tens of billions of pounds of European tax-payers' money, often on the discretion of small groups of officials in essence accountable to no-one, except possibly a Commissioner who, as was shown by the scandals leading up to the mass-resignation of Commissioners in 1999, might be as open to corruption as anyone else.

Any informed study of the project's workings, however, would have to conclude that by far the most effective single interest group in ensuring that the 'project' was run to suit its own collective purposes was the government of just one member state: France.

Again and again, throughout the decades, it was France which showed that it best knew how to manipulate the 'project' and the Commission to its own national ends. It was France which fought to set up an agricultural policy, absorbing initially 90 percent of the Community's entire budget, designed solely for the purpose of protecting French farmers and the French state. It was France which, behind the scenes, initiated the *coup de main* which tricked Britain into handing over control of the world's richest fishing waters, primarily in the first place for the interests of French fishermen.

It was France which insisted that the Amsterdam treaty should enshrine forever the right of Strasbourg to share with Brussels the headquarters of the European Parliament, even though this created farcical logistical problems as the Parliament's staff and documents had to be ferried between the two cities and back again 12 times a year, at a price of injecting hundreds of millions of pounds a year into the Strasbourg economy.

It was France which flagrantly broke the state aid rules by giving Air France an unprecedented £2.4 billion subsidy and which then, when this was ruled illegal by the ECJ, simply persuaded the Commission to sanction the subsidy in another form. It was France which in 2003 was unashamedly playing a similar game in bailing out one of its largest national firms, Alstom. When it arranged a £5 billion deal to save from bankruptcy the company which built Eurostar trains, France's TGVs and the world's largest liner, the QMII (the contract for which itself had only been secured through massive hidden subsidies), the French government simply ignored the Commission, which it knew would be bound to declare the payments illegal.

But in so doing France merely continued a pattern of conduct which had not varied since the Community was launched, and which no other member state would have dared emulate. For France the rules of the Community were there to be imposed on other countries when this served French interests, and ignored by France herself whenever it suited her. It was no accident that it was France which in the run-in to the launch of the euro was first to object to the Maastricht criteria to which she had insisted that everyone else must be bound; which negotiated herself the most favourable exchange rate when the values of the currency were fixed; and which was then among the first to breach the rules of the growth and stability pact on which she had insisted the success of the euro would depend. It was no accident that it was France which, having most flagrantly breached UN sanctions against Saddam Hussein's Iraq in the 1990s, was then in 2003 leading the opposition to the Anglo-American coalition to topple him. And it was no coincidence that, in the great debate over the future shape of 'Europe', it was France's president who should have led the way in pushing for that *'directoire'* form of intergovernmentalism which would legitimise France's right to play top dog in settling Europe's affairs, and to ensure they would continue to be run in France's interests as they had been for 50 years.

From Monnet to de Gaulle, from Delors to Mitterand, from Chirac to Giscard, the 'European project' had all along been as much a project for promoting the power, wealth, influence and glory of France as anything else. By comparison, the role played by Germany, tucked in alongside France as her closest ally but inhibited by her wish to show she had forsworn her old nationalistic arrogance and the shame of her earlier record, was insignificant.

Behind the lofty ideals of supranationalism in short, evoking an image of Commissioners sitting like Plato's Guardians, guiding the affairs of Europe on some rarified plane far above the petty egotisms and rivalries of mere nation states, the project Monnet had set on its way was a vast, ramshackle, self-deluding monster: partly suffocating in its own bureaucracy; partly a corrupt racket, providing endless opportunities for individuals and collectives to outwit and exploit their fellow men; partly a mighty engine for promoting the national interests of those countries which knew how to 'work the system': among whom the Irish and the Spanish had done better than most, but of whom France was the unrivalled master.

The one thing above all the 'project' could never be, because by definition it had never been intended to be, was in the remotest sense democratic. The whole purpose of a supranational body is to stand above the wishes of individual nations and peoples. When Monnet and Salter first conceived their idea of a supranational 'United States of Europe' it never entered their minds that the wishes of the people should be consulted. They were technocrats, who thought that the future of Europe would best be served by placing it under the role of a government of technocrats like themselves, men whose only interest was efficient co-operation to pursue a common goal, unsullied by any need to resort to all the messy, unpredictable business of elections.

Democracy is for nation states, for people who still live under the illusion that human affairs are best decided through rivalry and conflict between competing political parties. And just as the supranational technocracy has transcended rivalries between nations, so it has moved on from that openly declared disputing for power between different groups and ideologies in society which is the essence of democracy.

The Communist Spinelli had his own version of the same transcendent vision. For him the role of the 'people' was to wait patiently while the chosen elite gradually assembled the new 'government of Europe', and then, when a 'constituent assembly' had unveiled its constitution, to acclaim it as just what they had wanted all along.

Such was the model on which 'Europe' was built through the decades, by an elite of politicians, technocrats, academics and professional experts, all bound together by the same shared ideology. It was fascinating to see how, each time the 'project' extended its reach into new countries, the same kind of elite would form and be recruited to the cause, sharing the same ideology and looking down in condescension on all those outsiders who remained outside the magic circle.

Of course, since the whole purpose of the 'project' was to take over the reins of governance from nation states and peoples who still thought of themselves as being in the 'democratic' stage of human development, it was necessary to delude them by surrounding the 'project' with a façade of democratic legitimacy. Such was the purpose of the European Parliament, with its sham debates, in which speakers might be allowed 90 seconds to read out a prepared speech to which no one listened, followed by voting sessions in which MEPs might be expected to record 400 votes in an hour and a half, frenziedly jabbing at electronic buttons to decide on issues of which they had not the faintest knowledge. Yet all this was to achieve nothing of any substance, since the members of this pretend-Parliament had very little power and no real role except to act out a self-important charade of democracy.

The Parliament's layout, with its 'hemicycles' on the continental model, gave another symbolic clue. To anyone watching the different groupings of MEPs sitting round in their horseshoe-shaped chamber, it soon became obvious that there was no 'opposition', other than occasional outbursts from eccentric malcontents. The whole purpose of the Parliament, as of every other gathering of ministers, delegates, officials or Commissioners in the 'project' was to arrive at a 'consensus'. There was no sense of ministers being challenged; of an executive being opposed; of politicians being called trenchantly to account for their policies and actions. In the world of 'consensus', everyone must in the end be seen to be on the same side. When Giscard looked round that room in Brussels in June 2003, after 17 months of debate and discussion, he was allowed to sniff the air, without taking a vote, and to divine his 'consensus' as to what had been agreed. What the convention had agreed to, what the entire 'project' had over the years shown itself to be, with its almost pathological intolerance of any kind of dissent, was in effect a one-party state.

Inevitably this prompted a question: how was it that Britain, the nation which gave to the world the idea that democracy relies on the right of the people to dismiss a government which has failed them, had willingly allowed herself to become subjected to a form of government which was essentially a one-party state, in which the same unaccountable ruling body would be permitted to remain in power for ever?

Britain's Euro-schizophrenia

The odd thing about British attitudes to 'Europe' was how schizophrenic they were. If Scott Fitzgerald was right in his ironic observation that a test of intelligence is the ability to hold two contradictory ideas in one's mind at the same time, he could not have wanted a better example than Britain's response to membership of the European Community.

On the one hand, President de Gaulle had been entirely right in that passage of his 'veto speech' in 1963, when he suggested that the British simply did not fit in with the continental way of looking at the world:

'England, in effect is insular. She is maritime. She is linked through her trade, her markets, her supply lines to the most distant countries … She has, in all her doings, very marked and very original habits and traditions. In short England's nature, England's structure, England's very situation differs profoundly from those of the Continentals.'

Despite the shrewdness of his comments, there was nevertheless a widespread misconception, often deliberately fostered as part of the 'pro-European' orthodoxy, that before entering the Common Market the 'insular' British had generally stood aloof from involvement in the affairs of their next-door neighbours. The truth was that, throughout her history, Britain could scarcely have been more intimately engaged with Europe. After two world wars when she and her Commonwealth had contributed a million and a half lives to sorting out problems which arose from continental politics, Britain in the immediate post-war era could not have been more active in trying to organise European co-operation on an intergovernmental basis.

For centuries, however, Britain's policy on Europe had been driven by one central principle: the need to preserve the 'balance of power'. Whenever power had become concentrated in the hands of one or more nations, whether 16th century Spain, the France of Louis XIV and Napoleon or early 20th century Germany, Britain had seen it as her interest to provide a counterbalance. What was unprecedented about Britain's decision to join her destiny with that of the Six was that this was the first time when, after a new concentration of power had arisen in Europe, she had opted to join it.[8]

The problem was that, from that moment on, everything would ensure that Britain remained the 'odd man out'. As a legacy of the fact that she had been the centre of a global empire, she was linked by kinship and shared values to a family

8 Of course in the thinking of many, including Macmillan, part of the purpose of Britain's original decision to apply for entry was that she could help to maintain 'the balance of power' from within the Community, most notably as a balance to de Gaulle's France. This was a factor which weighed not just in Britain's own calculations, but in those of Adenauer, Washington and even Monnet himself.

of English-speaking nations across the world. She had exported her form of adversarial parliamentary democracy to scores of countries, including America. From the tradition of common law to her non-metric weights and measures, everything about Britain's ways of thought and doing things marked her out as different from her new partners. If she was now to 'harmonise' her ways with theirs, this would inevitably require Britain to abandon much more than would be asked of them.

For this reason alone, as we have seen, from the moment Britain entered the Community she found herself cast as 'the awkward partner'. What made it worse was that neither her leaders nor her people ever really understood or accepted the basic principle on which the Community had been founded, that its chief purpose was to move forward to ever greater integration. Having joined what most of her citizens assumed was only a trading arrangement, based on a desire for friendly co-operation, Britain was thus disconcerted to find herself under constant pressure to give up ever more of her power to govern herself.

This led to the only too familiar pattern which was to be re-enacted again and again, as British politicians found themselves confronted by their partners with some radical new proposal which they did not regard as necessary. Their archetypal response was outlined by *The Times* in the summer of 2003, analysing Britain's response to the proposed constitution:

'It is at first denied that any radical new plan exists; it is then conceded that it exists but ministers swear blind that it is not even on the political agenda; it is then noted that it might well be on the agenda but is not a serious proposition; it is later conceded that it is a serious proposition, but that it will never be implemented; after that it is acknowledged that it will be implemented but in such a diluted form that it could make no difference to the lives of ordinary people; and at some point it is finally recognised that it has made such a difference, but it was always known that it would and voters were told so from the outset.'[9]

In this way, as we have seen, Britain had for 30 years given the impression that she was always the 'reluctant partner', the 'slowest ship in the convoy', being dragged along to concede further sacrifices of her power against her wishes. And this had eventually culminated, of course, in the emergence of one issue, the currency, on which Britain's reluctance was so great that for once she had to be allowed to opt out (although at the time her 'reprieve' was regarded as only temporary).

In compensation, however, there was another side to Britain's involvement with 'Europe' so startlingly different that it might have seemed hard to believe it was coming from the same country.

Firstly there was the rise of that 'pro-European orthodoxy' in Britain's ruling circles which dictated that it was unthinkable to challenge her membership of the Community; so that anyone daring to question it must immediately be anathematised as a 'head banger', 'little Englander', or any of the other familiar litany of pejorative phrases. Often the very people who were reluctant to allow further

---

9 *The Times* (editorial: 'Brussels and Damascus – Straw's improbable conversion to an EU constitution'), 28 August 2002.

concessions of Britain's powers of self-government would be the first to dismiss any thought that there might be some fundamental contradiction between the 'project' and Britain's interests. They might show no understanding of the nature of supranational government. But they covered up their constant misreading of its operations by attempting to suppress any intelligent discussion of the issue. Thus it was often the 'Europhiles' themselves who appeared the true 'little Englanders', uncomprehending of what their continental partners were up to, but projecting onto it their own insular daydreams of a 'Europe' essentially dedicated to no more than peaceful co-operation between nation states.

Britain's other startling response to Community membership was the exceptional zeal shown by her politicians and civil servants in how they implemented and enforced the Community's laws. By the mid-1990s no other country in the EU had such a reputation for the rigour with which it applied Community legislation to its own citizens: firstly by 'gold-plating', adding on all sorts of onerous new requirements not included in the original Brussels directives, and then by the ruthless manner in which they were enforced. In no other country in Europe would public officials have been so willing to close down three quarters of its abattoirs for no reason other than their inability to comply with absurdly misconceived rules which were in many cases not even based on law. No other country would have been willing to close down much of its fishing industry; or to drive tens of thousands of other firms out of business, in the name of enforcing 'EC regulations' which bore no relation to practical reality. In no other country would officials have been prepared to bring criminal charges against a market stallholder for selling a 'pound of bananas', when polls showed more than 90 percent of Britain's population opposed to the law which had made the selling of goods in non-metric weights and measures a criminal offence.

Yet this relentless drive to tie up businesses in more and more regulations, at costs amounting to tens of billions of pounds a year, was insisted on by the Foreign Office as necessary to show that the British were 'good Europeans'. Behind the scenes, FCO officials brought constant pressure on other government departments to ensure that Britain was complying with her 'Treaty obligations', apparently unconcerned as to whether other countries were doing the same. The contrast with France could not have been greater. While the French regarded the Community as having set up a system to be exploited to their advantage, British officialdom viewed it as a sacred edifice of obligations to be blindly obeyed, irrespective of what British interests might suffer as a result. This attitude was only reinforced by the willingness of ministers to defend the system regardless of justice or common sense, so that they might end up offering excuses as cynically implausible as the famous explanation that hundreds of slaughterhouses had closed their doors solely because their owners had 'taken a commercial decision not to invest in the future of their business'.

So glaring was the contradiction between these two sides to Britain's attitude to membership of the EU, that, particularly as the tide of 'Eurosceptic' feeling began in the 1990s to run ever more strongly, some committed supporters of British membership eventually began to lose patience. Why did Britain always have to play the role of 'reluctant partner' in this embarrassing fashion, presenting as many difficulties to her colleagues as it did to Britain herself? Had the time not come for the British to make up their minds about 'Europe' one way or another? In a speech in 1999, Lord Jenkins could not have put the point more bluntly:

'There are only two coherent British attitudes to Europe. One is to participate fully ... and to endeavour to exercise as much influence and gain as much benefit as possible from the inside. The other is to recognise that Britain's history, national psychology and political culture may be such that we can never be other than a foot-dragging and constantly complaining member; and that it would be better, and certainly would produce less friction, to accept this and to move towards an orderly, and if possible, reasonably amicable withdrawal.' [10]

By now there was no issue which exemplified Jenkins's point more starkly than the euro, formally launched just a few weeks before his speech. Here was the supreme symbol of the desire of Britain's partners to subject their national interests to supranational control. And here was Britain still playing the 'foot-dragging' member in refusing to join them. How could she pretend to want to play a central part in the 'project', yet continue refusing to sign up to the most crucial condition of membership of all?

No one, of course, was more painfully aware of this than Britain's prime minister himself. Blair knew he could not hope to play his 'leading role' unless he could somehow contrive to get Britain into the single currency. Yet he was completely hamstrung by his commitment to put the decision to the British people in a referendum, knowing that his chances of reversing popular hostility to the euro, now running at two-to-one against, had all but vanished.

More and more, in all his relations with 'Europe', Blair was now to give the impression of a small boy standing on the touchline, longing to join the bigger boys on the field, but without understanding the rules of the game they were playing.

The greatest irony of Britain's membership of the EU in the early years of the 21st century lay in contrasting her economic performance with that of her Continental partners. Back in the 1960s and 1970s she had above all wanted to join them because they seemed to have discovered the secret of economic success which she had lost. In the 1980s and early 1990s while Britain's economy had been restructured and liberated, for reasons unconnected with her membership of the EC, those of the original Six had lost their dynamism. They had begun to sink under a dead weight of ever higher taxes, labour costs and regulations, the so-called 'European social model', which the coming of the euro had only made worse.

By 2003, in terms of unemployment, growth rates, inward investment and trade, the contrast between Britain and the eurozone had become more striking than ever. A list of the world's top 1,000 companies by market capitalisation showed that, although the USA was way out ahead of anyone else, British firms now came second, ahead of Japan and with their value more than twice that of the

10 Speech made on 22 March at Queen Elizabeth II Conference centre, London, reported in the *Sunday Telegraph*, 28 March 1999.

top German and French firms combined.[11] In 1996 a majority of European finance directors predicted that by 2001, unless Britain joined the euro, Frankfurt would have overhauled London as Europe's leading financial centre. In 2003 it emerged that London had in fact surged even further ahead, and that many international banks had actually relocated from Frankfurt to London.[12]

Until now Britain had only benefited from her failure to join the euro. The successful economy bequeathed by a Conservative government to Labour in 1997 had so far continued to prosper, despite the willingness of the Blair government to sign the Social Chapter and to accept from the Community ever more costly regulatory burdens, such as a succession of working time directives. But rolling up over the horizon were all sorts of dark clouds to threaten this, most of them attributable in part or whole to Britain's EU membership.

One was the energy crisis which could soon face Britain when, with the running down of her North Sea oil and gas reserves, she would by 2010 become 90 percent dependent on imported energy, much of it from politically unstable regions of the world such as Russia and North Africa. This was particularly significant since, having closed down her coal industry, Britain's only other significant source of electricity was her ageing nuclear power stations, still supplying 23 percent of her needs but most now nearing the end of their life. Instead of facing up honestly to the immense threat this represented, the Blair government had been beguiled by the EU's 'renewable energy' policy into imagining that it could replace the obsolete nuclear power stations by a huge wind power programme. Ministers seemed wholly blind to the fact that wind turbines were an absurdly expensive and inefficient source of electricity, which could not replace Britain's nuclear power even if half the UK and its surrounding seas were covered in giant windmills. Britain's only hope of maintaining regular supplies of electricity lay with France, still producing 80 percent of her electricity from nuclear power. But to allow a country which had once led the world in nuclear technology and enjoyed western Europe's largest energy reserves, to become economically so vulnerable was likely to prove a blunder of the first magnitude.

Equally alarming was Britain's fast-approaching waste crisis, resulting from her agreement under the Single European Act to hand control of her waste management policy to Brussels. Not only had the EU produced a series of directives making it increasingly difficult and costly to dispose of every kind of waste, from old vehicles and fridges to millions of tons a year of unwanted food products. It had also introduced a virtual ban on burying waste in landfill sites, on which Britain relied significantly more than any other EU country. Now faced with an obligation by 2016 to dispose of almost all her waste by other means, Britain would need to install new plants, including 165 giant incinerators, at a rate of one a week for 14 years. The chances of this happening were zero.

A whole string of further EU laws were due to come into force over the next few years, imposing crippling new costs on British industry. These ranged from the

11 *Business Week*, 14 July 2003.
12 *Wall Street Journal Europe*, 11–13 July 2003.

WEEE directive on disposing of electrical waste and the 'physical agents directive' drastically limiting the time workers would be allowed to spend using machine tools, tractors or any form of machinery, to the proposed REACH directive regulating the use of 170,000 varieties of chemical and chemical products. The cost to Britain's chemical industry alone, Europe's largest, was estimated in 2003 at £6 billion a year, more than cancelling out the industry's entire £5.5 billion a year export earnings. But Britain would find it hard to protest, because the directive had been proposed by her own environment minister Michael Meacher under the UK's EU presidency in 1998.[13]

All this alone might have provoked the British people into wondering whether the UK's interests were best served by remaining in the European Union, quite apart from the growing shadow cast by the constitution due to be signed in 2004. But as that moment approached the ruling orthodoxy remained as insistent as ever that any consideration of British withdrawal was out of the question. Although opinion polls continued to show between 30 and 50 percent of the British people agreeing that Britain should leave the EU, still not one of the 659 MPs who represented them in Parliament was prepared publicly to echo that view. Although the Conservative leader, Duncan Smith, had been elected by his party's membership as much as anything for his strongly Eurosceptic views and on a suspicion that he privately favoured British withdrawal, the most obvious consequence of his election in 2001 had been to suppress discussion of EU-related issues within his party even further, for fear of reopening the divisions which had reduced it to such a parlous plight in the 1990s.

Equally, the practical difficulties involved in any British withdrawal from the EU would now be enormous. The problem did not lie, as supporters of the 'project' liked to suggest, in any threat such a withdrawal would pose to Britain's continued trade with her former EU partners. So one-sided had become the advantage they derived from their trade with Britain that in their own interests this would continue, apart from the fact that, under WTO rules, it would now be virtually impossible to shut British exports out by raising tariffs. Norway and Switzerland both sent a much larger share of their exports than Britain to the EU, and Britain could negotiate the type of free-trading agreement the EU had signed with Mexico.

Much more intractable would be the problem of unravelling all those areas of British law and public administration which had now become inextricably entangled with the EU, as so much of her national system of government had become enmeshed with the supranational system centred on Brussels. For a start there would be those 97,000 pages of directives and regulations, all of which were now in force in Britain, in many cases replacing pre-existent national laws. The task of rewriting a substantial part of Britain's statute book would in itself be monumental; quite apart from having to rethink and reorganise vast areas of national policy, from agriculture and fisheries to regional government.

But the real question beginning to loom in 2003, not just over Britain but over the whole of Europe, was what was to be the future of the European Union itself?

---

13 Information from CBI and the *Sunday Telegraph*, 23 August 2003.

How long could it realistically be expected to survive in anything like a recognisable form? For 50 years it had gone on evolving step by step towards that distant goal of full integration. But now that far-off point seemed almost within reach, suddenly a new set of question marks were emerging, more challenging than any it had faced before.

For 50 years the 'project' had been able to live comfortably in that hypothetical future, where to every problem the answer had been to use it as justification for another step forward in the integration process. But now, in all directions, that future was no longer hypothetical. Once the 10 new applicant countries had entered in 2004, it would no longer be possible to look to 'enlargement' as merely the excuse for another round of integration. They would bring with them a host of very serious new problems of their own, demanding practical solutions.

For decades it had been possible to dream of the distant prospect of monetary union as one of the crowning achievements of integration. But now the euro had arrived, it also was bringing with it immense new problems to which it would be remarkably difficult to find a remedy. So profound were those problems that scarcely a serious economist in the world in 2003 was prepared to rule out the possibility that, within a few years, the whole euro experiment would collapse in chaos, as the infinitely more modest ERM had done before it.

Indeed the countries of the eurozone had still to face up to the grim message of the previous decade that their economies appeared to be in a state of advanced structural decline, to which no glimmer of an answer appeared to be yet in view. Expert forecasts of the EU's economic future were now shrouded in almost universal pessimism, such as that from the French Institute of International Relations predicting that, by the middle of the century, the EU's projected GDP would be growing at one percent a year, compared with over two percent in North America and 2.5 percent in China. Combined with demographic forecasts showing that most eurozone countries would soon be facing shrinking populations, where the proportion of pensioners and other dependents would be too great for the active workforce to support, the French report gloomily concluded that the EU appeared to be facing 'a slow but inexorable' exit from history.[14]

Perhaps the most likely scenario was one to which the debate of the previous few years had already given plenty of clues. This was the idea that the EU's future should lie in an *avant-garde* of countries, centred on the original Six, moving forward to even fuller integration on their own. The 'Union' would thus divide into two groups: an inner club, dominated by the Franco-German axis, and an outer ring of 'second class' members, including the new entrants and all those countries, led by Britain, which remained outside the euro. If agreement could not be reached on the constitution – and even Giscard's rambling draft presented little more than a messy compromise, leaving the core contradictions still unresolved – there seemed to be no alternative but for the EU to become in some way a 'two tier' organisation, split between inner and outer rings, the nature of the relationship between them yet to be worked out.

14 'Europe's Population Implosion', the *Economist*, 17 July 2003.

There was nothing novel about this. Key players in the debate, led by Delors, with support from Chirac, Fischer and even Giscard, had been repeatedly discussing it ever since 1999. It was viewed by the French and Germans as the only solution to the insuperable problems posed both by the arrival of those poorer entrant countries who could not possibly be admitted to full 'first-class' membership, and the refusal of Britain, Denmark and Sweden to join that *sine qua non* of full membership, the currency.

How such a radical realignment of the EU might be achieved was a matter for the future. The one thing the events of 2003 had made certain was that the 'project' as it had evolved continuously through half a century, on an ever broader front, was at last reaching the end of the road. That famous 'train' no one was supposed to miss was nearing the buffers. Whatever 'Europe' was to evolve into in the years that lay ahead would mark an entirely new phase in its development: one characterised more by retreat and retrenchment than by any further broad-front advances along the old, familiar lines.

What had begun with 'the Six' would now in essence return to the 'Six'. The Monnet project was dead.

Two 20th century dreams

Those same years back in the 1920s when Monnet and Salter were first conceiving the ideology which would eventually lead to the European Union, had also seen the coming to birth of another of the 20th century's most influential ideas.

In Paris the French-Swiss architect Le Corbusier was conceiving his vision of 'the Radiant City'. His belief was that many of the ills besetting mankind derived from having to live in unhygienic, unplanned cities which had grown up over the centuries, as he put it, 'the pack donkey way'. The future demanded that these cities, starting with Paris, should be swept away and replaced with his 'city of the future', planned down to the tiniest detail. Everyone should live and work in immense concrete buildings, laid out on a geometric transport grid of motorways and surrounded by areas of 'public open space', planted with grass and trees.

For two decades Le Corbusier's dream remained unrealised, no more than a curiosity, known only to a handful of young architects and would-be town planners. But it had awakened in them an evangelical enthusiasm, because it offered them the chance of playing the central role in what would amount to one of the greatest revolutions in history.

Their opportunity to put the vision into practice was created by the Second World War. In the 1940s, particularly in Britain, it was those same architects and planners who were entrusted with planning how the blitzed cities would be rebuilt. In the 1950s and 1960s, the results could be seen rising over many of Britain's cities: vast estates of concrete towers and slab blocks, surrounded by public open space, cut through by new urban motorways.

Similar gargantuan developments were being constructed all across Europe, notably in the Communist countries to the east. The 'modernist' ideology so persuasively synthesised by Le Corbusier in the 1920s had become the ruling orthodoxy of the age, subscribed to by politicians of all parties, acclaimed by the media, scarcely questioned by anyone.

Quite suddenly in the late 1960s and early 1970s, just when the fashion for tower blocks and vast comprehensive redevelopment schemes had reached its height, a dramatic reaction set in. Faced with the reality of what the vision had led to, people suddenly decided they had seen the future and that it didn't work. Far from creating the gleaming, efficient cities promised by the architects' drawings and planners' models, these mighty structures were inhuman, soulless, oppressive, dirty and ugly, their concrete disfigured with graffiti, their walkways the haunt of muggers and drug addicts, their surrounding spaces just dead areas of worn grass, covered in litter and belonging to no one.

The disillusionment which set in towards all Le Corbusier's vision had stood for was like waking up from a dream. It was hard to recall just how powerfully the prevailing orthodoxy had dictated that this vision represented the only possible future; when to question it had been like the small boy trying to insist the emperor was wearing no clothes.

The trouble was that the vision of a perfectly planned world created by efficient technocrats might have seemed beguiling in theory. In practice, however, it eventually became clear that it did not relate to human reality in any way. Nothing about it worked in the way it was intended, because this rigid technocratic vision could only work on paper and in people's heads. Once gigantic resources were put into bringing about the abstract vision in the real world, it soon became apparent that the dream had led only to a nightmare.

For Monnet the equivalent of Le Corbusier's wish to pull down the old cities of the past was his detestation of the nation state. His shining dream was of that supranational government of the future, run by technocrats, rising above all the messy complications of nationalism and democracy. As with Le Corbusier, the unexpected opportunity for his dream to be brought to realisation was created by the Second World War. And as with Le Corbusier his dream eventually became the inspiration for a whole new generation of technocrats and civil servants, supported by the political elites of western Europe, for whom the 'project' offered the chance to play a central role in the greatest political adventure of their time.

As with Le Corbusier's vision, there was a time when the new orthodoxy seemed to carry all before it, demolishing the structures of the nation states and erecting in their place all the rigid technocratic structures of the new system. There was no book which would convey more clearly the nature of the Monnet project than the European Commission's 1200-page *Directory of Community Legislation Currently In Force*, listing in small print all the tens of thousands of directives, regulations and decisions which embodied the outward form of what the project had achieved: its sacred *acquis communautaire*.

Here in these endless lists of the laws which set up the Common Agricultural Policy, the Common Fisheries Policy, the Competition Policy and the rest were the mighty tower blocks of the 'European project', stretching to the horizon. It was symbolically apt that, just as Le Corbusier's vision was rooted in his reverence for concrete as the supreme building material, so for the technocrats of the European

Commission they had no higher term of praise for their achievements than to describe them as 'concrete'.

All that was wrong with Le Corbusier's tower blocks became obvious when real people had to live in them, to discover that they defied human realities and human needs. It was the same with the tower blocks created by Monnet's technocrats. The nation state and democracy were too fundamental to human needs and human nature simply to be eliminated by technocratic diktat. Just as when people woke up to the soulless inhumanity of Le Corbusier's utopian dream they hankered for all the warmth and vitality and human reality of the old cities they had lost, so the same was becoming true of all that had been swept away by the Utopian dream of M. Monnet. Only when people discovered that they had lost their democracy and the power of their countries to govern themselves did they begin to appreciate in a new way just how valuable was that which had been taken away from them without their knowing it.

They had become the victims of one of the greatest collective acts of make-believe of the 20th century: fit in that respect to rank alongside the self-deceiving dreams of Communism.

Sooner perhaps rather than later, the fantasy of the great 'European project' would crumble into reality: destroyed by all those contradictions which in its mad ambition it had failed to foresee and which it could never have hoped to resolve. But like the vision of Le Corbusier and on a much grander scale, it would leave a terrible devastation behind it: a wasteland from which it will take many years for the people of Europe to emerge.

Index